TRANSLATOR AND SENIOR EDITOR:
Rabbi Israel V. Berman

MANAGING EDITOR:
Baruch Goldberg

EDITOR:
Rabbi Moshe Sober

ASSOCIATE EDITOR:
Dr. Jeffrey M. Green

COPY EDITOR:
Michael Plotkin

BOOK DESIGNER:
Ben Gasner

GRAPHIC ARTIST:
Michael Etkin

TECHNICAL STAFF:
Abby Berman
Moshe Greenvald
Meir Hanegbi
Yona Ratzon
Inna Schwartzman

Random House Staff

PRODUCTION MANAGER:
Lou Bilka

ART DIRECTOR:
Bernard Klein

CHIEF COPY EDITOR:
Amy Edelman

THE TALMUD

THE STEINSALTZ EDITION

VOLUME IX

TRACTATE KETUBOT

PART III

Volume IX
Tractate Ketubot
Part III

Random House
New York

THE TALMUD

תלמוד בבלי

THE STEINSALTZ EDITION

Commentary by Rabbi Adin Steinsaltz (Even Yisrael)

Published in the United States by Random House, Inc., New York, and simultaneously in Canada by Random House of Canada Limited, Toronto.

This work was originally published in Hebrew by the Israel Institute for Talmudic Publications, Jerusalem. Copyright by the Israel Institute for Talmudic Publications, Jerusalem, Israel.

Library of Congress Cataloging-in-Publication Data

Talmud. English.
The Talmud : the Steinsaltz edition / the Talmud with commentary by
Adin Steinsaltz
p. cm.
ISBN 0-679-42694-9 (v. III)
1. Talmud—Commentaries I. Steinsaltz, Adin. II. Title.
BM499.5.E4 1993 296.1'250521—dc20 89 42911

Manufactured in the United States of America
98765432
First U.S. Edition

This volume is dedicated

to the memory of

Celia and Hyme Zorensky

and

Ida and Saul Gendler

our parents, our teachers

with love, respect and gratitude

by

Mary and Louis I. Zorensky

The Steinsaltz Talmud in English

The English edition of the Steinsaltz Talmud is a translation and adaptation of the Hebrew edition. It includes most of the additions and improvements that characterize the Hebrew version, but it has been adapted and expanded especially for the English reader. This edition has been designed to meet the needs of advanced students capable of studying from standard Talmud editions, as well as of beginners, who know little or no Hebrew and have had no prior training in studying the Talmud.

The overall structure of the page is similar to that of the traditional pages in the standard printed editions. The text is placed in the center of the page, and alongside it are the main auxiliary commentaries. At the bottom of the page and in the margins are additions and supplements.

The original Hebrew-Aramaic text, which is framed in the center of each page, is exactly the same as that in the traditional Talmud (although material that was removed by non-Jewish censors has been restored on the basis of manuscripts and old printed editions). The main innovation is that this Hebrew-Aramaic text has been completely vocalized and punctuated, and all the terms usually abbreviated have been fully spelled out. In order to retain the connection with the page numbers of the standard editions, these are indicated at the head of every page.

We have placed a *Literal Translation* on the right-hand side of the page, and its punctuation has been introduced into the Talmud text, further helping the student to orientate himself. The *Literal Translation* is intended to help the student to learn the meaning of specific Hebrew and Aramaic words. By comparing the original text with this translation, the reader develops an understanding of the Talmudic text and can follow the words and sentences in the original. Occasionally, however, it has not been possible to present an exact literal translation of the original text, because it is so different in structure from English. Therefore we have added certain auxiliary words, which are indicated in square brackets. In other cases it would make no sense to offer a literal translation of a Talmudic idiom, so we have provided a close English equivalent of the original meaning, while a note, marked "lit.," explaining the literal meaning of the words, appears in parentheses. Our purpose in presenting this literal translation was to give the student an appreciation of the terse and enigmatic nature of the Talmud itself, before the arguments are opened up by interpretation.

Nevertheless, no one can study the Talmud without the assistance of commentaries. The main aid to understanding the Talmud provided by this edition is the *Translation and Commentary,* appearing on the left side of the page. This is Rabbi Adin Steinsaltz's highly regarded Hebrew interpretation of the Talmud, translated into English, adapted and expanded.

This commentary is not merely an explanation of difficult passages. It is an integrated exposition of the entire text. It includes a full translation of the Talmud text, combined with explanatory remarks. Where the translation in the commentary reflects the literal translation, it has been set off in bold type. It has also been given the same reference numbers that are found both in the original text and in the literal translation. Moreover, each section of the commentary begins with a few words of the Hebrew-Aramaic text. These reference numbers and paragraph headings allow the reader to move from one part of the page to another with ease.

There are some slight variations between the literal translation and the words in bold face appearing in the *Translation and Commentary.* These variations are meant to enhance understanding, for a juxtaposition of the literal translation and the sometimes freer translation in the commentary will give the reader a firmer grasp of the meaning.

The expanded *Translation and Commentary* in the left-hand column is intended to provide a conceptual understanding of the arguments of the Talmud, their form, content, context, and significance. The commentary also brings out the logic of the questions asked by the Sages and the assumptions they made.

Rashi's traditional commentary has been included in the right-hand column, under the *Literal Translation.* We have left this commentary in the traditional "Rashi script," but all quotations of the Talmud text appear in standard square type, the abbreviated expressions have all been printed in full, and Rashi's commentary is fully punctuated.

Since the *Translation and Commentary* cannot remain cogent and still encompass all the complex issues that arise in the Talmudic discussion, we have included a number of other features, which are also found in Rabbi Steinsaltz's Hebrew edition.

At the bottom of the page, under the *Translation and Commentary,* is the *Notes* section, containing additional material on issues raised in the text. These notes deepen understanding of the Talmud in various ways. Some provide a deeper and more profound analysis of the issues discussed in the text, with regard to individual points and to the development of the entire discussion. Others explain Halakhic concepts and the terms of Talmudic discourse.

The *Notes* contain brief summaries of the opinions of many of the major commentators on the Talmud, from the period after the completion of the Talmud to the present. Frequently the *Notes* offer interpretations different from that presented in the commentary, illustrating the richness and depth of Rabbinic thought.

The *Halakhah* section appears below the *Notes.* This provides references to the authoritative legal decisions reached over the centuries by the Rabbis in their discussions of the matters dealt with in the Talmud. It explains what reasons led to these Halakhic decisions and the close connection between the Halakhah today and the Talmud and its various interpreters. It should be noted that the summary of the Halakhah presented here is not meant to serve as a reference source for actual religious practice but to introduce the reader to Halakhic conclusions drawn from the Talmudic text.

English commentary and expanded translation of the text, making it readable and comprehensible

Hebrew/Aramaic text of the Talmud, fully vocalized, and punctuated

Literal translation of the Talmud text into English

REALIA

קַלְתָּה **Her basket.** The source of this word is the Greek κάλαθος, kalathos, and it means a basket with a narrow base.

Illustration from a Greek drawing depicting such a basket of fruit.

CONCEPTS

פֵּאָה *Pe'ah.* **One of the presents left for the poor** (מַתְּנוֹת עֲנִיִּים). The Torah forbids harvesting "the corners of your field," so that the produce left standing may be harvested and kept by the poor (Leviticus 19:9).

The Torah did not specify a minimum amount of produce to be left as *pe'ah*. But the Sages stipulated that it must be at least one-sixtieth of the crop.

Pe'ah is set aside only from crops that ripen at one time and are harvested at one time. The poor are allowed to use their own initiative to reap the *pe'ah* left in the fields. But the owner of an orchard must see to it that each of the poor gets a fixed share of the *pe'ah* from places that are difficult to reach. The poor come to collect *pe'ah* three times a day. The laws of *pe'ah* are discussed in detail in tractate *Pe'ah*.

Marginal notes provide essential background information

TRANSLATION AND COMMENTARY

[1]**and her husband threw her a bill of divorce into her lap or into her basket**, which she was carrying on her head, [2]would you say **here, too,** that **she would not be divorced**? Surely we know that the law is that she *is* divorced in such a case, as the Mishnah (*Gittin* 77a) states explicitly!

אֲמַר לֵיהּ [3]Rav Ashi **said** in reply **to** Ravina: The woman's **basket is** considered to be **at rest, and it is she who walks beneath it.** Thus the basket is considered to be a "stationary courtyard," and the woman acquires whatever is thrown into it.

MISHNAH הָיָה רוֹכֵב [4]If a **person was riding on an animal and he saw an ownerless object** lying on the ground, **and he said to another person** standing nearby, **"Give that object to me,"** [5]if **the other person took** the ownerless object **and said, "I have acquired it for myself,"** [6]he has **acquired it** by lifting it up, even though he was not the first to see it, and the rider has no claim to it. [7]But **if, after he gave** the object **to** the rider, the person who picked it up **said, "I acquired** the object **first,"** [8]**he** in fact **said nothing.** His words are of no effect, and the rider may keep it. Since the person walking showed no intention of acquiring the object when he originally picked it up, he is not now believed when he claims that he acquired it first. Indeed, even if we maintain that when a person picks up an ownerless object on behalf of someone else, the latter does *not* acquire it automatically, here, by *giving* the object to the rider, he makes a gift of it to the rider.

GEMARA תְּנַן הָתָם [9]**We have learned elsewhere** in a Mishnah in tractate *Pe'ah* (4:9): **"Someone who gathered *pe'ah*** — produce which by Torah law [Leviticus 23:22] is left unharvested in the corner of a field by the owner of the field, to be gleaned by the poor — **and said, 'Behold, this** *pe'ah* which I have gleaned **is** intended **for so-and-so the poor man,'** [10]**Rabbi Eliezer says:** The person who gathered the *pe'ah* **has acquired it**

בִּרְשׁוּת הָרַבִּים [1]וְזָרַק לָהּ גֵּט לְתוֹךְ חֵיקָהּ אוֹ לְתוֹךְ קַלְתָּהּ — [2]הָכָא נַמִי דְּלָא מִגָּרְשָׁה? [3]אֲמַר לֵיהּ: קַלְתָּהּ מֵינָח נַיְיחָא, וְאִיהִי דְּקָא מְסַגְּיָא מִתּוּתָהּ.

מִשְׁנָה [4]הָיָה רוֹכֵב עַל גַּבֵּי בְהֵמָה וְרָאָה אֶת הַמְּצִיאָה, וְאָמַר לַחֲבֵירוֹ "תְּנָה לִי", [5]נְטָלָהּ וְאָמַר, "אֲנִי זָכִיתִי בָּהּ", [6]זָכָה בָּהּ. [7]אִם, מִשֶּׁנְּתָנָהּ לוֹ, אָמַר, "אֲנִי זָכִיתִי בָּהּ תְּחִלָּה", [8]לֹא אָמַר כְּלוּם.

גְּמָרָא [9]תְּנַן הָתָם: "מִי שֶׁלִּיקֵּט אֶת הַפֵּאָה וְאָמַר, 'הֲרֵי זוֹ לִפְלוֹנִי עָנִי', [10]רַבִּי אֱלִיעֶזֶר

LITERAL TRANSLATION

in a public thoroughfare [1]and [her husband] threw her a bill of divorce into her lap or into her basket, [2]here, too, would she not be divorced?

[3]He said to him: Her basket is at rest, and it is she who walks beneath it.

MISHNAH [4][If a person] was riding on an animal and he saw a found object, and he said to another person, "Give it to me," [5][and the other person] took it and said, "I have acquired it," [6]he has acquired it. [7]If, after he gave it to him, he said, "I acquired it first," [8]he said nothing.

GEMARA [9]We have learned there: "Someone who gathered *pe'ah* and said, 'Behold this is for so-and-so the poor man,' [10]Rabbi Eliezer says:

RASHI

קלתה — סל שעל ראשה, שנותנת בה כלי מלאכתה וטווי שלה. הכי נמי דלא הוי גיטא — והאנן תנן במסכת גיטין (עז,א): זרק לה גיטה לתוך חיקה או לתוך קלתה — הרי זו מגורשת!

משנה לא אמר כלום — דאפילו אמרינן המגביה מציאה לחבירו לא קנה חבירו, כיון דיהבה ליה — קנייה ממה נפשך. אי קנייה קמא דלא מתכוין להקנות לחבירו — הא יהבה ניהליה במתנה. ואי לא קנייה קמא משום דלא היה מתכוין לקנות — הויא ליה הפקר עד דמטא לידיה דהאי, וקנייה האי במאי דעקרה מידיה דקמא לשם קנייה.

גמרא מי שליקט את הפאה — אדם בעלמא שאינו בעל שדה. דאי בבעל שדה — לא אמר רבי אליעזר זכה. דליכא למימר "מגו דזכי לנפשיה", דאפילו הוא עני מוזהר הוא שלא ללקט פאה משדה שלו, כדאמר בשחיטת חולין (קלא,ב): "לא תלקט לעני" — להזהיר עני על שלו.

Hebrew commentary of Rashi, the classic explanation that accompanies all editions of the Talmud

Numbers link the three main sections of the page and allow readers to refer rapidly from one to the other

NOTES

מִי שֶׁלִּיקֵּט אֶת הַפֵּאָה **If a person gathered *pe'ah*.** According to *Rashi*, the Mishnah must be referring to someone other than the owner of the field. By Torah law the owner of a field is required to separate part of his field as *pe'ah*, even if he himself is poor, and he may not take the *pe'ah* for himself. Therefore the "since" (מגו) argument

HALAKHAH

קַלְתָּה **A woman's basket.** "If a man throws a bill of divorce into a container that his wife is holding, she thereby acquires the bill of divorce and the divorce takes effect." (*Shulḥan Arukh, Even HaEzer* 139:10.)

הַמְלַקֵּט פֵּאָה עֲבוּר אַחֵר **A person who gathered *pe'ah* for someone else.** "If a poor person, who is himself entitled to collect *pe'ah*, gathered *pe'ah* for another poor person, and said, 'This *pe'ah* is for X, the poor person,' he acquires the *pe'ah* on behalf of that other poor person. But if the person who collected the *peah* was wealthy, he does not acquire the *pe'ah* on behalf of the poor person. He must give it instead to the first poor person who appears in the field," following the opinion of the Sages, as explained by Rabbi Yehoshua ben Levi. (*Rambam, Sefer Zeraim, Hilkhot Mattenot Aniyyim* 2:19.)

Notes highlight points of interest in the text and expand the discussion by quoting other classical commentaries

On the outer margin of the page, factual information clarifying the meaning of the Talmudic discussion is presented. Entries under the heading *Language* explain unusual terms, often borrowed from Greek, Latin, or Persian. *Sages* gives brief biographies of the major figures whose opinions are presented in the Talmud. *Terminology* explains the terms used in the Talmudic discussion. *Concepts* gives information about fundamental Halakhic principles. *Background* provides historical, geographical, and other information needed to understand the text. *Realia* explains the artifacts mentioned in the text. These notes are sometimes accompanied by illustrations.

The best way of studying the Talmud is the way in which the Talmud itself evolved - a combination of frontal teaching and continuous interaction between teacher and pupil, and between pupils themselves.

This edition is meant for a broad spectrum of users, from those who have considerable prior background and who know how to study the Talmud from any standard edition to those who have never studied the Talmud and do not even know Hebrew.

The division of the page into various sections is designed to enable students of every kind to derive the greatest possible benefit from it.

For those who know how to study the Talmud, the book is intended to be a written Gemara lesson, so that, either alone, with partners, or in groups, they can have the sense of studying with a teacher who explains the difficult passages and deepens their understanding both of the development of the dialectic and also of the various approaches that have been taken by the Rabbis over the centuries in interpreting the material. A student of this kind can start with the Hebrew-Aramaic text, examine Rashi's commentary, and pass on from there to the expanded commentary. Afterwards the student can turn to the Notes section. Study of the *Halakhah* section will clarify the conclusions reached in the course of establishing the Halakhah, and the other items in the margins will be helpful whenever the need arises to clarify a concept or a word or to understand the background of the discussion.

For those who do not possess sufficient knowledge to be able to use a standard edition of the Talmud, but who know how to read Hebrew, a different method is proposed. Such students can begin by reading the Hebrew-Aramaic text and comparing it immediately to the *Literal Translation*. They can then move over to the *Translation and Commentary*, which refers both to the original text and to the *Literal Translation*. Such students would also do well to read through the *Notes* and choose those that explain matters at greater length. They will benefit, too, from the terms explained in the side margins.

The beginner who does not know Hebrew well enough to grapple with the original can start with the *Translation and Commentary*. The inclusion of a translation within the commentary permits the student to ignore the *Literal Translation*, since the commentary includes both the Talmudic text and an interpretation of it. The beginner can also benefit from the *Notes*, and it is important for him to go over the marginal notes on the concepts to improve his awareness of the juridical background and the methods of study characteristic of this text.

Apart from its use as study material, this book can also be useful to those well versed in the Talmud, as a source of additional knowledge in various areas, both for understanding the historical and archeological background and also for an explanation of words and concepts. The general reader, too, who might not plan to study the book from beginning to end, can find a great deal of interesting material in it regarding both the spiritual world of Judaism, practical Jewish law, and the life and customs of the Jewish people during the thousand years (500 B.C.E.-500 C.E.) of the Talmudic period.

Contents

The Talmud

The Steinsaltz Edition

Volume IX

Tractate Ketubot

Part III

Introduction to Chapter Three

אֵלּוּ נְעָרוֹת

"And if a man seduces a virgin who has not been betrothed and lies with her, he shall surely make her his wife. If her father will surely refuse to give her to him, he shall pay money according to the dowry of virgins." (Exodus 22:15–16.)

"If a man finds a virgin na'arah who has not been betrothed, and seizes her and lies with her, and they are found, then the man who lay with her shall give to the father of the na'arah fifty pieces of silver, and she shall be his wife, for he has humbled her. He cannot let her go all his days." (Deuteronomy 22:28–29.)

The laws concerning the seducer or the rapist of a girl between twelve and twelve-and-a-half years old are stated explicitly in the Torah. However, because these laws are written in a very terse style, many questions demanding practical Halakhic solutions remain open.

One fundamental question relates to the precise meaning of the Biblical verses containing these laws. Do the laws concerning the seducer and the rapist apply only in the precise cases described by the Torah, or are the laws that are explicitly stated here meant to be applied in other cases? Many details, too, must be considered. Do these laws apply only to a virgin girl of that specific age, or do they also apply to a girl who is minor and to an adult woman? Do these laws apply only when the girl's father is living? And what is the law if she is an orphan? Does the right to refuse this marriage belong solely to the girl's father, and only in the case of seduction?

Another fundamental question, related to the first, is this: What is the law when, in addition to the prohibition against the seduction or the rape itself, there is a further prohibition against these sexual relations? It is possible to conceive of circumstances in which the rape victim is forbidden to the rapist by Rabbinic law, or by a positive Torah commandment, or by a Torah prohibition — even a prohibition punishable by death. In all such cases must the wrongdoer marry the girl? Must he pay a fine? Is he punished in another way? Or is he perhaps subject to both punishments? This problem necessitates a more comprehensive clarification of the laws of punishment in general, in order to establish what the law is when a transgression incurs more than one type of penalty.

Another major question is the clarification of the substance of the payment made by the seducer or the rapist. Is this fixed sum a general compensation for injury, or is it a special fine in addition to which other compensation must be paid? And if there are other payments, how are they assessed and to whom are they made? These broad issues constitute the main topics of this chapter.

TRANSLATION AND COMMENTARY

MISHNAH אֵלּוּ נְעָרוֹת [1]The Mishnayot of this chapter deal with the laws relating to a girl who is between twelve and twelve-and-a-half years old (called in Hebrew נַעֲרָה — *na'arah*) and who was seduced (Exodus 22:15-16) or raped (Deuteronomy 22:28-29) when she was a virgin. The Torah requires that the seducer or the rapist must pay the father of the *na'arah* a fine of fifty silver shekalim. This Mishnah and the next one (below, 36b) consider several problematic cases in which it is not clear whether the fine is applicable or not. The Mishnah declares that **the following** virgin ***ne'arot*** **are entitled to a fine,** even though their cases are problematic. [2]**If someone rapes** an unmarried young virgin who is between twelve and twelve-and-a-half years old and whom an ordinary Jew is not permitted to marry, such as **a** ***mamzeret*** (a child who was born from an incestuous or an adulterous relationship), [3]**or**

LITERAL TRANSLATION

MISHNAH [1]These are the *ne'arot* who have a fine: [2][If] someone [forcibly] has intercourse with a *mamzeret,* [3]or

אֵלּוּ

[1]נְעָרוֹת שֶׁיֵּשׁ לָהֶן קְנָס: [2]הַבָּא עַל הַמַּמְזֶרֶת, [3]וְעַל

RASHI

משנה אלו נערות — דוקא נערה, משהביאה שתי שערות עד שתבגר, והם ששה חדשים שבין נערות לבגרות. אבל קטנה ובוגרת — אין להם קנס. שיש להן קנס — אם אנסה אדם — נותן לאביה חמשים כסף, כדכתיב "ונתן האיש השוכב וגו'" (דברים כב). הבא על הממזרת — בגמרא פריך: אבל כשירות לא? ומשני: פסולות איצטריכא ליה לאשמועינן.

NOTES

אֵלּוּ נְעָרוֹת These are the *ne'arot.* Most of the Mishnayot of this chapter and the next deal with the laws of the virgin *na'arah.* Virgin *ne'arot* are subject to several special laws in the Torah. The primary topic of this chapter is the virgin *na'arah* who was seduced (Exodus 22:15-16) or raped (Deuteronomy 22:28-29). In both cases, the Torah requires the offender to pay a fine to the girl's father. In the case of the rapist, this fine is set at fifty silver shekalim; in the case of the seducer, it is described as "the dowry of the virgins." The Gemara (below, 29b) demonstrates, however, that these two sums are in fact identical. Indeed, the laws applying to seduction and rape are generally assumed to be the same, unless it is proved otherwise (below, 39b), with one notable exception: The Torah requires the rapist to marry his victim (if she agrees), and forbids him to divorce her without her consent. Moreover, regardless of whether he marries her or not, he must pay the fine to her father. By contrast, in the case of seduction, the Torah merely recommends that the seducer marry the *na'arah*, but he is not compelled to do so, and his right of divorce is in no way limited. Moreover, the fine must be paid only if he does not marry her. There are a few other differences in the laws governing rape and seduction, and they are stated in the Mishnah (below, 39a).

The Torah requires the fine to be paid if the girl is a virgin *na'arah*. The term *na'arah* refers to a stage in the girl's physical development, between the point when she produces two pubic hairs (presumed to occur at the age of twelve), and the point when she achieves full sexual maturity (presumed to occur at the age of twelve-and-a-half). During this period, the girl is considered legally competent, like an adult, but is still part of her father's household, particularly regarding financial matters. This is why the fine is paid to the *na'arah*'s father, rather than to the *na'arah* herself.

אֵלּוּ נְעָרוֹת These are the *ne'arot.* Our translation and commentary follow the text of the standard Vilna Talmud. In *Rif*'s version of the Talmud, this chapter begins: "*And these are the ne'arot*" — starting with the conjunction vav. Now, when a Mishnah begins with the conjunction vav, it usually implies that the Mishnah should be read in connection with a previous Mishnah. In this case, however, this is the first Mishnah dealing with the subject of the virgin *na'arah*. Accordingly, *Rosh* argues that the version appearing in our text is correct, and the conjunction vav should be omitted.

Shittah Mekubbetzet, however, supports *Rif*'s version, arguing that our Mishnah should be read in conjunction with the Mishnayot in the first chapter of the tractate (above, 10b and 11a). These Mishnayot declare that a woman who has already performed the first stage of marriage (*kiddushin* — "betrothal"), or a convert, a captive, or a slave who were converted, or ransomed, or freed before the age of three, are considered virgins for the purpose of deciding the amount of their ketubah, whereas a woman who has performed the second stage of marriage (*nissuin*), or a convert, a captive, or a slave, who were converted, or ransomed, or freed after the age of three, are not considered virgins for this purpose. On the basis of these earlier Mishnayot, our Mishnah declares that a similar rule applies to the fine that is awarded to a virgin *na'arah* who was raped.

Melekhet Shlomo adds that *Shittah*'s explanation makes it easier to understand why our Mishnah listed the women in this particular order, mentioning the *mamzeret,* the *netinah,* and the *kutit* before the proselyte, the captive, and the freed slave. The latter women have already been discussed in the first chapter, and our Mishnah is merely stating that the same distinctions that applied to the ketubah in the first chapter apply to the fine as well. But the other categories of women have not yet been discussed; hence our Mishnah places them first.

הַבָּא עַל הַמַּמְזֶרֶת If someone forcibly has intercourse with a ***mamzeret.***

Shittah Mekubbetzet raises the following question: Why

HALAKHAH

אֵלּוּ נְעָרוֹת These are the ***ne'arot.*** "If someone rapes or seduces a virgin *na'arah* whom he is forbidden to marry, whether by a commandment carrying the penalty of lashes or by a commandment carrying the penalty of excision, if

LANGUAGE

קְנָס A fine. According to some scholars, this word is not of Hebrew origin. It appears to be connected with the Latin word *census* or with the function of the *censor,* a high Roman official responsible for meting out punishment for undesirable behavior.

CONCEPTS

קְנָס A fine. A sum that a person must pay as a punishment. In various laws the Torah stipulates that a transgressor must pay a fine; for example, a rapist or a seducer — fifty shekalim of silver; a thief — double the value of the object or four or five times its value; compensation for another person's Canaanite slave killed by one's animal; half the damage in certain cases of damage caused by animals; and so on. A fine can be distinguished from normal compensation for damage in that the sum involved is either more than would be required to compensate (e.g., double the value) or is a fixed sum unrelated to the damage (e.g., in the case of rape). The regulations concerning fines differ from those of normal compensation in several respects. For example, only a court of fully ordained Rabbis, not of ordinary Rabbis or of laymen, may impose a fine. Furthermore, a person who admits his transgression before he is convicted in court is not liable to a fine, though he must pay compensation for any damage caused. Because of the law requiring fully ordained Rabbis, fines could not be imposed in Babylonia during Talmudic times and cannot be imposed today.

מַמְזֵר, מַמְזֶרֶת A *mamzer,* a *mamzeret.* A child born from relations between a married woman and a man other than her husband, or between relatives who are forbidden to marry by Torah law, where the participants in such a relationship are subject to excision. An exception to this rule is a menstruating woman, with whom sexual relations are forbidden under penalty of excision, but whose offspring is not a *mamzer.* The offspring of an

TRANSLATION AND COMMENTARY

a *netinah* (a descendant of the Gibeonites, a people who had converted to Judaism during the days of Joshua, but were later declared forbidden to marry other Jews), [4] **or a *kutit*** (a Samaritan, whose Jewish status is in question), in each of these cases the *na'arah* is entitled to a fine of fifty shekalim from the rapist.

The Torah ordinarily requires the rapist to marry the girl he raped, but in this case he is not permitted to do so. Hence we might have thought that the fine is not applicable. Accordingly, the Mishnah informs us that the girl is still entitled to

הַנְּתִינָה, [4] וְעַל הַכּוּתִית.

LITERAL TRANSLATION

with a *netinah*, [4] or with a *kutit*.

RASHI

נתינה — מן הגבעונים, והיא אסורה לקהל, דדוד גזר עליהם, כדאמרינן ביבמות (עח,ב). ועל שם "ויתנם יהושע חוטבי עצים ושואבי מים וגו'" (יהושע ט) קרי להו נתינים. **כותית** — קסבר: גירי אריות הן, וישנן בלאו "לא תתחתן בם" (דברים ז).

NOTES

does the Mishnah write: "If someone has intercourse, etc."? It should simply say: "The following *ne'arot* are entitled to a fine: The *mamzeret*, etc."

Shittah Mekubbetzet quotes the answer given by *Tosafot* that the Mishnah used this device in order to divide the *ne'arot* into three categories: Those whom the man is forbidden to marry, those who are suspected of having lost their virginity, and those who are forbidden to the man on pain of excision.

מַמְזֶרֶת A *mamzeret*. The Hebrew term *mamzer* (feminine: *mamzeret*) refers to a person born from relations between a married woman and a man other than her husband, or from relations between relatives who are forbidden to marry by Torah law, where the participants in such a relationship are subject to excision.

The Torah states (Deuteronomy 23:3) that a *mamzer* is not permitted to enter the congregation of the Lord unto the tenth generation (meaning forever; *Yevamot* 78b). This is understood to mean that a *mamzer*, male or female, may not marry a Jew of unblemished lineage. A *mamzer* is permitted, however, to marry a Jew of blemished lineage, since such a person is not considered to be a member of "the congregation of the Lord." Therefore, a *mamzer* may marry another *mamzer* or a *natin* (see next note), or a convert to Judaism (*Kiddushin* 69a). The offspring of such a marriage, however, are themselves *mamzerim*, not because the marriage is improper, but because of the Torah's decree that the status of the *mamzer* should remain unchanged.

A *mamzer* is considered his father's son in all respects, and is entitled to a full share in his inheritance, just like any other son (*Yevamot* 22a). Except for marriage (and a few matters directly related to lineage), the *mamzer* suffers no discrimination under Jewish law. Indeed, the Mishnah (*Horayot* 13a) rules that a *mamzer* who is a Torah scholar should be treated with even more respect than an ignorant High Priest.

הַנְּתִינָה A *netinah*. In the Book of Joshua (9:3-27), the story is told that one of the Canaanite tribes living in the vicinity of the town of Gibeon approached Joshua and tricked him into signing a treaty of friendship with them. Even after the scheme was discovered, the treaty was honored. But the Gibeonites were punished for their ruse by being "given" (וַיִּתְּנֵם — *vayitenem*, from the Hebrew root נתן — *natan*, meaning "to give"; verse 27) to the Temple as hewers of wood and drawers of water for perpetuity. The *netinim* (from the same Hebrew root), the descendants of the Gibeonites, appear to have survived as a distinct group until well after the destruction of the second Temple (see *Yevamot* 79b). The status of the *netinim* is mentioned in several places in the Talmud and is discussed in detail in tractate *Yevamot* (78b).

הַכּוּתִית A *kutit*. In II Kings (17:24-41) it is related that after the King of Assyria exiled the Ten Tribes of the northern kingdom of Israel (Samaria), he settled a mixed group of people from several other provinces of his empire on the land. These people met with difficulties at first, and suffered from an attack by lions. They decided that this was because they were not worshipping the local god, who dwelt in their new land. They then asked the King of Assyria to send them a priest from the Ten Tribes, to teach them about the local religion. The priest came and taught them the Torah, and as a result, they converted to Judaism. But they did not abandon all their former practices, and as a result, the Samaritan religion was a mixture of Judaism and pagan practices. The Samaritans themselves insisted that they were the legitimate heirs of the Ten Tribes, and attempted to be recognized as such by the Judeans at the beginning of the Second Temple period (Ezra 4:1-3). Perhaps by way of response, the Talmud always refers to these people as *kutim*, referring to the Asiatic province from which most of them originated, rather than as Samaritans. There is a collection of Baraitot, called "Tractate *Kutim*" (printed in the standard editions of the Talmud with the other so-called minor tractates at the end of the Order of *Nezikin*), which describes this sect's practices and how Jews should behave toward them. It begins: "*Kutim* sometimes behave like non-Jews and sometimes like Jews, but mostly they behave like Jews."

There is a Tannaitic dispute (*Kiddushin* 75b) as to whether the original conversion of the Samaritans to Judaism was valid, in spite of its unusual circumstances, or whether it was invalid (the term for this is אֲרָיוֹת — "converts by lions," referring to the attack which led to the conversion). According to the first view, the Samaritans are legally Jewish, although their behavior is extremely deviant. They are thus in a similar category to that of the Sadducees and other sectarian groups. According to the latter view, the Samaritans are legally non-Jews, although their practices are reminiscent of Jewish practices in many ways. In the end, it was decided during the Amoraic period that the Samaritans were to be treated like non-Jews in every way (*Hullin* 6a). But it is not entirely clear if this was because the Halakhah follows the view that they were never Jewish, or if this was the result of a later Rabbinic

HALAKHAH

witnesses failed to warn him, so that he is not lashed, he must pay the fine," following our Mishnah. (*Rambam, Sefer Nashim, Hilkhot Na'arah Betulah* 1:11; *Tur, Even HaEzer* 177.)

unmarried couple is not a *mamzer*. A *mamzer* inherits from his natural father and is Halakhically considered his father's son in all respects. A *mamzer* may marry only a *mamzeret* or a convert to Judaism. Likewise, a *mamzeret* may marry only a *mamzer* or a convert. The offspring of any of these unions is a *mamzer*.

CONCEPTS

כּוּתִית A *kutit*. A term used to describe the Samaritans, the non-Jews who settled in Samaria and the surrounding territory after the exile of the Ten Tribes. Though they converted to Judaism, they had ulterior motives for doing so (see II Kings 17), and were not scrupulous in their observance of the commandments. Accordingly, it was a matter of debate among the Sages whether they were considered Jews. In the Mishnah the Samaritans are given an intermediate status between Jews and non-Jews. In later generations they totally abandoned Jewish practices and the Sages decreed that they should be treated as non-Jews.

¹הַבָּא עַל הַגִּיּוֹרֶת, וְעַל הַשְּׁבוּיָה, וְעַל הַשִּׁפְחָה, ²שֶׁנִּפְדּוּ וְשֶׁנִּתְגַּיְּירוּ וְשֶׁנִּשְׁתַּחְרְרוּ פְּחוּתוֹת מִבְּנוֹת שָׁלֹשׁ שָׁנִים וְיוֹם אֶחָד.

LITERAL TRANSLATION

[1] [If] someone [forcibly] has intercourse with a female proselyte, or with a female captive, or with a female slave, [2] who were redeemed or were converted or were freed [when they were] less than three years and one day old.

RASHI

ועל השבויה — ישראלית שנפדית פחותה מבת שלש שנים, דבחזקת בתולה היא. שאפילו נבעלה בשביה — בתולים חוזרים.

TRANSLATION AND COMMENTARY

the fine, even though she must not marry the man.

הַבָּא עַל הַגִּיּוֹרֶת [1] The Mishnah continues: A *na'arah* is entitled to the fine provided that she was a virgin at the time she was raped. Therefore, **if someone rapes a** *na'arah* who has been **converted to Judaism, or a** *na'arah* who was taken **captive** but was later redeemed from her captors, **or a** non-Jewish **female slave** who was set free by her master, thereby becoming Jewish, [2] **and the conversion, or the release from captivity, or the emancipation took place when they were less than three years and one day old,** the *na'arah* is entitled to a fine of fifty shekalim from the rapist. The Torah imposes the fine only if the seduced girl or the raped girl was a virgin, but the women mentioned here are normally presumed to have lost their virginity: Proselytes are presumed to have engaged in sexual relations before converting; captive women are presumed to have been raped by their captors; and female slaves are presumed to have engaged in sexual relations. Nevertheless, the Mishnah rules that the *ne'arot* mentioned here are entitled to the fine. This is because they were converted, ransomed, or freed when they were no more than three years old. Under Torah law, a girl less than three years old is presumed to be physically incapable of intercourse. Moreover, any damage suffered by her hymen before that time is presumed to heal. Accordingly, the Mishnah informs us that they are entitled to the fine if they are raped, because since they attained the status of ordinary Jewish girls before their third birthday, they have not lost their legal presumption of virginity.

NOTES

decree. In the Mishnah and in tractate *Kutim*, however, the opinion that the Samaritans are deviant Jews predominates.

Rashi explains that our Mishnah follows the view that the Samaritans are non-Jews. But this explanation poses a difficulty, because the Gemara (above, 11a) clearly states that the fine for rape or seduction is not paid to a non-Jewish *na'arah*, even if she believed that she was Jewish at the time and behaved accordingly. This objection is addressed by later commentators (see *Meiri* and *Hafla'ah*).

Most Rishonim follow *Tosafot*, who explains that our Mishnah reflects the view that Samaritans are deviant Jews. This explanation finds support in the fact that the Gemara declares (below) that our Mishnah is in accordance with the viewpoint of Rabbi Meir, and in tractate *Bava Kamma* (38b) the Gemara concludes that Rabbi Meir is of the opinion that the Samaritan conversion was valid. This explanation also finds support in the Jerusalem Talmud. The difficulty with it is that, according to the opinion that the Samaritans are Jewish, it is obvious that they are entitled to a fine, since they were forbidden only because of their lineage and their status is no more unfavorable than the status of *mamzerim*. Thus there was no need to mention them separately. On the basis of the passage in *Bava Kamma, Tosafot* explains that in a number of cases the Samaritans were denied the status of Jews for the purpose of Jewish monetary laws, to punish them for their deviant behavior. Hence we might have thought that here too they should be treated as non-Jews, to make it clear that it is forbidden to intermarry with them. In fact, however, the Rabbis did not apply this principle in this case, because they did not wish to reward the rapist or the seducer for his crime.

הַבָּא עַל הַגִּיּוֹרֶת If someone forcibly has intercourse with a female proselyte. *Rashash* asks: The Mishnah considers three categories of problematic cases: Women whom the rapist is forbidden to marry, women whose virginity is in doubt, and women who are forbidden to the rapist on pain of excision. Why were these categories listed in this order? Would it not be more logical to list the women who are forbidden on pain of excision immediately after the other women whom the rapist is forbidden to marry, and only afterwards list the women whose virginity is in doubt?

Rashash answers that the women whose virginity is in doubt were placed immediately after the *mamzeret,* the *netinah,* and the *kutit* to teach us that although women in these categories are forbidden to marry Jews, they are in no way suspected of immodest behavior, and their virginity is not in doubt.

הַגִּיּוֹרֶת וְהַשְּׁבוּיָה וְהַשִּׁפְחָה A female proselyte, and a female captive, and a female slave. These three classes of *ne'arot* are not entitled to a fine if they were converted, ransomed, or freed after the age of three, because they are not considered virgins. This law is not to be confused with the law that a woman who converted to Judaism is disqualified from marrying a priest (*Yevamot* 61a). That is a matter of legal status that has nothing to do with the presumed

HALAKHAH

הַבָּא עַל הַגִּיּוֹרֶת If someone forcibly has intercourse with a female proselyte. "If someone rapes or seduces a *na'arah* who is a proselyte or a ransomed captive or a freed slave, and she was converted or ransomed or freed when she was less than three years and one day old, he must pay the fine," following our Mishnah. (*Rambam, Sefer Nashim, Hilkhot Na'arah Betulah* 1:10; *Tur, Even HaEzer* 177.)

BACKGROUND

הַגִּיּוֹרֶת וְהַשְּׁבוּיָה וְהַשִּׁפְחָה A female convert, and a female captive, and a female slave. Because of their past status, it is considered likely that these three types of women are no longer virgins, and a man who marries one of them cannot lodge a claim against her if she is not a virgin. The status of a captive is self-evident, given the neglect with which captives were treated, as beings subject to the will of their captors. It was assumed that the captor would rape all the women and girls he seized. As for the convert, the assumption is that while she was a non-Jewess she was in a society that did not observe a modest and moral way of life, because the values of her society did not recognize modesty as a moral or religious virtue. Thus, any kind of sexual contact might have been possible at any age, sometimes with the mutual consent of the parties involved. This was even more characteristic of women slaves, who did not practice true marriage, for the society of slaves was unrestrictedly promiscuous.

[1] הַבָּא עַל אֲחוֹתוֹ, וְעַל אֲחוֹת אָבִיו, וְעַל אֲחוֹת אִמּוֹ, וְעַל אֲחוֹת אִשְׁתּוֹ, וְעַל אֵשֶׁת אָחִיו, וְעַל אֵשֶׁת אֲחִי אָבִיו, וְעַל הַנִּדָּה, יֵשׁ לָהֶם קְנָס. [2] אַף עַל פִּי שֶׁהֵן בְּהִכָּרֵת, אֵין בָּהֶן מִיתַת בֵּית דִּין.

LITERAL TRANSLATION

[1] [If] someone [forcibly] has intercourse with his sister, or with his father's sister, or with his mother's sister, or with his wife's sister, or with his brother's wife, or with his father's brother's wife, or with a menstruating woman, they have a fine. [2] Although they are [punished] by excision, the death [penalty] of the court is not [imposed] on them.

RASHI

ועל אשת אחיו – שנתקדשה לו לאחיו, וגירשה, שאין בה מיתה אלא כרת. **ועל אשת אחי אביו** – שנתקדשה לו וגירשה. **אף על פי שהן בהכרת הרי אין בהם מיתת בית דין** – וכרת לא פטר ליה מן התשלומין.

TRANSLATION AND COMMENTARY

הַבָּא עַל אֲחוֹתוֹ [1] The Mishnah continues: Even if the seduction or rape of the *na'arah* was also a serious crime of another kind, such as incest, the fine is nevertheless imposed. In general, a person who commits a capital crime is not subject to any other penalties stemming from the same crime, and the next Mishnah (below, 36b) rules that if the illicit intercourse involved a category of incest that is subject to the death penalty, the fine is not imposed. Nevertheless, our Mishnah rules that **if someone rapes his sister, or his father's sister, or his mother's sister, or his wife's sister, or his brother's** widow or his brother's divorced **wife, or his father's brother's** widow or his father's brother's divorced **wife,** while any one of these forbidden relations was a *na'arah,* he must pay the fine, since these categories of incest are not subject to the death penalty. Likewise, if someone rapes **a menstruating *na'arah*, he must pay the fine,** because it is not a capital offense under Torah law to have intercourse with a menstruating woman, even though it is a serious sin that is compared to incest. The Mishnah explains that the cases listed here are different from the capital cases listed in the next Mishnah, [2] because **although** these transgressions **are punishable by** the severe penalty of **excision,** which is considered comparable to a death penalty, **they are not punishable by execution**, and the rule that a person who commits a capital crime cannot be forced to pay a fine for the same crime does not apply in a case of excision. Hence a man who rapes a menstruating woman or one of the relatives listed in this Mishnah while they are *ne'arot,* must pay the fine.

CONCEPTS

כָּרֵת **Excision.** A divine punishment for serious transgressions. The precise definition of the term is a matter of debate among the commentators. Among the characteristics of כָּרֵת mentioned are: (1) premature or sudden death; (2) barrenness and the death of the sinner's children; (3) the "cutting off" of the soul in the World to Come. The tractate *Keritot* mentions thirty-six transgressions punishable by כָּרֵת. With the exception of two — failure to bring the Paschal sacrifice and failure to perform circumcision — all the others are violations of negative commandments. כָּרֵת applies only to a person who intentionally commits a transgression. In certain instances, if the transgression was committed in the presence of witnesses, the transgressor is liable to execution by an earthly court, or to the penalty of lashes (מַלְקוֹת). Anyone who inadvertently transgresses one of the negative commandments punishable by כָּרֵת must bring a sin-offering as atonement.

NOTES

behavior of the woman in question, and it applies even if the girl converted before she was three years old (*Yevamot* 60b).

For most purposes, a freed slave has the same status as a convert. In this case, however, it is not entirely clear why we presume that a slave who was freed after the age of three has already lost her virginity, since the slave of a Jewish master, unlike a non-Jew, is subject to the laws of the Torah. The Gemara (*Gittin* 13a) states that in general slaves are known to be promiscuous. The Rishonim argue, however, that this law applies even where the slave was known to have behaved modestly, and they cite the Jerusalem Talmud to that effect.

A woman who was taken captive by bandits is presumed to have been raped by them unless she can prove otherwise (above, 22a). Hence a captive woman who was freed after the age of three is presumed to have lost her virginity. This law is one of the major subjects of the second chapter of this tractate.

The Halakhah considers a girl to be physically capable of intercourse from the age of three, and a boy from the age of nine (*Niddah* 44b-45a). Hence, a girl who was raped before the age of three is still considered a virgin, and any damage done to her hymen is assumed to have healed. Likewise, a boy who has intercourse before the age of nine is considered to have done nothing Halakhically significant. Because of this rule, if before the age of three a non-Jewish girl converted, or a slave was freed, or a captive woman was ransomed, they are considered virgins, as it was physically impossible for them to have lost their virginity before that time.

אֲחוֹתוֹ וַאֲחוֹת אָבִיו **His sister and his father's sister.** This is a partial list of the relationships of consanguinity and affinity that the Torah forbids as incestuous (Leviticus 18:3-19). All acts of incest are subject to the penalty of excision, but in some cases of incest the Torah imposes a death penalty as well (Leviticus 20:11-14). The idea of the double penalty is that if for some reason the court does not execute the offenders, God will punish them with excision. Our Mishnah follows the opinion that the fine for rape is imposed even if the forbidden intercourse is punishable by excision, but not if it is punishable by death. Accordingly, our Mishnah, which considers cases where the fine is applicable, lists the types of incest that are not subject to the death penalty, whereas the types of incest that are subject to the death penalty are listed in the next Mishnah, which considers cases where the fine is not applicable.

אֵשֶׁת אָחִיו וְאֵשֶׁת אֲחִי אָבִיו **His brother's wife and his father's brother's wife.** These two cases present a special problem: The fine is paid only if the raped woman was a virgin *na'arah*, whereas these women are married, and presumably no longer virgins. Under Jewish law a situation exists in which a married woman could remain a virgin. If she has performed the first stage of the marriage (*kiddushin* or "betrothal"), but not the second (*nissuin*), the woman is considered legally married, with all the consequences regarding adultery and incest, but she does not actually live with her husband. Accordingly, we must explain that the Mishnah is referring to a woman who had been betrothed to the rapist's brother or uncle and was divorced or widowed before being raped.

There is a second problem with these two cases: The Torah specifically refers to a man who rapes an *unbetrothed*

TRANSLATION AND COMMENTARY

GEMARA הָנֵי נְעָרוֹת [1]The Gemara begins by noting that the Mishnah wrote that "these are the *ne'arot* who have a fine," thus suggesting that only the *ne'arot* in this list and no others are entitled to the fine. But the Mishnah listed only problematic cases — women who are not permitted to marry ordinary Jews, or who are not thought to be virgins, or who are forbidden on the grounds of incest. On this point the Gemara asks: Are **these unfit *ne'arot*** the only ones who **are entitled to a fine,** [2]**whereas** *ne'arot* who are **permitted** to marry **are not?**

הָכִי קָאָמַר [3]The Gemara explains: The Mishnah has not prepared an exhaustive list of all the *ne'arot* who are entitled to a fine. **This is what** the Mishnah **is saying:** Permitted *ne'arot* who are raped are certainly entitled to a fine, but among those who are unfit, some are entitled and some are not, [4]and **the following are the unfit *ne'arot* who are entitled to a fine:** [5]**If someone rapes a *mamzeret*, or a *netinah*, or a *kutit*,** etc.

נַעֲרָה [6]The Gemara now makes another inference from the language used by the Mishnah. The Torah requires the fine to be paid if the raped girl was a virgin *na'arah*. This term refers to a stage in the girl's development between the age of twelve, when she becomes legally competent, and the age of twelve-and-a-half, when she achieves full sexual maturity. It is accepted by all authorities that fully mature women who are raped or seduced are not entitled to a fine, but it is not clear whether the Torah meant the law to apply only to *ne'arot* or also to girls under the age of twelve. The Mishnah, however, writes that "these are the *ne'arot* who have a fine." This clearly indicates that the author of the Mishnah is of the opinion that the offender must pay the fine only if he raped or seduced **a *na'arah*,** but **not** if he raped or seduced a **minor.** [7]On this point the Gemara asks: **Which Tanna** is the author of our Mishnah? Which Tanna is of the opinion that a man who rapes or seduces a minor does not pay a fine?

גמרא [1]הָנֵי נְעָרוֹת פְּסוּלוֹת אִית לְהוּ קְנָס, [2]כְּשֵׁירוֹת לָא? [3]הָכִי קָאָמַר: [4]אֵלּוּ נְעָרוֹת פְּסוּלוֹת שֶׁיֵּשׁ לָהֶם קְנָס: [5]הַבָּא עַל הַמַּמְזֶרֶת, וְעַל הַנְּתִינָה, וְעַל הַכּוּתִית. [6]נַעֲרָה — אִין; קְטַנָּה — לָא. [7]מַאן תַּנָּא?

LITERAL TRANSLATION

GEMARA [1]These unfit *ne'arot* have a fine, [2][but] fit ones [do] not?

[3]This is what he is saying: [4]These are the unfit *ne'arot* who have a fine: [5][If] someone [forcibly] has intercourse with a *mamzeret*, or with a *netinah*, or with a *kutit*.

[6]A *na'arah* — yes; a minor girl — no. [7]Who is the Tanna?

NOTES

virgin *na'arah*, and, according to some Tannaim, a woman who is already betrothed is not entitled to the fine, even if her marriage has not been consummated. Our Mishnah, however, follows the view of Rabbi Akiva, who rules (below, 38a), that a man who rapes a widowed or divorced virgin *na'arah* does pay the fine. According to Rabbi Akiva, the verse is to be interpreted as teaching us that where the virgin *na'arah* is not betrothed, the rapist pays the *na'arah*'s father, but where she is betrothed, he pays the *na'arah* herself rather than her father. *Tosafot* notes, however, that even according to Rabbi Akiva, the fine is paid only in cases of rape, not of seduction. *Rashi* points out that even according to Rabbi Akiva no fine is imposed so long as the woman is still married, as intercourse with such a woman is adulterous and subject to the death penalty, and we have already learned that the fine is not imposed where the death penalty applies.

There is yet another problem with the case of the man who rapes his brother's widow: The Jerusalem Talmud points out that since this widow is a virgin, it is obvious that she does not have any children. But if a man dies childless and his brother rapes his widow, the rape is not subject to a fine, as it amounts to a levirate marriage (Deuteronomy 25:5-10). For the Mishnah (*Yevamot* 53b) rules that a levirate marriage is effected by the sexual act alone, even if the parties do not wish to marry, or even if they are not aware of each other's identity. The Jerusalem Talmud explains that the Mishnah is referring to a case where the brother had children from another wife. Alternatively, *Tosafot* points out that it may be referring to a case where the brother has not died, but has divorced his wife.

הָנֵי נְעָרוֹת פְּסוּלוֹת **These unfit *ne'arot*.** *Shittah Mekubbetzet* asks: What is the Gemara's difficulty here? Surely it is obvious that the Mishnah is listing the problematic cases where we might have thought that the fine does not apply, and is not dealing with the straightforward cases where the fine clearly applies.

Ritva explains that the Mishnah began by saying: "*These* are the *ne'arot* who have a fine" — implying that all other *ne'arot* are not entitled to a fine. Hence the Gemara asks why ordinary, fit *ne'arot* were not included in the list.

Ramban asks: Not all the women in the Mishnah are unfit. The female proselyte is not normally described in this way, and the relatives are certainly completely fit. Why, then, does the Gemara describe them as unfit? *Shittah Mekubbetzet* suggests that the Gemara's question may have been directed at the first section of the Mishnah, dealing with the *mamzeret*, the *netinah*, and the *kutit*, rather than at the entire Mishnah. Support for this explanation can be found in the Gemara's answer, which explicitly mentions these three women, and does not include the word, "etc." Support can also be found in the language of *Rashi*.

Ramban answers that the Gemara uses the term "unfit" loosely, and means women whose status is problematic. This explanation is also followed by *Ritva*, and is followed in our commentary.

נַעֲרָה — אִין; קְטַנָּה — לָא **A *na'arah* — yes; a minor girl — no.** The Gemara's hypothesis is puzzling. For the Torah explicitly states that the girl was a *na'arah*, and yet, according to the Sages who disagree with Rabbi Meir, the

CONCEPTS

קְטַנָּה **A female minor.** A girl before puberty (Halakhically, puberty begins with the appearance of two pubic hairs), generally until the age of twelve. A female minor, like a male minor, is not considered a responsible person in the full juridical sense, and a number of particular laws apply to her. As long as she is a minor, her father may sell her to be a Hebrew maidservant; he may arrange a marriage for her, even without her consent (even while she is a *na'arah*), and such a marriage is valid in every respect. The father may also receive his minor daughter's marriage settlement and he alone has the right to accept her bill of divorce on her behalf. The father's rights over his daughter cease once she is fully married, even though she may still be a minor. The Sages decreed that the relatives (the mother or brothers) of a minor girl whose father has died may arrange a marriage for her but such a marriage is not entirely valid, and the minor girl may sever the bond by refusing to remain married. Sexual intercourse with a girl under three years old is not considered true intercourse for any legal purpose, but sexual intercourse with a minor girl above that age is considered Halakhically significant. Thus, a man who commits incest with a minor girl over the age of three is punishable, though the girl herself is not punished since she is not yet legally responsible for her acts. Intercourse with a girl over the age of three is a legally effective method of betrothal. The seduction of a girl who is a minor is not considered as seduction but as rape.

BACKGROUND

אֵלּוּ נְעָרוֹת פְּסוּלוֹת **These are the unfit *ne'arot*.** *Tosafot* notes that there are several types of unfit *ne'arot* who are entitled to a fine but who are not listed in our Mishnah. Likewise, several types of *ne'arot* who are not entitled to a fine are not listed in the next Mishnah. *Tosafot* explains that our Mishnah and the next are merely citing prominent examples, they are

LITERAL TRANSLATION

[1] Rav Yehudah said in the name of Rav: [2] It is Rabbi Meir, for it has been taught: [3] "A minor girl, from one day old until she produces two [pubic] hairs, [4] is subject to (lit., "has") sale, but does not have a fine.

[1] אָמַר רַב יְהוּדָה אָמַר רַב:
[2] רַבִּי מֵאִיר הִיא, דְּתַנְיָא:
[3] "קְטַנָּה, מִבַּת יוֹם אֶחָד וְעַד שֶׁתָּבִיא שְׁתֵּי שְׂעָרוֹת, [4] יֵשׁ לָהּ מֶכֶר, וְאֵין לָהּ קְנָס.

RASHI

גמרא רבי מאיר היא — כדמייתי ברייתא לקמיה. יש לה מכר — יש לאביה בה זכייה למכרה לשפחות. ואין לה קנס — שהבא עליה אינו חייב קנס.

TRANSLATION AND COMMENTARY

אָמַר רַב יְהוּדָה [1] **Rav Yehudah said in the name of Rav:** [2] **It is Rabbi Meir,** whose view **was taught** in the following Baraita, which draws a comparison between the law that a man who seduces or rapes a *na'arah* must pay a fine and the law that a father who is under great financial pressure can sell his daughter into semi-slavery, on the understanding that his daughter's master will either marry her himself or marry her to his son (Exodus 21:7-11). The Gemara (*Nedarim* 76a) proves that the latter law applies only to minors, but not to *ne'arot* or to mature girls, whereas it is clear from the Torah that the fine for rape applies specifically to *ne'arot.* [3] The Baraita states: "These two laws are mutually exclusive. **A minor girl, from one day old until she produces two pubic hairs** (at about the age of twelve), [4] **is subject to sale** by her father, **but she is not entitled to a fine** if she is raped. A *na'arah,* on the other hand,

not intended to be exhaustive lists. *Tosafot* notes that the Gemara (*Kiddushin* 16b) declares that when a Mishnah uses the expression, "these...," it is intended to be an exhaustive list. However, it would appear from another passage (*Zevaḥim* 84a) that this rule does not apply when the Mishnah gives two contrasting lists, as in our case.

SAGES

רַב יְהוּדָה **Rav Yehudah.** A Babylonian Amora of the second generation. See *Ketubot,* Part I, p. 8.

רַב **Rav.** A Babylonian Amora of the first generation. See *Ketubot,* Part I, pp. 42-43.

רַבִּי מֵאִיר **Rabbi Meir.** A Tanna of the generation before the completion of the Mishnah. See *Ketubot,* Part I, pp. 61-62.

NOTES

Torah did not mean to exclude minors, but only adult women, who are not entitled to a fine according to all opinions. Perhaps the Mishnah is following the same convention, and only means to exclude adults. Why should we assume that minors are excluded as well?

The commentators offer several solutions to this problem. *Tosafot* and other Rishonim explain that the Gemara is aware that the author of our Mishnah maintains that minors are not entitled to a fine, because this is stated explicitly in a later Mishnah in our chapter (below, 40b). The Gemara is merely using our Mishnah's wording as a convenient way of raising this question here.

Alternatively, *Ramban* explains that the Gemara here may be suggesting that our Mishnah chose the term *na'arah* expressly, because there is no syntactical need for this word at all in our Mishnah, which could have simply stated: "These have a fine." Hence we can assume that this word was included for purposes of definition, and it is unlikely that it was inserted merely in order to exclude adult women, since they are clearly excluded by the Torah. *Ḥokhmat Shlomo* adds that if the Mishnah had meant only to exclude adults and to include minors and *ne'arot,* it could have used the word "virgins" rather than *ne'arot.* Adult women are not considered complete virgins for many Halakhic purposes, because a certain amount of damage is sustained by the hymen as a result of the natural maturation process (below, 36a).

מַאן תַּנָּא **Who is the Tanna?** *Shittah Mekubbetzet* asks: Why does our Gemara find it necessary to establish that Rabbi Meir was the author of this anonymous Mishnah? We have a tradition that most anonymous Mishnayot follow the view of Rabbi Meir (*Gittin* 4a). Moreover, *Tosafot* (*Moed Katan* 2a) explains that the Gemara never asks who the author of a Mishnah is unless it has reason to assume that it was *not* written by Rabbi Meir (e.g., *Gittin* 3a). Why, then, does our Gemara ask this question here?

Shittah Mekubbetzet explains that there is, in fact, reason to believe that our Mishnah does not reflect the viewpoint of Rabbi Meir. According to *Rashi,* the clause in our Mishnah which refers to the *kutit* does not represent the viewpoint of Rabbi Meir, because it follows the view that Samaritans are not Jews, and Rabbi Meir is of the opinion that they are Jews. For this reason, the Gemara felt that it was important to establish explicitly that the clause in our Mishnah that excludes minors reflects Rabbi Meir's view.

מֶכֶר **Sale.** The Torah mentions two types of slaves: Canaanite slaves and Hebrew servants. A Canaanite slave is a non-Jew who was sold into slavery to a Jew, or the offspring of a Canaanite slave. They are considered their master's possessions, and they lose many of the rights that the Torah accords to non-Jews. The master may sell them to other people, and everything they acquire automatically belongs to their master. Whenever the word "slave" appears alone, the reference is always to Canaanite slaves.

Hebrew servants, by contrast, never enter into a state of absolute bondage, as do Canaanite slaves. In fact, they are somewhat like hired workers contracted for a long period. They retain all their obligations and rights as free people even while they are slaves. They may not be bought and sold, and they retain a right of acquisition of their own. But they are obliged to work for their master until their period of servitude ends.

A male Jew can become a Hebrew servant in one of two ways: Voluntarily, as a way of escaping poverty; or as a punishment for theft, if he is too poor to repay the stolen goods. In either case, the servant must serve for no more than six years, after which he is released. Upon his release, his former master must give him a sum of money to enable him to start a new life.

There is only one way for a Jewish woman to become a Hebrew maidservant, and that is if her father sells her into servitude (in order to give her a chance to escape a

HALAKHAH

יֵשׁ לָהּ מֶכֶר **Is subject to sale.** "A minor girl, from the day of her birth until she is twelve years old and has produced two pubic hairs, may be sold as a Hebrew maidservant by her father. However, after her twelfth birthday, if she has produced two pubic hairs, she may no longer be sold." (*Rambam, Sefer Kinyan, Hilkhot Avadim* 4:1.)

TRANSLATION AND COMMENTARY

[1] **from** the time **when she produces two pubic hairs** (at the age of twelve) **until she becomes mature** (at twelve-and-a-half), [2] **is entitled to the fine, but is not subject to sale.** [3] **This is the opinion of Rabbi Meir, for Rabbi Meir used to say:** [4] **Wherever there is a sale** — i.e., whenever the girl is of an age that entitles her father to sell her — **there is no fine** if she is raped, [5] **and wherever there is a fine, there is no sale.** According to Rabbi Meir, the fine and the sale are mutually exclusive. Just as the sale does not apply to *ne'arot,* the fine does not apply to minors. [6] **But the Sages say:** The two laws are not mutually exclusive. Rather, **a minor girl, from three years and one day old until she becomes mature,** at the age of twelve-and-a-half, **is entitled to the fine,** even though she can no longer be sold by her father once she reaches the age of twelve." This Baraita shows that there is a dispute between Rabbi Meir and the Sages as to whether a girl between three and twelve years old is entitled to a fine, and that our Mishnah, which states that only a *na'arah* is entitled to a fine, reflects the viewpoint of Rabbi Meir.

קְנָס [7] Before continuing its analysis of our Mishnah, the Gemara seeks to clarify the Baraita it has just cited. Rabbi Meir ruled in that Baraita that a minor girl up to the age of twelve is subject to sale by her father, and a *na'arah* from the age of twelve is entitled to the fine if she is raped. The Sages responded that the fine applies to a girl from the age of three until she reaches sexual maturity at the age of twelve-and-a-half. Perhaps the Sages agree with Rabbi Meir that the fine and the sale are mutually exclusive, but disagree with him about how old the girl must be when the sale ends and the fine begins — Rabbi Meir maintaining that the sale applies until the age of twelve, and the Sages maintaining that it applies only until the age of three. But if so, it would follow that, according to the Sages, a minor girl from the age of three is entitled to the **fine,** but is **not** subject to **sale!** But surely everyone agrees that a minor girl is subject to sale, until she becomes a *na'arah* at the age of twelve!

אֵימָא [8] The Gemara answers: We cannot infer from the wording of the Baraita that the Sages disagree with Rabbi Meir about the termination of the period during which a father is permitted to sell his daughter. Indeed, we cannot infer anything about the sale of a young girl from this Baraita, because the topic of the Baraita was the imposition of the fine, and the issue of the sale was introduced only for the sake of comparison. Rabbi Meir ruled that the fine applies only when the sale is not applicable, whereas the Sages **said** that the two laws are not connected. Therefore, a minor girl or a *na'arah,* from the age of three until the age of twelve-and-a-half, is entitled [29B] to **a fine, irrespective of whether there is a sale**. Thus the ages of three and twelve-and-a-half, specified by the Sages in the Baraita, relate

[1] וּמִשֶּׁתָּבִיא שְׁתֵּי שְׂעָרוֹת וְעַד שֶׁתִּיבָּגֵר, [2] יֵשׁ לָהּ קְנָס, וְאֵין לָהּ מֶכֶר. [3] דִּבְרֵי רַבִּי מֵאִיר. שֶׁהָיָה רַבִּי מֵאִיר אוֹמֵר: [4] כָּל מָקוֹם שֶׁיֵּשׁ מֶכֶר, אֵין קְנָס, [5] וְכָל מָקוֹם שֶׁיֵּשׁ קְנָס, אֵין מֶכֶר. [6] וַחֲכָמִים אוֹמְרִים: קְטַנָּה, מִבַּת שָׁלֹשׁ שָׁנִים וְיוֹם אֶחָד וְעַד שֶׁתִּיבָּגֵר, יֵשׁ לָהּ קְנָס״.

[7] קְנָס — אִין; מֶכֶר — לָא?

[8] אֵימָא: [29B] אַף קְנָס בִּמְקוֹם מֶכֶר.

LITERAL TRANSLATION

[1] And from when she produces two [pubic] hairs until she becomes mature, [2] she has a fine, but is not subject to sale. [3] [These are] the words of Rabbi Meir. For Rabbi Meir used to say: [4] Wherever there is a sale, there is no fine, [5] and wherever there is a fine, there is no sale. [6] But the Sages say: A minor girl, from three years and one day old until she becomes mature, has a fine."

[7] A fine — yes; a sale — no?

[8] Say: [29B] [There is] also a fine wherever there is a sale.

RASHI

ואין לה מכר — כדתניא (ערכין כט,ג): יכול ימכור אדם את בתו כשהיא נערה? אמרת קל וחומר: מכורה — כבר יוצאה, עכשיו שאינה מכורה — אינו דין שלא תמכר? **מבת שלוש שנים ויום אחד** — שהיא ראויה לביאה. **מכר לא** — בתמיה. **אף קנס במקום מכר** — ומשום קנס נקט בת שלש, אבל למכר — מבת יום אחד ועד שתביא שתי שערות.

CONCEPTS

וּמִשֶּׁתָּבִיא שְׁתֵּי שְׂעָרוֹת וְעַד שֶׁתִּיבָּגֵר And from when she produces two pubic hairs until she becomes mature. The Halakhah defines legal majority in terms of sexual maturity. Hence it is signalled by the growth of pubic hair ("two hairs"). Although this sign usually appears close to the age of adolescence (thirteen for a boy, twelve for a girl), it is merely the beginning of a process, which continues for a certain time until the child has indeed attained full sexual maturity (not, however, the completion of his or her physical or spiritual growth). According to the Halakhah, we assume that this period lasts no longer than six months. During the transitional stage children, especially girls, have a special Halakhic status. The girl is called a *na'arah,* and her father retains some authority over her, as when she was a minor. Special laws (regarding rape, or sexual promiscuity) also apply to the *na'arah* with respect to her sexual status. After six months have elapsed, the girl becomes mature (בּוֹגֶרֶת) and is entirely independent, and the laws applying to adult women apply to her.

NOTES

life of extreme poverty). The father may sell his daughter in this way only while she is still a minor, before she reaches the age of twelve. The master is expected either to marry the Hebrew maidservant himself or to marry her to his son. If he fails to do so before she reaches the age of twelve, or the six years of servitude expire, she must be given money and released, just like the male Hebrew servant (see Exodus 21:7-11, and see *Kiddushin* 14b-22b).

HALAKHAH

יֵשׁ לָהּ קְנָס Has a fine. "A virgin is entitled to a fine, if she is raped or seduced, from her third birthday until she achieves full sexual maturity at the age of twelve-and-a-half," following the Sages against the minority

TRANSLATION AND COMMENTARY

to the fine and not to the sale, and in fact the Sages agree with Rabbi Meir that the girl may be sold by her father from birth until the age of twelve.

וְהָנֵי [1] The Gemara now considers the substance of our Mishnah. The Mishnah ruled that a man who rapes a *na'arah* who is a *mamzeret* or a forbidden relative must pay a fine, even though he is not permitted to marry either one. **But,** the Gemara objects, **are these** forbidden *ne'arot* indeed **entitled to a fine,** as the Mishnah ruled? [2] **Why** should they be? [3] Surely we should **apply here** the Mishnah's interpretation of the following verse (Deuteronomy 22:29) which deals with a man who rapes a virgin *na'arah*. The verse says: **"And she shall be his wife,"** and this means that the rapist must marry the girl, even if he does not want to. Concerning this verse, the Mishnah (below, 39a) rules that the rapist must marry the *na'arah* even if he finds her unattractive, [4] but he may marry her only if she is **a woman who is fit** (Halakhically permitted) **for him.** But if a man rapes a *na'arah* who is a *mamzeret* or a relative whom he is forbidden to marry, this law does not apply. Now, since the law requiring the rapist to marry the girl does not apply, it would seem logical that the fine mentioned in the same passage should not apply either. Why, then, does our Mishnah state that the fine does apply in the case of a girl whom the rapist is forbidden to marry?

אָמַר רֵישׁ לָקִישׁ [5] The Gemara cites two quite similar solutions to this problem. Each of them interprets a seemingly superfluous word in the Biblical passages dealing with the rapist and the seducer as teaching us that the fine applies even in cases where the law requiring the rapist to marry the girl does not apply. **Resh Lakish said: *"Na'arah," "na'arah,"* "the *na'arah."*** The Hebrew word *"na'arah"* (נַעֲרָה), appears twice in the passage dealing with the rapist (Deuteronomy 22:28-29), once with the definite article and once without it ("If a man finds a virgin *na'arah*"; "and the man who lay with her shall give to the father of the *na'arah*"). [6] Resh Lakish explains: **One** mention of the word *na'arah* **is** needed **for itself,** to teach us that this law applies specifically to a girl between twelve and twelve-and-a-half years old, and if the passage had mentioned the word *"na'arah"* only once, we would have concluded that the fine need be paid only when the rapist is permitted to marry the *na'arah*. But the word appears a second time in the next verse, and

[1] וְהָנֵי בְּנֵי קְנָסָא נִינְהוּ? [2] וְאַמַּאי? [3] אִיקְּרֵי כָּאן: ״וְלוֹ תִהְיֶה לְאִשָּׁה״ — [4] אִשָּׁה הָרְאוּיָה לוֹ! [5] אֲמַר רֵישׁ לָקִישׁ: ״נַעֲרָה״, ״נַעֲרָה״, ״הַנַּעֲרָה״. [6] חַד לְגוּפֵיהּ,

LITERAL TRANSLATION

[1] But are these [*ne'arot*] entitled to a fine? [2] But why? [3] Read here: "And she shall be his wife" — [4] a woman who is fit for him!

[5] Resh Lakish said: *"Na'arah," "na'arah,"* "the *na'arah."* [6] One is for itself,

RASHI

ואמאי — יש להן קנס לנערות פסולות? **איקרי כאן כו'** — אמתניתין מקשי. הכי גרסינן: **נערה נערה הנערה** — באונס כתיב "כי ימצא איש נערה בתולה וגו'". וכתיב בתריה "ונתן האיש השוכב עמה לאבי הנערה", ודרשינן "נערה" יתירה, וה"א יתירה ד"הנערה", דמלי למיכתב "ונתן לאביה". **חד לגופיה** — לכשרה.

NOTES

וְהָנֵי בְּנֵי קְנָסָא נִינְהוּ But are these *ne'arot* entitled to a fine? *Shittah Mekubbetzet* notes that these words are lacking in many versions of the Talmud, including, apparently, *Rashi*'s. According to *Rashi*'s explanation (followed by our commentary), this clause does not seem to add anything to the Gemara's question. It would have been sufficient for the Gemara to say: "But why? Read here: 'And she shall be his wife' — a woman who is fit for him!" The introductory question: "But are these *ne'arot* entitled to a fine?" that appears in the standard version of the Talmud, seems to be superfluous.

Shittah Mekubbetzet suggests that these words may in fact be effecting a transition from the previous passage, in which we established that our Mishnah reflects the viewpoint of Rabbi Meir, who maintains that a minor is not entitled to a fine.

אִיקְּרֵי כָּאן וְלוֹ תִהְיֶה לְאִשָּׁה Read here: "And she shall be his wife." Our Gemara reflects the Mishnah (below, 39a) in citing this verse as the source of the law that the rapist must not marry the *na'arah* if she is forbidden to him. *Ritva* notes, however, that it is clear from a later passage (below, 40a), that the true source of this law is not this verse at all. On the contrary, the Gemara argues there that if we were to base our ruling on this verse alone, we would infer that the man is commanded to marry the *na'arah* in every case, even where she is forbidden. In fact, the source

HALAKHAH

opinion of Rabbi Meir. This is the ruling of *Rif, Rambam,* and *Rosh,* and it is followed by *Shulḥan Arukh. Rabbenu Ḥananel* and *Ra'avad,* however, rule that she is entitled to the fine only from the time she produces two pubic hairs until she achieves full sexual maturity, following Rabbi Meir, whose viewpoint is represented by the anonymous Mishnah. (*Rambam, Sefer Nashim, Hilkhot Na'arah Betulah* 1:8; *Shulḥan Arukh, Even HaEzer* 177:1.)

TRANSLATION AND COMMENTARY

moreover, it appears with the definite article. [1] **One** (the second mention of the word) **is** needed **to include those who are liable** to the penalty **for transgression of a negative commandment,** such as intercourse with a *mamzeret.* The additional mention of the word *"na'arah"* teaches us that the fine must also be paid if the girl was forbidden to the rapist, even though the law commanding him to marry her cannot apply because of the prohibition. This, however, is still not sufficient to teach us the law in all the cases mentioned in our Mishnah. For marriages prohibited by Torah law fall into two categories: Marriages that are legally binding but forbidden, and marriages that are null and void. If a man marries a woman who is forbidden to him by an ordinary negative (or positive) commandment, such as a *mamzeret,* the marriage is legally valid, and the woman cannot marry anyone else, on pain of the penalty for adultery. Nevertheless, the couple are forbidden to remain married, and the court will force them to divorce. But if a man goes through a marriage ceremony with a woman, such as a relative, who is forbidden to him under the severe penalty of excision or death, the marriage is null and void and no divorce is required. Our Mishnah ruled that the fine must be paid in both these cases, and if the word *"na'arah"* had appeared superfluously only once in the verse, we might have inferred that the fine must also be paid in those cases where the rapist could have married the *"na'arah"* but was forbidden to, but not in those cases where the rapist could not have married her at all. [2] However, the word *"na'arah"* appears the second time with an apparently unnecessary definite article, **and** we learn from this that **one** further mention of the word (i.e., the definite article, which is counted as an additional superfluous word) **is needed to include those who are liable to excision,** such as someone who has intercourse with a forbidden relative. The superfluous definite article teaches us that the fine applies even where the rapist cannot marry the girl at all, because such a marriage is null and void, and this is the source of our Mishnah's ruling.

רַב פַּפָּא [3] **Rav Pappa said: "Virgin," "virgins," "the virgins."** Rav Pappa's method of exegesis is identical to that of Resh Lakish, except that Resh Lakish focuses on the word *"na'arah"* in the passage dealing with the rapist, whereas Rav Pappa focuses on the word "virgin" (בְּתוּלָה), which appears twice in the Biblical passage dealing with the seducer (Exodus 22:15-16) — once with the definite article and once without it ("And if a man seduces a virgin"; "he shall pay money according to the dowry of the virgins"). [4] Rav Pappa explains: **One**

LITERAL TRANSLATION

[1] and one is to include [those who are] forbidden by negative commandments, [2] and one is to include [those who are] punished by excision.

[3] Rav Pappa said: "Virgin," "virgins," "the virgins." [4] One

[1] וְחַד לְאַתּוּיֵי חַיָּיבֵי לָאוִין,
[2] וְחַד לְאַתּוּיֵי חַיָּיבֵי כָּרֵיתוֹת.
[3] רַב פַּפָּא אֲמַר: "בְּתוּלָה", "בְּתוּלוֹת", "הַבְּתוּלֹת". [4] חַד

RASHI

בתולה בתולות הבתולות – במפתה כתיב "וכי יפתה איש בתולה". וקרא אחרינא בתריה "כסף ישקול כמוהר הבתולות". ומצי למיכתב "כמוהר בתולות" – הא תלת. דדרשינן ה"א יתירה, ו"בתולות", דמצי למיכתב "כמוהר" ולשתוק.

NOTES

of the law forbidding such marriages is a general principle that applies in many cases: The requirement to marry the *na'arah* conflicts with the prohibition against marrying her, and in such Halakhic conflicts the rule is that if there is some way to fulfill both requirements, the Torah expects us to do so. Now, in this case, the rapist is commanded to marry the *na'arah* only if she agrees. Hence the Torah in effect expects her to refuse permission, so that both requirements can be fulfilled. *Ritva* explains that our Gemara, and the Mishnah below (39a), cite this verse not as a genuine exegetical derivation but as a homiletic device, since it is less complex and easier to remember than the true source of the law (see also *Tosefot Rid*).

בְּתוּלָה בְּתוּלוֹת הַבְּתוּלוֹת "Virgin," "virgins," "the virgins." Our commentary follows *Rashi,* who explains that the exegesis is based on the repetition of the word "virgin" in the passage in Exodus, and on the fact that the second, superfluous mention of the word appears with the definite article. The Rishonim note that the second mention of the word is in the plural ("the dowry of virgins"), even though it could just as easily have been written in the singular ("the dowry of a virgin"), yet we learn nothing from the plural form. *Ritva* explains that the plural form is often used by the Torah, and exegetically nothing can be derived from it. Here, too, *Rabbenu Ḥananel* gives an alternative interpretation, according to which only the second mention of the word is being considered, and the exegesis is based on the Torah's use of the plural (cf. *Rabbenu Ḥananel*'s explanation in the previous note).

It is interesting that the Jerusalem Talmud quotes Resh Lakish (who in our Gemara derives these laws from the word *"na'arah"*) as deriving these laws from the plural form of the word "virgins." According to the Jerusalem Talmud, the argument is not based on superfluous words at all. Rather, Resh Lakish argues that if the word "virgin" had been in the singular, we would have said that the fine need be paid only if the virgin is a woman whom he is permitted to marry. But since the word appears in the plural, we may infer that all types of virgins fall within its purview.

BACKGROUND

חַיָּיבֵי לָאוִין וְחַיָּיבֵי כָּרֵיתוֹת Those forbidden by negative commandments and those punished by excision. There is a fundamental difference of opinion between Abaye and Rava at the beginning of tractate *Temurah* (4b) as to whether a prohibited act has legal validity. Indeed, in several places it is proved that according to all opinions — even those most rigorous in their interpretation of the ruling of Rabbi Akiva — not all forbidden marriages are null and void, and some forbidden marriages do have legal validity, so that the wife is not permitted to marry anyone else until she has been divorced from her husband.

The division between prohibitions that are forbidden by a negative commandment and prohibitions that carry a more severe penalty (excision or capital punishment) is not clear-cut (see *Yevamot* 5a).

It must be emphasized that the term *mamzer* is not defined in the Torah at all, and its meaning derives solely from the tradition of the Oral Law. Since the matter was not well-defined, there were great differences in understanding the term, from the extreme approach taken by Rabbi Akiva, who sees almost every child born of a forbidden marriage as a *mamzer,* to the view of Rabbi Yehoshua (in tractate *Yevamot*), that only the child of a union punishable by execution decreed by a court is defined as a *mamzer.*

SAGES

רַב פַּפָּא Rav Pappa. One of the leading Babylonian Amoraim of the fifth generation, Rav Pappa was a student of Abaye and of Rava, and was a colleague of Rav Huna the son of Rav Yehoshua. After Rava's death Rava's yeshivah was divided: part went to Pumbedita with Rav Naḥman bar Yitzḥak, and the other part went to Neresh with Rav Pappa. Rav Pappa's yeshivah was famous and had many students, and among his disciples were Rav Ashi and Ravina. He served as head of his yeshivah for nineteen years.

לְגוּפֵיהּ, [1]וְחַד לְאַתּוּיֵי חַיָּיבֵי לָאוִין, [2]וְחַד לְאַתּוּיֵי חַיָּיבֵי כָרֵיתוּת.
[3]וְרַב פַּפָּא מַאי טַעֲמָא לָא אָמַר כְּרֵישׁ לָקִישׁ?
[4]הַהוּא מִיבָּעֵי לֵיהּ לִכְדְאַבַּיֵי.
[5]דְּאָמַר אַבַּיֵי: בָּא עָלֶיהָ וּמֵתָה, פָּטוּר, [6]שֶׁנֶּאֱמַר: ״וְנָתַן לַאֲבִי הַנַּעֲרָה״. [7]לַאֲבִי נַעֲרָה, וְלֹא לַאֲבִי מֵתָה.
[8]וְרֵישׁ לָקִישׁ מַאי טַעֲמָא לָא אָמַר כְּרַב פַּפָּא?
[9]הַהוּא מִיבָּעֵי לֵיהּ לִגְזֵירָה שָׁוָה. [10]דְּתַנְיָא: ״׳כֶּסֶף יִשְׁקֹל

LITERAL TRANSLATION

is for itself, [1]and one is to include [those who are] forbidden by negative commandments, [2]and one is to include [those who are] punished by excision. [3]And what is the reason that Rav Pappa did not say like Resh Lakish? [4]That [verse] is needed by him for what Abaye [said]. [5]For Abaye said: [If] he had intercourse with her and she died, he is exempt, [6]as it is said: "And he shall give to the father of the *na'arah*." [7]To the father of a *na'arah*, but not to the father of a dead [person]. [8]And what is the reason that Resh Lakish did not say like Rav Pappa? [9]That [verse] is needed by him for a *gezerah shavah*. [10]For it has been taught: "'He shall pay money according

TRANSLATION AND COMMENTARY

mention of this word is needed **for itself,** to teach us that this law applies only to a virgin, and if the passage had mentioned the word "virgin" only once, we would have concluded that the fine has to be paid only if the seducer is permitted to marry the virgin. But the word appears a second time, in the next verse, and moreover, it appears there with the definite article. [1]**One** (the second mention of the word) **is** needed **to include those who are liable** to the penalty **for transgression of a negative commandment,** such as the commandment forbidding intercourse with a *mamzeret.* [2]Moreover, as with the term *"hana'arah"* in Resh Lakish's exegesis, the word "virgins" appears the second time with an unnecessary definite article, **and** we learn from this that **one** further mention of the word (i.e., the definite article, which is counted as an additional superfluous word) **is needed to include those who are liable to excision,** such as someone who has intercourse with a forbidden relative. The superfluous definite article teaches us that the fine applies even when the seducer cannot marry the virgin at all, and this is the source of our Mishnah's ruling.

וְרַב פַּפָּא [3]The two exegeses are identical, except for the series of words on which they focus. On this point the Gemara asks: **Why is it that Rav Pappa did not explain** our Mishnah **like Resh Lakish** did? Why did he focus on the word "virgin" rather than on the word *"na'arah"?*

הַהוּא מִיבָּעֵי לֵיהּ [4]The Gemara explains that Rav Pappa **needed** the extra mention of the word *"na'arah,"* including the definite article, **for** the following law **which Abaye says** is derived from this word. [5]**For Abaye said: If** the rapist or seducer **has intercourse with** the *na'arah,* **but** before he is ordered by the court to pay the fine **she dies, he is exempt** from paying, even though the girl's father, who was supposed to receive the fine, is still alive. [6]**For the verse says** (Deuteronomy 22:29): **"And he shall give** the fine **to the father of the *na'arah.*"** The verse could simply have said: "To her father." [7]The extra mention of "the *na'arah*" is intended to teach us that the rapist must pay the fine **to** the father only if he is still **the father of a *na'arah,* but not** if he is **the father of a dead girl.** Thus we learn that if the *na'arah* who has been raped dies before the payment of the fine, the fine need not be paid. Thus the second mention of the word *"na'arah"* is needed in order to teach us this important law, and is not superfluous, as Resh Lakish claimed.

וְרֵישׁ לָקִישׁ [8]The Gemara asks: **And why is it that Resh Lakish did not explain** our Mishnah **like Rav Pappa?** Why did he focus on the word *"na'arah"* rather than on the word "virgin"?

הַהוּא מִיבָּעֵי לֵיהּ [9]The Gemara explains that Resh Lakish **needed** the extra mention of the word "virgin," including the definite article, **for** the following ***gezerah shavah*** (a method of exegesis, according to which, when the Torah uses very similar words in two contexts, it intends to compare the subject matter in the two contexts, and to transfer information from one to the other). [10]**For it has been taught** in the following Baraita: "The Biblical verse (Exodus 22:16) requires a seducer to **'pay money according**

RASHI

ההוא מיבעי ליה — ההוא ״הנערה״, הא דלא כתיב ״ונתן לאביה״, מיבעי ליה לכדאביי, שאם לא הספיק האב להעמידו בדין עד שמתה — פטור. **לאבי הנערה** — משמע שהיא קיימת. **מיבעי ליה לגזירה שוה** — ״בתולה״ דכתיב גבי מפתה מיבעי ליה לגזירה שוה ״בתולה״ ״בתולה״. לגזירה שוה: מה ״כסף״ האמור באונס — חמשים אף מפתה — חמשים. ומה מפתה — שקלים, דכתיב ביה ״ישקול״, אף חמשים של אונס — שקלים קאמר.

HALAKHAH

בָּא עָלֶיהָ וּמֵתָה **If he had intercourse with her and she died.** "If someone rapes or seduces a *na'arah*, and before the court can consider the case the girl dies, he is exempt from paying the fine to her father." (*Rambam, Sefer Nashim, Hilkhot Na'arah Betulah* 1:15; *Tur, Even HaEzer* 177.)

SAGES

רֵישׁ לָקִישׁ **Resh Lakish.** Otherwise known as Rabbi Shimon ben Lakish, Resh Lakish was a leading Palestinian Amora of the second generation and a student, colleague, and brother-in-law of Rabbi Yoḥanan. See *Ketubot,* Part II, p. 59.

CONCEPTS

גְּזֵירָה שָׁוָה ***Gezerah shavah.*** This is a fundamental Talmudic principle of Biblical interpretation, appearing in all the standard compilations of exegetical rules. If the same word or phrase appears in two places in the Torah, and a law is explicitly stated in one of those places, we may infer, on the basis of a *gezerah shavah* ("verbal analogy") that the same law applies in the other case as well. Thus the inferences drawn on the basis of a *gezerah shavah* rely on verbal identity rather than on conceptual similarity. Usually inferences can be drawn by means of a *gezerah shavah* only if the same word (or phrase) appears in both of the verses being compared, although a *gezerah shavah* may occasionally be drawn even if the words being compared are not identical, provided that their meanings are similar (see *Yevamot* 17b). The *gezerah shavah* is not merely a type of linguistic interpretation, whereby the meaning of an obscure word or phrase is inferred on the basis of another occurrence of the same word or phrase in a clearer context. The *gezerah shavah* is used to "transfer" entire Halakhot from one place to another. It is therefore essential that it be used only when appropriate, if unfounded conclusions are not to be drawn. Accordingly, there are certain limitations on its use. Most significantly, "one cannot infer a *gezerah shavah* on one's own." Only a *gezerah shavah* based on ancient tradition is valid (*Pesaḥim* 66a; see also *Rashi*). A second condition required for making a *gezerah shavah* is that at least one of the words on which the *gezerah shavah* is based must be מוּפְנֶה — lit., "free, empty," i.e., unnecessary in its own context. In such cases we may justifiably assume

כְּמֹהַר הַבְּתוּלֹת׳. [1]שֶׁיְּהֵא זֶה כְּמוֹהַר הַבְּתוּלוֹת, וּמוֹהַר הַבְּתוּלוֹת כָּזֶה״.
[2]וְרֵישׁ לָקִישׁ נַמִי מִיבָּעֵי לֵיהּ לְכִדְאַבַּיֵי, [3]וְרַב פַּפָּא נַמִי מִיבָּעֵי לֵיהּ לִגְזֵירָה שָׁוָה!
[4]אֶלָּא, שִׁיתָּא קְרָאֵי כְּתִיבִי: [5]״נַעֲרָה״, ״נַעֲרָה״, ״הַנַּעֲרָה״, ״בְּתוּלָה״, ״בְּתוּלוֹת״, ״הַבְּתוּלֹת״. [6]תְּרֵי לְגוּפַיְיהוּ, [7]חַד לְכִדְאַבַּיֵי, [8]וְחַד לִגְזֵירָה שָׁוָה.

LITERAL TRANSLATION

to the dowry of virgins.' [1]That this should be like the dowry of virgins, and the dowry of virgins [should be] like this."

[2]But Resh Lakish also needs it for [the same purpose] as that of Abaye, [3]and Rav Pappa also needs it for a *gezerah shavah!*

[4]Rather, six expressions (lit., "verses") are written: [5]*"Na'arah," "na'arah", "the na'arah,"* "virgin," "virgins," "the virgins." [6]Two are for themselves, [7]one is for what Abaye [said], [8]and one is for a *gezerah shavah.*

RASHI

כמוהר הבתולות — חמשים כסף שהאונס נותן לאבי הבתולה. **שיהא זה** — חמשים כמוהר הבתולות. **ומוהר הבתולות** — יהיו שקלים כזה. **וחד לגזירה שוה** — ותהי מופנה מלד אחד, ולמידים הימנה.

TRANSLATION AND COMMENTARY

to the dowry of virgins.' [1]From here we learn **that this** fine **should be like the dowry of virgins, and that the dowry of virgins should be like this** fine." In other words, the verse teaches us that the fine paid by the seducer is the same as the fine paid by the rapist. In the passage in Deuteronomy dealing with rape, the Torah sets the fine of the rapist at fifty pieces of silver. Thus the *gezerah shavah* teaches us that both the seducer and the rapist must pay a fine of fifty silver shekalim. From this Baraita we learn, therefore, that the second mention of the word "virgin" is needed to teach us this important law, and is not superfluous, as Rav Pappa claimed.

וְרֵישׁ לָקִישׁ נַמִי [2]**But,** the Gemara objects, **Resh Lakish must also need** the second mention of the word *"na'arah"* **for the same purpose as that of Abaye,** who derived from this word that the fine is not paid if the *na'arah* dies. [3]**And,** continues the Gemara, **Rav Pappa must also need** the second mention of the word "virgin" **for the *gezerah shavah*** mentioned in **the Baraita,** which teaches us that the fine is fifty silver shekalim in both cases. How can Resh Lakish and Rav Pappa claim that the words they use for exegesis are superfluous when they are needed to teach us these important laws?

אֶלָּא [4]The Gemara answers: We must say **instead** that there is in fact no dispute between Resh Lakish and Rav Pappa, and each of them cited only half of a single complete exegesis. In fact, **six** pertinent **expressions are written** in the two passages: [5]***"Na'arah," "na'arah," "the na'arah"*** (the word *"na'arah"* appears twice in the passage dealing with the rapist, the second time with a definite article), and **"virgin," "virgins," "the virgins"** (the word "virgin" appears twice in the passage dealing with the seducer, the second time with a definite article). [6]Now, **two** mentions of these words (one of each) **are** needed **for themselves,** to teach us that these laws apply only to a *na'arah* who is a virgin. And if the passages had mentioned the words *"na'arah"* and "virgin" only once, I would have said that the fine has to be paid only where the rapist or seducer is permitted to marry the virgin *na'arah*. However, both words appear a second time, and moreover, they appear with definite articles, which is the equivalent of four superfluous words. [7]**One** mention **is** needed to teach us the law **that Abaye said** is derived from this word (that the fine need not be paid if the girl dies), [8]**and one** mention **is** needed **for the *gezerah shavah*** referred to in the Baraita cited above (which teaches us that the fine is set at fifty silver shekalim in both cases).

that this word was included for the express purpose of inferring a *gezerah shavah.* Where one or both of the words are not מוּפְנֶה, there is a Tannaitic dispute as to the effectiveness of the *gezerah shavah* (*Niddah* 22b). A third general rule governing the application of this principle states that אֵין גְּזֵירָה שָׁוָה לְמֶחֱצָה — "There cannot be half a *gezerah shavah*" (*Zevaḥim* 48a). In other words, there is no limit to the amount of information that can be transferred by a *gezerah shavah*, and if inferences are drawn from case A to case B, we may also draw conclusions from case B to case A. There is, however, an unresolved question as to whether a *gezerah shavah* can be used to transfer teachings that were not explicitly included in the original verse but were themselves derived by some other hermeneutic rule (*Zevaḥim* 51a).

NOTES

שֶׁיְּהֵא זֶה כְּמוֹהַר הַבְּתוּלוֹת That this should be like the dowry of virgins. Our commentary follows *Rashi*, who explains that the *gezerah shavah* teaches us that the laws appearing in the verse dealing with the rapist and in the verse dealing with the seducer should be equated. According to this explanation, the expression "this" refers to the fine paid by the rapist, which is to be equated with "the dowry of virgins," the fine paid by the seducer. *Rashi* explains that we derive the *number* of coins to be paid from the verse dealing with the rapist, and the *value* of the coins from the verse dealing with the seducer, and apply the combined result to both cases, using the *gezerah shavah*. The Rishonim explain that the *gezerah shavah* is also the source of the rule (stated explicitly by the Gemara below, 39b) that all the laws that apply to the seducer apply to the rapist, and vice versa (see *Rashi, Tosafot, Ritva*).

HALAKHAH

שֶׁיְּהֵא זֶה כְּמוֹהַר הַבְּתוּלוֹת That this should be like the dowry of virgins. "Whether a man seduces a *na'arah* or rapes her, the fine is the same: fifty sela'im of pure silver." (*Rambam, Sefer Nashim, Hilkhot Na'arah Betulah* 1:1; *Tur, Even HaEzer* 177).

LITERAL TRANSLATION

[1] Two remain superfluous. [2] One is to include [those who are] forbidden by negative commandments, [3] and one is to include [those who are] punished by excision.

[4] And it [our Mishnah] is to exclude [the opinion] of the following Tanna. [5] For it has been taught: "'And she shall be his wife.' [6] Shimon HaTimni says: A woman in whom there is 'being.' [7] Rabbi Shimon ben Menasya says: A woman who is fit [for him] to retain her."

[1] אִיַּיתְרוּ לֵיהּ תְּרֵי. [2] חַד לְאַתּוּיֵי חַיָּיבֵי לָאוִין, [3] וְחַד לְאַתּוּיֵי חַיָּיבֵי כָּרֵיתוֹת.

[4] וּלְאַפּוּקֵי מֵהַאי תַּנָּא. [5] דְּתַנְיָא: "'וְלוֹ תִהְיֶה לְאִשָּׁה'. [6] שִׁמְעוֹן הַתִּימְנִי אוֹמֵר: אִשָּׁה שֶׁיֵּשׁ בָּהּ 'הֲוָיָה'. [7] רַבִּי שִׁמְעוֹן בֶּן מְנַסְיָא אוֹמֵר: אִשָּׁה הָרְאוּיָה לְקַיְּימָהּ".

RASHI

ולאפוקי מהאי תנא — מתניתין דקתני: יש קנס לממזרת ולאחותו — לאפוקי מהאי תנא. **שיש בה הויה** — שקדושין תופסין לו בה, פרט לאחותו ולכל חייבי כריתות, דילפינן בקדושין שאין קדושין תופסין בהן, בפרק שלישי (סז,ב). ומשמע ליה "תהיה" לשון הוית קדושין. ורבי שמעון בן מנסיא משמע ליה "תהיה" — לשון קיום.

TRANSLATION AND COMMENTARY

[1] We thus find that the equivalent of **two superfluous words remains.** [2] **One** word **is** needed **to include those who are liable** to the penalty **for transgression of a negative commandment,** such as the commandment forbidding intercourse with a *mamzeret*. The additional mention of the word teaches us that the fine must also be paid if the rapist or the seducer is forbidden to marry the virgin *na'arah*. However, we might have thought that this applies only if he could have married the forbidden girl, albeit illegally. [3] Therefore, we have the equivalent of **one** more superfluous word whose purpose **is to include those who are subject to excision,** such as someone who has intercourse with a relative. The last superfluous word teaches us that the fine applies even if the rapist or the seducer cannot enter into a marital relationship with the *na'arah* at all. Accordingly, we learn that the fine must be paid even when the law requiring the rapist to marry the *na'arah* does not apply, and this is the source of our Mishnah's ruling.

וּלְאַפּוּקֵי מֵהַאי תַּנָּא [4] We have now established that according to our Mishnah a man who seduces or rapes a virgin *na'arah* must pay the fine, even if he is forbidden to marry her. The Gemara notes that the Tanna whose viewpoint is represented in our Mishnah **disagrees with the following Tannaim** about this matter, because they maintain that a man who rapes or seduces a girl whom he is forbidden to marry need not pay the fine. [5] **For it has been taught** in the following **Baraita:** "The Biblical verse (Deuteronomy 22:29) states: **'And she shall be his wife.'** This means that the rapist must marry the girl he raped. [6] Commenting on this verse, **Shimon HaTimni says:** This law applies only to **a woman in whom there is 'being.'** The term 'being' is traditionally understood to refer to a marriage taking effect. Thus Shimon HaTimni understands the verse to be saying that this law applies only if the man could have married the girl, albeit illegally. But if the girl is a relative, with whom a marriage would be null and void, this law does not apply and the fine need not be paid. [7] **Rabbi Shimon ben Menasya says:** We should not interpret the expression 'being' in this verse as referring to a marriage taking effect, but we should interpret the verse as commanding the man to keep the girl as a wife. Thus the law applies only to **a woman who is fit for him to retain** — a woman whom he is legally permitted to marry and is not required to divorce, but not to a woman who is forbidden to him. Thus, according to Rabbi Shimon ben Menasya, the fine need not be paid if the marriage would be illegal even though it would be binding.

SAGES

שִׁמְעוֹן הַתִּימְנִי Shimon HaTimni. A Tanna of the generation of Rabbi Akiva, Shimon HaTimni is named after his native town, Timnah, in Judea. He was one of the most important Sages of the Sanhedrin in Yavneh and numbered among the few who understood seventy languages. His teachers were Rabbi Yehoshua and Rabbi Akiva, and we sometimes find him disagreeing with them.

Most of the reletively few teachings presented in his name in the Mishnah and in Baraitot refer to matters of Halakhah, and only a few of them are Aggadic.

Shimon HaTimni was apparently an important Sage in his hometown of Timnah, though he seems to have spent much of his time in the House of Study in Yavneh.

רַבִּי שִׁמְעוֹן בֶּן מְנַסְיָא Rabbi Shimon ben Menasya. A Tanna of the fifth generation. See *Ketubot*, Part I, p. 193.

NOTES

אִשָּׁה שֶׁיֵּשׁ בָּהּ הֲוָיָה A woman in whom there is "being." According to all opinions, certain forbidden marriages are null and void from the outset and do not require a formal divorce to be dissolved. The Mishnah (*Kiddushin* 66b) links this idea with the concept of *mamzerim*, declaring that the offspring of a marriage are *mamzerim* only if the marriage is null and void. *Tosafot* notes that it is clear from many sources in the Talmud that, according to all opinions, if an illegal relationship is such that the offspring are *mamzerim*, the marriage is null and void with no need for divorce. The converse, however, is not true: It is possible for a marriage to be null and void, and for the offspring not to be *mamzerim* (indeed, the Mishnah in *Kiddushin* mentions such a case).

In tractate *Yevamot* (49a), there is a Tannaitic dispute (which forms the background to our passage) as to which illegal relationships produce *mamzerim* and which do not. To understand the implications of this dispute for our Gemara, it is important to keep in mind the assymmetrical relationship between *mamzerim* and void marriages: all marriages that produce *mamzerim* are void, but not all void marriages necessarily produce *mamzerim*. According to Rabbi Akiva, even the offspring of relationships that are forbidden by an ordinary negative commandment are *mamzerim*; hence it follows that such marriages are void. According to Rabbi Yehoshua, only the offspring of adulterous and incestuous relationships punishable by the death penalty are *mamzerim*, although Rabbi Yehoshua agrees that incestuous marriages that are penalized by excision alone are also void. According to the accepted Halakhah, which follows Shimon HaTimni, the offspring of all adulterous or incestuous relationships that are punishable by excision or by the death penalty are *mamzerim*, and all such marriages are void. However, even according

TRANSLATION AND COMMENTARY

מַאי בֵּינַיְיהוּ **[1]The Gemara asks: These two** Tannaim both disagree with our Mishnah, and they evidently disagree with each other as well. **What is the substantive issue over which they differ?** In which case would Shimon HaTimni say that the fine applies and Rabbi Shimon ben Menasya say that it does not?

אָמַר רַבִּי זֵירָא **[2]Rabbi Zera said** in reply: **They differ over a** *mamzeret* **and a** *netinah,* women whom a Jew is forbidden to marry under penalty of transgressing a negative commandment. Such marriages are forbidden but valid. **[3]Hence, according to** Shimon HaTimni, **who says:** "He need pay the fine only if she is **a woman in whom there is 'being,'"** a man who rapes a *mamzeret* or a *netinah* must pay the fine, **[4]since there is "being" in** a *mamzeret* and a *netinah.* Although forbidden, the marriage is valid, and the couple must divorce. Thus, according to Shimon HaTimni, this case is not excluded by the verse. **[5]But according to** Rabbi Shimon ben Menasya, **who says:** "He need pay the fine only if she is **a woman who is fit for him to retain,"** a man who rapes a *mamzeret* or a *netinah* need not pay the fine, **[6]since a** *mamzeret* **and a** *netinah* **are not fit for him to retain.** Although a marriage with a *mamzeret* or a *netinah* is not void, it is nevertheless strictly forbidden and the couple must divorce. Thus, according to Rabbi Shimon ben Menasya, such women are excluded from the purview of this law.

וּלְרַבִּי עֲקִיבָא **[7]The Gemara asks:** This explanation is satisfactory provided that Shimon HaTimni and Rabbi Shimon ben Menasya accept the majority viewpoint that marriages that are forbidden under an ordinary negative commandment (such as a marriage between an unblemished Jew and a *mamzeret* or a *netinah*) are valid though illegal. **But according to Rabbi Akiva, who** in a minority opinion **said: "Betrothal** (the first stage of marriage) **does not take effect** at all where **those** involved **are liable** to the penalty **for transgressing a negative commandment,** and such unions are null and void and require no divorce," **[8]what is the issue over which they differ?** According to Rabbi Akiva, there is no difference between women forbidden by an ordinary negative commandment and women forbidden on pain of excision. In either case, the union is null and void without any need for divorce. Therefore, if Shimon HaTimni and Rabbi Shimon ben Menasya were to agree with Rabbi Akiva, there would be no case where a woman would "have 'being'" but would be forbidden to be retained.

LITERAL TRANSLATION

[1]What is [the difference] between them? [2]Rabbi Zera said: There is [a difference] between them [regarding] a *mamzeret* and a *netinah.* [3][According] to the one who says: "[A woman] in whom there is 'being,'" [4]in this one too there is "being." [5][According] to the one who says: "[A woman] who is fit [for him] to retain her," [6]this one is not fit [for him] to retain her. [7]But [according] to Rabbi Akiva who said: "Betrothal does not take effect between those who are forbidden by negative commandments," [8]what is [the difference] between them?

מַאי בֵּינַיְיהוּ?

²אָמַר רַבִּי זֵירָא: מַמְזֶרֶת וּנְתִינָה אִיכָּא בֵּינַיְיהוּ. ³לְמַאן דְּאָמַר: "יֵשׁ בָּהּ 'הֲוָיָה'", ⁴הָא נַמִי יֵשׁ בָּהּ "הֲוָיָה". ⁵לְמַאן דְּאָמַר: "רְאוּיָה לְקַיְּימָהּ", ⁶הָא אֵינָהּ רְאוּיָה לְקַיְּימָהּ. ⁷וּלְרַבִּי עֲקִיבָא דַּאֲמַר: "אֵין קִדּוּשִׁין תּוֹפְסִין בְּחַיָּיבֵי לָאוִין", ⁸מַאי בֵּינַיְיהוּ?

RASHI

הָא נַמִי אִית בָּהּ הֲוָיָה — דְּקִדּוּשִׁין תּוֹפְסִין בְּחַיְיבֵי לָאוִין, וְהַס יַלִּיף לָהּ. וּלְרַבִּי עֲקִיבָא דְּאָמַר אֵין קִדּוּשִׁין תּוֹפְסִין בְּחַיְיבֵי לָאוִין — בִּיבָמוֹת בְּ"הָחוֹלֵץ" (מד,ב) בִּבְרַיְיתָא: הַמֵּזִיר גְּרוּשָׁתוֹ, רַבִּי עֲקִיבָא אוֹמֵר: אֵין לוֹ בָהּ קִדּוּשִׁין. מַאי בֵּינַיְיהוּ — מִשּׁוּם רַבִּי שִׁמְעוֹן בֶּן מְנַסְיָא קָא פָרֵיךְ לָהּ. דְּאִילוּ שִׁמְעוֹן הַתִּימְנִי שַׁמְעִינַן לֵיהּ בִּיבָמוֹת (מט,א) דְּפָלִיג עֲלֵיהּ דְּרַבִּי עֲקִיבָא בְּהָא. דִּתְנַן: אֵיזֶהוּ מַמְזֵר — כָּל שְׁאֵר בָּשָׂר שֶׁהוּא בְּ"לֹא יָבֹא", דִּבְרֵי רַבִּי עֲקִיבָא. שִׁמְעוֹן הַתִּימְנִי אוֹמֵר: כָּל שֶׁחַיָּיבִין עָלָיו כָּרֵת בִּידֵי שָׁמַיִם. אֶלָּא לְרַבִּי שִׁמְעוֹן בֶּן מְנַסְיָא קָא בָעֵינַן לָהּ, אִי סְבִירָא לֵיהּ כְּרַבִּי עֲקִיבָא — מַאי אִיכָּא בֵּין מַשְׁמָעוּתָא דְּ"תְּהֵיהּ" לְשׁוֹן קִיּוּם, לְמַשְׁמָעוּתָא דִּשְׁמְעוֹן הַתִּימְנִי? אִי נַמִי, מִשְׁמַע לֵיהּ לְרַבִּי שִׁמְעוֹן בֶּן מְנַסְיָא לְשׁוֹן הֲוָיָה אִימְּעֵיטָא לָהּ מַמְזֵר, וּמַה בֵּין רְאוּיָה לְקַיְּימָהּ לְיֵשׁ בָּהּ הֲוָיָה?

NOTES

to Shimon HaTimni, there are some marriages that are void without the offspring being *mamzerim.* Thus a marriage between a Jew and a non-Jew or between a Jew and a slave is void, yet the Halakhah is that their offspring are not *mamzerim* (*Yevamot* 45a). In addition, according to some Amoraim, if a woman who is subject to a levirate marriage marries someone else before being released by her brother-in-law through the *ḥalitzah* ceremony, the marriage is void, yet the offspring of such a relationship are not *mamzerim,* according to Shimon HaTimni (*Yevamot* 92b).

וּלְרַבִּי עֲקִיבָא **But according to Rabbi Akiva.** The Gemara investigates whether the dispute between Shimon HaTimni and Rabbi Shimon ben Menasya can be explained according to all opinions. *Rashi* and *Tosafot* ask: Why does the Gemara attempt to explain this Baraita according to Rabbi Akiva? It is obvious that the Tannaim cited in this Baraita disagree with Rabbi Akiva, since Shimon HaTimni himself took part in the dispute with Rabbi Akiva about the validity of forbidden marriages (*Yevamot* 49a), arguing that only the offspring of relationships penalized by excision are *mamzerim.* Why, then, should the Gemara attempt to reconcile his view here with that of Rabbi Akiva?

SAGES

רַבִּי זֵירָא **Rabbi Zera.** An Amora of the third generation. See *Ketubot,* Part I, p. 46.

רַבִּי עֲקִיבָא **Rabbi Akiva.** The great Tanna of the fourth generation. See *Ketubot,* Part II, p. 206.

TERMINOLOGY

מַאי בֵּינַיְיהוּ **What is the difference between them?** When the Gemara records a difference of opinion about the reason for a law or the definition of a legal concept, it often asks: "What practical difference is there between the reasons or definitions cited in the previous passage?" The answer to this question is introduced by the expression אִיכָּא בֵּינַיְיהוּ — "The difference between them is...."

[1]אִיכָּא בֵּינַיְיהוּ אַלְמָנָה לְכֹהֵן גָּדוֹל, כְּרַבִּי סִימַאי. [2]דְּתַנְיָא: "רַבִּי סִימַאי אוֹמֵר: [3]מִן הַכֹּל עוֹשֶׂה רַבִּי עֲקִיבָא מַמְזֵרִין, [4]חוּץ מֵאַלְמָנָה לְכֹהֵן גָּדוֹל, [5]שֶׁהֲרֵי אָמְרָה תּוֹרָה: 'לֹא יִקָּח....וְלֹא יְחַלֵּל'. [6]חִילּוּלִין הוּא עוֹשֶׂה, וְאֵין עוֹשֶׂה מַמְזֵרִין".

LITERAL TRANSLATION

[1]There is [a difference] between them [regarding] a widow in relation to a High Priest, in accordance with Rabbi Simai. [2]For it has been taught: "Rabbi Simai says: [3]Rabbi Akiva makes *mamzerim* of all, [4]except for [the child of] a widow and a High Priest, [5]for the Torah said: 'He shall not take....And he shall not profane.' [6]He makes [his children] profane, but he does not make [them] *mamzerim*."

TRANSLATION AND COMMENTARY

אִיכָּא בֵּינַיְיהוּ [1]The Gemara answers: Even according to Rabbi Akiva, **there is a difference between them regarding a widow** who was raped by **a High Priest** or a divorcee who was raped by an ordinary priest. There is a negative commandment forbidding a High Priest from marrying a widow, or an ordinary priest from marrying a divorcee (Leviticus 21:7,14), and in this case even Rabbi Akiva agrees that if the priest violates the law and marries the forbidden woman, the marriage is valid, even though the couple must divorce. Hence we have one instance of a woman who "has 'being,'" but whom it is forbidden to retain, even according to Rabbi Akiva. Therefore, if a High Priest were to rape a widow, or an ordinary priest were to rape a divorcee, both would be liable to pay the fine, according to Shimon HaTimni, but not according to Rabbi Shimon ben Menasya. The Gemara continues to explain why the case of the widow and the High Priest and the case of the divorcee and the ordinary priest are different from those of all other women who are forbidden by an ordinary negative commandment. In this explanation, says the Gemara, we are **following Rabbi Simai's** interpretation of the viewpoint of Rabbi Akiva. [2]**For it has been taught** in the following Baraita: **"Rabbi Simai says:** [3]**From every** illegal relationship **Rabbi Akiva makes *mamzerim*.** Not only does Rabbi Akiva say that the offspring of incestuous or adulterous relationships are *mamzerim* (as is the case according to the accepted Halakhah), but even the children of relationships that are forbidden by negative commandments fall in this category. [4]This is true of all relationships that are forbidden by negative commandments, **except for** that of **a widow** who marries **a High Priest**, or that of a divorcee who marries an ordinary priest. [5]**For** in the case of the High Priest **the Torah said** (Leviticus 21:14-15): **'He shall not take** a widow....**And he shall not profane** his children.' [6]And from here we learn that if he does take a widow as a wife, **he makes his children profane** (i.e., they become *ḥalalim* — disqualified from the priesthood) **but he does not make them *mamzerim*."** Since the offspring are not *mamzerim*, the marriage itself is not void, and can be dissolved only by means of a divorce. Therefore, if a High Priest marries a widow, the marriage is valid although it is illegal, even according to Rabbi Akiva. Hence, in such a case, we have a woman who "has 'being,'" but is forbidden to be retained, even according to Rabbi Akiva. Therefore, if a High Priest were to rape a widow, or an ordinary priest were to rape a divorcee, they would be liable to pay the fine, according to Shimon HaTimni, but not according to Rabbi Shimon ben Menasya.

RASHI

אלמנה לכהן גדול — דמודה בה רבי עקיבא שקדושין תופסין לו בה, ואף על פי שהיא בלאו, וכרבי סימאי. והוא הדין גרושה להדיוט. **מן הכל** — כל הנולדים מחייבי לאוין. **לא יקח** — וסמיך ליה "ולא יחלל זרעו" — מדין כהונה הוא מחללו, ולא שם ממזרים עליהם.

SAGES

רַבִּי סִימַאי Rabbi Simai. A Tanna mentioned in Baraitot and Midrashim, Rabbi Simai was apparently one of the last Tannaim, a young contemporary of Rabbi Yehudah HaNasi. His Halakhic and Aggadic teachings are found in both the Babylonian and the Jerusalem Talmud. He seems to have outlived Rabbi Yehudah HaNasi, for some of the early Amoraim were his disciples and transmit his teachings. Rabbi Simai's son, Rabbi Menaḥem, was also a Sage, and he was known as בְּנָן שֶׁל קְדוֹשִׁים — "the son of holy men."

NOTES

Rashi and *Tosafot* answer that the Gemara is primarily interested in Rabbi Shimon ben Menasya, who may well agree with Rabbi Akiva. *Ra'ah* adds that this is actually quite likely, since Rabbi Shimon ben Menasya's opponent in this Baraita is Shimon HaTimni, who is the main opponent of Rabbi Akiva on questions of marital status. Hence the Gemara asks: According to Rabbi Akiva, there is no difference between a woman who is fit to be retained and a woman in whom there is "being." So if Rabbi Shimon ben Menasya agrees with Rabbi Akiva, why does he make a point of disagreeing with Shimon HaTimni's exegesis?

Alternatively, *Ra'ah* explains that the Gemara is not objecting to the Baraita per se, since the Gemara knows that the Baraita does not reflect the viewpoint of Rabbi Akiva. Rather, the Gemara is asking whether those who rule in favor of Rabbi Akiva would find the exegetical dispute in this Baraita relevant, or whether it would have no significance for them.

חִילּוּלִין הוּא עוֹשֶׂה He makes his children profane. Among the women whom a priest is forbidden to marry (as related in Leviticus 21:7) is the *ḥalalah* (lit., "profane woman"). A few verses later (21:15), the Torah states that a High Priest must not violate these commandments, "so that he shall not profane his children." From here we learn that the father of the *ḥalalah* is a priest who has married a woman whom a priest is forbidden to marry (*Kiddushin* 77a).

In our explanation of Rabbi Simai's viewpoint, we have followed *Rashi*, who explains that although the Baraita mentioned only a High Priest who marries a widow, and the Gemara follows the same convention throughout the passage, Rabbi Simai's argument also applies to an ordinary priest who marries a divorcee, whose offspring are also not *mamzerim*. *Shittah Mekubbetzet* explains that

TRANSLATION AND COMMENTARY

וּלְרַבִּי יְשֵׁבָב [1]The Gemara asks: This explanation is satisfactory provided that Shimon HaTimni and Rabbi Shimon ben Menasya both accept the viewpoint of Rabbi Simai, who maintains that even Rabbi Akiva agrees that the children of a priest who marries a divorcee or of a High Priest who marries a widow are not *mamzerim*. **But** this is only one version of Rabbi Akiva's position. What can we say **according to Rabbi Yeshevav, who said: "Come and let us cry out against Akiva ben Yosef** for unjustly categorizing people as *mamzerim*. [2]**For he has been saying: The offspring of any couple who must not have intercourse according to Jewish law** — i.e., the offspring of any forbidden relationship, including a priest with a divorcee or a High Priest with a widow — **is a *mamzer*.'"** Rabbi Yeshevav understood Rabbi Akiva as saying that the offspring of any illegal marriage is a *mamzer*. Although Rabbi Yeshavav personally disagreed with this viewpoint, he clearly insisted that this was Rabbi Akiva's authentic position. [3]According to Rabbi Yeshevav's understanding of Rabbi Akiva, **what is the difference between** Shimon HaTimni, who says that only women "in whom there is no 'being'" are not entitled to the fine, and Rabbi Shimon ben Menasya, who says that any woman whom the rapist is forbidden to retain is not entitled to the fine? For according to Rabbi Yeshevav's understanding of Rabbi Akiva, every woman whom the rapist is forbidden to retain "has no 'being'" and vice versa, and this includes even a relationship between a widow and a High Priest!

אִיכָּא בֵּינַיְיהוּ [4]The Gemara answers: Even according to Rabbi Yeshevav's extreme presentation of Rabbi Akiva's position, Rabbi Akiva annulled only those marriages that are forbidden by a negative commandment, such as the marriage of a priest to a divorcee, or of an ordinary Jew to a *mamzeret*. But Shimon HaTimni, who says that only women "in whom there is no 'being'" are not entitled to the fine, and Rabbi Shimon ben Menasya, who says that any woman whom the rapist is forbidden to retain is not entitled to the fine, continue to **differ regarding** [30A] **those** relationships **that are liable to a prohibition implied by a positive commandment.** Generally, when the Torah forbids something, it does so explicitly, by saying: "You shall not...." Occasionally, however, a prohibition is implied by a statement phrased in positive language. Such prohibitions-by-implication are considered less severe than explicit negative commandments. In the light of this distinction, the Gemara argues that Rabbi Akiva would agree, even according to Rabbi Yeshevav's more extreme version of his position, that a marriage forbidden on the basis of a positive commandment is valid, though illegal, and the couple must divorce. Such a union offers an instance of a woman who "has 'being,'" but is forbidden to be retained, even according to Rabbi Akiva. [5]Relationships that are forbidden on the basis of a positive commandment include the case of a Jew who marries **an Egyptian or Edomite** convert. The Torah states in a positive form (Deuteronomy 23:9) that Edomite and Egyptian converts are permitted to marry Jews after three generations, implying that for the first two generations such marriages are forbidden. Therefore, if a Jew rapes or seduces an Egyptian or Edomite convert of the first or second generation, he is liable to pay the fine, according to Shimon HaTimni, since these women "have 'being,'"

LITERAL TRANSLATION

[1]But [according] to Rabbi Yeshevav who said: "Come and let us cry out against Akiva ben Yosef, [2]who used to say: 'Anyone who must not have intercourse in Israel, the offspring is a *mamzer*,'" [3]what is [the difference] between them?

[4]There is [a difference] between them [30A] [regarding those who] are forbidden by [a prohibition implied by] a positive commandment, [5][such as] an Egyptian or an Edomite.

[1]וּלְרַבִּי יְשֵׁבָב, דְּאָמַר: ״בּוֹאוּ וְנִצְוַח עַל עֲקִיבָא בֶּן יוֹסֵף, [2]שֶׁהָיָה אוֹמֵר: ׳כָּל שֶׁאֵין לוֹ בִּיאָה בְּיִשְׂרָאֵל, הַוָּלָד מַמְזֵר׳״, [3]מַאי בֵּינַיְיהוּ?

[4]אִיכָּא בֵּינַיְיהוּ [30A] חַיָּיבֵי עֲשֵׂה, [5]מִצְרִי וַאֲדוֹמִי.

RASHI

בואו ונצוח על עקיבא בן יוסף — שמרבה ממזרים בישראל חנם. **שהוא אומר כל שאין לו ביאה בישראל** — הבא על אשה שאין לו בה היתר ביאה — הולד ממזר, אפילו אלמנה לכהן גדול נמי. **חייבי עשה מצרי ואדומי** — בתוך שלשה דורות, דכתיב (דברים כג) ״דור שלישי יבא להם״, דור שני — לא, ולאו הבא מכלל עשה — עשה.

SAGES

רַבִּי יְשֵׁבָב Rabbi Yeshevav. A Tanna of the fourth generation, Rabbi Yeshevav was a contemporary and friend of Rabbi Akiva, and he is frequently mentioned as differing with his famous colleague. Very little is known about Rabbi Yeshevav's life. According to the Midrash, Rabbi Yeshevav was one of the ten martyrs killed during the Hadrianic persecutions (c.135 C.E.). The Midrash also relates that he was a scribe by profession.

NOTES

Rabbi Simai mentioned a High Priest who married a widow rather than an ordinary priest who married a divorcee, because the verse from which he makes his inference explicitly refers to the High Priest. Subsequently, the Gemara continues to use the language of Rabbi Simai's Baraita throughout the passage.

חַיָּיבֵי עֲשֵׂה Those who are forbidden by a prohibition implied by a positive commandment. Generally, when the Torah forbids something, it does so explicitly. In some instances, however, a prohibition may be implied by a statement phrased in positive language. Such prohibitions-by-implication are generally not subject to punishment; hence they are considered less severe than explicit negative commandments, which are usually punished by lashes (*Yevamot* 7a). Nevertheless, when there is a conflict between a positive commandment and a single

ⁱהָנִיחָא לְרַבִּי יְשֵׁבָב, ²אִי לְאַפּוּקֵי מִטַּעֲמָא דְּרַבִּי סִימַאי קָאָתֵי — שַׁפִּיר. ³אֶלָּא אִי טַעֲמָא דְנַפְשֵׁיהּ קָאָמַר — ⁴כָּל שֶׁאֵין לוֹ בִּיאָה בְּיִשְׂרָאֵל, הַוָּלָד מַמְזֵר, ⁵וַאֲפִילּוּ חַיָּיבֵי עֲשֵׂה — ⁶מַאי בֵּינַיְיהוּ?

⁷אִיכָּא בֵּינַיְיהוּ בְּעוּלָה לְכֹהֵן גָּדוֹל.

LITERAL TRANSLATION

[1] This is well according to Rabbi Yeshevav, [2] if he is coming to exclude the argument of Rabbi Simai — it is well. [3] But, if he is stating his own argument — [4] anyone who must not have intercourse in Israel, the offspring is a *mamzer*, [5] and even [those who] are forbidden by [a prohibition implied by] a positive commandment — [6] what is [the difference] between them?

[7] There is [a difference] between them [regarding the prohibition against marriage between] a non-virgin and a High Priest.

TRANSLATION AND COMMENTARY

but he is not liable according to Rabbi Shimon ben Menasya, since it is forbidden to retain these women and they must be divorced.

הָנִיחָא [1] The Gemara objects to this answer: There are two possible interpretations of Rabbi Yeshevav's presentation of Rabbi Akiva's position. **This** explanation **is satisfactory,** even **according to Rabbi Yeshevav's** presentation of Rabbi Akiva's viewpoint, [2] **if** Rabbi Yeshevav's **purpose is to disagree with the reasoning of Rabbi Simai** mentioned above. If Rabbi Yeshevav's intention was to disagree with Rabbi Simai's moderate presentation of Rabbi Akiva's statement, we may take his words as a slight exaggeration to make a point. On this assumption, Rabbi Yeshevav maintains that Rabbi Akiva considers even the offspring of a relationship between a widow and a High Priest to be a *mamzer*. If so, it is possible that a marriage forbidden by a positive commandment is valid — although illegal — even according to Rabbi Yeshevav's extreme presentation of Rabbi Akiva's position. [3] **But** Rabbi Yeshevav's statement can be read in another way. **If** Rabbi Yeshevav **is stating his own reasoning** — if his purpose is to attack what he sees as Rabbi Akiva's authentic position — [4] we must take him literally when he says that if a man has relations with **"anyone who must not have intercourse according to Jewish law** — any woman who is forbidden to him for any reason at all — **the offspring is a *mamzer*."** [5] **And** if so, this would apply **even to relationships that are liable to the penalty for non-observance of a positive commandment,** such as a marriage between a Jew and an Egyptian or Edomite woman, since such women are forbidden to have intercourse with Jews. But if this second version of the argument is correct, [6] **what difference is there between** Shimon HaTimni, who says that only women "in whom there is no being" are not entitled to the fine, and Rabbi Shimon ben Menasya, who says that any woman whom it is forbidden to retain is not entitled to the fine? For according to the viewpoint just presented, every woman whom it is forbidden to retain "has no 'being.'"

אִיכָּא בֵּינַיְיהוּ [7] The Gemara answers: Even according to this interpretation of Rabbi Yeshevav's presentation of Rabbi Akiva's position, Rabbi Akiva declared void only those marriages that are forbidden on the basis of a negative commandment (such as an ordinary priest marrying a divorcee), or marriages that are forbidden to ordinary Jews on the basis of a positive commandment (such as marriages with an Egyptian or an Edomite). But **there** remains **a difference between** Shimon HaTimni, who says that only women "in whom there is no 'being'" are not entitled to the fine, and Rabbi Shimon ben Menasya, who says that any woman whom it is forbidden to retain is not entitled to the fine, **regarding the** positive commandment **prohibiting a High Priest from marrying a non-virgin.** The Torah requires a High Priest to

RASHI

הניחא — אי רבי ישבב האי "כל שאין לו היתר ביאה" דקאמר אליבא דרבי עקיבא לאו כללא כייל, אלא לאפוקי מדרבי סימאי לחודיה אתא, ואחייבי לאוין הוא דפליג, לאוסופי חייבי לאוין בכהונה, אבל שום חייבי עשה לא הוסיף. **שפיר** — מצינו למימר איכא בינייהו דשמעון התימני ורבי שמעון בן מנסיא חייבי עשה. **אלא** — אי לאו אדרבי סימאי קאי, וטעמא דנפשיה קאמר בשם רבי עקיבא, שכל שאין לו היתר ביאה באשה זו הולד ממזר — מאי איכא למימר? **בעולה לכהן גדול** — שאין בה לאו דאלמנות וגירושין אלא עשה ד"בתולה יקח" (ויקרא כא), ולא בעולה. ואם תאמר: יש כאן לאו דזונה! לא אשכחן תנא דאמר: פנוי הבא על הפנויה עשאה זונה אלא רבי אלעזר, ולית הלכתא כוותיה,

NOTES

ordinary negative commandment, the positive commandment generally takes precedence (*Yevamot* 3b). Occasionally, the Torah forbids something explicitly with a negative commandment as well as forbidding it by implication with a positive commandment. In such cases, the prohibition is considered to have been strengthened by the repetition, and is not set aside by other positive commandments (*Yevamot* 20a).

The Torah does not explicitly forbid marriage with Egyptian and Edomite converts. Instead, it states (Deuteronomy 23:8-9) that such marriages are permitted after three generations, implying that in the first two generations they are forbidden. Likewise, the Torah explicitly forbids (Leviticus 21:14) the High Priest to marry a widow, or a woman forbidden to an ordinary priest — a divorcee, a *ḥalalah*, or a *zonah* (a woman who has had intercourse

TRANSLATION AND COMMENTARY

marry only a virgin (Leviticus 21:13). By implication, therefore, the High Priest is forbidden, on the basis of a positive commandment, to marry a woman who is not a virgin, even if she is not a widow or a divorcee. If a High Priest were to marry such a woman, even Rabbi Akiva — and even according to our present understanding of Rabbi Yeshevav — would agree that the illegal marriage is valid. Thus we have found a case of a woman whom the rapist is forbidden to retain, but who "has 'being'", even according to Rabbi Akiva. Therefore, if a High Priest seduces or rapes a *na'arah* who is not a virgin, he is held liable to pay the fine, according to Shimon HaTimni, since this woman "has 'being,'" but not according to Rabbi Shimon ben Menasya, since he is forbidden to retain her.

וּמַאי שְׁנָא [1]The Gemara asks: **What is different** about the positive commandment forbidding a non-virgin from marrying a High Priest? How is it different from the other positive commandments forbidding intermarriage with Egyptian and Edomite converts?

דַּהֲוָה לֵיהּ עֲשֵׂה [2]The Gemara answers: **It is a positive commandment that does not apply equally to everyone,** since it applies only to a High Priest and not to ordinary Jews. Rabbi Yeshevav stated that Rabbi Akiva considers a *mamzer* the offspring of anyone who is not permitted to have intercourse *in Israel* (i.e., the offspring of a person who is forbidden to any Jew). Regarding women who are permitted to have intercourse with ordinary Jews, and are forbidden only to priests, he did not make a categorical statement. Admittedly, Rabbi Yeshevav insists that, in Rabbi Akiva's view, the offspring of women who are forbidden to priests on the basis of a negative commandment are *mamzerim*. But regarding an unmarried non-virgin who is forbidden to a High Priest only on the basis of a positive commandment, he agrees with Rabbi Simai that the marriage is not void, although it is illegal. Thus we have found a case of a woman who "has 'being,'" but whom it is forbidden to retain, even according to Rabbi Yeshevav's interpretation of Rabbi Akiva, and this is the case about which Shimon HaTimni and Rabbi Shimon ben Menasya disagreed.

אָמַר רַב חִסְדָּא [3]**Rav Ḥisda said:** Even though Shimon HaTimni and Rabbi Shimon ben Menasya disagree with the author of our Mishnah about many of the cases in the Mishnah, they **agree about** the last case, that concerns **a man who has intercourse with a menstruating woman,** which in our context means a man who raped a *na'arah* who was forbidden to have relations with any man while she was menstruating (Leviticus 18:19) but was otherwise permitted. In this case, they agree **that he must pay a fine,** even though

וּמַאי שְׁנָא? [1]

דַּהֲוָה לֵיהּ עֲשֵׂה שֶׁאֵינוֹ שָׁוֶה בַּכֹּל. [2]

אָמַר רַב חִסְדָּא: הַכֹּל מוֹדִים בְּבָא עַל הַנִּדָּה שֶׁמְּשַׁלֵּם קְנָס. [3]

LITERAL TRANSLATION

[1]And what is the difference?

[2]That this is a positive commandment that does not [apply] equally to everyone.

[3]Rav Ḥisda said: All agree about someone who has intercourse with a menstruating woman that he must pay a fine.

RASHI

ואין זונה אלא הנבעלת לפסול לה. ובבעולה שלא כדרכה איירי, דאי כדרכה – תו ליכא קנס. ומאי שנא – האי עשה מאחר עשה דמודה ביה רבי עקיבא. דהוה ליה עשה שאינו שוה בכל – שאינו נוהג אלא בכהן גדול, אבל עשה דמצרי ואדומי נוהג בכל הקהל.

SAGES

רַב חִסְדָּא Rav Ḥisda. A Babylonian Amora of the second generation. See *Ketubot,* Part II, p. 64.

NOTES

with a man whom she is forbidden to marry). It does not explicitly forbid the High Priest to marry a woman who has never been married and is not a *zonah* but has nevertheless lost her virginity. Instead, it states (Leviticus 21:13) that the High Priest must marry a virgin, implying that a woman who has lost her virginity in any way is forbidden. (A woman who has lost her virginity through marriage, or through intercourse with someone she is forbidden to marry, is forbidden to the High Priest both on the basis of a negative commandment, as a widow, divorcee, or *zonah*, and on the basis of a positive commandment, as a non-virgin.)

עֲשֵׂה שֶׁאֵינוֹ שָׁוֶה בַּכֹּל A positive commandment that does not apply equally to everyone. In several places (e.g., *Yevamot* 5a), the Gemara considers commandments that apply to all Jews to be more severe than commandments that are addressed only to a single group or class (e.g., commandments that are addressed to men and not to women). The Rishonim note, however, that priestly marriage prohibitions are sometimes considered as applying equally to everyone, even though they are not addressed to laymen. *Tosafot* (*Yevamot* 5a) explains that the priestly marital prohibitions are considered to be "equal for everyone," since they apply to all Israelite women. For when an ordinary priest marries a divorcee, or a High Priest marries a widow, they are both liable to lashes.

In our case, however, the Gemara does consider the prohibition against a High Priest marrying a non-virgin to be "a positive commandment that does not apply equally to everyone." *Meiri* explains that this is because it applies only to the High Priest, and not even to ordinary priests. *Rabbi Akiva Eger* suggests that it is possible that the prohibition-by-implication against a High Priest marrying a non-virgin is different from the other priestly prohibitions in that it applies only to the High Priest and not to the woman he is marrying. But *Rashash* refutes this suggestion, and proves that the prohibition-by-implication against a High Priest marrying a non-virgin does indeed apply equally to the High Priest and to the non-virgin.

הַכֹּל מוֹדִים בְּבָא עַל הַנִּדָּה All agree about someone who has intercourse with a menstruating woman. The Rishonim object: It is not true that all Tannaim agree with

[1] לְמַאן דְּאָמַר: ״יֵשׁ בָּהּ ׳הֲוָיָה׳״, [2] הָא נַמִי יֵשׁ בָּהּ ״הֲוָיָה״. [3] לְמַאן דְּאָמַר: ״רְאוּיָה לְקַיְּימָהּ״, [4] הָא נַמִי רְאוּיָה לְקַיְּימָהּ.

LITERAL TRANSLATION

[1] [According] to the one who says: "[A woman] in whom there is 'being,'" [2] in this one too there is "being." [3] [According] to the one who says: "[A woman who is] fit [for him] to retain her," [4] this one is also fit [for him] to retain her.

RASHI

הא נמי יש בה הויה – המקדש אשה בימי נדותה מקודשת.

TRANSLATION AND COMMENTARY

the penalty for having intercourse with a menstruating woman is excision (Leviticus 20:18). For Shimon HaTimni and Rabbi Shimon ben Menasya disagree with our Mishnah only about cases in which marriage between the rapist and the *na'arah* is impossible (according to Shimon HaTimni) or illegal (according to Rabbi Shimon ben Menasya). But this problem does not apply to a menstruating woman. For although it is forbidden to have intercourse with a menstruating woman, it is permitted to marry her. [1] Thus, **according to** Shimon HaTimni, **who said** that the fine need be paid only if the *na'arah* was **"a woman in whom there is 'being,'"** [2] a menstruating woman **is also** "a woman in whom **there is 'being,'"** since a marriage with a menstruating woman is valid. [3] Likewise, **according to** Rabbi Shimon ben Menasya, **who said** that the fine need be paid only if the *na'arah* was **"a woman who is fit to be retained,"** [4] a menstruating woman **is also** "a woman who is **fit to be retained,"** since a marriage with a menstruating woman is perfectly legal and need not be dissolved by a divorce. Therefore, if a man rapes a menstruating virgin *na'arah*, who is otherwise permitted to him, he must pay the fine even according to Shimon HaTimni and Rabbi Shimon ben Menasya.

The Gemara now turns to another aspect of our Mishnah, which is a major topic of this chapter. Sometimes a person commits a single act which is forbidden for several different reasons. In such a case, the question arises: Is he subject to all possible penalties for his misdeed, or is only the most severe penalty imposed while the others are waived? The procedure to be followed differs from situation to situation, and there are several situations which are the subject of dispute. There is one case, however, that is clear: If a person commits a misdeed that involves two offenses, one of which is subject to the death penalty whereas the other creates a financial obligation, the criminal is exempt from the financial penalty, since he is subject to the more severe penalty of death. Moreover, the Gemara rules (below, 36a) that the offender is exempt from paying even when, because of a legal technicality, he is not in fact executed.

The Mishnah (below, 36b) derives this rule from a Biblical verse. The context in which this verse occurs deals with two quarreling men. The two are attempting to kill each other, and one of them accidentally

NOTES

Rav Ḥisda's ruling. For Rabbi Neḥunya ben Hakkanah states (below) that the fine is not imposed where intercourse between the rapist and the woman is subject to the penalty of excision — and intercourse with a menstruating woman, although it does not result in *mamzerim*, is definitely punished by excision (Leviticus 20:18). Moreover, in the Tosefta (*Ketubot* 3:5) Rabbi Neḥunya ben Hakkanah explicitly states that a man who rapes a menstruating girl is exempt from paying the fine because he is subject to the penalty of excision.

Our commentary follows *Ritva*, who explains that when Rav Ḥisda said "everyone," he was referring exclusively to Rabbi Shimon ben Menasya and Shimon HaTimni, who were previously described as disagreeing with the author of our Mishnah, and not to any other Tannaim. *Tosafot* suggests that the first line of the next section of the Gemara should be added to Rav Ḥisda's statement, so that it reads: "All agree about someone who has intercourse with a menstruating woman...excluding Rabbi Neḥunya ben Hakkanah, as was taught in a Baraita, etc."

In the parallel passage in the Jerusalem Talmud, Rabbi Shimon ben Menasya agrees with the position held by Rabbi Neḥunya ben Hakkanah in our Gemara, arguing that people punished by excision are exempt from any financial penalty connected with the same crime, and that a man who rapes a menstruating woman is not required to pay the fine for that reason. By contrast, Rabbi Neḥunya ben Hakkanah himself rules that the fine is imposed if a man rapes a menstruating woman or if he rapes his wife's sister, even though the fine is not imposed in other cases punishable by excision, because these two prohibitions have a unique mitigating characteristic, in that they are not permanent: A menstruating woman is permitted once that instance of menstruation ceases and she ritually purifies herself, and a wife's sister is permitted after the death of the wife (Leviticus 18:18).

הָא נַמִי יֵשׁ בָּהּ הֲוָיָה In this one too there is "being." The source of this law is a passage in tractate *Yevamot* (49b). There, the Gemara considers the difference of opinion between Rabbi Akiva, Shimon HaTimni, and Rabbi Yehoshua as to whether the offspring of all relationships forbidden by a negative prohibition are *mamzerim*, or only the offspring of relationships forbidden under penalty of excision, or only the offspring of relationships forbidden under penalty of death. Abaye states that according to all opinions the offspring of a man who has relations with a menstruating woman is not a *mamzer* — even though the intercourse itself is punishable by excision — because a marriage entered into with a woman while she is menstruating is valid, and we have a principle that *mamzerim* are produced only from relationships (incest and adultery) that cannot result in a valid marriage. Abaye learns this law

TRANSLATION AND COMMENTARY

strikes an innocent third party, a pregnant woman, causing her to miscarry. The Torah declares (Exodus 21:22–23) that "if there is no disaster [if the woman herself is not harmed], he [the man who struck her] must surely be punished [for inducing the miscarriage, with the payment of damages mentioned later in the verse]. But if there is a disaster [if the woman herself is accidentally killed], you shall give a life for a life." From here we learn that monetary punishment is imposed only when no "disaster" occurs and no one is killed, but if the offender is liable to the death penalty, there is no payment of damages.

The technical term for this principle is: קָם לֵיהּ בִּדְרַבָּה מִינֵּיהּ — "he is subject to the greater penalty." In accordance with this principle, the next Mishnah (below, 36b) rules that a man who rapes or seduces his daughter is exempt from paying the fine, even if his daughter was a virgin *na'arah*, because he is subject to the death penalty for incest with his daughter (Leviticus 20:14), and anyone who is liable to the death penalty does not pay monetary damages for his crime. Our Mishnah, on the other hand, rules that a man who rapes his sister must pay the fine, even though he is subject to the severe penalty of excision for incest with his sister (Leviticus 20:17). Excision is considered to be next in severity to the death penalty. It contains a promise of death at the hands of Heaven, as well as several other dire consequences, and is treated as the equivalent of execution for many purposes. Nevertheless, the author of our Mishnah is of the opinion that if a person commits an offense that is subject to excision as well as to a monetary penalty, he is not exempt from paying damages.

וּלְאַפּוּקֵי [1]The Gemara observes: Our Mishnah, which makes the point of distinguishing between incest that is punished by execution and incest that is punished by excision, **disagrees with the viewpoint of Rabbi Neḥunya ben Hakkanah,** who is of the opinion that a person who commits an offense that is subject to excision is exempt from paying damages for the same act, since there is no difference between the death penalty and excision in this context. [2]**For it has been taught** in a Baraita: **"Rabbi Neḥunya ben Hakkanah used to treat Yom Kippur** (the Day of Atonement) **like Shabbat for payments** of damages." The Torah (Exodus 35:2–3) forbids working (e.g., lighting a fire) on Shabbat, and decrees that violators of Shabbat prohibitions are to be executed. Precisely the same laws apply to Yom Kippur, except that the penalty for violating a prohibition relating to Yom Kippur is excision rather than death (Leviticus 23:28–30). Now, if someone sets

[1]וּלְאַפּוּקֵי מִדְּרַבִּי נְחוּנְיָא בֶּן הַקָּנָה. [2]דְּתַנְיָא: "רַבִּי נְחוּנְיָא בֶּן הַקָּנָה הָיָה עוֹשֶׂה אֶת יוֹם הַכִּפּוּרִים כְּשַׁבָּת לְתַשְׁלוּמִין.

LITERAL TRANSLATION

[1]And it is to exclude [the opinion] of Rabbi Neḥunya ben Hakkanah. [2]For it has been taught: "Rabbi Neḥunya ben Hakkanah used to treat (lit., 'make') Yom Kippur like Shabbat for payments.

RASHI

ולאפוקי מדרבי נחוניא — מתניתין דמחייב תשלומין לבא על אחותו, ואף על פי שמתחייב כרת בביאתו — מפקא מדרבי נחוניא. **את יום הכפורים כשבת** — לפטור המדליק את הגדיש ביום הכפורים כאילו הדליקו בשבת.

SAGES

רַבִּי נְחוּנְיָא בֶּן הַקָּנָה Rabbi Neḥunya ben Hakkanah. A Tanna who lived at the time of the destruction of the Second Temple, Rabbi Neḥunya ben Hakkanah was the teacher of the great Sage Rabbi Yishmael. Only a few of his Halakhic teachings have been preserved, and several Aggadic sayings are transmitted in his name.

The development of one of the hermeneutic principles used in Halakhic Midrash, in which inferences are drawn from a generalization and a specific detail, is attributed to him, and Rabbi Yishmael continued to develop this principle.

NOTES

from a verse (Leviticus 15:24) which describes the penalty imposed on a man who has intercourse with a menstruating woman, using the verb "to be."

Abaye's ruling itself is not disputed, but the practical application of his ruling is subject to a dispute between the Rishonim. According to all opinions, the first stage of marriage (*kiddushin*, or "betrothal") is valid if it is performed while the woman is menstruating. According to *Rambam*, however, the second stage of marriage, *nissuin*, does not take effect if it is performed while the woman is menstruating, since the essence of *nissuin* is the entry of the wife into the husband's domain, and this cannot take place when she is forbidden to him, such as when she is menstruating. *Rosh* and other Rishonim disagree, however, ruling that *nissuin* too may be performed while the woman is menstruating. In practice, the custom is to plan the wedding date to avoid this problem if possible, but to permit the marriage to take place if necessary (see *Ran*, *Ritva*).

וּלְאַפּוּקֵי מִדְּרַבִּי נְחוּנְיָא בֶּן הַקָּנָה And it is to exclude the opinion of Rabbi Neḥunya ben Hakkanah. Our commentary follows *Rashi*, who explains that the Gemara is informing us that the ruling of our Mishnah — that a man who rapes his sister must pay the fine — is in fact controversial, and does not reflect the opinion expressed by Rabbi Neḥunya ben Hakkanah in the Baraita. According to this explanation, the Gemara is here beginning a new topic, unrelated to the previous discussion.

Tosafot suggests that this line of the Gemara should be read in connection with Rav Ḥisda's statement in the previous discussion, so that the line reads: "Rav Ḥisda said: Everyone agrees that a person who has intercourse with a menstruating woman must pay the fine (since she has 'being' and it is permitted to retain her), excluding Rabbi Neḥunya ben Hakkanah, whose opinion was taught in the following Baraita, etc."

Shittah Mekubbetzet notes that the language of the Mishnah supports *Rashi*'s explanation. The Mishnah emphasizes that the man who rapes his sister must pay the fine even though he is punished by excision, since he is not punished by death at the hands of a court, and this suggests that the Mishnah is concerned about recording its disagreement with the opinion of Rabbi Neḥunya ben Hakkanah, who does not recognize the distinction between excision and death at the hands of a court.

רַבִּי נְחוּנְיָא בֶּן הַקָּנָה הָיָה עוֹשֶׂה אֶת יוֹם הַכִּפּוּרִים כְּשַׁבָּת Rabbi Neḥunya ben Hakkanah used to treat Yom Kippur like Shabbat. According to Rabbi Neḥunya ben Hakkanah, if a single offense incurs both excision and a monetary penalty,

TRANSLATION AND COMMENTARY

his neighbor's property on fire on Shabbat, he is exempt from paying damages, since lighting a fire on Shabbat is an offense subject to the death penalty. If, on the other hand, he sets his neighbor's property on fire on Yom Kippur, most authorities would rule that he is liable to pay damages, since the penalty for lighting a fire on Yom Kippur is excision, not death. Rabbi Neḥunya ben Hakkanah, however, makes no distinction between excision and death in this connection, arguing that someone who sets his neighbor's property on fire on Yom Kippur is also exempt from paying damages. [1]The Baraita explains his point of view: **"Just as by desecrating Shabbat he forfeits his life and is exempt from paying** damages, [2]**so too by desecrating Yom Kippur he forfeits his life** (since excision is considered to be the equivalent of death) **and is exempt from paying** damages." It follows from this Baraita that Rabbi Neḥunya ben Hakkanah would disagree with the author of our Mishnah, and rule that a man who rapes his sister is exempt from paying the fine, since he is punished by excision.

מַאי טַעֲמָא [3]The Gemara asks: **What is the reasoning** behind the ruling **of Rabbi Neḥunya ben Hakkanah?** The law that someone liable to the death penalty is exempt from paying damages is derived by the Mishnah (below, 36b) from the verse dealing with the man who accidentally killed a woman (Exodus 21:22). That verse expressly deals with a woman who is killed and a man who is punished by death. How can Rabbi Neḥunya ben Hakkanah extend this exemption and apply it to excision? For although excision is a severe penalty, it is not as severe as capital punishment.

אָמַר אַבַּיֵי [4]The Gemara offers two different solutions to this problem, one attributed to Abaye and the other (below, 30b) to Rava. **Abaye said:** The reasoning of Rabbi Neḥunya ben Hakkanah is based on a *gezerah shavah*. According to this hermeneutic rule, when the same word appears in two different contexts, the laws in the two contexts are equated. In this case, **the verse** from which we learn the exemption of a

[1]מַה שַּׁבָּת מִתְחַיֵּיב בְּנַפְשׁוֹ וּפָטוּר מִן הַתַּשְׁלוּמִין, [2]אַף יוֹם הַכִּפּוּרִים מִתְחַיֵּיב בְּנַפְשׁוֹ וּפָטוּר מִן הַתַּשְׁלוּמִין". [3]מַאי טַעֲמָא דְּרַבִּי נְחוּנְיָא בֶּן הַקָּנָה? [4]אָמַר אַבַּיֵי: נֶאֱמַר "אָסוֹן"

LITERAL TRANSLATION

[1]Just as [by desecrating] Shabbat he forfeits his life and is exempt from payments, [2]so too [by desecrating] Yom Kippur he forfeits his life and is exempt from payments."

[3]What is the reasoning of Rabbi Neḥunya ben Hakkanah?

[4]Abaye said: "Disaster"

RASHI

מה שבת – שהוא מיתת בית דין. **פטור מן התשלומין** – כדתנן במתניתין גבי בא על בתו, ויליף לה מ"ולא יהיה אסון ענוש יענש". **אף יום הכפורים** – שהוא בכרת, חיוב נפש הוא זה – ופטור מן התשלומין. **אסון בידי אדם** – "ולא יהיה

NOTES

the monetary penalty is waived, because excision is comparable to execution. According to the other Tannaim, however, this is true of offenses that are punishable by execution, but not of those that are punishable by excision.

Later in this chapter (35a), the Gemara concludes that if the offense is subject to the more severe penalty of execution, the offender is exempt from monetary payments, even if he is not in fact executed (e.g., if his transgression was inadvertent). If the offense is subject to lashes, however, the offender is exempted from monetary payments only if he is actually lashed. *Tosafot* and *Ba'al HaMa'or* explain that, according to Rabbi Neḥunya ben Hakkanah, excision is comparable to execution in this respect as well. According to him, someone who sets his neighbor's property on fire without realizing that it is Yom Kippur is exempt from all monetary penalties.

Ramban argues that Rabbi Neḥunya ben Hakkanah exempts the offender from monetary payment only if the transgression that is subject to excision was committed deliberately. This also appears to be the position of *Rashi* (*Pesaḥim* 29a).

The Gemara explains (below) that the ruling of Rabbi Neḥunya ben Hakkanah is based on an exegetical argument. According to Abaye, since excision is a kind of death penalty, albeit at the hands of Heaven, the rules applying to execution should apply to it as well. According to Rava, excision is expressly compared in the Torah to execution. The Gemara does not, however, explain the reasoning of the other Tannaim, who disagree with Rabbi Neḥunya ben Hakkanah and distinguish between excision and execution. *Ra'ah* explains that, although excision is very severe, in applying the rule that a person who is subject to the

HALAKHAH

מִתְחַיֵּיב בְּנַפְשׁוֹ וּפָטוּר מִן הַתַּשְׁלוּמִין He forfeits his life and is exempt from payments. "If the *na'arah* was forbidden to the rapist or the seducer on pain of excision, and the rapist or the seducer was not punished by lashes, he must pay the fine. But if she was forbidden to him on pain of death, he is exempt from paying the fine, even if the death penalty is ultimately not carried out. The same rule applies to any offense that is punishable by death and by a monetary penalty as well: The offender is always exempt from paying, even if the death penalty cannot be carried out. Therefore, someone who damages someone else's property in the course of a crime which should be subject to the death penalty is exempt from paying damages." (*Rambam, Sefer Nashim, Hilkhot Na'arah Betulah* 1:11-14 and *Sefer Nezikin, Hilkhot Genevah* 3:1; *Shulḥan Arukh, Ḥoshen Mishpat* 351:1.)

TRANSLATION AND COMMENTARY

person who is subject to the more severe penalty **uses** the word **"disaster,"** and refers to execution **by the hands of man,** [1]**and** another **verse** (Genesis 42:38) uses the same word, **"disaster,"** and refers to death **at the hands of Heaven.** The latter verse refers to a warning Jacob gave his sons, that they should not take their youngest brother Benjamin to Egypt with them, "lest a disaster befall him on the way in which you go." Utilizing the *gezerah shavah* principle, Rabbi Neḥunya ben Hakkanah equates the case of Jacob, which refers to a disaster at the hands of Heaven, with the other verse, which refers to a disaster at the hands of man, and argues that the same laws apply to both. [2]Hence, we learn from the *gezerah shavah* that **just as** a person who is subject to **"disaster" at the hands of man** (execution) **is exempt from payment** of damages, [3]**so too is** a person who is subject to **"disaster" at the hands of Heaven,** such as excision, **exempt from payment** of damages, even though excision is less severe than execution.

מַתְקִיף לָהּ [4]**Rav Adda bar Ahavah objected to** Abaye's explanation. This explanation is based on the assumption that when the verse in Genesis uses the word "disaster," it is referring to "disaster at the hands of Heaven" (i.e., some natural disaster beyond human control). [5]But **from where do we know that when Jacob warned his sons** about possible disasters, he **was** thinking **about colds and fevers** and the like, [6]**which are in the hands of Heaven?** [7]**Perhaps** he was concerned that Benjamin might be attacked **by lions or thieves** — [8]situations **that are in the hands of man!** If so, the verse in Genesis cannot serve as a source for the ruling of Rabbi Neḥunya ben Hakkanah that excision is equivalent to the death penalty.

אַטּוּ [9]The Gemara answers: **Was Jacob warning about the one but not about the other?** [10]**Jacob was warning about everything.** Jacob was concerned lest a disaster of any kind befall Benjamin. He included in the term "disaster" both disasters at the hands of Heaven, like colds and fevers, and disasters at the hands of man, like lions and thieves. Hence, even though the word "disaster," as it appears in Genesis, is not restricted to disaster at the hands of Heaven, it does have that connotation as well.

וְצִינִּים פַּחִים [11]Before considering the alternative explanation of Rabbi Neḥunya's reasoning given by Rava, the Gemara considers a point mentioned by Rav Adda bar Ahavah in the course of his objection to Abaye's explanation. Rav Adda bar Ahavah suggested that Jacob may have been referring only to disasters at the hands of man, such as lions and thieves, but not to disasters at the hands of Heaven, such as colds and fevers. **But,** the Gemara objects, **are colds and fevers** really **in the hands of Heaven,** as Rav Adda bar Ahava seems to imply? [12]**Surely it has been taught** in a Baraita: **"Everything is in the hands**

בִּידֵי אָדָם, [1]וְנֶאֱמַר ״אָסוֹן״ בִּידֵי שָׁמַיִם. [2]מָה ״אָסוֹן״ הָאָמוּר בִּידֵי אָדָם פָּטוּר מִן הַתַּשְׁלוּמִין, [3]אַף ״אָסוֹן״ הָאָמוּר בִּידֵי שָׁמַיִם פָּטוּר מִן הַתַּשְׁלוּמִין.

[4]מַתְקִיף לָהּ רַב אַדָּא בַּר אַהֲבָה: [5]מִמַּאי דְּכִי קָא מַזְהַר לְהוּ יַעֲקֹב לִבְנֵיהּ, עַל צִינִּים וּפַחִים, [6]דְּבִידֵי שָׁמַיִם נִינְהוּ? [7]דִּלְמָא עַל אַרְיָא וְגַנָּבֵי, [8]דְּבִידֵי אָדָם נִינְהוּ!

[9]אַטּוּ יַעֲקֹב אַהָא אַזְהַר, אַהָא לָא אַזְהַר? [10]יַעֲקֹב עַל כָּל מִילֵּי אַזְהַר.

[11]וְצִינִּים פַּחִים בִּידֵי שָׁמַיִם נִינְהוּ? [12]וְהָתַנְיָא: ״הַכֹּל בִּידֵי

LITERAL TRANSLATION

at the hands of man is said [in the verse], [1]and "disaster" at the hands of Heaven is said [in the verse]. [2]Just as "disaster" that is said at the hands of man is exempt from payments, [3]so too "disaster" that is said [to take place] at the hands of Heaven is exempt from payments.

[4]Rav Adda bar Ahavah objected to this: [5]From where [do you know] that when Jacob warned his sons, it was about colds and fevers, [6]which are in the hands of Heaven? [7]Perhaps it was about lions and thieves, [8]which are in the hands of man!

[9]Is it that Jacob warned about this, [and] did not warn about that? [10]Jacob warned about everything.

[11]But are colds [and] fevers in the hands of Heaven? [12]But surely it has been taught: "Everything is in the hands of

RASHI

אסון" דמשתעי — במיתת בית דין, למימר דהיכא דליכא מיתת בית דין — משלם דמי ולדות. אסון בידי שמים — "וקראהו אסון". צינים פחים — קור וחום. בידי שמים — אם באים פורעניות על האדם — גזירת המלך הוא.

TERMINOLOGY

מַתְקִיף לָהּ He objected to it. This term is used when an Amora objects to a statement of another Amora on logical grounds rather than on the authority of a primary Halakhic source (e.g., a Mishnah or a Baraita).

SAGES

רַב אַדָּא בַּר אַהֲבָה Rav Adda bar Ahavah. A Babylonian Amora of the first and second generations. See *Ketubot*, Part II, p. 26.

NOTES

greater penalty is exempt from payment, a court can only consider penalties imposed by the court, such as lashes, executions, or fines, and not penalties imposed by God.

וְהָתַנְיָא הַכֹּל בִּידֵי שָׁמַיִם But surely it has been taught: Everything is in the hands of Heaven. According to this Baraita, only colds and fevers can be prevented absolutely by taking precautions, but other woes and ailments cannot be prevented altogether. *Tosafot* explains that while there are considerable differences in the risks faced by careful and careless people, a person who is careful never to go

שָׁמַיִם חוּץ מִצִּינִּים פַּחִים,
[1]שֶׁנֶּאֱמַר: ״צִנִּים פַּחִים בְּדֶרֶךְ
עִקֵּשׁ; [2]שׁוֹמֵר נַפְשׁוֹ יִרְחַק
מֵהֶם״״.
[3]וְתוּ, אַרְיָא וְגַנָּבֵי בִּידֵי אָדָם
נִינְהוּ? [4]וְהָאָמַר רַב יוֹסֵף, וְכֵן
תָּנֵי רַבִּי חִיָּיא: [5]״מִיּוֹם שֶׁחָרַב
בֵּית הַמִּקְדָּשׁ, [6]אַף עַל פִּי
שֶׁבָּטְלוּ סַנְהֶדְרִין, אַרְבַּע מִיתוֹת
לֹא בָּטְלוּ״.

LITERAL TRANSLATION

Heaven except for colds [and] fevers, [1]as it is said: 'Colds and fevers are in the way of the stubborn; [2]he that guards his soul will be far from them.'" [3]And furthermore, are lions and thieves in the hands of man? [4]But surely Rav Yosef said, and similarly Rabbi Ḥiyya taught: [5]"From the day that the Temple was destroyed, [6]even though the Sanhedrin ceased, the four [methods of] execution did not cease."

RASHI

חוץ מצינים ופחים – שפעמים שבאין בפשיעה. **בידי אדם נינהו** – שלא מגזירת מלך.

TRANSLATION AND COMMENTARY

of Heaven, except for colds and fevers. It is impossible to protect oneself completely against all misfortunes, since so many factors are beyond human control, but it is possible to take precautions against catching a cold or a fever, and only careless people succumb to them. [1]**For there is a** Biblical **verse that says** (Proverbs 22:5): **"Colds and fevers are in the way of the stubborn;** [2]**he that guards his soul will be far away from them."** Thus we see that colds and fevers are by no means totally beyond human control.

וְתוּ [3]**And** furthermore, the Gemara continues, **are lions and thieves** really **in the hands of man,** as Rav Adda bar Ahavah contends? [4]**Surely** this is not so, as can be seen from the following statement of **Rav Yosef, and the same** point is made by the following Baraita **taught by Rabbi Ḥiyya:** [5]**"From the day that the Temple was destroyed,** [6]**even though the Sanhedrin ceased** to function as it had previously, and there were no courts empowered to deal with capital cases, nevertheless **the four methods of execution did not cease."** Executions were still carried out in accordance with the law, which mandates four different methods of execution, depending on the crime: stoning, burning, decapitation, and strangulation.

NOTES

outside in bad weather and always to wear suitable clothing can be sure that he will never catch a cold or a fever, whereas it is not possible to prevent other maladies and misfortunes altogether. But *Tosafot* notes that in all cases the dangers a person faces are a combination of his own carelessness and the working of Providence.

חוּץ מִצִּינִּים פַּחִים Except for colds and fevers. The Baraita's argument is based on a play on words, and is not faithful to the straightforward meaning of the verse in Proverbs, which, like the verses preceding it, contrasts the fate of stubborn fools with that of the wise. The word צִינִּים, which we have translated as "colds" (from the word צוֹנֵן), means "thorns," or more generally "troubles" in its original context (from the word צְנִינִים); and the word פַּחִים, which we have translated as "fevers" (from the word פֶּחָם, meaning "hot coals"), means "traps" in its original context. Thus, a contextual translation of the verse would read: "Troubles entrap only the stubborn, but he who guards his soul will succeed in keeping far away from them" (see *Rashi*'s commentary on the Book of Proverbs). Indeed, the Talmud's explanation of the verse is almost the opposite of its simple meaning, since it implies that troubles, other than colds and fevers, cannot be prevented by those who guard their souls. It is quite normal, however, for the Talmud to make a point in this way for homiletic purposes.

Our explanation of these terms in the context of our Gemara follows *Rashi* and most other Rishonim. *Rashbam* attempts to explain the verse in a way that does not depart so radically from the literal interpretation: "Colds entrap only the stubborn, etc.," but *Tosafot* points out that it is clear from other places in which this verse is cited that the Gemara understands "פַּחִים" as "fevers" and not as "traps."

מִיּוֹם שֶׁחָרַב בֵּית הַמִּקְדָּשׁ From the day that the Temple was destroyed. Under Torah law, capital cases were judged by regional courts and not by the central Sanhedrin. However, the regional courts were empowered to judge capital cases only during the period when the central Sanhedrin sat in its chamber within the courtyard of the Temple. Thus capital cases could no longer be judged after the destruction of the Temple, since the Sanhedrin was forced to leave Jerusalem and convene in Yavneh.

Tosafot points out that the language of the Baraita is not precise. Although the Sanhedrin did not leave Jerusalem until the Temple was destroyed, it left its chamber in the Temple courtyard forty years before the destruction, and capital cases ceased to be judged from that time (*Avodah Zarah* 8b). Our commentary follows *Shittah Mekubbetzet*, who explains that the Baraita was not concerned with the precise date, since the Sanhedrin's exile from the Temple occurred only a short period before the destruction of the Temple.

Ritva explains that until the destruction it was still theoretically possible for the Sanhedrin to reconvene and resume its authority over capital cases, but after the destruction this was no longer possible. *Tosafot* goes even further, suggesting that the Sanhedrin actually did move back into the Temple courtyard for brief periods during the forty years before the destruction.

Alternatively, *Tosafot* explains that so long as the Temple was standing, the sacrificial ritual offered a degree of atonement for sinners who were not punished by the court, so that divine execution by the four methods was not carried out as regularly as after the destruction.

TRANSLATION AND COMMENTARY

לֹא בָּטְלוּ [1]The Gemara at once interrupts the Baraita to challenge its wording. The Baraita said that the four methods of execution **did not cease.** But how can this be so? [2]**Surely** the courts were no longer authorized to administer the death penalty, and thus the four methods of execution *did* **cease!**

אֶלָּא [3]**Rather,** says the Gemara, we must emend the wording of the Baraita slightly to read: [30B] [4]**"The punishment** imposed **by the four methods of execution did not cease."** In other words, offenders are still punished by the Supreme Judge in accordance with the law, even though an earthly court is no longer able to impose a sentence of death. The Baraita goes on to explain how, in the absence of an earthly court, divine justice carries out the four methods of execution: [5]"By law, **someone who was liable to stoning** would be hurled from a cliff, and then heavy stones would be cast upon him (*Sanhedrin* 45a). In the absence of an earthly court to carry out such a sentence, God arranges for the offender to be punished in a similar way, [6]and he **either falls from a roof or is** fatally **mauled by wild beasts.** [7]Likewise, **someone who was liable to burning** [8]**either falls into a fire or is bitten by a snake.** By law, someone sentenced to be burned had molten metal poured down his throat (*Sanhedrin* 52a), and the pain caused by this punishment was somewhat similar to the effect of the bite of a venomous snake. [9]Likewise, by law, **someone who was liable to decapitation** was beheaded by means of a sword (*Sanhedrin* 52b). In the absence of an earthly court to carry out such a sentence, [10]**either** God arranges for the sinner **to be handed over to the** gentile **government,** which in Talmudic times beheaded offenders against its laws, **or** else **bandits come upon him,** and kill him with their swords. [11]Likewise, **someone who was liable to strangulation** was put to death by means of a garrotte (*Sanhedrin* 52b). In the absence of an earthly court to carry out such a sentence, [12]God arranges for the sinner **either to drown in a river, or** else **to die of diphtheria,** both deaths being forms of asphyxiation." We see from this Baraita that in the course of imposing divine punishment, God sends lions to kill a person who deserves the punishment of stoning, and bandits to attack a person who deserves the punishment of decapitation. Thus we see that death caused by lions and by bandits is in the hands of Heaven and not in the hands of man, as assumed by Rav Adda bar Ahavah in his objection.

אֶלָּא [13]**Rather,** says the Gemara, we must **reverse** the assumptions on which Rav Adda bar Ahavah's objection is based. [14]Death caused by **lions and thieves is in the hands of Heaven,** as we see from the

[1]לֹא בָּטְלוּ? [2]הָא בָּטְלוּ לְהוּ! [3]אֶלָּא, [30B] [4]"דִּין אַרְבַּע מִיתוֹת לֹא בָּטְלוּ. [5]מִי שֶׁנִּתְחַיֵּיב סְקִילָה [6]אוֹ נוֹפֵל מִן הַגַּג, אוֹ חַיָּה דּוֹרַסְתּוֹ. [7]וּמִי שֶׁנִּתְחַיֵּיב שְׂרֵיפָה [8]אוֹ נוֹפֵל בִּדְלֵיקָה, אוֹ נָחָשׁ מַכִּישׁוֹ. [9]וּמִי שֶׁנִּתְחַיֵּיב הֲרִיגָה [10]אוֹ נִמְסָר לַמַּלְכוּת, אוֹ לִיסְטִים בָּאִין עָלָיו. [11]וּמִי שֶׁנִּתְחַיֵּיב חֶנֶק [12]אוֹ טוֹבֵעַ בְּנָהָר, אוֹ מֵת בִּסְרוּנְכִּי".
[13]אֶלָּא, אֵיפּוּךְ: [14]אַרְיָא וְגַנָּבֵי

LITERAL TRANSLATION

[1]They did not cease? [2]Surely they did cease!

[3]Rather, [30B] [4]"the punishment of the four [methods of] execution did not cease. [5]Someone who was liable to stoning [6]either falls from the roof, or a wild animal mauls him. [7]And someone who was liable to burning [8]either falls into a fire, or a snake bites him. [9]And someone who was liable to decapitation [10]either is handed over to the government, or bandits come upon him. [11]And someone who was liable to strangulation [12]either drowns in a river, or dies of diphtheria."

[13]Rather, reverse [it]: [14]Lions and thieves

RASHI

דין ארבע מיתות — עונש דוגמתס.
נופל מן הגג — דומה לנסקל, שדוחפין אותו מבית הסקילה לארץ. דגבוה שתי קומות היה, כדאמרינן ב"נגמר הדין" (סנהדרין מה,א). **חיה דורסתו** — ארי מפילו לארץ והורגו בדריסה. **נחש מכישו** — והארס שורפו. **נמסר למלכות** — והן מתיזין ראשו בסייף, כי כן דרך המומתין על ידיהן, וזו היא מיתת סייף. **סרונכי** — אסכרא, והוא בגרון, *מלנ"ט.

BACKGROUND

אוֹ נָחָשׁ מַכִּישׁוֹ Or a snake bites him. Snakebite, especially the bite of the poisonous snakes (mainly vipers) found in the region, is considered death by fire, because the snake's venom causes a sensation of great heat accompanied by serious internal hemorrhaging.

LANGUAGE

סְרוּנְכִּי Diphtheria. This word is apparently derived from the root סנך (hence שנק, סרנך), meaning "to choke." Thus סְרוּנְכִּי apparently refers to diphtheria, which causes the trachea to contract, suffocating the victim.

LANGUAGE (RASHI)

*מלנ"ט (some manuscripts of Rashi read בו"ן מלנ"ט). From the Old French *bon malant,* which literally means "good wound," but is apparently a euphemism for diphtheria.

TERMINOLOGY

אֵיפּוּךְ Reverse it. Sometimes, when certain opinions are attributed to a pair of Sages in one context, and the opposite opinions are attributed to these Sages in another context, the Talmud may attempt to resolve the contradiction by suggesting that the viewpoints attributed to these Sages be "reversed." Subsequently, however, the Gemara may reject this suggestion, saying: לְעוֹלָם לָא תֵּיפּוּךְ — "in fact do not reverse the opinions, but instead explain as follows...."

NOTES

דִּין אַרְבַּע מִיתוֹת לֹא בָּטְלוּ The punishment of the four methods of execution did not cease. The Rishonim note that common experience shows us that even since the destruction of the Temple, wicked people do not always meet their deaths in the ways described by this Baraita, and some even die peacefully in their beds. *Tosafot* explains that God sometimes shows mercy to wicked people who show signs of repentance, or who have some merits to their credit. *Ritva* explains that God sometimes chooses not to execute the wicked, preferring to reserve judgment on them for the next world. *Shittah Mekubbetzet* explains that the Baraita is teaching us that when God does kill such people, He selects the method of execution that fits their crimes. *Tosafot* explains that the four methods of execution are listed in the order of their severity, and the Baraita teaches us that God does not kill people by a method of execution more severe than the one that should have been imposed by the court.

אַרְיָא וְגַנָּבֵי בִּידֵי שָׁמַיִם Lions and thieves are in the hands of Heaven. According to the Gemara's conclusion, mishaps that could not have been prevented are in the hands of Heaven, even if they are brought about through a human

בְּיְדֵי שָׁמַיִם; [1]צִינִּים וּפַחִים בִּידֵי אָדָם.
[2]רָבָא אֲמַר: טַעֲמָא דְּרַבִּי נְחוּנְיָא בֶּן הַקָּנָה מֵהָכָא: [3]"וְאִם הַעְלֵם יַעְלִימוּ עַם הָאָרֶץ אֶת עֵינֵיהֶם מִן הָאִישׁ הַהוּא, בְּתִתּוֹ מִזַּרְעוֹ לַמֹּלֶךְ, וְשַׂמְתִּי אֲנִי אֶת פָּנַי בָּאִישׁ הַהוּא וּבְמִשְׁפַּחְתּוֹ וְהִכְרַתִּי אֹתוֹ". [4]אָמְרָה תּוֹרָה: כָּרֵת שֶׁלִּי כְּמִיתָה שֶׁלָּכֶם. [5]מַה

LITERAL TRANSLATION

are in the hands of Heaven; [1]colds and fevers are in the hands of man.

[2]Rava said: The reason of Rabbi Neḥunya ben Hakkanah is from here: [3]"But if the people of the land surely hide their eyes from that man, when he gives of his seed to Molekh [and do not put him to death], then I will set My face against that man and against his family, and I will cut him off." [4]The Torah said: My excision is like your execution. [5]Just as [with]

RASHI

מן האיש ההוא — שהוא חייב מיתת בית דין. **ושמתי אני את פני והכרתי** — למדנו שהכרת במקום מיתה וחילופה.

TRANSLATION AND COMMENTARY

Baraita describing the four methods of execution. [1]**Colds and fevers,** by contrast, **are in the hands of man,** as we see from the verse in Proverbs, as explained in the Baraita above (30a). Thus Rav Adda bar Ahavah's objection to Abaye in its amended form was that Jacob may have been referring to disasters at the hands of man, such as colds and fevers, rather than to disasters at the hands of Heaven, such as lions and bandits. Abaye's response, however, remains the same: Jacob was referring to both types of disaster; and the verse in Genesis can therefore be used as part of a *gezerah shavah* to teach us that the law in Exodus applies to disasters at the hands of Heaven as well as to disasters at the hands of man.

רָבָא אֲמַר [2]Up to this point, the Gemara has been considering Abaye's explanation of Rabbi Neḥunya ben Hakkanah's reasoning. The Gemara now introduces an alternative interpretation: **Rava said: Rabbi Neḥunya ben Hakkanah's reasoning is** not based on a *gezerah shavah*, but on a passage in the Torah (Leviticus 20:4-5) which explicitly declares that excision is in essence a substitute for execution. The passage deals with an idolatrous practice in which a person handed over his child to the idol called Molekh in a ceremony involving a fire. The previous verse requires that the court stone to death anyone guilty of delivering his child to Molekh. [3]The Torah then says: **"But if the people of the land surely hide their eyes from that man, when he gives of his seed to Molekh, and do not put him to death, then I will set My face against that man and against his family, and I will cut him off."** Rava explains how Rabbi Neḥunya ben Hakkanah's principle is inferred from this passage. [4]**The Torah is saying** that **My** (i.e., God's) decree of **excision is like your** (i.e., the court's) sentence of **execution.** The one is a substitute for the other. Hence it follows that the same laws apply to both. [5]Therefore,

NOTES

agency, and only mishaps that are absolutely preventable are in the hands of man. The Rishonim comment: Abaye based his *gezerah shavah* on the assumption that the verse in Exodus (21:22), which refers to a woman who was accidentally struck by a quarreling man, was dealing with a disaster at the hands of man. But surely, according to the Gemara's conclusion, it should be considered a disaster at the hands of Heaven, since the woman could not have prevented it, and God may have put it into the man's mind to behave as he did.

Ramban and other Rishonim reply that this passage follows the opinion mentioned later by the Gemara (below, 35a) — that the disaster to which the verse refers is not the death of the woman, but rather the death penalty imposed on the man by the court. *Ra'ah* explains that execution by the court is considered to be in the hands of man, even according to the Gemara's conclusion that death at the hands of bandits or at the hands of the non-Jewish government is considered to be in the hands of God, because Jewish courts do not execute people capriciously, and it is within the power of the offender to prevent the execution, if he refrains from violating the laws of the Torah.

וְאִם הַעְלֵם יַעְלִימוּ עַם הָאָרֶץ אֶת עֵינֵיהֶם But if the people of the land surely hide their eyes. *Shittah Mekubbetzet* asks: Rava's exegesis is based on Leviticus 20:4. Why did Rava select this verse, rather than the immediately preceding verses (Leviticus 20:2-3), which say: "He who gives of his seed to Molekh shall be put to death by stoning. And I will set My face against that man and will cut him off." It is obviously not possible to excise ("cut off") a person who has already been executed. Thus the verse which warns of the punishment of excision must be referring to a condemned person who for some reason was not executed, and it is clear from these verses that excision is intended as a substitute for execution by the court!

Shittah Mekubbetzet answers that these previous verses refer to a case where the courts were unable to carry out the death sentence for legal reasons — for example, where the crime was not witnessed. In such a case, the Torah tells us that God will excise the criminal instead. But this is not a good proof that excision is the equivalent of execution, because it applies precisely in those situations in which the offender is not legally subject to execution, and not in the more serious situations in which the offender is subject to execution. Rava's verse, by contrast, speaks of a case in which the courts deliberately refrained from executing a criminal without legal grounds, and from the fact that the Torah still describes excision as a substitute, we can infer that it is of comparable severity.

TRANSLATION AND COMMENTARY

just as with your execution, a person who is subject to the more severe penalty of execution **is exempt from paying damages** for the losses he caused in the course of his crime, [1]**so too with My excision,** a person who is subject to the more severe penalty of excision **is exempt from paying** damages for the losses he caused in the course of his crime. Rabbi Neḥunya ben Hakkanah is of the opinion that a person who sets his neighbor's property on fire on Yom Kippur need not pay damages, just like a person who causes such a fire on Shabbat. Similarly, Rabbi Neḥunya ben Hakkanah disagrees with the author of our Mishnah, who ruled that someone who rapes his sister while she is a virgin *na'arah* must pay the fine, since the penalty for such incest is excision, and a person who is subject to excision does not make any monetary payments for the same crime.

מִיתָה שֶׁלָּכֶם, פָּטוּר מִן הַתַּשְׁלוּמִין, [1]אַף כָּרֵת שֶׁלִּי, פָּטוּר מִן הַתַּשְׁלוּמִין.
[2]מַאי אִיכָּא בֵּין רָבָא לְאַבַּיֵי?
[3]אִיכָּא בֵּינַיְיהוּ זָר שֶׁאָכַל תְּרוּמָה. [4]לְאַבַּיֵי פָּטוּר, [5]וּלְרָבָא חַיָּיב.

LITERAL TRANSLATION

your execution, he is exempt from payments, [1]so too [with] My excision, he is exempt from payments.
[2]What [difference] is there between Rava and Abaye?
[3]There is [a difference] between them [regarding] a non-priest who ate terumah. [4]According to Abaye, he is exempt, [5]but according to Rava, he is liable.

RASHI

זר שאכל תרומה — במזיד, הוא במיתה בידי שמים ולא בכרת. כרת — הוא וזרעו נענשין, דכתיב (ויקרא כ) "ערירים יהיו". **לאביי פטור** — מתשלומין, דנפקא ליה מאסון בידי שמים, וכל אסון במשמע, בין במיתה בין בכרת.

מַאי אִיכָּא [2]The Gemara asks: **What difference is there between** the explanations given by **Rava and** by **Abaye?** Both explanations agree that Rabbi Neḥunya ben Hakkanah derives his viewpoint from a Biblical verse. Does it make any practical legal difference whether he derives it from the *gezerah shavah* suggested by Abaye or from the passage cited by Rava?

אִיכָּא בֵּינַיְיהוּ [3]The Gemara answers: **There is a** practical legal **difference between** the two explanations of Rabbi Neḥunya ben Hakkanah's viewpoint, **and it concerns a non-priest who** deliberately **ate terumah** (the portion of the crop that is set aside for priests). The eating of terumah by a non-priest is a transgression which is not subject to excision, but to a slightly lesser penalty called "death at the hands of Heaven." The Torah states that unauthorized consumption of terumah is punished by death (Leviticus 22:9), and this is traditionally understood to mean death at the hands of Heaven. Thus a non-priest who deliberately eats terumah belonging to a priest should be subject to death at the hands of Heaven, and should also have to pay the priest for the terumah he ate without permission. [4]Nevertheless, **according to Abaye's** explanation of Rabbi Neḥunya ben Hakkanah's viewpoint, the non-priest **is exempt** from paying for the terumah, because death at the hands of Heaven is "a disaster at the hands of Heaven" and falls within the purview of Abaye's *gezerah shavah*, which teaches us that a disaster at the hands of Heaven is like a disaster at the hands of man. Therefore a person who is subject to the penalty of death at the hands of Heaven should be exempt from paying damages for the losses he caused in the course of his crime. [5]**According to Rava,** however, who explains the viewpoint of Rabbi Neḥunya ben Hakkanah on the basis of a verse which explicitly compares excision with execution, the non-priest **is liable,** because the verse compares execution to excision and not to the less severe penalty of death at the hands of Heaven, and the penalty for eating the terumah is death at the hands of Heaven and not excision. This, then, says the Gemara, is the case about which Abaye and Rava differ.

NOTES

זָר שֶׁאָכַל תְּרוּמָה A non-priest who ate terumah. Concerning terumah (the special portion that must be separated from produce and given to a priest), the Torah states (Leviticus 22:9): "And they shall keep My ordinance and shall not bear sin for it, lest they die if they profane it." As understood by the Sages, this verse means that any unauthorized consumption of terumah or of *tevel* (produce from which terumah has not yet been separated) is punished by death at the hands of Heaven (*Sanhedrin* 83a).

Excision is considered a more severe penalty than death at the hands of Heaven, because it involves death at the hands of Heaven together with other additional penalties. Accordingly, Rava would argue that we cannot extrapolate from the verse that teaches us that excision is a substitute for execution to the case of death at the hands of Heaven, because the latter is less severe. Abaye, by contrast, learns from the *gezerah shavah* that the exemption from payment granted a person who is subject to a more severe penalty applies to any "disaster" at the hands of Heaven, and this clearly includes death at the hands of Heaven.

[1]וּלְאַבַּיֵי פָּטוּר? [2]וְהָאָמַר רַב חִסְדָּא: מוֹדֶה רַבִּי נְחוּנְיָא בֶּן הַקָּנָה בְּגוֹנֵב חֶלְבּוֹ שֶׁל חֲבֵירוֹ וַאֲכָלוֹ, שֶׁהוּא חַיָּיב, [3]שֶׁכְּבָר נִתְחַיֵּיב בִּגְנֵיבָה קוֹדֶם שֶׁבָּא לִידֵי אִיסּוּר חֵלֶב! [4]אַלְמָא דְּמֵעִידָּנָא דְּאַגְבְּהֵיהּ קַנְיֵיהּ,

LITERAL TRANSLATION

[1]But according to Abaye, is he exempt? [2]But surely Rav Ḥisda said: Rabbi Neḥunya ben Hakkanah agrees concerning someone who steals his fellow's forbidden fat and eats it, that he is liable, [3]since he was already liable for theft, before he came to the prohibition [against] forbidden fat! [4]Consequently [we see] that from the time that he picked it up he acquired it,

RASHI

ולאביי פטור — בתמיה; נהי נמי דמיתה בידי שמים פוטרת מתשלומין, אבל היכא דאכיל תרומה דגזלה מי מיפטר? הא כיון דאגבהה קניה, וחייב בתשלומין, ואפילו תישרף, ומתחייב בנפשו לא הוי עד דאכיל לה.

TRANSLATION AND COMMENTARY

וּלְאַבַּיֵי פָּטוּר [1]**But,** the Gemara objects, **according to Abaye, is** a non-priest who deliberately ate terumah belonging to a priest really **exempt** from paying for the terumah? It seems reasonable to explain that Abaye and Rava disagree about a non-priest who ate terumah, because this is a transgression punishable by death at the hands of Heaven. However, this explanation cannot be correct, because it cannot be reconciled with the accepted principle that in all cases in which a person eats someone else's food without permission, he is not exempt from payment, even if he is subject to a more severe penalty. [2]For **surely Rav Ḥisda said: Rabbi Neḥunya ben Hakkanah**, who said that a person who is subject to excision is exempt from paying monetary damages for the same act, **agrees** with the other Sages **that if someone steals someone else's forbidden fat** (חֵלֶב — *ḥelev*) **and eats it, he must** pay for it, even though eating forbidden fat is a sin punishable by excision (Leviticus 7:25), and Rabbi Neḥunya ben Hakkanah maintains that excision is a more severe penalty that exempts a transgressor from monetary payment. The rule that a person who is subject to a more severe penalty is exempt from paying monetary compensation or a fine applies only if the act that incurred the death penalty (or excision according to Rabbi Neḥunya ben Hakkanah) was precisely the same act that incurred the monetary obligation. But if someone engages in a series of related actions, one of which is subject to the death penalty (or excision), and another of which involves a monetary obligation, he is liable for both, because each action is judged separately. [3]Thus the person who ate someone else's *ḥelev* **was already liable for theft before he was in a position to violate the prohibition against** eating ***ḥelev.*** This is why Rav Ḥisda ruled that Rabbi Neḥunya ben Hakkanah would agree that someone who eats his neighbor's *ḥelev* must pay for it, even though he is also subject to excision for eating it. [4]**Consequently,** says the Gemara, **we see that** the rule that a person who is subject to a more severe penalty need not pay monetary compensation does not generally apply to stealing and eating forbidden foods, because in all such cases the thief **acquires** the forbidden food and becomes liable for stealing it **from the time he picks it up,**

NOTES

מוֹדֶה רַבִּי נְחוּנְיָא בֶּן הַקָּנָה **Rabbi Neḥunya ben Hakkanah agrees.** *Ramban* asks: What is Rav Ḥisda teaching us that we did not already know? The principle that a person who is subject to a more severe penalty is exempted from a financial penalty only if the two penalties are incurred at precisely the same time is found in many places in connection with the death penalty. Why should we think that there would be any difference between the death penalty according to the Sages and excision according to Rabbi Neḥunya ben Hakkanah?

Ramban answers that Rabbi Neḥunya ben Hakkanah maintains that the more severe penalty exempts the offender from monetary payment, even in cases such as excision in which the other Tannaim maintain that he is liable. We might have thought that he would also exempt the offender from payment where the timing was not exact. Therefore Rav Ḥisda felt the need to inform us that Rabbi Neḥunya ben Hakkanah agrees with the other Sages on the question of timing.

Alternatively, *Ramban* explains — based on a passage further on in the Gemara (31a) — that Rav Ḥisda's point was not so much that the timing principle was accepted by Rabbi Neḥunya ben Hakkanah, but that it applies to food. For we might have defined eating as one continuous act that begins the moment the food is picked up and ends when the food is swallowed, and that in such cases the more severe penalty does indeed exempt from payment, even if the financial obligation is incurred at an early stage in the process. Therefore Rav Ḥisda felt the need to inform us that eating does not begin at the moment when food is picked up, since it is possible to eat without picking up the food.

דְּמֵעִידָּנָא דְּאַגְבְּהֵיהּ קַנְיֵיהּ **That from the time that he picked it up he acquired it.** The Talmud regularly refers to the

HALAKHAH

בְּגוֹנֵב חֶלְבּוֹ שֶׁל חֲבֵירוֹ וַאֲכָלוֹ **Concerning someone who steals his fellow's forbidden fat and eats it.** "Someone who steals his neighbor's *ḥelev* (forbidden fat) and eats it must pay for the *ḥelev*, even though he is punished with excision for eating it. *Sma* explains that this is because the thief became liable to pay when he picked up the *ḥelev*,

TRANSLATION AND COMMENTARY

[1]**and he does not forfeit his life** for eating forbidden food **until he** actually **eats it.** [2]It follows that **here too,** in the case of a non-priest who stole a priest's terumah and ate it, everyone would agree that he must pay compensation, even though he is subject to death at the hands of Heaven, because although **he acquired** the terumah **the moment he picked it up,** and became liable to pay for it, [3]**he did not forfeit his life until he ate it.** Hence, even though Abaye and Rava ought to disagree regarding a non-priest who ate terumah, since he is subject to death at the hands of Heaven, Abaye in fact agrees with Rava in this case, because of Rav Ḥisda's argument, and we have still not found a practical difference between Abaye and Rava.

הָכָא בְּמַאי עָסְקִינַן [4]The Gemara offers three solutions to this problem. (1) Normally, if a person steals forbidden food and eats it, he is not exempt from paying for it, since the two penalties are not incurred at precisely the same moment, as Rav Ḥisda ruled. But it is possible to construct an unusual case in which the two penalties *are* incurred at the same time. **With what are we dealing here?** [5]**For example, where** the person stealing the terumah had assistance from **someone else,** who **inserted** the terumah **into** the thief's **mouth.** In this situation, the person eating the terumah did not pick it up, and was not liable for the theft itself. Nevertheless, a person who derives benefit from someone else's loss must pay that other person for the benefit he has derived, even if, for some reason, he is not liable to pay for the loss itself. In our case, the eater must pay the owner of the terumah for having satisfied his hunger, and this financial obligation is incurred when he eats it. Thus the monetary obligation and the more severe penalty for eating terumah are incurred at the same time, and the person eating the terumah is exempt from paying damages.

סוֹף סוֹף [6]The Gemara raises an objection: **At all events, as soon as he chews it he acquires it,**

[1]מִתְחַיֵּיב בְּנַפְשׁוֹ לָא הֲוָה עַד דְּאָכֵיל לֵיהּ. [2]הָכָא נַמִי, בְּעִידָּנָא דְּאַגְבְּהֵיהּ קַנְיֵיהּ, [3]מִתְחַיֵּיב בְּנַפְשׁוֹ לָא הָוֵי עַד דְּאָכֵיל לֵיהּ! [4]הָכָא בְּמַאי עָסְקִינַן? [5]כְּגוֹן שֶׁתָּחַב לוֹ חֲבֵירוֹ לְתוֹךְ פִּיו. [6]סוֹף סוֹף, כֵּיוָן דִּלְעָסֵיהּ, קַנְיָיהּ,

LITERAL TRANSLATION

[1][but] he did not forfeit his life until he ate it. [2]Here too, at the time that he picked it up he acquired it, [3][but] he did not forfeit his life until he ate it!

[4]With what are we dealing here? [5]For example, where his fellow inserted it into his mouth.

[6]At all events, as soon as he chewed it, he acquired it,

RASHI

שתחב לו חברו — דלא אגבהה ולא קניה ולא מיחייב בתשלומין. אלא בבליעתו מתחייב דמי הניית מעיו, ולא דמי כולה. וההיא שעתא חיוב מיתה נמי איכא.

TERMINOLOGY

הָכָא בְּמַאי עָסְקִינַן With what are we dealing here? I.e., the case we are referring to here is.... This expression is used by the Gemara to introduce an אוֹקִימְתָּא — an explanation whose purpose is usually to answer a previously raised objection, and to limit the application of the Mishnah or the Baraita under discussion to one particular set of circumstances.

סוֹף סוֹף At all events (lit., "the end," "finally"). In the course of a Talmudic discussion, after an objection has been made to a statement and a response has been offered to that objection, the Gemara may then restate its original objection by pointing out the weak point of the answer: "However much I wish to accept your answer, *nevertheless* my previous objection still stands."

NOTES

moment when a thief becomes liable as the moment of "acquisition." From this point on, the thief is liable for any damage to the object — even if such damage was in no way caused by the theft — and he becomes subject to the penalty of double payment (Exodus 22:3). In effect, the thief is viewed as having acquired ownership of the stolen object, although he is obliged to return it. Indeed, if the object undergoes substantial change, the thief is not permitted to return it, and must pay for it instead (*Bava Kamma* 65a).

The rules relating to "acquisition" in this sense are similar to the rules regarding "acquisition" in the context of buying and selling. Thus the thief becomes liable when he physically takes possession of the object, by taking it from the owner's domain to a place under his own control, or by lifting it up even in the owner's domain. Later, the Gemara cites an Amoraic dispute as to whether the laws of acquisition regarding theft are defined as rigidly as those governing purchase, or whether a thief is liable even if his act of acquisition would not have been technically valid for a purchase (see below, 31b).

כֵּיוָן דִּלְעָסֵיהּ קַנְיֵיהּ As soon as he chewed it, he acquired it. Our translation and commentary follow the standard text of the Talmud. *Meiri* argues, however, that this phrase should be removed from the text of the Talmud, because a thief who holds food in his mouth and does not spit it out acquires it, since this shows that he has taken physical possession of it. Whether he chews the food or not is irrelevant. Excision, by contrast, is not incurred until the food is swallowed. *Meiri* suggests that the chewing may be required to indicate that the thief really intends to eat the food and not to spit it out (see also *Maharam Schiff*).

HALAKHAH

but became subject to excision only when he swallowed it (following Rav Ḥisda's statement in our Gemara). *Shakh* points out, however, that the discussion in our Gemara follows Rabbi Neḥunya ben Hakkanah, who maintains that excision is a more severe penalty which exempts from payment; but according to the Halakhah (which does not follow Rabbi Neḥunya ben Hakkanah), excision is not grounds for exemption under any circumstances, and the eater is in any event liable to pay for the *ḥelev.* Nevertheless, *Shakh* points out that Rav Ḥisda's statement and the subsequent discussion in our Gemara has relevance, even according to the Halakhah which does not follow Rabbi Neḥunya ben Hakkanah." (*Rambam, Sefer Nezikin, Hilkhot Genevah* 2:4; *Shulḥan Arukh, Ḥoshen Mishpat* 350:1.)

BACKGROUND

בֵּית הַבְּלִיעָה **Throat.** This apparently refers to the back of the mouth (in particular, the pharynx). Once food reaches this area, it is swallowed automatically by the involuntary swallowing mechanism, and only with great difficulty can one prevent this by vomitting up the food.

TRANSLATION AND COMMENTARY

[1] **but he does not forfeit his life until he swallows it!** The Torah imposes penalties for eating forbidden foods only when the food is swallowed. A person who chews forbidden food and then spits it out is exempt from any penalty. But a person who chews food that does not belong to him is immediately obligated to compensate the owner of the food (even if, for some reason, he is not liable for picking it up), regardless of whether he swallows it. Therefore a non-priest who eats a priest's terumah without picking it up is still required to pay for it, since he committed theft by chewing it before he was in a position to violate the prohibition against eating terumah, and the two liabilities were not incurred at the same moment.

כְּגוֹן [2] The Gemara answers: We can construct a case in which chewing is not involved: **For example, where** the thief's accomplice **inserted** the terumah **into** the thief's **throat,** so that he swallowed it without picking it up or chewing it. In this situation, the thief becomes liable to pay for the benefit he received when he swallows the terumah, and this is also the moment when he incurs the penalty of death at the hands of Heaven. Thus the monetary penalty and the more severe penalty are incurred at the same time, and the thief is exempt from paying compensation.

הֵיכִי דָּמֵי [3] The Gemara objects: **How do we visualize the case?** [4] **If** the thief **can cough up** the terumah, **let him cough it up** before he swallows it, and thus avoid any financial obligation. Until forbidden food is swallowed, the act is not an offense subject to excision or death at the hands of Heaven. But the eater in our case is obligated to compensate the owner even before he swallows the terumah, because he failed to return it when he could have done so. Thus this suggestion is no better than the first one, where the terumah was put in the thief's mouth: The two penalties are still not incurred at precisely the same moment. [5] And **if** the thief **cannot cough up** the terumah because it is so far down his throat that he cannot avoid swallowing it, [6] **why is he liable** to the penalty of death at the hands of Heaven for eating it? The entire action was done by his accomplice, and he played no active role at all in eating the terumah!

לָא צְרִיכָא [7] The Gemara answers: **No, it is necessary** to consider a case **where** the accomplice placed the terumah in the thief's throat, and it is not possible for him to cough it up easily, but **he can cough it up if he makes an effort.** In such a case, the moment he swallows it he becomes liable to pay for the benefit he derived from it. And at that very moment he also becomes subject to death at the hands of Heaven. Hence, according to Rabbi Neḥunya ben Hakkanah, he is exempt from paying compensation

[1] מִתְחַיֵּיב בְּנַפְשׁוֹ לָא הָוֵי עַד דְּבָלְעָהּ! [2] כְּגוֹן שֶׁתָּחַב לוֹ לְתוֹךְ בֵּית הַבְּלִיעָה. [3] הֵיכִי דָּמֵי? [4] אִי דְּמָצֵי לְאַהֲדוּרָהּ, נִיהֲדַר. [5] אִי לָא מָצֵי לְאַהֲדוּרָהּ, [6] אַמַּאי חַיָּיב? [7] לָא, צְרִיכָא דְּמָצֵי לְאַהֲדוּרָהּ עַל יְדֵי הַדְּחָק.

LITERAL TRANSLATION

[1] [but] he did not forfeit his life until he swallowed it!

[2] For example, where he inserted it into his throat.

[3] How do we visualize the case? [4] If he can cough it up (lit., "return it"), let him cough [it] up. [5] If he cannot cough it up, [6] why is he liable?

[7] No, it is necessary where he can cough it up with an effort.

RASHI

איבעי ליה לאהדורה — וכי לא אהדרה — מההיא שעתא איהו מזיק לה. דראשון לאו מידי עבד, ולא נתחייב לכהן כלום. **ואי דלא מצי לאהדורה אמאי חייב** — מיתה? אנוס הוא. **על ידי הדחק** — דאי נמי אהדרה — ממאסה ולא חזיא לבעלים, הלכך, מגזל לא גזלה, אמאי קא מחייבת ליה בתשלומין — אהנאת גרונו ומעיו, ההיא שעתא חיוב מיתה איכא.

NOTES

מִתְחַיֵּיב בְּנַפְשׁוֹ לָא הָוֵי עַד דְּבָלְעָהּ **He did not forfeit his life until he swallowed it.** *Rosh* asks: In tractate *Keritot* (7a), the Gemara cites a Baraita that rules that after a priest anoints himself with terumah oil, other people need not be concerned about touching the priest's hands. The Gemara explains that once use has been made of terumah, it ceases to be holy. Yet our Gemara declares that a person who chews terumah is not liable until he swallows it. Why does the terumah not lose its sanctity once it has been chewed?

Rosh answers that terumah loses its sanctity through use only when the use is complete and the full benefit has been derived from the terumah. But eating is not complete until the food has been swallowed; hence, the terumah remains sacred until then.

אִי לָא מָצֵי לְאַהֲדוּרָהּ אַמַּאי חַיָּיב **If he cannot cough it up, why is he liable?** The Gemara rejects the suggestion that the other person inserted the terumah so far down the eater's throat that he could not cough it up because we are trying to visualize a case in which the eater is exempt from monetary payment as a result of being subject to a more severe penalty. Hence we must find a case in which both penalties are applicable. In this case, however, one of the penalties does not apply. But it is not entirely clear which of the penalties the Gemara considers inapplicable when one person inserts terumah into another person's throat.

Our commentary follows *Rashi*, who explains that the Gemara is referring to the penalty of death at the hands of Heaven. *Rashi* explains that if the other person inserted the terumah so far down the eater's throat that he could not cough it up, the eater was in effect *forced* to swallow

TRANSLATION AND COMMENTARY

because he became subject to the more severe penalty of death at the hands of Heaven at the same moment. This is in accordance with Abaye's explanation of Rabbi Neḥunya ben Hakkanah, which maintains that death at the hands of Heaven is the equivalent of excision. Conversely, he *is* liable to pay compensation according to Rava's explanation, which maintains that death at the hands of Heaven is not the equivalent of excision.

[1]רַב פַּפָּא אָמַר: כְּגוֹן שֶׁתָּחַב לוֹ חֲבֵירוֹ מַשְׁקִין שֶׁל תְּרוּמָה לְתוֹךְ פִּיו.

[2]רַב אַשִׁי אָמַר: בְּזָר שֶׁאָכַל

LITERAL TRANSLATION

[1]Rav Pappa said: For example, where his fellow inserted liquids of terumah into his mouth.

[2]Rav Ashi said: [The case is referring] to a non-priest who ate

RASHI

משקין של תרומה — ולא תדחקה לשנויה בבית הבליעה, אלא מכיון שתחבה לתוך פיו אימאסא לה, ולא מצית לאיחיובי משום גזילה — דהא לא חזיא למידי, אלא אהניית גרונו ומעיו מיחייב, ומיתה ותשלומין באים כאחד.

רַב פַּפָּא אָמַר (2) [1]The Gemara now proposes a second solution to the problem of finding a case in which a non-priest who eats a priest's terumah can become subject to death at the hands of Heaven at the very moment he becomes liable to pay monetary compensation. **Rav Pappa said:** We can construct a case in which chewing is not involved: **For example, where** the terumah was a liquid such as wine, and **someone else poured the liquid terumah into his mouth.** In such a case, the eater cannot be expected to return the liquid, as it will not be fit for consumption a second time, and he is not liable for stealing it, because he did not pick the terumah up before drinking it, and liquid terumah need not be chewed. But he becomes liable to pay for the benefit he derived from drinking it as soon as he swallows the terumah. And since he also becomes liable to the penalty of death at the hands of Heaven at the same moment, he is exempt from paying monetary compensation, according to Abaye's explanation of Rabbi Neḥunya ben Hakkanah, which maintains that death at the hands of Heaven is the equivalent of excision, but he *is* liable to pay according to Rava, who maintains that death at the hands of Heaven is not the equivalent of excision.

רַב אַשִׁי (3) [2]The Gemara now gives a third answer to the problem of finding a case in which a non-priest who eats a priest's terumah can become subject to death at the hands of Heaven at the very moment he becomes liable to monetary compensation: **Rav Ashi said:** We can construct a simpler case in which Abaye would differ with Rava. In fact, says Rav Ashi, we are not referring to a case in which a non-priest stole a priest's terumah, but rather to **a case in which a non-priest ate his own**

NOTES

the terumah, and should not be punished for doing so. But the reduced payment for the benefit the eater derived by satisfying his hunger does apply, even though he was forced to swallow the terumah. Thus the Gemara is objecting that the more severe penalty of death at the hands of Heaven does not apply to this case, and there is therefore no reason to exempt the eater from making the monetary payment. But the Gemara responds that we are referring to a case where the eater could with difficulty have coughed up the terumah, and in such a situation he is required to cough it up, and is punished with death at the hands of Heaven if he swallows it instead. Hence, the financial obligation and the more severe penalty are both incurred at the moment he swallows the terumah, and he is therefore exempt from payment.

Tosafot notes that *Rashi*'s explanation is difficult to accept. For if the Gemara's objection was that the eater should have been exempt from death at the hands of Heaven because he was forced to swallow the terumah, why does the Gemara not explain that we are referring to a case where the eater asked the other man to insert the food into his throat, and cooperated with him? In such a case, he could not claim that he was forced to eat the terumah, and he would incur death at the hands of Heaven at the same moment as he became liable to pay — when he swallowed the terumah! *Ritva* suggests that the Gemara may not have proposed this solution because the Hebrew expression for "inserting into a throat" implies force. *Tosafot* suggests that if the food had been inserted into the eater's throat with his consent, he would have been liable to pay monetary compensation as soon as the food entered his mouth, since this would have been the equivalent of picking the food up. Therefore the Gemara assumes that we are referring to a case where it was inserted into his throat against his will.

Tosafot suggests an alternative to *Rashi*'s explanation: If the terumah were inserted so far into the eater's throat that he could not cough it up, he would not be required to make even the payment for the benefit he derived, because the entire act would have been done by the other man, and it would be the latter who would bear all the responsibility. According to this explanation, the Gemara is objecting that the monetary penalty does not apply to this case anyway, and therefore it is not the more severe penalty that exempts the eater from paying. But the Gemara responds that we are referring to a case where the eater could have coughed up the terumah with difficulty, and in such a situation the terumah is regarded as intact until the eater completes its destruction by swallowing it. Hence the eater should be required to pay for the benefit he derived at the owner's expense, but since the financial obligation and the more severe penalty were both incurred at the moment when he swallowed the terumah, he is exempt from payment.

LANGUAGE

שִׁירָאִין Silk garments. From the Greek σηρικόν, *serikon*, meaning "silk" or "silken robe."

TERMINOLOGY

גּוּפָא Returning to the previous statement (lit., "the body," "the thing itself"). An expression used to introduce a quotation from a source cited in passing in the previous discussion, which will now be analyzed at length. Generally, גּוּפָא introduces a new theme.

TRANSLATION AND COMMENTARY

terumah (which he had bought from a priest), thereby incurring death at the hands of Heaven without infringing anyone else's property rights. [31A] [1] However, while he was swallowing the terumah, he incurred an unrelated financial obligation by **tearing someone else's silk garments.** According to Rav Ashi, it is not necessary for the deed that incurs the financial penalty to be connected to the sin that incurs the more severe penalty, provided that they both occur at precisely the same moment. Hence it is easy to construct a case in which a person becomes liable to pay monetary compensation at the very moment he becomes liable to death at the hands of Heaven. In such a case, he is exempt from monetary penalties, following Abaye's explanation of Rabbi Neḥunya ben Hakkanah, according to which death at the hands of Heaven is the equivalent of excision; but he is not exempt from those penalties following Rava's explanation, according to which death at the hands of Heaven is not the equivalent of excision.

גּוּפָא [2] **Returning to a statement that was mentioned** in passing **earlier**, the Gemara now gives it further consideration. **Rav Ḥisda said:** Even though eating forbidden fat (חֵלֶב — *ḥelev*) is a sin punishable by excision, and Rabbi Neḥunya ben Hakkanah maintains that a person who is subject to excision need not pay monetary compensation, [3] **Rabbi Neḥunya ben Hakkanah agrees that if someone steals someone else's forbidden fat and eats it, he is obligated** to pay for it. For the rule that a person who is subject to a more severe penalty is exempt from paying monetary compensation applies only if the deed that incurred the death penalty (or excision, according to Rabbi Neḥunya ben Hakkanah) was precisely the same deed that incurred the monetary payment, but if the person engaged in a series of related actions, one of which incurred the death penalty (or excision) and another a monetary payment, he is not exempt from paying. Applying this principle, [4] Rav Ḥisda argues that a person who steals his neighbor's forbidden fat and eats it **is already liable for theft, before he violates the prohibition against** eating **forbidden fat.** The thief owes his neighbor money the moment he steals the forbidden fat — before he even puts it in his mouth — whereas the penalty of excision for eating it is incurred only when the forbidden food is consumed.

תְּרוּמָה מִשֶּׁלּוֹ, [31A] [1] וְקָרַע שִׁירָאִין שֶׁל חֲבֵירוֹ.
[2] גּוּפָא: אָמַר רַב חִסְדָּא: [3] מוֹדֶה רַבִּי נְחוּנְיָא בֶּן הַקָּנָה בְּגוֹנֵב חֶלְבּוֹ שֶׁל חֲבֵירוֹ וַאֲכָלוֹ, שֶׁהוּא חַיָּיב, [4] שֶׁכְּבָר נִתְחַיֵּיב בִּגְנֵבָה קוֹדֶם שֶׁיָּבֹא לִידֵי אִיסּוּר חֵלֶב.

LITERAL TRANSLATION

his own terumah, [31A] [1] and tore the silk [garments] of his fellow.

[2] Returning to the previous statement (lit., "the thing itself"): Rav Ḥisda said: [3] Rabbi Neḥunya ben Hakkanah agrees concerning someone who steals his fellow's forbidden fat and eats it, that he is liable, [4] since he was already liable for theft before he incurred (lit., "came into the hands of") the prohibition [against] forbidden fat.

RASHI

וקרע שיראים — בשעה שבולעה. ואף על גב דמיתה לאו משום ממונא דניזק אתיא ליה — מיפטר. וסבירא ליה לרב אשי מיתה לזה ותשלומין לזה — פטור.

NOTES

שֶׁאָכַל תְּרוּמָה מִשֶּׁלּוֹ Who ate his own terumah. *Rashba* and other Rishonim explain that Rav Ashi was not insisting that the terumah must belong to the person eating it in order that he be exempt from paying for the garments. Rather, Rav Ashi was saying that the terumah could *even* have been his, since the monetary obligation is connected to the garments and not to the terumah itself.

וְקָרַע שִׁירָאִין שֶׁל חֲבֵירוֹ And tore the silk garments of his fellow. Rav Ashi's explanation appears to have two novel aspects: (1) The sin on account of which the man forfeits his life is not connected in any way to the misdeed which made him liable to pay damages. They simply happened to take place at the same moment. (2) In Rav Ashi's case, the terumah belongs to the sinner himself while the silk garments belong to someone else, and it would appear from a passage in tractate *Sanhedrin* (10a) that the more severe penalty exempts one from the financial penalty only if both offenses were against the same person. (This is what happened in the case of the woman who was killed accidentally. Her assailant was exempt from the payment of damages for her miscarriage.)

Rashi explains that Rav Ashi disagrees with the author of the passage in *Sanhedrin*, and maintains that the more severe penalty cancels out the financial penalty, even if the offenses were against different people. *Shittah Mekubbetzet* adds that *Rashi* understands the two novel aspects of Rav Ashi's view as being connected: According to the Gemara in *Sanhedrin*, which maintains that the more severe penalty exempts one from the financial penalty only if both offenses were against the same person, the two offenses must also be intrinsically connected, but according to Rav Ashi, who maintains that the two offenses can be committed against different people, there is likewise no need for a logical connection. *Tosafot* cites an opinion that goes even further, according to which even the Gemara in *Sanhedrin* would agree that it is immaterial whether the two offenses are committed against the same person or against two different people, provided that the two offenses were accomplished by a single act, and the dispute between Rav Ashi and the Gemara in *Sanhedrin* concerns only cases like ours, in which the two offenses were logically distinct and were committed against different

¹לֵימָא פְּלִיגָא דְּרַבִּי אָבִין? ²דְּאָמַר רַבִּי אָבִין: הַזּוֹרֵק חֵץ מִתְּחִילַּת אַרְבַּע לְסוֹף אַרְבַּע, ³וְקָרַע שִׁירָאִין בַּהֲלִיכָתוֹ, פָּטוּר, ⁴שֶׁעֲקִירָה צוֹרֶךְ הַנָּחָה הִיא.

LITERAL TRANSLATION

¹Shall we say that he disagrees with [the following statement] of Rabbi Avin? ²For Rabbi Avin said: [If] someone shoots an arrow from the beginning of four [cubits] to the end of four [cubits], ³and it tore silk [garments] in its passage, he is exempt, ⁴because displacing is a necessary element of replacing.

RASHI

שעקירה צורך הנחה היא — הלכך, אף על גב דחיוב ממון מקמי הנחה אתיא ליה — פטור. הואיל ובין עקירה והנחה אתיא ליה, מיתה ותשלומין באין כאחד, שעקירה צורך הנחה היא, ומההיא שעתא אתחלה לה מלאכה.

TRANSLATION AND COMMENTARY

לֵימָא ¹The Gemara now suggests that Rav Ḥisda's viewpoint — that someone who eats someone else's forbidden food is always liable to pay, because the theft took place before the food was consumed — may not be accepted by everyone. **Shall we say that** Rav Ḥisda **disagrees with the following statement of Rabbi Avin?** Rabbi Avin's statement deals with someone who causes monetary damage and at the same time violates Shabbat — an offense punishable by death (Exodus 31:14). We have already seen (above, 30a) that in such a case the person is exempt from paying compensation, because he is subject to a more severe penalty. One of the ways in which a person can violate Shabbat is by throwing an object a distance of at least four cubits in the public domain (*Shabbat* 96b). ²Concerning this case, **Rabbi Avin said: If someone shoots an arrow a distance of at least four cubits** in the public domain on Shabbat, thereby committing a capital offense, ³**and** the arrow **tears** someone's **silk garments in its flight,** the archer **is exempt** from paying for the damage, because he is subject to the more severe penalty of violating Shabbat. Rabbi Avin explains: In this case, you might have thought that the liability to pay is incurred the moment the garment is torn, whereas the penalty for violating Shabbat does not apply until the arrow lands more than four cubits away from where it was shot. ⁴But in fact the archer is exempt from payment, **because the displacing** of the arrow **is a necessary element of** its **replacing.** Since carrying on Shabbat is defined as displacing an object from its place and replacing it somewhere else, the entire activity, from the moment the arrow is shot until it lands, is considered one single deed punishable by death. Hence the garment was torn during the Shabbat violation, and both penalties are considered to have been incurred at the same moment. The Gemara now

NOTES

people. *Tosafot Yeshanim* points out, however, that *Rashi's* explanation — that Rav Ashi disagrees with the author of the passage in *Sanhedrin* — is difficult to accept, because the author of the passage in *Sanhedrin* is none other than Rava, and Rav Ashi's purpose here is to explain the dispute in our Gemara between Rava and Abaye.

Tosafot disagrees with *Rashi*, pointing out that the ruling of the Gemara in *Sanhedrin* is difficult to understand according to *Rashi*, because it is clear from several sources that the more severe penalty does create an exemption from financial penalties, even if the two offenses were not directed against the same person. For example, the Mishnah (*Bava Kamma* 34b) rules that a person who burns someone else's property on Shabbat is exempt from payment because of the more severe penalty, even though the Shabbat offense is directed against God and the property offense is aimed against the man's neighbor. Accordingly, *Tosafot* explains that the Gemara in *Sanhedrin* does not disagree with Rav Ashi, and the rule about both offenses being directed against the same person applies only if the more serious offense was a sin against another person. But if the more serious offense was a religious sin directed at God alone (such as eating *ḥelev*), it is immaterial against whom the less serious offense was committed.

הַזּוֹרֵק חֵץ מִתְּחִילַּת אַרְבַּע לְסוֹף אַרְבַּע If someone shoots an arrow from the beginning of four cubits to the end of four cubits. Moving an object from one place to another is one of the thirty-nine categories of work that are forbidden on Shabbat (*Shabbat* 73a). A large part of tractate *Shabbat*, as well as tractate *Eruvin*, is devoted to this topic.

The Torah permits moving an object within the same room, or even from room to room in the same house. What is forbidden is the transfer of an object from a private domain to the public domain or vice versa, or the moving of an object four cubits in the public domain. It is also forbidden to move an object from one private domain to another via the public domain (*Shabbat* 96a-b).

The terms "private domain" and "public domain" have a unique definition for this purpose, which does not correspond to the definitions applicable to other Halakhot. Accordingly, the Rabbis forbade moving an object in certain other situations, which are permitted by the Torah definitions of the two domains but which appear forbidden to the casual observer (*Shabbat* 6a). They did not, however, forbid moving an object from place to place within a single private domain owned by one person.

Someone who moves an object from the public domain to a private domain or vice versa, or from one private

HALAKHAH

הַזּוֹרֵק חֵץ If someone shoots an arrow. "If someone shoots an arrow in the public domain on Shabbat, over a distance of at least four cubits, and the arrow tears a garment while in flight, the archer is exempt from paying for the garment, since he is subject to the more severe penalty for violating Shabbat," following Rabbi Avin in our Gemara. (*Rambam, Sefer Nezikin, Hilkhot Genevah* 3:2.)

SAGES

רַבִּי אָבִין Rabbi Avin. An Amora of the third and fourth generations, Rabbi Avin was apparently born in Babylonia and studied Torah in Eretz Israel. In most cases where his name appears in the Babylonian Talmud, it is abbreviated as Ravin. He returned to Babylonia several times, bringing with him the teachings of the Sages of Eretz Israel. He was one of the most important of the נְחוּתֵי דְּמַעֲרְבָא (the Sages who traveled from Eretz Israel to Babylonia). His son was also called Rabbi Avin, and it is difficult to know which teachings to attribute to one and which to the other. In Eretz Israel he was a disciple of the Sages of the third generation: Rabbi Abbahu, Rabbi Zera, and Rabbi Il'ai, from whom he learned many teachings of Rabbi Yoḥanan. Rabbi Avin's teachings were transmitted by the Sages of the fourth generation: Rava, Rabbi Yudan, and others. Rabbi Avin's son was one of the greatest Palestinian Amoraim of the fifth generation. According to tradition, the day Rav Adda bar Ahavah died, Rabbi Avin was born, and the day Rabbi Avin died, his son Rabbi Avin was born. The younger Rabbi Avin was the head of the yeshivah of Tiberias. His colleague was Rabbi Mana, the head of the yeshivah of Tzipori, and he transmitted the teachings of the Sages of the fourth generation: Rabbi Aḥa, Rabbi Berekhyah, Rabbi Pineḥas, and Rabbi Shammai.

TRANSLATION AND COMMENTARY

applies Rabbi Avin's reasoning to the case of the *ḥelev*. [1]**Here too** we can argue that **the picking up** of the *ḥelev* **was a necessary element** in the **eating** of it! Eating, like shooting an arrow, is one activity, from the moment the food is picked up until it is completely swallowed. Hence a person who eats someone else's *ḥelev* becomes liable to pay compensation while he is in the process of eating the *ḥelev*. Therefore we are justified in arguing that both penalties are incurred at the same moment, and the thief should be exempt from paying because he is subject to the more severe penalty of excision. Thus we see that Rabbi Avin apparently disagrees with Rav Ḥisda, who maintains that a person who steals his neighbor's *ḥelev* and eats it has to pay for it (even according to Rabbi Neḥunya ben Hakkanah).

הָכִי הָשְׁתָּא [2]The Gemara rejects this suggestion: **Now is this so?** How can you compare shooting an arrow on Shabbat with eating *ḥelev?* [3]In the case of the arrow, **it is impossible for** the arrow **to be replaced** in its new resting place **without** first having been **displaced** by being shot. The death penalty for violating Shabbat applies only when one person carries out the entire forbidden action from start to finish. In particular, there is no penalty for moving an object four cubits in the public domain, unless the same person who moved it both displaced it and replaced it. Therefore the entire sequence, from the shooting of the arrow to its landing, is all intrinsically connected. [4]By contrast, in the case of the *ḥelev*, **it is possible to eat** the *ḥelev* **without picking** it **up.** [5]**For if** a person **wants** to, **he can bend over and eat** the *ḥelev* without picking it up at all. Picking up the *ḥelev* is not an intrinsic part of the process of eating it, and since the monetary obligation precedes the penalty of excision, the eater is not exempt, as Rav Ḥisda ruled. Thus we see that Rav Ḥisda does not, in fact, disagree with Rabbi Avin.

[1]הָכָא נַמִי, הַגְבָּהָה צוֹרֶךְ אֲכִילָה הִיא! [2]הָכִי הָשְׁתָּא? [3]הָתָם, אִי אֶפְשָׁר לְהַנָּחָה בְּלֹא עֲקִירָה. [4]הָכָא, אֶפְשָׁר לַאֲכִילָה בְּלֹא הַגְבָּהָה, [5]דְּאִי בָּעֵי, גָּחֵין וְאָכֵיל.

LITERAL TRANSLATION

[1]Here too, picking up is a necessary element of eating!

[2]Now is this so? [3]There, a replacing is impossible without a displacing. [4]Here, eating is possible without picking up, [5]for if he wants, he can bend over and eat.

RASHI

דאי בעי גחין – למטה משלשה טפחים ואכיל. ובציר משלשה לאו הגבהה היא.

NOTES

domain to another via the public domain, is liable by Torah law for having violated Shabbat, even if the distance traversed by the object was very small (ibid.). But if someone moves an object within the public domain, he is liable only if he moved it at least the distance described as "four cubits" (which in this context is approximately three meters). The Torah permits moving an object less than that distance, and, according to some authorities, it is not even forbidden by Rabbinic enactment.

Regardless of whether the object was moved from the public domain to a private domain or vice versa, or was moved four cubits in the public domain, certain conditions must apply if the action is to be considered a violation of Shabbat by Torah law. (1) The object must be displaced from a stable position and replaced in another stable position. (2) The displacement, replacement, and transferral must all be done by the same person. The movement itself can be done in any way — by carrying, throwing, dragging, etc. — provided that the object is considered to have been in motion for the entire time from displacement to replacement.

דְּאִי בָּעֵי גָּחֵין וְאָכֵיל **For if he wants, he can bend over and eat.** According to *Rashi*, the Gemara means that the eater can avoid acquiring the *ḥelev* by bending his head to within three handbreadths (approximately 10 inches) from the food, and then picking it up and eating it. This explanation is consistent with *Rashi*'s view, expressed in several places in the Talmud (e.g., *Kiddushin* 26a), that it is not possible to acquire an object by picking it up, unless it is raised to a height of at least three handbreadths, since the Halakhah considers any object that is within three handbreadths from the ground to be resting on the ground.

Rashi's view on this matter has provoked debate among the commentators. *Ritva* disagrees with *Rashi*, citing several sources that prove that it is not necessary to lift an object three handbreadths in order to acquire it, but *Meiri* defends *Rashi*, arguing that in the places cited by *Ritva*, the Gemara is referring to cases where full acquisition is not necessary. *Ran* takes an intermediate position, suggesting that it may not be necessary to lift an object three handbreadths, but it is necessary to lift it at least one handbreadth.

Rashi's explanation of our Gemara presents an additional problem. *Tosafot* points out that even if we accept *Rashi*'s view that acquisition by lifting normally requires three handbreadths, it is clear from the previous passage, which stated that the eater acquires the food by chewing it, that the thief acquires the food when he puts it in his mouth, at the very latest. Accordingly, *Tosafot* explains that our Gemara means that the eater can bend over and insert the food into his throat without picking it up at all (as when the food is on a stick). *Tosafot* adds that the thief could have had someone else insert the *ḥelev* into his throat, as the Gemara explained in the previous passage.

According to this explanation, the Gemara does not mean that Rav Ḥisda was actually referring to a case where the eater bent over. What the Gemara is saying is that picking up food is not an intrinsic part of eating, in the way that shooting an arrow is an intrinsic part of the arrow's flight. *Tosafot*'s explanation is also accepted by *Rashba* and *Ra'ah*, and has been followed in our commentary.

TRANSLATION AND COMMENTARY

אִי נַמִי [1] **Alternatively,** continues the Gemara, there is another possible distinction between shooting an arrow and eating *ḥelev*. In the case of the arrow, once the archer starts the process, it continues automatically until its conclusion. [2] Even **if he wants to bring the arrow back, he cannot bring it** back once it has been shot. Hence the entire process, from displacing to replacing, from the shooting of the arrow to its coming to rest, is considered one continuous action. [3] By contrast, in the case of the *ḥelev*, after the eater has picked it up, **he can return it** to its place uneaten at any stage in the process until he swallows it. The process of eating the *ḥelev* cannot be considered one action, since there is no certainty that one stage will lead to the next. Therefore, since the monetary obligation and the penalty of excision are incurred at different stages, the eater is not exempt, just as Rav Ḥisda ruled. Thus we see again that Rav Ḥisda does not, in fact, disagree with Rabbi Avin, and his ruling stands unchallenged.

מַאי אִיכָּא [4] The Gemara asks: **What is the difference between these two alternative answers?** What practical difference does it make which way we distinguish between shooting an arrow and eating *ḥelev*, since according to both answers there is no contradiction between the statements of Rav Ḥisda and Rabbi Avin?

אִיכָּא בֵּינַיְיהוּ [5] The Gemara replies: **There is** indeed **a** practical **difference between these** two alternative answers. The first answer made a distinction between *carrying on Shabbat* and eating *ḥelev*: in the former case, the entire process is intrinsically connected, whereas in the latter the early stages in the process are not indispensable. The second answer made a distinction between *shooting an arrow* and eating *ḥelev*: in the former case, the process is irreversible, whereas in the latter it can be stopped. [6] This difference can be illustrated by the following case in which **someone was carrying a knife** for a distance of at least four cubits **in the public domain, and** the knife **tore** another person's **silk garment in its passage.** [7] **According to** the first **answer, in which you said** that shooting an arrow is different from eating *ḥelev* [8] because **it is** logically **impossible for** the arrow **to be replaced** in its new resting place **without** first having been **displaced** by being shot, this argument would apply to all cases of carrying on Shabbat. [9] Thus **here too**, in the case of the

[1] אִי נַמִי: [2] הָתָם, אִי בָּעֵי לְאַהֲדוּרָהּ, לָא מָצֵי מַהֲדַר לָהּ. [3] הָכָא, מָצֵי מַהֲדַר לָהּ.

[4] מַאי אִיכָּא בֵּין הַאי לִישָּׁנָא לְהַאי לִישָּׁנָא?

[5] אִיכָּא בֵּינַיְיהוּ [6] הַמַּעֲבִיר סַכִּין בִּרְשׁוּת הָרַבִּים, וְקָרַע שִׁירָאִין בַּהֲלִיכָתוֹ. [7] לְהַךְ לִישָּׁנָא דְּאָמְרַתְּ: [8] ״אִי אֶפְשָׁר לְהַנָּחָה בְּלֹא עֲקִירָה״, [9] הָכָא נַמִי

LITERAL TRANSLATION

[1] Or alternatively (lit., "if also"): [2] There, if he wants to return it, he cannot return it. [3] Here, he can return it.

[4] What [difference] is there between this version and that version?

[5] There is [a difference] between them [6] [regarding] someone who was carrying a knife in the public domain, and it tore silk [garments] in its passage. [7] According to that version in which you said: [8] "A replacing is impossible without a displacing," [9] here too

RASHI

לא מצי לאהדורה — משזרק את החץ. הלכך משעת עקירה סופו לקרוע לו סיראין. **הכא מצי מהדר ליה** — הלכך לא אמרינן משעת הגבהה אתחלה לה אכילה. **המעביר סכין** — בידו בהליכה.

NOTES

אִי בָּעֵי לְאַהֲדוּרָהּ If he wants to return it. According to the literal meaning of the Gemara (followed by our commentary), it appears that the entire sequence of shooting the arrow is considered one act, because an arrow cannot be turned back once it has been shot, whereas a person eating *ḥelev* or a person carrying a knife can stop at any time. According to this explanation, the Gemara's second answer is that the distinction between an arrow on the one hand and *ḥelev* or a knife on the other is entirely physical, unlike the first answer, which was essentially Halakhic. *Shittah Mekubbetzet* points out, however, that this explanation is difficult to accept, because Rabbi Avin explicitly stated that his reasoning was based on the idea that displacement is a necessary element of replacement, and this clearly implies a Halakhic dimension.

Shittah Mekubbetzet explains that, according to both of the Gemara's answers, the main reason for the archer being liable is because the displacement of the arrow is a necessary element of its replacement, so that the entire sequence, from beginning to end, is inherently one single Shabbat violation. According to the first answer of the Gemara, it is sufficient to establish that the entire sequence was one Shabbat violation, and it is not important at which stage the monetary damage took place. According to the second explanation, it is also important to establish that the action that would eventually cause the monetary damage was carried out at the same moment as the action that would eventually cause the Shabbat violation. Hence the Gemara explains that the arrow cannot be turned back, so that from the moment of displacement, when the arrow was shot, it was inevitable that the garment would be torn and Shabbat violated. Support for this explanation can be found in *Rashi*.

אִיכָּא בֵּינַיְיהוּ הַמַּעֲבִיר סַכִּין There is a difference between them regarding someone who was carrying a knife. *Ritva* notes that there is another practical difference

SAGES

רַב בִּיבִי בַּר אַבַּיֵי Rav Bivi bar Abaye. A Babylonian Amora of the fifth generation, Rav Bivi was the son of Abaye, Rava's colleague. His teachers were Rav Yosef and his own father. His contemporaries were Rav Pappi and Rav Huna the son of Rav Yehoshua. His Halakhic teachings and Aggadic sayings are found in many places in the Talmud.

אִי אֶפְשָׁר לְהַנָּחָה בְּלֹא עֲקִירָה. [1]לְהַךְ לִישָּׁנָא דְּאָמְרַתְּ: [2]"לָא מָצֵי מַהֲדַר לָהּ", [3]הָכָא מָצֵי מַהֲדַר לָהּ.

[4]גּוּפָא: [5]אָמַר רַבִּי אָבִין: הַזּוֹרֵק חֵץ מִתְּחִלַּת אַרְבַּע לְסוֹף אַרְבַּע, [6]וְקָרַע שִׁירָאִין בַּהֲלִיכָתוֹ, פָּטוּר, [7]שֶׁעֲקִירָה צוֹרֶךְ הַנָּחָה הִיא.

[8]מְתִיב רַב בִּיבִי בַּר אַבַּיֵי: [9]"הַגּוֹנֵב כִּיס בְּשַׁבָּת,

LITERAL TRANSLATION

a replacing is impossible without a displacing. [1]According to that version in which you said: [2]"He cannot return it," [3]here he can return it.

[4]Returning to the previous statement: [5]Rabbi Avin said: [If] someone shoots an arrow from the beginning of four [cubits] to the end of four [cubits], [6]and it tore silk [garments] in its passage, he is exempt, [7]because displacing is a necessary element of replacing.

[8]Rav Bivi bar Abaye objected: [9]"[If] someone steals a wallet on Shabbat,

RASHI

הגונב כיס בשבת — הגביהו ברשות הבעלים, והוליכו לרשות הרבים.

TRANSLATION AND COMMENTARY

knife, **it is impossible for** the knife **to be replaced without** first having been **displaced,** and the person carrying the knife should be exempt from paying damages, even though the garment was torn before he became subject to the death penalty. [1]But **according to** the second **answer, in which you said** that shooting an arrow is different from eating *ḥelev* [2]because the archer **cannot bring** the arrow **back** once it has been shot, whereas the person eating the *ḥelev* can stop the process at any point before it is swallowed, this argument does not apply to a case in which a person carries an object on Shabbat across a distance of four cubits in the public domain. [3]In the case of the knife, **he can return** the knife to its original place and be exempt from the penalty for violating Shabbat. According to this answer, damage caused by carrying a knife through the public domain on Shabbat is not treated like damage caused by an arrow, and the person carrying the knife is liable to pay for the damage caused by his knife, since the garment was torn before he became subject to the death penalty.

גּוּפָא [4]**Returning to the ruling** about the arrow **mentioned above**, the Gemara now gives it further consideration. [5]**Rabbi Avin said: If someone shoots an arrow a distance of at least four cubits** in the public domain on Shabbat, thereby committing a capital offense, [6]**and** the arrow **tears** someone's **silk garments in its passage,** the archer **is exempt** from paying for the damage, because he is subject to the more severe penalty of violating Shabbat. Although the damage was done and the liability to pay was incurred at the moment the garment was torn, and the penalty for violating Shabbat does not apply until the arrow lands at a point more than four cubits away, and although we know that the more severe penalty normally exempts a person from a financial penalty only when both penalties are incurred at precisely the same moment, nevertheless the archer is exempt, [7]**because the displacing** of the arrow **is a necessary element of its replacing.** Since carrying on Shabbat is defined as displacing an object from its place and replacing it somewhere else, the entire activity, from the moment the arrow is shot until it lands, is considered to be one single deliberate violation of Shabbat, punishable by death, from the moment the arrow is shot until it lands at least four cubits away. Hence the garment was torn in the course of a Shabbat violation, and both penalties are considered to have been incurred at the same moment. Therefore the archer is exempt from paying for the garment, since he is subject to the more severe penalty for violating Shabbat.

מְתִיב [8]**Rav Bivi bar Abaye** raised an **objection** to Rabbi Avin's ruling, from the following Tosefta (*Bava Kamma* 9:19). This Tosefta, like the ruling of Rabbi Avin, deals with a person who causes monetary damage while violating Shabbat. One of the ways in which Shabbat can be violated is by moving an object from a private domain into the public domain. This action, like throwing or shooting an object over a distance of at least four cubits in the public domain (which we considered earlier), is a transgression only if the object was displaced from its original resting place in the private domain and replaced in the public domain. Now, theft is carried out in much the same way — by picking up an object in its owner's house and taking it outside. Hence we might have thought that a thief who steals an object on Shabbat by taking it out of its owner's house into the public domain should be exempt from paying for it, since he is subject to a more severe penalty for violating Shabbat. [9]However, the Baraita rules that **"if someone steals a wallet on Shabbat**

NOTES

between the two solutions of the contradiction between Rav Ḥisda and Rabbi Avin: If the eater had an associate who inserted the *ḥelev* into his mouth, the eater should be exempt from paying for the *ḥelev*, according to the first solution, because we can argue that holding food in one's mouth is for the sake of swallowing, since it is not possible to swallow food unless it first enters the mouth. But according to the second solution, the eater should be liable, since he could have spit out the *ḥelev* instead of swallowing it. Thus it is like a knife being carried in the public domain, which can be put down at any time.

חַיָּיב, [1]שֶׁכְּבָר נִתְחַיֵּיב בִּגְנֵיבָה קוֹדֶם שֶׁיָּבֹא לִידֵי אִיסּוּר סְקִילָה. [2]הָיָה מְגָרֵר וְיוֹצֵא, מְגָרֵר וְיוֹצֵא, פָּטוּר, [3]שֶׁהֲרֵי אִיסּוּר שַׁבָּת וּגְנֵיבָה בָּאִין כְּאֶחָד״.

[4]וְאַמַּאי? [5]הָכָא נַמִי, לֵימָא הַגְבָּהָה צוֹרֶךְ הוֹצָאָה הִיא!

LITERAL TRANSLATION

he is liable, [1]since he was already liable for theft before he incurred the prohibition [punishable by] stoning. [2][If] he was dragging it out, dragging it out, he is exempt, [3]since the prohibition of Shabbat and theft come as one."

[4]But why? [5]Here too, let us say [that] picking up is a necessary element of taking out!

TRANSLATION AND COMMENTARY

in this way, **he is liable** to pay for the wallet, even though he is also subject to the death penalty for violating Shabbat, **since he became liable for theft** the moment he picked up the wallet in its owner's house, [1]**before he violated the** Shabbat **prohibition punishable by stoning.** The thief became liable for violating Shabbat only after he moved the wallet from the private domain to the public domain, whereas he was already liable for the theft from the moment he picked it up." [2]The Baraita illustrates its point by citing a contrasting case: **"If,** on the other hand, the thief **drags** the wallet **out** of its owner's house without picking it up, **he is exempt** from paying for it, **since** in this case **the violation of Shabbat and the theft were committed simultaneously."** A thief who drags an object along the ground without picking it up is liable for the theft only when the object leaves its owner's domain. Likewise, a person who drags an object from a private domain into the public domain on Shabbat without picking it up becomes liable when the object leaves the private domain. Therefore, a thief who steals a wallet on Shabbat by dragging it out of the house incurs both liabilities at precisely the same moment, and is exempt from paying for the wallet, since he is subject to the more severe penalty for violating Shabbat.

וְאַמַּאי [4]Rav Bivi bar Abaye now explains how this Tosefta contradicts Rabbi Avin. The Tosefta ruled that a thief who picks up a wallet and takes it out of a house on Shabbat is liable, because the monetary penalty and the Shabbat violation are not incurred at precisely the same stage in the process. **But** we may ask: **Why** should this be so, according to Rabbi Avin? [5]**Here too we should say that picking up** the wallet and displacing it from its original resting place in its owner's house **is a necessary element of taking** it **out!** When the thief picks up the wallet and becomes liable to pay for it, he is at the same time beginning the sequence of violating Shabbat, since there can be no penalty for violating Shabbat unless the wallet is displaced from its resting position in its owner's house, and the wallet was displaced in this case precisely by being picked up. Hence, we should consider the wallet to have been stolen in the course of a Shabbat violation, and the thief should be exempt from paying for it. Yet the Tosefta rules that the thief is liable, and in effect compares this case with the case of *ḥelev* considered above, in which we established that the two penalties must be incurred at precisely the same stage. Does this not prove that the Tosefta disagrees with Rabbi Avin's opinion, that the entire sequence of moving an object on Shabbat is considered a single action?

RASHI

חייב – בתשלומין, אף על פי שנהרג. **שכבר נתחייב בגניבה** – לשלם, דהגבהה קונה בכל מקום וקמה לה ברשותיה אף להתחייב באונסים. **היה מגרר ויוצא** – שלא הגביהו ברשות הבעלים. ולא קנאו אלא בהוצאה מרשות הבעלים – פטור, שאיסור שבת כו'. **ואמאי** – כי הגביהו ברשות הבעלים וקנאו אמאי חייב? נימא משעת הגבהה אתחלה לה הוצאה.

NOTES

הָיָה מְגָרֵר וְיוֹצֵא **If he was dragging it out.** From this Tosefta, it is clear that someone who drags an object from domain to domain is liable for violating Shabbat, even if he does not pick up the object. The Rishonim note that this idea appears to be contradicted by a passage in tractate *Shabbat* (8b), which declares that a person who moves a big bundle of sticks by rolling it over and over is exempt from the penalty for violating Shabbat, since he lifted one end of the bundle at a time, and did not displace it in its entirety. How, then, can the Tosefta rule that someone who drags an object without picking it up is liable?

The Rishonim give three basic answers to this question. *Ramban* explains that the Tosefta is referring to a situation in which the floor of the house was above street level, so

HALAKHAH

הַגּוֹנֵב כִּיס בְּשַׁבָּת **If someone steals a wallet on Shabbat.** "If someone steals a wallet on Shabbat by picking it up while it is still in its owner's domain, and he then takes it out to the public domain, he is liable to pay for the wallet, even though he is also subject to the death penalty for violating Shabbat, since the two penalties were not incurred at the same moment. But if he dragged the wallet out into the public domain, so that he acquired it at the moment he removed it from its owner's domain, he is exempt from payment, since the two penalties were incurred at the same moment. *Maggid Mishneh* notes that *Rambam* apparently rejects our Gemara's stipulation that the thief is not liable to pay for the wallet unless he stood still and took a rest before taking the wallet out." (*Rambam, Sefer Nezikin, Hilkhot Genevah* 3:2; *Shulḥan Arukh, Ḥoshen Mishpat* 351:1.)

SAGES

רַבִּי סִימוֹן Rabbi Simon. Rabbi Simon was a third-generation Palestinian Amora. In many places in the Babylonian Talmud he is known as Rabbi Shimon ben Pazzi. He was one of the younger students of Rabbi Yehoshua ben Levi, and he transmits many Halakhic teachings in his name. Rabbi Simon was a colleague of the greatest disciples of Rabbi Yoḥanan.

Rabbi Simon seems to have been affiliated with the House of the Nasi, where he wielded considerable influence. He was in charge of the sanctification of the New Moon and of adding the intercalary month to make a leap year. Many of his teachings are presented in the Babylonian Talmud, and many more in the Jerusalem Talmud and the Aggadic Midrashim. The Sages of the following generation in Eretz Israel present rulings in his name.

TRANSLATION AND COMMENTARY

הָכָא בְּמַאי עָסְקִינַן [1]The Gemara attempts to resolve this difficulty by suggesting that the Tosefta may be dealing with a special case in which Rabbi Avin's argument does not apply. **With what are we dealing here?** asks the Gemara. [2]With a case, **for example, where** the thief **picked up** the wallet, not in order to take it out, but **in order to hide it** somewhere inside the owner's domain, [3]**but** later he **changed his mind about it and took it out.** In such a case, the thief is guilty of theft the moment he picks the wallet up, but he does not begin the sequence of violating Shabbat until he changes his mind and decides to take it out, since the initial displacement was not for the sake of taking it out. Therefore, in the first case, where the thief picks the wallet up, he is liable to pay for it, since the act of theft occurred before the wallet was moved into the public domain. But in the second case, where the thief drags the wallet out, he is exempt from payment, since neither the act of theft nor the Shabbat violation take effect until he actually removes the wallet from the owner's home.

וְכִי הַאי גַּוְונָא [4]**But** the Gemara rejects this suggestion and asks rhetorically: **In such a case,** where the thief changes his mind, **is he liable** for violating Shabbat? A person who picks up an object with the intention of hiding it, and then changes his mind and takes it out, is not considered to be in violation of Shabbat from the moment he picked it up. In fact, he is not culpable at all, unless he puts the object down when he changes his mind and then picks it up again with the intention of taking it out. [5]For **surely Rabbi Simon said in the name of Rabbi Ammi in the name of Rabbi Yoḥanan:** [6]**If someone was**

[1]הָכָא בְּמַאי עָסְקִינַן? [2]כְּגוֹן שֶׁהִגְבִּיהוֹ עַל מְנָת לְהַצְנִיעוֹ, [3]וְנִמְלַךְ עָלָיו וְהוֹצִיאוֹ. [4]וְכִי הַאי גַּוְונָא, מִי חַיָּיב? [5]וְהָאָמַר רַבִּי סִימוֹן אָמַר רַבִּי אַמִּי אָמַר רַבִּי יוֹחָנָן: [6]הַמְפַנֶּה

LITERAL TRANSLATION

[1]With what are we dealing here? [2]For example, where he picked it up in order to hide it, [3]and changed his mind about it and took it out. [4]But in such a case, is he liable? [5]But surely Rabbi Simon said in the name of Rabbi Ammi in the name of Rabbi Yoḥanan: [6][If] someone was removing

RASHI

וכי האי גוונא מי חייב – משום שבת.

NOTES

that the thief did displace the wallet when it left the house.

Ra'avad explains that the Tosefta is referring to an object that was moved from a private domain to the public domain, whereas the Gemara in *Shabbat* is referring to an object that was moved four cubits in the public domain. According to *Ra'avad*, when an object is moved four cubits in the public domain, a violation occurs only if one picks up the object in its entirety, but when an object is moved from domain to domain, the transfer itself is considered a displacement, even if the object was not picked up.

Most Rishonim (*Rambam*, *Rashba*, *Ra'ah*, *Tosafot*) make a distinction between dragging and rolling. They explain that our Tosefta considers dragging to be a kind of displacement, since the entire object moves from its place. The Gemara in *Shabbat*, by contrast, was referring to rolling, where one end of the bundle remains in its place while the other one moves, after which both ends come to rest momentarily before the previously resting end begins to move again. This kind of movement is not considered displacement, since the movement of the two ends is interrupted by a moment of rest, and between moments of rest, one of the ends does not move at all.

הָכָא בְּמַאי עָסְקִינַן With what are we dealing here? The Gemara responds to the apparent contradiction between Rabbi Avin's ruling and the Tosefta by insisting that the Tosefta is referring to a special case. In the end, the Gemara is forced to conclude that the Tosefta reflects the viewpoint of Ben Azzai, which is not accepted as the Halakhah. *Maggid Mishneh* asks: *Rambam* (*Hilkhot Genevah* 3:2) rules in accordance with both Rabbi Avin and the Tosefta. Yet *Rambam* does not rule in favor of Ben Azzai (*Hilkhot Shabbat* 14:15), nor does he state that the Tosefta is referring to a special case. How, then, can *Rambam* rule in favor of both the Tosefta and Rabbi Avin, since our Gemara clearly states that without a special explanation, these rulings contradict each other?

Maggid Mishneh explains that this entire passage of the Gemara is rejected by the Halakhah. According to many Rishonim, this passage is not consistent with the second answer of the Gemara in the previous passage, whereby the difference between shooting an arrow and eating *ḥelev* is that shooting an arrow is irreversible. And according to many Rishonim, the first answer of the Gemara in the previous passage, which states that the difference between shooting an arrow and eating *ḥelev* is that it is possible to eat *ḥelev* by bending over, is not consistent with the passage on the previous page, in which the Gemara discussed the case of a non-priest who ate terumah. Therefore, if we accept the passage about terumah, we must reject the Gemara's first distinction between shooting an arrow and eating *ḥelev*, and accept the Gemara's second distinction. And if we accept the Gemara's second distinction, we must reject Rav Bivi bar Abaye's objection in our passage and the entire ensuing discussion. Consequently, *Rambam* rules in accordance with both Rabbi Avin and the Tosefta, since the case of the Tosefta is comparable to the case of *ḥelev*, and not to the case of the arrow.

TRANSLATION AND COMMENTARY

removing objects from one corner of a private domain **to another,** [1]**and** then **changed his mind about them and took them out** to the public domain, **he is exempt** from the death penalty for violating Shabbat, [2]**since the** act of **displacing** the objects **was not from the outset for the purpose** of removing them from the private to the public domain! By Torah law, Shabbat can be violated only by an act whose full implications are understood and which is planned from beginning to end. Thus, someone who moves an object from a private domain to the public domain is culpable only if he planned that action from the displacement to the replacement. If at any stage he changed his mind, he is exempt. In our case, since the thief did not intend to pick up this wallet in order to take it out, he is not subject to the penalty for violating Shabbat at all, and is obviously fully liable to pay for the wallet.

לָא תֵּימָא [3]Accordingly, the Gemara changes its interpretation of the Tosefta. **Do not say** that the thief picked up the wallet **in order to hide it,** and later changed his mind, [4]**but** rather **say** that he did so **in order to take it out,** as we understood originally. On this basis we can construct another special case in which Rabbi Avin's argument does not apply. [5]**With what are we dealing here** in the Tosefta? [6]With a case **in which** the thief picked up the object in the private domain in order to take it out, and then **stopped** for a moment in the private domain before taking the object out. In such a case, we consider the movement of the object to have been interrupted, and we regard the object as having been returned to a resting position wherever the thief is standing at the moment. When the thief moves again, the object is considered

חֲפָצִים מִזָּוִית לְזָוִית, [1]וְנִמְלַךְ עֲלֵיהֶם וְהוֹצִיאָן, פָּטוּר, [2]שֶׁלֹּא הָיְתָה עֲקִירָה מִשָּׁעָה רִאשׁוֹנָה לְכָךְ!

[3]לָא תֵּימָא: ״עַל מְנָת לְהַצְנִיעוֹ״, [4]אֶלָּא אֵימָא: ״עַל מְנָת לְהוֹצִיאוֹ״. [5]הָכָא בְּמַאי עָסְקִינַן? [6]כְּשֶׁעָמַד.

LITERAL TRANSLATION

objects from [one] corner to [another] corner, [1]and changed his mind about them and took them out, he is exempt, [2]since the displacing was not from the outset (lit., "from the first hour") for that [purpose]!

[3]Do not say: "In order to hide it," [4]but say: "In order to take it out." [5]With what are we dealing here? [6]When he stopped (lit., "stood").

RASHI

לכך — להוציאו. **לא תימא** בהגביהו על מנת להצניעו אלא הגביהו על מנת להוציאו — ודקשיא לך: נימא הגבהה לצורך הוצאה היא. **הכא במאי עסקינן בשעמד** — ועמידתו היא הנחה לעקירה ראשונה, ואין חיוב שבת באה לו על ידי עקירת חפץ הראשונה, אלא על ידי עקירת גופו שעוקר עצמו אחר העמידה על מנת להוציא, ועקירת גופו כעקירת חפץ.

BACKGROUND

וְנִמְלַךְ עֲלֵיהֶם וְהוֹצִיאָן And changed his mind about them and took them out. All the labors forbidden on Shabbat share a general principle: a person is not liable for the action by itself, unless it was done in premeditated fashion. There is, however, a dispute among the Tannaim regarding the degree of premeditation necessary for an act to be regarded as having been intentional from the outset. For example, if someone intended to pick a certain bunch of grapes and then mistakenly picked another bunch instead, is this regarded as a premeditated action? Regardless of their rulings in doubtful situations, all the Sages agree that prior intention to commit an act is necessary for that act to be considered forbidden by the Torah. Therefore someone who picks up an object without intending to transfer it to a different domain, even if he later changes his mind and does transfer it, is not liable for the action by Torah Law, since he did not originally intend to move the object from one domain to another on Shabbat.

NOTES

הַמְפַנֶּה חֲפָצִים מִזָּוִית לְזָוִית If someone was removing objects from one corner to another corner. The Torah (Exodus 31:12-17 and 35:1-3) inserts the commandment to observe Shabbat in the midst of the detailed instructions about building the Tabernacle (chapters 25-31 and 35-40). This is traditionally understood to be teaching us that it is forbidden to violate Shabbat even for the sake of important religious duties, such as the obligation to build the Tabernacle or the Temple (*Mekhilta*). The juxtaposition of these verses is further understood to be teaching us that the work involved in the construction of the Tabernacle is the paradigm for the types of work that are forbidden on Shabbat (*Shabbat* 49b).

Among the phrases that recur constantly in the story of the Tabernacle is "creative work" (מְלֶאכֶת מַחֲשֶׁבֶת). Because of the juxtaposition of the commandments in the Torah, this phrase is traditionally understood to apply to Shabbat as well. It is therefore a Halakhic principle that the Torah specifically forbade "creative work" on Shabbat, but work that is not creative is not a violation of Torah law (*Betzah* 13b).

Among the types of work that are not considered "creative" is work in which a person changes his mind in the middle (such as the case in our Gemara), and work done in an abnormal way (an example can be found below [31b], where a person drags a pocket-sized wallet out of a house without lifting it up). The principle of creative work may also be the basis for the rule that there can be no liability for moving an object unless it is displaced, moved, and replaced by the same person, and that an object is not considered to have been displaced or replaced unless it rests in a stable fashion on an area of at least four handbreadths by four handbreadths, or is held in a person's hand.

לָא תֵּימָא: עַל מְנָת לְהַצְנִיעוֹ Do not say: "In order to hide it." This phrase appears superfluous in the Gemara's discussion, and indeed does not appear in some versions of the Talmud. For it is not necessary for the Gemara to retract its previous explanation — according to which the Tosefta is referring to a thief who picked up a wallet in order to hide it and then changed his mind — in order to introduce its new explanation, according to which the

HALAKHAH

כְּשֶׁעָמַד When he stopped. "If someone is carrying an object in the public domain, and he stops and takes a rest before he has carried it a distance of four cubits, he is exempt from the penalty for violating Shabbat, even if the total distance he has carried the object is more than four cubits. This refers only to halts for the purpose of rest. But

TRANSLATION AND COMMENTARY

to have been displaced a second time. Therefore in our case, the thief displaced the wallet twice: Once, when he picked it up and became liable for theft, and a second time after he stood still. The first displacement did not constitute a violation of Shabbat, because the wallet was effectively replaced in the same domain. The thief became liable for violating Shabbat only after he displaced the wallet again and took it out to the public domain. Therefore, in the first case mentioned in the Tosefta, where the thief picked the wallet up, he is liable to pay for it, because the act of theft occurred when he first displaced the wallet (before he stood still), and he began to violate Shabbat only when he displaced the wallet again, when he began moving again after having stood still. But in the second case mentioned in the Tosefta, where the thief dragged the wallet out, he is exempt from payment, since the act of theft and the Shabbat violation took effect only when he actually removed the wallet from the owner's domain.

[1]עָמַד לְמַאי? [2]אִי לְכַתֵּף, אוֹרְחֵיהּ הוּא! [3]אֶלָּא, בְּעוֹמֵד לָפוּשׁ.
[4]אֲבָל לְכַתֵּף מַאי? [31B] פָּטוּר!

LITERAL TRANSLATION

[1]For what [purpose] did he stop? [2]If it was to shoulder [the wallet], it is his [normal] way! [3]Rather, it is where he stopped to rest.

[4]But what about shouldering? [31B] He is exempt!

RASHI

אורחיה הוא — ואין עמידתו הנחה לבטל עקירה ראשונה ממלאכת שבת. **פטור** — מתשלומין, דאתי עליה חיוב שבת מתחת הגבהה ראשונה שבה נקנה לו הכיס, ומיתה ותשלומין באין כאחד.

עָמַד לְמַאי [1]The Gemara now seeks to clarify this interpretation, and it asks: **Why did** the thief **stop?** [2]**If** we say that he stopped in order **to shoulder the wallet** to prevent it from falling to the ground, **this is the normal way** of acting! A person who removes an object from one domain to another, and who stands still for some purpose connected to the object itself, is not considered to have interrupted the object's motion. In such a case, we should consider the displacement to have been for the sake of the replacement, as Rabbi Avin ruled, and the thief should be exempt from payment. [3]**Rather,** we must say that the Tosefta **is** referring to a case **where** the thief **stood still** in order **to rest.** A person moving an object, who stands still for some purpose unconnected to the object itself, is considered to have interrupted the object's motion. In this case, the critical act of displacement with regard to violating Shabbat was the second one, when the thief began to move again. Since the thief was already liable for theft from the time of the first displacement, he is not exempt from payment because of the more severe penalty he incurred later for violating Shabbat.

אֲבָל לְכַתֵּף מַאי [4]But the Gemara objects to this interpretation as well. The Tosefta's distinction between a thief who picks up a wallet on Shabbat and a thief who drags it out applies only if the thief stopped to rest after the first displacement. **But** by implication, if the thief had, in fact, stopped in order **to shoulder** the wallet, or had not stopped at all, **what** would the law be? [31B] Clearly, according to Rabbi Avin's argument, **he would be exempt,** even in the first clause of the Tosefta, in which he is described as having

NOTES

Tosefta is referring to a thief who halted and took a rest before taking the wallet out. The law stated in the Tosefta is the same irrespective of whether the thief picked up the wallet to take it out or picked it up in order to hide it and then changed his mind, provided that he stopped and took a rest before taking the wallet out. In either case, he is liable for theft from the time he picked up the wallet, and he does not begin the sequence of violating Shabbat until he begins to move again.

Ritva points out, however, that it is clear from the discussion below that the Gemara does in fact retract its previous explanation. For the Gemara states that a thief who picks up a wallet and stops in order to shoulder it (or does not stop at all) is exempt from paying for the wallet, because he is subject to the death penalty. And if the Gemara were still following its previous explanation, the thief should be exempt from the death penalty (and hence liable to the financial penalty) because his action in stopping is not considered an interruption, and the purpose of his original displacement was to hide the wallet. It is, therefore, clear that the Gemara is now assuming that the thief picked up the wallet in order to take it out; hence he is liable to the death penalty from the time of the first displacement, since the fact that he stopped is not considered an interruption.

Shittah Mekubbetzet cites a tradition that this passage in the Gemara was a comment of *Rashi* that was mistakenly inserted in the text. In this comment, *Rashi* explains why the Gemara assumed that the thief would be exempt from payment if he stopped in order to shoulder the wallet. According to this tradition, *Rashi* was explaining that the Gemara had retracted its previous explanation, along the lines suggested by *Ritva*, and *Rashi*'s comment was inserted into the text by a scribal error.

HALAKHAH

if he stops in order to rearrange the load and immediately resumes his walk, the halt does not interrupt his walk, and if he carries the object a total distance of at least four cubits, he is liable," following our Gemara. (*Rambam, Sefer Zemanim, Hilkhot Shabbat* 13:10.)

[1]אַדְּתָנֵי: ״הָיָה מְגָרֵר וְיוֹצֵא, מְגָרֵר וְיוֹצֵא, פָּטוּר״, [2]נִפְלוֹג וְנִיתְנֵי בְּדִידָהּ: [3]״בַּמֶּה דְּבָרִים אֲמוּרִים? בְּעוֹמֵד לָפוּשׁ, [4]אֲבָל לְכַתֵּף, פָּטוּר״.

[5]אֶלָּא, הָא מַנִּי? [6]בֶּן עַזַּאי הִיא, דְּאָמַר: ״מְהַלֵּךְ כְּעוֹמֵד דָּמֵי״.

LITERAL TRANSLATION

[1]Rather than teaching: "[If] he was dragging it out, dragging it out, he is exempt," [2]let him distinguish and teach [it] in [the first clause] itself: [3]"In what [case] are these things said? When he stops to rest, [4]but [if he stops] to shoulder [it], he is exempt."

[5]Rather, whose [opinion] is this? [6]It is Ben Azzai's, who said: "Walking is like standing."

RASHI

ניפלוג בדידה — במגביה עצמו, יכול לשנות בו חיוב ופטור. **אלא** — לא תוקמה כשעמד, ואפילו הכי חיוב שבת דעקירה לאו מחמת עקירה ראשונה דהגבהה אתיא ליה, אלא בעקירת גופו של פסיעה אחרונה כשיוצא מן הבית, ובן עזאי היא. **דאמר** — בפרק קמא דשבת. **מהלך בעומד דמי** — ועקירת כל פסיעה הויא עקירה, והנחת הרגל היא הנחה, הלכך קניה משעת הגבהה, וחיוב מיתה בפסיעה בתרייתא קא אתיא ליה.

TRANSLATION AND COMMENTARY

picked the object up! For we are explaining the Tosefta's argument as applying only where the thief stood still to rest. But if he did not stop to rest, the original displacement which made the thief liable for theft also began the sequence of violating Shabbat, and the thief should be exempt, on the basis of Rabbi Avin's argument. [1]If the sole reason for the thief being liable in the first case was because he stopped to rest, then **instead of** selecting a contrasting case by **teaching** us that **if** the thief **dragged** the wallet **out** of its owner's house without picking it up, **he is exempt** from paying for it, [2]**let** the Tosefta **make a distinction and teach us about** this thief **in the first clause itself.** If the sole reason for the thief being liable is because he stopped to rest, the contrast should have been presented more starkly by selecting an otherwise identical case in which the thief did not stop to rest. Thus the Tosefta should have read as follows: "If someone steals a wallet on Shabbat, he is liable to pay for the wallet, even though he is also subject to the death penalty for violating Shabbat, since he became liable for theft the moment he picked up the wallet in its owner's house, before he was in a position to violate the prohibition that is subject to the death penalty. But this is not true in all cases. [3]**When does this ruling apply?** Only if the thief **stopped to rest,** since the act of theft and the violation of Shabbat by carrying took place at two different times, [4]**but if** the thief stopped in order **to shoulder** the wallet, or did not stop at all, **he would be exempt** from paying damages, since he would then be subject to the greater penalty at precisely the same moment, because the act of theft and the violation of Shabbat would both have occurred when the wallet was first picked up." Since the Tosefta did not illustrate its point with the straightforward case of a thief who does not take a rest, but selected instead the unusual case of a thief who drags a wallet out without picking it up, we must conclude that even a thief who does not take a rest is not exempt from payment, since the theft did not take place at precisely the same stage in the process as the Shabbat violation. Thus we see that the Tosefta contradicts Rabbi Avin's ruling that the entire sequence, from displacement to replacement, is considered one single action.

אֶלָּא [5]**Rather,** says the Gemara, we must reject this suggestion and seek another resolution of Rav Bivi bar Abaye's objection — one that does not involve the thief stopping. The Tosefta ruled that a thief who picks up a wallet and takes it out is not considered to be initiating a process of violating Shabbat, and this appears to contradict Rabbi Avin's ruling that displacement is a necessary element of replacement. **Who is** the author of **this** Tosefta? Whose view is reflected in it? [6]**It is Ben Azzai, who said** (*Shabbat* 5b): **"Walking is** considered **like standing."** We have seen that someone who stops to rest while carrying an object on Shabbat is considered to have interrupted the object's motion. According to Ben Azzai, the same is true of someone who walks from place to place on Shabbat while carrying an object. Each time he puts his foot down, he is considered as having interrupted the object's motion. Thus Ben Azzai maintains that someone who picks up an object in a private domain and walks with it, is considered to have replaced it

NOTES

מְהַלֵּךְ כְּעוֹמֵד דָּמֵי **Walking is like standing.** The Jerusalem Talmud asks: According to Ben Azzai, a person can be liable for carrying an object from the private domain to the public domain and vice versa. But how is it possible for someone to be liable for carrying an object a distance of four cubits in the public domain? With each step, it seems that he has interrupted the object's motion!

In our version of the Jerusalem Talmud, no answer to this question is given. *Tosafot* and other Rishonim, however, have a reading in the Jerusalem Talmud in which the Gemara answers that he would be liable if he were to leap forward more than four cubits.

The Rishonim offer two other answers to this question, according to which it is not necessary to construct a special case: (1) *Rashba* explains in the name of *Ra'avad* that Ben Azzai's ruling — that a walker is considered to have stood still with each step — applies only to places where the walker is permitted (by Torah law) to move the

TRANSLATION AND COMMENTARY

with every step, so that the critical displacement does not occur until he steps into the public domain. Thus, in the first clause of the Tosefta, the displacement of the object as far as Shabbat is concerned occurred when the thief stepped out of the owner's domain, whereas the act of acquisition created by the theft occurred when he first picked up the wallet. Therefore the thief was liable for stealing the wallet, since his liability for theft preceded the greater penalty for violating Shabbat. In the second clause of the Tosefta, however, the thief is exempt from payment, since the critical moment for both offenses was when he left the owner's house. Seen in this light, the Tosefta is consistent with Rabbi Avin's ruling.

¹אֲבָל זוֹרֵק מַאי? פָּטוּר! ²נִיפְלוֹג וְנִיתְנֵי בְּדִידָהּ: ״בַּמֶּה דְּבָרִים אֲמוּרִים? ³בִּמְהַלֵּךְ, אֲבָל זוֹרֵק, פָּטוּר״. ⁴מְגָרֵר וְיוֹצֵא אִיצְטְרִיכָא לֵיהּ.

LITERAL TRANSLATION

[1] But what about throwing? He is exempt! [2] Let him distinguish and teach [it] in [the first clause] itself: "In what [case] are these things said? [3] When he walks, but [if he] throws, he is exempt."

[4] He needed it for [the case of] dragging it out.

RASHI

אבל זורק מאי – הגביהו וזרקו. פטור – מתשלומין, דאתיא ליה חיוב שבת על ידי חיוב הגבהה, דתו ליתא עקירה אחריתי.

אֲבָל [1] **But** the Gemara objects to this solution as well. According to Ben Azzai, **what** would the law be if the thief were to **throw** the wallet outside, instead of walking with it? Clearly, according to Rabbi Avin's argument, **he would be exempt,** even in the first clause of the Tosefta, in which he is described as having picked the object up! For even according to Ben Azzai, if the thief were to throw the wallet out of the window immediately after picking it up, the critical displacement with regard to Shabbat would be the moment when he picked up the wallet. Therefore the original displacement, which would have made the thief liable for theft, would also have initiated the sequence of violating Shabbat, and the thief should be exempt. If the sole reason for the thief being liable in the first case was because he walked with the wallet, then instead of selecting a contrasting case by teaching us that a thief who dragged the wallet out of its owner's house without picking it up is exempt from paying for it, [2] **let** the Tosefta **make a distinction and teach us about** this thief **in the first clause itself.** If the sole reason for the thief being liable is because he was walking, the contrast should have been presented more starkly by selecting an otherwise identical case in which the thief threw the wallet. Thus the Tosefta should have read as follows: "If someone steals a wallet on Shabbat, he is liable to pay for the wallet, even though he is also subject to the death penalty for violating Shabbat, since he became liable for theft the moment he picked up the wallet in its owner's house, before he was in a position to violate the prohibition that carries the death penalty. But this is not true in all cases. [3] **When does this ruling apply?** Only if the thief **walked** outside with the wallet, thereby interrupting the sequence of violating Shabbat. **But if** the thief **threw** the wallet, **he would be exempt** from paying damages, since he would then be subject to the greater penalty at precisely the same moment." Since the Tosefta did not illustrate its point with the straightforward case of a thief who threw a wallet outside, but selected instead the unusual case of a thief who drags a wallet out without picking it up, we must conclude that even a thief who walks with the wallet is not exempt from payment, since the theft did not take place at precisely the same stage in the process as the Shabbat violation. Thus we see that the Tosefta contradicts Rabbi Avin's ruling that the entire sequence, from displacement to replacement, is considered one single action.

מְגָרֵר [4] The Gemara answers: The Tosefta does, in fact, reflect the viewpoint of Ben Azzai, and it could indeed have selected a case of throwing to illustrate its point rather than a case of dragging. But the Tosefta saw a greater **need** to teach us **about the case of** a thief who **drags** a wallet **out** than to teach us about

NOTES

object from place to place (i.e., a private domain and a neutral area). But in the public domain, where it is forbidden to move the object, a person who is walking is not considered to have stopped. (2) *Tosafot* and other Rishonim explain that Ben Azzai's ruling applies only to moving an object from domain to domain and not to moving it four cubits in the public domain. They cite a Gemara (*Shabbat* 96b) which declares that the law forbidding one to carry an object four cubits in the public domain is a basic Halakhic tradition (הֲלָכָה לְמשֶׁה מִסִּינַי) which is not subject to the usual rules that apply to other forms of carrying.

מְגָרֵר וְיוֹצֵא אִיצְטְרִיכָא לֵיהּ **He needed it for the case of dragging it out.** The Rishonim offer three different interpretations of this statement. *Tosafot* explains that, according to the Gemara's present argument, if the second clause of the Tosefta had selected the case in which the thief threw the wallet out of the window, it would indeed have illustrated its main point more clearly than it does at present, but it would not have taught us anything else. Hence the Tosefta preferred to select the case of dragging, in order to teach us that dragging is a normal way of moving a wallet.

Ritva notes that in some versions of this Talmudic

TRANSLATION AND COMMENTARY

the case of a thief who throws a wallet out of the window. [1]For if we had not been informed of the case of the thief dragging the wallet, **it might have entered our minds to think** that someone who drags a wallet out of a house on Shabbat without picking it up should not be liable at all for violating Shabbat, [2]since dragging **is not the normal way of taking** a wallet **out** of a house, and a violation of Shabbat committed in an unusual manner is not considered a complete violation, and is not punishable with death. Hence we might have thought that the thief should be liable for the theft, even though the theft and the Shabbat violation took place at the same moment, because the thief would not, in fact, be subject to the more severe penalty. [3]Accordingly, the Tosefta **informs us that this is not so.** Dragging is considered a normal way of removing a wallet, and a thief who drags a wallet out of a house on Shabbat without picking it up is liable for violating Shabbat, and is therefore exempt from paying damages.

[1]סָלְקָא דַּעְתָּךְ אָמִינָא: [2]אֵין דֶּרֶךְ הוֹצָאָה בְּכָךְ. [3]קָא מַשְׁמַע לָן.

[4]וּבְמַאי? [5]אִי בְּרַבְרְבֵי, אוֹרְחֵיהּ הוּא. [6]אִי בְּזוּטְרֵי, לָאו אוֹרְחֵיהּ הוּא!

[7]אֶלָּא, בְּמִיצְעֵי.

LITERAL TRANSLATION

[1]It might enter your mind to say: [2]This is not the [normal] way of taking out. [3][Therefore] he tells us [that this is not so].

[4]And with what [wallet are we dealing]? [5]If with big ones, it is his [normal] way. [6]If with little ones, it is not his [normal] way!

[7]Rather, with medium-sized ones.

RASHI

אין דרך הוצאה בכך — ואין כאן חיוב שבת. **ובמאי** — אצטריך לאשמועינן דדרך הוצאה בכך. **אי ברברבי** — כיס גדול שיש בו משוי להגביהו. **אורחיה הוא** — לגררו, ופשיטא דהוצאה היא. **לאו אורחיה הוא** — ואמאי חייב משום שבת?

וּבְמַאי [4]The Gemara is willing to accept this solution — that the first clause in the Tosefta reflects the view of Ben Azzai, and that the second clause was selected in order to teach us that dragging a wallet is considered a normal way of removing it. But first the case must be defined more sharply: **To what** kind of **wallet are we referring** when we say that the Tosefta was teaching us that dragging a wallet is a normal way of taking it out? [5]**If** we are referring **to a big** wallet, it is obvious that **it is normal** to drag it out, and the Tosefta is not teaching us anything new. It should instead have selected the case of throwing, to illustrate its first point more clearly. [6]**If,** on the other hand, we are referring **to a small** wallet, such as a person might put in his pocket, **it is not normal** to drag such a wallet out, and a thief who did so would indeed not be liable for violating Shabbat.

אֶלָּא [7]**Rather,** we must say that the Tosefta is referring **to a medium-sized** wallet, which is not usually dragged, but which is sufficiently heavy for the thief's action to be considered reasonable. Thus the Tosefta

NOTES

passage, the line, "he needed it for the case of dragging it out," is preceded by the word "rather" (אֶלָּא) — a technical term which tells us that the Gemara is conceding the validity of the immediately preceding objection and is beginning an entirely new explanation. Following this reading, *Ritva* explains that the Gemara is no longer claiming that the Tosefta reflects the viewpoint of Ben Azzai. Rather, the Gemara is returning to its original explanation — that the Tosefta is referring to a case in which the thief stopped in order to rest. The Gemara is explaining that the Tosefta did not illustrate its point with the much clearer contrast of the case in which the thief did not stop to rest, because the Tosefta wanted to make an additional point — that dragging a wallet out is considered a normal way of carrying it.

Rashba notes that the word "rather" (אֶלָּא) does not appear in most versions of the Gemara. Accordingly, *Rashba* explains that the Gemara is not insisting on its claim that the Tosefta reflects the view of Ben Azzai, nor is it withdrawing it and returning to its original explanation that the Tosefta is referring to a special case. Rather, it is presenting a single answer to the objections raised against both explanations. Thus the Gemara's conclusion is that the Tosefta may either be referring to a case in which the thief stopped, or else it may reflect the viewpoint of Ben Azzai. In either case, its main point is that the thief is liable because his act of theft in picking up the object was not an act of displacement with reference to Shabbat, and the reason the Tosefta illustrated its point with the case of dragging was in order to teach us the additional law — that dragging is considered a normal way of taking out.

אִי בְּזוּטְרֵי, לָאו אוֹרְחֵיהּ הוּא If with little ones, it is not his normal way! Our commentary follows *Rashi* and *Tosafot*, who explain that the Gemara is objecting that the thief should not be liable for violating *Shabbat*, if he dragged a small wallet out in an unusual manner, because Shabbat violations are not culpable unless they were done "creatively."

Ritva explains that the Gemara is also objecting that the thief should not be liable for *theft*, if he dragged a small wallet out in an unusual manner, because wallets are normally acquired by picking them up, and the Gemara in tractate *Bava Batra* (86a) rules that an object that is normally picked up cannot be acquired by pulling.

אֶלָּא בְּמִיצְעֵי Rather, with medium-sized ones. The Rishonim ask: In tractate *Bava Batra* (86a), the Gemara declares that pulling is not a valid mode of acquisition for objects that are normally picked up and carried. The

TRANSLATION AND COMMENTARY

is informing us that even though this wallet is not always dragged, and we might have thought that it is not normal to drag it, nevertheless it is considered sufficiently normal for the laws of Shabbat; hence the thief is liable for violating Shabbat and is exempt from paying for the wallet.

וּדְאַפְּקֵיהּ [1]The Gemara accepts this resolution of Rav Bivi bar Abaye's objection — that the Tosefta reflects the view of Ben Azzai. But having mentioned the Tosefta, the Gemara now considers its second clause, which stated that if the thief dragged the wallet out of the house without picking it up, he is exempt from paying damages, since the theft and the Shabbat violation took place at the same moment. We may infer from this clause that dragging an object out of a private domain is a violation of Shabbat, and that dragging a stolen object out of its owner's house is an act of acquisition which renders a thief liable for theft, and that both liabilities are incurred the moment the object leaves the house. But this presents a problem. The Gemara asks: **Where was** the thief **taking** the wallet when he dragged **it out?** [2]**If** you say that **he was taking it** from the owner's domain directly **to the public domain** (for example, where the door of the owner's house opened onto the road), [3]**there would** indeed **be a** violation of the **prohibition a**gainst working on **Shabbat,** since someone who drags an object directly from a private domain to the public domain on Shabbat is liable. [4]But **there would not be a** violation of the **prohibition against theft,** because a thief is not liable for theft until he performs a valid act of acquisition on the stolen object — either by picking it up or by pulling it — and pulling is a valid act of acquisition only in the acquirer's domain, or in a deserted alleyway, but not in the owner's house or in the public domain. Thus the thief would not be liable for theft until he brought the wallet home or picked it up. [5]**If,** on the other hand, you say that the thief **took** the wallet directly from one **private domain to** another (for example, where his own house or courtyard was next to the house of the owner of the wallet, and he dragged the wallet directly from the owner's house to his own without passing through the street), [6]**there would** indeed **be a** violation of the **prohibition against theft** the moment the wallet left the owner's house, since pulling is a valid act of acquisition in the acquirer's domain. [7]**But there would not be a** violation of the **prohibition** against working on **Shabbat,** since someone who moves an object on Shabbat from one private domain directly to another is not liable for violating Shabbat. Either way, there is no case in which the thief incurs both liabilities when he removes the wallet from the owner's house!

[1]וּדְאַפְּקֵיהּ לְהֵיכָא? [2]אִי דְּאַפְּקֵיהּ לִרְשׁוּת הָרַבִּים, [3]אִיסּוּר שַׁבָּת אִיכָּא, [4]אִיסּוּר גְּנֵיבָה לֵיכָּא. [5]אִי דְּאַפְּקֵיהּ לִרְשׁוּת הַיָּחִיד, [6]אִיסּוּר גְּנֵיבָה אִיכָּא, [7]אִיסּוּר שַׁבָּת לֵיכָּא.

LITERAL TRANSLATION

[1]And to where was he taking it out? [2]If he was taking it out to the public domain, [3]there is a Shabbat prohibition, [4][but] there is not a prohibition of theft. [5]If he was taking it out to a private domain, [6]there is a prohibition of theft, [7][but] there is not a Shabbat prohibition.

RASHI

איסור גניבה ליכא – דמשיכה בלא הגבהה, קסלקא דעתך דלא קניא ברשות הרבים. **לרשות היחיד** – לרשותו, שהיתה חצירו סמוכה לחצר הבעלים.

NOTES

Gemara notes that our Tosefta appears to contradict this, because it rules that dragging a wallet is a valid mode of acquisition. And the Gemara answers that the Tosefta is referring to a big bag with a rope attached, that is normally pulled along. Clearly the Gemara's conclusion there appears to conflict with our Gemara's statement here — that the wallet was a medium-sized one that is normally carried but occasionally dragged. Accordingly, *Ritva* explains that the two passages conflict with each other. *Ritva* rules that the passage in *Bava Batra* is more reliable, and our Gemara's statement here is to be rejected. *Ritva*'s explanation reflects his viewpoint that our Gemara is also considering the validity of the thief's act of acquisition (see previous note).

Ramban adds that the conclusions of both passages can be reconciled with the viewpoint of Rav Ashi, who explains below that our Gemara is referring to a case in which the thief dropped the wallet into his other hand, or with the viewpoint of Ravina, who explains below that the laws of theft and the laws of acquisition are two separate areas of Halakhah. But it is not possible to explain the entire passage in *Bava Batra* in this way, because the question and answer there are clearly based on the assumption that our Tosefta considers dragging a wallet to be a case of acquisition by pulling.

Tosafot, who explains that our Gemara was not concerned with the problem of acquisition but only with the problem of Shabbat (see previous note), has a simple solution to this problem. *Tosafot* explains that the wallet could have been small enough for it to be normal to pick it up, but still big enough for it not to have been unusual to drag it. Hence, regarding Shabbat laws, the thief is liable, since his action in dragging the wallet was not unusual, but regarding the laws of acquisition, the act of dragging the wallet is not valid, since pulling is not a valid mode of acquisition for objects that are normally picked up and carried.

¹לָא, צְרִיכָא דְּאַפְּקֵיהּ לְצִידֵּי רְשׁוּת הָרַבִּים. ²וּכְמַאן? ³אִי כְּרַבִּי אֱלִיעֶזֶר, דַּאֲמַר: "צִידֵּי רְשׁוּת הָרַבִּים כִּרְשׁוּת הָרַבִּים דָּמוּ", ⁴אִיסּוּר שַׁבָּת אִיכָּא, ⁵אִיסּוּר גְּנֵיבָה לֵיכָּא. ⁶אִי כְּרַבָּנַן, דְּאָמְרִי: "צִידֵּי רְשׁוּת הָרַבִּים לָאו כִּרְשׁוּת הָרַבִּים דָּמוּ", ⁷אִיסּוּר גְּנֵיבָה אִיכָּא, ⁸אִיסּוּר שַׁבָּת לֵיכָּא.

LITERAL TRANSLATION

[1] No, it is necessary where he took it out to the sides of the public domain.

[2] But according to whom? [3] If it is in accordance with Rabbi Eliezer, who said: "The sides of the public domain are like the public domain," [4] there is a Shabbat prohibition, [5] [but] there is not a prohibition of theft. [6] If it is in accordance with the Rabbis, who said: "The sides of the public domain are not like the public domain," [7] there is a prohibition of theft, [8] [but] there is not a Shabbat prohibition.

RASHI

צידי רשות הרבים – סמוך לכתים, שמניחין להלן מן הבתים אבנים ומכשולין להרחיק מיכוך העגלות. ומאותן חיפופי ולפנים קרי צידי רשות הרבים. פלוגתא דרבי אליעזר ורבנן בעירובין בפרק "כל גגות".

SAGES

רַבִּי אֱלִיעֶזֶר **Rabbi Eliezer.** See *Ketubot*, Part II, pp. 13–14.

TRANSLATION AND COMMENTARY

לָא [1] The Gemara answers: **No,** there is a case in which the thief removes the wallet from the owner's house and incurs both liabilities at the same moment. The Tosefta **needed** this clause to teach us that the thief is exempt **if he took** the wallet **to the sides of the public domain.** Between private houses and the street there was often an area where homeowners discouraged people from walking, by placing a row of stones and the like there, but people would nevertheless walk there when the street was crowded. This area's legal status was somewhat unclear, and the Gemara is now suggesting that it should be considered part of the public domain for the purpose of Shabbat laws, but not for the laws of acquisition. Thus the Tosefta can be explained as referring to a case in which the door of the owner's house opened on to the area next to the public domain. Hence, when the thief drags the wallet out of the door on Shabbat, he becomes liable for stealing the wallet and for violating Shabbat at precisely the same moment — when the wallet leaves the owner's house and enters the sides of the public domain.

וּכְמַאן [2] **But,** the Gemara objects, the status of the sides of the public domain is the subject of a Tannaitic dispute between Rabbi Eliezer and the Sages, and neither side in this dispute took this position. **According to which** Tanna are the sides of the public domain considered public for the purposes of Shabbat but not for the purposes of acquisition? [3] **If** you say that the Tosefta **is in accordance with Rabbi Eliezer, who said: "The sides of the public domain are like the public domain** itself, since the public sometimes walks there," [4] **there would** indeed **be a** violation of the **prohibition** against working on **Shabbat,** since Rabbi Eliezer maintains that someone who moves an object from a private domain to the sides of the public domain on Shabbat is liable. [5] **But there would not be a** violation of the **prohibition against theft.** Since Rabbi Eliezer is of the opinion that the sides of the public domain are like the public domain itself, he presumably also maintains that it is not possible to acquire an object there by pulling it, since pulling is not a valid act of acquisition in the public domain. [6] **If,** on the other hand, you say that the Tosefta **is in accordance with the Rabbis, who** disagreed with Rabbi Eliezer and **said: "The sides of the public domain are not like the public domain** itself, since people do not usually walk there," [7] **there would** indeed **be a** violation of the **prohibition against theft** the moment the wallet leaves the owner's domain, since pulling is a valid act of acquisition in a secluded alley, and the sides of the public domain have a similar status according to the Rabbis. [8] **But there would not be a** violation of the **prohibition** against working on **Shabbat,** since the Rabbis are of the opinion that someone who moves an object from a private domain to the sides of the public domain is not guilty of violating Shabbat. Either way, there is no case in which the thief incurs both liabilities when he removes the wallet from the owner's house!

NOTES

צִידֵּי רְשׁוּת הָרַבִּים **The sides of the public domain.** The definitions of "private" and "public" vary from one area of Halakhah to another. Regarding monetary laws, an area owned and controlled by an individual is considered to be "private"; an area open to the general public which must not be blocked by any individual is "public"; and an alleyway which does not belong to any individual person, but is not a through street and is used for unloading merchandise and the like, is in an intermediate category.

Regarding the laws of ritual impurity, an enclosure containing one or two competent adults is considered "private," whereas an enclosure containing at least three competent adults, or an open area, is considered "public." There is no intermediate category for the purposes of ritual impurity.

The most complicated rules of all apply to Shabbat. An area at least four handbreadths square (slightly more than a foot square) that is surrounded by walls at least ten handbreadths high (approximately three feet), or is on top of a mound at least ten handbreadths high, or is at the

TRANSLATION AND COMMENTARY

לְעוֹלָם [1]The Gemara answers: **In fact,** we can explain that the Tosefta **is in accordance with** the viewpoint of **Rabbi Eliezer,** who maintains that the sides of the public domain are considered like the public domain itself. Hence the thief is in violation of Shabbat. [2]**And** regarding the claim raised above — that the act of acquisition by the thief in pulling the wallet should be invalid at the sides of the public domain, since pulling is not effective in the public domain — this is not so, because Rabbi Eliezer does not consider the sides of the public domain to be like the public domain for all purposes. **When Rabbi Eliezer said that the sides of the public domain are like the public domain,** [3]**he said so** only **with regard to liability for Shabbat,** [4]**because sometimes** the members of the **public** crowd the street, people in the crowd **push** each other **and go up to there.** When the street is crowded, people walk on the sides as well; hence Rabbi Eliezer considers the sides to be part of the street which they border. [5]**But with regard to** the laws of **acquisition,** even Rabbi Eliezer would agree that the sides of the public domain are not treated like the street itself, but rather like a secluded alleyway, and someone who pulls an object there can **acquire** it in that way. [6]**What is the reason? Because the public is not often there.** Thus our Tosefta can be explained as reflecting the viewpoint of Rabbi Eliezer, and when the thief drags the wallet out of the door on Shabbat, he becomes liable for stealing the wallet and for violating Shabbat at precisely the same moment — when the wallet leaves the owner's house and enters the sides of the public domain.

רַב אַשִׁי אָמַר [7]**Rav Ashi said:** It is possible to explain the Tosefta without invoking the dispute between Rabbi Eliezer and the Rabbis regarding the sides of the public domain. [8]The Tosefta can be explained as referring, **for example,** to a case **where** the thief dragged the wallet out of the house into the public domain proper, and then **brought his hands together and received** the wallet at a height of **less than three handbreadths** from the ground. In other words, he pulled the wallet out with one hand and dropped it into the other, without at any time raising the wallet to a height of three handbreadths (approximately 10 inches) above the ground. An object that is less than three handbreadths above the ground is considered as resting

[1]לְעוֹלָם כְּרַבִּי אֱלִיעֶזֶר. [2]וְכִי אֲמַר רַבִּי אֱלִיעֶזֶר צִידֵּי רְשׁוּת הָרַבִּים כִּרְשׁוּת הָרַבִּים דָּמוּ, [3]הָנֵי מִילֵּי לְעִנְיַן חִיּוּבָא דְּשַׁבָּת, [4]דְּזִימְנִין דְּדַחֲקִי רַבִּים וְעַיְילֵי לְהָתָם. [5]אֲבָל לְעִנְיַן מִיקְנָא, קָנֵי. [6]מַאי טַעֲמָא? דְּהָא לָא שְׁכִיחִי רַבִּים.

[7]רַב אַשִׁי אָמַר: [8]כְּגוֹן שֶׁצֵּירַף יָדוֹ לְמַטָּה מִשְּׁלֹשָׁה וְקִיבְּלוֹ.

LITERAL TRANSLATION

[1]In fact, it is in accordance with Rabbi Eliezer. [2]And when Rabbi Eliezer said [that] the sides of the public domain are like the public domain, [3]these words [apply] with regard to liability for Shabbat, [4]because sometimes the public pushes and enters there. [5]But with regard to acquisition, he acquires. [6]What is the reason? Because the public is not often [there].

[7]Rav Ashi said: [8]For example, where he brought his hand together below three [handbreadths] and received it.

RASHI

דהא לא שכיחי רבים — והוי ליה כסימטא, דתיקון בה משיכה. **רב אשי אמר** — מגרר ויוצא דקאמר פטור — לעולם ברשות הרבים, ודקשיא לך: איסור גניבה ליכא. **כגון שצירף ידו** — השניה לפחות משלשה סמוך לקרקע, ובידו אחת גיררה, ונפלה לתוך חברתה, וידו קניא ליה.

NOTES

bottom of a pit at least ten handbreadths deep, is considered "private" regardless of its ownership or use. An open area where the large numbers of people pass through (according to some Rishonim, an area frequented by at least 600,000 people), such as a highway, or a town square, or a main street, is considered to be "public."

It is clear from the above that it is not at all difficult to construct a case in which an area is considered public as far as monetary laws are concerned and intermediate — or even private — as far as the laws of Shabbat are concerned. But it is not so easy to construct a case in which an area is considered public as far as the laws of Shabbat are concerned and intermediate or private in relation to monetary laws. In fact, the only possible case is an open area adjacent to the public domain, which is available to the public but is not ordinarily used by them. According to Rabbi Eliezer, this area is considered part of the public domain for the purposes of Shabbat, although it is comparable to an alleyway for the purposes of monetary laws. According to the Sages, however, the area adjacent to the public domain is considered intermediate for the purposes of Shabbat as well as for monetary laws, and there is no case where an area is considered public as far as the laws of Shabbat are concerned and intermediate or private as far as monetary laws are concerned.

כְּגוֹן שֶׁצֵּירַף יָדוֹ **For example, where he brought his hand together.** Our commentary follows *Rashi,* who explains

HALAKHAH

אֲבָל לְעִנְיַן מִיקְנָא, קָנֵי **But with regard to acquisition, he acquires.** "Pulling is a valid mode of acquisition for movable property, provided that the movable property is in the buyer's domain, or in an alleyway, but not if it is in

TRANSLATION AND COMMENTARY

on the ground. Hence the object was not acquired by being picked up. But it was acquired by being placed in the thief's other hand, and this, according to Rav Ashi, is itself a valid act of acquisition. [1] Rav Ashi continued: My explanation **follows Rava**. It is an extension of an idea expressed by Rava in another context, **for Rava said:** [2] **A person's hand is regarded as an area four** handbreadths long **by four handbreadths** wide. To be guilty of the prohibition against moving an object on Shabbat, one must have displaced it from, and replaced it in, an area at least four handbreadths square (slightly more than a foot square). If the object was in an area smaller than this, it is not considered to have been resting stably, and the displacer or replacer is not liable. Rava ruled that this law does not apply to an object resting in a person's hand. Such an object is treated as if it is resting in an area four by four handbreadths square. According to Rav Ashi, Rava's idea, which was expressed in connection with the laws of Shabbat, can be applied to the laws of acquisition as well. Therefore an object resting in a thief's hand is not considered to be resting on the ground — even if it is within three handbreadths of the ground — but is considered to be under the thief's control and to have been acquired, as though it had been raised to a height of three handbreadths. Therefore, when the thief deposits the wallet in his hand in the public domain, he is simultaneously violating Shabbat (by replacing the object in a significant place in the public domain) and acquiring the object (by performing an act that is legally the equivalent of picking it up). Hence he is exempt from paying for the wallet, since the act of theft and the violation of Shabbat take place at precisely the same moment.

רַב אַחָא [3] **Rav Aḥa explained this Tosefta** as we have been explaining it until now. He noted that the Tosefta seems to be of the opinion that a thief who drags a wallet from its owner's home into the public domain becomes liable for theft the moment it enters the public domain. He raised the objection that pulling is not a valid act of acquisition in the public domain. And he responded by saying either that the Tosefta is referring to the sides of the public domain and reflects the view of Rabbi Eliezer, or that the thief deposited the wallet in his other hand, which he held close to the ground. [4] But **Ravina explained** this

[1] כִּדְרָבָא, דְּאָמַר רָבָא: [2] יָדוֹ שֶׁל אָדָם חֲשׁוּבָה לוֹ כְּאַרְבָּעָה עַל אַרְבָּעָה.

[3] רַב אַחָא מַתְנֵי הָכִי. [4] רָבִינָא

LITERAL TRANSLATION

[1] [And this is] in accordance with Rava, for Rava said: [2] A person's hand is regarded for him as [a place] four by four [handbreadths].

[3] Rav Aḥa taught [the Tosefta] thus. [4] Ravina taught:

RASHI

כדרבא, דאמר רבא ידו של אדם חשובה — לענין הנחת שבת, כמקום ארבעה על ארבעה. וכי היכי דלענין שבת חשוב מקום — לענין מיקנא נמי חשוב מקום למיקני, כאילו הגביהה למעלה משלשה. ומיהו, ברשות היחיד לא אגבהה דתיקני ליה מקמי דליתי חיוב שבת עליה, וביאתה לרשות הרבים וקנייתה באין כאחד. ולהכי משני: כשצירף, דלא תיהוי הגבהה ברשות היחיד, כדקתני "מגרר ויוצא". **רב אחא מתני הכי** — כדאמרן, דמשיכה ברשות הרבים לא קני, ומוקים לה: כשצירף ידו וקיבלה לתוכה.

NOTES

that Rav Ashi's purpose is to deduce the laws of acquisition from Rava's ruling regarding Shabbat. Rav Ashi is extrapolating from Rava's argument that placing an object in a hand, even if the hand is resting on the ground, is the equivalent of lifting up the object to a height of at least three handbreadths for the purposes of the laws of acquisition.

Tosafot amends the text of the Gemara to read: "For example, where he brought his hands together below three handbreadths and received it, *or alternatively* it is in accordance with Rava, who said, etc." According to this explanation, it was obvious to Rav Ashi that a thief who deposits a stolen object in his hand is liable for theft, even if he is standing in the public domain, since an object in a person's hand does not need to be raised three handbreadths. But it was not entirely clear to Rav Ashi that the thief would be liable for violating Shabbat in such a case, since the object would not have been replaced on the ground of the public domain in an area larger than four by four. Therefore Rav Ashi explains that the Tosefta may be referring to a case where the thief's hand was within three handbreadths of the ground (even according to those Amoraim who disagree with Rava), or else it may follow Rava and be referring to a case where the hand was more than three handbreadths above the ground (for example, where the floor of the house was elevated).

Tosafot's explanation is straightforward and is favored by many Rishonim, but *Ramban* points out that most manuscripts do not support this textual emendation. Other explanations were given by other Rishonim (*Rabbenu Tam*, *Ramban*), and the Aḥaronim further discussed this matter (see, for example, *Ḥatam Sofer*, who attempts to address *Tosafot*'s objections to *Rashi*'s viewpoint).

HALAKHAH

the public domain, or in a courtyard belonging to a third party. *Rashi* explains that our Gemara considers the sides of the public domain like an alleyway for this purpose." (*Rambam*, *Sefer Kinyan*, *Hilkhot Mekhirah* 4:3-4; *Shulḥan Arukh*, *Ḥoshen Mishpat* 198:9,14.)

יָדוֹ שֶׁל אָדָם A person's hand. "A person's hand is regarded as the equivalent of an area of four by four handbreadths. Therefore, if an object is resting in the hand of a person

TRANSLATION AND COMMENTARY

Tosefta in accordance with its straightforward meaning. **In fact,** says Ravina, the Tosefta is referring to a case **where** the thief **took** the wallet **out to the public domain** and deposited it there. [1] **And** as for the objection that a thief is liable only if he performs an act of acquisition, and pulling is not a valid act of acquisition in the public domain, Ravina is of the opinion that the laws of theft do not reflect the laws of acquisition in this matter. According to Ravina, a thief **also acquires** if he pulls a stolen object from its owner's house **to the public domain,** even if he does not pick it up or pull it into his own property or into an alleyway.

וְתַרְוַיְיהוּ [2] The Gemara now explains the basis of the dispute between Rav Aḥa and Ravina about the relationship between the laws of acquisition and the laws of theft. **The two** Amoraim **disagree about** the **inference** that is **to be drawn from the following Mishnah** (*Bava Kamma* 79a). According to Rav Aḥa, the Mishnah implies that a thief, like a purchaser, can acquire an object by pulling it only if he takes it to his own property or to a secluded alleyway, but not if he takes it to the public domain. Ravina, however, analyzes the Mishnah somewhat differently, and infers that a thief can acquire by pulling, even in the public domain. [3] **For we have learned** in the Mishnah: **"If** a thief was stealing an animal from its owner's property, and as **he was pulling it out, it died** of natural causes **within the owner's domain,** the thief **is exempt** from paying for the animal. The thief was not responsible for the animal, because he had not yet taken possession of it. [4] But **if** the thief **lifted** the animal **up,** he would be liable for it, even if it died of natural causes before it was taken out, because a thief is liable for any damage to an object he steals, however caused, from the moment he acquires it, and a thief acquires stolen goods by picking them up, even on their owner's property, as we have seen above. Likewise, if the thief **took** the animal **out from the owner's domain,** even if he did not pick it up, **and** the animal **died** of natural causes, **he is liable,** because removing a stolen animal from its owner's property is also an act of acquisition with regard to theft."

מַתְנֵי: לְעוֹלָם דְּאַפְּקֵיהּ לִרְשׁוּת הָרַבִּים, [1] וּבִרְשׁוּת הָרַבִּים נָמֵי קָנָה.

[2] וְתַרְוַיְיהוּ בְּדִיוּקָא דְּהָא מַתְנִיתִין קָמִיפַּלְגִי. [3] דִּתְנַן: ״הָיָה מוֹשְׁכוֹ וְיוֹצֵא, וּמֵת בִּרְשׁוּת בְּעָלִים, פָּטוּר. [4] הִגְבִּיהוֹ אוֹ שֶׁהוֹצִיאוֹ מֵרְשׁוּת בְּעָלִים, וּמֵת, חַיָּיב.

LITERAL TRANSLATION

In fact, it is where he took it out to the public domain, [1] and in the public domain he also acquired.

[2] And both of them disagree about the inference [to be drawn] from this Mishnah. [3] For we have learned: "[If] he was drawing it and going out, and it died in the owner's domain, he is exempt. [4] [If] he lifted it up or took it out from the owner's domain, and it died, he is liable."

RASHI

היה מושכו — בגונב בהמה ברשות בעלים קאי, בפרק "מרובה". **ומת — השור. ברשות הבעלים פטור** — הגנב מלשלם כלום, דלא קני להתחייב באונסין. **הגביהו** — אפילו ברשות הבעלים.

NOTES

וּבִרְשׁוּת הָרַבִּים נָמֵי קָנָה And in the public domain he also acquired. *Tosafot* offers two explanations of Ravina's position. Our commentary follows *Ri*, who explains that Ravina agrees that a buyer cannot acquire an object in the public domain by pulling it, but disagrees with our Gemara's previous assumption that the laws of theft are entirely consistent with the laws of acquisition. *Riva* explains that Ravina agrees with our Gemara's assumption that the laws of theft follow the laws of acquisition, but disagrees with the accepted law (*Bava Batra* 76b and 84b) that a buyer cannot acquire an object in the public domain by pulling it.

Ritva and *Ra'ah* offer an intermediate explanation: Ravina agrees that an object that is already standing in the public domain cannot be acquired by pulling it, but maintains that an object that is on the owner's property can be acquired by pulling it into the public domain. It is not entirely clear, however, if according to this explanation Ravina was referring to all forms of acquisition or only to theft.

HALAKHAH

standing in the public domain, and another person picks it up and brings it into a private domain and places it in the hand of a third person standing in the private domain (or vice versa), the person moving the object is liable." (*Rambam, Sefer Zemanim, Hilkhot Shabbat* 13:2.)

וּבִרְשׁוּת הָרַבִּים נָמֵי קָנָה And in the public domain he also acquired. "If a thief drags a wallet out of its owner's house into the public domain on Shabbat, he is exempt from paying for it, because he incurs the more severe penalty for violating Shabbat at the same moment as he incurs the financial obligation. *Gra* explains that *Rambam* and *Shulḥan Arukh* rule in favor of Ravina, who maintains that pulling is a valid act of acquisition with reference to theft, even in the public domain, whereas *Tur* follows the explanation that Ravina and Rav Aḥa disagree about regular acquisition as well as about theft, and he rules in favor of Rav Aḥa, who maintains that pulling is never valid in the public domain." (*Rambam, Sefer Nezikin, Hilkhot Genevah* 3:2; *Shulḥan Arukh, Ḥoshen Mishpat* 351:1.)

אוֹ שֶׁהוֹצִיאוֹ מֵרְשׁוּת בְּעָלִים Or took it out from the owner's domain. "A thief who pulls an animal out of its owner's barn is fully liable for it, and must pay the double payment for it, as soon as it leaves its owner's domain." (*Rambam, Sefer Nezikin, Hilkhot Genevah* 2:16; *Shulḥan Arukh, Ḥoshen Mishpat* 348:4.)

TRANSLATION AND COMMENTARY

רָבִינָא [1]The Gemara explains how this Mishnah led to the difference of opinion between Rav Aḥa and Ravina. **Ravina made an inference from the first clause** of this Mishnah, [2]whereas **Rav Aḥa made an inference from the last clause** of the Mishnah.

רָבִינָא [3]The Gemara elaborates: **Ravina made an inference from the first clause** of the Mishnah, which reads: **"If** a thief stole an animal from its owner's property, and as **he was pulling it out, it died** before it left **the owner's domain,** the thief **is exempt** from paying for the animal." [4]And Ravina infers: **The reason** given by the Mishnah for the thief's exemption **is that** the animal **died** before it left **the owner's domain.** [5]**Thus** we may infer that **if it had died** after the thief **removed it from the owner's domain, he would have been liable,** regardless of where he took it. Thus we see that a thief acquires a stolen object as soon as he removes it from its owner's domain, and it is immaterial whether he takes it to his own domain or to the public domain. Hence Rav Bivi bar Abaye's Tosefta poses no problems, and can be explained literally as referring to a case where the thief dragged the wallet from the owner's house to the public domain.

רַב אַחָא [6]**Rav Aḥa,** however, **made an inference from the last clause** of the Mishnah. That clause reads: **"If** the thief **lifted up** the animal (even if he did not take it out), **or** if he **took it out** (even if he did not lift it), he is liable." [7]Rav Aḥa noted that the Mishnah **compares the removal of** an animal **from** its owner's domain **to lifting** it **up,** suggesting that the same rationale underlies these two ways by which the thief can acquire the animal. When a thief lifts up a stolen object, he acquires it because he is taking it into his physical possession. [8]Therefore, **just as lifting up** a stolen object **is** both an act of acquisition and **the means whereby it comes into** the thief's physical **possession,** [9]**so too is taking out** a stolen object both an act of acquisition and **the means whereby it comes into** the thief's physical **possession**. Thus, only if the stolen object is taken into the thief's own domain does he become liable, but not if it remains in the public domain. Hence our Tosefta, which refers to the thief dragging the wallet into the public domain, is difficult to understand, and Rav Aḥa is forced to explain it as referring to the sides of the public domain according to Rabbi Eliezer, or to a case in which the thief put his other hand down near the ground to receive it.

לְרַב אַחָא [10]The Gemara notes that this explanation is not complete. For **according to Rav Aḥa,** we draw our inferences from the last clause, but **the first clause is difficult** to understand. [11]And **according to Ravina,** we make our inferences from the first clause, but **the last clause is difficult** to understand. How do each of these Amoraim account for the other's proof clause?

רֵישָׁא [12]The Gemara answers: **The first clause presents no difficulty to Rav Aḥa.** The first clause, which seems to imply that the thief acquires the animal as soon as it is removed from its owner's domain, even if it is taken to the public domain, can be explained as follows: [13]As far as the Mishnah is concerned, **so long as** the animal **has not** been pulled in a way that brings it **into** the thief's physical **possession,** [14]**we** continue to **refer to it as** being in **"the owner's domain,"** even if it is actually standing in the public domain,

[1]רָבִינָא דָּיֵיק מֵרֵישָׁא; [2]רַב אַחָא דָּיֵיק מִסֵּיפָא. [3]רָבִינָא דָּיֵיק מֵרֵישָׁא: ״הָיָה מוֹשְׁכוֹ וְיוֹצֵא, וּמֵת בִּרְשׁוּת בְּעָלִים, פָּטוּר״. [4]טַעְמָא דְּמֵת בִּרְשׁוּת בְּעָלִים. [5]הָא הוֹצִיאוֹ מֵרְשׁוּת בְּעָלִים וּמֵת, חַיָּיב. [6]רַב אַחָא דָּיֵיק מִסֵּיפָא: ״הִגְבִּיהוֹ אוֹ שֶׁהוֹצִיאוֹ״. [7]הוֹצָאָה דּוּמְיָא דְּהַגְבָּהָה. [8]מָה הַגְבָּהָה דְּאָתֵי לִרְשׁוּתֵיהּ, [9]אַף הוֹצָאָה נַמִי דְּאָתֵי לִרְשׁוּתֵיהּ. [10]לְרַב אַחָא, קַשְׁיָא רֵישָׁא; [11]לְרָבִינָא, קַשְׁיָא סֵיפָא! [12]רֵישָׁא לְרַב אַחָא לָא קַשְׁיָא. [13]כַּמָּה דְּלָא אָתֵי לִרְשׁוּתֵיהּ, [14]״רְשׁוּת בְּעָלִים״ קָרֵינָא בֵּיהּ.

LITERAL TRANSLATION

[1]Ravina made an inference from the first clause; [2]Rav Aḥa made an inference from the last clause. [3]Ravina made an inference from the first clause: "[If] he was drawing it and going out, and it died in the owner's domain, he is exempt." [4]The reason is that it died in the owner's domain. [5]But, [if] he took it out from the owner's domain and it died, he is liable.

[6]Rav Aḥa made an inference from the last clause: "[If] he lifted it up or took it out." [7]Taking out is analogous to lifting up. [8]Just as lifting up is [the means] whereby it comes into his possession, [9]so too is taking out [the means] whereby it comes into his possession.

[10]According to Rav Aḥa, the first clause is difficult; [11]according to Ravina, the last clause is difficult!

[12]The first clause is not difficult according to Rav Aḥa. [13]So long as it has not come into his possession, [14]we call it "the owner's domain."

RASHI

הא הוציאו — כל היכא דלפקיה, ואפילו לרשות הרבים.

NOTES

כַּמָּה דְּלָא אָתֵי לִרְשׁוּתֵיהּ So long as it has not come into his possession. *Ritva* explains that, according to Ravina, the term רְשׁוּת בְּעָלִים should be translated as "the property of the owner" — i.e., his house — whereas according to Rav Aḥa, it should be translated as "the possession of the owner" — i.e., his legal control. Therefore Rav Aḥa can argue that so long as the object has not fully entered the thief's possession, it is regarded as not having left the owner's possession. Our translation and commentary follow this explanation.

TRANSLATION AND COMMENTARY

because the thief has not yet taken control of it. [1] Likewise, **the last clause presents no difficulty to Ravina.** The last clause, which seems to compare lifting the animal to taking it out, suggesting that both acts involve the thief taking physical possession, can be explained as follows: [2] According to Ravina, **we do not say that taking** the animal **out is analogous to lifting** it **up.** The Mishnah merely states that a thief is liable if he lifts up the animal or takes it out. It does not explicitly state that the rationale is the same in both cases. Rav Aha felt that he could read such an implication into the Mishnah, but Ravina felt that this was not warranted. Therefore Ravina explains that taking the animal out of its owner's property is sufficient by itself to render the thief liable, even if the animal is taken to a public place where the thief does not exert any control over it.

[1] סֵיפָא לְרָבִינָא לָא קַשְׁיָא. [2] הוֹצָאָה דּוּמְיָא דְהַגְבָּהָה לָא אָמְרִינַן.

[3] "הַבָּא עַל אֲחוֹתוֹ, וְעַל אֲחוֹת אָבִיו, כו'". [4] וּרְמִינְהוּ: "אֵלּוּ הֵן הַלּוֹקִין: הַבָּא עַל אֲחוֹתוֹ, וְעַל אֲחוֹת אָבִיו, וְעַל אֲחוֹת אִמּוֹ, וְעַל אֲחוֹת אִשְׁתּוֹ, [5] וְעַל אֵשֶׁת אָחִיו, וְעַל אֵשֶׁת אֲחִי אָבִיו,

LITERAL TRANSLATION

[1] The last clause is not difficult according to Ravina. [2] We do not say [that] taking out is analogous to lifting up.

[3] "[If] someone [forcibly] has intercourse with his sister, or with his father's sister, etc." [4] A contradiction was raised (lit., "cast them together"): "These are those who are lashed: [If] someone has intercourse with his sister, or with his father's sister, or with his mother's sister, or with his wife's sister, [5] or with his brother's wife, or with his father's brother's wife,

RASHI

אלו הן הלוקין — אם התרו בהן.

הַבָּא עַל אֲחוֹתוֹ [3] The Gemara now considers another aspect of the clause of our Mishnah (above, 29a), which refers to a man who rapes a close relative. The Mishnah rules that **"someone who has forcible intercourse with** a close relative, such as **his sister, or his father's sister,** or his mother's sister, or his wife's sister, or his brother's wife, or his father's brother's wife, or with a menstruating woman, is liable to pay the fine," even though intercourse with these women is punished by the severe penalty of excision, because the author of our Mishnah is of the opinion that someone who is subject to a more severe penalty is exempt from paying damages only if the more severe penalty is death, but not if it is excision (see above, 30a). [4] But, the Gemara objects, **a contradiction can be raised** against our Mishnah from the following Mishnah (*Makkot* 13a), which lists the offenses punishable by lashes (see Deuteronomy 25:2–3). The first part of that list is identical to the list of relations subject to excision mentioned in our Mishnah: "Those who commit **the following** sins **are** punished by **lashes,** if their deeds were deliberate and they were properly warned by witnesses: **Someone who has intercourse with his sister, or with his father's sister, or with his mother's sister, or with his wife's sister,** [5] **or with his brother's wife, or with his father's brother's wife,**

NOTES

וּרְמִינְהוּ A contradiction was raised. *Tosafot* asks: The Gemara is raising this objection against the last clause in our Mishnah, which ruled that excision is not a more severe penalty that exempts from payment. But surely the same objection can be raised against the first clause of the Mishnah, which rules that someone who rapes a virgin *na'arah* who is a *mamzeret* must pay the fine. In the case of the *mamzeret* — and possibly in the other cases as well — the Torah punishes intercourse with lashes. Why, then, did the Gemara wait until now to raise this objection?

Ramban adds that the Gemara's objection would have been more effective if it had been directed against the first clause of the Mishnah, since the objection aimed at the last clause is based on the ruling of the Mishnah in tractate *Makkot* that sins punishable by excision are also punishable by lashes, and this idea is the focus of a Tannaitic dispute (see following note), whereas there is no dispute that intercourse with a *mamzeret* is punishable by lashes.

Tosafot answers that the editors of the Gemara placed the objection here for stylistic reasons, because the Mishnah in *Makkot* lists the cases of excision first, whereas the case of the *mamzeret* is not listed until much later, following several cases that have no parallel in our Mishnah. Thus, it would have been necessary to quote the entire Mishnah in *Makkot* up to the clause referring to the *mamzeret* in order to raise an objection against the first clause in our Mishnah, and the editors of the Gemara felt that this would be unwieldy.

אֵלּוּ הֵן הַלּוֹקִין: הַבָּא עַל אֲחוֹתוֹ These are those who are lashed: If someone has intercourse with his sister. The Gemara (*Makkot* 13a–b) explains that this Mishnah reflects the viewpoint of Rabbi Akiva, who maintains that sins punishable by excision are also punished by lashes if the offense was witnessed and the offender was properly warned. Sins punishable by execution, however, are not punished by lashes, even if the offender was warned. Rabbi

HALAKHAH

אֵלּוּ הֵן הַלּוֹקִין These are those who are lashed. "If a person deliberately violates a negative commandment which is punishable by excision but not by execution, and his transgression was witnessed, and the witnesses gave him

וְעַל הַנִּדָּה״. [32A] [1]וְקַיְימָא לָן דְּאֵינוֹ לוֹקֶה וּמְשַׁלֵּם! [2]אֲמַר עוּלָּא: [3]לָא קַשְׁיָא. [4]כָּאן בַּאֲחוֹתוֹ נַעֲרָה. [5]כָּאן בַּאֲחוֹתוֹ בּוֹגֶרֶת.

LITERAL TRANSLATION

or with a menstruating woman." [32A] [1]But it is accepted by us that [a person] does not receive lashes and [also] pay!

[2]Ulla said: [3]There is no difficulty. [4]Here [it refers] to his sister [who is] a *na'arah*. [5]Here [it refers] to his sister [who is] an adult.

RASHI

וקיימא לן דאין לוקה ומשלם — דנפקא לן לקמן מ״כדי רשעתו״ משום רשעה אחת אתה מחייבו, ואי אתה מחייבו משום שתי רשעיות. **מתניתין באחותו נערה** — דאיכא קנס, וסבירא ליה דממונא משלם ולא לקי. והאיך דמכות — **בבוגרת**, דאין לה קנס.

TRANSLATION AND COMMENTARY

or with a menstruating woman." Thus, the Mishnah in *Makkot* teaches us that sins that are punished by excision (but not sins that are punished by the death penalty) are also punishable by lashes, if the sin was witnessed and the sinner warned. [32A] [1]**But,** says the Gemara, this Mishnah in *Makkot* contradicts our Mishnah, for **it is an established** Halakhic **principle that a person does not receive lashes and also pay** for the same crime. The verse describing the procedure to be followed when inflicting lashes (Deuteronomy 25:2) says: "And he shall be beaten in front of him [the judge] according to his wickedness by a certain number." The Gemara (below, 37a) infers from this verse that when someone is lashed, that punishment is considered a fair retribution for his wickedness, and there is no need for additional penalties. Thus we learn from that passage that someone who is lashed does not pay damages as well. Now, our Mishnah ruled that a man who rapes his relative must pay the fine, even though he is punished by excision, because excision is not a more severe penalty that exempts from payment. But while it is possible that excision is not in itself grounds for exemption from payment, the fact that cases of excision are punished by lashes as well, as we are informed by the Mishnah in *Makkot*, should be grounds for exemption. Therefore, the man who rapes his sister should be exempt from paying the fine because he is subject to the more severe penalty of lashes, even if we disregard the penalty of excision. Why, then, does our Mishnah rule that a man who rapes his sister must pay the fine?

אֲמַר עוּלָּא [2]The Gemara offers three solutions to this problem, each of which will be considered at length. (The second solution, presented by Rabbi Yoḥanan, begins below, on 32b; the third solution, set forth by Resh Lakish, begins on 33b.) The first solution is offered by **Ulla,** who **said:** The exegetical argument from the verse in Deuteronomy (25:2) does not teach us which penalty takes precedence. It merely rules out a compound punishment consisting of lashes and a monetary penalty. We can therefore argue that in those cases in which a monetary penalty is prescribed by the Torah — such as the case of the seduction or rape of a *na'arah* — the offender is required to pay the fine but is exempt from the lashes that he would otherwise be required to bear. [3]Hence **there is no difficulty** in resolving the contradiction between the two Mishnayot. [4]**Here,** in our Mishnah, **the case is** one in which the rapist's **sister was a *na'arah*,** and he is required to pay a fine for raping her. In such a case, the rapist is not lashed, in accordance with the principle that a person is not lashed and made to pay damages for the same offense. [5]**In the other** Mishnah, however, **the case is** one in which the rapist's **sister was an adult,** who is not entitled to a fine, because

SAGES

עוּלָּא Ulla. A Palestinian Amora of the second and third generations. See *Ketubot*, Part I, p. 103.

NOTES

Akiva explains that lashes cannot be imposed for an offense that is punishable by execution, as there cannot be two court-imposed penalties for the same crime. Excision, however, is fundamentally different from lashes and execution, since it is imposed by God, who frequently waives divine punishment if the offender mends his ways, whereas the court is not empowered to waive its penalties.

The Gemara in *Makkot* notes that there are two other Tannaitic views on this matter. Rabbi Yishmael maintains that sins punishable by execution are also punished by lashes if the offender was warned about lashes and not about execution. This is because the rule that prohibits two court-imposed penalties for the same crime excludes imposing both penalties together, but where one penalty is waived for technical reasons, the other can be imposed.

A third viewpoint is that of Rabbi Yitzḥak, who maintains that there is no difference between sins punishable by excision and sins punishable by execution. In neither case are lashes inflicted, even if the offender was warned. Rabbi Yitzḥak derives this from the fact that the Torah twice decrees that incestuous relations between a brother and a sister are punished by excision — once in conjunction with all the other cases of incest (Leviticus 18:29), and a second time independently (Leviticus 20:17). From the repetition of this penalty, Rabbi Yitzḥak learns that sins punishable by excision are not punished by lashes. Rabbi Yitzḥak's view is cited by the Gemara below (35b).

כָּאן בַּאֲחוֹתוֹ נַעֲרָה Here it refers to his sister who is a *na'arah*. In the parallel passage in the Jerusalem Talmud, Ulla's explanation is stated by Rabbi Natan bar Oshaya,

HALAKHAH

due warning, he is punished with lashes," following the Mishnah in *Makkot* cited here. (*Rambam, Sefer Shofetim, Hilkhot Sanhedrin* 18:1; see also 16:4 and 19:1, ibid.)

TRANSLATION AND COMMENTARY

the Torah imposed the fine only if the girl was a *na'arah* (or a minor). Thus the Mishnah in *Makkot* rules that the man is to be lashed, because there is no conflicting monetary penalty. According to Ulla, therefore, a person who commits incest that is subject to a fine must pay the fine (as our Mishnah ruled), and a person who commits incest that is exempt from the fine is lashed (as the other Mishnah ruled), and the two Mishnayot do not contradict each other.

LITERAL TRANSLATION

[1] Even [if] his sister is an adult, [2] surely there are [payments for] shame and blemish!

[1] אֲחוֹתוֹ בּוֹגֶרֶת נַמִי, [2] הָא אִיכָּא בּוֹשֶׁת וּפְגָם!

RASHI

בושת ופגם — דגבי קנס הוא דבעינן נערה, אבל בושת — ממונא הוא. **ופגם** — כאילו היא שפחה נמכרת בשוק, כמה פיחתה מדמיה להשיאה לעבד שיש לרבו קורת רוח הימנו, כדלקמן (כתובות מ,ב). והא בבוגרת נמי איתא.

אֲחוֹתוֹ בּוֹגֶרֶת נַמִי [1] But, the Gemara objects, **even if** the Mishnah in *Makkot* refers to a case in which **his sister is an adult** and no fine is imposed, we still impose a monetary penalty. [2] For **surely** the offender **must pay for shame and blemish!** The Mishnah (below, 39a) rules that someone who seduces a *na'arah* must not only pay the fifty-shekel fine set by the Torah but must also pay damages for the girl's ruined reputation ("shame" — בּוֹשֶׁת), and her loss of virginity ("blemish" — פְּגָם). A rapist must pay these categories of damage and in addition must pay for the pain (צַעַר) suffered by the girl during the rape. The fifty-shekel fine is a fixed sum, set by the Torah as a penalty for the crime itself, and it applies only if the girl was a *na'arah* (or a minor). But the additional payments mentioned here are assessed on an individual basis, just as for any other case of assault, and apply regardless of the woman's age. Therefore a man who rapes his adult sister is always liable to pay monetary damages of some kind. Hence he should always be exempt from lashes, according to Ulla, and this contradicts the Mishnah in *Makkot*.

NOTES

who explains that the Mishnah in *Makkot* is referring to a case in which the man's sister was an adult. The Gemara then objects that the rapist should still be liable to pay for her loss of reputation and virginity, and the Rabbis of Caesarea respond that the Mishnah is referring to a case of seduction, or to a case of rape in which the woman subsequently waived the financial penalty.

הָא אִיכָּא בּוֹשֶׁת וּפְגָם Surely there are payments for shame and blemish! The Mishnah (below, 39a) rules that a man who seduces or rapes a *na'arah* not only pays the fifty-shekel fine set by the Torah, but also pays compensation for the girl's ruined reputation and for her lost virginity. A rapist must, in addition to these payments, also pay for the pain suffered by the girl during the rape; but the seducer is exempt from this payment, since the seduced girl does not ordinarily suffer pain.

The fifty-shekel fine is a fixed sum, set by the Torah as a penalty for the crime itself, whereas these additional payments are assessed on an individual basis, just as in the case of any other assault. Accordingly, these additional payments apply in principle regardless of the woman's age, even though the fine applies only if the girl was a *na'arah* (or a minor, according to some Tannaim). In practice, however, an adult woman who was seduced is not entitled to any kind of payment, because she is considered to have waived any financial claims on her seducer when she agreed to have intercourse with him. She is entitled to compensation only if she was raped. A minor or a *na'arah*, by contrast, cannot waive her financial claims, since these are linked to rights that belong to the girl's father. Thus, the father is entitled to compensation whether the girl was raped or seduced.

Loss of reputation is an example of "shame" (בּוֹשֶׁת), one of the five categories of payment that are imposed in cases of assault. "Shame" must be paid whenever someone physically assaults another person in a humiliating way (e.g., by spitting, tearing off clothes, slapping, etc.), and rape clearly falls into this category. The Mishnah (below, 40a; see also *Bava Kamma* 83b) rules that the sum to be paid depends on the social status of the *na'arah* and on the status of her seducer or rapist. *Rambam* explains that we assess the amount of money the girl's relatives would have been prepared to pay to prevent this from happening to a member of their family.

Loss of virginity is an example of "blemish" (פְּגָם), which is usually classified under the heading of "damage" (נֶזֶק), another of the five payments that are imposed in cases of assault. "Blemish" must be paid whenever the rapist or the seducer causes permanent bodily damage to his victim. The Mishnah (below, 40a) rules that the sum to be paid is assessed by determining the reduction in value of a slave who suffered bodily damage of the same sort. In the case of loss of virginity, we assess the price that could have been obtained if this woman were a slave and her master sold her as a concubine. The seducer or the rapist must pay the difference between the price the master could have obtained if the girl was a virgin and the price he can obtain for her as a non-virgin.

"Pain" (צַעַר) is normally assessed by ascertaining the amount of money a person who knows he is about to be injured in this way would pay to suffer the injury without pain. Only the pain suffered by the victim during the assault itself is assessed, but not the emotional scars carried afterwards by the victim, nor the recurring pain suffered

HALAKHAH

הָא אִיכָּא בּוֹשֶׁת וּפְגָם Surely there are payments for shame and blemish! "Someone who rapes an adult woman does not pay the fifty-shekel fine, but he does pay for her damaged reputation, for the loss of her virginity, and for her pain and suffering. A man who seduces an adult woman, however, pays nothing at all," following our Gemara. (*Rambam*, *Sefer Nashim*, *Hilkhot Na'arah Betulah* 2:11.)

TRANSLATION AND COMMENTARY

בְּשׁוֹטָה [1] Ulla answers that the Mishnah in *Makkot* **is referring to** a case in which the man's sister was an adult and was also **an imbecile**. A girl who is an imbecile has no reputation to lose, and her virginity has no monetary value. But if she is a *na'arah*, she is still entitled to the fifty-shekel fine imposed by the Torah as a penalty for the crime itself. On the other hand, if she is already an adult, the fine does not apply, and she is not entitled to any monetary compensation at all. Hence her seducer or her rapist cannot escape the penalty of lashes. Thus, according to Ulla, the Mishnah in *Makkot* can be interpreted as referring to such a case without contradicting our Mishnah.

וְהָא אִיכָּא צַעֲרָא [2] **But,** the Gemara objects again, even if the Mishnah in *Makkot* refers to a case in which the sister is an adult imbecile, there is still an applicable monetary penalty in the case of the rapist, if not in the case of the seducer. For **surely there is payment for pain!** The Mishnah (below, 39a) rules that a rapist must pay for the pain suffered by his victim during the rape, in addition to the "shame" and "blemish" paid by both a seducer and a rapist, and in addition to the fifty-shekel fine imposed by the Torah. While it is true that an imbecile has no reputation to lose, and a monetary value cannot be placed on her virginity, she does suffer pain when she is raped. Therefore a man who rapes his sister is always obligated to pay monetary damages of some kind, even if his sister was an adult imbecile. Hence he should always be exempt from lashes, according to Ulla, and this contradicts the Mishnah in *Makkot*.

בִּמְפוּתָּה [3] Ulla answers that the Mishnah in *Makkot* **is referring to** a case in which the man's adult imbecile sister **was seduced** and not raped. The Mishnah (below, 39a) rules that only the rapist must pay for pain. The seducer is exempt. The Gemara (below, 39b) explains that a woman who is raped feels pain not felt by a woman who engages in intercourse voluntarily. Hence a brother who seduces his sister is not liable to pay for her pain. Ordinarily, he is still liable to pay for her damaged reputation and her lost virginity, in addition to the fifty-shekel fine imposed by the Torah, but if his sister is an imbecile, he is not liable to pay compensation for her reputation and her virginity, and if she is an adult, he is not required to pay the fine either. Under these circumstances, his sister is entitled to no financial compensation at all, and her seducer cannot escape the penalty of lashes. Thus, according to Ulla, the Mishnah in *Makkot* can be interpreted as referring to such a case, and this would not contradict our Mishnah.

[1] בְּשׁוֹטָה.
[2] וְהָא אִיכָּא צַעֲרָא!
[3] בִּמְפוּתָּה.

LITERAL TRANSLATION

[1] [It refers] to an imbecile.

[2] But surely there is [payment for] pain!

[3] [It refers] to one who was seduced.

RASHI

בשוטה — שאין לה בושת, ודמים למכור בשוק נמי אין לה. והא איכא צערא — דהכי תנן במתניתין: המפתה נותן בושת ופגם וקנס, מוסיף עליו האונס שנותן את הצער. במפותה — דאין לה צער, כדאמרינן לקמן בפירקין (כתובות לט,ב): פקחות שבהן אומרות מפותה אין לה צער.

CONCEPTS

שׁוֹטֶה **An imbecile.** A person so intellectually and emotionally unstable that he is not responsible for his actions. There are three classes of people who are not responsible for their behavior: חֵרֵשׁ — a deaf-mute; שׁוֹטֶה — an imbecile; and קָטָן — a minor. Of the three, a שׁוֹטֶה is considered the most severely incapacitated. He has no religious obligations and no act that he performs has legal validity. The Sages discussed the legal definition of a שׁוֹטֶה. They defined several levels of imbecility, and the extent to which a שׁוֹטֶה is considered criminally responsible for his actions.

NOTES

long after the injury. Accordingly, in the case of rape, the rapist must pay for the pain the *na'arah* suffered during the rape itself, but not for pain suffered later. The seducer is exempt from this payment, because the pain suffered by a woman during her first act of sexual intercourse is not assessed, since nearly every woman suffers this pain once. The rapist, by contrast, must pay for the pain he caused, because the Rabbis were aware that a woman who is raped suffers pain that is not felt by a woman who engages in intercourse voluntarily.

In other cases of assault, there are two further payments that the assailant must make: for medical treatment (רִיפּוּי), and for lost income (שֶׁבֶת). These, however, are not applied to rape or seduction.

שׁוֹטָה **An imbecile.** Normally, a woman who is raped is entitled to compensation for her damaged reputation and her lost virginity. But the Gemara is clearly of the opinion that an imbecile is not entitled to this compensation. The Gemara's reasoning regarding loss of reputation is relatively easy to understand, but the argument regarding lost virginity is more difficult.

Damage to a person's reputation is an example of "shame," one of the five categories of payment that are imposed in cases of assault. "Shame" must be paid whenever someone assaults another person in a humiliating way. The Mishnah (below, 40a and see *Bava Kamma* 83b) rules that the sum to be paid depends on the social status of the shamed person, and the Gemara (*Bava Kamma* 86b) rules that an imbecile cannot suffer "shame" at all. The Gemara explains that an imbecile does not

HALAKHAH

בְּשׁוֹטָה **It refers to an imbecile.** "Someone who rapes a *na'arah* who is an imbecile or a deaf-mute is exempt from paying the fine, and from paying for her damaged reputation and her lost virginity, but must pay compensation for her pain and suffering. But someone who seduces a *na'arah* who is an imbecile or a deaf-mute pays nothing at all. *Ra'avad* agrees with *Rambam*'s ruling regarding the imbecile's reputation, her lost virginity, and her pain and suffering, but disagrees regarding the fine, arguing that it applies to imbeciles and deaf-mutes as well." (*Rambam*, *Sefer Nashim*, *Hilkhot Na'arah Betulah* 1:9 and 2:11.)

LITERAL TRANSLATION

[1] Now that you have come to this, [2] you may even say [that it speaks of] his sister [who is] a *na'arah*, [and refers] to an orphan and a seduced [girl].

[1] הַשְׁתָּא דְּאָתֵית לְהָכִי, [2] אֲפִילּוּ תֵּימָא אֲחוֹתוֹ נַעֲרָה, בִּיתוֹמָה וּמְפוּתָּה.

RASHI

ביתומה — שקנסה ובושתה ופגמה שלה. ומפותה — כיון שהכל שלה — אין כאן חיוב ממון, דהא עבדא מדעתה, ואחולי אחלה גביה. שוטה לא גרסינן, דפקחת נמי אין שום חיוב ממון במפותה יתומה.

TRANSLATION AND COMMENTARY

הַשְׁתָּא דְּאָתֵית לְהָכִי [1] The Gemara notes that Ulla's resolution of the contradiction between the two Mishnayot can be simplified. **Now that you have come to this** solution and you explain the Mishnah in *Makkot* as referring to a case of seduction and not rape, it is no longer necessary to explain that the girl was an imbecile in order to find a case in which she is not entitled to any financial compensation. For the Gemara (below, 39b) explains that there is an additional difference between seduction and rape, apart from the fact that raped women feel pain that is not felt by seduced women. A *na'arah* who was seduced consented to the seduction and should really not be entitled to any compensation at all. Nevertheless, the seducer must normally pay for her damaged reputation and her lost virginity, in addition to the fifty-shekel fine, because these payments are made to the girl's father, and he has not waived his rights. But if the woman is an adult, financial compensation of any kind is paid to her directly, and if she consented to the illicit intercourse, her seducer owes her nothing. [2] **You may even say that** the Mishnah in *Makkot* **is speaking of** a case in which **his sister was a *na'arah*,** and he may still be exempt from payment. For the Mishnah in *Makkot* may **be referring to** a case in which this sister was **an orphan who was seduced.** A *na'arah* who is an orphan has the same status as an adult if she is seduced, because any payments must be made to her directly, in the absence of her father. Hence, if she is raped, the rapist must pay her directly for her damaged reputation and her lost virginity, and for her pain, and he must also pay her the fifty-shekel fine. But if she consented to the illicit intercourse, her seducer owes her nothing. Thus a brother who seduces his sister after their father's death is not required to pay any financial compensation at all, and he has no way of escaping the penalty of lashes, according to Ulla. Hence, the Mishnah in *Makkot* can be interpreted as referring to such a case, according to Ulla, without contradicting our Mishnah. But if the girl was raped, or if her father was alive (and she was not an adult), the rapist is held liable to pay compensation, and would therefore be exempt from lashes, according to Ulla.

NOTES

recognize that he is being humiliated, and his social status among his relatives and neighbors is also not affected, since the indignity of being an imbecile is so great that it is impossible to increase it.

The argument regarding lost virginity is more difficult to understand. Loss of virginity is an example of "blemish," another of the five payments that are imposed in cases of assault. "Blemish" must be paid whenever the assailant causes permanent bodily damage to his victim. The Mishnah (below, 40a) rules that the value of virginity is assessed by ascertaining the price the woman would have fetched on the slave market if she had been sold as a concubine. Why, then, should we not assess in the same way the market value of a woman who is an imbecile?

Rashi explains that a slave who is an imbecile is worth nothing on the slave market. Hence, since bodily damage inflicted on a free person is assessed by comparing it to similar bodily damage inflicted on a slave, there is no way of assessing bodily damage of any kind inflicted on an imbecile. *Rashash* points out that *Rashi*'s explanation is difficult to accept, because there is a Mishnah in tractate *Arakhin* (2a) which indicates that an imbecile is in fact considered to have some value on the slave market. Accordingly, *Rashash* explains that although a maidservant who is an imbecile has some value, no one would buy her as a concubine for his slave; hence the fact that she is or is not a virgin would have no effect on her price. Therefore someone who assaults an imbecile is normally required to pay damages, but a person who seduces or rapes an imbecile is not required to pay for her lost virginity.

בִּיתוֹמָה וּמְפוּתָּה And refers to an orphan and a seduced girl. Our translation and commentary follow the standard Vilna Talmud, whose text was the one favored by *Rashi*. There is a variant version which reads: "And refers to an orphan who was an imbecile and was seduced." According to this reading, the orphan *na'arah* is indeed not entitled to the fine if she engaged in intercourse voluntarily, but she is entitled to compensation for the loss of her virginity and for her damaged reputation, unless she was an imbecile. *Rashi* rejects this reading, arguing that an orphan *na'arah* who has been seduced is not entitled to compensation for the loss of her virginity and for her damaged reputation, even if she is normal. For just as a seduced woman is considered to have waived her claim to the fine, she is similarly considered to have waived her claim to compensation for the loss of her virginity and for her damaged reputation, even if she is normal. But if her father is alive, her waiver is invalid, since the money is owed to her father, but an orphan managing her own affairs has no monetary claims whatsoever against her seducer. *Ramban* supports *Rashi*'s rejection of this reading, citing a tradition in the name of *Rav Hai Gaon* that it is an error. Some Rishonim, however, justify the variant reading (see *Rabbi Shmuel HaNagid,* cited by *Ramban*, and see *Ritva*).

TRANSLATION AND COMMENTARY

אַלְמָא קָסָבַר עוּלָּא [1]Having found Ulla's explanation satisfactory, the Gemara now analyzes the reasoning underlying it. We have seen that the Gemara (below, 37a) infers from a Biblical verse that lashes are never imposed together with a monetary penalty, but it is not clear from the verse which penalty takes precedence. **It follows,** however, **from Ulla's** resolution of the contradiction between our Mishnah and the Mishnah in *Makkot* **that he maintains** [2]that **whenever** a single offense is subject to both **monetary payment and lashes,** [3]the offender **pays the money but is not lashed,** and this applies even in a case in which there is no technical legal barrier preventing the court from sentencing a person to lashes. We will see later that other Amoraim disagree with Ulla, and maintain that lashes take precedence over monetary penalties. This will naturally lead them to a different solution to the contradiction between the two Mishnayot.

מְנָא לֵיהּ לְעוּלָּא [4]The Gemara asks: **From where does Ulla learn this?** How does Ulla know that monetary penalties take precedence over lashes? Why does he not accept the view of the other Amoraim who are of the opinion that lashes take precedence over monetary penalties?

גָּמַר מֵחוֹבֵל בַּחֲבֵירוֹ [5]The Gemara now makes four attempts to prove that Ulla derives his principle from a Biblical source. In the first attempt, the Gemara argues that Ulla **derives it from** the case of **someone who injures someone else** — a case in which all agree that monetary penalties take precedence over lashes. Someone who injures another person violates a negative commandment (Deuteronomy 25:3). Moreover, under certain unusual circumstances, under which financial penalties cannot be applied, this offense is punishable by lashes (below, 32b). Nevertheless, the Torah (Exodus 21:19) explicitly requires the assailant to reimburse his victim for loss of income and for his medical bills (in addition to other payments adduced by the Rabbis from various passages in the Torah). It follows, therefore, that the assailant is not lashed, since we have already established that lashes and monetary penalties cannot both be imposed for the same offense. [6]We can extrapolate from this case and reason as follows: **Just as someone who injures someone else,** and who should be subject to both **monetary payment and lashes,** [7]only **pays the money but is not lashed,** [8]**so too, whenever** a single offense is punishable both by **monetary payments and** by **lashes,** [9]the offender only **pays the money but is not lashed,** even if there is no technical legal barrier preventing the court from inflicting the lashes.

מַה לְחוֹבֵל בַּחֲבֵירוֹ [10]The Gemara rejects this proof: **What is special about** the case of **someone who injures someone else is that** the punishment is unusually severe, since the assailant **is liable** to pay, not only for

[1]אַלְמָא קָסָבַר עוּלָּא: [2]כָּל הֵיכָא דְּאִיכָּא מָמוֹן וּמַלְקוּת, [3]מָמוֹנָא מְשַׁלֵּם, מִילְקָא לָא לָקֵי.

[4]מְנָא לֵיהּ לְעוּלָּא הָא?

[5]גָּמַר מֵחוֹבֵל בַּחֲבֵירוֹ. [6]מַה חוֹבֵל בַּחֲבֵירוֹ — דְּאִיכָּא מָמוֹן וּמַלְקוּת — [7]מָמוֹנָא מְשַׁלֵּם, מִילְקָא לָא לָקֵי, [8]אַף כָּל הֵיכָא דְּאִיכָּא מָמוֹן וּמַלְקוּת, [9]מָמוֹנָא מְשַׁלֵּם, מִילְקָא לָא לָקֵי.

[10]מה לְחוֹבֵל בְּחֲבִירוֹ שֶׁכֵּן חַיָּיב

LITERAL TRANSLATION

[1]Consequently Ulla maintains: [2]Wherever there is money [to be paid] and lashes, [3]he pays the money, [but] he is not lashed.

[4]From where does Ulla [learn] this?

[5]He learns [it] from one who injures his fellow. [6]Just as one who injures his fellow — for which there is money [to be paid] and lashes — [7]pays the money, [but] he is not lashed, [8]so too wherever there is money [to be paid] and lashes, [9]he pays the money, [but] he is not lashed.

[10]What is [special] about one who injures his fellow is that he is liable

RASHI

קסבר עולא — דאוקי מתניתין דמכות בבוגרת, ולא אוקמה למתניתין דהכא בשלא התרו בו — שמעת מינה: אפילו אתרו ביה נמי — ממונא משלם ולא לקי. **חובל בחבירו** — איכא מלקות ד״לא יוסיף״ (דברים כה), וממונא משלם כדכתיב (שמות כא) ״שבתו יתן״. ואפילו אתרו ביה נמי מרבי ליה לקמן בשמעתין בהדיא לתשלומין. **מה לחובל בחבירו** — דין הוא לידון בממון שהוא חמור ממלקות, שכן יש בו חומר אחר.

CONCEPTS

מַלְקוּת **Lashes.** A form of punishment. The offender is tied to a post in a leaning position and whipped on his back and his chest. The Sages interpreted the verse, "Forty stripes he may give him and not exceed" (Deuteronomy 25:3), to mean that the number of lashes administered per transgression is thirty-nine. But if the victim cannot survive that number of lashes, he receives the number he can bear. Negative commandments are usually punishable by lashes. However, there are a number of exceptions, notably: (1) a commandment that is violated without action (לָאו שֶׁאֵין בּוֹ מַעֲשֶׂה); (2) a transgression for which the Torah provided a means of reparation (לָאו הַנִּיתָּק לַעֲשֵׂה); (3) a collective prohibition that includes several different laws (לָאו שֶׁבִּכְלָלוֹת); and (4) a transgression that under certain circumstances could be subject to the death penalty (לָאו שֶׁנִּיתָּן לְאַזְהָרַת מִיתַת בֵּית דִּין). Lashes are not administered unless there were two witnesses to the transgression and unless the offender was warned immediately before his transgression. According to the Halakhah, a court of three is required in order to administer lashes.

NOTES

מַה לְחוֹבֵל בַּחֲבֵירוֹ **What is special about someone who injures his fellow.** The Rishonim ask: Even if it is true that we cannot extrapolate from the case of assault to all other cases where a monetary penalty and lashes conflict, Ulla's primary purpose is to prove that monetary penalties take precedence in the cases of rape and seduction. But rape is itself a type of assault. Why, then, should Ulla not be able to argue from the general case of assault to the special case of rape that money takes precedence over lashes in a case of rape just as it does in all cases of assault?

Ri in *Tosafot* explains that the Gemara here is asking about the fifty-shekel fine, which is not a form of compensation for assault. According to Ulla, the fine also takes precedence over lashes even in a case where the other payments are not applicable, and this cannot be learned from the case of ordinary assault.

CONCEPTS

הוּתַּר מִכְּלָלוֹ It was exempted from its general rule. This term denotes the relaxation of a Torah prohibition because of certain special circumstances. For example, though priests are generally forbidden to come in contact with dead bodies, the Torah relaxes that prohibition with regard to a priest's immediate family (Leviticus 21:2). A prohibition that is occasionally relaxed in this manner is considered less severe than one which is not.

LITERAL TRANSLATION

for five things. [1]And if money is more lenient, [2][we can argue] that it was exempted from its general rule [and permitted] in a court.

בַּחֲמִשָּׁה דְּבָרִים. [1]וְאִי מָמוֹנָא לְקוּלָּא, [2]שֶׁכֵּן הוּתַּר מִכְּלָלוֹ בְּבֵית דִּין.

RASHI

שחייב בחמשה דברים — נזק, לער, ריפוי, שבת, ובושת. **ואי ממונא לקולא הוא** — ואם תאמר: ממון קל מן המלקות, ואין זו תשובה שהשבנו, דכל שכן בעלמא, מה זה שאמור להתחייב בחמשה דברים נדון בקלה שבשני חיובין שבהן — קל וחומר לשאר חייבי ממון הקלין, שידונו בממון הקל. איכא למיפרך: מה לחובל בחבירו — שכן הותר מכללו בבית דין, דניתן רשות לבית דין להלקותו — תאמר בשאר חייבי ממון, כגון קנס דאונס ומפתה, שלא הותרו מכללן בבית דין.

TRANSLATION AND COMMENTARY

the damage he has caused, but also for pain, shame, medical costs, and loss of income — a total of **five things.** Hence we cannot extrapolate from this case to cases in which the relevant monetary penalty is for damage alone. This objection is based on the assumption that monetary penalties are at least comparable in severity to lashes. [1]**But if** we say that **monetary** penalties **are** substantially **more lenient** than lashes, and that Ulla is deriving from the case of assault that if there is a conflict between monetary penalties and lashes, the Torah imposes the lighter, monetary penalty, we can no longer raise this objection. We can, however, raise another objection, [2]for **we can argue** the opposite way **that** assault is in some sense a less severe crime than others, as we see from the fact that the Torah **permitted** assault in certain special cases which **were exempted from the general rule** — namely, **in a court.** The Torah forbids striking another person "excessively" (see Deuteronomy 25:3). A court, on the other hand, is specifically permitted to inflict up to thirty-nine lashes for a single offense. Since the court is permitted to "assault" a transgressor, it would seem that assault is a relatively minor crime. Hence we cannot extrapolate from the fact that the Torah imposed a financial penalty in this case, rather than lashes, that the same would apply to other, more severe cases in which the two penalties conflict. Thus we see that regardless of whether we take the position that monetary penalties are of comparable severity to lashes, or the position that they are considerably less severe, we cannot extrapolate from the laws of injury to other cases in which monetary penalties and lashes conflict.

NOTES

Rivam explains that the Gemara is objecting that rape is less severe than other cases of assault. For in all other cases of assault, it is at least potentially possible for the assailant to be liable to make five payments, whereas the rapist is at most liable to make three of them. *Shittah Mekubbetzet* adds in *Rashi*'s name that the rapist is not liable to pay for the woman's medical expenses, even though medical expenses are theoretically applicable, since the rapist did cause a wound.

וְאִי מָמוֹנָא לְקוּלָּא And if money is more lenient. Our commentary follows *Tosafot* and other Rishonim, who explain that the Gemara is in doubt whether lashes are in general a more severe penalty or a more lenient one than monetary penalties. *Tosafot* asks: How can we possibly say that according to Ulla a monetary payment is more lenient than lashes? Ulla maintains that monetary penalties take precedence over lashes in a case where the offender has committed two offenses. Now, if monetary penalties are more lenient than lashes, this would mean that the Torah treats a person who commits both offenses more leniently than a person who committed only the offense punishable by lashes! Why should the offender benefit from committing a double offense? *Ritva* adds that the Gemara rules (below, 32b) that a person who inflicts a very slight injury that is worth less than the coin of lowest value is lashed, since he cannot atone for his sin through payment. But if lashes were more severe than monetary payment, it would follow that the punishment for a slight injury is more stringent than for a severe one!

Tosafot and *Ritva* answer that it is still possible that lashes are the more severe penalty, even according to Ulla, who is of the opinion that monetary penalties take precedence over lashes. Ulla can argue that monetary penalties were nevertheless given precedence over lashes for the sake of the injured person. The Torah prefers to compensate the injured person for his injuries, rather than to inflict lashes on his assailant. But where this is not a consideration — for example, where the injury is too slight to justify monetary compensation, lashes are inflicted. Thus, paradoxically, slight injuries are punished more strictly than severe ones.

Ḥatam Sofer suggests that the Gemara may not in fact be questioning whether monetary payments are more severe or less severe than lashes in a general, abstract sense. Obviously a small money payment is less severe than lashes, and a very large one more severe, since the penalty of lashes is fixed whereas monetary penalties vary. Rather, the Gemara is pointing out that our objection to Ulla's argument must cover cases in which monetary compensation is more severe than lashes as well as cases in which it is less severe.

שֶׁכֵּן הוּתַּר מִכְּלָלוֹ בְּבֵית דִּין That it was exempted from its general rule and permitted in a court. *Ritva* asks: Normally, the expression "exempted from its general rule" refers to a case in which under special circumstances the Torah permits doing something forbidden. Thus the Torah normally forbids killing animals on Shabbat, but this is permitted for the Shabbat sacrifices in the Temple. By contrast, striking someone is not permitted under special circumstances; it is simply defined in such a way that it does not apply at all to a court. For the Torah did not forbid striking another person per se; it forbade striking another person "excessively." Hence the lashes inflicted by a court, which are not excessive, are not in this category at all. How, then, can they be described as being exempted from the general rule and permitted?

TRANSLATION AND COMMENTARY

אֶלָּא [1] **Rather,** the Gemara makes a second attempt to find a Biblical source for Ulla's principle that monetary penalties take precedence over lashes. According to this explanation, Ulla **derives it from** the case of **conspiring witnesses** (עֵדִים זוֹמְמִים — *edim zomemim*), in which monetary penalties also take precedence over lashes according to all opinions. Witnesses who conspire to testify falsely violate a negative commandment (Exodus 20:13): "You shall not bear false witness." Moreover, under certain unusual circumstances, in which the regular penalty cannot be applied, this offense is punishable by lashes (*Makkot* 2a-b). Nevertheless, the Torah (Deuteronomy 19:19) explicitly commands that witnesses who conspire to give false testimony must have the same punishment inflicted on them that they sought to inflict on the defendant. If the conspiring witnesses testify that the defendant was guilty of a monetary offense, they must pay him a sum equal to the amount he would have been required to pay had their testimony prevailed. From this it follows that they are not lashed, since we have already established that lashes and monetary penalties cannot both be imposed for the same offense. Thus we see that in the case of conspiring witnesses, monetary penalties take precedence over lashes. [2] We can extrapolate from this case and reason as follows: **Just as conspiring witnesses,** who should be subject to both **monetary payment and lashes,** [3] only **pay the money but are not lashed,** [4] **so too, whenever** a single offense is punishable both by **monetary payments and** by **lashes,** [5] the offender only **pays the money but is not lashed,** even if there is no technical legal barrier preventing the court from inflicting the lashes.

מַה לְּעֵדִים זוֹמְמִין [6] The Gemara rejects this proof: **What is special about** the case of **conspiring witnesses is that** their punishment is unusually severe, since **they do not need a warning.** Ordinarily, an offender cannot be punished with lashes or death unless his offense was witnessed and the witnesses warned him in advance that what he was about to do was a punishable offense. Conspiring witnesses, however, are punished even if they were never warned. Thus we see that the Torah is very severe toward conspiring witnesses, and this may be the reason why they are punished with the more severe monetary penalty, rather than with lashes. Hence we cannot extrapolate from this case to other cases. This objection is based on the assumption that monetary penalties are at least comparable in severity to lashes. [7] **But** even **if** we say that **monetary** penalties **are** substantially **more lenient** than lashes, [8] **we can argue that** conspiring to bear false witness is in some sense a less severe crime than others, since the conspiring witnesses **do not do an action.** The courts are

[1] אֶלָּא, גָּמַר מֵעֵדִים זוֹמְמִין. [2] מָה עֵדִים זוֹמְמִין — דְּאִיכָּא מָמוֹן וּמַלְקוֹת — [3] מָמוֹנָא מְשַׁלֵּם, מִילְקָא לָא לָקֵי, [4] אַף כָּל הֵיכָא דְּאִיכָּא מָמוֹן וּמַלְקוֹת, [5] מָמוֹנָא מְשַׁלֵּם, מִילְקָא לָא לָקֵי.

[6] מַה לְּעֵדִים זוֹמְמִין שֶׁכֵּן אֵינָן צְרִיכִים הַתְרָאָה. [7] וְאִי מָמוֹנָא לְקוּלָּא הוּא, [8] שֶׁכֵּן לֹא עָשׂוּ מַעֲשֶׂה.

LITERAL TRANSLATION

[1] Rather, he learns [it] from conspiring witnesses. [2] Just as [in the case of] conspiring witnesses — for which there is money [to be paid] and lashes — [3] [each witness] pays the money [but] is not lashed, [4] so too wherever there is money [to be paid] and lashes, [5] he pays the money, [but] he is not lashed.

[6] What is [special] about conspiring witnesses is that they do not need a warning. [7] And if money is more lenient, [8] [we can argue] that they did not do an action.

RASHI

אלא גמר מעדים זוממים — כמה מלינו. **דאיכא ממון** — ד"כאשר זמם". **ומלקות** — ד"לא תענה". **ממונא משלם** — לקמן יליף לה במתניתין. **שכן אין צריכין התראה** — ונענשין במיתה או במלקות או בממון, ודין הוא שידונו בחמורה כי איכא תרתי. **ואי ממונא קולא הוא** — אשכחן בהן צד הקל, ודין הוא שידונו בקלה. **שכן לא עשו מעשה** — אלא בדיבורא בעלמא מיענשי.

NOTES

Ritva answers that if a court inflicts more lashes than the thirty-nine authorized by the Torah, it too violates the prohibition against striking another person excessively. Yet the Torah commands the court to punish offenders in this way, in spite of the possibility of abuse, and this is considered the equivalent of permitting something under special circumstances. Alternatively, *Ritva* explains that assault is not, in fact, a prohibition "exempted from its general rule" and permitted, but rather a prohibition defined in a limited way. However, the Gemara is objecting to a proposed extrapolation, and such arguments must be flawless. Hence the Gemara is of the opinion that prohibitions defined in a limited way are somewhat less stringent than absolute prohibitions, even if they were not exactly "exempted from their general rule" and permitted.

שֶׁכֵּן לֹא עָשׂוּ מַעֲשֶׂה **That they did not do an action.** Our

HALAKHAH

מַה לְּעֵדִים זוֹמְמִין שֶׁכֵּן אֵינָן צְרִיכִים הַתְרָאָה **What is special about conspiring witnesses is that they do not need a warning.** "Conspiring witnesses can be convicted and punished, even if they were not warned," as stated by our Gemara. (*Rambam, Sefer Shofetim, Hilkhot Edut*, 18:4.)

CONCEPTS

עֵדִים זוֹמְמִים **Conspiring witnesses.** These are witnesses who have perjured themselves to make someone lose a monetary dispute or to cause him to be punished by the court. There are two ways in which the testimony of witnesses can be invalidated: (1) If two other witnesses testify that something did not happen as described by the first pair of witnesses. In such a case, the testimony of neither pair is accepted, and the matter is left undecided. (2) If two witnesses testify that the first pair of witnesses, whose testimony condemned the defendant, were elsewhere (with the second pair of witnesses) when the incident transpired, and could not have witnessed the events about which they testified. The second pair of witnesses are not contradicting the evidence of the first pair (which may indeed be true). They are testifying that the first pair were not present and therefore were not in a position to know. In such a case, the testimony of the second pair of witnesses is accepted, and the testimony of the first pair is rejected. Furthermore, the first pair of witnesses, the עֵדִים זוֹמְמִים, pay the penalty they sought to inflict on the defendant (see Deuteronomy 19:16-19). Thus if their testimony would have resulted in the execution of the defendant, they are both executed. If their testimony would have resulted in his receiving lashes, they are both lashed. If their testimony would have led to a penalty that cannot be applied to them (if, for example, their evidence would have disqualified the defendant from the priesthood), they are given lashes. The acceptance of the testimony of the second pair of witnesses is a חִידּוּשׁ, a unique law not necessarily following from existing Torah principles. Accordingly, many limitations are placed on its application. Among them: (1) *Both* the first pair of witnesses (or *all* the witnesses, if there are more than two) must be proven to be conspiring witnesses before the retaliatory punishment is meted out to any of them. (2) עֵדִים זוֹמְמִים are not punished unless the defendant has already been convicted on the basis of their testimony. (3) In capital cases, the death penalty is administered to the conspiring witnesses only if it has *not* been administered to the defendant. If, however, the defendant *has* already been executed, the conspiring witnesses are not executed.

CONCEPTS

הַתְרָאָה **Warning.** A formal warning given to a person who is about to commit a prohibited act. The warning must state that the act is forbidden and must describe the punishment a violator would receive. Capital and corporal punishment cannot be administered unless such a warning was given beforehand and acknowledged by the transgressor. In only a few instances (e.g., מֵסִית — one who incites to idol worship; and עֵדִים זוֹמְמִים — conspiring witnesses) is punishment administered even though no warning was given.

TRANSLATION AND COMMENTARY

normally authorized to impose penalties only on forbidden activities. Mere words or thoughts, although sometimes strictly forbidden, are not usually punishable by a court. One of the few exceptions to this rule is the case of conspiring witnesses, who are punished by the court even though they merely uttered false words. Thus it is possible that the reason the Torah was lenient with them and imposed a monetary penalty on them, instead of punishing them with lashes, was because they did not commit an action. Hence we cannot extrapolate from the fact that the Torah imposed a financial penalty in this case, rather than lashes, that the same would apply to other, more severe cases in which the two penalties conflict. Thus we see that regardless of whether we take the position that monetary penalties are of comparable severity to lashes, or the position that they are considerably less severe, we cannot extrapolate from the case of conspiring witnesses to other cases in which monetary penalties and lashes conflict.

אֶלָּא [1]**Rather,** the Gemara makes a third attempt to find a Biblical source for Ulla's principle that monetary penalties take precedence over lashes. According to this explanation, Ulla **derives it from** the common factor in **both of** the previously discussed cases — assault and conspiring witnesses. One of the traditional methods of scriptural exegesis is the hermeneutic principle called "the common factor" (הַצַּד הַשָּׁוֶה). According to this principle, if a general rule is based on two or more cases in the Torah, it applies to all other cases, even if there are objections to each individual analogy, provided that there are no objections that apply equally to both or all analogies. In our case the general rule that monetary penalties take precedence over lashes is based on two cases — that of the assailant and that of the conspiring witnesses. Each of these cases was inadequate to establish a general principle for a different reason: The case of the assailant, because of his obligation to make five payments, or because assault is permitted to a court; and that of the conspiring witnesses, because they do not require to be warned, or because they commit their crime through words rather than deeds. But there are no objections that apply equally to both cases. [2]Therefore, we can extrapolate from the factor that is common to both these cases and reason as follows: **Just as the common factor between** the assailant and the conspiring witnesses **is that** they should be subject to both **monetary payment and lashes,** [3]**and** yet **they** only **pay the money but are not lashed,** even if there are no technical legal barriers preventing the court from inflicting the lashes, [4]**so too, whenever** a single offense is punishable both by **monetary payments and** by **lashes,** [5]the offender only **pays the money but is not lashed**, even if there are no technical legal barriers preventing the court from inflicting the lashes.

מַה לְּהַצַּד הַשָּׁוֶה שֶׁבָּהֶן [6]The Gemara rejects this proof: **What is special about the common factor between** assault and conspiring witnesses **is that** the punishment imposed in both cases is unusually severe, since **they** both **have a stringent aspect.** It is possible to extrapolate from a common factor only if there is no objection that applies to both cases. But in both of the cases mentioned here there is a common objection. In both cases, the Torah was unusually stringent, imposing penalties that would not ordinarily be imposed: five categories of damages on the assailant, and punishment without warning on the conspiring witnesses. Thus we see that the Torah was very strict with assailants and with conspiring witnesses, and this may

[1]אֶלָּא, גָּמַר מִתַּרְוַיְיהוּ. [2]מַה הַצַּד הַשָּׁוֶה שֶׁבָּהֶן דְּאִיכָּא מָמוֹן וּמַלְקוֹת, [3]מָמוֹנָא מְשַׁלֵּם מִילְקָא לָא לָקֵי, [4]אַף כָּל הֵיכָא דְּאִיכָּא מָמוֹן וּמַלְקוֹת, [5]מָמוֹנָא מְשַׁלֵּם, מִילְקָא לָא לָקֵי.
[6]מַה לְהַצַּד הַשָּׁוֶה שֶׁבָּהֶן שֶׁכֵּן יֵשׁ בָּהֶן צַד חָמוּר.

LITERAL TRANSLATION

[1]Rather, he learns [it] from both of them. [2]Just as the common factor between them is that there is money [to be paid] and lashes, [3][and] he pays the money [but] is not lashed, [4]so too wherever there is money [to be paid] and lashes, [5]he pays the money, [but] he is not lashed.

[6]What is [special] about the common factor between them is that they have a stringent aspect.

RASHI

מתרווייהו – כי פרכת: מה לחובל בחבירו שכן חייב בחמשה דברים – עדים זוממין יוכיחו, מה לעדים זוממין שכן אין צריכין התראה – חובל יוכיח; וחזר הדין.

NOTES

commentary follows *Rashi* and most Rishonim, who explain that the conspiring witnesses sinned through their words rather than through deeds.

Rashba suggests an alternative interpretation of this phrase of the Gemara, based on the law (*Makkot* 5b) that conspiring witnesses are punished only if their testimony resulted in the defendant's conviction. But if the conspiring witnesses were not exposed until after the sentence was carried out, they are not punished. According to this explanation, our Gemara means that the sin of conspiring witnesses is less severe, because they are punished only if they did not do an action — in other words, if their false testimony had no practical effect.

שֶׁכֵּן יֵשׁ בָּהֶן צַד חָמוּר **They have a stringent aspect.** The Rishonim ask: How can the Gemara raise this kind of objection against an extrapolation from a common factor?

TRANSLATION AND COMMENTARY

be the reason why they are punished with the more severe monetary penalty, rather than with lashes. Hence, we cannot extrapolate from these two cases to other cases, in which the Torah is not so strict. This objection is based on the assumption that monetary penalties are at least comparable in severity to lashes. [1]**But** even **if** we assume that **monetary** penalties **are** substantially **more lenient** than lashes, [2]**we can argue that** beating a person and conspiring to bear false witness are in some sense less severe crimes than others, since these two transgressions **have a lenient aspect.** In both cases, the offense has a particular lenient characteristic — beating being permitted to a court and conspiring to bear false witness being mere words without action. This may be the reason why the Torah was lenient with them and decreed only a monetary penalty instead of lashes. Hence, we cannot extrapolate from the fact that the Torah imposed a financial penalty in these cases, rather than lashes, that the same would apply to other, more severe cases in which the two penalties conflict. Thus we see that regardless of whether we take the position that monetary penalties are of comparable severity to lashes, or the position that they are considerably less severe, we cannot extrapolate from the common factor found in assault and conspiring witnesses to other cases in which monetary penalties and lashes conflict.

אֶלָּא [32B] [3]**Rather,** the Gemara makes a fourth attempt to find a Biblical source for Ulla's principle that monetary penalties take precedence over lashes. According to this explanation, Ulla applied the exegetical rule called *gezerah shavah* (see above, 29b), according to which, when the Torah uses the same words in two contexts, it intends to compare the subject matter in the two contexts, and to transfer information from one to the other. [4]The Gemara explains: **Ulla infers** his principle **from** a comparison of the expression **"for"** (תַּחַת in Hebrew), which appears in the verse dealing with the fine paid by a rapist, and the expression **"for,"** which appears in the verse dealing with the payments made by an assailant who injures someone. [5]**Here,** in the case of the rapist, **it is written** (Deuteronomy 22:29) that the fine has to be paid **"for he has humbled her,"** [6]**and there,** in the case of the assailant, **it is written** (Exodus 21:24) that the person inflicting the injury must compensate his victim in full, **"an eye for an eye."** Therefore, says Ulla, we can apply the *gezerah shavah* rule and transfer the laws applying to assault to the case of the rapist. We have already seen that in the case of assault monetary payments take precedence over lashes. [7]Hence it follows that **just as there** the assailant, who should be subject to monetary payments and lashes, is in fact only required to **pay the money but is not lashed,** [8]**so too whenever** a single offense is punishable both by **monetary payments and** by **lashes,**

[1]וְאִי מָמוֹנָא לְקוּלָּא הוּא, [2]שֶׁכֵּן יֵשׁ בָּהֶן צַד הַקַּל.
[32B] [3]אֶלָּא, [4]עוּלָּא ״תַּחַת״, ״תַּחַת״, גָּמַר. [5]כְּתִיב הָכָא: ״תַּחַת אֲשֶׁר עִנָּהּ״, [6]וּכְתִיב הָתָם: ״עַיִן תַּחַת עַיִן״. [7]מָה הָתָם מָמוֹנָא מְשַׁלֵּם מִילְקָא לָא לָקֵי, [8]אַף כָּל הֵיכָא דְּאִיכָּא מָמוֹנָא וּמַלְקוֹת,

LITERAL TRANSLATION

[1]And if money is more lenient, [2][we can argue] that they have a lenient aspect.

[32B] [3]Rather, [4]Ulla learns [it from] "for," "for." [5]It is written here: "For he has humbled her," [6]and it is written there: "An eye for an eye." [7]Just as there he pays the money [but] is not lashed, [8]so too wherever there is money [to be paid] and lashes,

RASHI

תחת תחת גמר — וגזירה שוה מופנה היא, ולמדין ואין משיבין.

NOTES

The whole point of this kind of exegesis is that each of the cases used as the basis for the exegesis is subject to an objection of some kind, but there is no single objection that applies equally to both of them. But if it is sufficient to object that each of the cases has a stringent or lenient aspect, even though the two stringencies or leniencies have nothing in common, how can we ever extrapolate from a common factor?

Our commentary follows *Tosafot,* who explains that the Gemara is not merely objecting that these two cases have stringent or lenient aspects, but rather that the Torah went out of its way to display unusual stringency or leniency toward these two cases. For a person who injures another is the only offender who pays the four additional penalties beyond "damage," and conspiring witnesses are the only offenders who are punished without receiving warning. Likewise, very few offenses are permitted under exceptional circumstances, like assault, and very few punishable offenses can be committed without performing an action, like false testimony. Thus it is clear that these cases are exceptional and cannot serve as precedents. *Tosafot* cites other examples where the Gemara raises this objection against exegesis based on a common factor, and *Tosafot* also attempts to explain them in this way. *Ramban,* however, questions whether *Tosafot*'s explanation is adequate to explain all the instances where the Gemara raises this particular objection.

Further explanations were given by *Rabbenu Tam* (differing versions can be found in *Tosafot* and in *Ritva*) and by other Rishonim (see *Ritva* and others).

אַף כָּל הֵיכָא דְּאִיכָּא מָמוֹנָא So too wherever there is money to be paid. Our translation and commentary follow the text of the standard Vilna Talmud. According to this reading, even at this stage in the argument the Gemara

SAGES

רַבִּי יוֹחָנָן Rabbi Yoḥanan (bar Nappaḥa). See *Ketubot*, Part II, pp. 15–16.

TRANSLATION AND COMMENTARY

[1] the offender only **pays the money but is not lashed.** This fourth argument is not refuted by the Gemara, although Rabbi Yoḥanan, in the next section, argues that it is not conclusive. Therefore, according to Ulla, whenever monetary penalties and lashes both apply, the monetary penalties take precedence, just as they do in cases of assault. He explains the Mishnah in *Makkot*, which rules that a man who has intercourse with his sister is lashed, as referring to a special case in which the fine imposed by the Torah on rapists and seducers — as well as the other relevant monetary penalties — was not applicable; and he explains our Mishnah, which rules that a man who rapes his sister must pay the fine, as referring to all other cases.

The Gemara (above, 31b) objected that our Mishnah, which rules that someone who rapes his sister must pay a fine, conflicts with the Mishnah in *Makkot*, which rules that he is lashed. The Gemara's objection was that we have an established Halakhic principle that a person can never be punished by lashes and by a monetary penalty for the same crime. Therefore a man who seduces or rapes his sister should be exempt from paying the fine because he is subject to the more severe penalty of lashes. Why, then, does our Mishnah rule that a man who rapes his sister must pay the fine?

We have seen Ulla's solution to this problem. He maintains that the principle that we do not inflict lashes and impose a monetary penalty for the same crime does not teach us which penalty takes precedence; it merely rules out a punishment that combines both penalties. Hence we can argue that in those cases in which a monetary penalty is imposed by the Torah — such as the seduction or rape of a *na'arah* — this penalty takes precedence over lashes, and the offender is required to pay damages and a fine but is exempt from the lashes. According to Ulla, the Mishnah in *Makkot* must be interpreted as dealing with a special case in which the fine imposed by the Torah on rapists and seducers, as well as the other relevant financial penalties, are not applicable for technical reasons (because the victim in these cases was an adult, or an orphan who was seduced), whereas our Mishnah is referring to all other cases.

The Gemara will now consider the viewpoint of Rabbi Yoḥanan, who maintains that lashes take precedence over monetary payments, just as the death penalty (or excision, according to Rabbi Neḥunya ben Hakkanah) takes precedence over monetary payments. According to this viewpoint, the Mishnah in *Makkot*, which rules that lashes are inflicted, needs no special explanation, but we must construct a special case to explain our Mishnah, which rules that a fine *is* paid, thereby implying that lashes are *not* inflicted.

רַבִּי יוֹחָנָן אָמַר [2] **Rabbi Yoḥanan said:** It is unnecessary to construct a special case to explain the Mishnah in *Makkot*. Rather, **you may even say that it applies to** all cases, including the case in which **his sister was a *na'arah*** who was entitled to the fine. The Mishnah in *Makkot*, which lists the cases in which lashes are actually inflicted, **is** referring to a case [3] **where** witnesses had **warned** the rapist that intercourse with one's sister is punishable by lashes. In such a case, the rapist is indeed lashed and does not pay the fine, since

[1] מָמוֹנָא מְשַׁלֵּם, מִילְקָא לָא לָקֵי.

[2] רַבִּי יוֹחָנָן אָמַר: אֲפִילּוּ תֵּימָא אֲחוֹתוֹ נַעֲרָה. [3] כָּאן שֶׁהִתְרוּ בּוֹ;

LITERAL TRANSLATION

[1] he pays the money, [but] he is not lashed.

[2] Rabbi Yoḥanan said: You may even say [that it speaks of] his sister [who is] a *na'arah*. [3] Here it is where they warned him;

RASHI

אפילו תימא — ההיא דמכות באחותו נערה, וכשהתרו בו — דאיכא ממון ומלקות, ואשמעינן דלקי ולא משלם. **ומתניתין דכתובות** — בשלא התרו בו, דליכא מלקות.

NOTES

continues to maintain that Ulla is of the opinion that monetary penalties take precedence over lashes, whenever the two penalties conflict. This reading and interpretation are supported by *Rashi* in a comment later in the passage.

Some Rishonim reject this interpretation. *Tosafot* and *Ritva* point out that at this stage in the argument Ulla is deriving his ruling from a *gezerah shavah* rather than from a logical deduction, as was argued earlier. A logical deduction extends to all cases that are logically similar, whereas a *gezerah shavah* establishes a connection between two specific verses — in this case, between the verse dealing with rape and the verse dealing with injury. Thus Ulla's *gezerah shavah* proves only that just as monetary penalties take precedence over lashes in a case of ordinary assault, so too do they take precedence in a case of rape. However, we have no general proof that monetary penalties take precedence. Accordingly, *Ritva* amends the text very slightly to read: אַף הָכָא דְּאִיכָּא מָמוֹן — "So too *here* (i.e., in the case of rape) where there is money to be paid, etc."

Tosefot Sens takes an intermediate position, arguing that after Ulla used the *gezerah shavah* to prove that monetary penalties take precedence over lashes in cases of rape and seduction, he in effect had a third precedent for the general rule that monetary penalties take precedence over lashes, in addition to the earlier precedents of assault and conspiring witnesses. Accordingly, he was then able to extrapolate the general rule from the common factor among these three precedents, since the Gemara's previous objection to the common factor — that both cases had unusually severe or unusually lenient aspects — does not apply to rape or seduction.

TRANSLATION AND COMMENTARY

it is an established principle that we do not mete out lashes and impose a monetary penalty for the same crime. Our Mishnah, by contrast, which imposes a fine (and by implication does not decree lashes) must therefore be explained as referring to a special case, in which lashes are not applicable for technical legal reasons, [1]such as **where** witnesses **did not warn** the rapist in advance that intercourse with one's sister is an offense punishable by lashes. According to the Halakhah, a court cannot inflict lashes or a death penalty unless the offense was witnessed and unless the witnesses had warned the offender of the punishment he would receive if he committed the crime. Thus a man who seduces or rapes his sister is not lashed unless he was duly warned that incest is punishable by lashes (in which case he is exempt from the fine), but if he was not warned, he is exempt from the lashes, and is accordingly required to pay the fine. There is, therefore, no contradiction between the two Mishnayot: The Mishnah in *Makkot* expressly refers to a case in which lashes are applicable, whereas our Mishnah can be explained as referring to a case in which lashes are not applicable, for some technical reason. Thus, according to Rabbi Yoḥanan, a man who rapes his sister is lashed for his act of incest (as the Mishnah in *Makkot* ruled) and is accordingly exempt from the fine for rape, unless he was exempt from the lashes for technical reasons, in which case he must pay the fine (as our Mishnah ruled).

[1]כָּאן שֶׁלֹּא הִתְרוּ בּוֹ. [2]אַלְמָא קָסָבַר רַבִּי יוֹחָנָן: כָּל הֵיכָא דְּאִיכָּא מָמוֹן וּמַלְקוּת, [3]וְאַתְרוּ בֵּיהּ, [4]מִילְקָא לָקֵי, מָמוֹנָא לָא מְשַׁלֵּם. [5]מְנָא לֵיהּ לְרַבִּי יוֹחָנָן הָא? [6]אָמַר קְרָא: ״כְּדֵי רִשְׁעָתוֹ״. [7]מִשּׁוּם רִשְׁעָה אַחַת אַתָּה

LITERAL TRANSLATION

[1]here it is where they did not warn him.
[2]Consequently Rabbi Yoḥanan maintains: Wherever there is money [to be paid] and lashes, [3]and they warned him, [4]he is lashed, [but] he does not pay the money.
[5]From where does Rabbi Yoḥanan [learn] this?
[6]The verse says: "According to his wickedness." [7]Because of one wickedness you

אַלְמָא קָסָבַר [2]The Gemara now analyzes the reasoning underlying Rabbi Yoḥanan's explanation. We have seen that the Gemara infers from a verse (Deuteronomy 25:2) that the punishment of lashes is never meted out together with a monetary penalty, but it is not clear from the verse which penalty takes precedence. But **it follows from Rabbi Yoḥanan's** resolution of the contradiction between our Mishnah and the Mishnah in *Makkot* **that he is of the opinion** that **whenever** an offense is punishable both by **monetary payments and** by **lashes,** [3]**and** witnesses **gave** the offender a proper **warning,** so that there are no technical legal barriers preventing the lashes being inflicted, [4]the offender **is lashed but does not pay the money.** The ruling of the Mishnah in *Makkot*, which lists the cases in which lashes are actually administered, applies even if there is also a monetary penalty, such as the fine to be paid by a seducer or a rapist. It is only when lashes are not applicable that monetary penalties are imposed. It is thus clear that Rabbi Yoḥanan maintains that lashes take precedence over monetary compensation, and a person who is subject to lashes and a monetary penalty is lashed and is exempt from the payment. Hence the Mishnah in *Makkot* rules that a man who rapes his sister is lashed but does not pay the fine.

מְנָא לֵיהּ [5]The Gemara asks: **From where does Rabbi Yoḥanan learn this?** What primary Halakhic source is the basis for his ruling that lashes take precedence over monetary penalties?

אָמַר קְרָא [6]The Gemara finds a source in the Torah for this view. **The verse** describing the procedure to be followed when a court inflicts lashes (Deuteronomy 25:2) **says:** "And he shall be beaten in front of him a number of times, **according to his wickedness.**" [7]The Gemara (below, 37a) interprets the use of the word "wickedness" in the singular as follows: **Because of one** act of **wickedness you punish him,**

NOTES

מְנָא לֵיהּ לְרַבִּי יוֹחָנָן הָא **From where does Rabbi Yoḥanan learn this?** The Rishonim ask: On the previous page, the Gemara demanded to know what source in the Torah supported Ulla's opinion that monetary penalties take precedence over lashes. Presumably the Gemara then felt that without such a source our natural assumption would be that lashes should take precedence. Yet here the Gemara demands a Torah source for Rabbi Yoḥanan's opinion that lashes take precedence over monetary penalties. Why does Rabbi Yoḥanan need a source? Why is it not sufficient for him simply to reject Ulla's source (as he does below, 33a)?

Tosafot Yeshanim and *Rosh* explain that it was not sufficient for Rabbi Yoḥanan to reject Ulla's *gezerah shavah* and use the term "for" to learn another law; for this term is regularly used as part of a *gezerah shavah* in

TRANSLATION AND COMMENTARY

[1] **but you do not punish him because of two** acts of **wickedness.** In other words, when a person is lashed, it is considered a fair retribution for his wickedness, and there is no need for additional penalties. This interpretation informs us that a person who is lashed does not pay damages, and vice versa. But it is not clear which penalty takes precedence — the monetary one (as Ulla argued) or the lashes (as Rabbi Yoḥanan maintains). [2] To answer that question, we must look at the verse **immediately following** this one (Deuteronomy 25:3), **which says: "He shall strike him forty times."** From here we learn, according to Rabbi Yoḥanan, that whenever there are "two acts of wickedness," we inflict the lashes and waive the other penalty. Hence we can conclude that whenever lashes conflict with a monetary penalty, we inflict the lashes and waive the monetary penalty.

וַהֲרֵי [3] **But** the Gemara cites a contrary example to refute the idea that lashes always take precedence over monetary penalties. We know that **in the case of someone who injures another person,** monetary penalties take precedence over lashes according to all opinions. [4] Now, according to Rabbi Yoḥanan, a person who commits an offense punishable both by **monetary obligations and** by **lashes** is lashed, **yet** in this case the assailant only **pays the money but is not lashed!** Thus we see that in the case of the person who injures his fellow, monetary penalties take precedence over lashes.

וְכִי תֵּימָא [5] **And,** continues the Gemara, **if you** try to explain away this example, as you did the contradiction between the two Mishnayot, by **saying:** The Torah's requirement that one person who injures another must pay damages **applies** only when there is a technical barrier that rules out a sentence of lashes, [6] such as **where** witnesses **did not warn** the assailant, [7] **but if they did warn him, he is lashed but does not pay the money**, you will be in conflict with an accepted tradition, transmitted by Rabbi Yoḥanan himself. [8] For **Rabbi Ammi said in the name of Rabbi Yoḥanan:** [9] **If** the assailant **struck a blow that** caused such slight injury that the blow **was not worth** even **a perutah** in damages, **he is lashed.** According to the Halakhah, the perutah is the smallest coin with legal significance. Financial obligations worth less than one perutah are considered to be nonexistent. Therefore, if a person causes an injury to another person that is assessed for the purposes of compensation at less than one perutah, he pays nothing at all. But he was nevertheless guilty of the sin of striking another person. Hence in such a case there is no conflict between the financial penalty and lashes, and the assailant is punished for his sin by lashes.

מְחַיְּיבוֹ, [1] וְאִי אַתָּה מְחַיְּיבוֹ מִשּׁוּם שְׁתֵּי רִשְׁעִיּוֹת. [2] וּסְמִיךְ לֵיהּ: ״אַרְבָּעִים יַכֶּנּוּ״.
[3] וַהֲרֵי חוֹבֵל בַּחֲבֵירוֹ, דְּאִיכָּא מָמוֹן וּמַלְקוּת, [4] מָמוֹנָא מְשַׁלֵּם, מִילְקָא לָא לָקֵי!
[5] וְכִי תֵּימָא: הָנֵי מִילֵּי הֵיכָא דְּלָא אַתְרוּ בֵּיהּ, [6] אֲבָל אַתְרוּ בֵּיהּ, [7] מִילְקָא לָקֵי, מָמוֹנָא לָא מְשַׁלֵּם, [8] וְהָאָמַר רַבִּי אַמִּי אָמַר רַבִּי יוֹחָנָן: [9] הִכָּהוּ הַכָּאָה שֶׁאֵין בָּהּ שָׁוֶה פְּרוּטָה, לוֹקֶה.

LITERAL TRANSLATION

punish him, [1] but you do not punish him because of two wickednesses. [2] And next to it [is written]: "He shall strike him forty [times]."

[3] But consider [the case of] someone who injures his fellow, where there is money [to be paid] and lashes, [4] [and yet] he pays the money, [but] he is not lashed!

[5] And if you say: This applies (lit., "these words") where they did not warn him, [6] but [if] they did warn him, [7] he is lashed, [but] he does not pay the money, [8] but surely Rabbi Ammi said in the name of Rabbi Yoḥanan: [9] [If] he struck him a blow that does not have the value of a perutah, he is lashed.

RASHI

וסמיך ליה ארבעים יכנו — דהיכא דאיכא שתי רשעיות ניעבד ביה הכאה.

SAGES

רַבִּי אַמִּי **Rabbi Ammi.** A Palestinian Amora of the third generation. See *Ketubot*, Part II, p. 195.

BACKGROUND

שָׁוֶה פְּרוּטָה **A perutah's worth.** The perutah was the lowest coin in circulation, and in the Halakhah it is particularly meaningful. The perutah is considered the lowest monetary unit with any Halakhic significance; anything worth less than a perutah is not regarded as being worth money at all, and none of the commandments concerning money apply to it. Naturally, something worth less than a perutah does have some value, for the value of a perutah can be made up of many tiny objects. However, so long as their total value does not reach that basic amount, one may have moral responsibility for the objects but they are not recognized as having monetary value.

NOTES

several other instances (*Bava Kamma* 5a and 84a, and *Bekhorot* 12a), according to all opinions. Hence we would normally expect to use it to construct a *gezerah shavah* here as well, as Ulla argued, unless there was an additional scriptural argument to suggest otherwise.

HALAKHAH

הִכָּהוּ הַכָּאָה שֶׁאֵין בָּהּ שָׁוֶה פְּרוּטָה **If he struck him a blow that does not have the value of a perutah.** "Striking another person contravenes a negative commandment and is punishable by lashes. But if there is a possibility of payment, the assailant is not lashed, since the court does not inflict lashes and a monetary penalty for the same offense. If the injury was so slight that it was not worth a perutah, the assailant is lashed (if his crime was witnessed and he had been duly warned), following the statement of Rabbi Ammi in the name of Rabbi Yoḥanan in our Gemara. (*Rambam, Sefer Nezikin, Hilkhot Ḥovel U'Mazzik* 5:1,3; *Shulḥan Arukh, Ḥoshen Mishpat* 420:1,2.)

TRANSLATION AND COMMENTARY

הֵיכִי דָּמֵי [1]The Gemara now explains how this ruling of Rabbi Yoḥanan contradicts his previous statement that lashes always take precedence over monetary penalties if the offender was warned. **How do we visualize the case** to which Rabbi Yoḥanan was referring in his ruling about injuries worth less than a perutah? [2]**If** the ruling refers to a case in which witnesses **did not warn** the assailant that his assault, slight as it was, was punishable with lashes, **why is he lashed?** Lashes can never be inflicted unless the offender was warned in advance! [3]**Rather, it is obvious that** Rabbi Yoḥanan must have been referring to a case in which witnesses **warned** the assailant that he would be lashed. [4]**And** yet **the reason** given by Rabbi Yoḥanan for inflicting lashes rather than a monetary penalty **was because** the injury **was not worth a perutah** in damages, and restitution could not be made with money. [5]**But** the implication of this is that in an otherwise identical case where the injury **was worth a perutah** in damages, [6]the assailant **pays the money but is not lashed!** But surely this contradicts Rabbi Yoḥanan's first statement, that lashes take precedence over monetary penalties whenever they are both applicable.

כִּדְאָמַר רַבִּי אִילְעָא [7]The Gemara replies to this objection as follows: Rabbi Yoḥanan admits that monetary payments take precedence over lashes in a few exceptional instances, such as assault, where the Torah specifically decreed that monetary payments take precedence. **It is** in a wide range of other cases that he maintains that lashes take precedence. For just **as Rabbi Il'a said** that **the Torah explicitly** required **conspiring witnesses** to be punished by making a monetary **payment,** rather than by lashes, [8]**similarly here,** in the case of assault, **the Torah explicitly** commanded that **someone who injures his fellow** must be punished by making a monetary **payment,** rather than by lashes. The case of assault, like that of conspiring witnesses, is exceptional. But if a man rapes his sister, for example, he is punished by lashes for incest, and the fine for rape is not imposed unless there is a technical legal barrier preventing the court from inflicting the lashes.

[1]הֵיכִי דָּמֵי? [2]אִי דְּלָא אַתְרוּ בֵּיהּ, אַמַּאי לוֹקֶה? [3]אֶלָּא פְּשִׁיטָא דְּאַתְרוּ בֵּיהּ. [4]וְטַעְמָא דְּלֵית בָּהּ שָׁוֶה פְּרוּטָה. [5]הָא אִית בָּהּ שָׁוֶה פְּרוּטָה, [6]מָמוֹנָא מְשַׁלֵּם, מִילְקָא לָא לָקֵי! [7]כִּדְאָמַר רַבִּי אִילְעָא: בְּפֵירוּשׁ רִיבְּתָה תּוֹרָה עֵדִים זוֹמְמִין לְתַשְׁלוּמִין. [8]הָכָא נַמִי, בְּפֵירוּשׁ רִיבְּתָה תּוֹרָה חוֹבֵל בַּחֲבֵירוֹ לְתַשְׁלוּמִין.

LITERAL TRANSLATION

[1]How do we visualize the case? [2]If they did not warn him, why is he lashed? [3]Rather, it is obvious that they warned him. [4]And the reason is because it does not have the value of a perutah. [5]But [if] it does have the value of a perutah, [6]he pays the money, [but] he is not lashed!

[7][It is] as Rabbi Il'a said: The Torah explicitly included conspiring witnesses for payments. [8]Here too, the Torah explicitly included someone who injures his fellow for payments.

RASHI

בפירוש ריבתה – לקמיה מפרש היכא.

BACKGROUND

בְּפֵירוּשׁ רִיבְּתָה תּוֹרָה The Torah explicitly included. The precise meaning of this expression is that there is an explicit proof contained in the Torah regarding a particular law, and that this proof is derived from the principle of **רִבּוּי** — "amplification." "Amplification" is a fundamental Midrashic form of exegesis (used in particular by Rabbi Akiva and his disciples) whose purpose is to extend the scope of a subject on the basis of the interpretation of certain linguistic expressions. In the case discussed here, the Torah could merely have made the general statement, "And you shall do to him as he conspired to do." The fact that the Torah goes on to use the expression, "a hand for a hand," which is seemingly superfluous, indicates that its purpose is to extend or amplify the law and to give it a more universal application — that the conspiring witness pays money specifically for damage that he sought to do to his fellow.

SAGES

רַבִּי אִילְעָא Rabbi Il'a. A famous Palestinian Amora of the third generation, Rabbi Il'a was a disciple of Rabbi Yoḥanan. He transmitted the teachings of his teacher, of Resh Lakish, and of the students of Rabbi Yoḥanan: Rabbi Elazar, Rabbi Ammi, and Rabbi Abbahu. Several Sages of the fourth generation were his students.

NOTES

הָכָא נַמִי בְּפֵירוּשׁ רִיבְּתָה תּוֹרָה Here too, the Torah explicitly included. The Rishonim ask: Granted that the Torah explicitly commanded that monetary penalties should take precedence over lashes in cases of assault and in cases of conspiring witnesses, whereas in other cases the Torah did not say this explicitly. But why should we not regard these two cases as precedents, and extrapolate from them that monetary penalties take precedence over lashes in all cases?

Rabbi Crescas Vidal explains that we do not do so because of the Gemara's objections in the previous passage. Assault has a unique severe aspect in that it is punished by five payments, and a unique lenient aspect in that it is permitted to a court. Likewise, conspiring witnesses have a unique severe aspect in that they are punished without having received a warning, and a unique lenient aspect in that they have committed a sin that did not involve action on their part. Accordingly, we cannot extrapolate from either of them, nor from their common factor, since they are both treated with exceptional severity and with exceptional leniency by the Torah.

Rashba and *Ritva* explain that the source of Rabbi Yoḥanan's ruling — that lashes take precedence over monetary penalties — was a verse in the passage in the Torah dealing with lashes. Since Rabbi Yoḥanan's verse appears in the passage dealing with lashes, whereas the

HALAKHAH

בְּפֵירוּשׁ רִיבְּתָה תּוֹרָה חוֹבֵל בַּחֲבֵירוֹ לְתַשְׁלוּמִין The Torah explicitly included someone who injures his fellow for payments. "In general, someone who commits an offense that is punishable by lashes is not required to pay damages for the same offense, if his offense was witnessed and he was duly warned that he would be lashed, since lashes take precedence over monetary penalties. But if the offense was an assault, such as where one person injured another on Yom Kippur (an offense considered to be a violation of Yom Kippur, punishable by excision and by lashes), he makes the customary five payments for the assault and is exempt from lashes, even if the assault was witnessed and he had been warned. For the Torah expressly demands that assault be punished by a monetary payment whenever feasible." (*Rambam, Sefer Nezikin, Hilkhot Ḥovel U'Mazzik* 4:9; *Shulḥan Arukh, Ḥoshen Mishpat* 424:2.)

LITERAL TRANSLATION

[1] And where was [the ruling] of Rabbi Il'a stated? [2] With reference to this: [3] "[If witnesses said:] 'We testify about so-and-so that he owes his fellow two hundred zuz,' [4] and they were found to be conspiring [witnesses], [5] they are lashed and pay, [6] because it is not the factor (lit., 'name') that brings them to lashes [that] brings them to payment. [7] [These are] the words of Rabbi Meir.

[1] וְהֵיכָא אִיתְּמַר דְּרַבִּי אִילְעָא? [2] אַהָא: [3] ״מְעִידִין אָנוּ אֶת אִישׁ פְּלוֹנִי שֶׁחַיָּיב לַחֲבֵירוֹ מָאתַיִם זוּז׳, [4] וְנִמְצְאוּ זוֹמְמִין, [5] לוֹקִין וּמְשַׁלְּמִין, [6] שֶׁלֹּא הַשֵּׁם הַמְבִיאָן לִידֵי מַכּוֹת מְבִיאָן לִידֵי תַשְׁלוּמִין. [7] דִּבְרֵי רַבִּי מֵאִיר.

RASHI

שלא השם המביאו לידי מכות כו׳ — המקרא המביאו לידי מלקות אינו מביאו לתשלומין. מלקות מ״לא תענה״, תשלומין מ״כאשר זמם״, וכיון דשני שמות הן — חייב על שניהם.

TRANSLATION AND COMMENTARY

וְהֵיכָא אִיתְּמַר [1] Before explaining where the Torah explicitly requires that monetary payments take precedence over lashes in cases of assault, the Gemara pauses to consider the statement of Rabbi Ila'a that we have just quoted. The Gemara asks: **In what context was Rabbi Il'a's statement made?**

אַהָא [2] The Gemara answers: Rabbi Il'a made his statement **with reference to the following** Mishnah (*Makkot* 4a): [3] **"If witnesses** come forward and **say: 'We testify about so-and-so that he owes this other person two hundred zuz,'** [4] **and they are fund to be conspiring witnesses,** [5] **they are lashed and** they also **pay** the two hundred zuz, [6] **because the prohibition that imposes** the penalty of **lashes on them is not** the same as the **prohibition that imposes** the penalty of **payment on them.** The negative commandment that is punishable by lashes is derived from a verse in Exodus (20:13), and the law that conspiring witnesses must be punished by the same punishment that they sought to impose on the defendant is derived from a different verse (Deuteronomy 19:19), and in such cases we impose both penalties. [7] **This is the opinion of Rabbi Meir,** who maintains that the principle that lashes are not inflicted together with a monetary penalty applies only when the offender committed a single offense subject to a monetary penalty (for example, an assailant). But if someone commits two separate offenses, one of which is subject to lashes and the other to a monetary penalty (for example, a man who rapes his sister), Rabbi Meir maintains that both penalties are imposed. Moreover, even conspiring witnesses, who

NOTES

commandments that monetary penalties should take precedence appear in the passages dealing with assault and with conspiring witnesses respectively, it stands to reason that Rabbi Yoḥanan's verse is the general rule, applying to all cases, and the other verses are exceptions, applicable only to the cases in question.

מְעִידִין אָנוּ אֶת אִישׁ פְּלוֹנִי We testify about so-and-so. The Gemara (*Makkot* 4b) explains that the dispute between Rabbi Meir and the Sages revolves primarily around the commandment, "you shall not bear false witness." According to Rabbi Meir, this is a separate negative commandment, and violators of it receive the punishment of lashes, which is independent of the punishment imposed on conspiring witnesses, "and you shall do to him as he conspired." According to the Sages, "you shall not bear false witness" is simply the negative commandment whose punishment is enjoined in "and you shall do to him". Hence, according to Rabbi Meir, a conspiring witness who sought to inflict lashes on a defendant is punished with two sets of lashes, and a conspiring witness who sought to inflict a monetary payment is punished by lashes and a monetary payment. *Meiri* explains that the Sages are of the opinion that "you shall not bear false witness" is not punishable by lashes, since it is a sin that does not involve an action, whereas Rabbi Meir maintains that negative commandments violated without action are also punished by lashes. Other Rishonim give other explanations of this dispute (see *Tosafot* and others).

In addition to the primary dispute about "you shall not bear false witness," it is clear that Rabbi Meir and the Sages also disagree about cases where lashes and monetary penalties coincide. The Sages argue that a person who pays money is never lashed, and vice versa, whereas Rabbi Meir clearly rejects this argument. The Gemara explains this dispute between Rabbi Meir and the Sages as follows: According to the Sages, we are bound by a Halakhic principle that lashes cannot be inflicted together with other penalties. Rabbi Meir, however, rejects this rule, because there is a contrary example: A man who falsely accuses his wife of adultery is punished by lashes, as well as by a fine of one hundred silver shekalim. Thus we see that lashes are inflicted together with a monetary penalty. The Sages, however, insist that the case of the man who falsely accuses his wife is exceptional.

שֶׁלֹּא הַשֵּׁם הַמְבִיאָן לִידֵי מַכּוֹת מְבִיאָן לִידֵי תַשְׁלוּמִין Because it is not the factor that brings them to lashes that brings them to payment. Our commentary follows *Rashi,* who explains that Rabbi Meir agrees that lashes are not imposed together with a monetary penalty where both penalties are derived from the same verse. But if a person

HALAKHAH

״שֶׁחַיָּיב לַחֲבֵירוֹ מָאתַיִם זוּז״, וְנִמְצְאוּ זוֹמְמִין "That he owes his fellow two hundred zuz," and they were found to be conspiring witnesses. "If a plaintiff brings witnesses who testify that the defendant owes him money, and the witnesses are later found to have been conspiring witnesses, they must pay the defendant the sum they sought

TRANSLATION AND COMMENTARY

seem to have committed only the single offense of testifying falsely, are punished by two penalties, since the two penalties are derived from different verses. [1]**But the Sages say:** The general principle that **whoever pays is not lashed** applies even if two separate offenses were committed. Thus the conspiring witnesses are required to pay the two hundred zuz but are not lashed."

וְנֵימָא [2]The following question was asked concerning this Mishnah: Granted that according to the Sages the conspiring witnesses cannot be punished twice. **But surely** the Sages **should say: Whoever is lashed does not pay,** rather than: Whoever pays is not lashed! The wording of the Sages' opinion in the Mishnah clearly implies that monetary penalties take precedence. Why, then, do they not apply our principle in the way suggested by Rabbi Yoḥanan, who maintains that lashes take precedence over monetary penalties?

אָמַר רַבִּי אִילְעָא [3]It was in response to this objection that **Rabbi Il'a said:** The Sages in the Mishnah were dealing with a case of conspiring witnesses, which is exceptional. They phrased their position in the way they did because in the case of conspiring witnesses monetary payments do indeed take precedence over lashes. The reason for this is that **the Torah explicitly** commmanded that **conspiring witnesses** should be punished with a monetary **payment** rather than with lashes. But in other cases, lashes are a more severe penalty that exempts from payment, according to the Sages.

LITERAL TRANSLATION

[1]But the Sages say: Whoever pays is not lashed." [2]But let us say: Whoever is lashed does not pay? [3]Rabbi Il'a said: The Torah explicitly included conspiring witnesses for payments.

[1]וַחֲכָמִים אוֹמְרִים: כָּל הַמְשַׁלֵּם אֵינוֹ לוֹקֶה". [2]וְנֵימָא: כָּל הַלּוֹקֶה אֵינוֹ מְשַׁלֵּם? [3]אָמַר רַבִּי אִילְעָא: בְּפֵירוּשׁ רִיבְּתָה תּוֹרָה עֵדִים זוֹמְמִין לְתַשְׁלוּמִין.

RASHI

נימא כל הלוקה אינו משלם — ונידייניה במלקות, מאי שנא ממון דפסיטא להו?

NOTES

commits two separate offenses by the same act, he is punished for both of them, even if one is punishable by lashes and the other by a monetary penalty.

Ritva objects to this explanation. For in tractate *Bava Metzia* (91a), the Gemara considers the case of someone who borrows a neighbor's ox to thresh grain and muzzles it, in violation of the Torah's prohibition against muzzling an ox while it threshes grain (Deuteronomy 25:4). The Gemara there rules that according to the Sages he is lashed for muzzling the ox but he is exempt from paying the ox's owner for the grain he prevented the ox from eating, since both penalties cannot be imposed for the same offense. But according to Rabbi Meir, he is lashed for muzzling the ox and must also pay the ox's owner for the grain. In this case both penalties are derived from the same verse, which teaches us that an ox must be allowed to eat from the grain it is threshing, and yet the Gemara says that Rabbi Meir would impose both penalties. How, then, can this passage be reconciled with *Rashi*'s explanation here?

Ritva suggests that Rabbi Meir's position, as expressed in the Mishnah cited by our Gemara, may not be consistent with his actual position, as explained by the Gemara in *Bava Metzia*. According to *Ritva,* Rabbi Meir really disagrees entirely with the rule that lashes and a monetary penalty cannot be imposed at the same time, and it makes no difference to him if the two punishments are derived from the same verse or from two different verses. In the Mishnah, however, Rabbi Meir is conceding for the sake of argument that there is such a rule, and he is arguing that nevertheless it should apply only to cases in which the two penalties are derived from the same verse, but not to cases in which the two penalties are derived from different verses.

Alternatively, *Ritva* points out that there are two independent issues in dispute between Rabbi Meir and the Sages: whether the verse forbidding false testimony is a separate commandment punishable by lashes, and whether lashes and a monetary penalty can be imposed at the same time. According to this explanation, Rabbi Meir maintains that there is never a problem with imposing a compound sentence of lashes and a monetary penalty, and when he justified the double penalty by explaining that the two punishments are derived from different verses, he was not referring to this question at all. He was simply explaining that in his opinion the two verses should be treated separately, with one penalty for each verse, and that he differs from the Sages who maintain that the two verses are referring to the same commandment. According to this explanation, it is the Sages who are conceding to Rabbi Meir's opinion for the sake of argument. For according to the Sages' own opinion, there can be no question of punishing the conspiring witnesses with lashes, since the verse that forbids false testimony is not a separate commandment and is not punishable by lashes. However, say the Sages, even if we were to concede for the sake of argument that this verse is a separate commandment punishable by lashes, we would still reject Rabbi Meir's conclusion that both penalties are imposed, because we maintain that lashes and monetary penalties are not imposed at the same time. Other Rishonim give other explanations (see *Tosafot*, *Ramban*, and *Ra'ah*).

HALAKHAH

to make him pay, dividing the payment between them. But they are not lashed for testifying falsely, as there is a Halakhic principle that we do not inflict lashes together with a monetary penalty," following the Sages in the Mishnah cited in our Gemara. (*Rambam, Sefer Shofetim, Hilkhot Edut* 18:1; *Tur, Ḥoshen Mishpat* 38.)

הֵיכָן רִיבְּתָה תּוֹרָה?[1] מִכְּדִי כְּתִיב: "וַעֲשִׂיתֶם לוֹ כַּאֲשֶׁר זָמַם לַעֲשׂוֹת לְאָחִיו",[2] "יָד בְּיָד" לָמָּה לִי?[3] דָּבָר הַנִּיתָּן מִיָּד לְיָד.[4] וּמַאי נִיהוּ? מָמוֹן.[5]

חוֹבֵל בַּחֲבֵירוֹ נַמִי.[6] מִכְּדִי כְּתִיב: "כַּאֲשֶׁר עָשָׂה כֵּן יֵעָשֶׂה לוֹ",[7] "כֵּן יִנָּתֶן בּוֹ" לָמָּה לִי?[8] דָּבָר שֶׁיֵּשׁ בּוֹ נְתִינָה.[9] וּמַאי נִיהוּ? מָמוֹן.[10]

LITERAL TRANSLATION

[1] Where did the Torah include [them]? [2] Now since it is written: "And you shall do to him as he conspired to do to his brother," [3] why do I [need]: "A hand for a hand"? [4] A thing that is given from hand to hand. [5] And what is that? Money.

[6] [This] also [applies to] someone who injures his fellow. [7] Now since it is written: "As he did, so shall it be done to him," [8] why do I [need]: "So shall it be given to him"? [9] A thing in which there is giving. [10] And what is that? Money.

RASHI

יד ביד — דסמיך ליה "לא תחוס עינך נפש בנפש וגו'". **כן ינתן** — "כאשר יתן מום באדם וגו'".

TRANSLATION AND COMMENTARY

הֵיכָן רִיבְּתָה תּוֹרָה [1] But, the Gemara asks, **where did the Torah widen** the scope of the law and state that monetary payment is the penalty to be imposed on conspiring witnesses? Where do we find an explicit commandment that monetary penalties take precedence over lashes in a case of conspiring witnesses? The verse requiring that the witnesses be punished by the same punishment they wished to inflict on the defendant may perhaps refer to the death penalty and lashes and the like. On the other hand, if the witnesses tried to make the defendant pay money, is it possible that they are punished by lashes and are not required to pay, in accordance with Rabbi Yoḥanan's principle?

מִכְּדִי כְּתִיב [2] The Gemara now explains that Rabbi Il'a inferred this law from the verse which describes the penalty to be imposed on conspiring witnesses. **Now since the** Biblical **text says** (Deuteronomy 19:19–21): **"And you shall do to him** [the conspiring witness] **as he conspired to do to his brother,** and you shall remove the evil from your midst. And those who remain will hear and see and will not continue to do like this evil thing in your midst. And your eye shall not pity — a life for a life, an eye for an eye, a tooth for a tooth, a hand for a hand, a foot for a foot," [3] **why do we need** the expression **"a hand for a hand"?** We have already learned that the conspiring witness is punished with the same punishment as he sought to inflict, even if that means to taking his life. What purpose does this additional, seemingly superfluous phrase serve? [4] It teaches us that this penalty also applies to **something that is given from hand to hand.** [5] **And what is that? Money.** Thus we see that the Torah commands that in cases of money, too, this penalty is to be imposed. Accordingly, Rabbi Il'a explains that according to the Sages, who maintain that the two penalties cannot be imposed together, the monetary penalty takes precedence, and the witnesses are not lashed.

חוֹבֵל בַּחֲבֵירוֹ נַמִי [6] Rabbi Il'a has explained that there is a special reason why monetary penalties take precedence over lashes in the case of conspiring witnesses. We can argue that **this** reasoning **also applies to** the case of **someone who injures his fellow.** [7] For regarding one person who injures another, **since the verse states** (Leviticus 24:19–20): "And if a man shall inflict a blemish on his fellow, **as he did, so shall it be done to him**....as he inflicted a blemish on a person, so shall it be given to [i.e., inflicted on] him," [8] **why do we need** the expression **"so shall it be given to him"?** Surely this is superfluous, because we have already learned that the assailant must pay his victim adequate compensation. [9] The superfluous phrase, "so shall it be given to him," teaches us that the proper penalty is **something that can be given.** [10] **And what is that? Money.** This additional emphasis on the monetary penalty tells us that this type of penalty applies even under circumstances when it is legally possible to inflict lashes. Thus we see that the Torah explicitly commands that even where witnesses have warned the assailant, the monetary penalty is imposed. Accordingly, we can apply Rabbi Ila's reasoning and explain that the financial penalty takes precedence and the assailant is not lashed. The case of an assailant who injures someone is exceptional, and Rabbi Yoḥanan's argument — that in general lashes take precedence over monetary penalties — stands.

NOTES

"יָד בְּיָד" לָמָּה לִי Why do I need: "A hand for a hand"? *Tosafot* asks: Why do we need a special verse to teach us that witnesses who conspire to force a defendant to pay money are punished by being made to pay the defendant money? We already know from the previous verse that conspiring witnesses are punished with the same punishment that they sought to inflict on the defendant. Surely it is obvious that this applies to monetary penalties as well!

Tosafot explains that if we did not have a special verse to teach us that the general law of conspiring witnesses applies to monetary penalties as well, we would have thought that this law is overridden by the principle that lashes take precedence over money, and that the rule that conspiring witnesses are punished with the same punishment that they sought to inflict on the defendant applies only where they sought to have the defendant killed or to

[1]וְרַבִּי יוֹחָנָן מַאי טַעֲמָא לָא אֲמַר כְּעוּלָּא? [2]אִם כֵּן, בִּטַּלְתָּ: [3]״עֶרְוַת אֲחוֹתְךָ לֹא תְגַלֵּה״.

LITERAL TRANSLATION

[1]And what is the reason [that] Rabbi Yoḥanan did not say as Ulla?

[2]If so, you have annulled [the law]: [3]"The nakedness of your sister you shall not uncover."

RASHI

מאי טעמא לא אמר כעולא — דגמר גזירה שוה לעונשו ממון ולא מלקות לכל חייבי ממון ומלקות. **אם כן** — דפטרת בא על אחותו ממלקות — בטלת לאו שבה, שעונש לאו במלקות.

TRANSLATION AND COMMENTARY

וְרַבִּי יוֹחָנָן [1]Having explained Rabbi Yoḥanan's resolution of the contradiction between our Mishnah and the Mishnah in *Makkot*, the Gemara now compares his solution to that of Ulla, considered above. **Why is it that Rabbi Yoḥanan did not explain** the two Mishnayot **as Ulla** did? Why did he prefer his exegesis over Ulla's, and conclude that lashes take precedence over monetary penalties in cases of rape? Why did he not adopt Ulla's exegesis and rule that monetary penalties take precedence over lashes?

אִם כֵּן [2]The Gemara answers: Rabbi Yoḥanan does not accept Ulla's exegesis. He argues that **if** we accept it, **we annul the law** prescribing the penalty of lashes which is derived from the following verse (Leviticus 18:9): [3]**"The nakedness of your sister...you shall not uncover."** According to the Halakhah, any negative commandment of the Torah which forbids an action and is not subject to the death penalty is punishable by lashes. But according to Ulla, a man is punished by lashes for committing incest with his sister only if his sister was an adult or a seduced orphan. But if his sister was a *na'arah* and her father was alive, the law contained in this verse would not apply at all. Since, according to Rabbi Yoḥanan, this would constitute a gross distortion of the plain meaning of the verse, he prefers his own exegesis, whereby all the verses apply to the standard cases: The verse punishing incest with lashes applies whenever lashes are applicable, and the verse punishing rape or seduction with a fine applies to non-relatives all the time, and even to relatives, if lashes are not inflicted for technical reasons.

NOTES

have him lashed. Now that the Torah has added that the conspiring witnesses are punished "hand for hand" (i.e., with a monetary penalty), we know that the general law of conspiring witnesses applies to monetary penalties as well, and that money takes precedence over lashes in this case.

וְרַבִּי יוֹחָנָן מַאי טַעֲמָא לָא אֲמַר כְּעוּלָּא And what is the reason that Rabbi Yoḥanan did not say as Ulla? The Rishonim ask: What is the Gemara's question? Obviously, Rabbi Yoḥanan does not accept Ulla's *gezerah shavah*.

Tosafot answers that the Gemara knows that Rabbi Yoḥanan was fully aware of Ulla's *gezerah shavah*, since a similar *gezerah shavah* appears in other places, according to all opinions. Hence the Gemara reasons that Rabbi Yoḥanan would not have rejected it without a reason.

Ramban asks: Why did the Gemara not also seek a reason for Ulla's disagreement with Rabbi Yoḥanan? He answers that Ulla's reason is obvious: He has a *gezerah shavah*, and this form of exegesis is generally better than the argument of juxtaposition of verses used by Rabbi Yoḥanan (see also *Rashba*).

Shittah Mekubbetzet points out that, according to *Rashi*, who explains that Ulla and Rabbi Yoḥanan disagree about every case in which lashes and monetary penalties coincide, Ulla's *gezerah shavah* and Rabbi Yoḥanan's argument of juxtaposition of verses contradict each other, and it is important to determine which exegesis is correct. However, according to *Tosafot*, who explains that Ulla agrees with Rabbi Yoḥanan about cases other than rape and seduction, there is no question of rejecting Rabbi Yoḥanan's argument of juxtaposition of verses entirely, even if we accept the *gezerah shavah*.

אִם כֵּן בִּטַּלְתָּ If so, you have annulled. The Gemara states that according to Ulla, who rules that a man who rapes his sister is not lashed, the verse forbidding incest between brother and sister loses its meaning. *Rashba* asks: Why does the Gemara consider nullification of the penalty of lashes to be a nullification of the verse? Granted that the verse no longer teaches us that lashes are to be inflicted, but it still teaches us that intercourse between brother and sister is forbidden as incest, and this has many ramifications, such as the punishment of the perpetrators by excision!

Rashba answers that even though the commandment still has importance according to Ulla, it is nevertheless severely weakened if the crime of incest is not punishable by lashes. *Rashi* explains that this prohibition was phrased as a negative commandment, whose primary function is to inflict lashes. Thus, if lashes are not inflicted, the negative commandment is in effect annulled.

Tosafot asks: According to the Gemara's reasoning, what is the significance of all those negative commandments that are never punished by lashes (for example, theft)? *Tosafot* answers that the Gemara has no difficulty in understanding commandments that the Torah excludes from the penalty of lashes. Clearly in such cases the Torah did not intend its use of the negative commandment to imply lashes in the first place. The issue concerns commandments that are theoretically supposed to be punishable by lashes, such as incest. Ulla insists that the lashes are overridden by his *gezerah shavah*, whereas Rabbi Yoḥanan argues that it is implausible to suggest that the Torah intended one of its commandments to be overridden in this way.

Rashba asks: Even according to Ulla, the verse imposing lashes for incest between brother and sister is not entirely annulled. For it does apply to cases where the sister is an adult or an orphan and her brother seduced her. Moreover,

TRANSLATION AND COMMENTARY

חוֹבֵל בַּחֲבֵירוֹ נַמִּי [33A] [1]The Gemara objects that this argument does not provide a good basis for preferring Rabbi Yoḥanan's exegesis over that of Ulla, for although it is true that according to Ulla the plain meaning of the verses dealing with incest is distorted, that is **also** true of the verses dealing with **someone who injures another person,** even according to Rabbi Yoḥanan. Everyone agrees that the penalty for assault is monetary payment. [2]Hence, **if** we accept Rabbi Yoḥanan's argument, we must conclude that **we have annulled the law** prescribing the penalty of lashes which is derived from the following verse (Deuteronomy 25:3): [3]**"He shall not exceed this, lest he continue"!** Someone who injures someone else violates a negative commandment against striking another person "excessively," and if monetary penalties cannot be applied, as in a case where the wound was not worth a perutah (see above, 32b), the offense is punishable by lashes. But assault is punished by lashes only in the rare situation in which the wound was not worth a perutah, whereas in most situations the law contained in this verse does not apply at all, and this would constitute a distortion of the plain meaning of the verse. [4]Moreover, the plain meaning of the verse is **also** distorted, according to all opinions, **in the case of conspiring witnesses** who testified about a monetary matter. Here, too, a monetary penalty applies according to everyone, [5]and **if** we accept Rabbi Yoḥanan's argument, we must conclude that **we have annulled the law** prescribing the penalty of lashes which is derived from the following verse (Deuteronomy 25:2): [6]**"And it shall be, if the wicked man is punishable by lashes"!** In tractate *Makkot* (2b), the Gemara infers from this verse that when conspiring witnesses cannot be punished with the penalty they sought to inflict on the defendant, they are lashed. But this verse applies only in those rare cases in which the regular punishment was inapplicable (for example, if the defendant was a priest and two non-priests sought to disqualify him). But in ordinary monetary cases the law contained in this verse does not apply at all, and this surely constitutes a gross distortion of the plain meaning of the verse.

[33A] [1]חוֹבֵל בַּחֲבֵירוֹ נַמִּי: [2]אִם כֵּן, בִּטַּלְתָּ: [3]״לֹא יֹסִיף, פֶּן יֹסִיף״! [4]עֵדִים זוֹמְמִין נַמִּי: [5]אִם כֵּן, בִּטַּלְתָּ: [6]״וְהָיָה, אִם בִּן הַכּוֹת הָרָשָׁע״!

LITERAL TRANSLATION

[33A] [1][But in the case of] someone who injures his fellow also [we can say]: [2]If so, you have annulled [the law]: [3]"He shall not exceed this, lest he continue"! [4][And in the case of] conspiring witnesses also [we can say]: [5]If so, you have annulled [the law]: [6]"And it shall be, if the wicked man is punishable by being lashed"!

RASHI

ופרכינן: חובל בחבירו, דעל כרחך **בממון נידון — תקשי:** בטלת לאו ד״לא יוסיף...פן יוסיף״, שהוא אזהרה למכה את חבירו! **והיה אם בן הכות** — במסכת מכות (ג,ג) מוקמינן לה בעדים זוממין.

NOTES

even according to Rabbi Yoḥanan, we cannot explain all the verses as applying to all cases, since according to him, the verse commanding the rapist or the seducer to pay the fine does not apply to a man who raped or seduced his sister and was warned that he would be lashed. Why is Ulla's position considered to be a nullification of the verse forbidding incest, whereas Rabbi Yoḥanan's is not considered to be a nullification of the verse commanding a fine to be paid in cases of rape and seduction?

Rashba answers that although it is true that all the verses cannot apply to all cases, they are not considered annulled unless they do not apply at all to certain people. Thus, according to Ulla, a *na'arah* whose father is alive is excluded from the law of incest entirely, as there is no possible way for her brother to be lashed for having intercourse with her. According to Rabbi Yoḥanan, however, there is no person to whom the law of rape and seduction does not apply if the rapist or the seducer was not warned. *Shittah Mekubbetzet* adds that it is not unreasonable to explain that the verse dealing with rape is not referring to relatives, but it is unreasonable to explain that the verse dealing with incest is not referring to a *na'arah*.

״וְהָיָה אִם בִּן הַכּוֹת הָרָשָׁע״ "And it shall be, if the wicked man is punishable by being lashed." In tractate *Makkot* (2b), the Gemara asks why Ulla found it necessary to seek an oblique reference in the Torah to this punishment, when there is a specific negative commandment in the Torah against bearing false witness (Exodus 20:13), and we know that violations of negative commandments are normally punished by lashes. The Gemara answers that bearing false witness is an offense committed by means of words without action, and such commandments are normally not punishable by lashes.

The Rishonim note that there are other problems about using the negative commandment against bearing false witness as the source for the punishment of lashes, since there is a dispute between Rabbi Meir and the Sages about this matter. According to the Sages, this verse (Exodus 20:13) is intended to serve as a negative commandment against false testimony in capital cases, in which the conspiring witnesses are put to death (*Makkot* 4b), and there is a Halakhic rule that verses that serve this purpose cannot be used to teach us that an offense is punished by lashes. *Tosafot* explains, however, that the Gemara did not mention this point because it is a problem only according to the Sages but not according to Rabbi Meir.

TRANSLATION AND COMMENTARY

אֶלָּא [1] **Rather,** says the Gemara, we must reject Rabbi Yoḥanan's argument and say that it is legitimate to limit the scope of a verse, provided that there remains at least one case to which it applies. Thus, **in the case of conspiring witnesses, it is possible to apply the punishment of lashes with regard to the son of a divorcee and the son of a woman who performed *ḥalitzah*.** A divorcee is forbidden by Torah law to marry a priest (Leviticus 21:7). The Rabbis extended this prohibition to include a widow whose husband died without children and who was released from levirate marriage through the *ḥalitzah* ceremony performed by her deceased husband's brother (Deuteronomy 25:9). If one of these women marries a priest in violation of the law, their descendants are disqualified from the priesthood for all future generations. If witnesses who are themselves not priests testify that the son of a priest is disqualified from the priesthood because his mother was not permitted to marry a priest, and these witnesses are later found to have testified falsely, they cannot be punished by receiving the same status that they sought to impose on the priest (disqualification from the priesthood). Since the standard punishment is not applicable, they are lashed, in accordance with the verse that requires conspiring witnesses to be lashed. [2] The Gemara continues: **In the case of someone who injures someone else, too, it is possible to apply** the punishment of lashes where, [3] **for example,** the assailant **struck** the other person **a blow that was not worth** even **a perutah,** because in this situation the regular monetary penalty is not applicable. [4] **And** by the same token, **in the case of** a man who commits incest with **his sister, it is possible to apply** the penalty of lashes **if his sister was an adult,** or an orphan who consented to the act, as explained by Ulla. Although this appears to be a distortion of the plain meaning of the verse, it is legitimate to interpret a verse in this way, as we see from the cases of assault and conspiring witnesses. Hence there is no basis for Rabbi Yoḥanan's rejection of Ulla's *gezerah shavah*.

אָמַר לָךְ [5] In the light of this argument, the Gemara now seeks another reason for Rabbi Yoḥanan's rejection of Ulla's explanation. **Rabbi Yoḥanan can say** that he rejected Ulla's *gezerah shavah* because it is flawed. A *gezerah shavah* connecting two verses, in which the same word or phrase appears, applies only if the word or phrase on which it is based is superfluous in both verses. But in this case, the phrase used by Ulla to construct his *gezerah shavah*, **"for he has humbled her,"** which appears in the verse dealing with rape (Deuteronomy 22:29), is not superfluous at all. **It is needed** to teach us the following important law **stated by Abaye.** [6] **For Abaye said** (below, 40b): The Mishnah (below, 40a) rules that the rapist or the seducer must pay for shame, blemish, and (in the case of the rapist) pain, in addition to paying the fifty-shekel fine imposed on him by the Torah. How do we know that this is so? Is it not possible that the fifty-shekel fine is intended to cover everything? [7] The answer, says Abaye, can be found in **the verse** used by Ulla, which **said** that the rapist must pay the father of the *na'arah* fifty shekels, **"for he has humbled her."** Why does the Torah need to explain the reason for the fine again? [8] It is to teach us that ***this*** fifty-shekel **fine is**

1 אֶלָּא, עֵדִים זוֹמְמִין אֶפְשָׁר לְקַיּוּמָהּ בְּבֶן גְּרוּשָׁה וּבֶן חֲלוּצָה. 2 חוֹבֵל בַּחֲבֵירוֹ נַמִי, אִיכָּא לְקַיּוּמָהּ, 3 כְּגוֹן שֶׁהִכָּהוּ הַכָּאָה שֶׁאֵין בָּהּ שָׁוֶה פְּרוּטָה. 4 אֲחוֹתוֹ נַמִי, אִיכָּא לְקַיּוּמָהּ בַּאֲחוֹתוֹ בוֹגֶרֶת.

5 אָמַר לָךְ רַבִּי יוֹחָנָן: הַאי ״תַּחַת אֲשֶׁר עִנָּהּ״ מִיבָּעֵי לֵיהּ לְכִדְאַבַּיֵי. 6 דְּאָמַר אַבַּיֵי: 7 אָמַר קְרָא: ״תַּחַת אֲשֶׁר עִנָּהּ״. 8 הַאי

LITERAL TRANSLATION

[1] Rather, [in the case of] conspiring witnesses it is possible to apply it [the punishment of lashes] with regard to the son of a divorcee and the son of a woman who performed *ḥalitzah*. [2] [And in the case of] someone who injures his fellow also, it is possible to apply it, [3] for example, where he struck him a blow that does not have the value of a perutah. [4] [And in the case of] his sister also, it is possible to apply it with regard to his sister who is an adult.

[5] Rabbi Yoḥanan can say to you: This "for he has humbled her" is needed for what Abaye [said]. [6] For Abaye said: [7] The verse said: "For he has humbled her." [8] This [fine is payable]

RASHI

אלא – על כרחך, כיון דרבייה קרא לתשלומין, איכא לאוקמא לעונש מלקות דלאו דידיה, "במעידין אנו את איש פלוני כהן שהוא בן גרושה". דליכא לאוקמי "כאשר זמם" ולומר: יהא הוא בן גרושה תחתיו, אלא סופג את הארבעים. והכי תנן במסכת מכות. וחובל בחבירו נמי מוקמינן ליה בשאין בה שוה פרוטה בכל חמשה דברים שבה, כגון שלא פיחתו מכספו וממלאכתו, וריפוי לא הוצרך, ולא צער היה בה, ובשוטה שאין לה בושת. והכא נמי באחותו מצית לאוקמי מלקות דידה בבוגרת. אבל נערה – לישלם ולא לילקי, הואיל וריבתה גזירה שוה ד"תחת" "תחת" לתשלומין. **לכדאביי** – בשילהי פירקין. דפרכינן: ואימא חמשים אמר רחמנא מכל מילי? ושני אביי: חמשים כסף נתחדשו תחת קנס העינוי, אבל בושת ופגם שהוא בשאר חובלים – לא כלל כאן.

TRANSLATION AND COMMENTARY

imposed only **"for he has humbled her,"** and for no other reason. In other words, rape involves a number of different offenses, and the fifty-shekel fine is paid as compensation for the illicit intercourse. All other penalties that may be incurred by the rapist are in addition to the fifty shekels, and are assessed as for any other assault. [1] **This proves by implication that** a man who rapes or seduces a virgin *na'arah* is liable to **pay for** her **shame** (i.e., the damage to her reputation) **and blemish** (i.e., her lost virginity), in addition to paying the fifty-shekel fine. Thus we see that the phrase considered superfluous by Ulla is needed to teach us this important law, and it is therefore not available to construct a *gezerah shavah*. Accordingly, Rabbi Yoḥanan rejects Ulla's exegesis and prefers his own.

"תַּחַת אֲשֶׁר עִנָּהּ". [1] מִכְּלָל דְּאִיכָּא בּוֹשֶׁת וּפְגָם.
[2] וְעוּלָּא?
[3] נָפְקָא לֵיהּ מִדְּרָבָא. [4] דְּאָמַר רָבָא: [5] אָמַר קְרָא: "וְנָתַן הָאִישׁ הַשֹּׁכֵב עִמָּהּ לַאֲבִי הַנַּעֲרָה חֲמִשִּׁים כָּסֶף". [6] הֲנָאַת שְׁכִיבָה חֲמִשִּׁים. [7] מִכְּלָל דְּאִיכָּא בּוֹשֶׁת וּפְגָם.

LITERAL TRANSLATION

"for he has humbled her." [1] [This proves] by implication that there are [payments for] shame and blemish.

[2] And Ulla?

[3] He derives it from what Rava [said]. [4] For Rava said: [5] The verse said: "And the man who lay with her shall give the father of the *na'arah* fifty [pieces of] silver." [6] [For] the pleasure of lying [with her he pays] fifty [pieces. [7] This proves] by implication that there are [payments for] shame and blemish.

RASHI

השוכב עמה — קרא יתירא הוא לדרשה, נימא: ונתן לאבי הנערה חמשים כסף. **מכלל דבושו; ופגם** — דלאו מחמת הנאת שכיבה נינהו, שהרי ישנן בשאר חובלים — לא כיילינהו בגווייהו דהכי.

וְעוּלָּא [2] The Gemara's explanation of Rabbi Yoḥanan's reason for rejecting Ulla's *gezerah shavah* is so satisfactory that it casts strong doubt on Ulla's own reasoning. How, then, could **Ulla** use that phrase to construct a *gezerah shavah* when the phrase was needed to teach us about shame and blemish?

נָפְקָא לֵיהּ מִדְּרָבָא [3] The Gemara answers that Ulla **derives** the law prescribing payment for shame and blemish **from** a different verse, in accordance with **a ruling** given **by Rava.** [4] **For Rava** (below, 40b) pointed to a different source in the Torah for the payments for shame and blemish, **saying:** How do we know that the fifty-shekel fine is not all that the offender must pay? [5] The answer can be found in the beginning of **the** same **verse** cited by Abaye, which **said: "And the man who lay with her shall give the father of the *na'arah* fifty pieces of silver."** Why does the Torah need to repeat the fact that it is "the man who lay with her" who pays the fine? [6] It is to teach us that these **fifty pieces** of silver **are** to be **paid** in compensation **for the** illicit **pleasure** he had when **lying with her,** and for nothing else. All other penalties that may be incurred by the rapist are in addition to the fifty shekels, and are assessed as for any other assault. [7] **This proves by implication that** a man who rapes or seduces a virgin *na'arah* is liable to **pay for** her **shame** (i.e., the damage to her reputation) **and blemish** (i.e., her lost virginity), in addition to paying the fifty-shekel fine. Thus we see that Abaye's law can be derived from a different part of the verse, and Ulla's phrase remains superfluous and therefore available for constructing a *gezerah shavah*. Therefore Ulla (who agrees with Rava) was entirely justified in constructing a *gezerah shavah* and inferring from it that monetary penalties take precedence over lashes in cases of rape and seduction. But Rabbi Yoḥanan (who agrees with Abaye) was equally justified in rejecting the *gezerah shavah*, because the phrase on which it is based is not superfluous according to Abaye. This is why Rabbi Yoḥanan rules that lashes take precedence over monetary penalties in all cases except assault and conspiring witnesses.

The Gemara has now concluded its consideration of the solutions offered by Ulla and Rabbi Yoḥanan regarding the contradiction between our Mishnah and the Mishnah in tractate *Makkot* (see above, 31b). Before proceeding to the third resolution, that of Resh Lakish (below, 33b), the Gemara pauses at this point to give detailed consideration to a subject that was mentioned in passing in the previous discussion. The Gemara objected earlier to Rabbi Yoḥanan's opinion — that lashes take precedence over monetary payments — by citing the two cases about which it is universally agreed that monetary payments take precedence: assault and conspiring witnesses. This objection was answered by citing a statement of Rabbi Il'a, who argued that the Torah explicitly directed that monetary payments should take precedence in these cases. Now the Gemara cites a different explanation for each of these rulings, first with regard to the case of conspiring witnesses, and then with regard to the case of assault.

CONCEPTS

בּוֹשֶׁת **Shame.** One of the five headings (חֲמִשָּׁה דְּבָרִים) under which a person may have to pay damages for an injury he caused another person. If the injured person has been shamed in the process, the person who caused the injury is obligated to compensate the person he injured for the shame he has caused him. The amount of the payment for בּוֹשֶׁת is evaluated according to the social standing of both the person who suffered the shame and the person who caused it. Payment is required under the heading of בּוֹשֶׁת even if no physical injury was inflicted, provided that the shame was caused by a physical act. A person who verbally puts another to shame has no financial obligation to him under the heading of בּוֹשֶׁת.

פְּגָם **Blemish.** One of the categories of compensation that must be paid by a man who seduces or rapes a woman. פְּגָם is assessed according to the reduction in the woman's value, caused by the loss of her virginity, if she were to be sold as a slave.

BACKGROUND

הֲנָאַת שְׁכִיבָה **The pleasure of lying with her.** This is not to say that the rapist or the seducer pays the fine as compensation for the pleasure he enjoyed from the act of intercourse. The intention here is to emphasize that the fine is imposed specifically in relation to the forbidden physical contact. By contrast, compensation for any other damage (physical or psychological) suffered by the woman as a result of the rape or the seduction comes under the heading of damages paid by anyone who commits an assault.

TRANSLATION AND COMMENTARY

רַבִּי אֱלְעָזָר אוֹמֵר [1] **Rabbi Elazar says:** There is no need for an explicit verse to teach us that **conspiring witnesses pay money but are not lashed.** It is obvious that this is so, [2] **because they are not subject to warning.** As we have seen above (32b), lashes are not usually inflicted unless the offender was warned in advance of the legal consequences of his impending action. But in the case of conspiring witnesses, this warning is not required. Therefore lashes are not an appropriate punishment for conspiring witnesses, and it is only by way of exception that they are imposed in certain unusual situations in which the regular penalty is inapplicable. But whenever it is possible to impose the regular penalty on conspiring witnesses, this penalty takes precedence over lashes, even if the regular penalty is monetary payment. Hence monetary penalties take precedence over lashes in the case of conspiring witnesses, even though lashes take precedence in other cases in which they are an appropriate penalty.

אָמַר רָבָא [3] **Rava said: The truth of the matter is** that the Torah waived the requirement that conspiring witnesses be warned because it is a practical impossibility to warn them. [4] For **when should we warn them?** [5] **Shall we warn them from the outset,** well before they testify? [6] **They can** then later **say: "We forgot."** For a warning to be legally valid, it must be issued immediately before the offense, so that the offender cannot claim that he forgot the warning. [7] **Shall we warn them at the time the** prohibited **act** was about to be committed? Are we to warn every pair of witnesses, when they come forward to testify, that if they are found to be testifying falsely they will be punished by the same punishment that they sought to inflict on the defendant? [8] This too cannot be acceptable, for if we admonish all witnesses in this way, **they will withdraw and not testify.** [9] **Shall we warn themat the end,** after they have finished testifying, that if

[1] רַבִּי אֱלְעָזָר אוֹמֵר: עֵדִים זוֹמְמִין מָמוֹנָא מְשַׁלְּמֵי וּמִילְקָא לָא לָקֵי, [2] מִשּׁוּם דְּלָאו בְּנֵי הַתְרָאָה נִינְהוּ.

[3] אֲמַר רָבָא: תֵּדַע. [4] נִיתְרֵי בְּהוּ אֵימַת? [5] נִיתְרֵי בְּהוּ מֵעִיקָּרָא? [6] אָמְרִי: ״אִישְׁתַּלִּין״. [7] נִיתְרֵי בְּהוּ בִּשְׁעַת מַעֲשֶׂה? [8] פָּרְשִׁי וְלָא מְסַהֲדֵי. [9] נִיתְרֵי בְּהוּ

LITERAL TRANSLATION

[1] Rabbi Elazar says: Conspiring witnesses pay money but are not lashed, [2] because they are not subject to warning.

[3] Rava said: Know [that this is true]. [4] When shall we warn them? [5] Shall we warn them from the outset? [6] They can say: "We forgot." [7] Shall we warn them at the time of the deed? [8] They will withdraw and not testify. [9] Shall we warn them

RASHI

רבי אלעזר אומר עדים זוממין דממונא משלמי ולא לקו — לא צריכי קרא, דסברא היא דמלקות לא שייך בהו. **דלאו בני התראה נינהו** — קודם עדות, כדמפרש רבא ואזיל. הלכך, אי איכא למענשינהו — לא תענשינהו אלא ממון, דאין עונש הגוף בלא התראה. ואף על גב דגבי בן גרושה ובן חלוצה ענשינן להו מלקות בלא התראה — התם גזירת הכתוב, דאשכחן בהו מלקות בהדיא "והיה אם בן הכות" ומוקמינן לקרא במידי דלא מצית למענשינהו מ"כאשר זמם". אבל היכא דמצית למיעבד בהו הזמה — לא שייך בהו מלקות. **תדע** — שאי אפשר להתרות בהם. **מעיקרא** — יום או שעה קודם שיעידו העדות. **אמרי אישתלין** — שכחנו ההתראה, הרי שבטלה ההתראה. **פרשי ולא מסהדי** — אפילו אמת, הואיל ואנו חשודים בעיניכם — מה לנו ולצרה?

NOTES

מִשּׁוּם דְּלָאו בְּנֵי הַתְרָאָה נִינְהוּ **Because they are not subject to warning.** Our commentary follows *Rashi* and other Rishonim (*Rashba*, *Ra'ah*), who explain that since we do not normally execute or lash an offender unless he has been warned, lashes are not an appropriate punishment for conspiring witnesses, who are punished without having been warned.

Maharsha asks: According to *Rashi*'s explanation, why do we execute or lash the conspiring witnesses if this was the penalty they sought to impose on the defendant? Why do we not impose a monetary penalty instead? *Maharsha* explains that there is no problem with executing these conspiring witnesses or lashing them when this is in fulfillment of the Torah's commandment to punish conspiring witnesses with the same punishment that they sought to inflict on the defendant. The problem arises when we wish to lash them for their false testimony in itself, as we would for other negative commandments. In such cases, lashes are not appropriate, since the witnesses were not warned; hence every other penalty takes precedence.

פָּרְשִׁי וְלָא מְסַהֲדֵי **They will withdraw and not testify.** Our commentary follows *Rashi*, who explains that we are afraid that genuine witnesses will be insulted if we treat them like criminals, and will refuse to testify. *Ritva* explains that if we stimulate the witnesses' imagination by telling them how they will be punished if they are caught lying, they will begin to panic, fearing that false witnesses may come forward and successfully convict them of conspiring to testify falsely.

The Rishonim ask: The Mishnah (*Sanhedrin* 37a) rules that in capital cases the court must warn the witnesses, before their testimony is investigated, about the dire

HALAKHAH

אָמְרִי: אִישְׁתַּלִּין **They can say: "We forgot."** "An offender cannot be lashed or executed unless he had been warned immediately before his offense. But if he was warned some time earlier, the warning is not valid, for he can claim that he forgot the warning," following our Gemara. (*Rambam*, *Sefer Shofetim*, *Hilkhot Sanhedrin* 12:2.)

לְבַסּוֹף? [1]מַאי דַּהֲוָה, הֲוָה.
[2]מַתְקִיף לָהּ אַבַּיֵי: [3]וְנִיתְרִי בְּהוּ בְּתוֹךְ כְּדֵי דִבּוּר!
[4]מַתְקִיף לָהּ רַב אַחָא בְּרֵיהּ דְּרַב אִיקָא: [5]וְנִיתְרִי בְּהוּ מֵעִיקָּרָא, [6]וְנִרְמַז בְּהוּ רְמוּזֵי!

LITERAL TRANSLATION

at the end? [1]Whatever was, was.

[2]Abaye objected to this: [3]But let us warn them within [the time of] speaking!

[4]Rav Aḥa the son of Rav Ika objected to this: [5]But let us warn them from the outset, [6]and let us hint hints to them!

RASHI

לבסוף – לאחר שהעידו. **מאי דהוה הוה** – דכיון שהגיד אינו חוזר ומגיד, ואין יכולין לחזור. **וניתרי בהו בתוך כדי דבור** – לאחר שהעידו, דתוך כדי דבור כדבור דמי, ויכולים לחזור. **תוך כדי דבור** – כדי שאילת שלום. **ונרמז רמוזי** – בשעת העדות נרמוז להם רמזים על ההתראה להזכירם, ובלשון רך, שלא יקפידו.

TRANSLATION AND COMMENTARY

they do not retract their testimony, and are found to have testified falsely, they will be punished? [1]This too is unsatisfactory, for **whatever has happened, has happened.** Warning witnesses after they have given evidence will be of no value, because witnesses are not permitted to retract their testimony (above, 18b). Thus we see that it is a practical impossibility to warn conspiring witnesses, and it is obvious that the Torah must have waived this requirement.

מַתְקִיף לָהּ [2]**Abaye objected to** Rava's proof: It is not correct to say that there is no practical way of warning conspiring witnesses. [3]**Let us warn them** immediately after they finish giving their testimony, **within the time it takes to say a few words!** Although witnesses are not ordinarily permitted to retract their testimony, if they do so immediately after they have given it, within the time it takes to say a few words, the retraction is valid. Thus, if we warn them immediately after they conclude their testimony, the warning is perfectly effective.

מַתְקִיף לָהּ [4]**Rav Aḥa the son of Rav Ika** raised a similar **objection to** Rava's argument: [5]**Let us warn them from the outset,** well before they testify, [6]**and** in order to overcome the danger that they may claim to have forgotten the warning, or the danger that repetition of the warning immediately before the testimony may frighten away legitimate witnesses, **let us give them** gentle **hints,** reminding them of the warning they have already received! Thus there is no practical obstacle to warning conspiring witnesses just like we warn any other offender.

NOTES

consequences of testifying falsely. Why, then, is the warning in our Gemara considered more demeaning or frightening than this exhortation? Why are we not equally concerned in both cases that genuine witnesses may be deterred from testifying?

Ritva explains that no exhortation is as frightening as telling someone that he will be executed if he is found to have given false testimony. This explanation is consistent with *Ritva*'s opinion that the witnesses are afraid that they will be falsely accused of testifying falsely.

Shittah Mekubbetzet explains that the exhortation in tractate *Sanhedrin* is balanced. Together with the dire consequences of testifying falsely, we tell the witnesses that if they testify truthfully they will be doing a worthy deed, and if they withhold their testimony they will be committing a sin. Hence, there is no danger of the witnesses being insulted, if they are testifying truthfully. In our Gemara, by contrast, we are referring to a warning that is issued prior to an offense, and for such a warning to be valid, it must be stated unequivocally. In such a situation we are afraid that the witnesses will be insulted, even if they are telling the truth.

מַאי דַּהֲוָה הֲוָה Whatever was, was. Our commentary follows *Rashi*, who explains that a warning issued after testimony has been completed is ineffective, because the witnesses cannot retract their testimony, even if they want to. *Shittah Mekubbetzet* explains that the warning is invalid, regardless of the witnesses' reaction to it, because it relates to a deed that has already been committed.

בְּתוֹךְ כְּדֵי דִבּוּר Within the time of speaking. In general, whenever words are considered Halakhically significant, a person may change his statement if he does so immediately, since that is not considered a retraction, but a correction of a slip of the tongue. Thus an oath may be annulled, witnesses may retract their testimony, a blessing may be corrected, etc. "Immediately" is defined as the time it takes to say three or four words. Likewise, two events that took place one after the other within the time taken to utter three or four words are considered to have taken place at the same time, even if they do not involve speech. The only exceptions to this rule are dedications to the Temple, blasphemy, marriage, and divorce, which cannot be retracted even if the retraction is immediate (*Nedarim* 87a).

The "time of speaking" does not begin until the original statement has been completed. Thus a person who utters an oath, for example, may withdraw it immediately after completing it, even if the oath itself was more than three or four words long. Indeed, according to *Rambam*, if other people who heard the man utter the oath immediately urged him to withdraw it, the "time of speaking" does not begin until the other people's urging is complete, even if their urging was more than three or four words long. Similarly in our case, Abaye is suggesting that the witnesses should be warned after completing their testimony and that they then should be given a few seconds to retract, even though the warning itself was more than three or four words long (*Tosafot*). *Rashba* adds that since, according to Abaye, the court is required to warn the witnesses, the warning becomes part of the court's investigation of the testimony; hence the testimony is not complete until the warning is given.

Ra'avad asks: If the warning is considered an essential part of the testimony, why is it necessary to give it within

CONCEPTS

תּוֹךְ כְּדֵי דִבּוּר Within the time of speaking. The amount of time it takes to say שָׁלוֹם עָלֶיךָ רַבִּי — "Peace unto you, my teacher." According to the Halakhah, certain acts are rendered invalid by an interruption only if the interruption is longer than תּוֹךְ כְּדֵי דִבּוּר. Moreover, most Halakhically significant statements (blessings, testimony, etc.) may be retracted or altered within this period without penalty.

SAGES

רַב אַחָא בְּרֵיהּ דְּרַב אִיקָא Rav Aḥa the son of Rav Ika. A fifth-generation Babylonian Amora, Rav Aḥa the son of Rav Ika was the nephew of Rav Aḥa bar Ya'akov (both Sages apparently lived in the same city, Papunya). Rav Aḥa the son of Rav Ika studied with many fourth- and fifth-generation Amoraim, and engaged in Halakhic discussions with Rav Pappa, and later with Rav Ashi. His teachings — some of which were transmitted by his student, Rav Huna bar Manoaḥ — are cited in various places in the Talmud.

[1]הֲדַר אֲמַר אַבַּיֵי: [2]לָאו מִילְּתָא הִיא דַּאֲמָרִי. [3]אִי סָלְקָא דַּעְתָּךְ עֵדִים זוֹמְמִין צְרִיכִין הַתְרָאָה, [4]כִּי לָא מַתְרִינַן בְּהוּ, לָא קָטְלִינַן לְהוּ. [5]מִי אִיכָּא מִידֵי דְּאִינְהוּ בָּעוּ קָטֵיל בְּלָא הַתְרָאָה, [6]וְאִינְהוּ בָּעוּ הַתְרָאָה? [7]הָא בָּעֵינַן: ״וַעֲשִׂיתֶם לוֹ כַּאֲשֶׁר זָמַם לַעֲשׂוֹת לְאָחִיו״, [8]וְלֵיכָּא.

[9]מַתְקִיף לָהּ רַב סַמָּא בְּרֵיהּ דְּרַב יִרְמְיָה: [10]אֶלָּא מֵעַתָּה, [11]בֶּן גְּרוּשָׁה וּבֶן חֲלוּצָה, [12]דְּלָא מִ״כַּאֲשֶׁר זָמַם״ קָא מִיתְרַבִּי, [13]לִיבָּעֵי הַתְרָאָה!

LITERAL TRANSLATION

[1]Abaye retracted [and] said: [2]It is not a [correct] thing that I said. [3]If it should enter your mind [that] conspiring witnesses need warning, [4][then] when we do not warn them, we do not kill them. [5]Can there be such a thing that they wanted to kill without warning, [6]and [yet] they need warning? [7]Surely we need: "And you shall do to him as he conspired to do to his brother," [8]and here it is lacking.

[9]Rav Samma the son of Rav Yirmeyah objected to this: [10]But if so (lit., "but from now"), [11][in the cases of] the son of a divorcee and the son of a woman who performed *ḥalitzah*, [12]which are not included in "as he conspired," [13]let them require a warning!

RASHI

לאו מילתא היא דאמרי — שיהו עדים זוממין צריכין התראה. הכי גרסינן: דאינהו בעו למיקטל בלא התראה ואינהו בעו התראה כו׳. **כאשר זמם** — והם זממו להרוג את זה בעדותן שלא היה ולא נברא, ולא התרו בו ההתראה שהעידו עליה. **אלא מעתה** — דהאי דלא בעו התראה משום ״כאשר זמם״ הוא, מלקות של זוממי עדות בן גרושה ובן חלוצה. **דלאו מכאשר זמם אתי** — עונש דידהו, שהרי לא זממו להלקותו אלא לחללו.

TRANSLATION AND COMMENTARY

הֲדַר אֲמַר אַבַּיֵי [1]But **Abaye** later **retracted** his objection (and that of Rav Aḥa the son of Rav Ika) **and said:** [2]**What I said** — that conspiring witnesses must be warned — **is not correct.** Although it may be technically possible to find a way to warn conspiring witnesses, as we suggested, Rabbi Elazar was correct in ruling that this is not required. [3]For **if it should enter your mind that conspiring witnesses must be warned,** it follows that according to the Torah we may not execute conspiring witnesses who testified that an innocent man committed a capital crime unless they were warned, [4]but if they were **not warned, we do not kill them,** but let them go without penalty. Surely this is untenable. [5]For **can it be that** false witnesses **must be warned** before a penalty can be imposed on them, [6]even **though they wanted to kill** the defendant **without** giving him **warning?** [7]**Surely,** when we punish conspiring witnesses, **we need** to apply the principle contained in the verse (Deuteronomy 19:19): **"And you shall do to him as he conspired to do to his brother."** We must inflict on them precisely the same punishment that they sought to inflict on the defendant. [8]**And** if we insist that they must be warned, **it is not** precisely the same punishment, for we are being less harsh with the witnesses than they were with the defendant! Thus Rabbi Elazar was quite right in stating that conspiring witnesses require no warning.

מַתְקִיף לָהּ [9]**Rav Samma the son of Rav Yirmeyah objected to** the reasoning underlying Abaye's retraction and he said: [10]**If** your reasoning **is correct,** and conspiring witnesses need not be warned because this would impair the equality decreed by the Torah between the punishment meted out to the witnesses and the punishment they sought to inflict on the defendant, it should follow that in those cases in which the Torah did not mete out an equal punishment to the conspiring witnesses, [11]such as **the cases of the son of a divorcee and the son of a woman who performed *ḥalitzah*,** the witnesses are not punished unless they were warned. [12]For the penalty inflicted on witnesses who testify that a priest is disqualified **is not included** in the Torah's requirement that a conspiring witness must be punished **"as he conspired** to do to his brother." The punishment imposed in these special cases is inferred from a different verse (Deuteronomy 25:2): "And it shall be, if the wicked man is punishable by being lashed," from which we learn that in circumstances in which the regular punishment for conspiring witnesses is inapplicable, such as where they testified that a priest was disqualified, they are lashed. [13]So **let** us say that **these** conspiring witnesses **require a warning,** in accordance with Abaye's previous suggestion, and that if they were not warned, they should not be punished!

NOTES

the time needed for speaking? Even after this time the warning should be valid, since the testimony is not complete without it! *Ra'avad* answers that if more time passes than the time needed for speaking, the witnesses can claim that they have forgotten their original testimony.

וְאִינְהוּ בָּעוּ הַתְרָאָה And yet they need warning? *Rambam* (*Hilkhot Edut* 20:4) rules that conspiring witnesses are punished even if they were genuinely unaware of the law, because the distinction between deliberate and inadvertent offenses applies only to forbidden deeds and not to forbidden words. This explanation, however, was not accepted by other commentators (*Ra'avad*, *Kesef Mishneh*).

Ketzot HaḤoshen rules that if the witnesses were genuinely unaware that it is forbidden to testify falsely, they

TERMINOLOGY

לָאו מִילְּתָא הִיא It is not a correct thing. The Talmud sometimes rejects a statement by saying: "It [the previous opinion] is incorrect." Sometimes an Amora may use this expression in connection with a statement of his own if he feels he has erred.

SAGES

רַב סַמָּא בְּרֵיהּ דְּרַב יִרְמְיָה Rav Samma the son of Rav Yirmeyah. This Sage is mentioned in the Talmud only here, and we know nothing about the details of his life. He may possibly have been the son of the famous Amora Rabbi Yirmeyah who immigrated to Eretz Israel from Babylonia.

¹אָמַר קְרָא: ״מִשְׁפַּט אֶחָד יִהְיֶה לָכֶם״, ²מִשְׁפָּט הַשָּׁוֶה לְכוּלְּכֶם.
³רַב שֵׁישָׁא בְּרֵיהּ דְּרַב אִידִי אֲמַר: ⁴חוֹבֵל בַּחֲבֵירוֹ נַמִי מָמוֹנָא מְשַׁלֵּם, וּמִילְקָא לָא לָקֵי.
⁵מֵהָכָא: ״וְכִי יִנָּצוּ אֲנָשִׁים, וְנָגְפוּ אִשָּׁה הָרָה וְיָצְאוּ יְלָדֶיהָ״.
⁶וְאָמַר רַבִּי אֶלְעָזָר: בְּמַצּוּת שֶׁבְּמִיתָה הַכָּתוּב מְדַבֵּר, ⁷דִּכְתִיב: ״וְאִם אָסוֹן יִהְיֶה, וְנָתַתָּה נֶפֶשׁ תַּחַת נָפֶשׁ״.
⁸הֵיכִי דָּמֵי? ⁹אִי דְּלָא אַתְרוּ

TRANSLATION AND COMMENTARY

אָמַר קְרָא [1]The Gemara replies: This objection is without foundation, because **the verse** (Leviticus 24:22) **said: "There shall be one judgment for you,"** [2]which teaches us that the Torah requires **a judgment that is equal for all of you.** Witnesses who conspire to testify falsely are guilty of essentially the same crime, whether they testify about the qualifications of a priest or about other matters. Therefore, since conspiring witnesses are normally punished without having received a warning, witnesses who conspire to taint a priest's lineage are also punished without having received a warning, even though Abaye's argument does not apply to them directly.

רַב שֵׁישָׁא [3]The Gemara objected earlier to Rabbi Yoḥanan's opinion, that lashes take precedence over monetary payments, by citing the two cases in which it is universally agreed that monetary payments take precedence: assault and conspiring witnesses. The Gemara responded by citing a statement of Rabbi Il'a that the Torah explicitly required that monetary payments should take precedence in these cases. The Gemara has just considered a different explanation for this anomaly in the case of conspiring witnesses. It will now do so in the case of assault. **Rav Shesha the son of Rav Idi said:** There is no need for an explicit verse to teach us that monetary penalties take precedence in cases of assault. Just as it is obvious that monetary penalties take precedence regarding conspiring witnesses, [4]it is **also** obvious that **someone who injures somebody pays money but is not lashed.**

מֵהָכָא [5]Rav Shesha the son of Rav Idi explains that **we can infer this** idea **from** the following verse (Exodus 21:22): **"And if** two **men struggle, and** one of **them strikes a pregnant woman so that she loses her unborn child,** but no disaster befalls the woman herself, the assailant shall be punished, as the woman's husband shall impose upon him." The punishment in this case is traditionally understood to be a monetary penalty, equal to the value of an unborn child on the slave market. [6]**And Rabbi Elazar** gave an authoritative interpretation of this verse and **said: The verse is speaking about a quarrel to the death,** in which the men involved were trying to kill each other, and one of them struck the woman instead. [7]**For it is written** in the next verse: **"But if a disaster** befalls the woman herself [i.e., she is killed by the accidental blow], **you shall give a life for a life,"** and the man who struck the deathblow is guilty of murder. The verse teaches us that someone who was seeking to commit murder but accidentally killed someone other than his intended victim is regarded as guilty of premeditated murder and not of accidental manslaughter. Hence it must have been referring to a case in which the original quarrel was a fight to the death, for had there been no intent to kill anybody, the death would have been treated as accidental.

הֵיכִי דָּמֵי [8]Rav Shesha the son of Rav Idi now explains how Rabbi Elazar's authoritative interpretation of this verse proves that an assailant who injures somebody pays money but is not lashed. **How do we visualize the case?** Under what circumstances is a man who was intent on murder, but who accidentally killed an innocent bystander, executed for murder? [9]**If** we are referring to a case in which witnesses **did not warn**

LITERAL TRANSLATION

[1]The verse said: "There shall be one judgment for you," [2]a judgment that is equal for all of you.

[3]Rav Shesha the son of Rav Idi said: [4][Someone who] injures his fellow too pays money, [but] he is not lashed.

[5][This is derived] from here: "And if men struggle, and they strike a pregnant woman so that her children go out." [6]And Rabbi Elazar said [about this]: The verse is speaking about a quarrel to the death, [7]for it is written: "But if there will be a disaster, then you shall give a life for a life."

[8]How do we visualize the case? [9]If they did not warn

RASHI

משפט השוה – וכיון דרוב זוממין לאו בני התראה נינהו, הכי נמי לא בעו התראה. **במצות שבמיתה** – שמתכוין היה להורגו. **הכתוב מדבר** – דכתיב "אם אסון יהיה" – שמתה האשה, "ונתת נפש" ואף על פי שלא נתכוון אלא לחבירו. ואשמעינן: נתכוון להרוג את זה והרג את זה – חייב.

NOTES

would indeed be exempt. The only requirements that are relaxed in the case of conspiring witnesses are the additional precautions, normally required by the Torah, to be absolutely certain that the offender was not lacking any information whatsoever.

TRANSLATION AND COMMENTARY

him that murder is punishable by death, **why is he put to death** for killing the woman accidentally? Even if he had killed the man he planned to kill, we would still not have executed him if he had not been warned! [1]**Rather, it is obvious that** the Torah is referring to a case in which witnesses **warned him** that if he murdered the man he was planning to kill, he would be executed, but he paid no attention and struck the deathblow regardless, killing the woman by mistake. From this we can infer that when the Torah commanded the man to pay a financial penalty if the woman survived and miscarried, it was referring to a case in which the witnesses warned the man that if he murdered the person he was planning to kill, he would be executed. Admittedly, he was warned against killing, not against causing injury, [2]but it stands to reason that **someone who is warned** that the action he is about to take is subject to **a serious** penalty **is considered warned about** any **lighter** penalties that may also be incurred by this same action. Thus, when the witnesses warned the man that murder is a capital crime, they were in effect also warning him that if his victim survived the attack, he would be subject to whatever penalties apply to attempted murder, including lashes for assault. And although he injured the pregnant woman and not the man he was attacking, the Torah teaches us that the same penalty applies. Thus we would expect the man to be lashed for injuring the woman. [3]**And** yet **the Torah said: "And if there is no disaster, he shall surely be punished"** by a monetary penalty. Hence, in the case of assault, monetary penalties take precedence over lashes, even if the assailant was warned that he would be lashed.

מַתְקִיף לָהּ [4]**Rav Ashi objected to** the argument of Rav Shesha the son of Rav Idi: This argument is based on an unsupported assumption. [5]**From where do we know that someone who is warned** that the action he is about to take is subject to **a serious** penalty **is considered warned about** any **lighter** penalties that may also be incurred through this same action? [6]**Perhaps it is not so!** [7]Moreover, even **if we admit** for the sake of argument **that it is true** that a warning regarding a serious penalty is considered as including any lighter penalties that may be associated with the same action, [8]**from where do we know that** the person who is being warned considers **the death penalty a more serious** punishment than lashes? [33B] [9]**Perhaps** he considers that **lashes are more serious,** and claims that if he had been warned explicitly about the penalty

בֵּיהּ, אַמַּאי מִיקְטִיל? [1]אֶלָּא פְּשִׁיטָא דְּאַתְרוּ בֵּיהּ. [2]וּמוּתְרֶה לְדָבָר חָמוּר הָוֵי מוּתְרֶה לְדָבָר הַקַּל. [3]וְאָמַר רַחֲמָנָא: "וְלֹא יִהְיֶה אָסוֹן, עָנוֹשׁ יֵעָנֵשׁ". [4]מַתְקִיף לָהּ רַב אַשִׁי: [5]מִמַּאי דְּמוּתְרֶה לְדָבָר חָמוּר הָוֵי מוּתְרֶה לְדָבָר הַקַּל? [6]דִּלְמָא לָא הָוֵי! [7]אִם תִּמְצָא לוֹמַר הָוֵי, [8]מִמַּאי דְּמִיתָה חֲמוּרָה? [33B] [9]דִּלְמָא מַלְקוֹת חָמוּר!

LITERAL TRANSLATION

him, why is he killed? [1]Rather, it is obvious that they warned him. [2]And someone who is warned regarding a serious matter is [considered] warned regarding a light matter. [3]And the Torah (lit., "the Merciful One") said: "And [if] there is no disaster, he shall surely be punished."

[4]Rav Ashi objected to this: [5]From where [do we know] that someone who is warned regarding a serious matter is [considered] warned for a light matter? [6]Perhaps it is not so! [7]If you would say [that] it is so, [8]from where [do you know] that [the] death [penalty] is [more] serious? [33B] [9]Perhaps lashes are [more] serious!

RASHI

אי דלא אתרו ביה — אם תמיתנו תהרג. **לדבר חמור** — מיתה. **הוי מותרה לדבר הקל** — שאם יכנו ולא ימות ילקה,

NOTES

מִמַּאי דְּמוּתְרֶה לְדָבָר חָמוּר **From where do we know that someone who is warned regarding a serious matter.** From the plain text of the Gemara, it would appear that the two points in dispute between Rav Shesha the son of Rav Idi and Rav Ashi both involve psychological factors. Rav Shesha the son of Rav Idi argues that since death is more serious than lashes, a person who is so determined to commit an offense that he is prepared to give his life will not be deterred by the penalty of lashes. Hence, when the quarreler decided to strike a murderous blow after having been warned that he would be executed, he was also, in effect, deciding to commit assault, after being been warned that he would be lashed. Against this, Rav Ashi responds that it is not possible to determine a person's feelings with absolute certainty. Thus it is possible that someone may fear lashes more than death.

The Rishonim agree that although this explanation may be correct regarding the question whether a person takes lashes more seriously than death, it is not correct regarding the question whether a warning for a serious penalty is considered to be a warning for a lighter penalty as well.

Tosafot explains that the dispute revolves around the law that the offender must explicitly state that he wants to commit the crime, even though he knows that he will suffer the punishment mentioned in the warning. According to Rav Shesha the son of Rav Idi, it is sufficient for the offender to acknowledge the most severe punishment applicable to him, whereas Rav Ashi argues that the Torah requires the offender to acknowledge the punishment that is actually inflicted on him.

דִּלְמָא מַלְקוֹת חָמוּר **Perhaps lashes are more serious!** *Tosafot* points out that it is obvious that execution is more

SAGES

רַב סַמָּא בְּרֵיהּ דְּרַב אַסִי Rav Samma the son of Rav Assi. This Babylonian Amora was probably the son of the sixth-generation Babylonian Amora Rav Assi, who was a colleague of Rav Ashi. Rav Samma was Rav Ashi's disciple.

רַב סַמָּא בְּרֵיהּ דְּרַב אַשִׁי Rav Samma the son of Rav Ashi. This Babylonian Amora was Rav Ashi's youngest son and close disciple. He was also on close terms with Ravina (the second). His statements are recorded in a number of places in the Babylonian Talmud.

[1]דְּאָמַר רַב: אִילְמָלֵי נַגְדוּהּ לַחֲנַנְיָה מִישָׁאֵל וַעֲזַרְיָה, [2]פָּלְחוּ לְצַלְמָא!

[3]אֲמַר לֵיהּ רַב סַמָּא בְּרֵיהּ דְּרַב אַסִי לְרַב אַשִׁי, וְאָמְרִי לָהּ רַב סַמָּא בְּרֵיהּ דְּרַב אַשִׁי לְרַב אַשִׁי: [4]וְלָא שָׁנֵי לָךְ בֵּין הַכָּאָה שֶׁיֵּשׁ לָהּ קִצְבָּה לְהַכָּאָה שֶׁאֵין לָהּ קִצְבָּה?

LITERAL TRANSLATION

[1]For Rav said: If they had whipped Ḥananyah, Mishael, and Azaryah, [2]they would have worshipped the idol!

[3]Rav Samma the son of Rav Assi said to Rav Ashi, and some say Rav Samma the son of Rav Ashi [said] to Rav Ashi: [4]But is there no difference to you between a beating that has a limit and a beating that does not have a limit?

RASHI

ואפילו הכי אמר רחמנא דכי אין שם חיוב מיתה — יענש דמי ולדות, ואף על גב דאיכא התראה למלקות. אלמא: משלם ואינו לוקה. נגדוה — יסורין. ולא שני לך כו׳ — יסורי המלכות — הכאה שאין לה קצבה היא, אבל מלקות יש לה קצבה — ארבעים.

TRANSLATION AND COMMENTARY

of lashes as well as about the death penalty, he would have refrained from striking the blow that injured the woman! [1]**For Rav said:** In the Book of Daniel (chapter 3), we are told that three Jewish princes, Ḥananyah, Mishael, and Azaryah (called by their Babylonian names, Shadrakh, Meshakh, and Abednego), refused to bow down before King Nebuchadnezzar's idol, even though Nebuchadnezzar threatened to punish them by throwing them into a fiery furnace. **If,** instead of threatening them with death, the Babylonians **had whipped Ḥananyah, Mishael, and Azaryah** mercilessly, [2]**they would have** been compelled to **worship the idol,** because such torture is worse than death! Thus we see that lashes can be an even more severe punishment than death, and the argument of Rav Shesha the son of Rav Idi is refuted.

אֲמַר לֵיהּ [3]The Gemara rejects the point just made. **Rav Samma the son of Rav Assi said to Rav Ashi, and some say** that **Rav Samma the son of Rav Ashi said to Rav Ashi:** [4]**Do you not** see **the difference between a beating that has a limit,** like the thirty-nine lashes that are inflicted by a Jewish court, **and a beating that**

NOTES

serious than lashes in a legal sense, because lashes are inflicted for the violation of every ordinary negative commandment, whereas execution is reserved for the most serious offenses. Moreover, *Tosafot* notes that the Gemara (*Sanhedrin* 49b) uses just this kind of argument to determine which methods of execution are more severe. It is, therefore, difficult to understand Rav Ashi's uncertainty on this point.

Our commentary follows *Shittah Mekubbetzet,* who explains that although death is objectively a more severe punishment than lashes, Rav Ashi had doubts about the subjective feelings of the assailant, who may perhaps believe that lashes are more severe than death, along the lines suggested by Rav in connection with the story of Ḥananyah, Mishael, and Azaryah. For death is quick, whereas lashes cause prolonged suffering and humiliation. On this basis, the assailant could say that he would have refrained from attacking his victim if he had been warned explicitly about the penalty of lashes, and as a consequence Rav Shesha's argument would be negated. In support of this explanation, *Shittah Mekubbetzet* notes that Rav Ashi prefaced his question with the word "perhaps," suggesting that the point he was making was speculative and not clear-cut.

Ritva explains that Rav Ashi was not suggesting that lashes could be more severe than execution, even in the mind of the assailant. Rather, he was arguing that the assailant might have been prepared to die had he succeeded in killing his enemy, but he was not willing to be lashed if he could only have succeeded in injuring him.

אִילְמָלֵי נַגְדוּהּ לַחֲנַנְיָה מִישָׁאֵל וַעֲזַרְיָה If they had whipped Ḥananyah, Mishael, and Azaryah. Rav's statement appears to imply that it is permitted to worship idols in order to escape torture. *Tosafot* objects: The Gemara (*Sanhedrin* 74a) rules that it is forbidden to worship idols even on pain of death. How, then, could Ḥananyah, Mishael, and Azaryah have been prepared to worship Nebuchadnezzar's idol in public under any circumstances?

Shittah Mekubbetzet explains that although we are required to give our lives rather than worship idols, we are not required to suffer tortures that are worse than death. Most Rishonim, however, reject this explanation, since the Gemara (*Berakhot* 61b) relates that when Rabbi Akiva died a martyr's death, he cited the law that we must give our lives rather than worship idols, even though he was killed with the utmost cruelty.

Rashba cites an explanation by *Rashi* (not found in our texts), according to which Rav's statement is to be read as a rhetorical question: "Even if they had whipped Ḥananyah, Mishael, and Azaryah, instead of trying to kill them, would they have worshipped the idol?" According to this explanation, Ḥananyah, Mishael, and Azaryah would not have worshipped the idol under any circumstances, and Rav Ashi's proof is based on Rav's language, which assumes that whipping is worse than death.

Most Rishonim follow *Tosafot,* who explains that Nebuchadnezzar's idol was not, in fact, an idol at all, but rather a statue of Nebuchadnezzar, to which everyone was expected to bow down as an act of respect for the king. The Torah forbids bowing down to statues in this way, but it does not consider such an act idolatry, and does not demand martyrdom for it. Hence Ḥananyah, Mishael, and Azaryah were technically permitted to bow down to the idol, but chose to sacrifice their lives rather than give people the impression that Jews were prepared to worship idols in order to save their lives. And Rav teaches us that although they were prepared to give their lives, they would not have submitted to torture for this purpose.

הַכָּאָה שֶׁאֵין לָהּ קִצְבָּה A beating that does not have a limit. *Shittah Mekubbetzet* explains that the threat of a

TRANSLATION AND COMMENTARY

has no limit, like the torture inflicted by tyrants like Nebuchadnezzar? Thus the second part of Rav Ashi's objection falls away, and the argument of Rav Shesha the son of Idi stands.

מַתְקִיף לָהּ [1]**Rav Ya'akov from Nehar Pekod** raised another **objection** to the argument advanced by Rav Shesha the son of Rav Idi: Your argument was based on the verse dealing with the pregnant woman (Exodus 21:22), as explained by Rabbi Elazar. But this verse is the subject of a difference of opinion among Tannaim, and Rabbi Elazar's explanation applies only according to one opinion. [2]Your argument **is satisfactory according to the Rabbis, who say that** when the Torah requires the man who accidentally killed the woman to "give a life for a life," **the word "life" is meant** to be taken **literally.** According to the Rabbis, the verse teaches us that the killer is executed for murder, for even though he did not intend to kill this woman, he did intend to kill someone else. [3]**But** your argument is not satisfactory **according to Rabbi Yehudah HaNasi,** [4]**who said that** when the Torah requires the man who accidentally killed the woman to "give a life for a life," the word "life" is to be explained as **meaning money,** just as we explain all the other places in which the Torah uses the expression "an eye for an eye" as meaning money. According to Rabbi Yehudah HaNasi, someone who was intent on committing murder and accidentally killed the wrong person is considered guilty of manslaughter and not of premeditated murder. Hence there is no difference between a case in which the men were fighting to the death and a case in which the death of the woman was entirely accidental; in both cases, the Torah requires the woman's killer to pay her heirs a sum of money in compensation. According to this viewpoint, since there is no proof that the woman's assailant was warned that he would be executed, there is no basis for arguing that he should also be regarded as having been warned that he would be lashed. [5]So **what is there to say** according to the viewpoint of Rabbi Yehudah HaNasi? Is it possible to construct a version of Rav Shesha's argument that would apply even according to Rabbi Yehudah HaNasi?

אֶלָּא [6]**Rather,** says the Gemara, we must reject Rav Shesha's source for the rule that monetary penalties take precedence over lashes in cases of assault. But **Rav Ya'akov from Nehar Pekod said in the name of Rava:** It is still possible to advance a similar argument, but it must be based on a different verse. [7]There is a Baraita which states: "The principle that monetary penalties take precedence over lashes in cases of assault **can be inferred from** the following verse (Exodus 21:19), which describes the case of a person who attempts to murder someone and injures him. The verse says that **'if** the injured person **gets up and walks outside on his staff** (i.e., his life is no longer in danger), **then the person who hit him shall be cleared'** from the threat of the death penalty to which he would have been liable if his victim had died, and need only pay damages for his assault." [8]The Baraita notes that this verse appears superfluous: "For **would it enter your mind that** in a case in which the victim survived the attack and is **walking** about **in the marketplace,** his assailant **should be killed?** Surely attempted murder is not subject to the death penalty! [9]**Rather,**

[1]מַתְקִיף לָהּ רַב יַעֲקֹב מִנְּהַר פְּקוֹד: [2]הָנִיחָא לְרַבָּנַן, דְּאָמְרִי "נֶפֶשׁ" מַמָּשׁ. [3]אֶלָּא לְרַבִּי, [4]דְּאָמַר מָמוֹן, [5]מַאי אִיכָּא לְמֵימַר?

[6]אֶלָּא אֲמַר רַב יַעֲקֹב מִנְּהַר פְּקוֹד מִשְּׁמֵיהּ דְּרָבָא: [7]מֵהָכָא: "'אִם יָקוּם וְהִתְהַלֵּךְ בַּחוּץ עַל מִשְׁעַנְתּוֹ, וְנִקָּה הַמַּכֶּה'. [8]וְכִי תַּעֲלֶה עַל דַּעְתְּךָ שֶׁזֶּה מְהַלֵּךְ בַּשּׁוּק וְזֶה נֶהֱרָג? [9]אֶלָּא

LITERAL TRANSLATION

[1]Rav Ya'akov from Nehar Pekod objected: [2]It is well according to the Rabbis, who say [that the word] "life" is [meant] literally. [3]But [according] to Rabbi [Yehudah HaNasi], [4]who said [that it means] money, [5]what is there to say?

[6]Rather, Rav Ya'akov from Nehar Pekod said in the name of Rava: [7][It is derived] from here: "'If he gets up and walks outside on his staff, then he who hit him shall be cleared.' [8]But would it enter your mind that this one walks in the marketplace and that one is killed? [9]Rather,

RASHI

הניחא לרבנן דאמרי — בסנהדרין, ב"אלו הן הנשרפים" (עט,א): נתכוון להרוג את זה והרג את זה — חייב. והאי "ונתת נפש" — ממש קאמר, אית לן למידק ואוקמי קרא בשהתרו בו, ולמילף דאף על גב דאיכא התראה — יענש ממון כשאין שם מיתה. **אלא לרבי דאמר** — התם: נתכוון להרוג את זה והרג את זה אינו נהרג, אלא משלם דמי האשה ליורשיה, אם כן אפשר לאוקמי קרא בשלא התרו בו. ומשום הכי, כי אין אסון משלם דמי ולדות, וכי יש אסון משלם דמי אשה. אבל אתרו ביה — אימא לך לוקה ואינו משלם. **מאי איכא למימר** — מהיכא תיתי חובל בחבירו לתשלומין, ואף כשהתרו בו? **על משענתו** — כדמתרגמינן: "על בוריו", שב לכחו ולאיתנו הראשון.

SAGES

רַב יַעֲקֹב מִנְּהַר פְּקוֹד Rav Ya'akov from Nehar Pekod. A sixth-generation Babylonian Amora, Rabbi Ya'akov was a disciple and colleague of Ravina, but (as the Gemara here indicates) he also transmits teachings in the name of Rava. He was probably the most important Sage in the town of Nehar Pekod, and was responsible for introducing Rabbinic ordinances for the public benefit there.

NOTES

beating by a despotic government is always more frightening than death. Even if the government does not specify that it will beat the person without limit, there are no safeguards preventing the government from continuing the beating for as long as it likes.

TRANSLATION AND COMMENTARY

this verse was written to **teach us that** the assailant is not cleared of the murder charge until his victim is completely out of danger. Therefore the rule is that **we imprison** the assailant, [1] **and if the victim dies, we execute** the assailant, and exempt him from all monetary penalties, since he is subject to the more severe penalty. [2] **And if** the victim **does not die,** the assailant ceases to be threatened with the death penalty but becomes liable to pay damages, as the verse concludes: [3] **'He shall pay for his loss of time and he shall surely heal him.'** In other words, the assailant must pay the injured person's medical expenses and reimburse him for the income he lost while convalescing."

הֵיכִי דָּמֵי [4] Rav Ya'akov now explains how this interpretation of the verse proves that an assailant who injures somebody pays money and is not lashed. **How do we visualize the case?** [5] **If** we are referring to a case where the witnesses **did not warn** the assailant that murder is punishable by death, **why is he executed** if his victim dies later of his injuries? Even if the victim dies immediately, we still cannot execute the killer if he had not been warned! [6] **Rather, it is obvious that** the Torah is referring to a case where the assailant was **warned** that if he killed his intended victim he would be executed, but he disregarded the warning and struck the blow, inflicting an injury that would not kill the victim until later. Hence, when the Torah commanded the man to pay a financial penalty if the victim recovered from the attack, it follows that the Torah was referring to the same case — to a case of assault in which the assailant was warned. [7] Admittedly, he was warned against killing, not against causing injury, **but** it stands to reason that **someone who was warned** that the action he was about to take was subject to **a serious** penalty **is considered warned about** any **lighter** penalties that may also be incurred through this same action. [8] **And yet the Torah said: "He shall pay for his loss of time and he shall surely heal him."** In other words, he must pay a monetary penalty. Thus we see that in the case of assault, monetary penalties take precedence over lashes, even if the assailant was warned that he would be lashed.

מַתְקִיף לָהּ [9] Here, too, **Rav Ashi objected to** Rav Ya'akov's revised version of the argument used by Rav Shesha the son of Rav Idi: Your argument is based on unfounded assumption. [10] **From where do we know that someone who is warned** that the action he is about to take is subject to **a serious** penalty **is considered warned about** any **lighter** penalties that may also be incurred through this same action? [11] **Perhaps it**

מְלַמֵּד שֶׁחוֹבְשִׁין אוֹתוֹ, [1] וְאִי מִית קָטְלִינַן לֵיהּ; [2] וְאִי לָא מִית, [3] 'שִׁבְתּוֹ יִתֵּן וְרַפֹּא יְרַפֵּא'".

[4] הֵיכִי דָּמֵי? [5] אִי דְּלָא אַתְרוּ בֵּיהּ, אַמַּאי מִיקְטִיל? [6] אֶלָּא פְּשִׁיטָא דְּאַתְרוּ בֵּיהּ. [7] וּמוּתְרֶה לְדָבָר חָמוּר מוּתְרֶה לְדָבָר הַקַּל. [8] וְאָמַר רַחֲמָנָא: "שִׁבְתּוֹ יִתֵּן וְרַפֹּא יְרַפֵּא".

[9] מַתְקִיף לָהּ רַב אַשִׁי: [10] מִמַּאי דְּמוּתְרֶה לְדָבָר חָמוּר הָוֵי מוּתְרֶה לְדָבָר הַקַּל? [11] דִּלְמָא

LITERAL TRANSLATION

it teaches [us] that we imprison him, [1] and if he [the victim] dies, we kill him; [2] and if he does not die, [3] 'he shall pay for his loss of time and he shall surely heal him.'"

[4] How do we visualize the case? [5] If they did not warn him, why is he killed? [6] Rather, it is obvious that they warned him. [7] And someone who is warned regarding a serious matter is [considered] warned regarding a light matter. [8] And the Torah (lit., "the Merciful One") said: "He shall pay for his loss of time and he shall surely heal him."

[9] Rav Ashi objected to this: [10] From where [do we know] that someone who is warned regarding a serious matter is [considered] warned for a light matter? [11] Perhaps

RASHI

אלא מלמד שחובשין אותו — לא נאמר מקרא זה אלא ללמדך דהיכא דהכהו ולא מת ונפל למשכב — יחבשו את המכה ההוא בבית האסורין, עד שנראה "אם יקום והתהלך בחוץ", אז "ונקה המכה". מכלל דעד השתא — לא יצא מידי בית דין, אלא נחבש. **ואי מיית קטלינן ליה** — [כיון דאמרת חובשין, מכלל דאי מיית ניזק — קטלינן ליה להאי, דאי לאו לקטלא — למאי חבשינן ליה? **לדבר חמור** — מיתה. **לדבר הקל** — מלקות, ד"לא יוסיף" דחובל ולא מת]. **ואמר רחמנא** — להיכא דלא מת, דאיכא ממון ומלקות — נידון בממון, דכתיב "שבתו יתן".

HALAKHAH

מְלַמֵּד שֶׁחוֹבְשִׁין אוֹתוֹ **It teaches us that we imprison him.** "If someone attacks another person with a stone or with his fists, and the victim does not die immediately, but his injuries appear serious enough to endanger his life, we imprison the assailant until the fate of the victim is determined. If the victim dies of his injuries, we execute the assailant. Even if the victim appears to recover somewhat in the interim and then subsequently succumbs, the assailant is executed. But if the victim recovers completely, the assailant pays the five payments that are imposed on other assailants, and is exempt from the death penalty." (*Rambam, Sefer Nezikin, Hilkhot Rotze'aḥ* 4:3,5.)

TRANSLATION AND COMMENTARY

is not so! [1]Moreover, even **if we say** for the sake of argument **that it *is* so,** your argument is based on another unfounded assumption. [2]**From where do you know that** this man who is being warned considers **death to be a more serious penalty** than lashes? [3]**Perhaps** he considers that **lashes are more serious,** and if he had been warned about the penalty of lashes as well as about the death penalty, he would have refrained from striking the blow that injured the victim! [4]**For Rav said: If,** instead of threatening them with death, Nebuchadnezzar's men **had whipped Ḥananyah, Mishael, and Azaryah** mercilessly, [5]**they would have** been compelled to **worship the idol,** because such torture is worse than death! Thus we see that lashes can be an even more severe punishment than death, and Rav Ya'akov's revised version of Rav Shesha's argument is refuted.

אֲמַר לֵיהּ [6]The Gemara rejects the point just made. **Rav Samma the son of Rav Assi said to Rav Ashi, and some say that Rav Samma the son of Rav Ashi said to Rav Ashi:** [7]**Do you not see the difference between a beating that has a limit,** like the thirty-nine lashes that are inflicted by a Jewish court, **and a beating that has no limit,** like the torture inflicted by tyrants like Nebuchadnezzar? Thus the second part of Rav Ashi's objection is refuted, and Rav Ya'akov's revised version of Rav Shesha's argument stands.

מַתְקִיף לָהּ [8]**Rav Mari** raised another **objection** to Rav Ya'akov's argument: Your entire argument is based on the Baraita's statement that the man guilty of attempted murder is imprisoned pending his execution if the victim dies. But your interpretation of the Torah verse is unwarranted. [9]**From where do you know that** the verse is referring to **an assault** that **was deliberate,** [10]**and** that when the Torah says that the assailant **"shall be cleared,"** after the victim is out of danger, **it is referring** to the penalty of **execution** which is inflicted on someone who deliberately commits murder? [11]**Perhaps** the Torah was referring to an **inadvertent** assailant, who seriously hurt another person through negligence! In such a case, if the victim dies, the killer is not sentenced to death by the court, but is exiled to a city of refuge. [12]**And** if the victim recovers from his injuries, the assailant **"shall be cleared"** of the penalty of **exile,** and becomes liable to pay damages as

לָא הָוֵי! [1]וְאִם תִּמְצָא לוֹמַר הָוֵי, [2]מִמַּאי דְּמִיתָה חֲמוּרָה? [3]דִּלְמָא מַלְקוֹת חָמוּר! [4]דַּאֲמַר רַב: אִילְמָלֵי נַגְדוּהּ לַחֲנַנְיָה מִישָׁאֵל וַעֲזַרְיָה, [5]פָּלְחוּ לְצַלְמָא!

[6]אֲמַר לֵיהּ רַב סַמָּא בְּרֵיהּ דְּרַב אַסִי לְרַב אַשִׁי, וְאָמְרִי לָהּ רַב סַמָּא בְּרֵיהּ דְּרַב אַשִׁי לְרַב אַשִׁי: [7]וְלָא שָׁנֵי לָךְ בֵּין הַכָּאָה שֶׁיֵּשׁ לָהּ קִצְבָּה לְהַכָּאָה שֶׁאֵין לָהּ קִצְבָּה?

[8]מַתְקִיף לָהּ רַב מָרִי: [9]מִמַּאי דִּבְמֵזִיד, [10]וְ"נִקָּה" מִקְּטָלָא? [11]דִּלְמָא בְּשׁוֹגֵג, [12]וְ"נִקָּה" מִגָּלוּת!

LITERAL TRANSLATION

it is not so! [1]And if you say [that] it is so, [2]from where [do you know] that [the] death [penalty] is [more] serious? [3]Perhaps lashes are [more] serious! [4]For Rav said: If they had whipped Ḥananyah, Mishael, and Azaryah, [5]they would have worshipped the idol!

[6]Rav Samma the son of Rav Assi said to Rav Ashi, and some say Rav Samma the son of Rav Ashi [said] to Rav Ashi: [7]But is there no difference to you between a beating that has a limit and a beating that does not have a limit?

[8]Rav Mari objected: [9]From where [do you know] that [the assault was done] deliberately, [10]and "he shall be cleared" [means] from execution? [11]Perhaps [it was done] inadvertently, [12]and "he shall be cleared" [means] from exile!

RASHI

ממאי — דהאי "והכה איש את רעהו" במזיד קא משתעי, והאי "ונקה" דילפינן מיניה חבישה ונקה מקטלא קאמר, דמשמע מינה דאי מיית קטלינן ליה, ועל כרחין בהתרו בו. **דלמא בשוגג** — משתעי, ולא התרו בו. וחבישה לאו לקטלא, "ונקה" נמי לאו לקטלא, אלא מגלות דערי מקלט.

NOTES

דִּלְמָא בְּשׁוֹגֵג Perhaps it was done inadvertently. *Tosafot* asks: How can we possibly explain this verse as referring to an inadvertent blow? The verse requires the assailant to pay the victim's medical expenses and loss of income, whereas the Gemara (*Bava Kamma* 26b) rules that a person who injures another inadvertently must pay the "damage" payment, but not the other four payments (shame, pain, medical expenses, and loss of income). Clearly, then, the verse must be referring to a blow delivered deliberately!

Tosafot answers that "inadvertent" killing is not the same as "inadvertent" wounding. Thus, if a person injures another through extreme negligence, he is liable to pay all five payments, even though a person who kills another in this way is exiled and not executed.

Alternatively, *Tosafot* explains that Rav Mari may have been referring to a case in which the assailant delivered the blow quite deliberately, but had no intention whatsoever of killing his victim. In such a case, the assault is considered deliberate, but the death of the victim would be considered inadvertent.

וְ"נִקָּה" מִגָּלוּת And "he shall be cleared" means from exile. The Torah requires (Numbers 35:9-34) that six cities of refuge be established, three on each side of the Jordan

TRANSLATION AND COMMENTARY

in the case of any other assault, since damages are paid for inadvertent injuries just as they are paid for deliberate injuries. Now, if we interpret the verse in this way, it follows that the injury was entirely accidental. Hence we have no proof that the assailant was warned that he would be executed, and Rav Ya'akov's argument is refuted, because there is no basis for insisting that the assailant is considered to have been warned that he would be lashed. Hence we cannot infer from the case of attempted murder that monetary penalties take precedence over lashes in cases of assault.

קַשְׁיָא [1]The Gemara concludes that Rav Mari's objection **is difficult** to answer.

The Gemara now considers a third solution to its original objection (above, 31b) — that our Mishnah, which rules that a man who rapes his sister must pay a fine, conflicts with the Mishnah in *Makkot*, which rules that he is lashed. The Gemara objected that there is an established Halakhic principle that a person can never be punished both by lashes and by a monetary penalty for the same crime. Therefore the man who rapes his sister should be exempt from paying the fine because he is subject to the more severe penalty of lashes. Why, then, does our Mishnah rule that a man who rapes his sister must pay the fine?

We have seen Ulla's solution to this problem (above, 32a) — that the principle that we do not inflict both lashes and a monetary penalty for the same crime does not teach us which penalty takes precedence; it merely rules out inflicting both penalties for the same offense. Hence we can argue that in those cases in which a monetary penalty is imposed by the Torah — such as in the case of the seduction or rape of a *na'arah* — monetary penalties take precedence over lashes, and the offender is required to pay the money and is exempt from the lashes. According to Ulla, the Mishnah in *Makkot* must be interpreted as dealing with a special case in which the fine imposed by the Torah on rapists and seducers (as well as the other relevant monetary penalties) is not applicable for technical reasons (because the victim was an adult, or an orphan who was seduced), whereas our Mishnah refers to all other cases.

By contrast, Rabbi Yoḥanan argued (above, 32b) that lashes take precedence over monetary payments, just as the death penalty (or excision, according to Rabbi Neḥunya ben Hakkanah) takes precedence over monetary payments, but only if the lashes are actually inflicted. According to this viewpoint, the Mishnah in *Makkot*, which rules that lashes are inflicted, needs no special explanation, but our Mishnah, which rules that a fine is paid, must be explained as referring to a case in which there was a technical legal barrier preventing lashes from being inflicted, such as where the assailant was not warned.

[1]קַשְׁיָא.

LITERAL TRANSLATION

[1]It is difficult.

RASHI

וחבישה דילפינן מינה לגלות קאמר, ומשום הכי כי נקה מגלות — ישלם ממון. אבל היכא דאתרו ביה, אימא לך דכי לא מיית — לוקה ואינו משלם. ריש לקיש מהדר אשינויא דרומיא דרמינן ברים שמעתין מתניתין דמכות אדכתובות.

NOTES

River, in central, easily accessible locations. The Torah permits, and even commands, the relatives of a murdered person to kill the murderer. If the killing was deliberate, and the murderer was convicted in court and sentenced to death, a relative of the victim is invited to serve as executioner. If the killing was inadvertent, or the killer cannot be executed because of a legal technicality, the relative is permitted to kill him wherever he finds him. But if the inadvertent killer flees to one of the six cities of refuge, he must not be harmed, so long as he remains in the city. If he leaves the city, however, the relative may kill him with impunity. The killer's exile lasts until the death of the High Priest, at which time he is considered to have atoned for his sin, and he may return to his home without fear of retribution. The protection of the city of refuge extends only to inadvertent killing, but not to murder, even if the murderer was not executed because of legal technicalities. In such situations, the relative has the right to kill the murderer wherever he finds him, even after the High Priest dies, and the murderer's sole option is to live the life of a fugitive.

Shittah Mekubbetzet asks: Not every inadvertent killer goes into exile in a city of refuge. If the death was completely unforeseeable, the unintentional killer is entirely exempt; by contrast, if he deliberately endangered other people, he is not permitted to go into exile in the city of refuge. In the case described in the Torah, the assailant was deliberately endangering the other person. Why, then, is he allowed to go into exile?

Shittah Mekubbetzet answers that we can explain the verse as referring to a case in which a blow intended for one person hit another (see also *Ritva*). In such a case, the death of the second person would be considered a foreseeable accident that is subject to exile in a city of refuge.

Tosafot asks: How could the assailant discussed by the Gemara here possibly be sent into exile? The verse (Exodus 21:19) refers to a person who was seriously injured but who did not die until some time later. But the Gemara (*Gittin* 70b) rules that inadvertent killers are exiled only if the death took place immediately.

Tosafot answers that the passage in *Gittin* refers to situations in which there is a remote chance that other factors hastened the injured person's death, but if it is clear that no other factors were involved, the killer is exiled (see also *Rambam* and *Ra'avad*, *Hilkhot Rotze'aḥ* 5:2). Further explanations were given by other Rishonim.

[1]רֵישׁ לָקִישׁ אֲמַר: הָא מַנִּי? [2]רַבִּי מֵאִיר הִיא, דְּאָמַר: [3]לוֹקֶה וּמְשַׁלֵּם.

[4]אִי רַבִּי מֵאִיר, [5]אֲפִילוּ בִּתּוֹ נַמִי!

LITERAL TRANSLATION

[1]Resh Lakish said: Whose [opinion] is this? [2]It is [the opinion of] Rabbi Meir, who said: [3]He is lashed and he pays.

[4]If it is Rabbi Meir's [opinion], [5]it should even [apply in the case of] his daughter too!

RASHI

הא מני — מתניתין, דקתני בא על אחותו נותן קנס — רבי מאיר היא דאמר לעיל: לוקה ומשלם, שלא השם המביאו לידי מכות מביאו לידי תשלומין. אפילו בתו נמי — דמיקטיל עלה, לישלם. דהא לא סבירא ליה לרבי מאיר דפטור משום דרבה מיניה, ואמאי תנן מתניתין: הבא על בתו פטור מן הקנס?

TRANSLATION AND COMMENTARY

Although Ulla and Rabbi Yoḥanan disagree about whether lashes take precedence over monetary penalties or vice versa, they agree that a person can never be punished by both penalties for the same offense. The Gemara will now consider a third solution to this problem, that of Resh Lakish, who maintains that lashes take precedence over monetary payments even if the lashes are not inflicted in practice. According to this viewpoint, the Mishnah in *Makkot*, which rules that lashes are inflicted, needs no special explanation, but there is a clear contradiction between our Mishnah, which rules that a fine is paid, and the established principle that a person can never be punished by lashes *and* a monetary penalty for the same crime. Hence we must conclude that the author of our Mishnah does not accept this principle.

רֵישׁ לָקִישׁ אֲמַר [1]**Resh Lakish said: Who is** the author of our Mishnah? [2]**It is Rabbi Meir, who** disagrees with our accepted principle and **says:** Someone who commits an offense punishable by lashes is not thereby exempt from any monetary penalty that he may have incurred at the same time. [3]In such a case, both penalties are imposed, so that **he is lashed and pays** the monetary penalty as well.

Rabbi Meir's viewpoint was cited earlier (above, 32b), in connection with conspiring witnesses who testified that the defendant owed the plaintiff two hundred zuz, and who were then found to have testified falsely. Rabbi Meir ruled that the witnesses must pay the defendant two hundred zuz, in accordance with the law that conspiring witnesses are punished by the same punishment they sought to inflict on the defendant (Deuteronomy 19:19), and that they are also lashed for violating the negative commandment against testifying falsely (Exodus 20:13), because these two penalties are derived from different verses. The Sages, however, ruled that since the conspiring witnesses must pay the defendant two hundred zuz, they are exempt from lashes, in accordance with the principle that a person can never be punished by both lashes and a monetary penalty for the same crime. (The Halakhah follows the Sages.)

Thus we see that, according to Rabbi Meir, if someone commits two separate offenses at the same time, one of which is subject to lashes and the other to a monetary penalty, both penalties are imposed. Now, a man who seduces or rapes his sister is lashed on the authority of the verse (Leviticus 18:9) forbidding incest, and he is required to pay a fine on the authority of the verses (Deuteronomy 22:29 and Exodus 22:16) that prescribe this penalty if an unmarried virgin *na'arah* is violated. It follows, therefore, that Rabbi Meir would maintain that a man who seduces or rapes his sister while she is an unmarried virgin *na'arah* should suffer both penalties.

That this is the viewpoint of Rabbi Meir is indisputable. Resh Lakish's contribution is to argue that the contradiction between our Mishnah and the Mishnah in *Makkot* can be resolved by explaining that our Mishnah reflects the (rejected) view of Rabbi Meir. According to Resh Lakish, it is unnecessary to make a forced interpretation of our Mishnah, as Rabbi Yoḥanan did, or of the Mishnah in *Makkot*, as Ulla did. Instead, both Mishnayot are to be taken literally, as referring to all cases, but our Mishnah's ruling reflects the viewpoint of Rabbi Meir.

אִי רַבִּי מֵאִיר [4]Unfortunately, says the Gemara, this explanation is not without its own problems. For **if** our Mishnah reflects **the viewpoint of Rabbi Meir,** [5]the fine imposed by our Mishnah **should apply even to** a man who rapes **his daughter!** Rabbi Meir's opinion — that both penalties apply when the Biblical source imposing the monetary penalty is a different verse from the source imposing the lashes — seems to

NOTES

אִי רַבִּי מֵאִיר אֲפִילוּ בִּתּוֹ נַמִי **If it is Rabbi Meir's opinion, it should even apply in the case of his daughter too!** The Gemara objects to Resh Lakish's attempt to explain *our* Mishnah as reflecting the view of Rabbi Meir, who maintains that the more severe penalty does not exempt from payment, because the author of the *next* Mishnah clearly maintains that a person who is subject to a more severe penalty is indeed exempt from payment. Why can we not say that the two Mishnayot reflect the views of different Tannaim?

Shittah Mekubbetzet explains that the Gemara based its inference on the next Mishnah because that Mishnah

TRANSLATION AND COMMENTARY

undermine the entire concept of exempting from a less severe penalty a person who is subject to a more severe penalty. Thus, according to Rabbi Meir, even an offender who is subject to the death penalty should also be required to pay damages if the Biblical source imposing the monetary penalty is a different verse from the source imposing the death penalty. But the author of our Mishnah is clearly of the opinion that an offender who is subject to the death penalty is exempt from paying damages. For the following Mishnah rules (below, 36b) that a man who rapes or seduces his daughter is exempt from paying the fine, because a man who commits incest with his *daughter* is subject to the death penalty and is therefore exempt from paying damages for the same act, whereas a man who commits incest with his *sister* is subject only to excision, and is not exempt from paying damages. Hence Rabbi Meir cannot have been the author of our Mishnah, as Resh Lakish tried to explain.

וְכִי תֵּימָא [1] **And**, continues the Gemara, there is no problem **if you say that Rabbi Meir maintains that** an offender who commits two separate offenses at the same time, one of which is subject to lashes and the other to a monetary penalty, is punished by both penalties, so that **he is lashed and he pays** the monetary penalty as well, [2] **but** Rabbi Meir **does not maintain that** an offender who is subject to the death penalty and to a monetary penalty is punished by both penalties, with the result that **he dies and pays** the monetary penalty as well. [3] **But**, asks the Gemara, is it true that Rabbi Meir disagrees only about lashes and does **not** apply his argument to a person who is subject to the death penalty? [4] **Surely** there is evidence that Rabbi Meir has the same opinion in a case involving the death penalty, as **was taught** in a Baraita dealing with a person who stole an ox or a sheep and slaughtered it. The Torah (Exodus 21:37 - 22:3) requires that an ordinary thief must pay double compensation (by returning the stolen object plus another object of equivalent value), but a thief who stole an ox or a sheep and slaughtered it or sold it must pay four times the value of the sheep or five times the value of the ox. Now, says the Baraita, **"if** a thief **stole** an ox or a sheep **and slaughtered** it **on Shabbat,** he becomes liable to pay the additional fine for the ox or the sheep when he slaughters it, and at that same moment he becomes subject to the death penalty, because slaughtering an animal is a violation of the Shabbat laws. Similarly, if the thief **stole** an ox or a sheep **and slaughtered** it **for idol worship**, he also becomes liable to pay the additional fine for the ox or the sheep at the same moment he becomes subject to the death penalty, because offering a sacrifice to an idol is an offense punishable by death. Similarly, if the thief **stole and slaughtered an ox that is** sentenced **to be stoned,** he should be exempt from payment. The Torah commands that an ox that has killed a human being must be stoned to death (Exodus 21:28). Moreover, no use or pleasure may be derived from it, even if it dies or is killed in some other way before it can be stoned. Thus the ox is effectively valueless, and a thief who steals and slaughters such an ox has caused its owner no damage, and he should be exempt from paying any damages at all. [5] Nevertheless **he** must **pay the fourfold and fivefold payments** normally paid by a thief

[1] וְכִי תֵּימָא רַבִּי מֵאִיר לוֹקֶה וּמְשַׁלֵּם אִית לֵיהּ, [2] מֵת וּמְשַׁלֵּם לֵית לֵיהּ, [3] וְלָא? [4] וְהָתַנְיָא: "גָּנַב וְטָבַח בְּשַׁבָּת, גָּנַב וְטָבַח לַעֲבוֹדָה זָרָה, גָּנַב שׁוֹר הַנִּסְקָל וּטְבָחוֹ, [5] מְשַׁלֵּם תַּשְׁלוּמֵי

LITERAL TRANSLATION

[1] And if you say [that] Rabbi Meir maintains [that] he is lashed and he pays, [2] [but] does not maintain [that] he dies and pays, [3] but [does he] not? [4] But surely it was taught: "[If] he stole and slaughtered on Shabbat, [or] he stole and slaughtered for idol worship, [or] he stole an ox that is to be stoned and slaughtered it, [5] he pays the

RASHI

וטבח בשבת – איכא חיוב מיתה, וכן לעבודה זרה. **שור הנסקל** – לקמן פריך: הא לא שוה מידי.

CONCEPTS

שׁוֹר הַנִּסְקָל An ox that is to be stoned. An ox that has killed a person must be stoned to death, regardless of whether the ox had previously behaved maliciously or whether the victim was an adult, a child, or a Canaanite slave. It is forbidden to derive any benefit from an ox that has been stoned, not only after it has been killed, but from the moment the court, a tribunal of twenty-three members, has delivered its verdict. The term שׁוֹר הַנִּסְקָל is used for any domesticated or undomesticated animal that has killed someone, whether the animal be large or small, or even a bird.

תַּשְׁלוּמֵי אַרְבָּעָה וַחֲמִשָּׁה The fourfold or fivefold payments. A person who steals and then sells or slaughters an ox is obligated to reimburse its owner according to a rate of five times the value of the stolen animal. If the stolen animal is a sheep, the restitution is four times the animal's worth (Exodus 21:37). The Sages offered various explanations as to why the thief must pay more for an ox than for a sheep: (1) The theft of an ox causes additional loss to its owner, who cannot use it for work in plowing. (2) Someone who steals a sheep carries it on his shoulders, and at least suffers fatigue while committing the crime. (3) Someone who steals an ox, which is large and difficult to lead away and hide, may be assumed to be a habitual thief.

NOTES

explicitly states that a man who rapes his daughter is exempt from monetary penalties because he is subject to the death penalty. However, our Mishnah also makes the same point, albeit indirectly, because it concludes that a man who rapes his sister is not exempt.

In addition, it should be noted that the division of the Mishnah into tractates and chapters is authoritative, but the division of chapters into individual Mishnayot is arbitrary, and was largely done by the editors of the Talmud to facilitate the study of the Oral Law. It is, therefore, quite common for Mishnayot in different tractates to reflect different views, and this sometimes occurs even in different chapters in the same tractate. But Mishnayot in the same chapter do not normally conflict with each other.

HALAKHAH

גָּנַב וְטָבַח בְּשַׁבָּת If he stole and slaughtered on Shabbat. "If a thief stole an ox or a sheep and slaughtered it on Shabbat, or slaughtered it for idol worship, he is exempt from paying the fourfold and fivefold payments normally imposed on a thief who slaughters a stolen ox or sheep, because he is subject to the death penalty for violating Shabbat or for idolatry. This law applies even if the death penalty is not imposed for technical reasons.

TRANSLATION AND COMMENTARY

who steals and slaughters a sheep or an ox. [1]**These are the words of Rabbi Meir,** who is apparently of the opinion that someone who is subject to the death penalty (as in the cases of Shabbat and idolatry) must still pay damages. [2]**But the Sages** disagree with Rabbi Meir and **exempt** the thief from the additional payments (in the cases of Shabbat and idolatry) and from all payments (in the case of the ox that is condemned to be stoned), because they maintain that both someone who is subject to a more severe penalty, and also someone who steals a worthless object, are exempt from payment." We learn from this Baraita that Rabbi Meir maintains that the imposition of the death penalty does not exempt from monetary payments. Hence Rabbi Meir cannot have been the author of our Mishnah, as Resh Lakish proposed.

אַרְבָּעָה וַחֲמִשָּׁה. [1]דִּבְרֵי רַבִּי מֵאִיר. [2]וַחֲכָמִים פּוֹטְרִין״.
[3]הָא אִיתְּמַר עֲלָהּ, [4]אָמַר רַבִּי יַעֲקֹב אָמַר רַבִּי יוֹחָנָן, וְאָמְרִי לָהּ אָמַר רַבִּי יִרְמְיָה אָמַר רַבִּי שִׁמְעוֹן בֶּן לָקִישׁ: [5]רַבִּי אָבִין וְרַבִּי אִילְעָא וְכָל חֲבוּרָתָא מִשְּׁמֵיהּ דְּרַבִּי יוֹחָנָן אָמְרִי: [6]בְּטוֹבֵחַ עַל יְדֵי אַחֵר.
[7]וְכִי זֶה חוֹטֵא וְזֶה מִתְחַיֵּיב?

LITERAL TRANSLATION

fourfold and fivefold payments. [1][These are] the words of Rabbi Meir. [2]But the Sages exempt [him]."
[3]Surely it was stated concerning it: [4]Rabbi Ya'akov said in the name of Rabbi Yoḥanan, and some say Rabbi Yirmeyah said in the name of Rabbi Shimon ben Lakish: [5]Rabbi Avin and Rabbi Il'a and the whole group [of Sages] said in the name of Rabbi Yoḥanan: [6][It is] where he slaughters by the hands of another.
[7]But can this one sin and that one be liable?

RASHI

בטובח על ידי אחר — הגנב צוה לשלוחו לשחוט. **וכי** — שליח חוטא, ושולח מתחייב קנס דארבעה וחמשה? והא קיימא לן בקדושין (מב,ב): אין שליח לדבר עבירה. מכירה אי אפשר אלא על ידי אחר, שהלוקח לוקחו ממנו.

הָא אִיתְּמַר עֲלָהּ [3]The Gemara rejects this argument: **Surely** an authoritative explanation **was given** that the dispute in this Baraita (in the cases of Shabbat and idolatry) is not about the rule that an offender who is subject to the death penalty is exempt from monetary payment. [4]**Rabbi Ya'akov said in the name of Rabbi Yoḥanan, and some say that Rabbi Yirmeyah said in the name of Rabbi Shimon ben Lakish,** [5]that **Rabbi Avin and Rabbi Il'a and the whole group of Sages said in the name of Rabbi Yoḥanan:** [6]The Baraita **is** referring to a case **where** the thief who stole the ox or the sheep did not slaughter it himself, but had it **slaughtered by someone else,** and it was his agent who slaughtered it on Shabbat or for idol worship. In such a case, the agent is subject to execution, but the thief is not exempt from payment because of the more severe penalty, since he did not personally violate Shabbat or worship an idol.

According to this interpretation of the Baraita, there is no proof that Rabbi Meir applies his view regarding lashes to cases of the death penalty as well. It is possible that Rabbi Meir agrees that the death penalty exempts from payment, even though he maintains that lashes are inflicted together with a monetary penalty. Hence we can also accept Resh Lakish's explanation that our Mishnah, which rules that the fine must be paid by rapists who are lashed but not by rapists who are executed, reflects the view of Rabbi Meir. It is also possible to accept Resh Lakish's resolution of the contradiction between our Mishnah and the Mishnah in *Makkot*, and to explain that our Mishnah reflects the (rejected) view of Rabbi Meir. However, these conclusions are tenable only if we accept the Amoraim's explanation that the Baraita is referring to a case in which the thief instructed a butcher to slaughter the animal for him.

וְכִי זֶה חוֹטֵא [7]The Gemara now considers the explanation of the Amoraim in detail. There are several problems with it. Firstly, the Amoraim explained that the Baraita was referring to a case in which a thief stole an ox or a sheep and told a butcher to slaughter it, at which point the thief became liable to pay fourfold and fivefold damages. **But** how could the thief have become liable to pay because of the actions of the butcher? **Can one** person **sin and another** person **be liable?** According to an accepted Halakhic principle, there is no such thing as an agent for transgression (אֵין שָׁלִיחַ לִדְבַר עֲבֵירָה). In other words, if one person orders another to commit a sin for him, the actual perpetrator of the transgression is liable for all penalties, and the person issuing the command is exempt. Now, in this Baraita, as explained by the Amoraim, the thief ordered the butcher to slaughter the sheep or the ox for him in violation of the law,

TERMINOLOGY

הָא אִיתְּמַר עֲלָהּ **Surely it was stated concerning it.** The Talmud uses this expression to introduce an Amoraic statement reinterpreting a Tannaitic source, in order to solve problems arising from assumptions previously made in connection with it: "Now surely it was stated by the Amoraim as follows with regard to this Mishnah or Baraita...."

SAGES

רַבִּי יַעֲקֹב **Rabbi Ya'akov.** A third-generation Amora, Rabbi Ya'akov immigrated to Eretz Israel from Babylonia, studied under Rabbi Yoḥanan, and later returned to Babylonia. In his youth in Babylonia, he was a disciple of Rav Yehudah and Rav Ḥisda. His closest colleague was Rabbi Yirmeyah, and his most distinguished disciple was Rabbi Yirmeyah bar Taḥlifa.

רַבִּי יִרְמְיָה **Rabbi Yirmeyah.** An Amora of the third and fourth generations. See *Ketubot,* Part II, p. 231.

HALAKHAH

"If the thief did not personally slaughter the animal, but gave it to a butcher, *Rambam* rules that the thief is liable to pay the fourfold and fivefold payments, following the viewpoint of Rabbi Meir in the Baraita, as explained by the Amoraim. *Rosh*, however, rules that he is exempt, following the Sages. *Bet Yosef* explains that the Gemara attributes the opinion of the Sages to Rabbi Yoḥanan HaSandlar, whose view was rejected by the Halakhah in the view of *Rambam*, and accepted according to *Rosh*." (*Rambam*, *Sefer Nezikin*, *Hilkhot Genevah* 3:3,6; *Tur*, *Ḥoshen Mishpat* 350.)

SAGES

דְּבֵי רַבִּי יִשְׁמָעֵאל The School of Rabbi Yishmael. See *Ketubot,* Part I, p. 54.

חִזְקִיָּה Ḥizkiyah. See *Ketubot,* Part II, p. 225.

TRANSLATION AND COMMENTARY

and yet Rabbi Meir rules that it is the thief, and not the butcher, who is liable to pay the fourfold and fivefold penalties. How can this be so?

אָמַר רָבָא [1]The Gemara answers that the law regarding a thief who slaughters an ox or a sheep is exceptional, because the Torah holds the thief liable, even if he did not personally slaughter the animal. The Gemara offers three possible Biblical sources for this idea. **Rava said: The Torah said** about a thief who stole an ox or a sheep that **"he slaughtered it or sold it."** By placing the cases of slaughtering and selling in juxtaposition, the Torah is telling us that the laws in both cases are similar. [2]Thus, **just as** the Torah is referring to **a sale involving someone else,** because it is impossible to sell something without a buyer, [3]**so too** is the Torah referring to **slaughtering that involves someone else.** The Torah did not insist that the thief must slaughter the animal himself. Even if he gives it to a butcher to slaughter, he is still liable.

דְּבֵי רַבִּי יִשְׁמָעֵאל תָּנָא [4]A second Scriptural source was offered by **the School of Rabbi Yishmael. They taught** in a Baraita that **"the** superfluous **word 'or'** [או], appearing in the verse between the word 'slaughtered' and the word 'sold,' **was** added **to include** the case of an animal that was slaughtered by **an agent."**

דְּבֵי חִזְקִיָּה תָּנָא [5]A third Scriptural source was offered by **the School of Ḥizkiyah. They taught** that "the superfluous **word 'for'** (תַּחַת), that appears twice in this verse ('for the ox' and 'for the sheep'), **was** added **to include** the case of an animal that was slaughtered by **an agent.**

These three opinions differ only with regard to the source of this law in the Torah, but according to all of them the case of the thief who stole an ox or a sheep and gave it to another person to slaughter is exceptional, and the thief is liable for the actions of his agent. Hence our objection to the Amoraim's explanation of the Baraita is invalid.

[1]אָמַר רָבָא: אָמַר רַחֲמָנָא: ״וּטְבָחוֹ אוֹ מְכָרוֹ״. [2]מַה מְּכִירָה עַל יְדֵי אַחֵר, [3]אַף טְבִיחָה עַל יְדֵי אַחֵר.
[4]דְּבֵי רַבִּי יִשְׁמָעֵאל תָּנָא: ״׳אוֹ׳ לְרַבּוֹת אֶת הַשָּׁלִיחַ״.
[5]דְּבֵי חִזְקִיָּה תָּנָא: ״׳תַּחַת׳ לְרַבּוֹת אֶת הַשָּׁלִיחַ״.

LITERAL TRANSLATION

[1]Rava said: The Torah said: "And he slaughtered it or sold it." [2]Just as a sale is by the hand of another, [3]so too is slaughtering by the hand of another.

[4]In the School of Rabbi Yishmael it was taught: "[The word] 'or' is to include an agent."

[5]In the School of Ḥizkiyah it was taught: "[The word] 'for' is to include an agent."

RASHI

תחת השור – מלי למכתב ״ישלם בשור״.

NOTES

אָמַר רָבָא: אָמַר רַחֲמָנָא: וּטְבָחוֹ אוֹ מְכָרוֹ Rava said: The Torah said: "And he slaughtered it or sold it." *Tosafot* (*Bava Kamma* 71a) explains that the disagreement here between the schools of Rabbi Yishmael and Ḥizkiyah revolves around a Tannaitic dispute (*Bava Metzia* 94b) as to whether or not the word "or" is considered superfluous in cases like this. According to Rabbi Yoshiyah, were it not for the word "or," we would have understood the Torah to be teaching us that the thief is not liable unless he both sells and slaughters the animal, whereas Rabbi Yonatan maintains that lists of terms like these are assumed to be independent, unless the Torah specifies that they are to be read together. *Tosafot* explains that the School of Rabbi Yishmael, which derives the law of the agent from the word "or," follows Rabbi Yonatan, whereas the School of Ḥizkiyah follows Rabbi Yoshiyah, who maintains that the word "or" is needed to teach us that the two acts (slaughtering and selling) are treated separately.

Hafla'ah asks: Rabbi Yishmael was a late Tanna, and Ḥizkiyah an early Amora, and they both cited ancient traditions in the form of Baraitot. Why did Rava, a late Amora, need to offer his own source? Why did he not simply accept one of theirs?

Bet Ya'akov answers that Rava's exegesis was intended to supplement the two earlier Baraitot rather than to replace them. We need two Scriptural sources in order to teach us that the thief is liable both where the butcher was a legally competent adult who was fit to be an agent, as well as where the butcher was a person who was not fit to be an agent, such as a minor.

״אוֹ״ לְרַבּוֹת אֶת הַשָּׁלִיחַ The word "or" is to include an agent. *Shittah Mekubbetzet* explains that the Torah could have used the more customary conjunction "and," which is often used in the Torah in place of "or," and is written in

HALAKHAH

אַף טְבִיחָה עַל יְדֵי אַחֵר So too is slaughtering by the hand of another. "If a thief stole an ox or a sheep and did not sell or slaughter it himself, but rather gave it to an agent who sold it for him, or gave it to a butcher who slaughtered it for him, the thief is liable to pay the fourfold and fivefold payments normally imposed on a thief who sells or slaughters a stolen ox or sheep. This ruling does not conform to the principle that there is no agency for transgression, because this law is a special case, in which the Torah explicitly commanded that the thief be liable for the deeds of his agent," following the exegetical arguments in our Gemara. (*Rambam, Sefer Nezikin, Hilkhot Genevah* 2:10.)

TRANSLATION AND COMMENTARY

מַתְקִיף לָהּ [1] **Mar Zutra** raised another **objection to** the interpretation of the Baraita given by the Amoraim. According to this interpretation, Rabbi Meir agrees that death is a more severe penalty that exempts from payment. Hence it follows that if the thief had himself slaughtered the ox or the sheep on Shabbat or had slaughtered it for idolatrous purposes, he would have been exempt. But since it was the butcher and not the thief who slaughtered the animal, the penalty for violating Shabbat or for idolatry is inflicted on the butcher, and the liability for damages is imposed on the thief. Since the thief is not subject to the more severe penalty, he must pay the money. It would seem, then, that the thief is more liable if he gives the animal to a butcher to slaughter than if he slaughters it himself. [2] But **is it possible that, if** the thief **were to do** the deed **himself, he would not be liable,** [3] **but if his agent does it,** the thief **is liable?** Granted that in this exceptional case the thief is responsible for the deeds of his agent, but should the thief be more liable for the deeds of his agent than for his own deeds?

אִיהוּ לָאו [4] The Gemara answers: The reason the thief **is exempt** when he slaughters the animal himself is **not because he is not liable,** [5] **but because he is subject to a greater penalty.** In theory, the thief is just as responsible for his own deeds as for his agent's. It is just that, in practice, he cannot be required to pay the fine if he committed a capital offense at the same time. However, if the animal was slaughtered by his agent, this consideration does not apply, because the thief is not liable for the agent's violation of Shabbat or for his act of idolatry. Hence the thief can be required to pay damages.

אִי בְּטוֹבֵחַ [6] The Gemara now raises another objection to the interpretation of the Baraita given by the Amoraim: According to our original understanding of the Baraita, the disagreement between Rabbi Meir and the Sages was over the principle that an offender who is subject to a more severe penalty is exempt from monetary payments. But **if** the Baraita **is** referring to a case **where** the thief **slaughtered** the animal **by means of an agent,** as explained by the Amoraim, Rabbi Meir's ruling is correct, because it is clear that the thief cannot be rendered exempt from payment by the more severe penalty imposed on his agent. [7] So **what is the reasoning of the Rabbis who** disagree with Rabbi Meir and **exempt** the thief from payment if his agent slaughters the animal on Shabbat or for idolatrous purposes?

[1] מַתְקִיף לָהּ מָר זוּטְרָא: [2] מִי אִיכָּא מִידֵי דְּאִילּוּ עֲבַד אִיהוּ לָא מִיחַיַּיב, [3] וְעָבֵיד שָׁלִיחַ וּמִחַיַּיב?

[4] אִיהוּ לָאו מִשּׁוּם דְּלָא מִיחַיַּיב, [5] אֶלָּא מִשּׁוּם דְּקָם לֵיהּ בִּדְרַבָּה מִינֵּיהּ.

[6] אִי בְּטוֹבֵחַ עַל יְדֵי אַחֵר, [7] מַאי טַעֲמַיְיהוּ דְּרַבָּנַן דְּפָטְרִי?

LITERAL TRANSLATION

[1] Mar Zutra objected to this: [2] Is there anything that if he were to do [it] himself he would not be liable, [3] and [if] an agent does [it] he is liable?

[4] He himself [is exempt] not because he is not liable, [5] but because he is subject to a greater [penalty] than it.

[6] If it is where he slaughters by the agency of another, [7] what is the reasoning of the Rabbis that they exempt [him]?

RASHI

עבד איהו לא מיחייב – דהא מיקטיל. **לאו משום דלא מיחייב הוא** – דחיובא רמיא עליה, אלא משום דקם ליה בדרבה מיניה.

SAGES

מָר זוּטְרָא Mar Zutra. A colleague of Rav Ashi, Mar Zutra was one of the leading Sages of his generation, and his teachers, Rav Pappa and Rav Naḥman bar Yitzḥak, accepted him as their equal.
Apart from his greatness in Halakhah and Aggadah, Mar Zutra was noted as a preacher, and his sermons are cited throughout the Talmud. He apparently held an official position as scholar-in-residence and preacher in the Exilarch's house. In his old age, he was appointed head of the Pumbedita Yeshivah.
Meetings between Mar Zutra, Amemar, and Rav Ashi are frequently mentioned in the Talmud, and some of these meetings may well have been formal conferences of the leaders of Babylonian Jewry of that generation.

NOTES

Hebrew as a prefix of a single letter, vav. But instead, the Torah used "or," which is a separate word in Hebrew (או). Hence we can infer that the Torah was teaching us indirectly that we should include an additional case — that of an agent.

מַאי טַעֲמַיְיהוּ דְּרַבָּנַן What is the reasoning of the Rabbis? According to our original understanding of the Baraita, the thief slaughtered the animal himself, and the dispute between Rabbi Meir and the Rabbis was about whether or not a person who is subject to a more severe penalty must pay damages. But according to the Amoraim's explanation of the Baraita, everyone agrees that a person who is subject to the more severe penalty need not pay damages, and the Baraita is referring to a special case in which the more severe penalty was incurred by the butcher and the payment of damages by the thief. Hence the Gemara objects that there is no room for any dispute, because it is obvious that the more severe penalty imposed on the butcher cannot possibly exempt the thief from payment. What, then, is the reasoning of the Rabbis who rule that the thief is exempt?

The Rishonim ask: Earlier the Gemara raised an objection to the Amoraim's explanation of the Baraita, arguing that the thief should not be liable for the deeds of the butcher, because of the principle that there is no agency for transgression. And the Gemara answered that the case of a thief who stole an ox or a sheep is an exception to this general rule, and it then presented three exegetical arguments. Why does the Gemara not say that this is the issue in dispute between the Rabbis and Rabbi Meir? Perhaps the Rabbis reject the three exegetical arguments and maintain that the thief is not liable for the deeds of his agent!

Ra'ah answers that the dispute in the Baraita clearly revolves around Shabbat and idolatry. According to our original understanding of the Baraita, this makes sense, because the Rabbis exempted the thief from payment

[1] מַאן חֲכָמִים? [34A] [2] רַבִּי שִׁמְעוֹן הִיא, דְּאָמַר: [3] שְׁחִיטָה שֶׁאֵינָהּ רְאוּיָה לֹא שְׁמָהּ שְׁחִיטָה.

LITERAL TRANSLATION

[1] Who are the Sages? [34A] [2] It is Rabbi Shimon, who said: [3] Slaughtering that is not fit is not considered (lit., "its name is not") slaughtering.

RASHI

רבי שמעון — בפרק ״מרובה״ וב״כסוי הדם״ וב״אותו ואת בנו״.

TRANSLATION AND COMMENTARY

מַאן חֲכָמִים [1] The Gemara answers: According to the interpretation given by the Amoraim, the disagreement between Rabbi Meir and the Sages has nothing to do with the principle that an offender who is subject to a more severe penalty is exempt from monetary payments, because it is clear that the thief cannot be exempted from payment by the more severe penalty imposed on his agent. In fact, the disagreement is over the law that applies when a thief steals an ox or a sheep and has it slaughtered in an invalid way (such as on Shabbat, or for idol worship). There is a dispute between Rabbi Meir and Rabbi Shimon on this question (*Ḥullin* 85a). Rabbi Meir in the Baraita is expressing his own opinion, that a thief who slaughters an ox or a sheep in this way is liable. And **who are the Sages** who disagree with Rabbi Meir? Whose opinion do they reflect? [34A] [2] They reflect the opinion of **Rabbi Shimon, who** disagreed with Rabbi Meir and **said:** A thief who steals an ox or a sheep and has it slaughtered in an invalid way is exempt from paying the fourfold and fivefold penalty, [3] because **slaughtering that** does **not** render the meat **fit** to be eaten **is not considered slaughtering.** According to Rabbi Shimon, the term "slaughtering" refers specifically to slaughtering that makes the meat kosher, whereas according to Rabbi Meir, it refers to any slaughtering that was done in accordance with the laws of Jewish ritual slaughter, even if the animal was not kosher for some other reason. According to Rabbi Shimon, the Torah imposed the fourfold and fivefold penalty only if the thief had the animal slaughtered in a way that made it fit to be eaten, whereas Rabbi Meir is of the opinion that the law applies whenever the act of slaughtering itself was done properly. The Baraita can thus be explained as follows: The Rabbis, who reflect the opinion of Rabbi Shimon, exempt the thief from payment if the animal was slaughtered on Shabbat or for idol worship, or if the animal was an ox that had been sentenced to be stoned, because an animal slaughtered under these circumstances must not be eaten, regardless of how the slaughtering was done. By contrast, Rabbi Meir's statement reflects his own viewpoint, according to which the thief is liable in all cases.

NOTES

because of the death penalty associated with these transgressions. Likewise, according to the Gemara's conclusion that the Rabbis exempted the thief from payment because they maintain that he is not liable for invalid slaughtering, it also makes sense for the Baraita to refer to Shabbat and to idol worship, because slaughtering an animal either on Shabbat or as an act of idolatry renders the animal non-kosher. But if the Rabbis were to exempt the thief from payment because of the principle that there is no agency for transgression, there would be no point in telling us that the animal was slaughtered on Shabbat or for idol worship, since the same law would apply even if the thief's agent slaughtered the animal on a weekday (see also *Tosafot* and *Rosh*).

שְׁחִיטָה שֶׁאֵינָהּ רְאוּיָה Slaughtering that is not fit. There is a Tannaitic dispute between Rabbi Meir and Rabbi Shimon regarding several verses in the Torah in which it is mentioned that an animal was slaughtered (and the Hebrew root שחט or טבח is used). According to all opinions, the Torah is referring specifically to an animal that was slaughtered in accordance with the laws of Jewish ritual slaughter, but if the animal was killed in some other way, the law does not apply. A question arises, however, when an animal slaughtered in accordance with the laws of Jewish ritual slaughter was not kosher for some other reason (for example, where the animal had a physical defect, such as a punctured lung, that rendered it *terefah*). According to Rabbi Shimon, the term "slaughtering" refers only to slaughtering that makes the meat fit to be eaten, whereas according to Rabbi Meir, it refers to any slaughtering done in accordance with the laws of Jewish ritual slaughter, even if the animal was not kosher for some other reason.

The Talmud mentions five instances of this dispute: (1) The Torah (Leviticus 22:28) forbids the slaughter of an animal and its offspring on the same day. According to all opinions, if an animal was not killed in accordance with the laws of Jewish ritual slaughter, one is permitted to slaughter its offspring on the same day. According to Rabbi Shimon, the same law applies if the first animal was slaughtered properly but was found to be *terefah* (*Ḥullin* 81b). (2) The Torah (Leviticus 17:13) requires that when a

HALAKHAH

שְׁחִיטָה שֶׁאֵינָהּ רְאוּיָה Slaughtering that is not fit. "It is forbidden to slaughter an animal and its offspring on the same day, even if one of these animals is found not to be kosher because it has a defect that renders it *terefah* — following Rabbi Meir who maintains that slaughtering that is not fit is considered slaughtering. If a person slaughters a fowl, and it is found not to be kosher because it has a defect that renders it *terefah*, he need not cover its blood with dust — following Rabbi Shimon who maintains that slaughtering that is not fit is not considered slaughtering. These two rulings follow the Gemara's conclusion (*Ḥullin* 85a) that the Halakhah is in accordance with Rabbi Meir regarding an animal and its offspring, and in accordance with Rabbi Shimon regarding the covering of the blood.

TRANSLATION AND COMMENTARY

הָתֵינַח [1]The Gemara objects to this explanation: **This would be satisfactory** had the Baraita mentioned only **idol worship and an ox that is to be stoned.** For it is true that it is forbidden to eat, or derive benefit from, an animal slaughtered as an idolatrous sacrifice, or from an ox that has been condemned to be stoned, even if they were ritually slaughtered in a valid manner. [2]**But** if someone **slaughters** an animal **on Shabbat, the slaughtering is** considered **fit,** and the meat may be eaten, even though the act of slaughtering the animal was a violation of Shabbat. [3]**For we have learned** in a Mishnah (*Ḥullin* 14a): **"If someone slaughters** an animal in a valid manner **on Shabbat or on Yom Kippur,** [4]**even though he forfeits his life** for deliberately violating Shabbat or Yom Kippur by killing an animal, **his slaughtering is kosher."** Thus we see that the animal mentioned in the Baraita as being slaughtered on Shabbat is in fact kosher, and even Rabbi Shimon would agree that the thief should be liable. Why, then, do the Rabbis in the Baraita exempt the thief from payment (according to the Amoraim, who explained that the thief is not subject to the more severe penalty because the animal was slaughtered by an agent)?

[1]הָתֵינַח עֲבוֹדָה זָרָה וְשׁוֹר הַנִּסְקָל. [2]אֶלָּא שְׁחִיטַת שַׁבָּת שְׁחִיטָה רְאוּיָה הִיא, [3]דִּתְנַן: "הַשּׁוֹחֵט בְּשַׁבָּת וּבְיוֹם הַכִּפּוּרִים, [4]אַף עַל פִּי שֶׁמִּתְחַיֵּיב בְּנַפְשׁוֹ, שְׁחִיטָתוֹ כְּשֵׁרָה".

LITERAL TRANSLATION

[1]This would be satisfactory for idol worship and an ox that is to be stoned. [2]But slaughtering on Shabbat is fit slaughtering, [3]for we have learned: "[If] someone slaughters on Shabbat or on Yom Kippur, [4]although he forfeits his life, his slaughtering is kosher."

RASHI

התינח עבודה זרה — דזבחי מתים אסורים, וכן שור הנסקל, דמשנגמר דינו אסור בהנאה, כדאמרינן בבבא קמא (מא,א) ובפסחים (כב,ב): ממשמע שנאמר "סקול יסקל" איני יודע שהוא נבילה ונבילה כו'?

NOTES

kosher undomesticated animal or a kosher fowl is slaughtered, the blood must be covered with dust. According to Rabbi Shimon, this law does not apply if the animal or the fowl was found to be *terefah* (*Ḥullin* 85a). (3) It is forbidden to derive any benefit from an animal that was slaughtered in the Temple courtyard if it was not slaughtered as a sacrifice. But according to Rabbi Shimon, if the animal was found to be *terefah*, its meat may be sold to a non-Jew (*Ḥullin* 85b). (4) A thief who slaughters an ox or a sheep that he has stolen must pay the fourfold and fivefold penalty. According to Rabbi Shimon, if the animal was found to be *terefah*, the thief is exempt from this payment (*Bava Kamma* 70a). (5) This dispute also has implications regarding the slaughtering of sacrificial animals (*Ḥullin* 80a).

The Gemara (*Ḥullin* 85a) rules that the Halakhah is in accordance with Rabbi Meir in the first case (the animal and its offspring), and that it is in accordance with Rabbi Shimon in the second case (regarding the covering of the blood with dust). It is not clear whether in the other cases the Halakhah follows Rabbi Meir or Rabbi Shimon. *Rambam* rules in favor of Rabbi Shimon in the third case (*Sheḥitah* 2:2) and in favor of Rabbi Meir in the fourth (*Genevah* 2:8). *Tur* (*Ḥoshen Mishpat* 350) suggests that *Rosh* may have ruled in favor of Rabbi Shimon in the fourth case, although there is some doubt about this (see *Derishah*).

The Gemara (*Ḥullin* 85a) explains that there is an exegetical basis to the dispute between Rabbi Meir and Rabbi Shimon. Rabbi Shimon argues that the case of Joseph, who had animals slaughtered for food (Genesis 43:16), proves that the word "slaughtering" implies meat that is fit to eat. Rabbi Meir counters that in the case of an animal slaughtered as a sacrifice outside the Temple courtyard (Leviticus 17:1-9), the Torah forbids the meat and prescribes lashes for the person who slaughtered the animal; thus we see that the word "slaughtering" does not necessarily imply meat that is fit to eat. The Gemara explains that Rabbi Meir and Rabbi Shimon disagree about which Scriptural source is most like the case of the animal and its offspring. There are difficulties, however, in applying this argument to the other cases in dispute, such as that concerning the thief who slaughtered the ox or the sheep, and *Tosafot* addresses this problem.

HALAKHAH

"If a thief steals an ox or a sheep and slaughters it, and it is found not to be kosher because it has a defect that renders it *terefah*, *Rambam* rules that he is liable to pay the fourfold and fivefold penalty — following Rabbi Meir who maintains that slaughtering that is not fit is considered slaughtering. *Tur*, however, suggests that *Rosh* may have ruled in favor of Rabbi Shimon.

"It is forbidden to derive any benefit from an animal that was slaughtered in the Temple courtyard if it was not intended as a sacrifice, but if the animal was found to be *terefah*, its meat may be sold to a non-Jew — following Rabbi Shimon who maintains that slaughtering that is not fit is not considered slaughtering." (*Rambam, Sefer Kedushah, Hilkhot Sheḥitah* 2:2, 12:6, 14:10; *Rambam, Sefer Nezikin, Hilkhot Genevah* 2:8; *Shulḥan Arukh, Yoreh De'ah* 16:9, 28:17; *Tur, Ḥoshen Mishpat* 350.)

הַשּׁוֹחֵט בְּשַׁבָּת וּבְיוֹם הַכִּפּוּרִים If someone slaughters on Shabbat or on Yom Kippur. "If someone slaughters an animal on Shabbat or on Yom Kippur, his slaughtering is kosher and the meat may be eaten, even though slaughtering an animal on Shabbat is punishable by death, and slaughtering an animal on Yom Kippur is punishable by excision and lashes," following the Mishnah in *Ḥullin*. (*Rambam, Sefer Kedushah, Hilkhot Shehitah* 1:29; *Shulḥan Arukh, Yoreh De'ah* 11:2.)

SAGES

רַבִּי יוֹחָנָן הַסַּנְדְּלָר **Rabbi Yoḥanan HaSandlar.** A Tanna of the fourth generation, Rabbi Yoḥanan HaSandlar was one of the important disciples of Rabbi Akiva. His devotion to Rabbi Akiva was absolute, and he was prepared to risk his life to visit Rabbi Akiva when the latter was imprisoned by the Romans, and to carry out missions on his behalf.

Statements by Rabbi Yoḥanan HaSandlar are found in the Mishnah and in Baraitot, and his colleagues were mainly other disciples of Rabbi Akiva. The name "HaSandlar" may simply mean that Rabbi Yoḥanan was a shoemaker by profession, but it is also possible that the name is a corruption of the word "Alexandrian," reflecting the fact that, according to the Jerusalem Talmud, he was born in Alexandria in Egypt.

TRANSLATION AND COMMENTARY

סָבַר לָהּ [1]The Gemara answers: The author of our Baraita **agrees with Rabbi Yoḥanan HaSandlar,** [2]**as was taught** in the following Tosefta (*Shabbat* 3:3): **"If someone inadvertently cooked food on Shabbat** (because he was unaware that it was Shabbat or that it is forbidden to cook on Shabbat), **he may eat it** immediately, even on Shabbat, because the Rabbis imposed no penalties on inadvertent violations of Shabbat. [3]But if he cooked the food **deliberately, he may not eat it** until Shabbat is over, because the Rabbis did not wish him to profit from his deliberate violation of Shabbat. Nevertheless, the food remains kosher and he may eat it after the end of Shabbat. [4]**This is the opinion of Rabbi Meir.** [5]**Rabbi Yehudah says: If he** cooked the food **inadvertently, he may eat it,** but only **when Shabbat is over,** because the Rabbis did not wish him to profit from violating Shabbat, even inadvertently. [6]But if he did it **deliberately,**

[1]סָבַר לָהּ כְּרַבִּי יוֹחָנָן הַסַּנְדְּלָר, [2]דְּתַנְיָא: ״הַמְבַשֵּׁל בְּשַׁבָּת בְּשׁוֹגֵג, יֹאכַל; [3]בְּמֵזִיד, לֹא יֹאכַל. [4]דִּבְרֵי רַבִּי מֵאִיר. [5]רַבִּי יְהוּדָה אוֹמֵר: בְּשׁוֹגֵג, יֹאכַל לְמוֹצָאֵי שַׁבָּת; [6]בְּמֵזִיד,

LITERAL TRANSLATION

[1]He maintains in accordance with Rabbi Yoḥanan HaSandlar, [2]for it has been taught: "[If] someone cooked [food] on Shabbat inadvertently, he may eat [it]; [3]deliberately, he may not eat [it]. [4][These are] the words of Rabbi Meir. [5]Rabbi Yehudah says: [If he did it] inadvertently, he may eat [it] after Shabbat; [6]deliberately,

RASHI

בשוגג יאכל – אפילו בו ביום. **במזיד לא יאכל** – הוא לעולם, אבל אחרים ישראלים – אוכלים. **רבי יהודה אומר בשוגג יאכל** – הוא למוצאי שבת, ולא בו ביום. דקנסינן שוגג אטו מזיד.

NOTES

הַמְבַשֵּׁל בְּשַׁבָּת **If someone cooked food on Shabbat.** This Baraita is cited in several places in the Talmud. Our commentary follows *Rashi*'s explanation in tractate *Ḥullin* (15a), which is also followed by most other Rishonim. According to this explanation, when the food is permitted without reservation, it is permitted even to the person who cooked it, and when it is forbidden until after Shabbat, it is forbidden even to other people.

In our Gemara, *Rashi* offers a different explanation. According to *Rashi*, there is no dispute that if the person cooked the food deliberately, he is never permitted to eat it. The dispute concerns two points: the law in cases in which the food was cooked inadvertently, and the status of the food as regards other people. If the food was cooked inadvertently, Rabbi Meir maintains that even the cook may eat it immediately, whereas Rabbi Yehudah is of the opinion that the cook must wait until after Shabbat is over, and Rabbi Yoḥanan HaSandlar maintains that the cook is never permitted to eat the food, and on this point there is no difference whether he cooked it inadvertently or deliberately. Regarding the status of the food as regards other people, Rabbi Meir and Rabbi Yehudah maintain that there is no prohibition at all, even if the food was cooked deliberately, whereas Rabbi Yoḥanan HaSandlar forbids the food to other people until after Shabbat is over if it was cooked inadvertently, and forbids it totally if it was cooked deliberately.

בְּשׁוֹגֵג, יֹאכַל; בְּמֵזִיד, לֹא יֹאכַל **Inadvertently, he may eat it; deliberately, he may not eat it.** *Rashi* in tractate *Ḥullin* (15a) explains the reasoning of this Baraita as follows: There are two reasons to forbid the food: (1) To prevent people from profiting from Shabbat violations. This consideration applies equally to the cook and to other people and applies only until Shabbat is over. (2) In order to penalize the cook for violating Shabbat. This consideration applies only to the cook himself and remains in force for an unlimited time.

According to this explanation, Rabbi Meir is concerned only about the first consideration, and only if the violation was deliberate; Rabbi Yehudah is concerned about the first consideration even if the violation was inadvertent, and about the second consideration if the violation was deliberate; and Rabbi Yoḥanan HaSandlar is concerned about both considerations, even if the violation was inadvertent. Hence Rabbi Meir forbids the food to everyone until after Shabbat if the violation was deliberate; Rabbi Yehudah forbids the food to everyone until after Shabbat even if the violation was inadvertent, and to the cook himself forever if it was deliberate; and Rabbi Yoḥanan HaSandlar forbids the food to everyone until after Shabbat, and to the cook forever, if the violation was inadvertent.

In our Gemara, *Rashi* explains the reasoning of the Baraita as follows: The sole reason for forbidding the food is to penalize the person for violating Shabbat. But it is possible to impose a partial penalty until after Shabbat, or a penalty that applies only to deliberate violations, or a penalty that applies only to the cook and not to other people, and it is possible to be more strict, and forbid the food forever even if it was cooked inadvertently, or to forbid it to other people.

יֹאכַל לְמוֹצָאֵי שַׁבָּת **He may eat it after Shabbat.** In some places in the Talmud (e.g., *Betzah* 24b), the Gemara rules that food prepared in violation of Shabbat may not be eaten until after Shabbat is over and sufficient time has passed to prepare the food after Shabbat. *Rashi* explains that the purpose of this rule is to prevent a person from

HALAKHAH

הַמְבַשֵּׁל בְּשַׁבָּת **If someone cooked food on Shabbat.** "If a Jew prepares food in deliberate violation of Shabbat, he is never permitted to eat it, but other people may eat it as soon as Shabbat is over. If he cooks the food inadvertently, the food is forbidden to everyone until Shabbat is over, after which it is permitted to everyone, including the cook himself — following Rabbi Yehudah. *Gra* notes that many Rishonim rule in favor of Rabbi Meir — that the food is permitted immediately, if the violation was inadvertent, and permitted after Shabbat to everyone including the cook, if

לֹא יֹאכַל עוֹלָמִית. [1]רַבִּי יוֹחָנָן הַסַּנְדְּלָר אוֹמֵר: בְּשׁוֹגֵג, יֵאָכֵל לְמוֹצָאֵי שַׁבָּת לַאֲחֵרִים, וְלֹא לוֹ; [2]בְּמֵזִיד, לֹא יֵאָכֵל עוֹלָמִית, לֹא לוֹ וְלֹא לַאֲחֵרִים״.

[3]מַאי טַעֲמָא דְּרַבִּי יוֹחָנָן הַסַּנְדְּלָר?

TRANSLATION AND COMMENTARY

he himself **may not eat it forever.** The Rabbis penalized him but the food itself remains kosher and may be eaten by other people after Shabbat. [1]**Rabbi Yoḥanan HaSandlar says: If he** cooked the food **inadvertently, it** remains kosher and **may be eaten when Shabbat is over, but** only **by other** people, **not by** the inadvertent Shabbat violator **himself,** because the Rabbis penalized him. [2]But if he cooked on Shabbat **deliberately,** the food becomes non-kosher, and **no one is ever permitted to eat it — neither** the Shabbat violator **himself nor other** people." Thus we can explain that the Baraita reflects the viewpoint of Rabbi Yoḥanan HaSandlar that an animal slaughtered deliberately on Shabbat is not kosher. Hence our objection to the Amoraim's explanation of the Baraita is solved, and we can explain the dispute between Rabbi Meir and the Rabbis — as to whether a thief is exempt from the fourfold and fivefold payment if his agent slaughtered the sheep or the ox on Shabbat — as reflecting the dispute between Rabbi Shimon and Rabbi Meir. The Sages in the Baraita agree with Rabbi Shimon, who maintains that a thief who slaughtered an ox or a sheep in an invalid way is exempt from the fourfold and fivefold payment, whereas Rabbi Meir is consistent with his own viewpoint, that the thief is liable even if the slaughtering did not make the meat kosher.

מַאי טַעֲמָא [3]This explanation is satisfactory if Rabbi Yoḥanan HaSandlar is of the opinion that food prepared on Shabbat is not kosher by Torah law. If so, we can say that the Rabbis in the Baraita reflect the viewpoint of Rabbi Yoḥanan HaSandlar, who maintains that an animal slaughtered on Shabbat is not kosher, and the viewpoint of Rabbi Shimon, who maintains that a thief who slaughters an animal in an invalid way is exempt from payment. But if Rabbi Yoḥanan HaSandlar is of the opinion that food prepared on Shabbat is kosher by Torah law, and that it is the Rabbis who forbid it in order to penalize the Shabbat violator, this is not a good explanation. For even Rabbi Shimon would agree that a thief who slaughters an ox or a sheep in a way that is valid by Torah law but invalid by Rabbinic decree is liable to pay the fourfold and fivefold penalty, because this penalty is a Torah law that is not affected by a Rabbinic decree. Now, it is clear that all the partial prohibitions in the Tosefta are Rabbinic in character: The Rabbis quoted in the Tosefta do not allow anyone to eat the food until Shabbat is over, in order to prevent people from profiting from Shabbat violations, and they permanently bar the violator himself from eating the food, in order to penalize him for violating Shabbat. But it is not clear whether Rabbi Yoḥanan HaSandlar's total prohibition of food cooked deliberately on Shabbat, that covers all people over an unlimited period, is also a Rabbinic prohibition, albeit of unusual severity, or whether he maintains that food cooked in deliberate violation of Shabbat is forbidden by Torah law. Hence the Gemara asks: **What is the reason that Rabbi Yoḥanan HaSandlar** forbids the food permanently to everyone? Is it a Torah law or a Rabbinic prohibition? And if it is a Torah law, from what source does he derive it?

LITERAL TRANSLATION

he may not eat [it] forever. [1]Rabbi Yoḥanan HaSandlar says: [If he did it] inadvertently, it may be eaten after Shabbat by others, but not by him; [2]deliberately, it may not be eaten forever, neither by him nor by others."

[3]What is the reasoning of Rabbi Yoḥanan HaSandlar?

RASHI

במזיד לא יאכל — הוא עולמית, אלא אחרים. בדרבי יוחנן הסנדלר גרסינן יֵאָכֵל. **לאחרים** — לישראל. **לא לו ולא לאחרים** — ישראל, אבל מוכרו ונותנו לנכרים. **מאי טעמא דרבי יוחנן הסנדלר** — דאמר: מעשה שבת אסורין באכילה.

NOTES

profiting from the Shabbat violation by saving time. *Tosafot* explains that its purpose is to ensure that a person will not be encouraged to violate Shabbat again in this way.

In *Ḥullin* (15a), *Rashi* explains that this rule applies in our case as well, when the food is forbidden until Shabbat is over. But *Rambam* and most other Rishonim disagree with *Rashi* on this point, and permit the food immediately after Shabbat, with no need for a delay.

Bet Yosef (*Oraḥ Ḥayyim* 318) explains that the requirement to wait until sufficient time has passed applies only to cases like the one in tractate *Betzah*, which deals with violations of Shabbat committed by a non-Jew. But if a Jew violated Shabbat inadvertently, or succumbed to temptation and violated it deliberately, we are not concerned that he will be prepared to violate it deliberately in the future merely in order to save a little time.

HALAKHAH

the violation was deliberate. *Mishnah Berurah* rules that we may rely on this opinion in cases of great need. *Gra* further rules if the violation was Rabbinic, all authorities agree that the Halakhah is in accordance with Rabbi Meir." (*Rambam, Sefer Zemanim, Hilkhot Shabbat* 6:23; *Shulḥan Arukh, Oraḥ Ḥayyim* 318:1.)

[1]כִּדְדָרֵישׁ רַבִּי חִיָּיא אַפִּיתְחָא דְּבֵי נְשִׂיאָה: ״וּשְׁמַרְתֶּם אֶת הַשַּׁבָּת, כִּי קֹדֶשׁ הִיא לָכֶם״. [2]מַה קוֹדֶשׁ אָסוּר בַּאֲכִילָה, אַף מַעֲשֵׂה שַׁבָּת אֲסוּרִין בַּאֲכִילָה. [3]אִי מַה קוֹדֶשׁ, אָסוּר בַּהֲנָאָה, [4]אַף מַעֲשֵׂה שַׁבָּת, אָסוּר בַּהֲנָאָה! [5]תַּלְמוּד לוֹמַר: ״לָכֶם״. [6]שֶׁלָּכֶם יְהֵא. [7]יָכוֹל אֲפִילּוּ בְּשׁוֹגֵג. [8]תַּלְמוּד לוֹמַר: ״מְחַלֲלֶיהָ מוֹת יוּמָת״. [9]בְּמֵזִיד אֲמַרְתִּי לְךָ, וְלֹא בְּשׁוֹגֵג. [10]פְּלִיגִי בָּהּ רַב אַחָא וְרָבִינָא.

LITERAL TRANSLATION

[1][It is] as Rabbi Ḥiyya expounded at the entrance of the Nasi's house: "And you shall keep Shabbat, for it is holy to you." [2]Just as [something] holy is forbidden to be eaten, so too are deeds [profaning] Shabbat forbidden to be eaten. [3]If so, just as [regarding] holy [things], it is forbidden to [derive] benefit [from them], [4]so too [regarding] deeds [profaning] Shabbat, it is forbidden to [derive] benefit [from them]! [5]The verse states: "To you." [6]It shall remain yours. [7]I might have thought (lit., "could it be?") even [if it was done] inadvertently. [8][Therefore] the verse states: "Those that profane it shall be put to death." [9]About deliberate [violations] I was speaking to you, but not about inadvertent [violations].

[10]Rav Aḥa and Ravina disagree about it.

TRANSLATION AND COMMENTARY

כִּדְדָרֵישׁ רַבִּי חִיָּיא [1]The Gemara explains: According to Rabbi Yoḥanan HaSandlar, the prohibition against eating food cooked on Shabbat is in fact a Torah law, **as Rabbi Ḥiyya expounded at the entrance of Rabbi Yehudah HaNasi's house:** The verse (Exodus 31:14) says: **"And you shall keep Shabbat, for it is holy to you;** those that profane it shall be put to death." [2]From here we learn that **just as holy things** (items that have been dedicated to the Temple) **are forbidden to be eaten** by Torah law, **so too are items** prepared **in violation of Shabbat forbidden to be eaten** by Torah law. The Torah forbids consuming or deriving any benefit from Temple property, and Rabbi Ḥiyya explains that the same law applies to items prepared in violation of Shabbat, because the Torah calls them "holy." [3]**If so,** continues Rabbi Ḥiyya, you might argue that **just as it is forbidden to derive benefit from holy things,** [4]**so too should it be forbidden to derive benefit from things** prepared **in violation of Shabbat.** The prohibition against deriving benefit from Temple property extends beyond eating to all forms of benefit, and if food prepared on Shabbat has the same status, it should be forbidden to sell such food to a non-Jew, for example. Nevertheless, the Tosefta referred only to eating the food. It did not insist that it be destroyed unused, and even according to Rabbi Yoḥanan HaSandlar it may be sold to a non-Jew. Rabbi Ḥiyya answers this argument as follows: [5]In the same verse (Exodus 31:14) **the Torah states:** "It is holy **to you."** [6]From this expression we learn that food cooked on Shabbat **remains yours** — it is at your disposal for all purposes except for food. [7]Rabbi Ḥiyya continues: Since food prepared in violation of Shabbat is forbidden by Torah law, **you might think** that the food is forbidden **even if it was prepared inadvertently.** [8]**Therefore, the Torah states** in the same verse: **"Those that profane it shall be put to death."** [9]The fact that the death penalty is mentioned informs us that the Torah **is speaking to us about deliberate violations,** which are punishable by death, **but not about inadvertent violations,** which are not punished in this way. According to Rabbi Ḥiyya's explanation of this verse, we can argue that Rabbi Yoḥanan HaSandlar is of the opinion that by Torah law no one is ever permitted to eat food cooked deliberately on Shabbat, although such food may be sold to a non-Jew; whereas food cooked inadvertently on Shabbat is not forbidden by Torah law, although the Rabbis totally forbade it to the person who prepared it, and forbade it to other people until Shabbat is over. Since Rabbi Yoḥanan HaSandlar's viewpoint is indeed based on Torah law, it follows that a thief who instructed someone to slaughter an ox or a sheep on Shabbat is exempt from the fourfold and fivefold payment according to Rabbi Shimon, who maintains that the thief is not liable if the slaughtering was invalid by Torah law.

פְּלִיגִי בָּהּ [10]The Gemara is not convinced by Rabbi Ḥiyya's explanation, since **Rav Aḥa and Ravina**

RASHI

יכול אפילו בשוגג — תאסר באכילה, אם שגג בבישול, שלא ידע שהוא שבת. **מחלליה וגו'** — היכא דאיכא חיוב מיתה אסירי באכילה כי קודש. **במזיד אמרתי** — שהוא אסור כקודש, דהא גבי חיוב מיתה כתיב, ולא בשוגג.

NOTES

פְּלִיגִי בָּהּ רַב אַחָא וְרָבִינָא Rav Aḥa and Ravina disagree about it. Our commentary follows *Rashi*, who explains that Rav Aḥa and Ravina disagree about the reasoning underlying Rabbi Yoḥanan HaSandlar's position: One Amora agrees with Rabbi Ḥiyya's exegesis, whereas the other argues that even according to Rabbi Yoḥanan HaSandlar, the prohibition against eating food cooked on Shabbat is only Rabbinic.

Rif, however (*Shabbat* 38a), has a different understanding of this dispute. According to *Rif*, Rav Aḥa and Ravina disagree

TRANSLATION AND COMMENTARY

disagreed about this very matter. [1]**One** of these Amoraim **said:** According to Rabbi Yoḥanan HaSandlar, eating food prepared on **Shabbat is forbidden by Torah law,** in accordance with Rabbi Ḥiyya's exegesis. [2]**And the other said:** Even according to Rabbi Yoḥanan HaSandlar, eating food prepared on Shabbat is forbidden only **by Rabbinic decree**, in order to punish Shabbat violations in a very severe way. [3]Now, **according to the one who said** that eating food prepared on Shabbat is forbidden **by Torah law, it is as we said.** The source of the prohibition is the verse in Exodus stating that Shabbat is holy, as interpreted by Rabbi Ḥiyya. [4]But **according to the one who said** that eating food prepared on Shabbat is forbidden **by Rabbinic decree,** Rabbi Ḥiyya's exegesis was merely a homiletic device, not based on a genuine Scriptural source. According to the Amora (Rav Aḥa or Ravina) who maintains that food prepared in violation of Shabbat is not forbidden by Torah law, [5]**the verse** should be understood as follows: Since it **says "it is holy"** — using a grammatically unnecessary pronoun, suggesting emphasis — we learn that **it itself is holy,** like the Temple, because Shabbat is a day set apart for special purposes and may not be enjoyed in a mundane way, [6]**but** no other aspects of holiness are implied. Thus food prepared in violation of Shabbat **is not holy** in any way, and cannot be compared to Temple property, which *is* holy.

וּלְמַאן דְּאָמַר [7]Now, according to the opinion that food prepared in violation of Shabbat is forbidden by Torah law, the Amoraim's explanation of the case of the thief who instructed that the stolen animal be slaughtered on Shabbat is satisfactory, as we have explained. **But according to the** Amora (Rav Aḥa or Ravina) **who said** that even Rabbi Yoḥanan HaSandlar agrees that eating food prepared on Shabbat is forbidden only **by Rabbinic decree**, our problem reappears. The Rabbis in the Baraita exempted the thief from paying the fourfold and fivefold payments if the stolen animal was an ox condemned to be stoned or if it was slaughtered on Shabbat or for idol worship, and the Amoraim explained that this exemption was granted because the animal is not kosher by Torah law. This explanation reflects the opinion of Rabbi Shimon, who maintains that the thief is not liable if the animal was not slaughtered in a kosher way. The explanation is satisfactory in relation to the case of idol worship and the case of the ox condemned to be stoned, but not in relation to the case of the animal slaughtered on Shabbat, if everyone, including Rabbi Yoḥanan HaSandlar, agrees that the prohibition against eating an animal slaughtered on Shabbat is a Rabbinic one. [8]So **what is the reasoning of the Rabbis who exempted** the thief from payment if his agent slaughtered the animal on Shabbat? Why did they not agree with Rabbi Meir, who said that the thief is liable to make the fourfold and fivefold payment?

כִּי קָא פָּטְרִי רַבָּנַן [9]The Gemara answers: According to the argument just presented, we are forced to conclude that the Rabbis did not disagree with Rabbi Meir about the animal slaughtered on Shabbat. **When the Rabbis** disagreed with Rabbi Meir and **exempted** the thief from the fourfold and fivefold payments, **they**

[1]חַד אֲמַר: מַעֲשֵׂה שַׁבָּת דְּאוֹרַיְיתָא, [2]וְחַד אֲמַר: דְּרַבָּנַן. [3]מַאן דְּאָמַר: דְּאוֹרַיְיתָא, כְּדַאֲמָרַן. [4]מַאן דְּאָמַר: דְּרַבָּנַן, [5]אֲמַר קְרָא: ״קֹדֶשׁ הִיא״. הִיא קוֹדֶשׁ, [6]וְאֵין מַעֲשֶׂיהָ קוֹדֶשׁ. [7]וּלְמַאן דְּאָמַר: דְּרַבָּנַן, [8]מַאי טַעֲמַיְיהוּ דְּרַבָּנַן דְּפָטְרִי? [9]כִּי קָא פָּטְרִי רַבָּנַן, אַשְּׁאָרָא.

LITERAL TRANSLATION

[1]One said: Deeds [profaning] Shabbat are [forbidden] by Torah law, [2]and one said: By Rabbinic law. [3][According to] the one who says: By Torah law, it is as we said. [4][According to] the one who says: By Rabbinic law, [5]the verse says: "It is holy." It itself is holy, [6]but its deeds are not holy.

[7]But according to the one who says: By Rabbinic law, [8]what is the reasoning of the Rabbis that they exempt [him]?

[9]When the Rabbis exempt [him], [it is only] with regard to the other [cases].

RASHI

מעשה שבת — במזיד אסורין מן התורה באכילה, לרבי יוחנן הסנדלר. **מאי טעמא דרבנן** — דפליגי אדרבי מאיר, ופטרי מקנס ארבעה וחמשה, הואיל ובטובח על ידי אחר אוקימתא — הא שחיטה ראויה היא מדאורייתא. **אשארא** — אעבודה זרה ואשור הנסקל.

NOTES

about whether the Halakhah is in accordance with Rabbi Yoḥanan HaSandlar or in accordance with one of the other two Tannaim. Accordingly, *Rif* rules against Rabbi Yoḥanan HaSandlar, since we have a rule that in all disputes between Rav Aḥa and Ravina, the Halakhah follows the more lenient viewpoint.

וּלְמַאן דְּאָמַר דְּרַבָּנַן But according to the one who says: By Rabbinic law. The Gemara assumes that if the meat is forbidden by Rabbinic decree alone, the slaughtering is considered fit and the thief is liable to pay, even according to Rabbi Shimon. *Tosafot* (*Bava Kamma* 71a) notes that in other cases in which meat is forbidden by Rabbinic decree the Gemara considers the slaughtering to have been unfit. *Shittah Mekubbetzet* explains that it stands to reason that the Rabbis would not apply their decree in such a way that the laws of theft would become more lenient. The Aḥaronim discuss this matter further (see *Maharshal*, *Rashash*, *Kovetz Shiurim*).

[1]טוֹבֵחַ לַעֲבוֹדָה זָרָה, [2]כֵּיוָן דְּשָׁחַט בֵּיהּ פּוּרְתָּא, אִיתְּסַר לֵיהּ. [3]אֵידָךְ כִּי קָא טָבַח, לָאו דְּמָרֵיהּ קָא טָבַח!

[4]אֲמַר רָבָא: בְּאוֹמֵר בִּגְמַר זְבִיחָה הוּא עוֹבְדָהּ.

[5]שׁוֹר הַנִּסְקָל, [6]לָאו דִּידֵיהּ הוּא דְּקָטָבַח!

LITERAL TRANSLATION

[1] [If] someone slaughters for idol worship, [2] once he has slaughtered a little of it, it has become forbidden to him. [3] [So] when he slaughters the rest, he is not slaughtering its owner's [property]!

[4] Rava said: [It is] when he says [that] with the completion of the slaughtering he is worshipping it.

[5] [In the case of] the ox that is to be stoned, [6] he is not slaughtering his own [property]!

RASHI

כיון דשחט ביה פורתא איתסר ליה – דאמר מר (חולין מ,א): היתה בהמת חבירו רבוצה לפני עבודה זרה, כיון ששחט בה סימן אחד – אסרה. **לאו דמריה קא טבח** – דהא איתסרא עליה. וחיובא דתשלומי ארבעה וחמשה "טביחה" כתיב בהו, ועד גמר שחיטה לא מיחייב. ומקמי דמטי גמר שחיטה איתסרא בהנאה על בעליה, ומההיא שעתא אפסדה מיניה, דאי איתא – לא הדרא בעינא ולאו דמריה היא. **באומר בגמר זביחה הוא עובדה** – לעבודה זרה,

TRANSLATION AND COMMENTARY

were referring to the other cases mentioned by Rabbi Meir — the animal slaughtered for idol worship and the ox condemned to be stoned. In these cases, the animal is indeed not kosher, and according to Rabbi Shimon the thief is not liable. But in the case of the animal slaughtered on Shabbat, the Rabbis agree that the thief is liable. Thus the Baraita should read as follows: "If someone stole and later slaughtered on Shabbat, or stole and slaughtered for idol worship, or if he stole an ox that is to be stoned and slaughtered it, he is liable according to Rabbi Meir, but the Sages exempt the last two cases."

טוֹבֵחַ לַעֲבוֹדָה זָרָה [1]The Gemara has now answered all the objections to the Amoraim's explanation of the Baraita (above, 33b). Before proceeding to Rabbah's alternative explanation (below), the Gemara raises two more objections against the Baraita, objections that are not specifically related to the Amoraim's explanation. The first objection is this: According to the Baraita, if a thief steals an ox or a sheep and slaughters it for idol worship, Rabbi Meir maintains that the thief has to pay the fourfold and fivefold fine, whereas the Sages maintain that he is exempt — either because he is subject to the more severe penalty (as we maintained in our original explanation of the Baraita), or because the slaughtering is invalid (as the Amoraim explained). But with regard to idol worship, the thief should be exempt in any case. For the fourfold and fivefold penalty is imposed only if the animal still belongs to its owner when the thief sells it or slaughters it, but if the animal no longer belongs to the owner when it is slaughtered, the thief is exempt from the fourfold and fivefold penalty. Stolen property in the possession of a thief belongs to its rightful owner only to the extent that the thief is able to return it, but whenever this is not possible (for example, when a stolen animal dies), the stolen object ceases to be of legal interest, and the thief is obliged to repay its value to the owner. But **if someone slaughters** an animal **for idol worship,** [2]the animal **becomes forbidden as soon as he has begun to slaughter it** (i.e., the moment the knife begins to cut the animal's throat), because the Torah forbids deriving any benefit from an idolatrous sacrifice from the moment the act of slaughter is begun. [3]**Hence,** as soon as the thief begins to slaughter the animal for idol worship, it ceases to be returnable, and **when he completes the act of slaughtering, he is no longer slaughtering the owner's property.** But the fourfold and fivefold penalty is imposed only if the thief actually slaughters the animal, not if he merely begins the act of slaughtering. Hence, he should be exempt from the fourfold and fivefold payment, because the animal ceased to belong to the owner before it was slaughtered!

אֲמַר רָבָא [4]In answer to this objection, **Rava said:** The Baraita is referring to a case **in which** the slaughterer **said: "I will begin worshipping** this idol **when the act of slaughtering is complete."** If an idolator stipulates that an action he is about to take is not to be construed as idol worship, he is not liable for that action; and if he stipulates that he is not to be considered as worshipping the idol until he reaches a certain point in the ceremony, his stipulation is valid. Thus it is possible for the slaughterer to complete slaughtering the animal at the same moment as he begins to worship the idol, and in such a case the thief is liable to pay the fourfold and fivefold payment.

שׁוֹר הַנִּסְקָל [5]The Gemara now raises a second, general objection to the Baraita. According to the Baraita, if a thief steals an ox that has been sentenced to be stoned and he slaughters it, Rabbi Meir maintains that the thief is held liable to pay the fourfold and fivefold payment, whereas the Sages maintain that he is exempt. But surely, says the Gemara, **in the case of the ox that has** been sentenced **to be stoned,** the thief should be exempt in any case, even according to Rabbi Meir, who is of the opinion that a thief is liable for slaughtering that is invalid. For the Torah forbids deriving any benefit from an ox that has been sentenced to be stoned, even if it is slaughtered before it can be stoned. Thus, once an ox has been sentenced to be stoned, it is valueless and effectively ownerless, and the thief who steals it does its owner no harm. [6]Hence, when he

TRANSLATION AND COMMENTARY

slaughters it, **he is not slaughtering the property** of the owner at all, and he should be exempt from the fourfold and fivefold payment!

אָמַר רַבָּה [1] In reply to this objection, **Rabbah said: With what** case is the Baraita **dealing here?** With a special case, in which the ox was not worthless. [2] **For example, if** the animal's owner had previously **handed it over to a bailee.** The bailee took responsibility for the animal, and was liable to pay the owner if the animal was stolen or died. [3] Subsequently, the animal **did damage** and killed somebody while it was **in the bailee's house,** [4] **and** the animal's **trial was completed** and sentence was passed while it was still **in the bailee's house.** Now, if the sentence had been carried out, the bailee would have been liable to reimburse the owner for the death of the ox, since he should have guarded it more carefully. But if the bailee had returned the ox to the owner while it was still alive, he would have been exempt, since he would have returned the ox in good condition to the owner (even though it was now legally valueless). Hence it was in the bailee's interest to return the ox to its owner. [5] **But** before he could do so, **the thief stole it from the bailee's house**, and the bailee was forced to pay the owner for it. The thief was thus liable to make a double payment to the bailee for stealing the ox, even though it was legally worthless when he stole it, because it was of indirect value to the bailee, since he could have used it to save himself from having to pay the owner. Now, since the thief not only stole the ox but also slaughtered it, he is liable to pay fivefold damages — according to Rabbi Meir. But the Sages maintain that the thief is exempt from the fivefold payment (although he *is* liable to make the double payment), since the slaughtering was invalid. [6] The Gemara explains: **Rabbi Meir,** who maintains that the thief is liable, must **agree with** the viewpoint of **Rabbi Ya'akov and** must also **agree with** the viewpoint of **Rabbi Shimon.** [7] **He** must **agree with Rabbi Ya'akov, who said** that **a bailee** who **returns** an ox that is to be stoned **to its owner, even after its trial has been completed** and it has been sentenced to death, is exempt from payment (provided that he returns the ox while it is still alive), since the ox **was** duly **returned.** [8] Rabbi Meir must also **agree with Rabbi Shimon, who said: Something that can cause a loss of money,** such as a worthless object with indirect value, like an ox that has been sentenced to be stoned which is in the possession of a bailee, **is considered like money** and is subject to the same laws as an object that has intrinsic value. According to Rabbi Shimon, a thief who steals an ox that has been sentenced to death from a bailee who has a financial interest in it is held liable to pay the bailee double its value, and if he slaughters it, he must pay him five times its value.

The Gemara has now answered all the objections raised against the Amoraim's explanation of the Baraita. The Baraita can be explained as dealing with the problem of invalid slaughtering, rather than with

[1] אֲמַר רַבָּה: הָכָא בְּמַאי עַסְקִינַן? [2] כְּגוֹן שֶׁמְּסָרוֹ לְשׁוֹמֵר, [3] וְהִזִּיק בְּבֵית שׁוֹמֵר, [4] וְנִגְמַר דִּינֵיהּ בְּבֵית שׁוֹמֵר, [5] וּגְנָבוֹ גַּנָּב מִבֵּית שׁוֹמֵר. [6] וְרַבִּי מֵאִיר סָבַר לָהּ כְּרַבִּי יַעֲקֹב, וְסָבַר לָהּ כְּרַבִּי שִׁמְעוֹן. [7] סָבַר לָהּ כְּרַבִּי יַעֲקֹב, דַּאֲמַר: אַף מִשֶּׁנִּגְמַר דִּינוֹ, הֶחֱזִירוֹ שׁוֹמֵר לִבְעָלָיו, מוּחְזָר. [8] וְסָבַר לָהּ כְּרַבִּי שִׁמְעוֹן, דַּאֲמַר: דָּבָר הַגּוֹרֵם לְמָמוֹן כְּמָמוֹן דָּמֵי.

LITERAL TRANSLATION

[1] Rabbah said: With what are we dealing here? [2] For example, when he handed it over to a bailee [3] and it did damage in the bailee's house, [4] and its trial was completed in the bailee's house, [5] and a thief stole it from the bailee's house. [6] And Rabbi Meir agrees with Rabbi Ya'akov, and he agrees with Rabbi Shimon. [7] He agrees with Rabbi Ya'akov, who said: Even after its judgment is completed, [if] the bailee returned it to its owner, it was returned. [8] And he agrees with Rabbi Shimon, who said: Something that causes [loss of] money is considered as money.

RASHI

אינו עובד לעבודה זרה עד גמר זביחה. פלוגתא דרבי יעקב בבבא קמא. החזירו שומר לבעליו מוחזר — דאמר ליה: תורא אשלמת לי — תורא אשלימית לך. כממון דמי — והאי נמי, אף על גב דלא שוי מידי — גורם לממון הוא, דכי ליתא בעי לשלומי ליה תורא מעליא. דרבי שמעון בבבא קמא, בפרק "מרובה": קדשים שחייב באחריותן משלם ארבעה וחמשה,

NOTES

דָּבָר הַגּוֹרֵם לְמָמוֹן כְּמָמוֹן דָּמֵי **Something that causes loss of money is considered as money.** The source of this law is a Mishnah in tractate *Bava Kamma* (74b) which considers cases in which a thief is exempt from making the double payment, and from paying the fourfold and fivefold penalties. The Mishnah rules that a thief who steals

HALAKHAH

דָּבָר הַגּוֹרֵם לְמָמוֹן **Something that causes loss of money.** "The law that a thief must pay double the amount he stole, or four and five times the amount he stole, applies only if the owner of the stolen property is a private person. But a thief who stole property belonging to the Temple need repay only the principal. Likewise, if the animal belonged

TRANSLATION AND COMMENTARY

the exemption enjoyed by a person who is subject to the more severe penalty, if we explain that the thief did not slaughter the animal himself but gave it to a butcher to slaughter. This enables us to say that Rabbi Meir, who maintains that lashes do not exempt from payment, can still agree that death *is* a more severe penalty that exempts from payment. Therefore we can accept Resh Lakish's explanation that our Mishnah — which rules that a man who rapes his sister is liable to pay the fine, but that a man who rapes his daughter is exempt — reflects the viewpoint of Rabbi Meir.

רַבָּה אָמַר [1]The Gemara now considers an alternative explanation of the Baraita. According to this interpretation, we must return to our original understanding of the Baraita — that it deals with the exemption granted to a person who is subject to a more severe penalty. **Rabbah said: In fact,** the dispute in the Baraita between Rabbi Meir and the Sages, about a thief who stole an ox or a sheep and slaughtered it on Shabbat or for idol worship, **is referring to a case where** the thief **slaughtered** the animal **himself.** According to this explanation, the Sages exempted the thief from the fourfold and fivefold penalty because he became subject to the death penalty (for violating Shabbat or for committing an act of idolatry) at the same moment as he became liable to pay the penalty for slaughtering the ox or the sheep. [34B] However, says Rabbah, even though Rabbi Meir disagrees with the Sages in the Baraita about the case of a thief who slaughters an animal on Shabbat, he does not altogether reject the principle that an offender who is subject to a more severe penalty is exempt from paying damages. Instead, he distinguishes among three different situations: (1) If an offender commits two offenses at the same time, one of which is subject to lashes and the other to a monetary penalty of any kind, [2]**Rabbi Meir maintains that** he is punished with both penalties, so that he **is lashed and he pays** the monetary penalty as well. (2) If an offender commits two offenses at the same time, one of which is subject to the death penalty and the other to an ordinary

[1]רַבָּה אָמַר: לְעוֹלָם בְּטוֹבֵחַ עַל יְדֵי עַצְמוֹ, [34B] [2]וְרַבִּי מֵאִיר לוֹקֶה וּמְשַׁלֵּם אִית לֵיהּ,

LITERAL TRANSLATION

[1]Rabbah said: In fact, [it refers to a case] where he slaughtered [it] himself. [34B] [2]And Rabbi Meir maintains [that] he is lashed and he pays,

RASHI

משום דגורס לממון הוא. ואף על גב דהקדש לאו ממון בעלים הוא, ובהקדש לא שייך קנס, ד״רעהו״ כתיב. רבה גרסינן בכולהו. ותדע, מדאמר לקמן: אמר ליה רב פפא לאביי: לרבה דאמר חידוש הוא כו׳, ואם איתא דרבא גרסינן — הא רב פפא תלמידו של רבא היה, כדאמר לקמן: אמר ליה רב פפא לרבא: הי מכה. מאי שנא דשבקיה לרבא ולא שייליה [לתרוצי שמעתיה], ושייליה לאביי [שמעתא דרבא]? אלא רבה גרסינן. ורב פפא לא היה בימיו, ושייל לאביי שהיה תלמידו של רבה. **רבה אמר לעולם בטובח בעצמו ורבי מאיר** — בעלמא בתשלומי ממון לית ליה מת ומשלם, והכא תשלומי ארבעה וחמשה קנס הם, וכל משפט קנס חידוש הוא. הלכך, אף על גב דמיקטיל נמי לא מיפטר מיניה. ולקמן פריך: לרבה אליבא דרבי מאיר קשיא בתו, דמתניתין נמי קנס הוא, וקא פטר ליה אבתו.

NOTES

an animal that has been dedicated as a sacrifice is exempt from these payments, since sacrificial animals are considered the property of the Temple, and the law of double, fourfold, and fivefold payments applies only to property stolen from a private person, not to property stolen from the Temple. The Mishnah then considers a case in which the animal has been dedicated as a sacrifice, but the owner retains responsibility for it, so that he will be required to replace it if something happens to it. In this case, Rabbi Shimon rules that the thief is required to pay the double, fourfold, and fivefold payments, since the owner has a financial interest in the animal — the desire to save himself from having to dedicate another animal. The Rabbis, by contrast, rule that something that causes loss of money is not considered as money, and the thief is exempt in this case as well.

The issue in the dispute about "something that causes loss of money" is a question of property, not damage. According to Rabbi Shimon, if an ox that has been sentenced to be stoned can be used by a bailee to save himself from having to pay the owner, it is in a sense his property. Thus the thief is not paying for the indirect damage he caused the bailee by causing him to pay the owner for the ox, but rather for the ox itself, which in the eyes of the bailee was still an object of value. But if the thief were to steal a creditor's documents, for example, he would have caused the creditor damage, since the thief would have prevented him from collecting his debts, but he would have done negligible harm to his property (no more than the value of the paper), since the debts themselves were not the creditor's property (see *Ramban* and *Ra'ah*).

HALAKHAH

to a private person, but before it was stolen it was dedicated as a sacrifice, the thief need not pay the double payment, nor the fourfold and fivefold payments, because the animal is already considered the property of the Temple. This law applies even if the terms of the dedication were such that the owner accepted financial responsibility for the animal (i.e., he is required to bring another sacrifice if the dedicated animal dies or is stolen.) Even though the owner has a financial interest in the dedicated animal in such cases, the thief is still not required to pay the double payment or the fourfold and fivefold payments, because the animal is not the owner's property — following the Tannaim who disagree with Rabbi Shimon and maintain that something that causes loss of money is not considered money." (*Rambam*, *Sefer Nezikin*, *Hilkhot Genevah* 2:1.)

TRANSLATION AND COMMENTARY

damages payment, [1]Rabbi Meir **does not maintain that he** is punished with both **the death penalty and the payment** of damages. In such a case, the offender is exempt from the payment of damages since he is subject to the more severe penalty. The rule that a person who is subject to the death penalty is exempt from the payment of damages is derived from a different verse from the rule that a person subject to lashes is exempt from damage payments, so that it is possible for Rabbi Meir to accept the one rule and not the other. **And** (3) in the cases discussed in the Baraita — concerning a thief who slaughtered a stolen animal on Shabbat or for idolatrous purposes — [2]Rabbi Meir maintains that the offender is punished with both penalties because **these cases are special, since fines are an innovation that the Torah established.** Normally, damage payments correspond to the loss suffered by the victim. But punitive damage payments (called קְנָס — "a fine"), such as the double, fourfold, and fivefold payments that are imposed on thieves, do not correspond to any increased loss suffered by the victim. Rather, they are imposed in order to punish the offender for his behavior, and this is a novel idea that departs from the general practice of the Torah. Now, whenever the Torah states a novel requirement that is not consistent with the other laws of the Torah, we cannot assume that the regular laws apply unless the Torah explicitly states that they do. Hence, in the case of the double, fourfold, and fivefold fines imposed on thieves (discussed in the Baraita), and in the case of other fines imposed by the Torah as punishment in addition to normal damage payments (including the fines imposed on rapists and seducers discussed by our Mishnah), the rule that an offender who is subject to the death penalty is exempt from monetary payments does not apply, [3]**and even though** the offender **is killed** for violating Shabbat or for committing incest, [4]**he** must **pay** the fine as well.

Thus, according to Rabbah, the Baraita is to be explained as follows: If a thief stole an ox or a sheep and slaughtered it himself on Shabbat or for idol worship, the Sages maintain that he is exempt from the fourfold and fivefold penalty, because he is subject to the more severe penalty for violating Shabbat or worshipping idols. But Rabbi Meir is of the opinion that the thief is held liable to pay, because the fourfold and fivefold payment is a fine, and fines are imposed even on offenders who are subject to the death penalty. According to Rabbah, the dispute between Rabbi Meir and the Sages also applies in the case of a man who rapes or seduces his daughter, because the payment imposed by the Torah in this case is also a fine that goes beyond damage payments. According to Rabbah's interpretation of the Baraita, we must reject Resh Lakish's explanation that our Mishnah reflects the viewpoint of Rabbi Meir, because Rabbi Meir could not have written the subsequent clause (below, 36b) exempting a man who raped his daughter from payment of the fine, because he is of the opinion that a man who raped his daughter is liable to pay the fine, even though he is also subject to the death penalty.

[1]מֵת וּמְשַׁלֵּם לֵית לֵיהּ. [2]וְשָׁאנֵי הָנֵי, דְּחִידּוּשׁ הוּא שֶׁחִידְּשָׁה תּוֹרָה בִּקְנָס, [3]אַף עַל גַּב דְּמִיקְטִיל, [4]מְשַׁלֵּם.

LITERAL TRANSLATION

[1][but] does not maintain [that] he dies and pays. [2]And these [cases] are special, since it is an innovation that the Torah established regarding a fine, [3][and therefore] although he is killed, [4]he pays.

NOTES

דְּחִידּוּשׁ הוּא שֶׁחִידְּשָׁה תּוֹרָה בִּקְנָס **Since it is an innovation that the Torah established regarding a fine.** According to Rabbah, since fines have novel aspects, we cannot assume that they follow the established rules in other respects. It is not clear, however, what is so novel about fines. *Shittah Mekubbetzet* notes that from a straightforward reading of the text, we might have thought that Rabbah was referring not to all fines but merely to the fourfold and fivefold fine imposed by the Torah on a thief who slaughters an ox or a cow that he has stolen. This law has several unusual aspects: (1) The fine is much higher than other fines. (2) It applies only to oxen and sheep but not to other animals. (3) It bears no relationship to the damage suffered by the owner, who suffers no greater loss when the thief slaughters the animal than when he simply steals it.

Shittah Mekubbetzet points out, however, that this explanation is untenable, because the Gemara states explicitly (below, 35b) that according to Rabbah's interpretation of the Baraita (above, 33b) Rabbi Meir cannot agree with our Mishnah's ruling that a man who rapes his daughter is exempt from the fine, because he is of the opinion that the more severe penalty does not exempt from fines. But the fine imposed on a rapist is entirely reasonable, with none of the peculiarities of the fourfold and fivefold fine imposed on thieves. Hence when Rabbah said that the regular rules do not apply to fines because they have novel aspects, he was referring to all fines, not just to the fourfold and fivefold fine imposed on thieves. *Rashi*, followed by our commentary, also explains Rabbah's statement in this way.

Rashi does not explain what is so novel about fines. *Ḥatam Sofer* notes that if fines are seen as a kind of damage payment, they are indeed peculiar, since the amount paid has no relationship to the actual damage done. But fines are in fact not really a damage payment at all, but rather a form of punishment; hence, there is nothing incongruous about the amount of a fine being set at more than the damage done. *Ḥatam Sofer* suggests, however, that fines are unusual because they are paid to the victim

[1] וְאָזְדָא רַבָּה לְטַעֲמֵיהּ. [2] דְּאָמַר רַבָּה: הָיָה גְּדִי גָּנוּב לוֹ וּטְבָחוֹ בְּשַׁבָּת, חַיָּיב, [3] שֶׁכְּבָר נִתְחַיֵּיב בִּגְנֵיבָה קוֹדֶם שֶׁיָּבֹא לִידֵי אִיסּוּר שַׁבָּת. [4] גָּנַב וְטָבַח בְּשַׁבָּת, פָּטוּר, [5] שֶׁאִם אֵין

LITERAL TRANSLATION

[1] And Rabbah follows his [regular line of] argument. [2] For Rabbah said: [If] he had a kid that he had stolen and he slaughtered it on Shabbat, he is liable, [3] since he was already liable for theft before he came to [violate] the prohibition of Shabbat. [4] [If] he stole [it] and slaughtered [it] on Shabbat, he is exempt, [5] for if there is no

TRANSLATION AND COMMENTARY

וְאָזְדָא רַבָּה לְטַעֲמֵיהּ [1] The Gemara observes: In giving this explanation of Rabbi Meir's position, **Rabbah is following his** own **regular line of argument.** Unlike Resh Lakish, who tried to explain Rabbi Meir's position in such a way that Rabbi Meir could have been the author of our Mishnah, although Resh Lakish himself did not agree with the rulings that he attributed to Rabbi Meir, Rabbah explains Rabbi Meir's position in a way that is consistent with his own opinions, as we can see from another ruling that Rabbah himself issued on a related topic. [2] **For Rabbah said:** If a thief **had a kid** or a lamb in his possession **that he had stolen** beforehand, **and he slaughtered it on Shabbat, he is** held **liable** to pay the fourfold and fivefold penalty, even though he is subject to the death penalty for killing an animal on Shabbat, [3] **since he was already liable for theft before he was in a position to violate the prohibition** against doing work **on Shabbat.** The thief is liable to pay the regular double penalty for stealing the animal because he was already liable for theft before Shabbat. As the Gemara explained above (30b), the rule that a person who is subject to the more severe penalty is exempt from paying damages applies only if the deed that incurred the death penalty was precisely the same deed that incurred the damage payment. However, the additional fourfold and fivefold payment for slaughtering the animal was incurred on Shabbat itself, and according to the regular rules the thief should have been exempt from it. But Rabbah maintains (as he explained above) that the fourfold and fivefold fine is a novel requirement established by the Torah, and in this situation the regular rules do not apply. [4] **If,** on the other hand, the thief **stole and slaughtered** the animal **on Shabbat, he is exempt** from all payments, since the theft itself was a violation of Shabbat. In such a case, the thief is entirely exempt from paying for the animal, since he is subject to the more severe penalty for violating Shabbat, and the act of paying compensation for stolen property is not a novel requirement established by the Torah. We might have thought, however, that he should still be liable to pay the fines imposed by the Torah, less the value of the damage payment itself (i.e., the second half of the double payment for stealing, and an additional two or three payments for slaughtering a sheep or an ox, for a total of a threefold or fourfold payment), since these payments are an innovation established by the Torah, to which the exemption of the more severe penalty does not apply. [5] Rabbah explains that the thief is exempt from these payments as well, **for if there is no** penalty for **theft, there is** also **no** penalty for

RASHI

היה גדי גנוב לו – גנב גדי בחול ונתחייב הקרן, וטבחו בשבת, דלא אתי עליה חיובא דממון באיסור שבת, אלא חיוב קנס. **חייב** – ארבעה וחמשה. דקנס חידוש הוא, ורבה סבירא ליה כרבי מאיר. **גנב וטבח בשבת** – דחיוב ממון דקרן אתא עליה באיסור שבת. **פטור** – דקיימא לן: אין מת ומשלם. וכיון דאקרן לא מיחייב – קנס נמי לא משלם. דתשלומי ארבעה וחמשה אמר רחמנא, ולא תשלומי שלשה וארבעה. ולא סבירא לן כרבי נתן דאמר (שבת לד,א): חי נושא את עצמו. אי נמי: בכפות.

NOTES

of the offense, and it is not clear why he should profit from the offender's punishment, beyond being reimbursed for the damage he actually suffered. Logically, it would make more sense for them to be paid to charity or to the Temple. Hence fines are an innovation, whether they are classified as a kind of damage payment or as a punishment.

וְאָזְדָא רַבָּה לְטַעֲמֵיהּ **And Rabbah follows his regular line of argument.** Our commentary follows *Rashi,* who explains that Rabbah himself ruled in accordance with Rabbi Meir, as we can see from another ruling Rabbah himself issued on a related topic. Thus, whereas Resh Lakish tried to explain Rabbi Meir's position in such a way that Rabbi Meir could have been the author of our Mishnah, even though Resh Lakish himself did not agree with the rulings that he attributed to Rabbi Meir, Rabbah maintains that Rabbi Meir could not have been the author of our Mishnah, but agrees with Rabbi Meir's rulings.

Tosafot disagrees with *Rashi* and explains that Rabbah did not rule in accordance with Rabbi Meir, and that his rulings in the case of the kid were not rulings at all, but merely illustrations of Rabbi Meir's opinions.

גָּנַב וְטָבַח בְּשַׁבָּת פָּטוּר **If he stole it and slaughtered it on Shabbat, he is exempt.** According to *Rashi,* the theft and the slaughtering were carried out at different times, but both were violations of Shabbat. Accordingly, the thief is exempt from regular damage payments, since the theft was committed in violation of Shabbat, and the thief is also exempt from the double, fourfold, and fivefold penalties — not because he is subject to a more severe penalty for slaughtering the animal, since fines may be imposed on a person who is subject to the death penalty, but rather because these penalties cannot be imposed when the regular damage payment does not apply.

Rashba objects to this explanation, for according to *Rashi* the fact that the slaughtering was done on Shabbat is irrelevant. Why, then, did Rabbah say that the animal

גְּנֵיבָה, אֵין טְבִיחָה וְאֵין מְכִירָה.
[1]וְאָמַר רַבָּה: הָיָה גְּדִי גָּנוּב לוֹ וּטְבָחוֹ בַּמַּחְתֶּרֶת, חַיָּיב, [2]שֶׁכְּבָר נִתְחַיֵּיב בִּגְנֵיבָה קוֹדֶם שֶׁיָּבֹא לִידֵי אִיסּוּר מַחְתֶּרֶת.

LITERAL TRANSLATION

theft, there is no slaughtering and there is no sale. [1]And Rabbah [also] said: [If] he had a kid that he had stolen and he slaughtered it while breaking in, he is liable, [2]since he was already liable for theft before he came to [violate] the prohibition [against] breaking in.

RASHI

שאם אין גניבה — כלומר, שמאחר שפטור על הקרן משום מיתה. **אין טביחה ואין מכירה** — אינו מחויב קנס, כדפירשתי, דתשלומי ארבעה וחמשה כתיב ולא תשלומי שלשה וארבעה. **מחתרת** — שחתר בית והוציאו. **וטבחו במחתרת** — עצמה, דההיא שעתא בר קטלא הוא אי הוה אשכחיה בעל הבית, כדכתיב (שמות כב) ״אין לו דמים״.

TRANSLATION AND COMMENTARY

slaughtering or sale. The Torah imposed the double, fourfold, and fivefold payments as additional penalties, not as substitutes for the standard damage payment. Therefore this thief, who is exempt from paying for the value of the stolen animal itself, is also exempt from the double, fourfold, and fivefold penalties — not because he is subject to the death penalty for slaughtering the animal on Shabbat, but because he was subject to the death penalty for violating Shabbat when he stole.

וְאָמַר רַבָּה [1]The Gemara notes that **Rabbah also** issued another ruling, based on the same reasoning, regarding a burglar caught breaking into his victim's house. The Torah (Exodus 22:1) states that a burglar caught breaking into a house is presumed to be armed and dangerous, and may therefore be killed without further investigation. In effect, this amounts to a temporary death sentence, applicable as long as the burglar persists in his attempt to burgle the house. In such a case, the burglar need not pay for any damage he caused while breaking in, since he was subject to a more severe penalty at the time. Rabbah **said: If** a burglar **had a kid** or a lamb in his possession **that he had stolen** from a house in a previous burglary, **and he** broke into the same house a second time and **slaughtered** the animal **while breaking in, he is** held **liable** to pay the fourfold and fivefold penalty, even though he was temporarily subject to the death penalty while breaking in, [2]**since he was already liable for theft before he was in a position to violate the prohibition against breaking in.** But Rabbah maintains that the fourfold and fivefold fine is an innovation established by the Torah, and in this situation the regular rule, that an offender is exempt from monetary payment if he is subject to a more severe penalty, does not apply. Hence the thief is liable to pay the fourfold and fivefold penalty, even though he was temporarily

NOTES

was slaughtered on Shabbat? The thief should be exempt from all the penalties, even if the animal was slaughtered on a weekday, so long as it was stolen on Shabbat. Accordingly, *Rashba* rejects *Rashi*'s interpretation and maintains that the thief stole the animal by slaughtering it.

Ritva, however, argues that according to *Rashi* only if the entire sequence of acts took place on the same Shabbat is the thief exempt, but if the thief stole the animal on Shabbat and slaughtered it on a weekday, he would be liable. For although the thief would not be liable for the original theft that took place on Shabbat, his act of slaughtering the animal on a weekday is itself an additional act of theft, and the thief should be liable for all the penalties at that point.

The Aḥaronim discuss the reasoning behind the dispute between *Rashba* and *Ritva* (see *Rabbi Akiva Eger*, *Or Same'aḥ*, *Kovetz Shiurim*).

שֶׁאִם אֵין גְּנֵיבָה אֵין טְבִיחָה וְאֵין מְכִירָה For if there is no theft, there is no slaughtering and there is no sale. The Rishonim explain that Rabbah is saying that the Torah imposes the double, fourfold, and fivefold fines on thieves only if the regular damage payment is payable, but if the thief is exempt from the regular payment because he is subject to a more severe penalty, he need not pay any of the fines either.

It is not entirely clear why this should be so. Why should the thief be exempt from all the fines just because he is exempt from the regular damage payment? After all, if a man seduces a *na'arah* who is an imbecile, he is not exempt from paying the fine, even though the regular damage payments are not applicable (see above, 32a)!

Rashi and other Rishonim explain that Rabbah's ruling is based on a passage in the Gemara in *Bava Kamma* (75b), which rules that a thief who is exempt from the double penalty for technical reasons need not pay the fourfold or fivefold penalty either, even if the technical reasons are not applicable to these penalties. The Gemara explains that the Torah referred to these penalties by number, as fourfold and fivefold penalties. Hence they cannot be paid when the double payment is deducted, and they are in effect threefold and fourfold penalties. Following the same argument, the double, fourfold, and fivefold penalties are all inapplicable when the regular damage payment does not apply, since they would be, in effect, single, threefold, and fourfold penalties.

וּטְבָחוֹ בַּמַּחְתֶּרֶת And he slaughtered it while breaking in. The Torah (Exodus 22:1) permits the owner of a house to kill a burglar while he is breaking in to the house. The Mishnah (*Sanhedrin* 72a) explains that this is not because of the severity of the crime actually committed by the burglar, but because of the severity of the crime he was about to commit. The Gemara explains that a burglar who breaks in to a house may be assumed to be armed and dangerous. Hence the owner of the house is entitled to view the burglar as a potential murderer, and he is permitted to preempt the murderer by killing him first.

The Mishnah in *Sanhedrin* further rules that since it is permitted to kill the burglar, he is regarded as being

TRANSLATION AND COMMENTARY

subject to the death penalty while breaking in. [1] If, on the other hand, the burglar **stole and slaughtered** the animal **while breaking in, he is exempt** from all payments. The burglar is exempt from paying for the animal since he is subject to the more severe penalty for breaking in, and the simple payment of compensation for theft is not an innovation established by the Torah. We might have thought, however, that he should still be liable to pay the fines imposed by the Torah, minus the value of the damage payment itself, since these fines are an innovation established by the Torah, to which the exemption of the more severe penalty does not apply. But Rabbah explains that the burglar is exempt from these payments as well, [2] **for if there is no** penalty for **theft, neither is there** a penalty for **slaughtering or sale.**

[1] גָּנַב וְטָבַח בַּמַּחְתֶּרֶת, פָּטוּר, [2] שֶׁאִם אֵין גְּנֵיבָה, אֵין טְבִיחָה וְאֵין מְכִירָה.
[3] וּצְרִיכָא. [4] דְּאִי אַשְׁמַעִינַן שַׁבָּת, [5] מִשּׁוּם דְּאִיסּוּרָהּ אִיסּוּר עוֹלָם, [6] אֲבָל מַחְתֶּרֶת, דְּאִיסּוּר שָׁעָה הוּא, [7] אֵימָא לָא. [8] וְאִי אַשְׁמַעִינַן מַחְתֶּרֶת, [9] מִשּׁוּם דְּמַחְתַּרְתּוֹ זוֹ הִיא הַתְרָאָתוֹ,

LITERAL TRANSLATION

[1] [If] he stole [it] and slaughtered [it] while breaking in, he is exempt, [2] for if there is no theft, there is no slaughtering and there is no sale.

[3] And it is necessary. [4] For if he had informed us [about] Shabbat, [5] [it would have been] because its prohibition is a permanent prohibition, [6] but [regarding] breaking in, which is a temporary (lit., "hourly") prohibition, [7] I would say not. [8] And if he had informed us about breaking in, [9] [it would have been] because his breaking in is itself his warning,

RASHI

משום דאסוריה איסור עולם — כל זמן שיעידו עליו שחילל שבת ימיתוהו בית דין. הלכך חמירא מיתה דילה לפוטרו ממון. **דאיסור שעה** — אי לא משכח ליה ההיא שעתא — תו לא מיקטיל.

וּצְרִיכָא דְּאִי [3] The Gemara has now cited two rulings of Rabbah in which he makes the same two points: (1) When a thief slaughters an animal under circumstances which make the act a capital crime, he is also liable to pay the fourfold and fivefold penalties, since these payments are an innovation. (2) If the act of theft was itself a capital offense, the thief is exempt from all payments, since the payment of compensation for theft is not an innovation, and the double, fourfold, and fivefold penalties can be imposed only in addition to the regular damage payment. **And** the Gemara adds that although Rabbah was making the same distinction in both rulings, **it was necessary** for Rabbah to issue both rulings in order to clarify his position. [4] **For if he had told us** only **about** the case of a thief who stole on **Shabbat, we might have thought** that the second half of Rabbah's ruling — exempting the thief when the theft itself involved a capital offense — applies only to offenses like violating **Shabbat,** [5] **because the prohibition** against violating Shabbat **is permanent.** Violating Shabbat is an offense punishable by death administered by a court, without any limitation of time. [6] **But the prohibition against breaking in** to a house **is** a **temporary** one. A burglar who is caught breaking in to a house may be killed only if he is found breaking in. [7] Therefore **I would say** that the rule that a person who is subject to the more severe penalty is exempt from payment does **not** apply in such a case. Hence, were it not for Rabbah's explicit ruling, I might have thought that the burglar who slaughtered an animal while breaking into a house should be liable in all cases. [8] **And if he had told us** only **about** the case of a burglar who steals while **breaking in,** we might have thought that the second half of Rabbah's ruling — exempting the thief when the theft itself involved a capital offense — applies only to capital offenses like breaking in, because the death penalty in such a case, although temporary, is absolute and unconditional, but that the ruling does not apply to other cases in which the death sentence can be avoided because of legal technicalities. In most capital cases, the death penalty can be imposed only if the offender was explicitly warned by witnesses. [9] But a burglar caught breaking in to a house may be killed without warning, **because his** action in **breaking in is itself** considered **his warning.** The very fact that he is

NOTES

וּצְרִיכָא. דְּאִי אַשְׁמַעִינַן שַׁבָּת And it is necessary. For if he had informed us about Shabbat. Our commentary follows *Rashi* who explains that both parts of the Gemara's argument refer to the second part of Rabbah's statement, in which he ruled that the thief is exempt from paying the

subject to a death sentence and he is exempt from any damage he may have done while breaking in. However, once the burglar turns around and begins to leave the house, it is forbidden to kill him, and he becomes liable for any damage he may have caused.

HALAKHAH

גָּנַב וְטָבַח בַּמַּחְתֶּרֶת If he stole it and slaughtered it while breaking in. "If a thief causes damage while breaking in to a house, he is exempt from payment, since it is permitted to kill him at that time. Likewise, if he steals an

TRANSLATION AND COMMENTARY

breaking in to a house is considered proof enough that he is knowingly violating the law and is fully aware of the consequences. This is the equivalent of a warning in other cases. Thus the owner of the house is allowed to impose his personal death sentence on the intruder without hesitation. [1] **But** violation of **Shabbat,** like other capital crimes, **requires a warning.** [2] Therefore **I would say** that the rule that a person who is subject to the more severe penalty is exempt from payment does **not** apply in the case of a thief who steals on Shabbat, because the death sentence is not unconditional. [3] **Therefore it was necessary** for Rabbah to issue **both** rulings, so that we would understand that his distinction between a thief who was subject to the more severe penalty for the theft itself, and a thief who was subject only

LITERAL TRANSLATION

[1] but [regarding] Shabbat, which requires a warning, [2] I would say not. [3] [Therefore both are] necessary. [4] Rav Pappa said: [If] he had a cow that he had stolen and he slaughtered it on Shabbat, he is liable, [5] since he was already liable for theft before he came to [violate] the prohibition of Shabbat. [6] [If] he had a cow that he had borrowed, and he slaughtered it on Shabbat, he is exempt.

אֲבָל שַׁבָּת, דְּבָעֲיָא הַתְרָאָה, [1]
אֵימָא לָא. [3] צְרִיכָא. [2]
אָמַר רַב פַּפָּא: הָיְתָה פָּרָה [4]
גְּנוּבָה לוֹ וּטְבָחָהּ בְּשַׁבָּת, חַיָּיב,
שֶׁכְּבָר נִתְחַיֵּיב בִּגְנֵיבָה קוֹדֶם [5]
שֶׁיָּבֹא לִידֵי אִיסּוּר שַׁבָּת.
הָיְתָה פָּרָה שְׁאוּלָה לוֹ, [6]
וּטְבָחָהּ בְּשַׁבָּת, פָּטוּר.

RASHI

הָיְתָה פָּרָה שְׁאוּלָה לוֹ וּטְבָחָהּ בְּשַׁבָּת
פָּטוּר — דְּהָשְׁתָּא שַׁעְתָּא דְּקָא טָבַח לָהּ
גָּזֵיל לָהּ מַמְרַהּ, וּמִיתָה וּמָמוֹן בָּאִין
כְּאֶחָד. וְלֹא גַּרְסִינַן: שֶׁאָם אֵין גְּנֵיבָה אֵין טְבִיחָה וְאֵין מְכִירָה. דְּגַבֵּי
שׁוֹאֵל לֹא שַׁיָּיךְ לֹא כֶּפֶל וְלֹא אַרְבָּעָה וַחֲמִשָּׁה, שֶׁהֲרֵי חַיָּיב בְּקֶרֶן
לְעוֹלָם, אֲפִילּוּ טוֹעֵן טַעֲנַת גַּנָּב. וְאֵין קֶנָס אֶלָּא אוֹ בְּגַנָּב, אוֹ בְּשׁוֹמֵר
חִנָּם הַפּוֹטֵר עַצְמוֹ בְּטוֹעֵן טַעֲנַת גַּנָּב, שֶׁאוֹמֵר "נִגְנְבָה".

to the more severe penalty for slaughtering the animal, applies both to Shabbat and to breaking in.

אָמַר רַב פַּפָּא [4] **Rav Pappa said:** Rabbah's distinction between a thief who is subject to the more severe penalty for the theft itself, and a thief who is subject to the more severe penalty only for slaughtering the animal, applies to yet another case. If a thief **had a cow** in his possession **that he had stolen** beforehand **and he slaughtered it on Shabbat, he is** held **liable** to pay the fourfold and fivefold penalty, even though he is subject to the death penalty for killing an animal on Shabbat, [5] **since he was already liable for theft before he was in a position to violate the prohibition** against doing work **on Shabbat.** Rav Pappa agrees with Rabbah that the fourfold and fivefold fine is an innovation established by the Torah. Hence the thief is liable to pay the fourfold and fivefold penalty, even though he is also subject to the death penalty for violating Shabbat. [6] **If,** on the other hand, **he had a cow** in his possession **that he had borrowed** legally, **and he slaughtered it on Shabbat, he is exempt** from all payments. For he misappropriated the borrowed cow when he slaughtered it, and since the act of misappropriation was done by slaughtering, which is a violation of Shabbat, he is exempt altogether from paying for the animal. For the borrower is subject to the more severe penalty for violating Shabbat, and the payment of compensation for misappropriated property is not an innovation established by the Torah.

NOTES

principal if he was subject to the more severe penalty. According to *Rashi*, the Gemara is questioning the very idea that an offender who is subject to a more severe penalty is exempt from payment, and is saying that were it not for Rabbah we might have thought that this principle applies only in the case of Shabbat, or only in the case of the burglar caught breaking in.

Tosafot and *Ramban* explain that both parts of the Gemara's argument refer to the first part of Rabbah's statement, in which he ruled that an offender who is

subject to a fine is not exempt even if he was subject to a more severe penalty, because a fine is an innovation. According to this explanation, the Gemara is suggesting that Rabbah's ruling, that fines are not set aside by a more severe penalty, may apply only in the stricter cases. Hence we might have thought that it would apply only in the case of Shabbat, or only in the case of the burglar caught breaking in (since each of these offenses has a stringency that does not apply to the other), and it was necessary for Rabbah to repeat his ruling.

HALAKHAH

animal and slaughters it while breaking in, he is exempt from payment." (*Rambam, Sefer Nezikin, Hilkhot Genevah* 9:13; *Tur, Ḥoshen Mishpat* 351.)

הָיְתָה פָּרָה שְׁאוּלָה לוֹ וּטְבָחָהּ בְּשַׁבָּת **If he had a cow that he had borrowed, and he slaughtered it on Shabbat.** "If someone steals a cow before Shabbat and slaughters it on Shabbat, he is exempt from the fourfold and fivefold penalty, since the fine and the death penalty for violating

Shabbat were incurred at the same time, and the Halakhah is not in accordance with Rabbah who says that the more severe penalty does not exempt from fines. If someone borrows a cow before Shabbat and steals it on Shabbat by slaughtering it, he is totally exempt from paying for it, since the theft itself and the death penalty for violating Shabbat were incurred at the same time." (*Rambam, Sefer Nezikin, Hilkhot Genevah* 3:4; *Tur, Ḥoshen Mishpat* 350.)

SAGES

רַב אַחָא בְּרֵיהּ דְּרָבָא Rav Aḥa the son of Rava. A Babylonian Amora of the sixth generation. See *Ketubot*, Part I, p. 74.

TRANSLATION AND COMMENTARY

אָמַר לֵיהּ רַב אַחָא [1] **Rav Aḥa the son of Rava said to Rav Ashi:** Why did Rav Pappa teach us this additional case? [2] **Was Rav Pappa's purpose to inform us about a cow?** What difference is there between Rav Pappa's ruling and Rabbah's, other than the trivial one that Rabbah mentioned a kid and Rav Pappa a cow?

אָמַר לֵיהּ [3] In reply, Rav Ashi **said to** Rav Aḥa the son of Rava: **Rav Pappa's purpose was to inform us about borrowed** property. The significance of Rav Pappa's case lies not in his choice of animals, but in the way the thief became liable for the original theft on Shabbat. Rabbah selected a straightforward case in which the thief stole the animal from its owner's home on Shabbat, whereas Rav Pappa selected a case in which the thief took possession of the animal before Shabbat, but did not misappropriate it until he slaughtered it on Shabbat. Thus Rav Pappa teaches us that Rabbah's ruling can apply if the animal came into the thief's possession before Shabbat, provided that he held it legally until Shabbat. [4] Rav Ashi explains that Rav Pappa felt it necessary to make this point because otherwise **it might have entered your mind to say** that the borrower who later misappropriated the animal is liable for the regular damage payment from the moment he first borrowed the cow — before Shabbat — rather than from the time of the misappropriation on Shabbat. For both a borrower and a thief must either return the animal in good condition or pay for its full value. Even if the animal dies or is injured by some unavoidable accident, the thief and the borrower are both liable. Since the thief is considered to have incurred his liability from the moment of theft, we might have thought that the borrower also incurred his liability from the moment of borrowing, even though, as long as the object is intact, he is required to return the borrowed object and need not pay for it. [5] We might have thought this, says Rav Ashi, **since** it was **Rav Pappa** himself who **said** (*Bava Metzia* 91a) **that** someone who borrows an animal **is liable for its food from the time of *meshikhah*** (the symbolic pulling of the animal, by means of which the borrower acquires the right to use it). Thus we see that a borrower assumes his responsibilities

[1] אֲמַר לֵיהּ רַב אַחָא בְּרֵיהּ דְּרָבָא לְרַב אַשִׁי: [2] רַב פַּפָּא פָּרָה אֲתָא לְאַשְׁמוּעִינַן? [3] אֲמַר לֵיהּ: רַב פַּפָּא שְׁאוּלָה אֲתָא לְאַשְׁמוּעִינַן. [4] סָלְקָא דַּעְתָּךְ אָמִינָא: [5] הוֹאִיל וְאָמַר רַב פַּפָּא: מִשְּׁעַת מְשִׁיכָה הוּא דְּאִתְחַיַּיב לֵיהּ בִּמְזוֹנוֹתֶיהָ,

LITERAL TRANSLATION

[1] Rav Aḥa the son of Rava said to Rav Ashi: [2] Did Rav Pappa come to inform us [about] a cow? [3] He said to him: Rav Pappa came to inform us [about] a borrowed [animal]. [4] It might have entered your mind to say: [5] Since Rav Pappa said: It is from the time of *meshikhah* that he became liable for its food,

RASHI

פרה אתא לאשמועינן — בתמיה: מה למדנו ממנה שלא למדנו מגדי דקאמר רבה?! **שאולה אתא לאשמועינן** — דטובחה בשבת פטור. **סלקא דעתך אמינא הואיל ואמר רב פפא** — ב״השוכר את הפועלים״.

NOTES

מִשְּׁעַת מְשִׁיכָה From the time of *meshikhah*. In general, when someone buys an object, the ownership of the object is transferred through a symbolic act of acquisition. Animals are acquired by *meshikhah* — the symbolic pulling of the animal until it moves (*Kiddushin* 25b). The act of acquisition determines the legal status of the animal, should it die suddenly or should one of the parties seek to renege on the agreement. Until the act of acquisition is performed, the animal belongs to the seller; afterwards, it belongs to the buyer.

Acts of acquisition have importance regarding other laws as well. Thus we have seen (above, 30b and 31b) that a thief becomes liable for theft only after he performs an act of acquisition on the stolen object; until then, if he damages the stolen object, he is subject to the laws governing vandals. Accordingly, the Gemara rules (*Bava Metzia* 99a) that borrowers and other bailees become subject to the special laws governing them only after they have performed an act of acquisition, such as *meshikhah*.

Rosh rules that when the Gemara declares that a bailee must perform *meshikhah*, it is referring only to the bailee's obligation to care for the object and the owner's obligation to permit the bailee to use the object: Once *meshikhah* has been performed, the parties may no longer renege. But the bailee's liability to make restitution if the object is damaged, and his obligation to feed the animal, are incurred even if the parties neglect to perform a formal act of acquisition. The bailee's liability begins as soon as he is given the object and the owner walks away. *Rambam*, however, rules that liability for damages is also dependent

HALAKHAH

מִשְּׁעַת מְשִׁיכָה הוּא דְּאִתְחַיַּיב לֵיהּ בִּמְזוֹנוֹתֶיהָ It is from the time of *meshikhah* that he became liable for its food. "Someone who borrows an animal is responsible for feeding it from the moment it comes into his possession through *meshikhah* until his rights as a borrower expire. *Shakh* adds that the same law applies to the other responsibilities of the borrower, so that if the animal dies suddenly, the borrower is liable if he has already performed *meshikhah* and is exempt if he has not yet done so. *Rema* rules (following *Rosh*) that these obligations are incurred from the moment the owner departs, even if the borrower has not yet performed *meshikhah*." (*Rambam*, *Sefer Mishpatim*, *Hilkhot She'ilah U'Fikkadon* 1:4; *Shulḥan Arukh*, *Ḥoshen Mishpat* 340:4.)

TRANSLATION AND COMMENTARY

for a borrowed animal as soon as he borrows it. [1]Therefore I might have said that **here too** the borrower's **liability for any accident** that may befall the animal begins **from the time he borrows it.** If this were so, the borrower who misappropriated the animal in violation of Shabbat would not have been exempt from paying damages, since he had already incurred liability to pay for the borrowed animal from the moment of borrowing. [2]**Accordingly,** says Rav Ashi, Rav Pappa **informs us that this is not so.** Although a borrower is liable for the animal's food from the time he borrows the animal, he does not assume liability to pay for the animal itself, until it can no longer be returned. Hence the borrower who misappropriated the cow became liable to pay damages only when he slaughtered the cow, and since this occurred on Shabbat, he is exempt, because he is subject to the more severe penalty.

אָמַר רָבָא [3]The Gemara now cites a statement made by Rava which is related to Rav Pappa's ruling. **Rava said: If a father** dies leaving his property to his children, and among the other articles in the estate he **leaves them a cow** which had been **borrowed** from someone else, the children are not required to return the cow immediately. [4]Instead, **they may make use of it for the entire borrowing period** originally allotted to the father. But even though the children are permitted to use the animal, they are not themselves considered borrowers; rather, they are bailees who have a lesser degree of responsibility than borrowers. [5]Accordingly, **if the cow dies accidentally, they are not liable for it,** since only borrowers are responsible in cases of unavoidable accident, and the father, who would indeed have been responsible, is dead. [6]Rava continued: If the heirs **were under the impression that** the borrowed cow **was their father's** own property, **and they slaughtered it and ate its** meat, they are not held fully responsible. Therefore they need not pay

[1]הָכָא נַמִי מִשְּׁעַת שְׁאֵלָה אִתְחַיַּיב בְּאוֹנָסֶיהָ. [2]קָא מַשְׁמַע לַן.

[3]אָמַר רָבָא: הִנִּיחַ לָהֶן אֲבִיהֶן פָּרָה שְׁאוּלָה, [4]מִשְׁתַּמְּשִׁין בָּהּ כָּל יְמֵי שְׁאֵלָתָהּ. [5]מֵתָה, אֵין חַיָּיבִין בְּאוֹנְסָהּ. [6]כִּסְבוּרִין שֶׁל אֲבִיהֶם הִיא וּטְבָחוּהָ וַאֲכָלוּהָ,

LITERAL TRANSLATION

[1]here too from the time of borrowing he became liable for its accidents. [2][Therefore] he informs us [that this is not so].

[3]Rava said: [If] their father left them a borrowed cow, [4]they may make use of it all the days of its borrowing. [5][If] it died, they are not liable for its accident. [6][If] they thought that it was their father's and they slaughtered it and ate it,

RASHI

הכא נמי — נימא משעת שאלה רמיא עליה חיוב קרן, וכי טבחה בשבת ליחייב. **קא משמע לן** — כיון דכל כמה דאיתא הדרא בעינא, ההיא שעתא דקא טבח לה — קא גזיל לה. **כל ימי שאלתה** — כל ימי משך הזמן ששאלה אביהן מן הבעלים. **אין חייבין באונסה** — דאינהו לאו שואלין נינהו ונלה.

NOTES

on the performance of an act of acquisition. Rav Pappa's use of the word *meshikhah* in his ruling lends support to *Rambam*'s ruling. But *Leḥem Mishneh* explains that Rav Pappa may merely have been referring to the normal situation, in which *meshikhah* is performed when the animal is handed over, but in fact the borrower is liable even if he has not performed a formal act of acquisition.

מִשְׁתַּמְּשִׁין בָּהּ כָּל יְמֵי שְׁאֵלָתָהּ They may make use of it all the days of its borrowing. In general, once a borrower takes possession of a borrowed object through *meshikhah*, the owner may not renege on his agreement and demand the borrowed object back. Rava is teaching us that this law applies even if the borrower dies. His rights are inherited by his heirs, and the owner cannot demand the borrowed object back before the date that had been agreed upon by the parties. *Rosh* (*Bava Kamma* 112a) rules, however, that the owner may demand that the heirs assume full responsibility for the animal or return it immediately.

מֵתָה, אֵין חַיָּיבִין בְּאוֹנְסָהּ If it died, they are not liable for its accident. From the plain meaning of Rava's statement, it would appear that the heirs of the borrower enjoy all the benefits of the borrowed animal yet have none of the

HALAKHAH

הִנִּיחַ לָהֶן אֲבִיהֶן פָּרָה שְׁאוּלָה If their father left them a borrowed cow. "If someone borrows an animal or a utensil for a specified period of time and takes formal possession of the object, the owner cannot change his mind and demand the object back before the specified time is up. Moreover, even if the borrower dies, the owner still cannot demand the object back; rather, he must permit the borrower's heirs to use the object until the time is up. However, even though the heirs are entitled to use the borrowed object, they are not responsible for accidents as regular borrowers are. On the other hand, they do have the liabilities of a paid bailee or a hirer. Hence they are responsible if the object is lost or stolen. Some authorities (*Rosh*) say that this applies only if the owner said nothing to the heirs, but if the owner demanded that the heirs accept the responsibilities of a borrower or else return the object, they must do what he demands." (*Rambam*, *Sefer Mishpatim*, *Hilkhot She'ilah U'Fikkadon* 1:5; *Shulḥan Arukh*, *Ḥoshen Mishpat* 341:1,3.)

כִּסְבוּרִין שֶׁל אֲבִיהֶם הִיא If they thought that it was their father's. "If someone dies leaving a cow that he has borrowed, and the heirs are under the impression that the

TRANSLATION AND COMMENTARY

the owner the full value of the cow, but need only reimburse him for the benefit they derived from it. [1]Hence **they** must **pay** him for the cow according to **the price of cheap meat,** which is two-thirds of the average price of meat in the market. [2]Rava concluded: **If their father left them real estate,** which serves as a lien for any debts left by the father, [3]**they are** held **liable to pay** for the full value of the cow. Although the heirs are not themselves borrowers, their father was, and although he is now dead, his obligations are covered by a lien on his estate. Hence the owner of the cow can collect directly from the estate.

אִיכָּא דְּמַתְנֵי לָהּ [4]The conclusion of Rava's statement is somewhat unclear. Did he mean that if the father left real estate, his property is liable for any accidental damage to the cow (as in the first part of Rava's statement, in which the heirs knew that the cow was borrowed, and the cow died accidentally)? Or was he referring to damage inflicted deliberately, albeit innocently, by the heirs themselves (as in the second part of Rava's statement, in which the heirs did not know that the cow was borrowed, and they slaughtered it and ate it)? **There are those who explain** that Rava's concluding statement was made **in connection with the first clause,** in which the damage was accidental, [5]**and there are those who explain** that **it** was made **in connection with the second clause,** in which the damage was deliberate.

[1]מְשַׁלְּמִין דְּמֵי בָשָׂר בְּזוֹל. [2]הִנִּיחַ לָהֶן אֲבִיהֶן אַחֲרָיוּת נְכָסִים, [3]חַיָּיבִין לְשַׁלֵּם. [4]אִיכָּא דְּמַתְנֵי לָהּ אַרֵישָׁא, [5]וְאִיכָּא דְּמַתְנֵי לָהּ אַסֵּיפָא.

LITERAL TRANSLATION

[1]they pay the value of the meat at the cheap [rate]. [2][If] their father left them real estate (lit., "an obligation of property"), [3]they are liable to pay.

[4]There is [one] who teaches it in connection with the first clause, [5]and there is [one] who teaches it in connection with the last clause.

RASHI

דמי בשר בזול — כל זוזא חשבינן בארבעה דנקי. הכי אמרינן בפרק "מי שמת" (בבא בתרא קמו,ב), והעור יחזירו לבעלים. **אחריות נכסים** — קרקעות. **איכא דמתני ארישא** — להאי "הניח להן אביהן אחריות נכסים חייבין לשלם", ואמרינן דחייבין באונסין, דאישתעבוד נכסים דאבוהון מחיים, משעת שאלה.

NOTES

responsibilities. But *Tosafot* and other Rishonim rule that the heirs have the obligations of a paid bailee, because they derive benefit from the animal, and they must pay for it if it is lost or stolen. *Baḥ* adds that the Rishonim's ruling can be inferred directly from Rava's language, since he specifically mentions that the heirs are not liable for accidents, and does not mention other types of damage.

Rashba and *Meiri* cite another opinion, in the name of the Sages of Narbonne, which goes even further, arguing that the heirs are exempt from accidental damage only if they did not use the animal, but if they did use it, they themselves become borrowers. Most Rishonim, however, follow *Ra'avad*, who rules that the heirs never incur the liabilities of a borrower, even if they use the animal.

דְּמֵי בָשָׂר בְּזוֹל The value of the meat at the cheap rate. In tractate *Bava Batra* (146b), the Gemara explains that the cheap rate for meat is two-thirds of the regular market price. Accordingly, *Rashi* and *Rid* explain that the heirs here must pay for the meat they ate at two-thirds of the market price. Most Rishonim follow *Rashi* in this matter, and his viewpoint was accepted by *Shulḥan Arukh*.

Ritva rejects *Rashi*'s explanation, citing a tradition in the name of *Ramban* that the clause in *Bava Batra* defining "cheap" as two-thirds of the ordinary price of meat, was a Geonic insertion in the Gemara that was not intended to be applied outside the context of the case considered there. *Ritva* explains that there is no fixed amount that the heirs must pay for the meat. Rather, we assess the benefit they derived as the value of the meat they would have eaten if this animal had not been available to them, and they had had to go out and buy meat.

Rashi rules that the heirs must return the inedible parts of the animal, such as its hide. *Sma* infers from the language of the *Shulḥan Arukh* that the heirs are not required to return the hide itself, because the animal was changed substantially when it was slaughtered, and ceased to belong to its owner. Rather, they are permitted to return the hide if they wish, but they also have the option of keeping it and paying its full value to the owner, if they prefer. *Ketzot HaḤoshen*, however, maintains that the heirs must return the hide itself, if it is still in their possession.

אַחֲרָיוּת נְכָסִים Real estate. According to Talmudic law, all real estate owned by a debtor is mortgaged for his debts, but his movable property is not. Therefore, if a debtor sells his real estate after the debt has been created, the creditor may seize the property from the buyer, since the buyer

HALAKHAH

cow belongs to them, and they slaughter it and eat its meat, they need not pay the owner for the full value of the cow, since they were not themselves borrowers. Rather, they pay him for the meat they ate, at two-thirds of the market rate for meat, and return the hide to him intact or pay for its full value." (*Rambam, Sefer Mishpatim, Hilkhot She'ilah U'Fikkadon* 1:5; *Shulḥan Arukh, Ḥoshen Mishpat* 341:4.)

הִנִּיחַ לָהֶן אֲבִיהֶן אַחֲרָיוּת נְכָסִים If their father left them real estate. "The heirs of someone who died and who left a borrowed cow do not themselves have the responsibilities of a borrower, but if the original borrower left real estate, the heirs are fully responsible to the extent of the value of the real estate. According to *Rambam*, even if the animal dies accidentally, the heirs must pay for it in full from the real estate, following the first version of Rava's

TRANSLATION AND COMMENTARY

מַאן דְּמַתְנֵי לָהּ [1]**Those who explain** that Rava's statement was made **in connection with the first clause** agree that **it applies all the more so to the second clause,** because if the estate is liable for accidental damage to the borrowed object, it is certainly liable for deliberate damage to it. Thus Rava was saying, in effect, that both his statements apply only if the father left no real estate, but if he left real estate, the obligations of the father as a borrower are effectively transferred to his estate. [2]This opinion **conflicts with Rav Pappa's** view (above) that a borrower assumes liability to pay for the borrowed object only when it can no longer be returned. For according to Rav Pappa, the father had no financial obligation to the owner when he died, and hence there was no lien on his estate. [3]**But those who explain** that Rava's statement was made

[1]מַאן דְּמַתְנֵי לָהּ אַרֵישָׁא כָּל שֶׁכֵּן אַסֵּיפָא, [2]וּפְלִיגָא דְּרַב פַּפָּא. [3]וּמַאן דְּמַתְנֵי לָהּ אַסֵּיפָא

LITERAL TRANSLATION

[1]The one who teaches it in connection with the first clause [applies it] all the more so to the last clause, [2]and disagrees with Rav Pappa. [3]But the one who teaches it in connection with the last clause

RASHI

כל שכן אסיפא — כשטבחוה ואכלוה. **ופליגא דרב פפא** — דאמר לעיל: הויא שעתא דמטו לה אונסין הוא דאתי חיובא עליה, ולא משעת שאלה. **ואיכא דמתני לה אסיפא** — היכא דטבחוה, אם הניח להן אביהן אחריות נכסים — משלמין תשלומי מעליא ולא בזול, דאיבעי להו למידק.

NOTES

may seize the property from the buyer, since the buyer should have known that it was subject to a lien, and he should not have bought it before determining that the debtor was able to repay his debts by other means. But if the debtor sells his movable property, the creditor may not seize it. Hence, real estate is described in the Talmud as "property that can be mortgaged."

According to Jewish law, heirs do not inherit their forebears' debts, and have the status of buyers vis-à-vis the property that they have inherited. Thus, if the heirs have inherited real estate, the creditor may seize it since it was subject to a lien, but if the heirs have inherited movable property, the creditor may not seize it. The heirs do have a moral obligation to repay their forebears' debts with the movable property they have inherited, but according to Talmudic law this moral obligation is not enforceable in court. The Geonim instituted that movable property inherited by heirs should be considered subject to a lien, like real estate. Hence the law as it was codified later states that a creditor may seize any kind of property inherited from the debtor, except for movable property sold to a buyer.

Accordingly, when *Rambam* stated our Gemara's ruling, he removed the reference to "property that can be mortgaged," and simply ruled that the heirs of the borrower are liable if their father left them property of any kind. In this, *Rambam* followed the decree of the Geonim (*Maggid Mishneh*). This is also the view of *Rosh*, *Tur*, and *Shulḥan Arukh* (*Ḥoshen Mishpat* 341:4). *Ritva*, however, maintains that the decree of the Geonim applies only to loans but not to damage payments. Hence Talmudic law remains in force in our case, and the owner may obtain restitution only from real estate left by the borrower.

וּמַאן דְּמַתְנֵי לָהּ אַסֵּיפָא But the one who teaches it in connection with the last clause. According to this version, Rava agrees with Rav Pappa that a borrower's financial obligation for accidents is not incurred until the accident occurs. Hence Rava's first ruling, exempting the heirs from liability for accidental damage, applies even if the father left real estate, because the heirs themselves were not borrowers and the father was not liable when he died. Hence when the father died, he had no financial obligations to the owner for accidents, and there was no lien on the property he left to his heirs. But Rava's second statement — exempting the heirs from full liability if they thought that the cow was their own and they slaughtered it deliberately — does not apply if the father left real estate, even according to the version in which Rava agrees with Rav Pappa. *Rashi* explains that in this case the heirs are considered to have been negligent in their care of the cow, since they should have realized that the animal was borrowed and should not therefore have slaughtered it. Therefore the heirs are liable, since they have the status of bailees who are liable for negligence.

The Rishonim question *Rashi*'s explanation. If the heirs are considered negligent for not investigating the ownership of the cow, why are they liable only if the father left property (*Ramban*, *Ritva*)? Because of this objection, *Rashash* suggested that there may be a scribal error in *Rashi*'s text.

Most Rishonim agree that the heirs cannot be considered negligent if their father failed to inform them about the borrowed cow. *Tosafot* explains that it was the father who was considered negligent for passing the cow on to his heirs without telling them that it was borrowed. Rav Pappa's ruling — that a borrower is not liable for accidents until they occur — applies only to accidents, but the borrower is liable for damage caused by his negligence from the moment he was negligent. Hence the father was liable for his negligence when he died, and there was a lien on the property he left to his heirs, even according to Rav Pappa.

Remah has another explanation, based on a passage in tractate *Bava Kamma* (111b) which rules that if the children of a deceased thief eat stolen property left to them by their father, they need not pay the owner unless their

HALAKHAH

applies only if the heirs slaughtered the animal thinking that it was theirs. If the original borrower left real estate, they must pay for the animal in full, and may not pay the value of cheap meat, but if the animal died by accident, they are not liable at all, following the second version of Rava's statement." (*Rambam*, *Sefer Mishpatim*, *Hilkhot She'ilah U'Fikkadon* 1:5; *Shulḥan Arukh*, *Ḥoshen Mishpat* 341:4.)

TRANSLATION AND COMMENTARY

in connection with the second clause maintain that it applies only to deliberate damage,[1] **but** in cases of accidental damage, as **in the first clause, it does not apply,** because the estate is less liable for accidental damage than for deliberate damage. Thus Rava was saying, in effect, that his second statement, about deliberate damage, does not apply if the father left real estate, but his first statement, about accidental damage, applies even if the father left real estate, because the heirs themselves were not borrowers, and the father was not liable when he died. [2]This opinion **is consistent with Rav Pappa's,** cited above, for according to Rav Pappa, a borrower does not assume liability to pay for the borrowed object until it can no longer be returned. Hence the father had no financial obligation to the owner when he died, and there was no lien on his estate. But if the heirs caused injury to the cow deliberately, because they did not know that the cow was borrowed, the estate is liable, since the father was negligent in not informing his heirs that the cow was borrowed. Even Rav Pappa agrees that when a borrowed object is damaged through negligence, the borrower assumed liability to pay for the object from the time of his negligence, even before the object was damaged. Hence the father became liable for his negligence while he was still alive, and this obligation created a lien on his estate.

[1]אֲבָל אַרֵישָׁא לָא, [2]וְהַיְינוּ דְּרַב פַּפָּא.

LITERAL TRANSLATION

[1]does not [apply it] in connection with the first clause, [2]and this is in accordance with Rav Pappa.

RASHI

אבל ארישא — אם מתה, לא מיחייבי לשלומי, ולא אמרינן אישתעבוד נכסי דאבוהון משעת שאלה. והיינו דרב פפא — דאמר לעיל: לא אמרינן משעת שאלה רמו עליה תשלומין, אלא משעת אונסין ואילך. והאי שעתא ליתיה לשואל דליחייב.

The Gemara now returns to the main problem it raised above (31b) — that our Mishnah, which rules that someone who rapes his sister must pay a fine, conflicts with a Mishnah in tractate *Makkot*, which rules that he is lashed. Since there is an established Halakhic principle that a person can never be punished by lashes and by a monetary penalty for the same crime, the man who rapes his sister should be exempt from paying the fine because he is subject to the more severe penalty of lashes. Why, then, does our Mishnah rule that a man who rapes his sister must pay the fine?

Three solutions to this problem have been presented. The first was stated by Ulla (above, 32a). He argued that, although we cannot inflict both lashes and a monetary penalty for the same crime, we do not know which penalty takes precedence. According to Ulla, the Mishnah in *Makkot* must be interpreted as dealing with a special case in which the fine imposed by the Torah on rapists and seducers, as well as the other relevant financial penalties, are not applicable for technical reasons (because the victim was an adult, or an orphan who was seduced), whereas our Mishnah is referring to all other cases.

The second solution was offered by Rabbi Yoḥanan (above, 32b). He argued that lashes take precedence over monetary payments, much as the death penalty does, but only if they are actually inflicted. According to this viewpoint, the Mishnah in *Makkot* which rules that lashes are inflicted needs no special explanation, but our Mishnah, which rules that a fine is paid, must be explained as referring to a case in which there was a technical legal barrier preventing the court from imposing lashes, such as when the assailant had not been warned.

The third solution was offered by Resh Lakish (above, 33b). He argued that lashes do indeed take precedence over monetary payments, and this is the viewpoint accepted by the Halakhah. Our Mishnah, however, reflects the view of Rabbi Meir, who maintains that someone who is subject to the death penalty is exempt from monetary penalties, but someone who is subject both to lashes and to a monetary penalty is punished by both penalties. According to this viewpoint, our Mishnah, which rules that a fine is paid, and the Mishnah in *Makkot,* which rules that lashes are inflicted, do not contradict each other, and there is no need for any special explanation of either Mishnah.

NOTES

father also left them real estate. *Remah* explains that Rava's compromise, whereby the heirs pay only two-thirds of the value of the meat they ate, applies only if the heirs had no inkling that they might have to pay for the animal. But heirs must always take into account the possibility that the property they inherited did not belong to their father. Hence, if they inherited real estate, they knew when they ate the cow that they might have to pay for it from the real estate. Therefore the compromise does not apply, and even though the animal was borrowed and not stolen, they must pay for it in full.

Shittah Mekubbetzet suggests that *Rashi*'s explanation may be based on a similar idea: The heirs are considered negligent for not investigating the ownership of the cow only if they would have been required to pay for it if it had been stolen; but if they inherited no real estate and have no liabilities for stolen property, they are not considered negligent for failing to determine that the cow was not theirs.

TRANSLATION AND COMMENTARY

The Gemara has already explained (above, 32b and 33a) that Ulla's interpretation is based on a *gezerah shavah*, which is not accepted by Rabbi Yoḥanan (nor, presumably, by Resh Lakish). The Gemara now seeks to explain the basis of the difference of opinion between Rabbi Yoḥanan and Resh Lakish.

Rabbi Yoḥanan and Resh Lakish agree that lashes take precedence over monetary payments, according to the Sages who disagree with Rabbi Meir. Rabbi Yoḥanan and Resh Lakish also agree that Rabbi Meir is of the opinion that a sentence of lashes may be imposed together with monetary payments, and that Rabbi Meir maintains that the death penalty exempts from payments of all kinds, including fines. Hence Rabbi Meir could have been the author of our Mishnah. Why, then, did Rabbi Yoḥanan and Resh Lakish give different explanations of the Mishnah? Why did Rabbi Yoḥanan not explain the Mishnah as reflecting the viewpoint of Rabbi Meir, and why did Resh Lakish not explain the Mishnah as referring to a case in which the rapist was not warned?

[1]בִּשְׁלָמָא רַבִּי יוֹחָנָן לָא אָמַר כְּרֵישׁ לָקִישׁ, [2]דְּקָא מוֹקִים לָהּ כְּרַבָּנַן. [3]אֶלָּא רֵישׁ לָקִישׁ מַאי טַעֲמָא לָא אָמַר כְּרַבִּי יוֹחָנָן? [4]אָמַר לָךְ: כֵּיוָן דְּאִילּוּ אַתְרוּ בֵּיהּ פָּטוּר, [5]כִּי לָא אַתְרוּ בֵּיהּ נַמִי פָּטוּר.
[6]וְאָזְדוּ לְטַעֲמַיְיהוּ. [7]דְּכִי אֲתָא רַב דִּימִי, אָמַר: [8]חַיָּיבֵי מִיתוֹת

LITERAL TRANSLATION

[1]Granted that Rabbi Yoḥanan did not say like Resh Lakish, [2]because he explains it according to the Rabbis. [3]But what is the reason [that] Resh Lakish did not say like Rabbi Yoḥanan?

[4]He can say to you: Since, if they warned him, he is exempt, [5]when they did not warn him he is also exempt.

[6]And they follow their own arguments. [7]For when Rav Dimi came, he said: [8]Those who inadvertently [commit offenses that] are subject to the death penalty,

RASHI

בשלמא רבי יוחנן — דמוקי מתניתין בשלא התרו כו'. **לא אמר כריש לקיש** — דאוקמיה כרבי מאיר. **כי לא אתרו ביה נמי פטור** — הואיל ואיכא בר מלקות.

בִּשְׁלָמָא רַבִּי יוֹחָנָן [1]The Gemara now takes up this point: **It is understandable that Rabbi Yoḥanan did not explain** the Mishnah **as Resh Lakish** did, [2]**because** Resh Lakish was forced to explain the Mishnah as reflecting the minority viewpoint of Rabbi Meir, which was rejected by the Halakhah, whereas Rabbi Yoḥanan preferred to **explain** the Mishnah **as reflecting** the accepted viewpoint of **the Rabbis.** Even though Rabbi Yoḥanan could have explained the Mishnah as reflecting the viewpoint of Rabbi Meir, it is clearly better, if possible, to explain the Mishnah without invoking a rejected minority view. [3]**But why did Resh Lakish not explain** the Mishnah **as Rabbi Yoḥanan** did? Presumably Resh Lakish agrees with Rabbi Yoḥanan that, according to the Rabbis who disagree with Rabbi Meir, lashes take precedence over monetary payments, for otherwise Resh Lakish would have adopted Ulla's explanation. What, then, forced Resh Lakish to invoke a minority opinion? Why did he not simply say that our Mishnah is referring to a case in which the brother who raped his sister was exempt from lashes for technical legal reasons?

אָמַר לָךְ [4]The Gemara answers: Resh Lakish **can say to you:** I disagree with the basic idea underlying Rabbi Yoḥanan's explanation — that someone who is subject to lashes is exempt from payment only if the lashes are actually inflicted. On the contrary, I maintain that **since** the offender who was subject to lashes **would have been exempt** from monetary payments (according to the Rabbis) **if** the witnesses **had warned him** and the lashes had been inflicted, [5]**he is also exempt** from monetary payments **if they did not warn him,** even though he was not lashed. In my opinion, an offense that is subject to a more severe penalty is exempt from all monetary penalties even if the more severe penalty is not actually carried out. Therefore there is a clear contradiction between our Mishnah, which rules that a man who rapes his sister must pay a fine, and the established principle that someone who is subject to lashes cannot be punished by a financial penalty. Hence we must say that our Mishnah reflects the viewpoint of Rabbi Meir, who rejects this principle.

וְאָזְדוּ לְטַעֲמַיְיהוּ [6]We have now established that Rabbi Yoḥanan and Resh Lakish disagree as to whether someone who has committed an offense that is subject to both lashes and a monetary payment is exempt from payment if the lashes are not actually inflicted. Rabbi Yoḥanan maintains that in such cases the offender must pay the monetary penalty, whereas Resh Lakish is of the opinion that he is exempt. **And** in this dispute, Rabbi Yoḥanan and Resh Lakish **follow their own lines of argument.** Their positions regarding our Mishnah are consistent with the positions they took in the following dispute: [7]**For when Rav Dimi came** from Eretz Israel to Babylonia and met with the Babylonian Amoraim, he reported to them the views of Rabbi Yoḥanan and Resh Lakish, who lived in Eretz Israel, **saying:** [8]Rabbi Yoḥanan and Resh Lakish disagree about a person **who inadvertently commits an offense that is subject to the death penalty,**

שׁוֹגְגִין, [1]וְחַיָּיבֵי מַלְקִיּוֹת שׁוֹגְגִין, וְדָבָר אַחֵר — [2]רַבִּי יוֹחָנָן אָמַר: חַיָּיב, [3]וְרֵישׁ לָקִישׁ אָמַר: פָּטוּר.

[4]רַבִּי יוֹחָנָן אָמַר: חַיָּיב, [5]דְּהָא לָא אַתְרוּ בֵּיהּ.

[6]רֵישׁ לָקִישׁ אָמַר: פָּטוּר. [7]כֵּיוָן דְּאִילּוּ אַתְרוּ בֵּיהּ פָּטוּר, [8]כִּי לָא אַתְרוּ בֵּיהּ נַמִי פָּטוּר.

[9]אֵיתִיבֵיהּ רֵישׁ לָקִישׁ לְרַבִּי יוֹחָנָן: [10]״וְלֹא יִהְיֶה אָסוֹן, עָנוֹשׁ יֵעָנֵשׁ״. [35A] [11]מַאי לָאו אָסוֹן מַמָּשׁ?

LITERAL TRANSLATION

[1]or who inadvertently [commit offenses that] are subject to lashes, and [the offense is also subject to] something else — [2]Rabbi Yoḥanan said: He is liable, [3]and Resh Lakish said: He is exempt.

[4]Rabbi Yoḥanan said: He is liable, [5]because they did not warn him.

[6]Resh Lakish said: He is exempt. [7]Since, if they warned him, he is exempt, [8]when they did not warn him he is also exempt.

[9]Resh Lakish objected to Rabbi Yoḥanan: [10]"And [if] there is no disaster, he shall surely be punished." [35A] [11]Is it not a real disaster?

RASHI

שוגגין — שלא התרו בהן. **ודבר אחר** — ממון. ואכולה מילתא קאי, כלומר: חייבי מיתות שוגגין וממון, או חייבי מלקיות שוגגין וממון. **רבי יוחנן אומר חייב** — בתשלומין. **דהא לא אתרו ביה** — ואין אתה מחייבו אלא משום רשעה אחת דממון. **כי לא אתרו ביה נמי פטור** — ולקמן יליף טעמא. **מאי לאו אסון ממש** — אם לא מתה האשה — יענש הנוגף בדמי ולדות. הא אם מתה — לא יענש, ואפילו לא התרו בו, וקשיא לרבי יוחנן.

TRANSLATION AND COMMENTARY

[1]**or who inadvertently commits an offense that is subject to lashes, if the offense is also subject to another** penalty — the payment of damages. [2]**Rabbi Yoḥanan said:** In such a case the offender **is liable** and must pay the monetary penalty, since the more severe penalty of death or lashes is not applicable because the offense was inadvertent. [3]**But Resh Lakish said:** Even in such a case, the offender **is exempt** from all monetary payments, since his offense was subject to the more severe penalty of death or lashes.

רַבִּי יוֹחָנָן אָמַר [4]**Rabbi Yoḥanan explained:** In such a case the offender **is liable** and must pay the monetary penalty, [5]**because** in practice he is not subject to a more severe penalty. The penalties of lashes and death can be inflicted only if the offense was deliberate and the offender had been warned, but in this case witnesses **did not warn him,** since the offense was inadvertent. Hence the more severe penalty cannot be inflicted, and there is no reason for him to be exempt from the monetary penalty.

רֵישׁ לָקִישׁ אָמַר [6]**Resh Lakish explained:** Even in such a case the offender **is exempt** from payment, because an offense that is subject to a more severe penalty is exempt from all monetary penalties, even if the more severe penalty is not administered in practice. [7]Therefore, **since** this offender **would have been exempt** from payment **if** the offense had been deliberate and witnesses **had warned him,** [8]**he is also exempt** from payment **when** the sin was inadvertent and witnesses **did not warn him.**

אֵיתִיבֵיהּ [9]The Gemara now considers this dispute in more detail. **Resh Lakish raised** the following **objection against** the viewpoint of **Rabbi Yoḥanan:** The law that a person is exempt from paying damages if he is subject to the death penalty is derived by the Mishnah (below, 36b) from the Biblical passage (Exodus 21:22-23) dealing with a man who tries to kill another person with whom he is quarreling, and strikes a pregnant woman by mistake (see above, 33a): [10]"And if two men struggle, and one of them strikes a pregnant woman so that she loses her unborn child, **but no disaster befalls her** [the woman miscarries but survives the blow], the assailant **shall surely be punished,** as the woman's husband shall impose upon him." This is traditionally understood to mean a monetary penalty, equal to the value of an unborn child on the slave market. Thus the verse teaches us that damages are paid only if the woman is not killed. From this we learn that someone who commits a crime subject to the death penalty (such as murder) is not required to pay damages for the same act. According to this verse, the assailant is exempt from paying damages whenever he is theoretically subject to the death penalty, regardless of whether he is actually executed. [35A] [11]**Is** the verse **not** to be interpreted as referring to **a real disaster** that befalls the woman?

NOTES

חַיָּיבֵי מִיתוֹת שׁוֹגְגִין וְחַיָּיבֵי מַלְקִיּוֹת שׁוֹגְגִין Those who inadvertently commit offenses that are subject to the death penalty, or who inadvertently commit offenses that are subject to lashes. *Ritva* points out that until now Rabbi Yoḥanan has been referring to cases in which the offender deliberately committed his offense, but was not lashed because he had not been properly warned by witnesses. Rav Dimi, however, is referring to cases in which the offense was committed inadvertently. *Ritva* explains that the same rule applies to both cases: According to Rabbi Yoḥanan, if the warning was not delivered properly, even a deliberate offender is treated like an inadvertent offender and is liable to pay, whereas according to Resh Lakish, even a genuinely inadvertent offender is exempt from payment, just like a deliberate offender.

מַאי לָאו אָסוֹן מַמָּשׁ? Is it not a real disaster? Our commentary follows *Rashi*, who explains that the expression "a real disaster" refers to the death of the woman, and

TRANSLATION AND COMMENTARY

This implies that the monetary penalty is not paid if the woman is killed, regardless of how the fatality occurred. If so, the assailant is exempt from payment even if he was not warned and even if he had no intention of killing anyone and struck the blow inadvertently!

לָא, דִּין אָסוֹן [1]Rabbi Yoḥanan replied: **No,** the word "disaster" must be interpreted as referring to **a penalty of disaster** — to a death penalty imposed on the assailant. According to Rabbi Yoḥanan, the verse means: "If no disaster occurs that would justify imposing the death penalty on the woman's assailant, he shall surely be punished" by a monetary penalty for causing her to miscarry. Thus the verse teaches us that damages are paid whenever the assailant is not executed, whether this is because the woman survived the attack or because of technical legal reasons. Hence we can infer that someone who commits a crime subject to the death penalty (such as murder) is required to pay damages for his action, if the death penalty is not imposed in practice.

אִיכָּא דְּאָמְרִי [2]**There are some who** transmit a slightly different version of this dispute between Rabbi Yoḥanan and Resh Lakish. According to this version, **Rabbi Yoḥanan** raised an **objection** to the viewpoint of **Resh Lakish** from the verse that says: [3]**"But if no disaster befalls her,** the assailant **shall surely be punished"** by a monetary penalty for causing her to miscarry. By implication, therefore, the monetary penalty is not imposed if the assailant is executed. [4]**Is** the verse **not** to be interpreted as referring to **a penalty of disaster** — to a death penalty imposed on the assailant? If so, it would follow that the assailant must pay whenever he is not executed. Hence we can infer that someone who commits a crime subject to the death penalty (such as murder) is required to pay damages for his action if the death penalty is not imposed in practice.

לָא אָסוֹן מַמָּשׁ [5]Resh Lakish replied: **No,** the word "disaster" is to be interpreted as referring to **a real disaster** that befalls the woman. And we may infer from this verse that the monetary penalty is not paid if the woman is killed, regardless of how the fatality occurred. Therefore it follows that if the woman is killed the assailant is exempt from payment even if he was not warned and even if he had no intention of killing anyone and struck the blow inadvertently.

[1]לָא, דִּין אָסוֹן.
[2]אִיכָּא דְּאָמְרִי: אֵיתִיבֵיהּ רַבִּי יוֹחָנָן לְרֵישׁ לָקִישׁ: [3]"וְלֹא יִהְיֶה אָסוֹן, עָנוֹשׁ יֵעָנֵשׁ". [4]מַאי לָאו דִּין אָסוֹן?
[5]לָא, אָסוֹן מַמָּשׁ.

LITERAL TRANSLATION

[1]No, a penalty of disaster.
[2]There are [some] who say: Rabbi Yoḥanan objected to Resh Lakish: [3]"And [if] there is no disaster, he will surely be punished." [4]Is it not a penalty of disaster?
[5]No, a real disaster.

RASHI

לא דין אסון – הכי קאמר קרא: אם אין משפט מות לנוגף, כגון שלא מתה האשה, או מתה ולא התרו בו – ענוש יענש.

BACKGROUND

אָסוֹן וְדִין אָסוֹן A disaster and a penalty of disaster. The meaning of the word "disaster" as used in this passage (Exodus 21:22-23) is ambiguous. The context implies that "disaster" means death, but it is not clear whether the connotation is actual death or a transgression carrying the penalty of death.

NOTES

and the expression "a penalty of disaster" refers to the sentence of death passed on her assailant. Thus, according to Resh Lakish, the verse is informing us that the assailant pays damages for the aborted pregnancy only if the woman was not killed; but if she was killed — even inadvertently — no damages are paid, because the killer is theoretically subject to the more severe penalty. According to Rabbi Yoḥanan, however, the verse is informing us that the assailant must pay damages for the aborted pregnancy unless he himself is put to death. But if he is not put to death — either because the woman survived, or because he was not warned — he is liable to pay damages, because the more severe penalty exempts only if it is inflicted in practice.

Tosafot points out that it is difficult to reconcile this explanation with the next verse, which says: "But if there is a disaster, then you shall give life for life." We have seen above (33b) that there is a Tannaitic dispute about this latter verse between Rabbi Shimon and the Sages. According to the Sages, someone who tries to kill one person and accidentally kills another is executed; hence this verse is to understood literally. According to Rabbi Shimon, however, someone who tries to kill one person and accidentally kills another is exempt; hence the expression "life for life" is to be explained as referring to monetary compensation. Now, according to the Sages, the word "disaster" in the second verse clearly means "a penalty of disaster," because the law applies only if the man is executed. How, then, could Resh Lakish argue that the word "disaster" in the first verse is to be taken literally?

Tosafot explains that Resh Lakish admits that, according to the Sages, the word "disaster" means "a penalty of disaster" in the second verse, even though it should be taken literally in the first verse. According to Rabbi Shimon, however, it is possible to explain the word "disaster" in a literal manner in the second verse as well, because he is of the opinion that the man pays money for having killed the woman and is not executed, and it is possible that he must pay this money whatever the circumstances, even if the killing was entirely inadvertent. *Ritva*, however, argues that in the second verse the word "disaster" can only mean "a penalty of disaster," even according to Rabbi Shimon. Hence Resh Lakish is forced to explain the word "disaster" differently in each verse, both according to Rabbi Shimon and according to the Sages, whereas according to Rabbi Yoḥanan the word means "a penalty of disaster" in both verses.

אִיכָּא דְּאָמְרִי There are some who say. *Hafla'ah* asks: What difference does it make if Resh Lakish raised the objection to Rabbi Yoḥanan and Rabbi Yoḥanan replied, or if it was

1 אֲמַר רָבָא: וּמִי אִיכָּא לְמַאן דְּאָמַר חַיָּיבֵי מִיתוֹת שׁוֹגְגִין חַיָּיבִים? 2 וְהָא תָּנָא דְּבֵי חִזְקִיָּה: 3 ״מַכֵּה אָדָם וּמַכֵּה

LITERAL TRANSLATION

[1] Rava said: But is there anyone who says [that] those who inadvertently [commit offenses that] are subject to the death penalty are liable? [2] But surely it was taught in the School of Ḥizkiyah: [3] "[Regarding] someone who strikes a person and someone who strikes

RASHI

מכה אדם ומכה בהמה – מכה בהמה ישלמנה ומכה אדם לא ישלם, אלא יומת. הקיש פטור ממון דמכה אדם לחיוב ממון דמכה בהמה: מה מכה בהמה אין לך בו חילוק לחיוב, אף מכה אדם אין לך בו חילוק לפטור. מכה בהמה לעולם

TRANSLATION AND COMMENTARY

אֲמַר רָבָא [1] The Gemara has now explained the difference of opinion between Rabbi Yoḥanan and Resh Lakish, as reported by Rav Dimi. But the Gemara rejects this interpretation. For Rav Dimi explained the dispute between Rabbi Yoḥanan and Resh Lakish, in which an offense subject to lashes was committed inadvertently, as part of a wider dispute about every case in which a more severe offense was committed inadvertently. **Rava said: But is there anyone who** takes the position attributed by Rav Dimi to Rabbi Yoḥanan? Granted that Rabbi Yoḥanan maintains that someone who inadvertently commits an offense that is subject to both lashes and a damage payment must pay the monetary penalty, but he could not possibly have maintained this opinion regarding the death penalty as well. For how can any Amora **say that someone who inadvertently commits** an **offense that is subject to** both **the death penalty** and a damage payment **is** held **liable** to pay the monetary penalty merely because he is not actually executed? [2] **Surely** such a viewpoint is contradicted by the following Baraita, which **was taught in the School of Ḥizkiyah.** The Baraita is commenting on the following verse (Leviticus 24:21): "And he that strikes an animal shall pay for it, and he that strikes a man shall be put to death." [3] The Baraita states: "The verse places the law regarding **someone who strikes a person** in juxtaposition to the law regarding **someone who strikes an animal.** On the surface, the two laws

NOTES

the other way around? According to both opinions, Rabbi Yoḥanan maintains that the word "disaster" means a penalty of disaster while Resh Lakish maintains that it is to be taken literally.

Hafla'ah answers that according to some opinions it would be possible to explain Resh Lakish's viewpoint even if we were to interpret the word "disaster" as a penalty. Hence Rabbi Yoḥanan could not have asked the question, and it must have been the other way around.

Ritva answers that in situations such as these the person with the more straightforward explanation generally asks the question, and the person who is giving a somewhat forced explanation answers. In this case, however, Resh Lakish's explanation appears simpler at first glance, because he understands the word "disaster" literally, but Rabbi Yoḥanan's explanation is more consistent with the way this word is used in the next verse. Hence the Gemara phrases the question both ways.

וּמִי אִיכָּא לְמַאן דְּאָמַר But is there anyone who says. From the wording of Rava's objection, it would appear that the Baraita taught by the School of Ḥizkiyah was so authoritative that it would have been inconceivable for Rabbi Yoḥanan to have disagreed with it. *Tosafot* remarks that there are several Tannaim who are known to have disagreed with this Baraita. In tractate *Sanhedrin* (79b) the Gemara cites the Tannaitic dispute between Rabbi Shimon and the Rabbis as to whether someone who intended to kill one person but who killed another is executed or pays a ransom, and the Gemara states that the Baraita taught by the School of Ḥizkiyah disagrees with both opinions. *Tosafot* explains that the Gemara in *Sanhedrin* is drawing an inference from the clause in the Baraita referring to "unintentional" killing, a clause which disagrees with both Rabbi Shimon and the Sages, but the clause of the Baraita dealing with "inadvertent" killing, which contradicts Rabbi Yoḥanan's view as reported by Rav Dimi, is accepted by everyone.

Tosafot points out, however, that in tractate *Bava Kamma* (42a) there is a Baraita that appears to disagree with the Baraita taught by the School of Ḥizkiyah. Likewise, in *Sanhedrin* (84b) the Gemara states explicitly that there is an authority who rejects the Baraita taught by the School of Ḥizkiyah entirely, including the clause dealing with "inadvertent" killing.

Accordingly, *Tosafot* explains that there were indeed Tannaim who disagreed with the Baraita taught by the School of Ḥizkiyah. Nevertheless, Rava still considered this Baraita authoritative, since it was thoroughly investigated by the School of Ḥizkiyah, whereas the other opinions appear in Baraitot that were not scrutinized in this way.

וְהָא תָּנָא דְּבֵי חִזְקִיָּה But surely it was taught in the School of Ḥizkiyah. The Rishonim ask: Why does Rava need to cite the Baraita taught by the School of Ḥizkiyah to prove that Rabbi Yoḥanan's position, as reported by Rav Dimi, is untenable? The same point can be inferred directly from our Mishnah. For our Mishnah distinguishes between a man who commits incest with his daughter, who is exempt from payment, and a man who commits incest with his sister, who is liable, and according to Rabbi Yoḥanan our Mishnah is referring to a case in which the man was not punished for his incest because witnesses failed to warn him. It is thus clear that our Mishnah is of the opinion that a man who commits a capital offense (such as incest with his daughter) is exempt from payment even if the death penalty is not imposed in practice because he had not been warned.

Tosafot and *Rashba* answer that Rava preferred to cite the Baraita for two reasons: It is more explicit, and it cites the source in the Torah for this rule. Other explanations were given by other Rishonim (see *Ramban*, *Ritva*, *Shittah Mekubbetzet*).

מַכֵּה אָדָם וּמַכֵּה בְּהֵמָה Regarding someone who strikes a person and someone who strikes an animal. *Rashi* explains that the Baraita is applying a hermeneutical rule

TRANSLATION AND COMMENTARY

are being contrasted: Someone who kills an animal is punished by a monetary payment, whereas someone who kills a human being pays no money but is put to death. However, according to traditional hermeneutic rules, when the Torah juxtaposes two different laws in this way, it teaches us that they are subject to the same rules. Hence we apply the same rules to the penalty imposed on someone who kills an animal as we do to the penalty imposed on someone who kills another human being, and we say: **In the case of someone who strikes an animal we make no distinction between** cases in which the act **was done inadvertently and** those in which it was done **deliberately,** for the Mishnah (*Bava Kamma* 26b) rules that a human being is always culpable for the damage he does directly, even if the damage was entirely accidental. [1] And likewise we make no distinction **between** cases in which the animal was struck **intentionally and** cases in which the assailant intended to strike one animal but **unintentionally** struck another, for the person who killed the animal must pay for it even if he had no intention of striking it. [2] And likewise we make no distinction **between** cases in which the animal was killed **while** the man was **'going down'** (when the blow was struck accidentally, but the striker of the blow was negligent) **and** cases in which the animal was killed **while** the man was **'going up'** (when the striker of the

בְּהֵמָה, מַה מַּכֵּה בְהֵמָה לֹא חִילַּקְתָּ בּוֹ בֵּין בְּשׁוֹגֵג בֵּין בְּמֵזִיד, [1] בֵּין מִתְכַּוֵּין לְשֶׁאֵין מִתְכַּוֵּין, [2] בֵּין דֶּרֶךְ יְרִידָה לְדֶרֶךְ

LITERAL TRANSLATION

an animal, just as [in the case of] someone who strikes an animal you made no distinction between [doing it] inadvertently and deliberately, [1] between [doing it] intentionally and unintentionally, [2] between [doing it] while going down and while

RASHI

חייב, דאמרינן בבבא קמא (כו,ב): ״פצע תחת פצע״ — לחייב על השוגג כמזיד, ואונס כרצון. שאין מתכוין — אין בו חיוב מיתה באדם. דרך עלייה — שהכהו בהגבהת ידו, או שהתכו בחרבו מלמטה למעלה. בין דרך ירידה לדרך עלייה — משום דגבי גלות דהורג בשוגג איכא חילוק בין דרך ירידה לדרך עלייה, כדאמרינן במכות (ז,ב): כל שבדרך ירידתו גולה, דכתיב ״ויפל עליו״, עד שיפול כדרך נפילה.

NOTES

called *hekesh* (הֶיקֵּשׁ — "juxtaposition" or "analogy") When the Torah juxtaposes two laws in a way that suggests that they are closely related (as when they appear in the same verse), we may infer that the regulations governing the two laws are analogous. Thus the Baraita argues that since the Torah teaches the law about killing animals in juxtaposition to the law about killing people, we may infer that just as damage payments must *always* be made if an animal was killed, irrespective of whether it was killed deliberately or inadvertently, so too damage payments are *never* made if a person was killed, irrespective of whether he was killed deliberately or inadvertently.

Ritva adds that the verse cited by the Baraita (Leviticus 24:21) is entirely superfluous. For verse 17 of that chapter has already mentioned the law that a person who kills another person must be executed, and verse 18 has already mentioned the law that a person who kills an animal must pay for it. The reason why the Torah repeated these two laws was precisely in order to place them in juxtaposition, so that we would make an analogy between the regulations governing them.

Tosafot and *Ritva* ask: Why should the juxtaposition of the two laws in this verse not itself be a source for the rule that a person who is subject to the death penalty is exempt from payment? Why do we need to derive this rule from the verse dealing with the quarreling man who struck the pregnant woman?

The Rishonim cite a comment of *Rashi* (below, 38a) that when a verse juxtaposes two laws in this way, we are supposed to draw the strongest possible analogy between them. Hence, were it not for the verse dealing with the pregnant woman, I would have drawn a strict analogy between homicide and the killing of an animal, and I would have said that just as damage payments must always be made if an animal is killed, irrespective of whether it was killed deliberately or inadvertently, so too damage payments must always be made if a person is killed, irrespective of whether he was killed deliberately or inadvertently. But since we have already learned from the verse dealing with the pregnant woman that someone who is subject to a more severe penalty is exempt from payment, we interpret this verse as comparing the *obligation to pay* when an animal is killed with the *exemption from paying* when a person is killed.

לֹא חִילַּקְתָּ בּוֹ בֵּין בְּשׁוֹגֵג בֵּין בְּמֵזִיד **You made no distinction between doing it inadvertently and deliberately.** According to *Tosafot* (*Sanhedrin* 79b), the three distinctions made by the Baraita are all independent. Only the first clause of the Baraita — which distinguishes between deliberate and inadvertent killing — has a bearing on the dispute between Rabbi Yoḥanan and Resh Lakish, whereas the other two clauses are actually referring to cases in which the killing was deliberate. According to this explanation, it is possible that the first clause of the Baraita is completely authoritative, as Rava seems to be suggesting, but that the other clauses of the Baraita are controversial, as would appear from other places where this Baraita is cited.

בֵּין מִתְכַּוֵּין לְשֶׁאֵין מִתְכַּוֵּין **Between doing it intentionally and unintentionally.** The Gemara (*Sanhedrin* 79b) asks: What does the Baraita mean by "killing someone unintentionally"? What is the difference between "inadvertently" and "unintentionally"? And the Gemara answers that the Baraita is referring to a case in which the assailant fully intended to kill one person but accidentally killed another (as in the case of the quarreling man who killed the pregnant woman).

Tosafot notes that, according to the Gemara's explanation, this clause of the Baraita is dealing with deliberate killing and has no bearing on the dispute between Rabbi Yoḥanan and Resh Lakish.

TRANSLATION AND COMMENTARY

blow was not even negligent). [1]**Just as** in all these cases we do not argue that the man should be **exempt from paying money** for the animal if he was not at fault, **and we oblige him to pay money** in all cases, [2]**so too in the case of someone who strikes a person, we should make no distinction between** cases in which the act **was done inadvertently and** those in which it was done **deliberately,** even though someone who kills a person deliberately is executed and someone who kills a person inadvertently is sent into exile. [3]And likewise we should make no distinction **between** cases in which the person who was killed was struck **intentionally and** cases in which the assailant intended to strike a particular person but **unintentionally** struck another. [4]And likewise we should make no distinction **between** cases in which the person was killed accidentally **while** his killer was **'going down'** — in which case the killer is sent into exile for his negligence — **and** cases in which the person was killed accidentally **while** his killer was **'going up,'** in which case the killer was not even negligent and is not even required to go into exile. [5]In all these cases we should not argue **that** the killer should be **obliged to pay money** when he is not subject to the death penalty in practice, **and** we should **exempt him from paying money** in all cases, since he committed an offense that is subject to the death penalty."

עֲלִיָּיה, [1]לְפוֹטְרוֹ מָמוֹן, אֶלָּא לְחַיְּיבוֹ מָמוֹן, [2]אַף מַכֵּה אָדָם לֹא תַחֲלוֹק בּוֹ בֵּין בְּשׁוֹגֵג בֵּין בְּמֵזִיד, [3]בֵּין מִתְכַּוֵּין לְשֶׁאֵין מִתְכַּוֵּין, [4]בֵּין דֶּרֶךְ יְרִידָה לְדֶרֶךְ עֲלִיָּיה, [5]לְחַיְּיבוֹ מָמוֹן, אֶלָּא לְפוֹטְרוֹ מָמוֹן".

LITERAL TRANSLATION

going up, [1]in order to exempt him [from paying] money, but to oblige him [to pay] money, [2]so too, [in the case of] someone who strikes a person, you should make no distinction between [doing it] inadvertently and deliberately, [3]between [doing it] intentionally and unintentionally, [4]between [doing it] while going down and while going up, [5]in order to oblige him [to pay] money, but to exempt him [from paying] money."

NOTES

בֵּין דֶּרֶךְ יְרִידָה לְדֶרֶךְ עֲלִיָּיה Between doing it while going down and while going up. Inadvertent killing resulting from negligence is punished by Torah law with exile in one of the six cities of refuge (Numbers 35:9-34). Not every inadvertent killer goes into exile in a city of refuge. If the death was completely unavoidable, the accidental killer is entirely exempt, and if he deliberately endangered other people, he is not permitted to go into exile in the city of refuge but must permanently live the life of a fugitive.

The Mishnah (*Makkot* 7a-b) rules that the accidental killer goes into exile only if he killed the other person "while going down, not while going up." For example, if he fell off a ladder and crushed someone to death, he is exiled only if he was climbing down the ladder, but not if he was climbing up. Likewise, if he was chopping wood and killed someone with his axe, he is exiled only if he killed the person with a downstroke, not with an upstroke. The Gemara derives this law from a verse. *Rambam* (*Hilkhot Rotzeaḥ* 6:13) explains that the law has a logical basis as well, since the accident is easier to prevent — and the negligence is greater — if he was "going down" rather than "going up."

The distinction between "going up" and "going down" applies only to accidental killing but not to deliberate murder. Accordingly, *Remah* explains that the Baraita taught by the School of Ḥizkiyah is also distinguishing between two kinds of inadvertent killing. For the Baraita rules that someone who inadvertently kills someone else is exempt from damage payments just like a deliberate killer, even though he is not in practice subject to the more severe penalty. But we might have thought that this applies only if he was at least subject to the penalty of exile, as would be the case, for example, if the killing took place while he was "going down." Hence the Baraita informs us that the same law applies even if he is exempt from all penalties (for example, if the killing took place while he was "going up"), since the verse compares the *exemption* of a person who kills another person with the *obligation* of a person who kills an animal, and regarding animals, even someone who killed an animal accidentally, while "going up," is held liable to pay damages. (This also appears to be the view of *Rashi*, and we have followed it in our commentary.)

Tosafot and *Ritva*, however, base themselves on a passage that appears later in the Gemara (below, 38a), and insist that this clause of the Baraita is not referring to inadvertent killing at all, but rather to a deliberate killer who tries to save himself from execution by paying a ransom. The Torah forbids the court to accept this (Numbers 35:31). But we might have thought that this prohibition would apply only if the killing was done deliberately while the killer was "going up," since there is

HALAKHAH

אַף מַכֵּה אָדָם לֹא תַחֲלוֹק בּוֹ בֵּין בְּשׁוֹגֵג בֵּין בְּמֵזִיד So too, in the case of someone who strikes a person, you should make no distinction between doing it inadvertently and deliberately. "Someone who commits an offense that is subject to the death penalty is exempt from any monetary penalty or damage payment that he may have incurred by his action. This law applies even if the death penalty is not inflicted in practice. Therefore someone who strikes a pregnant woman and causes her to miscarry need not pay damages for the aborted pregnancy if the woman dies, following the Baraita taught by the School of Ḥizkiyah.

"This law applies only when the death penalty was at least applicable in theory. But if the man did not intend to strike the woman at all, *Rambam* and *Shulḥan Arukh* rule

TRANSLATION AND COMMENTARY

אֶלָּא [1] **Rather,** says the Gemara, we must reject as untenable Rav Dimi's version of Rabbi Yoḥanan's position, and we must seek another explanation of his dispute with Resh Lakish. The Gemara now relates that **when Ravin came** from Eretz Israel to Babylonia, he brought a different version of the dispute, **saying:** [2] There is no dispute between Rabbi Yoḥanan and Resh Lakish **regarding someone who inadvertently commits an offense that is subject to** both **the death penalty** and a damage payment. [3] **Both** Rabbi Yoḥanan and Resh Lakish **agree that** such a person **is exempt,** in accordance with the Baraita taught by the School of Ḥizkiyah. [4] The case **about which** Rabbi Yoḥanan and Resh Lakish **disagree is where someone inadvertently commits an offense that is subject to lashes, and** by the same act he **also** becomes liable for **something else** (the payment of damages). [5] About such a case **Rabbi Yoḥanan said:** The offender **is** held **liable** to pay damages because in practice he is not subject to a more severe penalty, since an inadvertent offender cannot be lashed. On the other hand, a deliberate offender, who is actually lashed, is exempt from paying damages. Even though Rabbi Yoḥanan agrees with Resh Lakish that an offender who is subject to the death penalty is exempt from payment, even if he is not executed in practice, we cannot extrapolate from the laws governing the death penalty to a case of lashes. For there is a Scriptural source, cited by the Baraita taught by the School of Ḥizkiyah, exempting from payment an offender who is subject to the death penalty. [6] The Torah explicitly **juxtaposed** offenders **who are subject to the death penalty** to the killers of animals, and thereby informed us that these laws are to be compared. From this juxtaposition, we learn that just as there is no distinction between deliberate and inadvertent offenses involving the killing of animals, similarly there is no distinction between deliberate and inadvertent offenses involving people who are subject to the death penalty. [7] By contrast, offenders **who are subject to lashes were** not mentioned in the verse and were **not** placed in **juxtaposition** to the killers of animals. Hence the exegetical argument of the Baraita taught by the School of Ḥizkiyah does not apply to offenses punishable by lashes. We must therefore return to our original assumption and argue that the more severe penalty of lashes exempts from payment only when it is inflicted in practice. [8] **Resh Lakish,** however, disagreed and **said:** Even if the offense was committed inadvertently, and lashes are not inflicted in practice, the offender **is exempt** from payment. For although offenses that are subject to

[1] אֶלָּא, כִּי אֲתָא רָבִין, אֲמַר: [2] חַיָּיבֵי מִיתוֹת שׁוֹגְגִין, [3] כּוּלֵּי עָלְמָא לָא פְּלִיגֵי דִּפְטוּרִין. [4] כִּי פְּלִיגֵי בְּחַיָּיבֵי מַלְקוֹת שׁוֹגְגִין, וְדָבָר אַחֵר. [5] רַבִּי יוֹחָנָן אָמַר: חַיָּיב. [6] חַיָּיבֵי מִיתוֹת אִיתְקוּשׁ; [7] חַיָּיבֵי מַלְקִיּוֹת לָא אִיתְקוּשׁ. [8] רֵישׁ לָקִישׁ אָמַר: פָּטוּר.

LITERAL TRANSLATION

[1] Rather, when Ravin came, he said: [2] [Regarding] those who inadvertently [commit offenses that] are subject to the death penalty, [3] no one disputes that they are exempt. [4] Where they disagree is about those who inadvertently [commit offenses that] are subject to lashes and something else. [5] Rabbi Yoḥanan said: He is liable. [6] Those who are subject to the death penalty were juxtaposed; [7] those who are subject to lashes were not juxtaposed. [8] Resh Lakish said: He is exempt.

RASHI

כולי עלמא לא פליגי דפטור — מדתנא דבי חזקיה. **חייבי מיתות איתקוש** — למכה בהמה.

TERMINOLOGY

כִּי אֲתָא רָבִין When Ravin came.... The expression כִּי אֲתָא introduces a tradition or a legal ruling quoted by a particular Sage when he came to the academy, usually when he came to Babylonia from Eretz Israel.

NOTES

no framework for atoning for inadvertent killing of this kind. But if the killing was committed deliberately while the killer was "going down," we might have thought that deliberate killing could be ransomed as well, since there is a framework for atoning for inadvertent killing of this kind. Accordingly, the Baraita teaches us that just as there is no difference regarding monetary matters between an animal killed "going up" or "going down," so too there is no difference regarding monetary matters between a person killed deliberately "going up" or "going down." According to this explanation, this clause of the Baraita is dealing with deliberate killing, and has no bearing on the dispute between Rabbi Yoḥanan and Resh Lakish.

HALAKHAH

that he must pay for the aborted pregnancy, since there is no death penalty for someone who tries to kill one person and accidentally kills another. On the other hand, *Ra'avad* and *Rema* rule that he is exempt from payment in all cases, following the wording of the Baraita taught by the School of Ḥizkiyah." (*Rambam, Sefer Nashim, Hilkhot Na'arah Betulah* 1:13, and *Sefer Nezikin, Hilkhot Ḥovel U'Mazik* 4:5-7 and *Hilkhot Genevah* 3:1; *Shulḥan Arukh, Ḥoshen Mishpat* 423:4 and 424:1,2.)

כִּי פְּלִיגֵי בְּחַיָּיבֵי מַלְקוֹת שׁוֹגְגִין וְדָבָר אַחֵר Where they disagree is about those who inadvertently commit offenses that are subject to lashes and something else. "Someone who commits an offense that is subject to lashes is exempt from any monetary penalty or damage payment that he may have incurred by his action, but only if he is actually lashed in practice. But if for technical reasons he is not lashed, he must pay the monetary penalty, following the view of Rabbi Yoḥanan against Resh Lakish, as explained by Ravin." (*Rambam, Sefer Nashim, Hilkhot Na'arah Betulah* 1:11, and *Sefer Nezikin, Hilkhot Genevah* 3:1.)

TRANSLATION AND COMMENTARY

lashes were not specifically mentioned in the verse cited by the Baraita taught by the School of Ḥizkiyah, we can extrapolate from the laws governing the death penalty to the laws governing lashes, [1]since **the Torah explicitly** commanded us to **include** offenders **who are subject to lashes** in the same category as offenders **who are subject to the death penalty.**

הֵיכָן רִיבְּתָה תּוֹרָה [2]The Gemara asks: According to Ravin, Resh Lakish's viewpoint is based on an exegetical argument. But what is the source in the Torah to which he alludes? **Where did the Torah** teach us that offenders who are subject to lashes **are included** in the same category as offenders who are subject to the death penalty?

אָמַר אַבַּיֵי [3]The Gemara offers two answers. **Abaye said:** Resh Lakish's inference is based on a *gezerah shavah* connecting these two laws. According to this hermeneutic rule, when the Torah uses very similar words in two different contexts, it intends to compare the subject matter in the two contexts, and to transfer information from one to the other. [4]In this case, Resh Lakish's ruling **is derived from** the word **"wicked"** which appears in the verse (Numbers 35:31) dealing with someone subject to the death penalty ("who is wicked enough to die"), while another verse (Deuteronomy 25:2) uses the same word **"wicked"** in connection with a person subject to lashes ("And it shall be, if the wicked man is punishable by being lashed"). Hence we must compare the death penalty with lashes and apply the same laws to both. The *gezerah shavah* informs us, therefore, that since the death penalty exempts from payment even if it is not inflicted in practice, the same applies to lashes.

רָבָא אֲמַר [5]The Gemara now cites the answer of Rava, who disagrees with Abaye's exegesis. **Rava said:** It is clear that Resh Lakish does not derive his ruling in the case of lashes from the case of the death penalty. Rather, he derives it directly from the case of someone who kills an animal, arguing that the laws governing someone who kills an animal should be compared with the laws governing someone who is lashed (along the same lines as the Baraita taught by the School of Ḥizkiyah). Moreover, Resh Lakish's ruling is not based on the established *gezerah shavah* cited by Abaye. [6]Rather, **it comes from** the Torah's use of the word **"strikes."**

[1]בְּפֵירוּשׁ רִיבְּתָה תּוֹרָה חַיָּיבֵי מַלְקִיּוֹת כְּחַיָּיבֵי מִיתוֹת. [2]הֵיכָן רִיבְּתָה תּוֹרָה? [3]אֲמַר אַבַּיֵי: [4]אָתְיָא "רָשָׁע", "רָשָׁע". [5]רָבָא אֲמַר: [6]אָתְיָא "מַכֵּה", "מַכֵּה".

LITERAL TRANSLATION

[1]The Torah explicitly extrapolated those who are subject to lashes [to be] like those who are subject to the death penalty.

[2]Where did the Torah extrapolate [them]?

[3]Abaye said: [4]It is derived [from] "wicked," "wicked."

[5]Rava said: [6]It is derived [from] "strikes," "strikes."

RASHI

אתיא רשע רשע — נאמר בחייבי מיתות "אשר הוא רשע למות" ונאמר בחייבי מלקות "והיה אם בן הכות הרשע". **רבא אמר אתיא מכה מכה** — דמלקות נמי איתקוש למכה בהמה, ולאו מגזרה שוה דחייבי מיתות ילפינן.

NOTES

אָתְיָא "רָשָׁע", "רָשָׁע" It is derived from "wicked," "wicked." This *gezerah shavah* comparing the death penalty with lashes appears in several places in the Talmud. In two instances (*Makkot* 5b and *Bava Kamma* 86b), it is cited anonymously as the authoritative interpretation of a Mishnah and a Baraita respectively. In all the other instances (*Makkot* 5a; *Sanhedrin* 10a, 33b), it is cited in the name of Abaye and is disputed by Rava. In general, the rules applying to execution apply to lashes as well (at least according to Abaye). Hence Abaye argues that just as an offender who is theoretically subject to execution is exempt from payment, even if the penalty is not inflicted in practice, so too an offender who is theoretically subject to lashes is exempt from payment, even if the penalty is not inflicted in practice.

Tosafot asks: If this *gezerah shavah* is accepted by everyone, why does Rava not utilize it to infer the case of lashes from the case of execution? *Tosafot* suggests that it is possible that in some of the instances, at least, Rava would have accepted Abaye's *gezerah shavah*, but he preferred to cite an alternative Scriptural source. In our Gemara, however, this is not a good explanation, for according to Abaye the *gezerah shavah* is Resh Lakish's source in his dispute with Rabbi Yoḥanan. But if the *gezerah shavah* is accepted by everyone, how could Rabbi Yoḥanan disregard it and disagree with Resh Lakish?

Tosafot answers that in the two instances in which this *gezerah shavah* is cited anonymously, the *gezerah shavah* is being used to make a direct comparison between lashes and execution. The Mishnah in *Makkot* declares that the circumstances under which conspiring witnesses are punished apply equally to lashes and to the death penalty. The Baraita in *Bava Kamma* declares that, according to one Tanna, offenders who are blind are exempt both from lashes and from the death penalty. Abaye, however, wishes to apply this *gezerah shavah* more generally to laws related to lashes and the death penalty, such as the rule that someone who is subject to a more severe penalty is exempt from payment — and this rule does not necessarily fall within the scope of the *gezerah shavah*. Abaye argues that this is precisely the issue in dispute between Resh Lakish and Rabbi Yoḥanan: Resh Lakish applies the *gezerah shavah*, whereas Rabbi Yoḥanan does not. But Rava argues that the exemption from payment of someone who is

[1] אֲמַר לֵיהּ רַב פַּפָּא לְרָבָא: הֵי "מַכֵּה"? [2] אִילֵימָא: "וּמַכֵּה בְהֵמָה יְשַׁלְּמֶנָּה, וּמַכֵּה אָדָם יוּמָת", [3] הַאי בְּקְטָלָא כְּתִיב! [4] אֶלָּא הַאי "מַכֵּה": "מַכֵּה נֶפֶשׁ בְּהֵמָה יְשַׁלְּמֶנָּה, נֶפֶשׁ תַּחַת נָפֶשׁ", [5] וּסְמִיךְ לֵיהּ: "וְאִישׁ כִּי יִתֵּן מוּם בַּעֲמִיתוֹ [כַּאֲשֶׁר עָשָׂה כֵּן יֵעָשֶׂה לוֹ]". [6] וְהַאי לָאו "מַכֵּה" הִיא!

LITERAL TRANSLATION

[1] Rav Pappa said to Rava: Which "strikes"? [2] If we say: "And he who strikes an animal shall pay for it, and he who strikes a person shall be put to death," [3] this is written about killing! [4] Rather, [it refers to] this "strikes": "He who strikes the soul of an animal shall pay for it, soul for soul," [5] and next to it: "And if a man shall inflict a blemish on his fellow, [as he did, so shall it be done to him]." [6] But this [does] not [mention] "strikes"!

TRANSLATION AND COMMENTARY

אֲמַר לֵיהּ [1] Rava's explanation is unclear. From his language, it would appear that he too is constructing a *gezerah shavah*, albeit with a different key word. But this explanation is difficult to accept. For Abaye's word, "wicked," does indeed appear in two verses, one dealing with someone who is put to death, and the other dealing with someone who is lashed. Rava's word, "strikes," however, is used to describe the killing of the animal, but it is never used to describe an offense punishable by lashes. Hence **Rav Pappa said to Rava: Which** word **"strikes"** do you mean? In which pair of verses does this word appear? [2] **If we say** that the reference is to the two halves of the verse from which the Baraita derived its law (Leviticus 24:21): **"And he who strikes an animal shall pay for it, and he who strikes a person shall be put to death," this** verse does indeed use the word "strikes" twice, but not in connection with lashes. [3] Rather, it **is used in the context of killing.** The meaning of the word "strikes" in this verse is "kills," and the verse is teaching us that the laws governing someone who kills an animal are to be compared with the laws governing someone who kills a human being (as explained by the Baraita). We learn nothing here about lashes! [4] **Rather,** continues Rav Pappa, you **must have been referring to this** pair of verses in which the word **"strikes"** appears (Leviticus 24:18-19): **"He who strikes the soul of an animal shall pay for it, soul for soul,"** which refers to the killing of an animal, [5] **and** the verse **next to it: "And if a man shall inflict a blemish on his fellow, as he did, so shall it be done to him,"** which teaches us that a person who injures another person must himself be injured — by lashes. [6] Now, says Rav Pappa, **this** second verse does indeed refer to lashes, **but** it **does not mention** your key word, **"strikes"!** How can you construct a *gezerah shavah?* And how do you know that the two verses should be compared?

RASHI

ואיש כי יתן מום בעמיתו כאשר עשה כן יעשה לו — והאי "יעשה לו" — מלקות קאמר, ולקמן פריך: והא חובל בחבירו, בתשלומין ולא מלקות! **וחאי** מלקות לאו מכה כתיב, אלא "כי יתן מום", ומאי אתיא "מכה" "מכה" דקאמר רבא?

NOTES

subject to a more severe penalty clearly does not fall within the scope of this *gezerah shavah*, and even Resh Lakish would not have applied it.

אָתְיָא "מַכֵּה", "מַכֵּה" It is derived from "strikes," "strikes." It is not entirely clear what kind of exegetical argument Rava is applying. From Rava's own words it would appear that he too is constructing a *gezerah shavah*, similar to Abaye's but based on a different key word. From Rav Pappa's words "and next to it," however, it would seem that Rava is applying a hermeneutic rule called *semukhim* (סמוכים — "closeness"), whereby the rules governing the laws in one verse may be inferred from the verse immediately following. An example of *semukhim* can be found above (32b), where Rabbi Yoḥanan uses this argument to prove that lashes take precedence over monetary penalties. This rule should not be confused with the much more powerful hermeneutic rule called *hekesh* — "juxtaposition," which applies only when the Torah juxtaposes two laws in a way that strongly indicates that they are to be compared, such as when the two laws appear in the same verse.

Tosafot notes that in tractate *Bava Kamma* (83b) the Gemara cites Rava's exegesis anonymously as the source for the tradition that terms like "an eye for an eye" are not to be interpreted literally but as referring to monetary compensation. There, too, the Gemara asks (as it does here): "Which 'strikes'" — and concludes that the reference is to the verse dealing with injuries and the immediately preceding verse dealing with animals, and that the exegesis is based on the concept of "blows" rather than on the word "strikes."

Based on this parallel passage, *Tosafot* explains that Rava's exegesis is in fact a *gezerah shavah*. According to this explanation, Rav Pappa objects to the *gezerah shavah* because the key word "strikes" does not appear in the verse dealing with assault. But Rava responds that it is possible to construct a *gezerah shavah* between a key word and its synonym, as the Gemara states in several places (e.g., Ḥullin 85a). According to this explanation, it is difficult to account for the words "and next to it." *Tosafot* suggests that the text here should be amended to remove these words. *Rosh*, however, suggests that these words may not be part of the exegesis itself, and that the Gemara may simply be indicating the location of the two verses upon which the *gezerah shavah* is constructed. (Our commentary follows this explanation.)

Ritva explains that Rav Pappa himself was not certain which exegetical method Rava was applying — *gezerah*

LITERAL TRANSLATION

[1] We were referring to "striking," "striking."

[2] But surely when it is written, it is written about someone who injures his fellow, [3] and someone who injures his fellow is subject to payment!

[4] If it has no relevance to "striking" that has the value of a perutah, [5] then let it have relevance to "striking" that does not have the value of a perutah.

[1] אֲנַן "הַכָּאָה", "הַכָּאָה" קָאָמְרִינַן.

[2] וְהָא כִּי כְּתִיב, בְּחוֹבֵל בַּחֲבֵירוֹ הוּא דִּכְתִיב, [3] וְחוֹבֵל בַּחֲבֵירוֹ בַּר תַּשְׁלוּמִין הוּא!

[4] אִם אֵינוֹ עִנְיָן לְ"הַכָּאָה" שֶׁיֵּשׁ בָּהּ שָׁוֶה פְּרוּטָה, [5] תְּנֵהוּ עִנְיָן לְ"הַכָּאָה" שֶׁאֵין בָּהּ שָׁוֶה פְּרוּטָה.

RASHI

הכאה הכאה קאמרינן — ומוס על ידי הכאה הוא ניתן. **וחובל בחבירו בר תשלומין הוא** — והיכי מוקמת ליה את במלקות ופטור ממון? **אם אינו ענין** — האי קרא. **להכאה שיש בה שוה פרוטה** — ולתשלומין, דהא מקרא דבתריה ילפינן, דכתיב ביה "כן ינתן בו" — דבר הניתן מיד ליד. **תנהו ענין** — להאי "כן יעשה לו". **להכאה שאין בה שוה פרוטה** — ולמלקות, ואיתקיש למכה בהמה שלא תחלוק בו.

TRANSLATION AND COMMENTARY

אֲנַן הַכָּאָה [1] Rava answered Rav Pappa: **I was referring to** the concept of **"striking"** that appears in both these verses. It is not necessary for a *gezerah shavah* to use precisely the same word in the two contexts, provided that the same concept is present. Here, one verse characterizes the killing of an animal as a form of assault, and the other verse discusses regular assault, which is subject to the penalty of lashes. Hence we can construct a *gezerah shavah* and compare the laws in these two verses. We can infer that just as the monetary penalties in the case of the killing of the animal are independent of the intentions of the assailant and apply equally to both deliberate and inadvertent killing, so too does the exemption from payment in the case of an assault that is punishable by lashes apply equally to deliberate and inadvertent assault.

וְהָא כִּי כְּתִיב [2] But the Gemara objects to this exegesis. Rava's argument is based on the assumption that the second verse, which refers to a person who injures someone, is dealing with an offense punishable by lashes. **But surely** this verse **was written about someone who injures another person,** [3] **and someone who injures another person is subject to payment,** not lashes. Despite the plain meaning of the verse, there is an established Halakhic tradition that in fact assailants are punished monetarily, not physically. Hence Rava's *gezerah shavah* connects the killing of an animal with an offense subject to a monetary penalty, and not with an offense subject to lashes!

אִם אֵינוֹ עִנְיָן לְהַכָּאָה [4] In defense of Rava, the Gemara answers: The content of this verse is repeated in the next verse (Leviticus 24:20): "As he inflicted a blemish on a person, so shall it be given to him." The Gemara (above, 32b) explains that we learn from this repetition that someone who injures another person is punished by a monetary penalty. Thus the second verse teaches us that if someone injures his fellow, and the injury is worth at least one perutah (the smallest coin considered significant by the Talmud), he must pay damages. So what does the first verse teach us? **If it does not teach us anything relevant about an assault** that inflicts an injury **worth a perutah,** which is subject to a damage payment, [5] **then let it teach us something relevant about an assault** that inflicts an injury **that is not worth a perutah**, which is punished by lashes. Thus we interpret the first verse as referring to an assault causing less than a perutah's worth of damage, and the second verse as referring to an assault causing at least a perutah's worth of damage. The command to give the offender "a blemish," in the second verse, is to be interpreted as referring to a damage payment, and the command in the first verse, "as he did so shall it be done to him," is to be interpreted

NOTES

shavah or *semukhim*. According to this explanation, Rav Pappa is asking: What did you mean when you said: "Strikes," "strikes"? If you meant that you were constructing a *gezerah shavah* between the two appearances of the word "strikes" in the verse cited by the Baraita, you are mistaken, because the word "strikes" in that verse refers to killing. And if you meant that an argument of *semukhim* applies to the two adjacent verses dealing with assault, why did you mention the key word "strikes" at all? But Rava replies that he has been misquoted, and that what he actually said was that he was applying an argument of *semukhim* to the two verses dealing with assault, and that he did not cite any key words in his statement.

Rashi explains that Rava was constructing a full argument of juxtaposition (*hekesh*) similar to the one used by the Baraita itself. According to this explanation, Rava was saying that just as the Torah juxtaposed the killing of people with the killing of animals, so too the Torah juxtaposed assault on people with assault on animals. Hence, just as the Baraita inferred from the case of the animal that there is no difference between the monetary penalties imposed for inadvertent and deliberate killing, so too may we infer from the case of the animal that there is no difference between the monetary penalties imposed for striking someone inadvertently and those imposed for striking someone deliberately. In *Bava Kamma*, however, *Rashi* explains the exegesis as a *gezerah shavah*, like *Tosafot*.

TRANSLATION AND COMMENTARY

literally as referring to lashes. Hence we can construct a *gezerah shavah* between killing an animal and inflicting an injury worth less than a perutah on another person — an offense punishable by lashes. And we can conclude that just as the financial obligations for the killing of an animal are independent of the intentions of the killer and apply equally to deliberate and inadvertent killing, so too the financial exemptions for inflicting an injury worth less than a perutah are independent of the intentions of the offender, and they apply equally to deliberate and inadvertent assault.

LITERAL TRANSLATION

[35B] [1] Ultimately (lit., "end, end") he is not subject to payment!

[2] No, it is needed [for a case] where while he was hitting him he tore his silk garments.

[35B] סוֹף סוֹף לָאו בַּר תַּשְׁלוּמִין הוּא! [1]

לָא, צְרִיכָא דְּבַהֲדֵי דְּמַחְיֵיה קָרַע שִׁירָאִין דִּילֵיה. [2]

RASHI

סוֹף סוֹף — הָאי לֹא מַחֲלוֹק בּוּ לְחַיֵּיבוּ מָמוֹן, טַעֲמָא מְשׁוּם דְּאֵין בּוּ כְּדֵי תַשְׁלוּמִין, וְלֹא מְשׁוּם הֶיקִּישָׁא. אֲבָל הֵיכָא דִּיֵש בַּהּ שָׁוֶה פְּרוּטָה — אֵימָא מַחֲלוֹק. לֹא צְרִיכָא — לְהָכִי אִיתְקַשׁ. דְּבַהֲדֵי דְמַחְיֵיה קָרַע שִׁירָאִין וְכוּ' — כְּלוֹמַר, וְאַשְׁמְעִינָן דְּלוֹקֶה מְשׁוּם חַבָּלָה, וּפָטוּר מִתַּשְׁלוּמֵי קְרִיעָה. לֹא שְׁנָא הַתְרוּ בּוֹ, וְלֹא שְׁנָא לֹא הַתְרוּ, דְּלֹא לָקֵי — פָּטוּר מִתַּשְׁלוּמִין מֵהֶיקִּישָׁא דְלֹא מַחֲלוֹק.

סוֹף סוֹף [35B] [1] But, the Gemara objects, we are trying to prove that someone who commits an offense that is subject both to lashes and to payment is exempt from payment, even if the offense was inadvertent. However, in the case of a person who inflicts an injury worth less than one perutah, **ultimately** the reason why he does not pay is not because he is subject to a more severe penalty but because **he is not subject to payment** at all, since he did not cause an injury that was worth any money. Hence we still do not have a verse that proves that someone is rendered exempt from a monetary penalty by the penalty of lashes.

לָא, צְרִיכָא [2] The Gemara answers: **No,** the verse **is needed** to teach us the law **in a case where** the assailant strikes a blow that is not worth a perutah, and is therefore punished with lashes, and **while he was hitting his victim he tore** the latter's **silk garment.** In such a case, the assailant is exempt from paying for the garment, because he is subject to the more severe penalty of lashes for the blow he struck. Thus the verse was written in order to teach us to construct a *gezerah shavah* between the case of someone who strikes a blow that is not worth a perutah and causes incidental damage at the same time, and the case of someone who kills an animal. Just as the killer of the animal is liable to pay, whether he killed it deliberately or inadvertently, so too the person who struck a blow that was not worth a perutah is exempt from paying for incidental damage, whether he struck the blow deliberately or inadvertently.

Having explained the dispute between Rabbi Yoḥanan and Resh Lakish according to Ravin, the Gemara returns to the Baraita that caused us to reject the rival tradition of Rav Dimi. Rav Dimi had reported that Rabbi Yoḥanan maintains that the death penalty (like lashes) exempts from payment only if it is actually carried out. Rava objected that this view is contradicted by the Baraita taught in the School of Ḥizkiyah, which clearly maintains that the death penalty exempts from payment even if the offense was committed inadvertently. And the Gemara responded by rejecting Rav Dimi's tradition in favor of Ravin's.

NOTES

לָא, צְרִיכָא דְּבַהֲדֵי דְּמַחְיֵיה קָרַע שִׁירָאִין דִּילֵיה **No, it is needed for a case where while he was hitting him he tore his silk garments.** *Maharshal* remarks that *Tosafot* explains Rav Pappa as agreeing with Ulla that monetary penalties take precedence over lashes, if they are incurred for the same offense, but that lashes take precedence over incidental damages incurred at the same time, even if the lashes are not actually inflicted. Following this reasoning, *Maharshal* suggests that someone who strikes a blow worth more than a perutah, and tears garments at the same time, should be exempt from paying for the garments. For although the assailant is not lashed for his assault, because he pays damages for the injury, he is still theoretically subject to lashes, much like someone who committed an offense inadvertently. Hence the theoretical lashes should set aside the incidental damages for the garments, even though they are themselves set aside in practice by the damage payment for the assault itself.

Pnei Yehoshua rejects this argument. The rule that lashes take precedence over damage payments which are incurred at the same time, even if the lashes are not actually inflicted, applies only to offenses that are punishable by lashes, when the punishment is not inflicted because of legal technicalities (because the offender was not warned or the offense was inadvertent). But assault worth more than one perutah is subject to a monetary penalty, and is not even theoretically punishable by lashes. Hence someone who tears a garment in the course of striking a blow worth one perutah is required to pay — both for the injury and for the garment; but if the blow was not worth one perutah, he is not required to pay, either for the injury or for the garment, because he is subject to lashes. Moreover, according to Resh Lakish, who maintains that lashes exempt from payment even if the offense was inadvertent, this would be true even if the lashes were not actually inflicted.

TRANSLATION AND COMMENTARY

אֲמַר לֵיהּ [1] **Rav Ḥiyya said to Rava:** [2] Granted that **according to** the Baraita **taught in the School of Ḥizkiyah** the death penalty exempts from payment even if the offense was committed inadvertently, but how did the author of the Baraita know that this is so? For the Baraita advanced the following exegetical argument: "The verse (Leviticus 24:21: 'And he who strikes an animal shall pay for it, and he who strikes a man shall be put to death') juxtaposed the law of **someone who strikes a person** with the law of **someone who strikes an animal.**" Hence we must make a comparison between the monetary penalty imposed on someone who kills an animal and the monetary penalty that is not imposed on someone who kills another person, and say: Just as in the case of someone who strikes an animal we make no distinction between cases in which the deed was done inadvertently and cases in which it was done deliberately, so too, regarding someone who strikes another person, you should make no such distinction. But this argument assumes that someone who kills an animal is always required to pay for it, and this assumption is not necessarily valid. Rav Ḥiyya explains: It is possible to construct a case in which he is subject to a more severe penalty and is exempt — for example, if he killed the animal on Shabbat. [3] So **from where does** the author of the Baraita **know that** this verse **is describing** a case in which an animal was killed on **a weekday,** [4] that the killer is required to pay damages, **and** that **there is** indeed **no basis to make a distinction** between deliberate and inadvertent killing? [5] **Perhaps** this verse **is describing** a case in which an animal was killed on **Shabbat,** and the killer is exempt from paying damages because he is subject to the more severe penalty? [6] If so, **there is a basis to make a distinction** between inadvertent and deliberate killing regarding **the animal itself,** since we have no proof yet that the exemption from payment because of a more severe penalty applies even when the offense was committed inadvertently. Instead, we can say that both in the case of the animal killed on Shabbat and in the case of the murdered person the financial obligation applies when the capital offense was committed deliberately, but not when it was committed inadvertently.

לָא סָלְקָא דַּעְתָּךְ [7] Rava replied: **This** interpretation of the verse **is untenable.** [8] **For** the verse **states: "And he who strikes an animal shall pay for it, and he who strikes a man shall be put to death,"** thereby placing these two cases in juxtaposition. The purpose of this juxtaposition is to show that the killing of the animal and the killing of the man were done under the same circumstances — in other words, either both offenses were punishable or both were not. [9] Now, if you say that the verse **is** referring to an animal killed on Shabbat, **how do we visualize the case?** [10] **If** we say the verse **is** referring to a case **in which** both offenses were not punishable because witnesses **did not warn him,** the verse is incomprehensible. [11] For **why** should the verse state that **"he who strikes a man shall be put to death,"** if he was not warned? The death penalty is never imposed without warning! [12] **Rather, it is obvious that** the verse is referring to a case in

[1] אֲמַר לֵיהּ רַב חִיָּיא לְרָבָא: [2] וְלַתַּנָּא דְּבֵי חִזְקִיָּה, דְּאָמַר: ״מַכֵּה אָדָם וּמַכֵּה בְהֵמָה״, [3] מִמַּאי דְּבַחוֹל כְּתִיב, [4] וְלֵיכָּא לְאִיפְלוּגֵי? [5] דִּלְמָא בְּשַׁבָּת כְּתִיב, [6] דְּבִבְהֵמָה גּוּפָהּ אִיכָּא לְאִיפְלוּגֵי?

[7] לָא סָלְקָא דַּעְתָּךְ. [8] דִּכְתִיב: ״וּמַכֵּה בְהֵמָה יְשַׁלְּמֶנָּה, וּמַכֵּה אָדָם יוּמָת״. [9] הֵיכִי דָּמֵי? [10] אִי דְּלָא אַתְרוּ בֵּיהּ, [11] מַכֵּה אָדָם אַמַּאי יוּמַת? [12] אֶלָּא, פְּשִׁיטָא

LITERAL TRANSLATION

[1] Rav Ḥiyya said to Rava: [2] And according to the Tanna of the School of Ḥizkiyah, who said: "[Regarding] someone who strikes a person and someone who strikes an animal, [etc.]" [3] from where [does he know] that it is written about a weekday, [4] and no distinction is to be made? [5] Perhaps it is written about Shabbat, [6] where a distinction can be made about the animal itself?

[7] This cannot enter your mind. [8] For it is written: "And he who strikes an animal shall pay for it, and he who strikes a man shall be put to death." [9] How do we visualize the case? [10] If it is when they did not warn him, [11] why should someone who strikes a man be put to death? [12] Rather, it is obvious

RASHI

ממאי דבחול כתיב — דפשיטא ליה דמכה בהמה בין שוגג בין מזיד חייב לשלם. **דלמא בשבת כתיב** — ועל כרחך אשוגג כתיב קרא, דאי במזיד — הוה ליה מתחייב בנפשו, ופטור מן התשלומין. **איכא לאיפלוגי** — בין שוגג למזיד. **לא סלקא דעתך** — דבשבת כתיב, ובשוגג.

NOTES

דִּלְמָא בְּשַׁבָּת כְּתִיב **Perhaps it is written about Shabbat.** From the language of *Rashi* and *Tosafot,* it would appear that the Gemara is suggesting that the verse is referring specifically to an animal killed on Shabbat and not on a weekday. *Ritva,* however, suggests that the verse may be referring to an animal killed on any day, Shabbat or weekday. According to *Ritva,* the Gemara's objection is that the *hekesh* between the killing of an animal, which is always subject to payment, and the killing of a person, which is never subject to payment, is invalid, because the

דְּאַתְרוּ בֵּיהּ. [1]וְאִי בְּשַׁבָּת, מַכֵּה בְהֵמָה יְשַׁלְּמֶנָּה?! [2]אֶלָּא לָאו בַּחוֹל?

[3]אֲמַר לֵיהּ רַב פַּפָּא לְאַבַּיֵי: לְרַבָּה, דְּאָמַר: חִידּוּשׁ הוּא שֶׁחִידְּשָׁה תּוֹרָה בִּקְנָס, [4]וְאַף עַל גַּב דְּמִיקְטִיל, מְשַׁלֵּם, [5]מַתְנִיתִין כְּמַאן מוֹקִים לָהּ?

LITERAL TRANSLATION

that they warned him. [1]And if it was on Shabbat, shall someone who strikes an animal pay for it?! [2]Rather, is it not on a weekday?

[3]Rav Pappa said to Abaye: According to Rabbah, who said: It is an innovation that the Torah established regarding a fine, [4]and although he is killed, he pays, [5]in accordance with whom does he explain our Mishnah?

RASHI

ואי בשבת מכה בהמה ישלמנה — בתמיה. **אלא לאו בחול** — דליכא לפלוגי, ואיתקש לה מכה אדם, שלא תחלוק בו, ואפילו אינו חייב מיתה. **לרבה דאמר** — לרבי מאיר חדוש הוא כו׳. **מתניתין כמאן מוקים** — לשנויי רומיא דרמינן עלה דאלו הן הלוקין, וקיימא לן דאין לוקה ומשלם.

TRANSLATION AND COMMENTARY

which both offenses were punishable because witnesses **warned him.** [1]But if so, **if** the animal **was** killed **on Shabbat,** why does the verse state that **"he who strikes an animal shall pay for it"?** According to all opinions, someone who kills an animal on Shabbat after witnesses have warned him that he will be executed for violating Shabbat is exempt from payment, since the more severe penalty to which he is subject is inflicted in practice! [2]**Rather, it is** clear that this interpretation is **not** correct, and the verse is referring to an animal killed **on a weekday,** and the killer is required to pay damages under all circumstances. Hence the author of the Baraita was able to compare the monetary penalty imposed on someone who kills an animal on a weekday with the monetary penalty that is not imposed on homicide, and he could say: Just as in the case of someone who strikes an animal on a weekday you make no distinction between cases in which it was done inadvertently and cases in which it was done deliberately, similarly in the case of someone who strikes a person no such distinction should be made.

The Gemara is now about to conclude its explanation of the contradiction between our Mishnah and the Mishnah in *Makkot* (see above, 31b). It will be recalled that three explanations were offered above — by Ulla (32a), by Rabbi Yoḥanan (32b), and by Resh Lakish (33b). The Gemara has explained why Ulla disagrees with the other two opinions — because of a *gezerah shavah* that he accepts and they reject (above, 33a). The Gemara has also explained why Rabbi Yoḥanan and Resh Lakish disagree with each other — because Resh Lakish maintains that lashes, like the death penalty, are a more severe penalty that exempts from payment even when they are not actually inflicted, whereas Rabbi Yoḥanan is of the opinion that this is true of the death penalty, but that lashes exempt only when they are actually inflicted (above, 35a). In the course of this discussion, there has been a thorough consideration of the view of Rabbi Meir, who maintains that lashes do not exempt from payment at all, but are imposed together with monetary penalties (above, 32b). Two versions of Rabbi Meir's viewpoint regarding the death penalty have been presented. One, attributed to a number of Amoraim including Rabbi Yoḥanan and Resh Lakish, explains that Rabbi Meir disagrees only about lashes, but he agrees that the death penalty exempts from all forms of payment (above, 33b). The other, attributed to Rabbah, explains that Rabbi Meir disagrees about the death penalty as well, maintaining that it exempts from regular damage payments but not from fines (above, 34b).

אֲמַר לֵיהּ [3]Before leaving this topic, the Gemara resolves a number of difficulties presented by these various views. **Rav Pappa said to Abaye:** We have seen how Ulla, Rabbi Yoḥanan, and Resh Lakish explain the contradiction between our Mishnah and the Mishnah in *Makkot*. But we have not been told how the contradiction is explained **according to Rabbah, who said** that Rabbi Meir is of the opinion that someone subject to the death penalty is exempt from paying regular damages but not from paying fines, because **fines are an innovation established by the Torah,** and we have a principle that whenever the Torah issues a novel commandment that is not consistent with the other laws of the Torah, we cannot assume that the regular laws apply, unless the Torah explicitly states that they do. Hence the rule that an offender who is subject to the death penalty is exempt from monetary payments does not apply to fines, [4]**and** therefore **even though** the offender **is killed** (for violating Shabbat or for committing incest with his daughter), **he must** still **pay** the fine as well. [5]On the basis of Rabbah's viewpoint, **in accordance with whom does he explain our Mishnah?** Whose opinion does it reflect?

NOTES

killing of an animal is sometimes not subject to payment, if it was done on Shabbat.

מַתְנִיתִין כְּמַאן מוֹקִים לָהּ In accordance with whom does he explain our Mishnah? The Rishonim ask: From the language of the Gemara, it would appear that the Gemara is having difficulties explaining our Mishnah in accordance

[1] אִי כְּרַבִּי מֵאִיר, קַשְׁיָא בִּתּוֹ; [2] אִי כְּרַבִּי נְחוּנְיָא בֶּן הַקָּנָה, קַשְׁיָא אֲחוֹתוֹ; [3] אִי כְּרַבִּי יִצְחָק, קַשְׁיָא מַמְזֶרֶת.

LITERAL TRANSLATION

[1] If it is in accordance with Rabbi Meir, [the case of] his daughter is difficult; [2] if it is in accordance with Rabbi Neḥunya ben Hakkanah, [the case of] his sister is difficult; [3] if it is in accordance with Rabbi Yitzḥak, [the case of] a *mamzeret* is difficult.

TRANSLATION AND COMMENTARY

אִי כְּרַבִּי מֵאִיר [1] Rav Pappa explains the problem: Rabbah cannot resolve the contradiction between the two Mishnayot (as did Resh Lakish) by saying that our Mishnah **is in accordance with** the viewpoint of **Rabbi Meir,** because the Mishnah rules that a man who rapes **his daughter** is exempt from paying the fine, since he is subject to a more severe penalty, and according to Rabbah's interpretation of Rabbi Meir this explanation **poses a difficulty,** since Rabbi Meir is of the opinion that a more severe penalty does not exempt from fines. On the other hand, Rabbah cannot resolve the contradiction between the two Mishnayot by saying that our Mishnah follows some other Tanna who does not have a problem with the clause dealing with the daughter and maintains that a man who rapes his sister is not exempt from payment because of the penalty of lashes. There are two such Tannaim — Rabbi Neḥunya ben Hakkanah, who agrees with Rabbi Meir that lashes do not exempt from payment but agrees with the Sages that the death penalty does exempt from fines, and Rabbi Yitzḥak, who agrees with the Sages both regarding lashes and regarding fines but maintains that a man who commits incest with his sister is not punished by lashes. [2] Rabbah cannot say that our Mishnah **is in accordance with** the viewpoint of **Rabbi Neḥunya ben Hakkanah,** because the Mishnah rules that a man who rapes **his sister** is held liable to pay the fine, since incest between brother and sister is subject to excision, not death, and according to Rabbi Neḥunya ben Hakkanah this explanation **poses a difficulty,** since Rabbi Neḥunya ben Hakkanah maintains that excision exempts from payment, just like the death penalty (see above, 30a). [3] Moreover, Rabbah cannot say that our Mishnah **is in accordance with** the viewpoint of **Rabbi Yitzḥak,** who disagrees with the Mishnah in *Makkot* (14a) and rules that offenses subject to excision are not punishable by lashes, because our Mishnah rules that a man who rapes **a *mamzeret*** is held liable to pay the fine, and everyone — including Rabbi Yitzḥak — agrees that intercourse with a *mamzeret* is punishable by lashes. Hence it **is difficult** to reconcile our Mishnah's ruling regarding a *mamzeret* with the principle that someone who is punished by lashes is not required to pay a monetary penalty for the same offense.

RASHI

אי כרבי מאיר — דאמר: לוקה ומשלם, וכדשנינהו ריש לקיש. **קשיא בתו** — דבשלמא לריש לקיש דאוקמה להאי דגנב וטבח בשבת בטובח על ידי אחר, אבל בטובח על ידי עצמו — לא משלם, לא קשיא; דמת ומשלם לית ליה לרבי מאיר אפילו בקנס. אלא לרבה קשיא בתו, דקנס הוא, וקתני מתניתין פטור. **ואי כרבי נחוניא בן הקנה** — דאית ליה נמי לוקה ומשלם כרבי מאיר, מדקאמר יום הכפורים כשבת. יום הכפורים הוא דפטור מתשלומין, ומשום כרת דאית ביה, ומגזירה שוה ד״אסון״ ״אסון״, אבל משום לאו ומלקות דאית ביה — לא פטר. ומתניתין נמי דאית ליה לוקה ומשלם — דידיה הוא, ומת ומשלם — לית ליה, אפילו בקנס. **קשיא אחותו** — נהי נמי דמשום מלקות לא פטר ליה, ליפטריה משום כרת. **ואי כרבי יצחק** — תוקמה, דאמר במסכת מכות (יד,א): אין חייבי כריתות בכלל מלקות ארבעים. ולית ליה האי ד״אלו הן הלוקין״: הבא על אחותו, ומשום הכי חייבין בתשלומין. **קשיא ממזרת** — דהכל מודים שהוא במלקות, וקתני: אית לה קנס.

SAGES

רַבִּי יִצְחָק Rabbi Yitzḥak. A Palestinian Amora of the second and third generations. See *Ketubot*, Part I, p. 97.

NOTES

with any known opinion. If so, why does the Gemara list these three minority opinions specifically? Why does it not cite the opinion followed by the Halakhah — that of the Sages who disagree with Rabbi Meir?

Tosafot answers that the Gemara did not mention the viewpoint of the Sages because they would have difficulty both with the clause dealing with a man who rapes his sister and with the clause dealing with a man who rapes a *mamzeret*. Instead, it mentioned only Rabbi Neḥunya ben Hakkanah and Rabbi Yitzḥak, each of whom has difficulty with one of the clauses but not with the other.

Shittah Mekubbetzet adds that the Gemara lists these three Tannaim in order, moving backwards through the clauses of the Mishnah. According to Rabbi Meir, the last clause, dealing with the daughter, is difficult, but all the earlier clauses are satisfactory. According to Rabbi Neḥunya ben Hakkanah, there is no problem with the clause dealing with the daughter, but there is a problem with the preceding clause dealing with the sister. According to Rabbi Yitzḥak, there is no problem with either of the later clauses dealing with the sister or the daughter, but there is a problem with the first clause dealing with the *mamzeret*. The Sages, however, for whom both of the earlier clauses are difficult, do not fit naturally in this list.

Our commentary follows *Rashi*, who explains that the Gemara is not trying to determine the authorship of our Mishnah, but is rather inquiring how Rabbah would resolve the conflict between our Mishnah and the Mishnah in *Makkot*. According to this explanation, it is obvious that the Gemara could not invoke the accepted view of the Sages who disagree with Rabbi Meir, since the whole point of this passage is to seek a minority view, along the lines suggested by Resh Lakish, because the accepted view of the Sages leads to a contradiction between the Mishnayot.

קַשְׁיָא אֲחוֹתוֹ The case of his sister is difficult. The Rishonim ask: How does the Gemara know that the clause in the Mishnah requiring a man who rapes his sister to pay the fine is not in accordance with the viewpoint of Rabbi

TRANSLATION AND COMMENTARY

הָנִיחָא [1] Thus we see that Rabbah cannot explain our Mishnah as being in accordance with Rabbi Meir, as did Resh Lakish, nor can he explain it as being in accordance with either Rabbi Neḥunya ben Hakkanah or Rabbi Yitzḥak. Hence there is no way to resolve the contradiction between our Mishnah and the Mishnah in *Makkot* by saying that they reflect a viewpoint that maintains that the sentence of lashes imposed on a man who rapes his sister does not exempt him from paying the fine. Instead, Rabbah must construct a special case, in which either the fine or the lashes do not apply. **This would pose no problem if** Rabbah were to **agree with Rabbi Yoḥanan** that lashes exempt from monetary penalties only if they are actually inflicted, or if he were to agree with Ulla that a man who rapes his sister is lashed only if the fine is inapplicable. [2] On this basis, Rabbah **too could explain** our Mishnah, **as Rabbi Yoḥanan** did, as referring to a case in which the offender was not warned, or else he could explain the Mishnah in *Makkot*, as Ulla did, as referring to a case in which the sister was an adult who was seduced. Explained in this way, our Mishnah can be reconciled with the Mishnah in *Makkot*. [3] **But if** Rabbah were to **agree with Resh Lakish** that lashes exempt from monetary penalties even if they are not actually inflicted, **how could he explain** the contradiction between our Mishnah — which rules that a man who rapes his sister or who rapes a *mamzeret* must pay a fine — and the Mishnah in *Makkot*, which rules that these offenses are punishable by lashes? For, according to the opinion of Resh Lakish, there is no way to construct a case in which the lashes do not conflict with the fine, and there are only three Tannaim who maintain that a man who rapes his sister is not exempt from paying the fine because of lashes, and none of these could have been the author of our Mishnah. How, then, would Rabbah have resolved the contradiction?

LITERAL TRANSLATION

[1] It is well if he agrees with Rabbi Yoḥanan. [2] He too can explain it like Rabbi Yoḥanan. [3] But if he agrees with Resh Lakish, how can he explain it?

[1] הָנִיחָא אִי סָבַר לָהּ כְּרַבִּי יוֹחָנָן. [2] הוּא נַמִּי מְתָרֵץ לָהּ כְּרַבִּי יוֹחָנָן. [3] אֶלָּא אִי סָבַר כְּרֵישׁ לָקִישׁ, הֵיכִי מְתָרֵץ לָהּ?

RASHI

הניחא אי סבר — רבה כרבי יוחנן, כשלא התרו בו, דמשלם, דחייבי מלקיות שוגגין ודבר אחר חייב. **איהו נמי** — מוקי למתניתין בשלא התרו בו, כרבי יוחנן. **אלא אי סבר לה** — בממון ומלקות דאפילו לא התרו בו פטור מממון, ופליג אדרבי יוחנן, וכל שכן אדעולא, דאמר אפילו התרו בו משלם ממון ואינו לוקה. **היכי מתרץ לה** — לא כרבי יוחנן ולא כעולא ולא כריש לקיש.

NOTES

Neḥunya ben Hakkanah? Perhaps the Mishnah is referring to a case in which the man raped his sister without being aware of her identity, and Rabbi Neḥunya ben Hakkanah maintains that offenses that are subject to excision are exempt from payment only if the offense was committed deliberately.

Three answers are given to this question:

(1) *Ba'al HaMa'or* explains that since Rabbi Neḥunya ben Hakkanah compares excision to the death penalty, he is of the opinion that they are both governed by the same rules. Hence an offense that is subject to excision is exempt from monetary penalties, even if it was committed inadvertently — even according to Rabbi Yoḥanan, who maintains that lashes do not exempt from payment unless they are actually inflicted. (Our commentary follows this view.)

(2) *Ra'ah* explains that, according to Rabbi Neḥunya ben Hakkanah, excision has the same status as lashes. For according to Rabbi Yoḥanan, the exegetical argument of the Baraita taught by the School of Ḥizkiyah, which teaches us that the death penalty exempts from payment even if the offense was inadvertent, applies to the death penalty and to nothing else. Hence, according to Rabbi Neḥunya ben Hakkanah, excision has the same status as lashes, and does not exempt from payment if the offense was inadvertent. According to Resh Lakish, who maintains that lashes exempt from payment even if the offense was inadvertent, the same applies to excision according to Rabbi Neḥunya ben Hakkanah. Thus we could have explained that the Mishnah is in accordance with the viewpoint of Rabbi Neḥunya ben Hakkanah — but only by invoking Rabbi Yoḥanan, who maintains that inadvertent offenses do not exempt from payment, and at this stage in the argument the Gemara is trying to explain Rabbah according to Resh Lakish.

(3) *Ramban* explains that, according to Rabbi Neḥunya ben Hakkanah, excision does not exempt from payment if the offense was inadvertent — even according to Resh Lakish, who maintains that lashes do exempt if the offense was inadvertent. *Ramban* maintains that it would have been possible to explain the Mishnah's ruling according to Rabbi Neḥunya ben Hakkanah, by saying that it refers to an inadvertent offense. However, the Mishnah states that a man who rapes his sister must pay the fine, "even though he is punished with excision, since he is not punished with death," and this language suggests that we are referring to a case in which the penalty of excision is applicable.

אִי כְּרַבִּי יִצְחָק, קַשְׁיָא מַמְזֶרֶת If it is in accordance with Rabbi Yitzḥak, the case of a *mamzeret* is difficult. The Rishonim note that it is possible to solve the problem of the *mamzeret,* and to explain the Mishnah according to Rabbi Yitzḥak, by saying that the Mishnah is referring to a rapist who was permitted to marry a *mamzeret* (e.g., a male *mamzer*, or a convert). Indeed, the Jerusalem Talmud explains our Mishnah in this way. *Ramban* argues that the Babylonian Talmud rejected this solution because the Mishnah is listing problematic cases, and the case of the *mamzeret* would not be problematic at all if she was raped by someone who was permitted to marry her.

The Rishonim ask: The Gemara's objection is based on the assumption that Rabbi Yitzḥak agrees with the accepted opinion that if a sentence of lashes is definitely imposed (such as in the case of the *mamzeret*), the rapist

SAGES

רַב מַתְנָא **Rav Matena.** Rav Matena's name is normally spelled with a final heh (ה), and it may be a shortened form of the Biblical name Matanyah. He was a second-generation Babylonian Amora and studied with the Amoraim of the first generation in Babylonia. He was a disciple of Shmuel, though he also transmits teachings in the name of Rav. Rav Matena's colleague, Rav Yehudah, was also a disciple of Rav and Shmuel. Many of the Amoraim of the third generation were Rav Matena's pupils and transmit teachings in his name. He lived in Papunya, near Pumbedita. He was the Rabbi of that town and may also have been the head of a small yeshivah there. According to a Geonic tradition, he was the son of the great Palestinian Amora Rabbi Yoḥanan, ten of whose sons died during his lifetime, and he was sent by Rabbi Yoḥanan to Babylonia to study with Shmuel.

TRANSLATION AND COMMENTARY

עַל כָּרְחָךְ [1] The Gemara answers: **We are forced to say that** Rabbah **must agree with Rabbi Yoḥanan** that lashes exempt from monetary penalties only if they are inflicted in practice, or that he agrees with Ulla that monetary penalties take precedence over lashes.

אָמַר לֵיה [2] Before concluding the subject, the Gemara resolves one final difficulty. **Rav Matena said to Abaye:** We have seen that according to the accepted Halakhah, which is not in accordance with Rabbi Neḥunya ben Hakkanah, excision is not a more severe penalty that exempts from payment. We have also seen that according to the accepted Halakhah, which is not in accordance with Rabbi Yitzḥak, offenses that are subject to excision are also punished by lashes. And we have also seen that according to the accepted Halakhah, which is not in accordance with Rabbi Meir, an offender who is punished by lashes is exempt from payment. It thus follows that even according to the accepted Halakhah, which is not in accordance with Rabbi Neḥunya ben Hakkanah, an offender who is subject to excision is exempt from payment — because of the lashes, if not because of the excision. According to Rabbi Yoḥanan, however, there is still a practical difference between this viewpoint and that of Rabbi Neḥunya ben Hakkanah. For Rabbi Yoḥanan is of the opinion that there is a difference between the rules governing lashes and the rules governing the death penalty — an offender who is theoretically subject to the death penalty is exempt from paying damages, even if the death penalty is not actually inflicted, whereas an offender who is subject to lashes must pay damages, unless the lashes are actually inflicted. Rabbi Neḥunya ben Hakkanah maintains that the rules governing excision are the same as those governing the death penalty. Thus, according to Rabbi Neḥunya ben Hakkanah, an offender who is theoretically subject to excision is exempt from paying damages even if the offense was inadvertent, whereas according to the accepted Halakhah he is not exempt unless he was warned and lashes were administered. [3] However, **according to Resh Lakish, who said** that any offense that is theoretically subject to lashes is exempt from payment, even if the offense was committed inadvertently and the lashes were not actually inflicted, [4] since **the Torah explicitly** commanded us to **include** offenders **who are subject to lashes in the same category as** offenders **who are subject to the death penalty**, there is no practical difference between the accepted opinion and that of Rabbi Neḥunya ben Hakkanah, regarding offenses punishable by excision. For the accepted opinion would agree with Rabbi Neḥunya ben Hakkanah that an offender who is theoretically subject to excision is exempt from payment, since all such offenses are punishable by lashes. But our Mishnah (above, 29a) rules that someone who is punished by excision is not exempt from payment. And another Mishnah (*Shevuot* 33a) rules that someone who burns his neighbor's crops on Yom Kippur is not exempt from payment, even though he is punished by excision. [5] So **who is the Tanna who disagrees with Rabbi Neḥunya ben Hakkanah** in these two Mishnayot?

LITERAL TRANSLATION

[1] You must [say that] he agrees with Rabbi Yoḥanan.

[2] Rav Matena said to Abaye: [3] [According] to Resh Lakish, who said: [4] The Torah explicitly extrapolated those who are subject to lashes [to be] like those who are subject to the death penalty, [5] who is the Tanna who disagrees with Rabbi Neḥunya ben Hakkanah?

עַל כָּרְחָךְ כְּרַבִּי יוֹחָנָן סְבִירָא [1]
לֵיה.
[2] אָמַר לֵיה רַב מַתְנָא לְאַבַּיֵי:
[3] לְרֵישׁ לָקִישׁ, דְּאָמַר: [4] בְּפֵירוּשׁ
רִיבְּתָה תּוֹרָה חַיָּיבֵי מַלְקִיּוֹת
כְּחַיָּיבֵי מִיתוֹת, [5] מַאן תַּנָּא
דְּפָלִיג עֲלֵיה דְּרַבִּי נְחוּנְיָא בֶּן
הַקָּנָה?

RASHI

עַל כָּרְחָךְ — אִי סְבִירָא לֵיה כְּמַמוֹן וּמַלְקוֹת דְּלוֹקֶה וְאֵינוֹ מְשַׁלֵּם — כְּרַבִּי יוֹחָנָן סְבִירָא לֵיה בְּשׁוֹגְגִים דְּמְשַׁלֵּם מָמוֹן, וּמוֹקֵי לָה בְּשֶׁלֹּא הִתְרוּ בּוֹ. לְרֵישׁ לָקִישׁ **דְּאָמַר בְּפֵירוּשׁ רִיבְּתָה תּוֹרָה כו'** — דְּמַיְירֵי מַלְקִיּוֹת שׁוֹגְגִין פְּטוּרִין מְּשַׁלֵּם. מַאן תַּנָּא דְּפָלִיג אַדְּרַבִּי נְחוּנְיָא — וּמַחְיֵיב תַּשְׁלוּמִין בְּחַיָּיבֵי כְּרִיתוֹת, כְּגוֹן הַהִיא דִשְׁבוּעוֹת, וְהַדְּלִיק גָּדִישׁ בְּיוֹם הַכִּפּוּרִים — מַיְירִין, בְּפֶרֶק "שְׁבוּעַת הָעֵדוּת" (שבועות לג,א). וּמַתְנִיתִין דְּהָכָא דְּקִנְסָה בְּאַלְמוּתוֹ. וְהַאי נַמִּי דְּלֵית לֵיה "אָסוֹן" "אָסוֹן" לְמִיפְטְרֵיה מִשּׁוּם כָּרֵת — לִיפְטְרֵיה מִשּׁוּם לָאו, בֵּין הִתְרוּ בּוֹ בֵּין לֹא הִתְרוּ בּוֹ. דְּאֵין כָּרֵת בְּלֹא לָאו חוּץ מִפֶּסַח וּמִילָה. דְּבִשְׁלָמָא רַבִּי יוֹחָנָן — מוֹקֵי לָהּ אֲפִילּוּ כְּרַבָּן דְּפָלִיגֵי עֲלֵיה דְרַבִּי מֵאִיר, דְּאָמְרֵי: אֵין לוֹקֶה וּמְשַׁלֵּם, וְהַנֵּי — בְּשֶׁלֹּא הִתְרוּ בּוֹ. אֶלָּא לְרֵישׁ לָקִישׁ כְּמַאן מוֹקֵי לָהּ?

NOTES

is exempt from payment. But how do we know that this is so? Perhaps Rabbi Yitzḥak agrees with Rabbi Meir that lashes do not exempt from payment. If he does, it is possible to explain the Mishnah according to Rabbi Yitzḥak, and the clause dealing with the *mamzeret* poses no problem!

Rashba answers that the Gemara did not wish to assume that Rabbi Yitzḥak agrees with the minority opinion of Rabbi Meir without proof. *Shittah Mekubbetzet* adds that

Rashi and *Tosafot* infer from the ruling of Rabbi Neḥunya ben Hakkanah regarding Yom Kippur that he agrees with Rabbi Meir. But in the case of Rabbi Yitzḥak there is no reason to assume that he departs from the consensus on this matter.

עַל כָּרְחָךְ כְּרַבִּי יוֹחָנָן סְבִירָא לֵיה **You must say that he agrees with Rabbi Yoḥanan.** The Rishonim ask: Three explanations were submitted to resolve the original

TRANSLATION AND COMMENTARY

אִי רַבִּי מֵאִיר [1]Abaye replied: According to Resh Lakish, these Mishnayot, which maintain that someone who is punished with excision is not exempt from payment, can reflect the opinions of only two Tannaim: **Either Rabbi Meir,** who is of the opinion that lashes do not exempt from payment, **or Rabbi Yitzḥak,** who maintains that offenses subject to excision are not punishable by lashes. But according to the accepted view — that offenses subject to excision are punishable by lashes, and lashes are a more severe penalty that exempts from payment — we are forced to agree with Rabbi Neḥunya ben Hakkanah's ruling, if not with his reasoning, according to Resh Lakish.

תָּנוּ רַבָּנַן [2]Having completed its analysis of our Mishnah, which listed the *ne'arot* whose cases are problematic but who are nevertheless entitled to a fine for rape or seduction, the Gemara now cites a Baraita on a related topic. **Our Rabbis taught** the following Baraita: "If a man rapes or seduces a **woman** with whom he is **forbidden** to have intercourse under the law forbidding incest (i.e., a close relative), or if he rapes or seduces a **woman** with whom he is **forbidden** to have intercourse under the law forbidding **secondary** incest (i.e., a more distant relative), these women **are not entitled to a fine for rape, or** to a fine

LITERAL TRANSLATION

[1]Either Rabbi Meir, or Rabbi Yitzḥak.

[2]Our Rabbis taught: "Forbidden relations and secondary forbidden relations do not have [a claim to] a fine [for rape] or [for] seduction.

[1]אִי רַבִּי מֵאִיר, אִי רַבִּי יִצְחָק. [2]תָּנוּ רַבָּנַן: ״עֲרָיוֹת וּשְׁנִיּוֹת לַעֲרָיוֹת אֵין לָהֶן לֹא קְנָס וְלֹא

RASHI

אי רבי מאיר – דאמר: לוקה ומשלם. **אי רבי יצחק** – דאמר: לא שייך מלקות בחייבי כריתות. וגזירה שוה ד״אסון״ ״אסון״ לית ליה, ובמאי ליפטר? הילכך מתניתין דהכא על כרחך רבי מאיר היא ולא רבי יצחק, משום דקשיא ממזרת. אבל ההיא דשבועות – בין כרבי מאיר בין כרבי יצחק. **עריות ושניות** – לקמן מפרש להו. **קנס** – דאנוסה.

NOTES

contradiction between our Mishnah and the Mishnah in *Makkot* — Ulla's, Rabbi Yoḥanan's, and Resh Lakish's. The Gemara has now proved that Rabbah cannot agree with Resh Lakish, but why does the Gemara draw the conclusion that Rabbah agrees with Rabbi Yoḥanan? Perhaps he agrees with Ulla.

Our commentary follows *Ramban* who explains that the Gemara could indeed have explained that Rabbah follows Ulla, but did not mention it since Ulla's view was rejected by the Halakhah, and the Gemara was mainly concerned with the dispute between Rabbi Yoḥanan and Resh Lakish.

שְׁנִיּוֹת לַעֲרָיוֹת Secondary forbidden relations. The Rabbis forbade, as "secondary forbidden relations," a number of relatives, both by blood and by marriage, who are not included in the list of forbidden relations mentioned in Leviticus, chapter 18, but who are related in a similar way. Thus the Torah forbids sexual relations between a man and his mother or his granddaughter, but sexual relations between a man and his grandmother are forbidden by Rabbinic decree. The complete list of secondary forbidden relations can be found in tractate *Yevamot* (21a).

By definition, every case of incest described as "secondary" is not punishable by Torah law. A marriage that is secondarily incestuous is valid, although forbidden, and cannot be dissolved without a bill of divorce. The offspring of such a relationship is not a *mamzer* and is permitted to marry a priest. Likewise, a woman who has intercourse with a man who is forbidden to her Rabbinically in this way is not disqualified from the priesthood. A couple who marry in this way, however, are compelled to divorce, and no ketubah need be paid.

אֵין לָהֶן קְנָס וְלֹא פִּיתּוּי Do not have a claim to a fine for rape or for seduction. Our translation and commentary are in accordance with the standard Vilna Talmud, which follows *Rashi* and *Tosafot*. According to this reading, the penalty paid by a rapist is called a "fine," whereas the penalty paid by a seducer is called "seduction." This is somewhat puzzling, since the compensation for seduction is no less a fine than the compensation for rape. Both are fixed payments made above and beyond regular damages, and their purpose is to punish the offender.

Tosafot explains that the compensation paid by a rapist is more of a fine, because he is compelled to marry his victim as well, whereas a seducer is merely requested to marry his victim, not compelled to do so. *Shittah Mekubbetzet* explains that *Tosafot* means to say that the rapist must pay the fine under all circumstances, whereas the seducer pays only if he does not marry his victim. Thus the fine paid by a rapist is more absolute than that paid by a seducer.

It should be noted, however, that some versions of the Talmud have a variant reading, in which the word אוֹנֶס ("compensation for rape") appears in place of the word קְנָס ("fine"). According to this reading, the Baraita is simply saying that these women "do not have a claim either to compensation for rape or to compensation for seduction" — and neither payment is singled out as more of a fine than the other.

HALAKHAH

אֵין לָהֶן קְנָס וְלֹא פִּיתּוּי Do not have a claim to a fine for rape or for seduction. "A girl who refuses marriage (מְמָאֶנֶת) and a girl who had an evil reputation before she was raped or seduced are not entitled to a fine. *Rambam* rules that a sexually undeveloped woman is also not entitled to a fine, but *Ra'avad* disagrees, since the Halakhah follows the Sages who maintain that minor girls are also entitled to a fine like *ne'arot*, and a sexually undeveloped woman under the age of twenty is considered a minor. *Tur* rules in favor of *Ra'avad*, but *Bet Yosef* attempts to justify *Rambam*." (*Rambam, Sefer Nashim, Hilkhot Na'arah Betulah* 1:9; *Tur, Even HaEzer* 177.)

CONCEPTS

עֲרָיוֹת Forbidden sexual relations, whether incestuous or adulterous. Leviticus (chapters 18 and 20) lists these severely prohibited relationships. Indeed, they are among the three categories of sins regarding which a person is commanded to sacrifice his life rather than commit. Among the עֲרָיוֹת are: One's mother, one's father's wife, one's father's sister, one's mother's sister, one's own sister, one's daughter, one's daughter-in-law, one's brother's wife, one's wife's sister (during one's wife's lifetime), one's wife's mother, and any married woman. In some contexts, a menstruating woman (נִדָּה) is also included in this category. Some of these prohibitions are punishable by execution by the court, and all are punishable by כָּרֵת — excision. These prohibitions apply equally to the man and the woman involved, and both are punished equally.

שְׁנִיּוֹת Secondary forbidden relations. Relationships forbidden as incestuous by Rabbinic decree. The Torah (Leviticus, chapters 18 and 20) lists many incestuous relationships (עֲרָיוֹת). The Sages expanded this list to include one's maternal and paternal grandmother; the mother of one's maternal and paternal grandfather; the wife of one's maternal and paternal grandfather (even though she is not one's grandmother); the wives of one's father's maternal brothers (his paternal brothers' wives are forbidden by Torah law); the wives of one's maternal uncles; one's son's or daughter's daughter-in-law; one's great-granddaughters; one's wife's great-granddaughters from previous marriages; and one's wife's maternal and paternal great-grandmothers. A man who marries a woman related to him in one of these ways is obligated to divorce her and need not pay her marriage settlement. Violation of these prohibitions is punished by מַכַּת מַרְדּוּת — lashes administered for the transgression of a Rabbinic decree.

LITERAL TRANSLATION

[1] A girl who refuses [marriage] does not have [a claim to] a fine [for rape] or [for] seduction. [2] A sexually undeveloped woman does not have [a claim to] a fine [for rape] or [for] seduction. [3] And a woman who is divorced (lit., 'goes out') because of a bad name does not have [a claim to] a fine [for rape] or [for] seduction."

פִּיתּוּי. [1] הַמְמָאֶנֶת אֵין לָהּ לֹא קְנָס וְלֹא פִּיתּוּי. [2] אַיְילוֹנִית אֵין לָהּ לֹא קְנָס וְלֹא פִּיתּוּי. [3] וְהַיּוֹצֵאת מִשּׁוּם שֵׁם רַע אֵין לָהּ לֹא קְנָס וְלֹא פִּיתּוּי".

TRANSLATION AND COMMENTARY

for seduction." This Baraita clearly disagrees with our Mishnah, which rules that a man who rapes a close relative, such as his sister, must pay the fine. From the language of the Baraita it would appear that not only is a man who rapes his sister exempt from the fine; the same is true even of a man who rapes a woman who is forbidden to him by Rabbinic decree (the so-called "secondary forbidden relations"). [1] The Baraita continues: **A girl who refuses marriage is** also **not entitled to a fine for rape or** to a fine **for seduction."** A "girl who refuses marriage" (מְמָאֶנֶת — *mema'enet)* is a minor orphan girl who was given in marriage by her mother or her brothers, under a Rabbinic arrangement, and then decided that she preferred not to remain married. Since the entire marriage was Rabbinic, the Rabbis instituted that she should be able to dissolve the marriage on her own initiative, without need for a bill of divorce, provided that she announced her refusal while she was still a minor. The marriage is considered annulled retroactively, and the girl has in effect the same status as any other unmarried girl. Nevertheless, if she is subsequently raped or seduced, she is not entitled to a fine, since she is not considered a virgin, because it is possible that she had intercourse with her husband before she annulled her marriage. [2] The Baraita continues: **"A sexually undeveloped woman is** also **not entitled to a fine for rape or** to a fine **for seduction."** According to Jewish law, legal majority is dependent on various physical developments associated with puberty. Normally, a girl's legal status changes from that of a minor to that of a *na'arah* when her puberty begins, and she achieves full legal adulthood at a later stage in her development. But the legal status of a sexually undeveloped woman is not determined in this way. Instead, she attains legal majority when she develops the physical signs associated with barren women. Hence she is never considered a *na'arah*. She legally remains a minor until she is declared an adult. Therefore she is not entitled to a fine if she is raped or seduced, because the author of this Baraita is of the opinion that the fine is paid only to *ne'arot*, not to minors or adults (see above, 29a). [3] The Baraita concludes: **"A woman who has been divorced because of an evil reputation is** also **not entitled to a fine for rape or** to a fine **for seduction,** because she does not have the status of a virgin."

RASHI

פיתוי — דמפותה. **הממאנת** — בבעלה, כגון יתומה קטנה שהשיאתה אמה ומיאנה בבעלה. **אין לה קנס** — שאינה בחזקת בתולה, הואיל וניסת. **איילונית** — שאין לה סימני נערות לעולם, ואינה יולדת. לשון איל זכר, דוכרניתא דלא ילדה (כתובות יא,א). **אין לה קנס** — לפי שאין קנס אלא לנערה, וזו שלא תביא שערות לעולם — כל עשרים שנה היא בחזקת קטנה, ומשם ואילך — בוגרת. **והיוצאת משום שם רע** — קסלקא דעתך שלא מצא לה בעלה בתולים. ולקמן פריך: בת סקילה היא!

CONCEPTS

הַמְמָאֶנֶת A girl who refuses marriage. A girl under the age of twelve can be married off by her father. If, however, her father is no longer alive, then according to Torah law she cannot get married while still a minor. Nevertheless, the Sages decreed that her mother or her brothers may marry her off with her consent. The girl may terminate this marriage before she reaches the age of twelve by performing מֵיאוּן, or "refusal," i.e., declaring that she does not want the marriage. In such cases, no bill of divorce is necessary. When a girl performs מֵיאוּן, the marriage is nullified retroactively, and she is considered never to have been married at all. Most of the laws of מֵיאוּן are discussed in tractate *Yevamot.*

אַיְילוֹנִית A sexually undeveloped woman, an *aylonit.* From the detailed discussions in the Talmud, especially in tractate *Yevamot,* it seems that an *aylonit* is a woman with a genetic flaw preventing her from giving birth. In contrast to a barren woman, who generally suffers from some secondary disability though her physical and sexual development is normal, an *aylonit* is characterized by abnormal physical development (such as failure to develop secondary sexual traits). From the descriptions in Talmudic literature it seems that there are various kinds of *aylonit,* ranging from those with excess male hormones to those who suffer from Turner's syndrome. In the Halakhah there are many laws relating to the status of the *aylonit,* mainly because she either completely lacks secondary sexual traits or because these appear only at a later age. Consequently various questions arise regarding the age at which an *aylonit* reaches legal majority.

NOTES

הַמְמָאֶנֶת A girl who refuses marriage. Under Torah law, a minor girl is not legally competent to marry. However, a father can marry off his daughter to any man he pleases, without her participation or even consent, until she becomes a full adult (at the age of twelve-and-a-half). This marriage is valid by Torah law, and can be dissolved only by a proper divorce or by the death of the husband. This power to give a minor girl in marriage resides only with the father. Neither the mother nor any other relative has this authority.

It would seem that child marriages of this type were quite common in Talmudic times. Indeed, the Rabbis felt the need to arrange marriages for minor girls who were orphans. They therefore instituted a procedure whereby a minor orphan girl would be permitted to marry with the consent of her close relatives. The marriage has Rabbinic status; by Torah law, it is void. When the girl reaches the age of majority, the marriage automatically becomes valid by Torah law.

By Torah law, the power to divorce resides entirely with the husband, and the wife cannot divorce him (although she may petition the court to compel him to divorce her). But when a minor girl was married under the Rabbinic procedure described above, the Rabbis further instituted a special simplified divorce procedure whereby the wife could divorce her husband. She was required to summon two witnesses, and to say: "I refuse to remain with my husband any longer," and the marriage was automatically dissolved. This procedure is called "refusal" (מֵיאוּן) and the wife is described as "a refuser" (מְמָאֶנֶת — *mema'enet*). Technically, refusal is a sort of annulment, rather than a divorce, because the marriage is considered never to have taken place.

The wife may refuse in this way only if she married as an orphan, and only as long as she is still a minor. If she was married off by her father, however, or if she remains with her husband until she becomes a *na'arah*, her marriage has Torah status, and may not be dissolved without a proper bill of divorce.

The witnesses would customarily write out a document testifying to the refusal procedure. But this document was not an intrinsic part of the refusal procedure itself, like a bill of divorce, but merely a record to serve as proof of the girl's unmarried status.

[1]מַאי ״עֲרָיוֹת״, וּמַאי ״שְׁנִיּוֹת לַעֲרָיוֹת״? [2]אִילֵימָא ״עֲרָיוֹת״ [36A] עֲרָיוֹת מַמָּשׁ, [3]״שְׁנִיּוֹת״ מִדִּבְרֵי סוֹפְרִים, [4]כֵּיוָן דְּמִדְּאוֹרַיְיתָא חַזְיָא לֵיהּ, [5]אַמַּאי אֵין לָהֶן קְנָס? [6]אֶלָּא, ״עֲרָיוֹת״ חַיָּיבֵי מִיתוֹת בֵּית דִּין, [7]״שְׁנִיּוֹת״ חַיָּיבֵי

TRANSLATION AND COMMENTARY

מַאי עֲרָיוֹת [1]The Gemara considers the first clause of the Baraita, which ruled that a man who rapes or seduces a woman with whom he is forbidden to have intercourse under the law forbidding incest, or under the law forbidding secondary incest, need not pay the fine. The Gemara asks: **What** does the Baraita mean by **"women with whom intercourse is incestuous** [עֲרָיוֹת]" **and** by **"women with whom intercourse is secondarily incestuous** [שְׁנִיּוֹת]"? Normally, the former term refers to those cases of incest forbidden by the Torah in Leviticus, chapter 18, and the latter term refers to more distant relatives forbidden by Rabbinic decree (*Yevamot* 21a). But is this what the Baraita means by these terms? [2]**If we say** that the Baraita is using these terms in their normal sense, so that the term **"women with whom intercourse is incestuous"** [36A] **is really referring to** those **women with whom intercourse is** forbidden as **incest** by the Torah in Leviticus, chapter 18, [3]**and** the term **"women with whom intercourse is secondarily incestuous"** is really referring to those women with whom intercourse is **forbidden by Rabbinic enactment** (the more distant relatives listed in *Yevamot*), then in that case the Baraita is ruling that a man who rapes a woman who is permitted to him by Torah law but forbidden by Rabbinic decree is exempt from paying the fine. But surely this is impossible! Granted that the Baraita disagrees with our Mishnah, which rules that even a man who rapes a close relative, such as his sister, must pay the fine; [4]but if the woman **is fit** to marry **him by Torah law** but forbidden by Rabbinic decree, the Torah clearly requires the fine to be paid, and it is unlikely that the Rabbis would reward the rapist for committing a sin forbidden by Rabbinic decree by exempting him from a fine that he is required to pay by Torah law. [5]So **why are** such women **not entitled to a fine?**

אֶלָּא, עֲרָיוֹת [6]**Rather,** says the Gemara, we must give the Baraita a different interpretation. In the context of this Baraita, the term **"women with whom intercourse is incestuous"** does not refer to all the cases of incest listed in Leviticus, chapter 18, but only to **those** cases of incest **that a court can punish by the death penalty.** All the cases of incest listed in Leviticus, chapter 18 are punished by excision, and some of them (listed in Leviticus, chapter 20) are also punishable by the death penalty, if the offense was witnessed and the offenders warned. [7]And the term **"women with whom intercourse is secondarily incestuous"** refers to all **those** other cases of incest **that are subject to excision** but not to the death penalty. Thus the Baraita

LITERAL TRANSLATION

[1]What are "forbidden relations," and what are "secondary forbidden relations"? [2]If we say [that] "forbidden relations" [36A] are really forbidden relations, [3][and] "secondary forbidden relations" are [forbidden] from the words of the Sages, [4]since by Torah law she is fit for him, [5]why do they not have a fine?

[6]Rather, "forbidden relations" are those who are subject to execution by the court, [7]"secondary forbidden relations" are those who are subject to

RASHI

עריות ממש — המפורש ב״אחרי מות״, והן בכריתות. **שניות** — שגזרו חכמים על שניות להן להרחיק מן העבירה, כגון אם אמו ואם אביו, ושאר עריות השנויות בפרק שני דיבמות (כא,א). **כיון דשניות חזיין ליה מדאורייתא** — קרינן ביה ״ולו תהיה לאשה״. **אמאי אין לה קנס** — בעלמא בעריות איכא למימר, כשמעון התימני, דלית ליה ״נערה״ ״נערה״ ״הנערה״. אלא שניות קשיא.

NOTES

כֵּיוָן דְּמִדְּאוֹרַיְיתָא חַזְיָא לֵיהּ **Since by Torah law she is fit for him.** *Rashi* explains that the law requiring a rapist to pay a fine is a Torah law, whereas the prohibition against marrying a "secondary relation" is a Rabbinic decree. Hence, even according to Shimon HaTimni and Rabbi Shimon ben Menasya, who rule that the fine need be paid only when the Torah's commandment to the rapist to marry the woman also applies, the fine should still be paid to a "secondary relation," since the rapist is permitted to marry her by Torah law.

Shittah Mekubbetzet points out that the Gemara (above, 29b) mentions that, according to Rabbi Shimon ben Menasya, a man who rapes a *na'arah* who is a *netinah* or a *mamzeret* is exempt from the fine, because the rapist is not permitted to marry her. Now, the *mamzeret* is indeed forbidden to be married by Torah law, but according to some Rishonim the *netinah* is forbidden only by Rabbinic decree. Thus we see that the rapist may conceivably be exempt if the victim is forbidden by Rabbinic decree. *Shittah Mekubbetzet* attempts to distinguish between the two Rabbinic prohibitions.

Tosafot explains, however, that according to the viewpoint that the *netinah* is forbidden by Rabbinic decree, the Gemara's statement above (29b) should not be taken literally, because the word *netin* or *netinah* is sometimes included together with the word *mamzer* or *mamzeret*, even though the law applies only to *mamzerim* and not to *netinim*.

TRANSLATION AND COMMENTARY

disagrees with our Mishnah, which rules that in cases of incest the fine must be paid unless there is a death penalty, in which case the rapist is exempt from the fine because he is subject to the more severe penalty. According to the Baraita, the rapist is exempt from the fine in all cases of incest, both the more severe kind exempted by the Mishnah and the "secondary" kind for which the Mishnah does not grant an exemption. [1]**But** according to this interpretation, women **who are** not listed at all in Leviticus, chapter 18, but **violate** Torah law by transgressing **an** ordinary **negative commandment** (e.g., a *mamzeret* or a divorcee who marries a priest), **are entitled to a fine,** even according to the Baraita. [2]The Gemara explains: According to this interpretation, **whose view is** reflected in the Baraita? Who is the Tanna who disagrees with our Mishnah and maintains that a man who rapes his sister is exempt from the fine, but agrees with our Mishnah that a man who rapes a *mamzeret* is not exempt, even though he is not permitted to marry her? [3]**It is Shimon HaTimni,** who ruled (above, 29b) that the fine is paid only if a marriage between the rapist and his victim would be valid, even if forbidden. But if such a marriage is invalid, the fine need not be paid. According to this viewpoint, a man who rapes a woman who is forbidden to him under penalty of excision or death is exempt from paying the fine, but a man who rapes a woman who is forbidden to him by an ordinary negative commandment is required to pay the fine.

אִיכָּא דְּאָמְרִי [4]**There are some** authorities **who** interpret the Baraita differently. According to their interpretation, the term **"women with whom intercourse is incestuous"** should be understood as **referring to** all the cases of incest listed in Leviticus, chapter 18, both **those that a court can punish by the death penalty and** those **that are subject to excision.** [5]But the term **"women with whom intercourse is secondarily incestuous"** in the context of this Baraita **refers to** women **who are** subject by Torah law to the penalty for **transgressing** a **negative commandment** (such as a *mamzeret,* or a divorcee who marries a priest). These women are described as "secondary," because the prohibition against marrying them, although a Torah law, is not as severe as the prohibition against marrying relatives. [6]The Gemara explains: According to this interpretation, **whose view is** reflected in the Baraita? Who is the Tanna who disagrees with our Mishnah completely and maintains that a man who rapes his sister or a man who rapes a *mamzeret* is exempt from the fine, because he is not permitted to marry her? [7]**It is Rabbi Shimon ben Menasya,** who ruled (above, 29b) that the fine is paid only if a marriage between the rapist and his victim would be permitted. But if such a marriage is forbidden, so that the Torah's commandment to the rapist to marry his victim cannot be carried out, the fine need not be paid. According to this viewpoint, a man who rapes a woman who is forbidden to him by Torah law for any reason is exempt from paying the fine.

הַמְמָאֶנֶת [8]The Gemara now considers the next clause of the Baraita: **"A girl who refuses marriage** — a minor orphan girl who was given in marriage by her mother or her brothers under a Rabbinic arrangement and who subsequently annulled her marriage — **is not entitled to a fine for rape or** to a fine **for seduction,** because she is not considered a virgin, since we suspect that she had intercourse with her husband before annulling her marriage." [9]**This implies,** says the Gemara, **that an ordinary minor girl** who was never married in this way ***is*** **entitled** to a fine if she is raped or seduced. For if a minor were not entitled to a fine at all, why would the Baraita need to inform us that she is not entitled to the fine if she marries and then annuls her marriage? The question of whether a minor girl is entitled to a fine is the subject of a Tannaitic

כָּרֵיתוֹת, [1]אֲבָל חַיָּיבֵי לָאוִין יֵשׁ לָהֶן קְנָס. [2]וּמַנִּי? [3]שִׁמְעוֹן הַתִּימְנִי הִיא.

[4]אִיכָּא דְּאָמְרִי: ״עֲרָיוֹת״ חַיָּיבֵי מִיתוֹת בֵּית דִּין וְחַיָּיבֵי כָּרֵיתוֹת, [5]״שְׁנִיּוֹת״ חַיָּיבֵי לָאוִין. [6]מַנִּי? [7]רַבִּי שִׁמְעוֹן בֶּן מְנַסְיָא הִיא.

[8]״הַמְמָאֶנֶת אֵין לָהּ לֹא קְנָס וְלֹא פִּיתּוּי״. [9]הָא קְטַנָּה בְּעָלְמָא

LITERAL TRANSLATION

excision, [1]but those who violate a negative commandment have a fine. [2]And whose [opinion] is it? [3]It is [the opinion of] Shimon HaTimni.

[4]There are [some] who say: "Forbidden relations" are those who are subject to execution by the court or who are subject to excision, [5]"secondary forbidden relations" are those who violate a negative commandment. [6][And] whose [opinion] is it? [7]It is [the opinion of] Rabbi Shimon ben Menasya.

[8]"A girl who refuses [marriage] does not have [a claim to] a fine [for rape] or [for] seduction." [9]This [implies that] an ordinary minor girl

RASHI

שמעון התימני — בריש פירקין, דאמר: אשה שיש בה הויה.
רבי שמעון בן מנסיא — דאמר: אשה הראויה לקיימה.

אִית לָהּ. [1]מַנִּי? [2]רַבָּנַן הִיא, דְּאָמְרִי: קְטַנָּה יֵשׁ לָהּ קְנָס.

[3]אֵימָא סֵיפָא: ״אַיְילוֹנִית אֵין לָהּ לֹא קְנָס וְלֹא פִּיתּוּי״. [4]אֲתָא לְרַבִּי מֵאִיר דַּאֲמַר: קְטַנָּה אֵין לָהּ קְנָס. [5]וְהָא מִקַּטְנוּתָהּ יָצְתָה לְבֶגֶר.

[6]רֵישָׁא רַבָּנַן [7]וְסֵיפָא רַבִּי מֵאִיר?

[8]וְכִי תֵּימָא: כּוּלָּהּ רַבִּי מֵאִיר הִיא, [9]וּבִמְמָאֶנֶת סָבַר לָהּ כְּרַבִּי יְהוּדָה, [10]וּמִי סָבַר לָהּ? [11]וְהָתַנְיָא: ״עַד מָתַי הַבַּת מְמָאֶנֶת? [12]עַד שֶׁתָּבִיא שְׁתֵּי שְׂעָרוֹת. [13]דִּבְרֵי רַבִּי מֵאִיר.

LITERAL TRANSLATION

does have [such a claim]. [1]Whose [opinion] is it? [2]It is [that of] the Rabbis, who say: A minor girl has a fine.

[3]Consider (lit., "say") the last clause: "A sexually undeveloped woman does not have [a claim to] a fine [for rape] or [for] seduction." [4]It is in accordance with (lit., "comes to") Rabbi Meir who says: A minor girl does not have a fine. [5]And this one went out from her minority to adulthood.

[6]The first clause [follows] the Rabbis [7]and the last clause [follows] Rabbi Meir?

[8]And if you say: All of it is Rabbi Meir, [9]and concerning a girl who refuses [marriage] he agrees with Rabbi Yehudah, [10]but does he agree [with him]? [11]But surely it was taught: "Until when can the daughter refuse? [12]Until she produces two [pubic] hairs. [13][These are] the words of Rabbi Meir.

TRANSLATION AND COMMENTARY

dispute between Rabbi Meir and the Rabbis, and the Gemara has explained (29a) that our Mishnah reflects the viewpoint of Rabbi Meir, who says that only *ne'arot* are entitled to a fine. [1]But, asks the Gemara, **whose opinion is** reflected in this Baraita? [2]**It is** the opinion **of the Rabbis, who** disagree with Rabbi Meir and **say: A minor girl is entitled to a fine** just like a *na'arah*, and only an adult woman is not entitled.

אֵימָא סֵיפָא [3]But, the Gemara objects, **consider the last clause** of the Baraita, which stated: **"A sexually undeveloped woman is** also **not entitled to a fine for rape or** to a fine **for seduction,** because sexually undeveloped women never have the status of *ne'arot."* [4]Clearly this clause **is in accordance with** the opinion of **Rabbi Meir, who says: A minor girl is not entitled to a fine.** [5]Hence a sexually undeveloped woman is not entitled to a fine, because she **proceeds** directly **from her minority to adulthood** without ever having the status of a *na'arah*. According to the Rabbis, however, such a woman should be entitled to a fine before she becomes an adult, like any other minor.

רֵישָׁא רַבָּנַן [6]Thus we see that the Baraita is inconsistent, with **the first clause** (dealing with the girl who refuses marriage) **following the Rabbis,** [7]**and the last clause** (dealing with the sexually undeveloped woman) **following Rabbi Meir!**

וְכִי תֵּימָא [8]Now, says the Gemara, **you may argue** that the **entire** Baraita can be explained as reflecting **Rabbi Meir's** viewpoint, that a minor is not entitled to a fine. But the Baraita needed to inform us that a girl who refuses marriage is not entitled to a fine, [9]because Rabbi Meir **agrees with Rabbi Yehudah about a girl who refuses marriage.** The Mishnah (*Niddah* 52a) rules that as soon as a girl produces two pubic hairs and becomes a *na'arah*, she is considered legally competent with regard to most of the laws of the Torah. The anonymous first Tanna in that Mishnah maintains that an orphan girl who was married off as a minor by her mother or her brothers (under the Rabbinic arrangement) may annul her marriage, but only until she produces two pubic hairs and becomes a *na'arah*. Rabbi Yehudah, however, maintains that she is entitled to annul her marriage in this way even after she becomes a *na'arah*, "until the black is more than the white" (i.e., until there is objective evidence that she is already a *na'arah*). If Rabbi Meir agrees with Rabbi Yehudah on this matter, it would follow that a girl who refuses marriage need not necessarily be a minor at the time of refusal. Hence it is possible that the Baraita is referring to a *na'arah* who annulled her marriage, and is teaching us that a *na'arah* who annuls her marriage in this way is not entitled to the fine, if she is subsequently raped or seduced. [10]**But** the Gemara rejects this line of argument: **Does** Rabbi Meir **agree with** Rabbi Yehudah on this point? [11]**But surely** the Tanna who disagrees with Rabbi Yehudah about this matter is none other than Rabbi Meir, as **has been taught** in the following Baraita: **"Until when may a girl refuse?** [12]**Until she produces two pubic hairs** — at the onset of puberty, at which point she becomes a *na'arah*. [13]**This is the opinion of Rabbi Meir.**

RASHI

רבנן היא — דפליגי אדרבי מאיר, בריש פירקין. **ובממאנת סבר לה כרבי יהודה** — דאמר: נערה ממאנת. והכי תידוק מינה: נערה ממאנת אין לה קנס, הא נערה בעלמא — יש לה קנס. **עד שתביא שתי שערות** — ומשהביאה אינה ממאנת, ואפילו לא בעל לאחר מיכן.

HALAKHAH

עַד מָתַי הַבַּת מְמָאֶנֶת Until when can the daughter refuse? "An orphan girl who married under the Rabbinic arrangement may annul her marriage by refusing to remain with her husband. She may refuse only as long as she remains a

TRANSLATION AND COMMENTARY

[1]But **Rabbi Yehudah says:** She may still annul her marriage even after she becomes a *na'arah*, **until the black is more than the white."** Thus we see that Rabbi Meir disagrees with Rabbi Yehudah about the case of the girl who refuses marriage, and it is impossible to explain the Baraita as reflecting his view.

אֶלָּא [2]**Rather,** says the Gemara, perhaps we can explain the entire Baraita as reflecting **Rabbi Yehudah's** opinion, that a girl is entitled to refuse even after she becomes a *na'arah*, and this would explain the ruling about the girl who refuses marriage. However, the Baraita ruled that a sexually undeveloped woman is not entitled to a fine because she is not a *na'arah,* [3]and perhaps Rabbi Yehudah **agrees with Rabbi Meir about a minor girl.** Hence the clause in the Baraita dealing with the girl who refuses marriage may still be understood as referring to a *na'arah* (following Rabbi Yehudah, as was explained above), and the clause about the sexually undeveloped woman may be informing us that a minor is not entitled to a fine, following Rabbi Meir (with whom Rabbi Yehudah happens to agree).

וּמִי סָבַר לָהּ [4]**But** the Gemara objects to this suggestion: **Does** Rabbi Yehudah **agree with** Rabbi Meir that a minor girl is not entitled to a fine? [5]**But surely** later in this chapter (40b) the Mishnah states that a minor is not entitled to a fine, and **Rav Yehudah** gave an authoritative interpretation **in the name of Rav, saying: This** Mishnah reflects the minority view **of Rabbi Meir,** but the other Sages disagree with him, and maintain that a minor *is* entitled to a fine. [6]**And if it were true** that Rabbi Yehudah agrees with Rabbi Meir on this point, why did Rav mention only Rabbi Meir? [7]**He should have said: "This** Mishnah reflects the viewpoints **of Rabbi Meir and Rabbi Yehudah."** If two eminent Tannaim were known to have expressed this view, why would Rav mention one and not the other?

הַאי תַּנָּא סָבַר לָהּ [8]The Gemara concludes that the only way the Baraita can be explained consistently is by saying that it reflects the viewpoint of an anonymous **Tanna** who happens to **agree with Rabbi Meir about** a minor girl who was raped, [9]**and** happens to **disagree with him about** a *na'arah* who wishes to annul her marriage by refusing to remain with her husband. Since the two issues are not logically connected, it is possible that the author of the Baraita rules in favor of Rabbi Meir regarding the rape of minors, and in favor of Rabbi Yehudah regarding the refusal of *ne'arot*.

[1]רַבִּי יְהוּדָה אוֹמֵר: עַד שֶׁיִּרְבֶּה שָׁחוֹר עַל הַלָּבָן״!

[2]אֶלָּא רַבִּי יְהוּדָה הִיא, [3]וּבִקְטַנָּה סָבַר לָהּ כְּרַבִּי מֵאִיר. [4]וּמִי סָבַר לָהּ? [5]וְהָאָמַר רַב יְהוּדָה אָמַר רַב: זוֹ דִּבְרֵי רַבִּי מֵאִיר. [6]וְאִם אִיתָא, [7]״זוֹ דִּבְרֵי רַבִּי מֵאִיר וְרַבִּי יְהוּדָה״ מִיבָּעֵי לֵיהּ.

[8]הַאי תַּנָּא סָבַר לָהּ כְּרַבִּי מֵאִיר בַּחֲדָא, [9]וּפָלֵיג עֲלֵיהּ בַּחֲדָא.

LITERAL TRANSLATION

[1]Rabbi Yehudah says: Until the black is more than the white"!

[2]Rather, it is Rabbi Yehudah, [3]and concerning a minor girl he agrees with Rabbi Meir.

[4]But does he agree [with him]? [5]But surely Rav Yehudah said in the name of Rav: These are the words of Rabbi Meir. [6]And if it were true, [7]he should have [said]: "These are the words of Rabbi Meir and Rabbi Yehudah."

[8]This Tanna agrees with Rabbi Meir about one [thing], [9]and disagrees with him about one [thing].

RASHI

רבי יהודה אומר — אם לא בעל. לאחר שגדלה — ממאנת. **עד שירבה שחור על הלבן** — ובנדה מפרש: שתי שערות שוכבות, ונראה כמו שירבה השחור. **אלא רבי יהודה היא** — ובממאנת נערה אשמעינן דאין לה קנס, ולא תדוק: הא קטנה יש לה קנס. וגבי אילונית, דתנא נמי: אין לה קנס — משום דבקטנה סבר כרבי מאיר, וזו מקטנותה יצאת לבגר. **זו דברי כו'** — לקמן בפרקין (מ,ב).

HALAKHAH

minor, but as soon as she becomes a *na'arah* her marriage takes on Torah status and cannot be dissolved without a proper bill of divorce, following Rabbi Meir, whose opinion in this case is accepted.

"A girl becomes a *na'arah* for this purpose only after she has produced two pubic hairs after her twelfth birthday. But if she has not produced two hairs, she may still refuse, even if she is already twelve years old. This applies only if the girl was examined and found not to have pubic hair. But if she was not examined, or even if she was examined and it seemed possible that she had produced hairs but they subsequently fell off, we assume that she became a *na'arah* on her twelfth birthday, and she is no longer permitted to annul her marriage.

"Nowadays we do not permit her to refuse after her twelfth birthday in any case, since we do not trust our ability to judge if she had pubic hairs which fell off. *Rema* adds that before her twelfth birthday she is permitted to refuse, even nowadays." (*Rambam, Sefer Nashim, Hilkhot Gerushin* 11:4-6; *Shulḥan Arukh, Even HaEzer* 155:12,19-22.)

[1] רַפְרָם אֲמַר: מַאי ״מְמָאֶנֶת״? [2] הָרְאוּיָה לְמָאֵן. [3] וְלִיתְנֵי: ״קְטַנָּה״! [4] קַשְׁיָא.
[5] ״אַיְילוֹנִית אֵין לָהּ לֹא קְנָס וְלֹא פִּיתּוּי״. [6] וּרְמִינְהִי: [7] ״הַחֵרֶשֶׁת, וְהַשּׁוֹטָה, וְהָאַיְילוֹנִית, יֵשׁ לָהֶן קְנָס [8] וְיֵשׁ לָהֶן טַעֲנַת בְּתוּלִים״. [9] וְהָא מַאי רוּמְיָא? [10] הָא רַבִּי מֵאִיר, הָא רַבָּנַן.

LITERAL TRANSLATION

[1] Rafram said: What is "a girl who refuses [marriage]"? [2] Someone who is entitled to refuse. [3] Then let it teach: "A minor girl"! [4] It is difficult.

[5] "A sexually undeveloped woman does not have [a claim to] a fine [for rape] or [for] seduction." [6] But a contradiction may be raised (lit., "cast them together"): [7] "A woman who is a deaf-mute, and an imbecile, and a sexually undeveloped woman, have a fine [8] and are subject to (lit., 'have') claims concerning [their] virginity." [9] But what sort of contradiction is this? [10] This is [the opinion of] Rabbi Meir, that is [the opinion of] the Rabbis.

TRANSLATION AND COMMENTARY

רַפְרָם אֲמַר [1] **Rafram said:** It is possible to explain the Baraita consistently according to Rabbi Meir, who maintains that only a minor can refuse, and that a minor is not entitled to a fine. We asked earlier why, in that case, the Baraita needed to teach us that a girl who refuses marriage is not entitled to a fine because she is suspected of not being a virgin, since every girl who refuses is a minor. But the answer is that the Baraita mentioned the girl who refuses as a way of illustrating its ruling about minors. **What** does the term **"a girl who refuses marriage"** mean in this Baraita? [2] It means **someone who is entitled to refuse** — i.e., any minor girl who would be entitled to refuse to remain with her husband if her father had died and she had been given in marriage by her mother or brothers under the Rabbinic arrangement.

וְלִיתְנֵי [3] The Gemara objects to this suggestion: Why, **then**, should the Baraita express itself in this unusual way? **Let it teach** explicitly that **a minor girl** is not entitled to a fine!

קַשְׁיָא [4] The Gemara concludes that Rafram's explanation **is difficult** to accept.

אַיְילוֹנִית [5] The Gemara now considers the next clause of the Baraita: **"A sexually undeveloped woman is not entitled to a fine for rape or** to a fine **for seduction,"** because sexually undeveloped women pass directly from minority to full adulthood and never have the status of *ne'arot*, and the author of this Baraita is of the opinion that only *ne'arot*, and not minors, are entitled to a fine (as the Gemara explained above). [6] **But,** the Gemara objects, **a contradiction may be raised** from the following Baraita, which indicates that barren women *are* entitled to a fine while they are still minors. [7] This second Baraita rules: **"A woman who is a deaf-mute or an imbecile** is entitled to a fine if she is raped or seduced. Under Jewish law, a deaf-mute is considered legally incompetent, like an imbecile. However, women suffering from these conditions are still presumed to be virgins, and we do not assume that they are so incapable of protecting themselves that they must already have lost their virginity. Likewise, **a sexually undeveloped woman is entitled to a fine** while she is still a minor," even though she never becomes a *na'arah* (as explained above), because the author of this second Baraita is of the opinion that a minor girl is entitled to the fine. [8] "For the same reason," continues the Baraita, "these women **are** also **subject to claims concerning their virginity."** If a man marries a woman who is supposedly a virgin, and discovers that she was not a virgin at the time of the marriage, he may divorce her without giving her her ketubah. This Baraita maintains that deaf-mutes, imbeciles, or minor women are still presumed to be virgins when they marry, and if they are not, the husband can argue that he was deceived.

וְהָא מַאי רוּמְיָא [9] We see that the author of the second Baraita is of the opinion that a sexually undeveloped woman is entitled to the fine, whereas the author of the first Baraita (above, 35b) maintains that such a woman (like any other minor) is not entitled to a fine. **But**, asks the Gemara, **what sort of contradiction is this?** We know that the question of minors is the subject of a Tannaitic dispute. [10] Perhaps **this** first Baraita **reflects the opinion of Rabbi Meir** that a minor is not entitled to a fine, whereas **that** second Baraita **reflects the opinion of the Rabbis** that a minor *is* entitled to a fine! How can you raise a contradiction from one Baraita to another without first determining that they reflect the same viewpoint!

RASHI

סבר לה כרבי מאיר – דקטנה אין לה קנס, משום הכי אין קנס באילונית. **ופליג עליה** – בממאנת, ואמר: עד שירבה השחור. וכי תנא: הממאנת אין לה קנס, הא הראויה למאן יש לה קנס, בנערה קאמר. **מאי ממאנת הראויה למאן** – כלומר, כל קטנה קאמר, וכולה רבי מאיר היא. **ויש להן טענת בתולים** – להפסידה כתובה. **הא רבי מאיר** – דאמר: קטנה אין לה קנס, ואילונית מקטנותה יצתה לבגר.

SAGES

רַפְרָם Rafram. A sixth- and seventh-generation Babylonian Amora, Rafram was a disciple of Rav Ashi and a colleague of Ravina II. The name Rafram is traditionally interpreted by the Geonim as an abbreviation of Rav Efrayim. Rafram lived in Pumbedita and became the head of the yeshivah in that city.

LITERAL TRANSLATION

[1] And he who asked it, why did he ask it? [2] Because he has another contradiction to raise against it: [3] "A woman who is a deaf-mute, and an imbecile, and an adult woman, and a woman who was injured by a stick, are not subject to claims concerning [their] virginity. [4] A blind woman and a sexually undeveloped woman are subject to

[1] וּדְקָאָרֵי לָהּ, מַאי קָאָרֵי לָהּ?
[2] מִשּׁוּם דְּאִית לֵיהּ לְמִירְמָא אַחֲרִיתֵי עִילָּוֵיהּ: [3] "הַחֵרֶשֶׁת, וְהַשּׁוֹטָה, וְהַבּוֹגֶרֶת, וּמוּכַּת עֵץ, אֵין לָהֶן טַעֲנַת בְּתוּלִים.
[4] הַסּוּמָא וְאַיְילוֹנִית יֵשׁ לָהֶן

TRANSLATION AND COMMENTARY

וּדְקָאָרֵי [1] The solution to the contradiction is so obvious that the Gemara cannot believe that it did not occur to the Amora who raised it. Hence the Gemara asks: **When this question was raised, what did the questioner think he was asking?** Surely he must have had some other point in mind!

מִשּׁוּם דְּאִית לֵיהּ [2] The Gemara answers: The questioner raised this objection **because he had another contradiction to raise against** the second Baraita from a third Baraita, and he used the original Baraita in order to introduce the problem of the two contradictory Baraitot. [3] The third Baraita states: **"A woman who is a deaf-mute or an imbecile is not subject to claims concerning her virginity."** If a man marries such a woman and discovers that she was not a virgin at the time of the marriage, he cannot divorce her without giving her her ketubah, as this Baraita (unlike the second Baraita) is of the opinion that women in this category are presumed not to be virgins. "Likewise," continues the Baraita, "if someone marries **an adult woman,** he is not entitled to divorce her if she shows no signs of virginity, because women often lose these signs as they grow to maturity; hence the signs are effective only as long as the girl is a minor or a *na'arah*. Likewise, if he marries **a woman who is** known to have **ruptured** her hymen because of an **injury** caused **by a stick** or the like, he is not entitled to divorce her, because women who have been injured in this way show no signs of virginity." [4] The Baraita continues: **"A blind woman and a sexually undeveloped woman,** on the other hand, **are subject to claims concerning their**

RASHI

ודקארי לה מאי קארי לה — מי שהשיב תשובה זו בבית המדרש, מה עלתה על רוחו, ולא סבירא ליה דאיכא לאוקמינהו כרבי מאיר ורבנן? **משום דאית ליה למירמא אחריתא עליה** — לא הביאה לבית המדרש אלא לפי שיש להשיב אחרת על זו; חרשת ושוטה אחרשת ושוטה. **בוגרת** — בתוליה כלים מאליהן.

BACKGROUND

מוּכַּת עֵץ **A woman who was injured by a stick.** Penetration of the vagina by a hard object, such as a stick, is liable to rupture the hymen. This can happen if a girl falls in such a way that some hard, projecting object directly strikes her vagina. In any event, this is not a likely occurrence, for a simple fall would not cause such a result.

NOTES

אֵין לָהֶן טַעֲנַת בְּתוּלִים **Are not subject to claims concerning their virginity.** *Rashi* explains that a man who marries a deaf-mute or an imbecile and discovers that she was not a virgin at the time of the marriage, is not entitled to divorce her without giving her her ketubah, because it is possible that she was raped between her betrothal and the consummation of her marriage. Even though the wife does not make this claim, we make it for her, since she is legally incompetent and incapable of representing herself.

Ramban explains that women who are deaf-mutes or imbeciles are not considered virgins, because we assume that they ruptured their hymens in some injury long before they were married or were raped. However, the Halakhah states that a deaf-mute or imbecile wife is not entitled to any ketubah whatsoever, but if the husband chooses to write her a ketubah, it is considered a gift and is valid. Hence, even though the husband claims that he wrote this ketubah on the assumption that his wife was a virgin, and has now discovered that she was not, he cannot claim that he was deceived, because he should have realized when

HALAKHAH

הַחֵרֶשֶׁת, וְהַשּׁוֹטָה,...וּמוּכַּת עֵץ, אֵין לָהֶן טַעֲנַת בְּתוּלִים **A woman who is a deaf-mute, and an imbecile,...and a woman who was injured by a stick, are not subject to claims concerning their virginity.** "A woman who was injured by a stick is entitled to a ketubah of a maneh, whether the husband was aware of this fact when he married her or not. The marriage of a deaf-mute has no validity by Torah law, but is valid by Rabbinic decree; but a deaf-mute is not entitled to any ketubah at all. The marriage of an imbecile has no validity at all, even by Rabbinic decree, and she too is not entitled to any ketubah. However, if the husband chooses to write a ketubah voluntarily for his deaf-mute or imbecile wife, it is valid.

"In all these cases, if the husband wrote a full ketubah as for a virgin, and then claimed that he discovered that his wife was not a virgin, his claim is not accepted, and she is entitled to the ketubah that he wrote." (*Rambam, Sefer Nashim, Hilkhot Ishut* 11:3,4,5,8; *Shulḥan Arukh, Even HaEzer* 67:5,7,8,9 and 68:1.)

הַבּוֹגֶרֶת **An adult woman.** "An adult woman is entitled to the full ketubah of a virgin, in accordance with the passage above (11b). If there was no bleeding as a result of the first intercourse, she is considered not to be a virgin, and her husband may divorce her without a ketubah, following our Gemara's conclusion." (*Rambam, Sefer Nashim, Hilkhot Ishut* 11:4,12,13; *Shulḥan Arukh, Even HaEzer* 67:6 and 68:1,3.)

סוּמָא יֵשׁ לָהּ טַעֲנַת בְּתוּלִים **A blind woman is subject to claims concerning her virginity.** "A virgin who is blind is entitled to the full ketubah of a virgin, and if she is found not to have been a virgin when she married, her husband may divorce her without a ketubah, following the first Tanna in the Baraita." (*Rambam, Sefer Nashim, Hilkhot Ishut* 11:4,8; *Shulḥan Arukh, Even HaEzer* 67:6 and 68:1.)

אַיְילוֹנִית יֵשׁ לָהּ טַעֲנַת בְּתוּלִים **A sexually undeveloped woman is subject to claims concerning her virginity.** "A virgin who is known to be sexually undeveloped is entitled to the full ketubah of a virgin, and if she is found not to

טַעֲנַת בְּתוּלִים. ¹סוּמָכוּס אוֹמֵר מִשּׁוּם רַבִּי מֵאִיר: סוּמָא אֵין לָהּ טַעֲנַת בְּתוּלִים״.

²אָמַר רַב שֵׁשֶׁת: לָא קַשְׁיָא. ³הָא רַבָּן גַּמְלִיאֵל, וְהָא רַבִּי יְהוֹשֻׁעַ.

⁴אֵימַר דְּשָׁמְעַתְּ לֵיהּ לְרַבָּן גַּמְלִיאֵל הֵיכָא דְּקָא טָעֲנָה אִיהִי. ⁵הֵיכָא דְּלָא קָא טָעֲנָה אִיהִי מִי שָׁמְעַתְּ לֵיהּ?

LITERAL TRANSLATION

claims concerning [their] virginity. ¹Summakhos says in the name of Rabbi Meir: A blind woman is not subject to claims concerning [her] virginity."

²Rav Sheshet said: There is no difficulty. ³This is [the opinion of] Rabban Gamliel, and that is [the opinion of] Rabbi Yehoshua.

⁴Say that you heard [the opinion of] Rabban Gamliel where she herself made a claim. ⁵Did you hear him [say this] where she herself did not make a claim?

TRANSLATION AND COMMENTARY

virginity. ¹**Summakhos** disagreed with the first Tanna, **saying in the name of Rabbi Meir: A blind woman is not subject to claims concerning her virginity,** because she may have lost her virginity without realizing it. Hence she is not guilty of deceit, and her husband cannot divorce her without giving her her ketubah."

Now, although these two Baraitot do not contradict each other regarding the sexually undeveloped woman — in fact, both of them maintain that she is subject to claims concerning her virginity, in apparent disagreement with the first Baraita (above, 35b) — they do contradict each other regarding the deaf-mute and the imbecile. The second Baraita maintains that these women are presumed to be virgins, whereas the third Baraita is of the opinion that they are not. What, asks the Gemara, is the basis of this disagreement?

אָמַר רַב שֵׁשֶׁת ²**Rav Sheshet said** in reply: **There is no difficulty.** ³The third Baraita **reflects the opinion of Rabban Gamliel, whereas** the second **one reflects the opinion of Rabbi Yehoshua.** In the first chapter of *Ketubot* there is a series of disputes between Rabban Gamliel and Rabbi Yehoshua as to whether a woman who is found not to be a virgin, and gives a plausible explanation (e.g., "I was raped after I was betrothed," or "I had an accident and ruptured my hymen"), is believed without proof, or whether the onus is on her to prove her explanation, or be divorced without receiving her ketubah. According to Rabban Gamliel, the wife is believed without proof, and the onus is on the husband to prove that she lost her virginity in a way that justifies divorcing her without giving her her ketubah, whereas according to Rabbi Yehoshua the burden of proof always falls on the wife. Now in our case, the imbecile or the deaf-mute is obviously incapable of proving how she lost her virginity. Hence Rabbi Yehoshua would maintain that we must assume it happened in a way that would cause her to lose her ketubah, whereas Rabban Gamliel would maintain that in our case, too, the burden of proof is on the husband.

אֵימַר ⁴But, the Gemara objects, you can **argue that you heard Rabban Gamliel's opinion** in a case **where** the wife **herself made a claim,** and the question was whether to believe her without proof. ⁵But in our case, the deaf-mute or imbecile **did not herself make a claim.** We are making an assumption that they lost their virginity in a way that would not cause them to lose their ketubah, unless the husband can prove otherwise. **Did you hear** that Rabban Gamliel applies his argument to such a case?

RASHI

הא רבן גמליאל — דאמר בפרק קמא (כתובות יב,ב): היא אומרת "משארסתני נאנסתי" — נאמנת. הכא נמי אין לה טענת בתולים להפסידה כתובתה, דאמרינן: אי הוה פקחת לטעון — הוה טוענה "משארסתני נאנסתי", ומהימנא. **הא רבי יהושע** — דאמר "לא מפיה אנו חיין" — הכא יש לה טענת בתולים, דאי נמי הוה טוענה קמן — לא מהימנינן לה.

SAGES

סוּמָכוּס Summakhos. His full name is Summakhos ben Yosef, and he was one of the Sages of the fifth and last generation of Tannaim. Summakhos was Rabbi Meir's most distinguished disciple and was responsible for transmitting much of his master's legacy of teachings. Even after Rabbi Meir's death, Summakhos devoted much effort to resolving possible contradictions in those teachings.

Like Rabbi Meir, Summakhos was famous for his חֲרִיפוּת — his acute powers of reasoning. The Talmud (*Eruvin* 13b) praises him as being capable of providing forty-eight explanations to substantiate every ruling he made in matters of ritual purity.

He was apparently considered one of the leading Sages of his generation, for we even find him recorded as contesting the Halakhic opinions of the greatest of the contemporaries of Rabbi Meir, including Rabbi Yose and Rabbi Eliezer ben Ya'akov. Even the distinguished Sage Rabbi Natan sought out Summakhos's opinion.

Summakhos appears to have lived to a great age, for even the Amora, Rav, met him and was taught by him.

רַבִּי יְהוֹשֻׁעַ Rabbi Yehoshua (ben Ḥananyah the Levite). See *Ketubot*, Part II, pp. 6-7.

רַבָּן גַּמְלִיאֵל Rabban Gamliel II (of Yavneh). See *Ketubot*, Part II, pp. 8-9.

LANGUAGE

סוּמָכוּס Summakhos. The source for this name is the Greek word σύμμαχος, *summakhos,* which means "ally."

NOTES

he wrote the ketubah that she was probably injured. And even though she did not make this claim, we make it for her, since she is legally incompetent and incapable of representing herself.

הָא רַבָּן גַּמְלִיאֵל וְהָא רַבִּי יְהוֹשֻׁעַ This is the opinion of Rabban Gamliel, and that is the opinion of Rabbi Yehoshua. Our commentary follows *Rashi*, who explains that the Gemara concludes that the second Baraita, which rules that an imbecile or a deaf-mute is subject to claims about her virginity, follows Rabbi Yehoshua, whereas the third Baraita, which rules that an imbecile or a deaf-mute is not subject to such claims, follows Rabban Gamliel. *Ritva* cites another explanation (followed by *Ba'al HaMa'or*), according to which the second Baraita follows Rabban Gamliel and the third follows Rabbi Yehoshua, but this explanation is not accepted by most other Rishonim.

HALAKHAH

have been a virgin when she married, her husband may divorce her without a ketubah, following the Baraita. *Shulḥan Arukh* adds that this applies only if the husband knew that she was sexually undeveloped when he married her, but if he was not aware of this, she is not entitled to any ketubah at all." (*Rambam, Sefer Nashim, Hilkhot Ishut* 11:4,8; *Shulḥan Arukh, Even HaEzer* 67:6 and 68:1.)

TRANSLATION AND COMMENTARY

אֵין [1] The Gemara answers: **Yes. Since Rabban Gamliel said** that the wife **is believed** if she made a claim, we are justified in assuming that he would be of the same opinion in cases in which she is not capable of making a claim. [2] For we have a rule that in monetary **cases such as this,** involving someone who is legally incompetent, the court assumes that the incapable party has made the best claim he could possibly have made, even if in fact he says nothing. This rule is based on a Biblical verse (Proverbs 31:8): **"Open your mouth for the dumb."** Hence in our case the wife who is a deaf-mute or an imbecile is considered to have claimed that she was raped after her betrothal, and since this claim is believed without proof, according to Rabban Gamliel, it is effectively impossible for a husband to claim that his deaf-mute or imbecile wife was not a virgin, unless he can prove that she committed adultery.

וְהַבּוֹגֶרֶת [3] Before returning to the first Baraita, the Gemara explains a few problematic clauses in the third Baraita it has just cited. The Baraita ruled that "an **adult woman is not subject to claims concerning her virginity."** In the first chapter of *Ketubot* (9a-b), the Gemara explains that a husband who claims immediately after consummating the marriage that his wife did not bleed from her hymen, or that he could detect from the ease of penetration that his wife was not a virgin, is believed and may divorce his wife without giving her her ketubah, since it is possible for a man to determine this with certainty, and a husband would not divorce his wife so quickly if he were not telling the truth. But the third Baraita teaches us that this ruling applies only to a man who marries a minor or a *na'arah*, but if the wife was an adult, we do not trust these claims, not because we question the husband's veracity, but because it is possible that his wife was a virgin and showed no signs of bleeding, since adult women often lose the signs of their virginity before marriage. [4] **But,** the Gemara objects, it is not true that adult women show no signs of virginity. For **surely Rav said: We give an adult woman the first night!** When a wife bleeds from her vagina, it is sometimes unclear if the blood is the result of an injury or if it is some type of menstrual flow. If it is the latter, the wife is forbidden on pain of excision (Leviticus 18:19) to have intercourse until she has purified herself. When a virgin has

LITERAL TRANSLATION

[1] Yes. Since Rabban Gamliel said [that] she is believed, [2] [a case] such as this is [an example of]: "Open your mouth for the dumb." [3] "And an adult woman is not subject to claims concerning [her] virginity." [4] But surely Rav said: We give an adult woman the first night!

אֵין. כֵּיוָן דַּאֲמַר רַבָּן גַּמְלִיאֵל מְהֵימְנָא, [2] כְּגוֹן זוֹ "פְּתַח פִּיךָ לְאִלֵּם" הוּא.

[3] "וְהַבּוֹגֶרֶת אֵין לָה טַעֲנַת בְּתוּלִים". [4] וְהָאָמַר רַב: בּוֹגֶרֶת נוֹתְנִין לָה לַיְלָה הָרִאשׁוֹן!

RASHI

נוֹתְנִין לָה לֵילָה הָרִאשׁוֹן — וּבוֹעֵל כַּמָּה בְּעִילוֹת, וְתוֹלִין כָּל דָּמִים שֶׁל אוֹתוֹ הַלַּיְלָה בְּדַם בְּתוּלִים. אַלְמָא: אִית לָה דַּם בְּתוּלִים לְבוֹגֶרֶת. דְּאִי לָא — לָא הֲוָה בָּעֵי לְמֵיתַב לָה אֶלָּא בְּעִילַת מִצְוָה. וְכֵיוָן דְּאִית לָה בְּתוּלִים — הֵיכָא דְּבָעַל וְלָא מָצָא דַּם מַפְסִיד כְּתוּבָּתָהּ, דְּהָא כַּנְּסָהּ בְּחֶזְקַת בְּתוּלָה וּמָצְאָהּ בְּעוּלָה.

REALIA

וְהַבּוֹגֶרֶת אֵין לָה טַעֲנַת בְּתוּלִים **And an adult woman is not subject to claims concerning her virginity.** Most women's hymens are perforated slightly, although the relationship between the size of the hole and the rest of the hymen varies from woman to woman. As a girl grows, so does the perforation in her hymen, and the perforation of an adult's hymen may be so large that the husband will be able to achieve penetration without rupturing the hymen at all. Alternatively, the hymen might be so small that the husband will not feel it, even if it ruptures and bleeds.

NOTES

כְּגוֹן זוֹ "פְּתַח פִּיךָ לְאִלֵּם" הוּא **A case such as this is an example of: "Open your mouth for the dumb."** This idea appears in two other places in the Talmud (*Gittin* 37b and *Bava Batra* 41a). In both instances, the Gemara is referring to a case in which a litigant made an incomplete and inadequate claim, and it appears very likely that he simply had difficulty finding the right words. Hence, although the court generally does not assist a litigant, the Gemara considers the possibility that we should do so in such circumstances. The Rishonim identify this idea with the concept, "We make claims for an orphan or for a purchaser" (see *Bava Batra* 23a and see *Rashi*'s comment on the Mishnah, below, 87a), whereby a claimant who is incapable of making a proper claim, because he is legally incompetent or because he is not in a position to know the facts, is considered to have made the best claim possible.

In our case, *Rashi* explains that no claims can be made about the virginity of the deaf-mute or imbecile wife, because we consider her to have claimed that she was raped after she was betrothed.

Tosafot objects to *Rashi*'s explanation: Even though it is true that a person who is incapable of making a claim is considered to have made the best claim possible, this applies only to reasonable claims, but not to claims that are far-fetched. Why, then, should we claim, without any evidence, that this woman was raped after her betrothal, and force her husband to pay a ketubah to which she is almost certainly not entitled?

Tosafot follows *Ramban*'s explanation, according to which we claim that the deaf-mute or the imbecile ruptured her hymen as the result of some injury long before she was betrothed. *Tosafot* explains that this is a reasonable claim, since it is quite common for women to hurt themselves in

HALAKHAH

בּוֹגֶרֶת נוֹתְנִין לָה לַיְלָה הָרִאשׁוֹן **We give an adult woman the first night.** "By Torah law, if a man marries an adult virgin woman who has never menstruated, and she bleeds during intercourse, they need not fear that she is menstruating,

because we assume that any blood appearing on the first night comes from the hymen. If the wife had begun to menstruate before marriage, the couple may complete the first act of intercourse, but after that the wife must behave

TRANSLATION AND COMMENTARY

intercourse for the first time, she is expected to bleed from the ruptured hymen. Hence a virgin who bleeds during the first intercourse is not suspected of having a menstrual flow, and is permitted to her husband. The Mishnah (*Niddah* 64b) discusses a case in which the wife continued to bleed after the first intercourse. Do we continue to assume that the bleeding is from the ruptured hymen, or do we suspect that she is menstruating? The Mishnah distinguishes between a minor, a *na'arah* who has never menstruated, and a *na'arah* who has already menstruated, giving each of these girls a shorter grace period before we begin to suspect that they are menstruating. Commenting on this Mishnah, Rav ruled that this law applies to an adult woman as well: If the adult woman has never menstruated, she may engage in intercourse during the entire first night of her marriage, and we attribute any bleeding that may occur to her ruptured hymen. If she has previously menstruated, however, we have a slight fear that the bleeding that occurred during the first intercourse may have been menstrual. Nevertheless, she may complete the first intercourse, and is not subject to the law governing a woman who menstruates in the course of intercourse (*Shevuot* 14b); but after the intercourse is completed, she must follow the purification procedure as though she had just menstruated. We see from Rav's ruling that an adult woman is expected to bleed from the first intercourse, and we assume that the blood came from the ruptured hymen. Thus we see that adult women retain the signs of virginity, in contradiction to the third Baraita's ruling.

אִי דְּקָא [36B] [1]The Gemara answers: There are two signs of virginity: Difficulty of penetration, which applies only to minors and to *ne'arot*, and bleeding, which applies to adult virgins as well. **If** the Baraita is referring to a case **where** the husband **claims** that he did not find any evidence of **bleeding, it is indeed the case** that the husband's claim is valid. The Baraita agrees that if a husband claims that his adult wife showed no signs of bleeding when they had intercourse for the first time, he may divorce her without giving her her ketubah, because there is no difference between adult women and *ne'arot* regarding bleeding from the hymen. [2]But, says the Gemara, **with what are we dealing here** in this Baraita? [3]We are dealing with a case **where** the husband was unable to determine whether or not his wife bled when they had intercourse for the first time, but he **claimed** that he found that his wife had **"an open opening,"** and he could detect

LITERAL TRANSLATION

[36B] [1]If it is where he puts forward a claim concerning blood, this is indeed so. [2]With what are we dealing here? [3]Where he puts forward a claim of "an open opening."

[36B] [1]אִי דְּקָא טָעֵין טַעֲנַת דָּמִים, הָכִי נַמִי. [2]הָכָא בְּמַאי עָסְקִינַן? [3]דְּקָטָעֵין טַעֲנַת ״פֶּתַח פָּתוּחַ״.

RASHI

הכי גרסינן: אי דקא טעין טענת דמים הכי נמי הכא במאי עסקינן דקטעין טענת פתח פתוח — אי דקאמר: בעלתי ולא מצאתי דם — ודאי טענה מעלייתא היא. והכא דקתני: אין לה טענת בתולים — דקטעין ואמר: פתח פתוח מצאתי, ודם לא בדקתי אם נמצא בה אם לאו. בנערה וקטנה — טענה היא,

BACKGROUND

פֶּתַח פָּתוּחַ וְדָמִים "An open opening" and blood. Most women have a perforation in their hymen, and its size varies from individual to individual, and is also dependent on the woman's age. When the opening is relatively large, full sexual intercourse can take place without rupturing the hymen and causing bleeding. Unlike bleeding, which can be verified objectively, an intact hymen may appear to be "open" when in fact it is not.

NOTES

this way. However, a girl who injures herself usually informs other people about it, and where nothing was said, we assume that she was not injured. Imbeciles and deaf-mutes, however, are not capable of informing other people, and so must be assumed to have been injured. Hence a man who rapes such a woman does not pay the fine, and even in the case of the husband, we claim for her that her husband was aware of this when he married her.

Ba'al HaMa'or has an entirely different explanation, according to which the second Baraita follows Rabban Gamliel and the third Baraita follows Rabbi Yehoshua, and the claim that we make for the deaf-mute or the imbecile concerns the fine paid by the rapist rather than the ketubah paid by the husband. This explanation avoids most of the logical problems associated with the other explanations, but *Ritva* finds it difficult to reconcile with the language of the Baraitot.

אִי דְּקָא טָעֵין טַעֲנַת דָּמִים If it is where he puts forward a claim concerning blood. Our translation and commentary follow *Rashi*'s text of the Gemara, which is followed by most Rishonim, including *Rambam* (*Hilkhot Ishut* 11:13). *Tosafot* cites a variant reading found in *Rabbenu Ḥananel*'s commentary on the Talmud, according to which a man who marries an adult woman is believed if he claims that he found "an open opening," but is not believed if he claims that he found no bleeding.

Ramban points out that *Rashi*'s text presents some difficulties, but he notes that the Jerusalem Talmud (1:1) clearly supports *Rashi*'s text.

According to *Rashi*, it is somewhat difficult to understand

HALAKHAH

as though she has menstruated, and she may not have any further physical contact with her husband until she purifies herself. However, the custom has arisen among Jewish women to be very strict about the laws of menstruation. Accordingly, in all cases the couple may complete the first act of intercourse, and after that they must behave as though the wife has menstruated." (*Rambam*, *Sefer Kedushah*, *Hilkhot Issurei Bi'ah* 5:19 and 11:8; *Shulḥan Arukh*, *Yoreh De'ah* 193:1.)

LITERAL TRANSLATION

[1] "Summakhos says in the name of Rabbi Meir: A blind woman is not subject to claims concerning [her] virginity." [2] What is Summakhos's reason? [3] Rabbi Zera said: Because she is struck against the ground.
[4] All of them also are struck!
[5] All of them see and show their mothers. [6] This one does not see and does not show her mother.
[7] "And a woman who is divorced because of a bad name does not have a fine [for rape] or [for] seduction."

[1] ״סוּמָכוֹס אוֹמֵר מִשּׁוּם רַבִּי מֵאִיר: סוּמָא אֵין לָהּ טַעֲנַת בְּתוּלִים״. [2] מַאי טַעֲמָא דְּסוּמָכוֹס?
[3] אָמַר רַבִּי זֵירָא: מִפְּנֵי שֶׁנֶּחְבֶּטֶת עַל גַּבֵּי קַרְקַע.
[4] כּוּלְּהוּ נַמִי חַבּוּטֵי מִיחַבְטִי!
[5] כּוּלְּהוּ רוֹאוֹת וּמַרְאוֹת לְאִמָּן.
[6] זוֹ אֵינָהּ רוֹאָה וְאֵינָהּ מַרְאָה לְאִמָּהּ.
[7] ״וְהַיּוֹצֵאת מִשּׁוּם שֵׁם רַע אֵין לָהּ לֹא קְנָס וְלֹא פִּיתּוּי״.

RASHI

כדאמרינן בפרק קמא. ואף על פי שאין יכול לברר דבריו בפנינו — אמרינן: חזקה אין אדם טורח בסעודה ומפסידה. אבל משבגרה, אין רחמה צר כבתחילה, ודומה לו כאילו פתח פתוח. **שנחבטה** — ובתוליה נשרין. **כולהו רואות** — אם נשרו בתוליהן [רואות דם]. **ומראות לאמן** — ופוסקות עליהן שאינן בתולות, ואם לא הודיעתו — הטעתו. **וזו אינה רואה ואינה מראה לאמה** — וזה שכנסה — בחזקת נחבטת כנסה, ואין אדם פוסק עליה, ולאו טעות הוא.

TRANSLATION AND COMMENTARY

from the ease of penetration that his wife was not a virgin. In such a case, if his wife was a minor or a *na'arah*, he would be believed. An adult woman, however, has a larger opening, and the husband will often have no difficulty in penetrating, even if his wife is a virgin. Hence the Baraita rules that the husband cannot claim that his adult wife was not a virgin, on the basis of a claim of "an open opening."

סוּמָכוֹס אוֹמֵר [1] The Gemara now considers another clause in the third Baraita. **"Summakhos says in the name of Rabbi Meir: A blind woman is not subject to claims concerning her virginity."** [2] The Gemara asks: **What is Summakhos's reasoning?** Why do we assume that a blind woman is not a virgin?

אָמַר רַבִּי זֵירָא [3] **Rabbi Zera said** in reply: It is **because she** is liable to **strike herself against the ground** and to rupture her hymen accidentally. Hence her husband must take into account the possibility that something like this happened, and she is not considered to have deceived him if she is found not to be a virgin when they marry.

כּוּלְּהוּ [4] But, the Gemara objects, **all** girls **collide** with things on occasion! Almost everyone falls down awkwardly at some time or another. If we assume that a woman can lose her virginity because of an accident of this kind, why are women whose vision is normal presumed to be virgins?

כּוּלְּהוּ רוֹאוֹת [5] The Gemara answers: **All** girls who have accidents involving bleeding from the vagina **see** the blood **and show their mothers,** and their mothers tell them what has happened. [6] But a blind girl **does not see** the blood, **and** so **does not show her mother.** Our concern is that she may have had an accident and ruptured her hymen, and, being blind, she will not have noticed the blood, and will not have found out that she has lost her virginity. Therefore a man who marries a blind woman must take into account the possibility that something like this has happened, and if she turns out not to be a virgin when they marry, he cannot accuse her of misleading him.

וְהַיּוֹצֵאת [7] Having completed its examination of the third Baraita, the Gemara now returns to the first Baraita quoted above (35b), and considers its last clause: **"And a woman who has been divorced because of an evil reputation is not entitled to a fine for rape or for seduction**, because she does not have the status

NOTES

why the husband in the Baraita would come to court to claim that he found "an open opening," but did not check whether his wife had suffered bleeding.

Rashi explains that we are referring to a case in which it was impossible to examine for blood for technical reasons. *Ramban* explains that we are referring to a case in which the husband insisted that the blood on the bedsheet had come from somewhere else. But *Rambam* argues that when the "open opening" test is effective (i.e., when the wife is a minor or a *na'arah*), it is better than the test of blood. Hence, if the husband found "an open opening," it is proof that his wife was not a virgin, even if she bled from her hymen.

כּוּלְּהוּ נַמִי חַבּוּטֵי מִיחַבְטִי **All of them also are struck.** The Rishonim ask: Granted that a blind woman may not know that she has ruptured her hymen through an injury, but why should we assume that she ruptured her hymen in this way? Indeed, the Jerusalem Talmud (2:1) mentions that it is unusual for a woman to rupture her hymen in this way.

Ritva explains that it is indeed unusual for a woman to rupture her hymen, but blind women are more likely to injure themselves than other women, because they tend to trip over things and to fall. According to this explanation, the Gemara's answer is twofold: (1) All of them see, whereas this one does not see (and therefore tends to fall). (2) All of them show their mothers, whereas this one does not show her mother (and therefore she never finds out).

Tosafot explains that the Babylonian Talmud maintains

TRANSLATION AND COMMENTARY

of a virgin." This is the literal meaning of this clause of the Baraita. [1]But the Gemara rejects this interpretation, saying: **A woman who is divorced because of an evil reputation is subject to stoning!** If this woman was caught committing adultery, she was obviously no longer a virgin. Why does the Baraita need to inform us that she is not entitled to a fine?

אָמַר רַב שֵׁשֶׁת [2]**Rav Sheshet said** in reply: This clause of the Baraita cannot be interpreted literally, and **this is what it is** really **saying:** [3]A *na'arah* who already **had an evil reputation in her childhood** (i.e., she was known to have been involved in sexually promiscuous behavior) **is not entitled to a fine for rape or for seduction**, because she is presumed not to be a virgin.

אָמַר רַב פַּפָּא [4]**Rav Pappa said: From** this Baraita's ruling in the case of the promiscuous girl, we may **infer that** compelling circumstantial evidence is generally sufficient to exempt a person from payment. Therefore a creditor who presents **a dubious document may not collect with it.** If a creditor presents a promissory note for collection, and the debtor denies its authenticity, the creditor must authenticate the signatures of the witnesses who signed it. Once this has been done, the burden of proof is on the debtor. If he can prove that the document was forged, he need not pay the debt; otherwise, the document is accepted and the debt may be collected. Normally, the debtor is required to produce witnesses to testify that the document was forged. Based on this Baraita, however, Rav Pappa argues that compelling circumstantial evidence is sufficient for this purpose.

[1]הַיּוֹצֵאת מִשּׁוּם שֵׁם רַע בַּת סְקִילָה הִיא!
[2]אָמַר רַב שֵׁשֶׁת: הָכִי קָאָמַר:
[3]מִי שֶׁיָּצָא עָלֶיהָ שֵׁם רַע בְּיַלְדוּתָהּ אֵין לָהּ לֹא קְנָס וְלֹא פִּיתּוּי.
[4]אָמַר רַב פַּפָּא: שְׁמַע מִינָּהּ הַאי שְׁטָרָא רִיעָא לָא מַגְבִּינַן בֵּיהּ.

LITERAL TRANSLATION

[1]A woman who is divorced because of a bad name is subject to stoning!

[2]Rav Sheshet said: This is what he says: [3]Someone who had a bad name (lit., "a bad name went out about her") in her childhood does not have a fine [for rape] or [for] seduction.

[4]Rav Pappa said: Deduce from this [that] we do not collect with an (lit., "this") unsound (lit., "shaken") document.

RASHI

ריעא — שילא עליו סם זיוף.

NOTES

that injury to the hymen is actually quite common. Other solutions are proposed by *Rashba* and other Rishonim.

הַיּוֹצֵאת מִשּׁוּם שֵׁם רַע בַּת סְקִילָה הִיא A woman who is divorced because of a bad name is subject to stoning. Our commentary follows *Tosafot,* who explains that the Baraita is initially understood to be referring to a girl who was divorced by her husband after betrothal but before the marriage was consummated, and who was subsequently raped or seduced. There is a dispute about this case later in this chapter (38a), and the Halakhah follows Rabbi Akiva, who maintains that such a *na'arah* is entitled to a fine. But if she was divorced because she was caught committing adultery, she is obviously not entitled to a fine, since she is definitely not a virgin. Hence the Gemara objects that the Baraita did not need to mention this case. And the Gemara answers that the Baraita is referring to a girl who was never married, but who was reputed to be a prostitute.

This explanation is somewhat difficult to understand, because the Gemara should have said: "Had intercourse" rather than: "Is subject to stoning," since the question as to whether the adulteress is punished is irrelevant. *Talmidei Rabbenu Yonah* suggests that the Gemara may be saying that it is obvious that we believe the witnesses who testify that she had intercourse, since their testimony is sufficient for us to sentence her to death (see also *Rosh*).

Tosafot Yeshanim explains that the Baraita is initially understood to be referring to a husband who caught his betrothed wife committing adultery. In this case, the Baraita rules that the adulterer is exempt from paying the fine for seduction. But the Gemara objects that it is obvious that he is exempt from paying the fine, because he is subject to the more severe penalty of stoning for committing adultery with a betrothed virgin *na'arah*.

מִי שֶׁיָּצָא עָלֶיהָ שֵׁם רַע בְּיַלְדוּתָהּ Someone who had a bad name in her childhood. Our commentary follows *Rashi,* who explains that since we know that this girl was involved in prostitution, we assume that she has already lost her virginity. *Rambam* (*Hilkhot Na'arah Betulah* 2:17) explains that since this girl was caught soliciting prostitution, we assume that the man who she claims raped or seduced her was in fact one of her clients. *Mishneh LeMelekh* explains that even if she really was raped, her rapist is exempt, because we presume that she offered herself to him as a prostitute, and was raped only because he refused to pay the price.

Rambam explains that the laws of rape and seduction were intended to punish unusual deviant behavior, not as a remedy for prostitution. He points out that applying these laws to prostitution would in effect be setting a market price for this behavior and regulating it, which is the opposite of the Torah's intention.

[1]הֵיכִי דָּמֵי? [2]אִילֵימָא דְּנָפַק קָלָא עֲלֵיהּ דִּשְׁטָרָא דְּזַיְיפָא הוּא — [3]דִּכְוָותָהּ הָכָא דְּנָפַק עֲלָהּ קָלָא דִּזְנַאי — [4]וְהָא אֲמַר רָבָא: יָצָא לָהּ שֵׁם מְזַנָּה בָּעִיר, [5]אֵין חוֹשְׁשִׁין לָהּ! [6]אֶלָּא, דְּאָתוּ בֵּי תְּרֵי וְאָמְרִי לְדִידְהוּ תְּבַעְתַּנְהִי בְּאִיסּוּרָא, [7]דִּכְוָותָהּ הָכָא דְּאָתוּ בֵּי תְּרֵי וְאָמְרִי לְדִידְהוּ אֲמַר לְהוּ: [8]״זַיְּיפוּ לִי״.

LITERAL TRANSLATION

[1]How do we visualize the case? [2]If we say that a rumor went out about it that it is a forged document — [3][and] similarly to it here that a rumor went out about her that she prostituted herself — [4]surely Rava said: If she had a [bad] name (lit., "a name went out about her") in the city as a prostitute, [5]we are not concerned about it!

[6]Rather, it is where two [witnesses] came and said [that] she solicited them to [have] forbidden [intercourse, [7]and] similarly to it here is that two [witnesses] came and said [that] he said to them: [8]"Forge for me."

TRANSLATION AND COMMENTARY

הֵיכִי דָּמֵי [1]The Gemara asks: **How do we visualize the case?** What kind of circumstantial evidence can the debtor produce that will be sufficient to invalidate the document? [2]**If we say** that it is sufficient for the debtor to show that **there is a rumor that the document was forged,** such an argument is untenable. For Rav Pappa deduced his ruling about the document from the ruling of the Baraita in the case of circumstantial evidence about promiscuous behavior. [3]Now, if he deduced that a rumor is sufficient, it follows that he inferred this from **the analogous** situation in the case of the promiscuous girl. In other words, Rav Pappa explained the Baraita as informing us that the rapist does not pay the fine **if there was a rumor concerning** this *na'arah* **that she had engaged in prostitution** while she was a child, even if there was no proof of this. [4]But **surely** such a ruling is impossible, because **Rava said: If a rumor** has **spread in the city** that a certain woman is **a prostitute,** but there is no proof of this, [5]**we are not concerned about it,** and she is even permitted to marry a priest. For there is a legal presumption that a Jewish man or a Jewish woman does not sin in this way, and we cannot set aside this presumption on the basis of mere rumor, but only on the basis of real proof.

אֶלָּא [6]**Rather,** argues the Gemara, we must say that the Baraita is referring to a case **where two witnesses came and said:** "This girl **solicited us** in the manner of a prostitute and suggested to us that **we have forbidden intercourse,** but we refused." In such a case, there is no concrete evidence that the girl engaged in prostitution, because, in the sole instance we know of, the solicitation was refused. Nevertheless, the circumstantial evidence is compelling that this girl was engaged in prostitution, and was presumably able to find other, willing customers. Hence she is presumed not to be a virgin, and if she is later the victim of rape, her rapist does not pay the fine. Now, continues the Gemara, Rav Pappa deduced his ruling in the case of the document from our Baraita. [7]If the Baraita is referring to a situation in which witnesses come forward and testify that they were solicited, **the analogous** situation in the case of the document **is where two witnesses came and said:** [8]"This creditor tried to persuade us to sign our names on this very document, **saying to us: 'Forge** a document **for me** that I can use against this debtor,' but we refused." In such a case, there is no concrete evidence that the document was forged, because, in the sole instance we know of,

RASHI

אין חוששין לה — אפילו לכהונה. אלא — יצא עליה שם רע
היכי דמי — כגון בעדים. ולא שאמרו עליה שנבעלה — דאם כן
מאי למימרא? הא לאו בתולה היא! אלא אמרי: לדידהו תבעתנהו
לאיסורא, הפקירה עצמה לכך, ולא שמענו לה.

NOTES

לְדִידְהוּ אֲמַר לְהוּ: זַיְּיפוּ לִי **He said to them: "Forge for me."** Our commentary follows *Rabbenu Ḥananel, Rif,* and most Rishonim, who explain that the "creditor" was caught trying to forge this very document. Hence his claim against this "debtor" is not believed. According to this explanation, if he were to present an entirely different promissory note against this debtor, he would be believed, if he succeeded in authenticating the signatures.

Rosh adds that although the creditor has clearly damaged his reputation, it does not follow that we assume that he was prepared to fabricate a completely nonexistent claim. Rather, it is possible that he had business with this

HALAKHAH

יָצָא לָהּ שֵׁם מְזַנָּה בָּעִיר **If she had a bad name in the city as a prostitute.** "If there is a rumor that a certain woman is a prostitute, we ignore it and permit her to marry a priest. Even if she has definitely behaved improperly, so that her husband has decided to divorce her, she is not forbidden, unless there is real testimony or unless she confesses." (*Rambam, Sefer Kedushah, Hilkhot Issurei Bi'ah* 17:21; *Shulḥan Arukh, Even HaEzer* 6:16.)

לְדִידְהוּ תְּבַעְתַּנְהִי בְּאִיסּוּרָא **She solicited them to have forbidden intercourse.** "If two witnesses testify that a certain girl solicited them for prostitution, she is not entitled to the fine if she is subsequently raped or seduced." (*Rambam, Sefer Nashim, Hilkhot Na'arah Betulah* 1:9; *Shulḥan Arukh, Even HaEzer* 177:4.)

לְדִידְהוּ אֲמַר לְהוּ: זַיְּיפוּ לִי **He said to them: "Forge for me."** "If a creditor presents a document and authenticates

[1] בִּשְׁלָמָא הָתָם שְׁכִיחִי פְּרוּצִין,
[2] אֶלָּא הָכָא, אִם הוּא הוּחְזַק,
כָּל יִשְׂרָאֵל מִי הוּחְזְקוּ?
[3] הָכָא נַמִי, כֵּיוָן דְּקָא מְהַדֵּר

LITERAL TRANSLATION

[1] Granted that there dissolute men are common, [2] but here, if he is established [as a fraud], are all Jews established as frauds?

[3] Here too, since he is looking for a forgery,

TRANSLATION AND COMMENTARY

the solicitation was refused. Nevertheless, the circumstantial evidence is compelling that this "creditor" was seeking to establish a fraudulent claim against the "debtor," and was presumably able to find other, willing "witnesses." Hence the document is presumed not to be authentic, and the "debtor" need not pay the debt.

בִּשְׁלָמָא הָתָם [1] The Gemara has now explained the Baraita and Rav Pappa's inference from it. But the Gemara objects to Rav Pappa's inference: Both in the case of prostitution and in the case of the forged document, the circumstantial evidence is based on the assumption that if the would-be forger or the prostitute approached these witnesses and was rejected, it proves that he or she was determined to commit a sin, and would eventually find willing accomplices. This assumption **is satisfactory** in the case of prostitution, because **immoral men are easily found,** and if a girl is determined to be a prostitute, she will certainly find a willing man. [2] **But** in the case of the forged document, this assumption is not satisfactory. The document presented in court was signed by witnesses, and even **if** it is true that this "creditor" **has established** a reputation **as a fraud, have all Jews established** a similar reputation? How can we assume that this "creditor" was able to find witnesses who were willing to conspire with him to defraud the "debtor"? The entire basis of the laws of documents is that we rely not on the credibility of the creditor himself, but on that of the witnesses. Presumably, just as these witnesses refused to conspire in forgery, everyone else who was approached responded in the same way. Hence the document that was eventually produced in court must be considered unconnected with the previous attempt at forgery. Therefore Rav Pappa's inference from the Baraita must be rejected, and we must accept the authenticity of the document on the basis of the signatures of the witnesses, unless the debtor can bring proof that this specific document was forged.

הָכָא נַמִי [3] The Gemara replies: **Here too,** in the case of the document, **since** we have established that the "creditor" **was looking** for ways **to forge** a document in order to make a false claim against this debtor,

RASHI

בשלמא התם כו' — היכי גמר רב פפא מינה דלא מגבינן בשטרא כי האי? בשלמא התם — שכיחי פרוצין, וכיון שיש עדים שהיתה מחזרת אחר הזנות — הרבה מצאה לה, משום הכי אין לה קנס לאחר זמן, דלאו בחזקת בתולה הואי. **אלא** — לגבי שטר. **אם הוא הוחזק** — לחזור אחר עידי שקר. **כל ישראל מי הוחזקו** — להיות שומעין לו לזייף.

NOTES

debtor, and felt that he owed him money, but could not prove his case in court and so stooped to forgery. But in other cases there is no reason to assume that a document he has succeeded in authenticating is a forgery. But if he asked the witnesses to collaborate with him in forgery, we must accept that he is willing to forge completely nonexistent claims, and we must reject all his documents.

Ritva disagrees with the other Rishonim, and rules that a creditor who is caught trying to forge a document is not believed at all, even regarding other debtors.

HALAKHAH

the signatures, and two witnesses come forward and testify that this creditor had previously asked them to forge a similar document against this debtor, we do not accept the document unless the witnesses who signed it come forward themselves and confirm its authenticity. *Sma* and *Shakh* agree that the document is rejected only if it is aimed against the same debtor and only if it concerns the same sum as the document that the creditor sought to forge. But the creditor's other documents — even against this debtor — are not rejected in this way. But if the creditor did not mention a sum at all, or did not mention a particular debtor, but simply asked the witnesses to forge a document, all his documents are rejected.

"*Shulḥan Arukh* proposes three methods of certifying such a document: (1) The witnesses who signed the document come forward and testify to the loan. (2) They testify that they recognize their own signatures. (3) Other witnesses come forward and testify that they saw these witnesses sign the document. In all these cases, we accept the document, since the witnesses' veracity has not been challenged. *Rema*, however, rules that it is not sufficient for the witnesses to recognize their own signatures if they do not remember the loan, since it is possible that the creditor forged their signatures sufficiently well to deceive them. But the other two methods are acceptable. *Sma* rules that, even according to *Rema*, it is sufficient if the witnesses testify that they remember signing the document, even if they do not remember its contents, but *Shakh* disagrees." (*Rambam, Sefer Shofetim, Hilkhot Edut* 22:5; *Shulḥan Arukh, Ḥoshen Mishpat* 63:1,2.)

TRANSLATION AND COMMENTARY

we do not trust the authentication of the witnesses' signatures. [1]For we can **say that** the creditor **wrote** the document without assistance **and forged** the signatures on **it himself.** Once the creditor realized that he could not find accomplices, he carefully forged the signatures of two witnesses and presented an entirely forged document, which passed the test of signature authentication. Ordinarily, we would not concern ourselves about such a possibility, but since there is evidence that this "creditor" was looking for ways to forge a promissory note for use against this "debtor," we accept the debtor's claim, and we do not order him to pay the debt — just as a rapist is not required to pay a fine if he rapes a *na'arah* who is known, on the basis of strong circumstantial evidence, to have engaged in prostitution.

אַזִּיּוּפָא, [1]אֵימַר זִיּוּפֵי זַיֵּיף וְכָתַב.

משנה [2]וְאֵלּוּ שֶׁאֵין לָהֶן קְנָס: הַבָּא עַל הַגִּיּוֹרֶת, וְעַל הַשְּׁבוּיָה, וְעַל הַשִּׁפְחָה, [3]שֶׁנִּפְדּוּ וְשֶׁנִּתְגַּיְּירוּ וְשֶׁנִּשְׁתַּחְרְרוּ יְתֵירוֹת עַל בְּנוֹת שָׁלֹשׁ שָׁנִים וְיוֹם אֶחָד.

[4]רַבִּי יְהוּדָה אוֹמֵר: שְׁבוּיָה שֶׁנִּפְדֵּית הֲרֵי הִיא בִּקְדוּשָּׁתָהּ, [5]אַף עַל פִּי שֶׁגְּדוֹלָה.

LITERAL TRANSLATION

[1]say [that] he forged and wrote [it himself].

MISHNAH [2]And these [are the *ne'arot*] who do not have a fine: [If] someone rapes a female proselyte, or a female captive, or a female slave, [3]who were redeemed or converted or freed [when they were] more than three years and one day old.

[4]Rabbi Yehudah says: A female captive who was redeemed, [5]is [still] in her holiness, even if she is an adult.

RASHI

אימר זיופי זייף — הוא עלמו למד לכוין כתב הדומה לכתב ידי עדים שחתמו בו.

משנה יתירות על בנות שלש שנים — דכיון דראויות לביאה — בחזקת הפקר הן, ונבעלות בנכריותן, והשבויה בשביותה.

MISHNAH וְאֵלּוּ [2]This Mishnah, like the previous one (above, 29a), considers problematic cases in which it is not obvious whether the fine for rape or seduction is applicable. The previous Mishnah listed several categories of *ne'arot* who are entitled to a fine, even though their cases are problematic. This Mishnah lists problematic cases of *ne'arot* who are not entitled to a fine, even though their situation is very similar to that of the *ne'arot* listed in the previous Mishnah. The Mishnah declares that **the following *ne'arot* are not entitled to a fine: If someone rapes** a girl who is not known to have had intercourse but who is legally considered not to be a virgin, such as **a *na'arah* who has been converted to Judaism, or a *na'arah* who was taken captive** and was later redeemed, **or a female** non-Jewish **slave** who was set free by her master, thus becoming Jewish. The Torah imposes the fine only if the seduced or raped girl was a virgin, and the women listed above are presumed to have lost their virginity: Proselytes are presumed to have engaged in sexual relations before converting, captive women are presumed to have been raped by their captors, and female slaves are presumed to have engaged in sexual relations. [3]Accordingly, the Mishnah rules that these *ne'arot* are not entitled to the fine, but this ruling applies only if the captive **was redeemed, or** the proselyte **was converted, or** the female slave **was freed when they were more than three years and one day old.** Under Torah law, a girl less than three years old is presumed to be incapable of intercourse. Moreover, any damage suffered by her hymen before that time is presumed to heal. But these girls have lost their legal presumption of virginity because they did not attain the status of ordinary Jewish girls before their third birthday. They are therefore not entitled to the fine if they are raped or seduced.

רַבִּי יְהוּדָה אוֹמֵר [4]**Rabbi Yehudah says:** Although I agree that a female proselyte or a freed female slave does not have the status of a virgin, I disagree about **a female captive who was redeemed** from captivity. I maintain that she **retains her status as a virgin** and is permitted to marry any Jewish man, including a priest, [5]**even if she was** held captive as **an adult.** According to Rabbi Yehudah, a female captive is not presumed to have been raped by her captors. Hence after her release she may marry a priest, even though a woman who was raped by a non-Jew may not marry a priest. By the same token, a *na'arah* who was held captive and was later released has the status of a virgin, and if she was raped or seduced after her release from captivity, she is entitled to the fine.

HALAKHAH

הַבָּא עַל הַגִּיּוֹרֶת **If someone rapes a female proselyte.** "A female proselyte who was converted to Judaism on or after her third birthday, or a woman who was held captive on or after her third birthday, or a female slave who was freed on or after her third birthday, are presumed not to be virgins. Hence, they are not entitled to a fine if they are subsequently raped or seduced," following the first Tanna in our Mishnah, who rejects Rabbi Yehudah's minority opinion. (*Rambam, Sefer Nashim, Hilkhot Na'arah Betulah* 1:10.)

TRANSLATION AND COMMENTARY

הַבָּא עַל בִּתּוֹ [1]The Mishnah continues: There is another situation in which the fine is not imposed — where the seduction or rape was also incest of the category that is subject to the death penalty. The previous Mishnah ruled that if the rape was also incest of the category that is subject to excision, the fine must be paid. However, we have seen that a person who commits a capital crime is not subject to monetary penalties for the same crime. Accordingly, our Mishnah rules that **if someone rapes his daughter, or his daughter's daughter, or his son's daughter, or his wife's daughter, or her son's daughter, or her daughter's daughter,** [2]**he does not pay** the **fine, because he forfeits his life** (i.e., he is subject to the death penalty). All categories of incest are subject to the penalty of excision (Leviticus 18:29). [3]But the cases listed in this Mishnah, as well as several others that are not listed, are punishable by **death at the hands of the court.** Hence a man who rapes a virgin *na'arah* who is related to him in one of these ways is exempt from paying the fine, because he is subject to the more severe penalty of execution.

וְכָל הַמִּתְחַיֵּיב בְּנַפְשׁוֹ [4]The Mishnah concludes: In general, **whoever forfeits his life** by incurring the death penalty **does not pay money** for the same offense, **for the verse** (Exodus 21:22) **says:** [5]"And if two men struggle, and one of them hits a pregnant woman so that her children go out, **but there is no disaster** [i.e., the woman miscarries but survives the attack], the assailant **shall surely be punished,** as the woman's husband shall impose upon him," which is traditionally understood to mean a monetary penalty. Thus the verse teaches us that damages are paid only if the woman was not killed. From this we learn that someone who commits a crime that is punishable by the death penalty (such as incest with his daughter) is not required to pay damages for the same act.

GEMARA The Gemara first considers the difference of opinion between Rabbi Yehudah and the first Tanna as to whether a female captive is presumed to have lost her virginity while in captivity. There is a dispute about this matter in a Mishnah in tractate *Eduyyot* (3:6). Rabbi Dosa rules there that a female captive who claims that she was not raped while in captivity remains qualified to marry a priest. The Sages, however, rule that this applies only if there were no witnesses that she was taken captive, and she came forward on her own initiative and said: "I was taken captive, but I was not raped." In such a case the woman is believed because we have no right to accept part of her statement and to reject the rest. But if we already know that she was a captive, she is not believed when she claims that she was not raped. Hence she may not marry a priest, because a woman who has had intercourse with a man whom she is forbidden to marry (such as a non-Jew) is disqualified from the priesthood, even if she was raped.

אָמַר רַבִּי יוֹחָנָן [6]**Rabbi Yoḥanan said: Rabbi Yehudah** in our Mishnah **and Rabbi Dosa** in the Mishnah in

[1]הַבָּא עַל בִּתּוֹ, עַל בַּת בִּתּוֹ, עַל בַּת בְּנוֹ, עַל בַּת אִשְׁתּוֹ, עַל בַּת בְּנָהּ, עַל בַּת בִּתָּהּ, [2]אֵין לָהֶן קְנָס, מִפְּנֵי שֶׁמִּתְחַיֵּיב בְּנַפְשׁוֹ, [3]שֶׁמִּיתָתָן בִּידֵי בֵּית דִּין. [4]וְכָל הַמִּתְחַיֵּיב בְּנַפְשׁוֹ אֵין מְשַׁלֵּם מָמוֹן, שֶׁנֶּאֱמַר: [5]"וְאִם לֹא יִהְיֶה אָסוֹן, עָנוֹשׁ יֵעָנֵשׁ".

גמרא [6]אָמַר רַבִּי יוֹחָנָן: רַבִּי יְהוּדָה וְרַבִּי דּוֹסָא אָמְרוּ

LITERAL TRANSLATION

[1][If] someone rapes his daughter, [or] his daughter's daughter, [or] his son's daughter, [or] his wife's daughter, [or] her son's daughter, [or] her daughter's daughter, [2]they do not have a fine, because he forfeits his life, [3]since their death is at the hands of the court. [4]And whoever forfeits his life does not pay money, as it is said: [5]"And if there is no disaster, he shall surely be punished."

GEMARA [6]Rabbi Yoḥanan said: Rabbi Yehudah and Rabbi Dosa said

RASHI

ולא יהיה אסון ענוש יענש — הא אם יהיה אסון — לא יענש.

BACKGROUND

מִפְּנֵי שֶׁמִּתְחַיֵּיב בְּנַפְשׁוֹ Because he forfeits his life. The language of the Mishnah indicates that the very fact that someone has committed a capital crime exposes him to the danger that the death penalty will be imposed on him, and this is why he is exempt from all other claims and punishments.

NOTES

הַבָּא עַל בִּתּוֹ If someone rapes his daughter. The Jerusalem Talmud asks: The fine paid by a man who rapes or seduces a *na'arah* is paid to the *na'arah*'s father. How, then, can a man who rapes his daughter ever be liable to pay the fine — even if we disregard the rule that an offender who is subject to the death penalty is exempt from payment?

The Jerusalem Talmud gives two answers: (1) The Mishnah may be referring to a case in which the father died after raping his daughter. In this case the daughter

HALAKHAH

הַבָּא עַל בִּתּוֹ If someone rapes his daughter. "A man who rapes or seduces a close relative with whom he is forbidden to have intercourse under penalty of death (e.g., his daughter or his stepdaughter) is exempt from paying the fine, because he is subject to the more severe penalty. This rule applies even if he is not actually executed for incest — for example, because the witnesses failed to warn him." (*Rambam, Sefer Nashim, Hilkhot Na'arah Betulah* 1:13.)

דָּבָר אֶחָד: [1]רַבִּי יְהוּדָה — הָא דַּאֲמָרַן; [2]רַבִּי דּוֹסָא — דְּתַנְיָא: "שְׁבוּיָה אוֹכֶלֶת בִּתְרוּמָה. [3]דִּבְרֵי רַבִּי דּוֹסָא. [4]אָמַר רַבִּי דּוֹסָא: וְכִי מָה עָשָׂה לָהּ עַרְבִי הַלָּז? [5]וְכִי מִפְּנֵי שֶׁמִּיעֵךְ לָהּ בֵּין דַּדֶּיהָ, פְּסָלָהּ מִן הַכְּהוּנָּה"? [6]אֲמַר רַבָּה: דִּלְמָא לָא הִיא. [7]עַד כָּאן לָא קָאָמַר רַבִּי יְהוּדָה הָכָא, אֶלָּא שֶׁלֹּא יְהֵא חוֹטֵא

LITERAL TRANSLATION

the same thing: [1]Rabbi Yehudah — what we [just] said; [2]Rabbi Dosa — as it was taught: "A female captive may eat terumah. [3][These are] the words of Rabbi Dosa. [4]Rabbi Dosa said: For what did that Arab do to her? [5]Because he squeezed her between her breasts, did he disqualify her from the priesthood?" [6]Rabbah said: Perhaps it is not so. [7]Rabbi Yehudah only said [this] here, that the sinner should not be

TRANSLATION AND COMMENTARY

Eduyyot **said the same thing.** Although Rabbi Yehudah was referring to the fine paid by a rapist, and Rabbi Dosa was referring to a female captive's qualification to marry a priest, these two minority opinions are in fact based on the same idea — that a female captive who claims that she was not raped is believed. Hence, says Rabbi Yoḥanan, Rabbi Yehudah and Rabbi Dosa accept each other's rulings, and would agree that a captive woman is assumed not to have been raped, and that this assumption applies to all aspects of Jewish law. [1]We know **Rabbi Yehudah**'s viewpoint from his ruling in our Mishnah **which we have just quoted.** [2]We know **Rabbi Dosa**'s viewpoint **from what was taught** in his name in the following Baraita, which elaborates on the Mishnah in tractate *Eduyyot*: **"A female captive may eat terumah.** The unmarried daughter of a priest or the wife of a priest is permitted to eat terumah (the portion of the crop set aside for the priests) unless she is disqualified from the priesthood. A woman who has been raped by a non-Jew is disqualified from the priesthood, but a woman who was kidnapped by non-Jews remains qualified for the priesthood, because we do not automatically assume that she was raped by her captors. [3]**This is the opinion of Rabbi Dosa,** who disagrees with the viewpoint of the Sages on this matter. [4]**Rabbi Dosa** explained his ruling by means of a rhetorical question, **saying: What** do you think **that Arab** (i.e., her non-Jewish captor) **did to her?** [5]Obviously she was ill-treated, but do you think that just **because he squeezed her between her breasts, he disqualified her from the priesthood?** Unless she admits that she was raped, or we have proof that she was raped, we may rely on the legal presumption that she remains qualified for the priesthood until the contrary is proved, and we accept her claim without proof." Thus, according to Rabbi Yoḥanan, Rabbi Yehudah's ruling in our Mishnah is identical to Rabbi Dosa's ruling in *Eduyyot*, and both rulings are disputed by the majority of the Sages.

אֲמַר רַבָּה [6]**Rabbah said: Perhaps** the assumption made by Rabbi Yoḥanan **is not correct.** Although Rabbi Yehudah's ruling in our Mishnah and Rabbi Dosa's ruling in *Eduyyot* are similar, they are not dependent on each other, and in fact these two Sages may not accept each other's rulings. [7]For it is possible that the ruling of **Rabbi Yehudah here** in our Mishnah — that a captive woman is entitled to a fine — **was made only in order that the sinner should not be rewarded** for his crime. Even though we assume that a captive

RASHI

גמרא שבויה — בת כהן. **אוכלת בתרומה** — ולא מחזקינן לה בחזקת בעולה לפסול לה, המחללה בביאתו. **מפני שמיעך לה** — כלומר, אין נוהגין בהן הפקר לאונסן בבעילה, אלא לשחק עמהן. [רבנן פליגי אדרבי דוסא, ואמרו: יש שבויה אוכלת ויש שאינה אוכלת. כיצד? האשה שאמרה: נשביתי וטהורה אני — אוכלת. ואם יש עדים שנשבית והיא אומרת: טהורה אני — אינה אוכלת, במסכת עדיות.]

SAGES

רַבִּי דּוֹסָא Rabbi Dosa (ben Horkinas). Rabbi Dosa ben Horkinas seems to have been a contemporary of Rabban Yoḥanan ben Zakkai and is said to have known the leading scholars of the generation of Yavneh (Rabbi Eliezer and Rabbi Yehoshua) when they were still in their infancy. It is probable that in the period during which the Sanhedrin convened in Yavneh, Rabbi Dosa was no longer active and did not take part in its sessions. But his opinions were still influential at that time. We know that he lived to a most advanced age and was very wealthy. Rabbi Dosa was one of the senior Sages of Bet Hillel, although he had a younger brother, Yonatan, who was one of the heads of Bet Shammai. It seems that references in the Mishnah to Rabbi Dosa without a patronymic are to Rabbi Dosa ben Horkinas.

BACKGROUND

עַרְבִי הַלָּז That Arab. The captor was assumed to have been an Arab because during the Mishnaic and Talmudic periods there were nomadic Arab tribes living in the area between the major centers of population and the desert. These tribes supported themselves by loot and pillage, and it was much more likely for a person to be kidnapped by one of them than as the result of a war of conquest. Since the purpose of the kidnapping was to extort ransom money, the Arabs were less inclined to rape their captives than to indulge in licentious behavior with them.

NOTES

would be entitled to press her claim against the estate of her criminal father, were it not for the rule that an offender who is subject to the death penalty is exempt from payment.

(2) The Mishnah may be referring to a case in which the *na'arah* was betrothed and divorced before her father raped her. This case is the subject of a Tannaitic dispute (below, 38a), and according to Rabbi Akiva a *na'arah* who was betrothed and divorced is entitled to receive the fine herself, even if her father is still alive. Hence, if a man rapes his betrothed and then divorced daughter, the daughter would be entitled to press her claim against her rapist father, were it not for the rule that an offender who is subject to the death penalty is exempt from payment.

HALAKHAH

שְׁבוּיָה אוֹכֶלֶת בִּתְרוּמָה. דִּבְרֵי רַבִּי דּוֹסָא A female captive may eat terumah. These are the words of Rabbi Dosa. "A woman who was taken captive by non-Jewish bandits is presumed to have been raped. For this reason she is disqualified from the priesthood, even if she insists that she was not raped. Accordingly, she is forbidden to marry a priest, and if she was already married to a priest, she must be divorced. If she is the daughter of a priest, she is forbidden to eat terumah. But if she comes forward and informs us that she was taken captive, before we have heard any testimony to that effect, her claim that she was not raped is believed, and she is permitted to marry a priest and to eat terumah. Likewise, if there is one witness who testifies that she was not raped, he is believed," following the Sages who disagree with Rabbi Dosa. (*Rambam, Sefer Zera'im, Hilkhot Terumot* 6:11 and *Sefer Kedushah, Hilkhot Issurei Bi'ah* 18:17,21.)

נִשְׂכָּר. [1]אֲבָל הָתָם, כְּרַבָּנַן סְבִירָא לֵיהּ. [2]אִי נַמִי, עַד כָּאן לָא קָאָמַר רַבִּי דּוֹסָא הָתָם אֶלָּא בִּתְרוּמָה דְּרַבָּנַן. [3]אֲבָל קְנָס דְּאוֹרַיְיתָא, כְּרַבָּנַן סְבִירָא לֵיהּ.

[4]אֲמַר לֵיהּ אַבַּיֵי: וְטַעֲמֵיהּ דְּרַבִּי יְהוּדָה הָכָא שֶׁלֹּא יְהֵא חוֹטֵא נִשְׂכָּר הוּא? [5]וְהָא תַּנְיָא: ״רַבִּי יְהוּדָה אוֹמֵר: שְׁבוּיָה שֶׁנִּשְׁבֵּית הֲרֵי הִיא בִּקְדוּשָּׁתָהּ. [6]אֲפִילּוּ בַּת עֶשֶׂר שָׁנִים, כְּתוּבָּתָהּ

LITERAL TRANSLATION

rewarded. [1]But there, he agrees with the Rabbis. [2]Alternatively, Rabbi Dosa only said [this] there about terumah which is Rabbinic. [3]But [about] the fine which is from the Torah, he agrees with the Rabbis.

[4]Abaye said to him: But is Rabbi Yehudah's reason here that the sinner should not be rewarded? [5]But surely it was taught: "Rabbi Yehudah says: A female captive who was redeemed is [still] in her holiness. [6]Even [if] she is ten years old, her ketubah

RASHI

אלא בתרומה בזמן הזה דרבנן — דכיון דאפילו נבעלה, איסורא דרבנן בעלמא הוא — לא גזרו על ספיקה. אבל קנס, דאפוקי ממונא הוא, אימא לך: ספק בעולה היא, ומספיקא לא מפקינן ממונא.

TRANSLATION AND COMMENTARY

woman was raped, we are not certain that this is so. It is possible that Rabbi Yehudah did not apply this assumption to a rapist in order not to exempt him from paying the fine. [1]**But there,** in the Mishnah in *Eduyyot*, Rabbi Yehudah **may** well **agree with the Rabbis** that we do not permit the female former captive to eat terumah, because she is probably disqualified from the priesthood. [2]**Alternatively,** says Rabbah, it is possible that even Rabbi Dosa does not rely absolutely on the legal presumption that a captive woman was not raped. Although he ruled that a captive woman is permitted to eat terumah, he may not necessarily agree with Rabbi Yehudah that in the case mentioned in our Mishnah we should be lenient with her in order to avoid rewarding the sinner. For it is possible that the ruling of **Rabbi Dosa there,** in the Mishnah in *Eduyyot* — that a captive woman is entitled to eat terumah — was made **only about terumah, which is** forbidden to non-priests by **Rabbinic** decree. According to many opinions, the laws of terumah and tithes were suspended by Torah law after the destruction of the Temple, and were maintained afterwards only by Rabbinic decree. Hence the captive woman would be permitted to eat terumah nowadays, even if she really were disqualified from the priesthood, because by Torah law that food is not terumah at all. And although the eating of terumah by non-priests is forbidden by Rabbinic decree, Rabbi Dosa may well have felt that a captive woman, whose disqualification is doubtful, should bc permitted to eat terumah. [3]**But** here in our Mishnah it is possible that Rabbi Dosa **agrees with the** other **Rabbis about the fine, which is** imposed **by Torah law,** and he also agrees that captive women are presumed to have been raped. Hence, even according to Rabbi Dosa, we compel this rapist to pay the fine only if the former captive can prove that she had not been raped by her captors. Thus, according to Rabbah, there is no proof that Rabbi Dosa and Rabbi Yehudah agree with each other's ruling.

אֲמַר לֵיהּ אַבַּיֵי [4]**Abaye said to** Rabbah: **But is Rabbi Yehudah's reason here** for awarding the female captive the fine in order **that the sinner should not be rewarded,** and does his ruling apply only to the fine for rape and seduction, as you have suggested? [5]**Surely it** Rabbi Yoḥanan is correct, and Rabbi Yehudah considers a female captive not to have been raped regarding other laws as well, **as was taught** in the following Baraita: **"Rabbi Yehudah says: A female captive who was redeemed** from captivity **retains her status as a virgin.** [6]She is assumed not to have been raped, **even if she was ten years old** when she was kidnapped. Hence **her ketubah**

NOTES

בִּתְרוּמָה דְּרַבָּנַן **About terumah which is Rabbinic.** The Torah ordains that various gifts and tithes must be taken from crops grown in Eretz Israel. Two of these donations are called terumah and are given to a priest: (1) An initial amount separated by the farmer from his crops (Numbers 18:12); and (2) an additional donation separated by the Levite, consisting of one tenth of the tithe he receives from the farmer (Numbers 18:26-28). By law, only a priest or a member of his household may eat terumah, and it may be eaten only in a state of ritual purity (Leviticus 22:10-13). Any unauthorized person who eats terumah is liable to death at the hands of Heaven (Leviticus 22:9).

Not all terumah has Torah status. When the Torah commands that terumah be given to the priests, it refers to "your grain, your wine, and your oil" (Deuteronomy 18:4). According to many Rishonim, terumah taken from any produce other than grain, grapes, and olives has Rabbinic status. According to all Rishonim, this is true of vegetables which are cultivated for their leaves and stems rather than for their fruit. In addition, there is a Tannaitic dispute (*Yevamot* 81a) as to whether terumah still applies by Torah law, even to grain, grapes, and olives, or whether it has Rabbinic status since the destruction of the Second Temple. Most Rishonim follow the view that terumah is of Rabbinic status today. According to *Rambam*, terumah lost its Torah status even earlier, before the destruction of the First Temple.

מָאתַיִם״. [1]וְהָתָם, מַאי ״שֶׁלֹּא יְהֵא חוֹטֵא נִשְׂכָּר״ אִיכָּא? [2]הָתָם נַמִי, דִּלְמָא מִימְנְעִי וְלָא נָסְבִי לָהּ.

[3]וְסָבַר רַבִּי יְהוּדָה בִּקְדוּשָּׁתָהּ קַיְּימָה? [4]וְהָתַנְיָא: ״הַפּוֹדֶה אֶת הַשְּׁבוּיָה יִשָּׂאֶנָּה. [5]מֵעִיד בָּהּ, לֹא יִשָּׂאֶנָּה. [6]רַבִּי יְהוּדָה אוֹמֵר: בֵּין כָּךְ וּבֵין כָּךְ, לֹא יִשָּׂאֶנָּה״. [7]הָא גּוּפָהּ קַשְׁיָא. [8]אָמְרַתְּ: ״הַפּוֹדֶה אֶת הַשְּׁבוּיָה יִשָּׂאֶנָּה״. [9]וַהֲדַר תָּנָא: ״מֵעִיד בָּהּ, לֹא

LITERAL TRANSLATION

is two hundred [zuz]." [1]But there, what [consideration of] "that the sinner should not be rewarded" is there?

[2]There too, perhaps they will refrain and will not marry her.

[3]But does Rabbi Yehudah maintain [that] she remains in her holiness? [4]But surely it was taught: "Someone who redeems a female captive may marry her. [5][If] he testifies about her, he may not marry her. [6]Rabbi Yehudah says: Whether so or so, he may not marry her."

[7]This itself is difficult. [8]You said: "Someone who redeems a female captive may marry her." [9]And then it taught: "[If] he testifies about her, he may not

RASHI

דלמא ממנעי ולא נסבי לה — אי פחתת כתובתה משוית לה בחזקת בעולה, ומרחקי לה אפילו ישראל. **מעיד בה** — קא סלקא דעתין דאפודה קאי, שאם היה מעיד בה שלא נבעלה לנכרי — לא ישאנה אם כהן הוא.

TRANSLATION AND COMMENTARY

is two hundred zuz, the full ketubah of a virgin, and not one hundred zuz, the ketubah of a non-virgin." [1]**But,** says Abaye, in the case described in this Baraita we are not dealing with rape or seduction. So **what consideration is** involved **here** that she should be considered a virgin **"in order that the sinner should not be rewarded,"** as you explained? Why should her husband, who has done no wrong, be required to pay a full ketubah? Surely it is obvious that Rabbi Yoḥanan is correct, and that Rabbi Yehudah considers a captive woman to be a virgin for all purposes, not because he wishes to avoid rewarding a sinner but because of Rabbi Dosa's argument that the legal presumption governing her status cannot be changed without proof.

הָתָם נַמִי [2]Rabbah replied: **There too,** in the Baraita dealing with the ketubah of a captive, it is possible that Rabbi Yehudah had a special reason for showing leniency. For if we assume that the captive woman lost her virginity while she was in captivity, **it is possible that** non-priests **will refrain from marrying her.** Even though we assume that a captive woman was raped, we are not certain that this is so. Hence Rabbi Yehudah did not apply this assumption to the laws governing the ketubah, in order not to discourage non-priests from marrying this captive. But regarding the priesthood, it is possible that Rabbi Yehudah agrees with the Rabbis that the captive woman is disqualified.

Although Rabbah has established that it is possible to distinguish between Rabbi Dosa's ruling and that of Rabbi Yehudah, Rabbi Yoḥanan's explanation — that both Tannaim are of the opinion that a captive woman is not presumed to have been raped — is more straightforward. From now on, throughout this passage, the Gemara will assume that this is Rabbi Yehudah's position.

וְסָבַר רַבִּי יְהוּדָה [3]The Gemara asks: **But does Rabbi Yehudah** really **maintain that** a captive woman **retains her status as a virgin** and is permitted to marry a priest, as Rabbi Yoḥanan explained? [4]**But surely** the following **was taught** in a Baraita: "A priest **who redeems a female captive may marry her.** [5]**If he testifies** that he personally observed **her** throughout her captivity, and he knows that she was never raped, **he may not marry her.** [6]**Rabbi Yehudah says:** No matter **whether** he redeemed her **or** he testified about her, **he may not marry her,"** because Rabbi Yehudah is of the opinion that a captive woman is presumed to have been raped, and therefore she is disqualified from the priesthood. From this Baraita it would appear that Rabbi Yehudah is of the opinion that a captive woman is *not* permitted to marry a priest!

הָא גּוּפָהּ קַשְׁיָא [7]Before answering this objection, the Gemara notes that **this** Baraita **itself is difficult** to understand, because it contains an apparent contradiction that demands explanation. [8]**You** — the author of the Baraita — **said:** "A priest **who redeems a captive may marry her."** [9]**And then** the Baraita **taught** that **"if he**

HALAKHAH

מֵעִיד בָּהּ, לֹא יִשָּׂאֶנָּה **If he testifies about her, he may not marry her.** "If a priest testifies that he observed a female captive throughout her captivity and knows that she was not raped, and there are no other witnesses, he is not permitted to marry the captive himself, because we suspect him of testifying falsely in order to marry her. *Ḥelkat Meḥokek* and *Bet Shmuel* add, however, that other priests may rely on his testimony to marry her, even if he was under the impression when he testified that he would be able to marry her himself. But if he spent money to redeem the captive, he is permitted to marry her, even if he is the only witness, because the fact that he spent money lends credibility to his testimony," following the Sages, who disagree with Rabbi Yehudah. (*Rambam, Sefer Kedushah, Hilkhot Issurei Bi'ah* 18:20; *Shulḥan Arukh, Even HaEzer* 7:3.)

TRANSLATION AND COMMENTARY

testifies about her, he may not marry her." It would seem, then, that a priest who redeems a captive may marry her, but not if he himself gives testimony about her status as a virgin. [1]But why should the fact that **he testified about her,** that he personally observed her throughout her captivity and knows that she was never raped, be a reason for **him not to marry her?**

הָא לָא קַשְׁיָא [2]The Gemara answers: **This** objection **poses no difficulty,** for it is based on the assumption that the priest who testified about the captive in the second clause also redeemed her, but this is not so. [3]Rather, says the Gemara, both clauses of the Baraita refer to a priest who testified about the captive, and **this is what** the Baraita **is saying:** "A priest **who redeems a female captive and testifies about her may marry her.** [4]But a priest **who testifies about** a female captive **but** did **nothing else, may not marry her,'** because we suspect him of lying in order to marry a captive woman whom he found attractive. But if he redeemed her, we believe him, because his efforts on her behalf lend credibility to his testimony.

מִכָּל מָקוֹם [5]Having resolved the internal difficulties in the Baraita, the Gemara now returns to its objection. **Nevertheless,** says the Gemara, this Baraita **is difficult** to understand **according to Rabbi Yehudah** as explained by Rabbi Yoḥanan. For Rabbi Yoḥanan said that Rabbi Yehudah's opinion that a female captive is presumed not to have been raped applies to all aspects of Jewish law, but in this Baraita Rabbi Yehudah rules that the captive is not permitted to marry a priest.

אֲמַר רַב פַּפָּא [6]**Rav Pappa said:** We must amend the Baraita to **read** as follows: [7]**"Rabbi Yehudah says:** No matter **whether** he redeemed her **or** he testified about her, **he may marry her,"** for Rabbi Yehudah maintains that a captive woman is presumed not to have been raped, and is not disqualified from the priesthood.

רַב הוּנָא בְּרֵיהּ דְּרַב יְהוֹשֻׁעַ [8]**Rav Huna the son of Rav Yehoshua said: In fact, it is** unnecessary to amend the Baraita, and it is possible to explain it **as** it **was** originally **taught.** [9]But **Rabbi Yehudah is** not expressing his own opinion in this Baraita; rather, he is **speaking to the Rabbis on the basis of their** own **opinion.** He is accepting the position of the Rabbis for the sake of argument, in order to formulate an objection against them. [10]Rabbi Yehudah is saying: **According to my** own position, there is certainly no room to distinguish between a case in which the priest redeemed a captive woman and a case in which he merely testified on her behalf, since a captive woman is not considered to have been raped, and no matter **whether** he redeemed her **or** he testified about her, **he is permitted to marry her.** Indeed, he may marry her even if he neither redeemed her nor testified about her, since you maintain that a captive is not assumed to have been raped. [11]**But according to you,** who assume that she was raped and that she is disqualified from the priesthood for that reason, why do you distinguish between a case where the priest redeemed her and a case where he

יִשָּׂאֶנָּה״. [1]מִשּׁוּם דְּמֵעִיד בָּהּ, לֹא יִשָּׂאֶנָּה?

[2]הָא לָא קַשְׁיָא. [3]הָכִי קָאָמַר: ״הַפּוֹדֶה אֶת הַשְּׁבוּיָה וּמֵעִיד בָּהּ יִשָּׂאֶנָּה. [4]מֵעִיד בָּהּ כְּדִי, לֹא יִשָּׂאֶנָּה״.

[5]מִכָּל מָקוֹם, קַשְׁיָא לְרַבִּי יְהוּדָה!

[6]אֲמַר רַב פַּפָּא: אֵימָא: [7]״רַבִּי יְהוּדָה אוֹמֵר: בֵּין כָּךְ וּבֵין כָּךְ, יִשָּׂאֶנָּה״.

[8]רַב הוּנָא בְּרֵיהּ דְּרַב יְהוֹשֻׁעַ אוֹמֵר: לְעוֹלָם כִּדְקָתָנֵי. [9]רַבִּי יְהוּדָה לְדִבְרֵיהֶם דְּרַבָּנַן קָאָמַר לְהוּ: [10]לְדִידִי, בֵּין כָּךְ וּבֵין כָּךְ, יִשָּׂאֶנָּה. [11]אֶלָּא לְדִידְכוּ,

LITERAL TRANSLATION

marry her." [1]Because he testifies about her, may he not marry her?

[2]This is no difficulty. [3]This is what he says: "Someone who redeems a female captive and testifies about her may marry her. [4][If] he testifies about her [and] nothing [else], he may not marry her."

[5]Nevertheless, it is difficult according to Rabbi Yehudah!

[6]Rav Pappa said: Say: [7]"Rabbi Yehudah says: Whether so or so, he may marry her."

[8]Rav Huna the son of Rav Yehoshua says: In fact, it is as taught. [9]Rabbi Yehudah is speaking to them according to the Rabbis' opinion (lit., "words"). [10]According to me, whether so or so, he may marry her. [11]But according to you,

RASHI

משום דמעיד בה וכו' – והא אמרו: הפודה את השבויה – ישאנה. **הפודה את השבויה ומעיד בה ישאנה** – דאי לאו דקים ליה בגוה – לא שדי זוזי בכדי, שהרי לישאנה פדאה. **מעיד בה כדי לא ישאנה** – שמא עיניו נתן בה.

SAGES

רַב הוּנָא בְּרֵיהּ דְּרַב יְהוֹשֻׁעַ Rav Huna the son of Rav Yehoshua. A fifth-generation Babylonian Amora. See *Ketubot,* Part II, p. 80.

NOTES

אֲמַר רַב פַּפָּא: אֵימָא: רַבִּי יְהוּדָה אוֹמֵר Rav Pappa said: Say: "Rabbi Yehudah says." At first glance, it would appear that Rav Pappa is amending the text of the Gemara to read the opposite of its original version. *Ritva* suggests that Rav Pappa may not be amending the text at all, but may be reading Rabbi Yehudah's statement as a rhetorical question: "In either case *may he not* marry her?"

SAGES

רַב פַּפָּא בַּר שְׁמוּאֵל **Rav Pappa bar Shmuel.** A Babylonian Amora of the third and fourth generations, Rav Pappa bar Shmuel studied with Rav Ḥisda and Rav Sheshet, and later engaged in Halakhic discussions with Abaye and Rava. Rav Pappa bar Shmuel lived in Pumbedita, where he was a Rabbinic judge. Indeed the Gemara states elsewhere (*Sanhedrin* 17b) that Talmudic references to "the judges of Pumbedita" refer to Rav Pappa bar Shmuel. The Gemara also relates that Rav Pappa bar Shmuel instituted a new unit of measurement, which was used in the city of Papunya.

TRANSLATION AND COMMENTARY

merely testified on her behalf? **You should have said:** "No matter **whether** he redeemed her **or** he testified about her, **he may not marry her,"** since you maintain that a captive woman is presumed to have been raped, and is therefore disqualified from the priesthood!

וְרַבָּנַן [1]The Gemara asks: **And** how would **the Rabbis** reply to Rabbi Yehudah's argument?

הַפּוֹדֶה אֶת הַשְּׁבוּיָה [2]The Gemara answers: The Rabbis would reply as follows: "A priest **who redeems a captive and testifies about her may marry her,"** because **a person does not throw away money for nothing,** and his efforts on her behalf lend credibility to his testimony. [3]On the other hand, "a priest **who testifies about** a captive **and** does **nothing else, may not marry her,"** [4]**lest he set his eyes upon her,** and testified falsely in order to marry her. Thus this Baraita does not contradict Rabbi Yoḥanan's explanation of Rabbi Yehudah, according to which he maintains that a captive woman is presumed not to have been raped, and that this presumption applies to all aspects of Jewish law.

רָמֵי לֵיהּ [5]**Rav Pappa bar Shmuel pointed out a contradiction to Rav Yosef:** [37A] [6]**But does Rabbi Yehudah** really **maintain that** a captive woman **retains her status as a virgin** for all Halakhic purposes, as Rabbi Yoḥanan explained? [7]**Surely it was taught** in a Baraita that there are two disputes between Rabbi Yehudah and Rabbi Yose regarding female proselytes. The first dispute concerns the laws that apply to menstruating women. Ordinarily, if a woman has a menstrual flow, however slight, she becomes ritually impure, and any objects she touches also become ritually impure. When a woman discovers that she has had a loss of blood, it is sometimes unclear when it began. Accordingly, the Sages decreed that any objects she touched during the twenty-four hours preceding her discovery must be considered ritually impure, unless she examined herself carefully within that time, in which case only those objects that she touched after the examination are considered ritually impure. This law applies only to Jewish women; non-Jews do not contract ritual impurity of any kind. "Accordingly," says the Baraita, "a question arises **if a female proselyte was converted and discovered** menstrual **blood** on her body or on her garments later on the day of her conversion. Clearly we cannot declare any objects she touched during the past twenty-four hours to be ritually impure, because she could not have been ritually impure before she converted to Judaism. Hence the question arises: Do we declare the objects she touched from the moment she converted to be ritually impure? Or do we waive this rule altogether, since it is impossible to apply it in the normal way? [8]On this point **Rabbi Yehudah says:**

"בֵּין כָּךְ וּבֵין כָּךְ, לֹא יִשָּׂאֶנָּה" מִבָּעֵי לֵיהּ.

[1]וְרַבָּנַן?

[2]"הַפּוֹדֶה אֶת הַשְּׁבוּיָה וּמֵעִיד בָּהּ יִשָּׂאֶנָּה". [3]לָא שָׁדֵי אִינִישׁ זוּזֵי בְּכְדִי. "מֵעִיד בָּהּ כְּדִי, לֹא יִשָּׂאֶנָּה". [4]שֶׁמָּא עֵינָיו נָתַן בָּהּ. [5]רָמֵי לֵיהּ רַב פַּפָּא בַּר שְׁמוּאֵל לְרַב יוֹסֵף: [37A] [6]וְסָבַר רַבִּי יְהוּדָה בִּקְדוּשָּׁתָהּ קָיְימָא? [7]וְהָתַנְיָא: "הַגִּיּוֹרֶת שֶׁנִּתְגַּיְּירָה וְרָאֲתָה דָּם, [8]רַבִּי יְהוּדָה אוֹמֵר:

LITERAL TRANSLATION

it should [have said]: "Whether so or so, he may not marry her."

[1]And the Rabbis?

[2]"Someone who redeems a female captive and testifies about her may marry her." [3]A person does not throw [away] money for nothing. "[If] he testifies about her [and] nothing [else], he may not marry her." [4]Lest he set his eyes upon her.

[5]Rav Pappa bar Shmuel pointed out a contradiction (lit., "cast") to Rav Yosef: [37A] [6]But does Rabbi Yehudah maintain [that] she remains in her holiness? [7]But surely it was taught: "[If] a female proselyte was converted and saw blood, [8]Rabbi Yehudah says:

RASHI

וראתה דם — נו כיוס.

NOTES

הַגִּיּוֹרֶת שֶׁנִּתְגַּיְּירָה וְרָאֲתָה דָּם **If a female proselyte was converted and saw blood.** By Torah law a woman who has a flow of menstrual blood is considered ritually impure in the highest degree. Any person or object touching her becomes ritually impure, and objects on which she sits impart ritual impurity to persons or other objects that touch them. This applies to a normal menstrual flow, to a menstrual flow occurring when the woman would not normally expect it (i.e., not during her regular period), and to the bleeding associated with childbirth (Leviticus 15:19-30 and 12:1-8). Even the smallest drop of blood renders the woman ritually impure, even if the blood remains in the uterus for some reason and has not yet passed through the vagina (*Niddah* 40a).

Accordingly, the Rabbis decreed that a woman who wishes to remain ritually pure should examine herself twice a day, morning and evening (*Niddah* 4b). This rule applies only in connection with the laws of ritual impurity, but the rules regarding sexual intercourse are less strict in this regard, even though the Torah forbids sexual intercourse with a menstruating woman on pain of excision (Leviticus 18:19). Hence, women are permitted to have intercourse without examination, except during the time of their periods, although it is considered praiseworthy behavior for them to examine themselves (*Rambam, Hilkhot Issurei Bi'ah* 4:16).

There is a Tannaitic dispute (*Niddah* 2a) between Hillel, Shammai, and the Sages with regard to the case of a woman who examines herself and discovers blood. Hillel

TRANSLATION AND COMMENTARY

We waive the twenty-four hour rule altogether, because it is impossible to apply it in the normal way. **It is enough for** the proselyte **to be** considered **ritually impure from this time forward** — from the moment she discovered the blood. [1]**Rabbi Yose** disagrees and **says: She is like all other women,** who **convey ritual impurity for twenty-four hours retroactively or from the last inspection** — whichever is closer to the time she discovered the blood. Although we cannot apply this rule fully, we declare the objects she touched from the moment she converted to be ritually impure." The second dispute in the Baraita, which has a bearing on the question of the captive woman mentioned in our Mishnah, concerns the waiting period imposed on a woman who wishes to marry, if there is a possibility that she is already pregnant. In general, the Rabbis wished to avoid doubts about paternity. Hence, whenever there is a possibility that a woman may be pregnant (for example, if she was recently widowed or divorced), she is required to wait three months before remarrying. [2]The Baraita rules that "a female proselyte **must** also **wait three months** after her conversion before she is permitted to marry. We take into account the possibility that this proselyte had

דַּיָּהּ שַׁעְתָּהּ. [1]רַבִּי יוֹסֵי אוֹמֵר: הֲרֵי הִיא כְּכָל הַנָּשִׁים, וּמְטַמְּאָה מֵעֵת לְעֵת וּמִפְּקִידָה לִפְקִידָה. [2]וּצְרִיכָה לְהַמְתִּין שְׁלֹשָׁה

LITERAL TRANSLATION

It is enough for her [to be ritually impure from] this time [forward]. [1]Rabbi Yose says: She is like all the [other] women, and she conveys ritual impurity for twenty-four hours (lit., 'from time to time') or from the last examination (lit., 'from examination to examination'). [2]And she must wait three

RASHI

דיה שעתה — ולא גזרו בה טומאת מעת לעת לטמא טהרות שנגעה בהן משעת טבילה עד שעת ראייה. דהא אפילו יצא דם זה מאתמול, והעמידוהו כותלי בית הרחם, שזהו הטעם של מעת לעת בבנות ישראל — הלא דם נכרית כדם בהמה. ואם תאמר: ניחוש שמא משטבלה נעקר ויצא מיד? טומאה למפרע דרבנן היא, והיכא דאיכא למיגזר מעת לעת שלם — גזור מפקידה לפקידה, והיכא דלא גזור מעת לעת — לא גזור מפקידה לפקידה. **וצריכה להמתין שלשה חדשים** — שלא תנשא, להבחין בין זרע הנזרע בקדושה לזרע הנזרע שלא בקדושה.

NOTES

rules that she must assume that any objects she has touched since her last examination may be impure, even if she has not examined herself for several days. For we are concerned that she may have had the flow some time earlier, but that the blood remained in her uterus and did not pass through the vagina. Shammai rules that she need not worry at all about objects she touched since her last examination, since it is unlikely that she had a flow and that the blood remained in the uterus, and we do not wish to impose additional restrictions on menstruating women, in case they apply them to the law forbidding sexual intercourse with a menstruating woman, and thereby cause marital problems. The other Sages take an intermediate position, ruling that she must assume that any objects she touched during the last twenty-four hours are ritually impure, unless she examined herself within that time, in which case she need only concern herself with objects she touched since that examination.

הַגִּיּוֹרֶת שֶׁנִּתְגַּיְּירָה וְרָאֲתָה דָּם If a female proselyte was converted and saw blood. By Torah law, the laws of ritual impurity apply only to Jews. Accordingly, a proselyte who had a menstrual flow before converting is not ritually impure, even if she converted the next day, unless the bleeding continues after her conversion.

Our commentary follows *Rashi* and most Rishonim, who explain that the proselyte in our Gemara discovers later on the day of her conversion that she has had a flow of blood. Hence she is definitely ritually impure from this point on. The question arises, however, regarding the Rabbinic decree that a woman who discovers that she is bleeding but does not know when the bleeding began should assume that any object she touched during the preceding twenty-four hours is ritually impure, because we suspect that she had the flow earlier and the blood remained in her uterus without passing through the vagina.

In the case of a newly-converted proselyte, it is impossible for her to have been ritually impure for twenty-four hours, since she only converted on that same day. Accordingly, Rabbi Yehudah rules that we do not apply this law at all, and she need only concern herself with objects that she touches from this point on. Rabbi Yose, however, rules that she must assume that objects she has touched since her conversion are ritually impure, because it is possible that she had a menstrual flow immediately after converting, and it did not pass through the vagina immediately.

Rashi's explanation is followed by the Rishonim. But it is a little difficult to reconcile it with the language of the Baraita, since Rabbi Yose rules that the proselyte is ritually impure retroactively *for twenty-four hours* (or since her last inspection), whereas according to *Rashi* she is ritually impure only from the time of her conversion — less than twenty-four hours earlier. *Rashi* explains that Rabbi Yose used the standard language applicable to Jewish women, and that his statement should not be taken literally. *Meiri* suggests that the Rabbis decreed that objects touched by the proselyte before her conversion should also be considered ritually impure.

Shittah Mekubbetzet suggests that this Baraita should be interpreted as referring to a proselyte who discovered blood several days after her conversion. According to this interpretation, Rabbi Yehudah maintains that the Rabbis viewed the first menstruation of a new proselyte like the first menstruation of a young Jewish girl. In such cases, the Rabbis do not apply their decree regarding retroactive ritual impurity, and permit the woman to concern herself only with objects she touches from this point on. Rabbi Yose, however, rules that a proselyte who has already had a menstrual flow before her conversion should be subject to the same laws that govern other Jewish women.

וּצְרִיכָה לְהַמְתִּין שְׁלֹשָׁה חֳדָשִׁים And she must wait three months. The law that a woman must wait three months

TRANSLATION AND COMMENTARY

intercourse shortly before her conversion, and in order to avoid future difficulties about paternity we insist that she wait three months before marrying. [1]**This is the opinion of Rabbi Yehudah.** [2]**Rabbi Yose,** however, **permits** the proselyte **to be betrothed and married immediately."** From this Baraita, concludes Rav Pappa bar Shmuel, we see that Rabbi Yehudah does not accept the female proselyte's uncorroborated testimony about herself. Is it not reasonable, then, to assume that he would also not believe a captive woman's uncorroborated testimony about herself, and would rule that we must assume that she was raped while in captivity? But if so, how could Rabbi Yoḥanan argue (above, 36b) that Rabbi Yehudah agrees with Rabbi Dosa that captive women are assumed not to have been raped?

אֲמַר לֵיהּ [3]Rav Yosef **said to** Rav Pappa bar Shmuel in reply: **Are you comparing a female proselyte with a female captive?** There is a psychological difference between the two cases. [4]The reason why we do not believe a female proselyte on this matter is because **a proselyte before her conversion does not protect herself** from sexual contact, and even though this proselyte insists that she did not engage in sexual relations, we do not believe her. **A captive woman,** by contrast, makes every effort to **protect herself** from the sexual advances of her captors. Hence, the captive woman's claim is more credible than that of the proselyte, and Rabbi Yehudah believes it.

וְרָמֵי [5]Rav Pappa the son of Shmuel **pointed out** another **contradiction between** the viewpoint of Rabbi Yehudah **on the subject of a female captive** as expressed in our Mishnah **and** his viewpoint **on the subject of a female captive** as expressed in the following Baraita, [6]in which **it was taught: "A female proselyte, or a female captive, or a female slave, who were ransomed or converted or freed when they were more than**

חֲדָשִׁים. [1]דִּבְרֵי רַבִּי יְהוּדָה. [2]רַבִּי יוֹסֵי מַתִּיר לֵיאָרֵס וְלִינָּשֵׂא מִיָּד״.

[3]אֲמַר לֵיהּ: גִּיּוֹרֶת אַשְּׁבוּיָה קָא רָמֵית? [4]גִּיּוֹרֶת לָא מְנַטְּרָא נַפְשָׁהּ; שְׁבוּיָה מְנַטְּרָא נַפְשָׁהּ.

[5]וְרָמֵי שְׁבוּיָה אַשְּׁבוּיָה. [6]דְּתַנְיָא: ״הַגִּיּוֹרֶת, וְהַשְּׁבוּיָה, וְהַשִּׁפְחָה, שֶׁנִּפְדּוּ וְשֶׁנִּתְגַּיְּירוּ וְשֶׁנִּשְׁתַּחְרְרוּ יְתֵירוֹת עַל בְּנוֹת שָׁלֹשׁ שָׁנִים וְיוֹם אֶחָד,

LITERAL TRANSLATION

months. [1][These are] the words of Rabbi Yehudah. [2]Rabbi Yose permits [her] to be betrothed and to be married immediately."

[3]He said to him: Are you comparing (lit., "throwing") a female proselyte with a female captive? [4]A female proselyte does not guard herself; a female captive guards herself.

[5]And he pointed out a contradiction between [one source dealing with] a female captive and [another source dealing with] a female captive. [6]For it was taught: "A female proselyte, or a female captive, or a female slave, who were redeemed or converted or freed [when they were] more than three years and one day old,

RASHI

רבי יוסי מתיר – לקמיה מפרש טעמא.

NOTES

before remarrying is mentioned in several places in the Talmud, and is discussed in detail in tractate *Yevamot*. The Gemara rules (*Yevamot* 41b) that the law requiring the widow to wait three months before remarrying applies even if the widow was a minor who could not possibly have been pregnant, because the Rabbis did not make any distinctions in this decree.

The Gemara (*Yevamot* 42a) explains that the purpose of this law is to determine paternity, and to prevent a situation of doubt from arising in the event that the woman remarries immediately and then gives birth seven or eight months later.

The Gemara gives two reasons why it is important to determine paternity in this way: (1) Rav Naḥman bar Shmuel cites a verse which suggests that it is a sign of holiness for the people of Israel to have accurate family trees. (2) Rava explains that it is a Rabbinic decree, designed to avoid possible problems of incest later.

According to either of these views, the Gemara cites a Baraita that rules that a husband and wife who converted together must also be separated for three months — even though there is no room for doubt about paternity — in order to distinguish between children conceived before conversion and children conceived afterwards.

יְתֵירוֹת עַל בְּנוֹת שָׁלֹשׁ שָׁנִים וְיוֹם אֶחָד When they were more than three years and one day old. Our translation and commentary follow the text of the standard Vilna Talmud, according to which Rabbi Yehudah maintains that even a minor proselyte, between the ages of three and twelve, must wait three months before marrying. *Tosafot* points out that this clause does not appear in the version of the Baraita cited in *Yevamot* (35b). Moreover, it is clear from the Gemara there that the dispute between Rabbi Yose and Rabbi Yehudah concerns an adult proselyte. Accordingly, *Tosafot* rejects our reading, and insists that Rabbi Yehudah permits a woman who converted as a

HALAKHAH

הַגִּיּוֹרֶת,...וְהַשִּׁפְחָה...צְרִיכוֹת לְהַמְתִּין שְׁלֹשָׁה חֳדָשִׁים A female proselyte...or a female slave...must wait three months. "A female proselyte who is converted, or a female slave who is freed, must wait ninety days before they are allowed to marry. *Shulḥan Arukh* rules, following *Maggid Mishneh*, that this applies only if the proselyte or the slave were married

TRANSLATION AND COMMENTARY

three years and one day old, [1]**must wait three months** before marrying, because we suspect that the proselyte and the slave previously engaged in sexual relations, and we suspect that the captive woman was raped before she was ransomed. And even if these women insist that they did not have intercourse, we do not believe them. [2]**This is the opinion of Rabbi Yehudah.** [3]**Rabbi Yose,** however, **permits** these women **to be betrothed and married immediately."** Do we not see from this Baraita, says Rav Pappa bar Shmuel, that Rabbi Yehudah does not believe the captive woman's uncorroborated testimony that she was not raped while in captivity? But if so, how could Rabbi Yoḥanan argue that Rabbi Yehudah agrees with Rabbi Dosa that captive women are assumed not to have been raped?

אִשְׁתִּיק [4]The Gemara relates that Rav Yosef **was silent,** not knowing how to solve the contradiction pointed out by Rav Pappa bar Shmuel. [5]**He** then **said to** Rav Pappa bar Shmuel: **Did you hear anything about this?** Perhaps you heard an answer to your objection from some other Sage.

אֲמַר לֵיהּ [6]Rav Pappa bar Shmuel **said to** Rav Yosef: **Rav Sheshet said** that the Baraita is not referring to a case in which the proselyte, the slave, or the captive claimed that they did not have sexual relations. [7]Rather, it is referring to a case **where** witnesses **saw them having intercourse** shortly before they were ransomed, converted, or freed. Therefore Rabbi Yehudah ruled that they must wait three months before marrying. But if we had not known whether they had had sexual relations (as in the case of our Mishnah), Rabbi Yehudah would have believed the captive if she claimed that she was not raped during her captivity.

אִי הָכִי [8]But, the Gemara asks, **if so** — if there are witnesses who saw them having intercourse — **what is** the basis for **Rabbi Yose's reasoning?** Why should they not be required to wait three months, just like any other woman who has had intercourse recently and may have become pregnant?

אֲמַר רַבָּה [9]**Rabbah said: Rabbi Yose maintains that** the three-month waiting period applies only to married women, who may have engaged in unprotected intercourse with the intention of becoming pregnant. But **a woman who is promiscuous** and engages in extramarital intercourse is always careful **to insert a soft cloth** into her vagina when she has intercourse, **in order not to become pregnant.** Therefore these women are permitted to get married immediately, without waiting three months.

[1]צְרִיכוֹת לְהַמְתִּין שְׁלֹשָׁה חֳדָשִׁים. [2]דִּבְרֵי רַבִּי יְהוּדָה. [3]רַבִּי יוֹסֵי מַתִּיר לֵיאָרֵס וְלִינָּשֵׂא מִיָּד״.
[4]אִשְׁתִּיק. [5]אֲמַר לֵיהּ: מִידִי שְׁמִיעַ לָךְ בְּהָא?
[6]אֲמַר לֵיהּ: הָכִי אֲמַר רַב שֵׁשֶׁת: [7]שֶׁרָאוּהָ שֶׁנִּבְעֲלָה.
[8]אִי הָכִי, מַאי טַעֲמָא דְּרַבִּי יוֹסֵי?
[9]אֲמַר רַבָּה: קָסָבַר רַבִּי יוֹסֵי אִשָּׁה מְזַנָּה מְשַׁמֶּשֶׁת בְּמוֹךְ שֶׁלֹּא תִּתְעַבֵּר.

LITERAL TRANSLATION

[1]must wait three months. [2][These are] the words of Rabbi Yehudah. [3]Rabbi Yose permits [them] to be betrothed and to be married immediately."

[4]He was silent. [5]He said to him: Did you hear anything about this?

[6]He said to him: Thus said Rav Sheshet: [7]Where they saw her having intercourse.

[8]If so, what is Rabbi Yose's reason?

[9]Rabbah said: Rabbi Yose maintains [that] a woman who is promiscuous uses a soft cloth so that she does not become pregnant.

RASHI

צריכות להמתין — ואף על פי שקטנה אינה מתעברת, גזירה קטנה אטו גדולה. **משמשת במוך** — נותנת מוך לאחר בעילה, ושואבת הזרע.

TERMINOLOGY

אִשְׁתִּיק He was silent. Sometimes a scholar is "silent" in the face of an objection raised against his viewpoint, either because he does not have a satisfactory answer or because he thinks the answer is so obvious that there is no need to reply.

NOTES

minor to marry without waiting, just as he permits other women who could not possibly have become pregnant to marry immediately. *Rashi*, however, supports the reading in our version, and insists that Rabbi Yehudah did not make any distinction between adults and minors regarding this law.

HALAKHAH

before they were converted or freed. But if they were unmarried, they need not wait the ninety days. A man and wife who convert to Judaism together must live apart for ninety days, to distinguish between children conceived before the conversion and children conceived afterwards." (*Rambam, Sefer Nashim, Hilkhot Gerushin* 11:21; *Shulḥan Arukh, Even HaEzer* 13:5.)

שְׁבוּיָה מוּתֶּרֶת לֵיאָרֵס וְלִינָּשֵׂא מִיָּד **A female captive is permitted to be betrothed and to be married immediately.** "A Jewish woman who has had extramarital intercourse — such as a woman who was raped or seduced, or a captive, or a prostitute — need not wait ninety days before marrying. This ruling follows the viewpoint of Rabbi Yose, who maintains that women who have extramarital intercourse take preventive measures to avoid becoming pregnant. *Rema* rules, however, that if they are adult women who are capable of becoming pregnant, they must wait ninety days, following *Rosh* who rules in favor of Rabbi Yehudah." (*Rambam, Sefer Nashim, Hilkhot Gerushin* 11:22; *Shulḥan Arukh, Even HaEzer* 13:6.)

TRANSLATION AND COMMENTARY

בִּשְׁלָמָא [1]But, the Gemara objects, although sexually active women generally take precautions to avoid pregnancy, ordinary non-Jewish women and female slaves do not do so. Nevertheless, **the case of the female proselyte can be** explained **satisfactorily,** [2]**because she intended to convert** to Judaism. [3]Hence, **she** would have **protected herself** during the months leading up to her conversion. [4]**The case of the captive woman can also be** explained **satisfactorily, because** she **does not know where** her captors **are taking her.** The captive woman knows that she may be brought to a Jewish community and ransomed without notice. Hence, although she cannot prevent herself from being raped, she takes precautions to prevent pregnancy. [5]**The case of the** freed **female slave can also be** explained **satisfactorily** if we are dealing with a slave who is freed voluntarily. In such a case, **she** is likely to **hear from the mouth of her master** that he is planning to free her, and she will take precautions to prevent pregnancy. [6]**But if she goes free** without notice, **as the result of losing a tooth or an eye, what is there to say?** The Torah (Exodus 21:26-27) commands that a master who knocks out his slave's tooth or puts out his eye must immediately set him free. Thus a female slave who was set free in this way would have no way of knowing in advance, and ordinarily would not take precautions against becoming pregnant. Why, then, is she permitted by Rabbi Yose to marry immediately, without waiting three months?

וְכִי תֵּימָא [7]**And if you say,** continues the Gemara, **that Rabbi Yose was not speaking about unexpected cases** like the cases just mentioned, and that he was referring only to regular cases, in which the slave (like the proselyte or the captive woman) has some advance warning that she is about to be freed, but if the slave was freed without warning, Rabbi Yose agrees that she must wait three months before marrying, this is not so. [8]For Rabbi Yehudah and Rabbi Yose disagree along the same lines as to whether **a woman who was raped or seduced** must wait three months before marrying, **even though this** case must also **be** classified as **unexpected.** A woman who is raped or seduced has no advance warning, yet Rabbi Yehudah and Rabbi Yose still disagree as to whether or not she must wait three months before marrying, [9]**as was taught** in the

[1]בִּשְׁלָמָא גִּיּוֹרֶת — [2]כֵּיוָן דְּדַעְתָּהּ לְאִיגַּיּוּרֵי, [3]מְנַטְּרָא נַפְשָׁהּ. [4]שְׁבוּיָה נַמִי, דְּלָא יָדְעָה הֵיכָא מַמְטוּ לָהּ. [5]שִׁפְחָה נַמִי דְּשָׁמְעָה מִפִּי מָרָהּ. [6]אֶלָּא יוֹצְאָה בְּשֵׁן וְעַיִן, מַאי אִיכָּא לְמֵימַר?

[7]וְכִי תֵּימָא כָּל מִמֵּילָא לָא אֲמַר רַבִּי יוֹסֵי, [8]הֲרֵי אֲנוּסָה וּמְפוּתָּה, דְּמִמֵּילָא, [9]וְתַנְיָא:

LITERAL TRANSLATION

[1][The case of the] female proselyte is satisfactory — [2]since her intention is to convert, [3]she guards herself. [4][The case of the] female captive is also [satisfactory], because she does not know where they are bringing her. [5][The case of the] female slave is also [satisfactory], for she heard from the mouth of her master. [6]But [if] she goes free through [loss of] a tooth or an eye, what is there to say?

[7]And if you say [that] Rabbi Yose was not speaking [about] any unexpected (lit., "automatic") case, [8]there is the case of a woman who was raped or seduced, which is unexpected, [9]and it has been taught:

RASHI

מנטרא נפשה — ומזמנת לה מוך. **דלא ידעה היכא ממטו לה** — שבאים למוכרה, וסברה דלמא ממטו לה לגבי ישראל ופרקו לה, ומנטרא נפשה לשמש במוך. **אלא יוצאה בשן ועין** — שפחה שסימא אדוניה את עינה ויצאה לחירות, מנא הות ידעה מעיקרא דתיפוק לחירות, דמנטרא נפשה לזמן מוך לשימושה? **כל ממילא** — מידי דליכא לאיזדהורי ביה מעיקרא דתיפוק לחירות — מודה רבי יוסי. **הרי אנוסה דממילא** — דלא הות ידעה דליסליק בה הכי, ותזמן לה מוך.

NOTES

יוֹצְאָה בְּשֵׁן וְעַיִן If she goes free through loss of a tooth or an eye. The Torah (Exodus 21:26-27) commands that a master who knocks out his non-Jewish slave's tooth or puts out his eye must immediately set him free. According to the accepted oral tradition, this commandment is understood to include a number of other parts of the body as well.

There is a Tannaitic dispute (*Kiddushin* 24b) as to whether the master is required to give the slave a formal bill of emancipation, or whether the slave goes free automatically, without a bill. The Rishonim rule in favor of the former position (*Rambam, Hilkhot Avadim* 5:4). Hence a female slave who goes free through loss of a tooth or an eye is not, in fact, freed automatically. Moreover, even according to the other Tannaim, the slave is not freed as soon as the tooth is knocked out or the eye is put out, but must take his master to court (*Ran*). This process, however, is quite rapid. Moreover, *Ran* rules that, even according to the viewpoint that the slave requires a bill of emancipation, the master can be compelled to write the bill immediately, and even before the bill of emancipation is delivered, the master cannot force his slave to work for him. Hence our Gemara considers this to be an automatic emancipation.

יוֹצְאָה בְּשֵׁן וְעַיִן, מַאי אִיכָּא לְמֵימַר If she goes free through loss of a tooth or an eye, what is there to say? Rabbi Yose does not actually say that a female slave who was freed in this way is exempt from the three-month waiting period, but he also does not say that she is treated differently from other freed slaves. Hence the Gemara assumes initially that she is no different from any other

TRANSLATION AND COMMENTARY

following Baraita: **"A woman who was raped or seduced must wait three months** before marrying. [1]**This is the opinion of Rabbi Yehudah.** [2]**Rabbi Yose,** however, **permits her to be betrothed and married immediately.**" Now, if Rabbi Yose maintains that only a woman who has advance notice that she is going to have the opportunity to get married is exempt from the three-month waiting period, because such a woman will use a soft cloth to prevent pregnancy, why should a woman who was raped or seduced be exempt from the waiting period? She had no advance warning to enable her to take such precautions!

"אֲנוּסָה וּמְפוּתָּה צְרִיכוֹת לְהַמְתִּין שְׁלֹשָׁה חֳדָשִׁים. [1]דִּבְרֵי רַבִּי יְהוּדָה. [2]רַבִּי יוֹסֵי מַתִּיר לֵיאָרֵס וְלִינָּשֵׂא מִיָּד".
[3]אֶלָּא אֲמַר רַבָּה: קָסָבַר רַבִּי יוֹסֵי: [4]אִשָּׁה מְזַנָּה מִתְהַפֶּכֶת כְּדֵי שֶׁלֹּא תִּתְעַבֵּר.
[5]וְאִידָךְ?
[6]חָיְישִׁינַן שֶׁמָּא לֹא נֶהֶפְכָה יָפֶה יָפֶה.

LITERAL TRANSLATION

"A woman who was raped or seduced must wait three months. [1][These are] the words of Rabbi Yehudah. [2]Rabbi Yose permits [her] to be betrothed and to be married immediately."

[3]Rather, Rabbah said: Rabbi Yose maintains [that] [4]a woman who is promiscuous turns herself over so that she does not become pregnant.

[5]And the other one?

[6]We are concerned in case she did not turn herself over carefully (lit., "well, well").

RASHI

מתהפכת – שיצא הזרע ולא יקלוט. והא אפילו במידי דממילא מנו למיעבד, וכולן עושות כן.

אֶלָּא [3]**Rather, Rabbah** modified his explanation slightly, **saying: Rabbi Yose maintains that** the three-month waiting period applies only to married women, who may have engaged in unprotected intercourse with the intention of becoming pregnant. [4]**But a woman who is promiscuous** and engages in extramarital intercourse is always careful **to turn herself over** immediately after intercourse, **in order not to become pregnant.** The same applies to a woman who is raped. Even under such circumstances a woman makes every effort to avoid becoming pregnant, and is therefore not required to wait three months before marrying.

וְאִידָךְ [5]And why, asks the Gemara, does **the other** Sage — Rabbi Yehudah — require a three-month waiting period?

חָיְישִׁינַן [6]The Gemara answers: Rabbi Yehudah maintains that even though a woman who engages in extramarital intercourse takes precautions to avoid pregnancy, we do not rely on this, because **we are concerned in case she did not turn herself over carefully.** There is no certainty that the measures taken by a woman after intercourse to prevent pregnancy are effective. Therefore we require these women to wait three months before marrying.

NOTES

freed slave. The Gemara then suggests that Rabbi Yose may have been referring only to regular freed slaves, but not to a slave who went free through loss of a tooth or an eye. And the Gemara responds by citing the case of a woman who was raped or seduced.

The Rishonim ask: Since the Gemara's objection is based, in the final analysis, on the case of a woman who was raped or seduced, why did it raise in the first place the problem of the female slave who went free through loss of a tooth or an eye? It should have immediately cited the Baraita about the woman who was raped or seduced!

Rashba and *Ritva* answer that the Gemara wished to raise an objection from within the Baraita cited by Rav Pappa bar Shmuel, before citing a Baraita from elsewhere. Hence it considered the case of a female slave freed through loss of a tooth or an eye, which can be included in the general category of the freed female slave, rather than raising the case of a woman who was raped or seduced, which was not mentioned in this Baraita at all.

קָסָבַר רַבִּי יוֹסֵי: אִשָּׁה מְזַנָּה מִתְהַפֶּכֶת **Rabbi Yose maintains that a woman who is promiscuous turns herself over.** *Tosafot* asks: This answer is satisfactory in the case of the woman who was raped or seduced. But how does it explain the case of the female slave who was freed through loss of a tooth or an eye? How could she possibly have known that she was about to be freed?

Tosafot answers that the Gemara did not withdraw its previous explanation that Rabbi Yose was referring only to a slave freed in the regular way, not to a slave who went free through loss of a tooth or an eye. The explanation that the woman turns herself over applies only to the case of a woman who was raped or seduced. In the case of the female slave who went free through loss of a tooth or an eye, however, Rabbi Yose would agree with Rabbi Yehudah that she is required to wait three months.

Rashi, however, maintains that the explanation that the woman takes precautions to avoid pregnancy applies to all women who are suspected of having had intercourse outside marriage, even to a female slave who went free through loss of a tooth or an eye. *Ritva* explains — on the basis of *Rashi*'s explanation in *Yevamot* (35a) — that a cloth would be used only by women who consider it very important to avoid pregnancy. Hence the Gemara assumes that a female slave would not use it unless she knew that she was about to be freed. But all women who engage in extramarital intercourse take the simple precaution of turning themselves over to avoid pregnancy, even female slaves.

חָיְישִׁינַן שֶׁמָּא לֹא נֶהֶפְכָה יָפֶה יָפֶה **We are concerned in case she did not turn herself over carefully.** *Rosh* asks: How do we know that Rabbi Yehudah is of the opinion that this method of preventing pregnancy is ineffective?

TRANSLATION AND COMMENTARY

שֶׁנֶּאֱמַר [1]The Gemara now turns to the last clause of the Mishnah, which rules that someone who is subject to the death penalty does not pay money for the same offense, **"as the verse** (Exodus 21:22) **says:** 'And if two men struggle and one of them hits a pregnant woman so that she loses her child, **but there is no disaster** [i.e., the woman miscarries but survives the attack], the assailant **shall surely be punished,** as the woman's husband shall put upon him.'" Thus the verse teaches us that damages are paid only if the woman is not killed, from which we learn the general principle that a person who commits a crime subject to the death penalty is not required to pay damages for the same act. [2]On this point the Gemara asks: **Is** the rule that a person who is subject to a more severe penalty is exempt from other penalties really **derived from** this verse? Surely it is derived from the following verse (Deuteronomy 25:2), which deals with the procedure to be followed when a court inflicts lashes: [3]"And [the judge] shall strike him in front of him a number of times, **according to his wickedness."** [4]The Gemara interprets this verse as follows: **"Because of one wickedness you make him liable, but you do not make him liable because of two wickednesses."** In other words, when a person is lashed, it is considered an appropriate retribution for his wickedness, and there is no need for additional penalties. From here we learn that a person is not given two punishments for the same offense.

חֲדָא [5]The Gemara answers: **One** verse (dealing with the pregnant woman) **informs us** that a person who is subject to the **death** penalty does not pay **money** for the same offense, [6]**and one** verse (dealing with the judge who inflicts lashes) **informs us** that a person who is subject to **lashes** does not pay **money** for the same offense.

[1]״שֶׁנֶּאֱמַר: ׳וְלֹא יִהְיֶה אָסוֹן, עָנוֹשׁ יֵעָנֵשׁ׳ וכו׳״. [2]וְהָא מֵהָכָא נָפְקָא? [3]מֵהָתָם נָפְקָא: ״כְּדֵי רִשְׁעָתוֹ״. [4]מִשּׁוּם רִשְׁעָה אַחַת אַתָּה מְחַיְּיבוֹ, וְאִי אַתָּה מְחַיְּיבוֹ מִשּׁוּם שְׁתֵּי רִשְׁעָיוֹת! [5]חֲדָא בְּמִיתָה וּמָמוֹן, [6]וַחֲדָא בְּמַלְקוֹת וּמָמוֹן.

LITERAL TRANSLATION

[1]"As it is said: 'And if there is no disaster, he shall surely be punished.'" [2]But is it derived from here? [3]It is derived from there: "According to his wickedness." [4]Because of one wickedness you make him liable, but you do not make him liable because of two wickednesses!

[5]One [informs us] about death and money, [6]and one [informs us] about lashes and money.

NOTES

Perhaps he forbids all women who have had intercourse to get married without waiting three months. For, according to the reading in our texts, he forbade a proselyte from remarrying without waiting, even if she converted as a minor and even though she could not possibly have become pregnant. *Rosh* uses this as proof that the reading in our texts is incorrect, and that Rabbi Yose and Rabbi Yehudah in fact disagree only about adult proselytes.

Pnei Yehoshua, however, explains that it is possible that Rabbi Yehudah forbids even a proselyte who was a minor from marrying without a waiting period. However, it would be unreasonable for him to have done so if there were no real grounds for concern regarding an adult proselyte, as this would amount to an unreasonable extension of the Rabbinic decree. But if Rabbi Yehudah is of the opinion that there are real grounds for concern regarding an adult proselyte, it would be reasonable for him to extend them to a minor as well, even though she could not possibly have become pregnant.

מֵהָתָם נָפְקָא **It is derived from there.** *Ritva* observes that the Gemara appears to be suggesting that the law that the more severe penalty exempts from payment should be derived entirely from the verse dealing with lashes, and not from the verse dealing with the pregnant woman. And the Gemara answers that we need two verses, because we could not have inferred from the fact that death is a more severe penalty that the same applies to lashes and vice versa. But surely, asks *Ritva*, the verse dealing with lashes only proscribes inflicting both penalties together; it does not inform us which penalty takes precedence. Thus we see that Rabbi Yoḥanan (above, 32b) was not able to prove from the verse dealing with lashes that lashes take precedence over monetary penalties, and he was forced to supplement it with an additional exegetical argument from another verse. Hence, even if we assume that we can extrapolate from death to lashes and vice versa, we still need the verse dealing with the pregnant woman to teach us that the more severe penalty (lashes or death) takes precedence over the monetary penalty.

Ritva replies that the Gemara could have answered its question in this way, but if it had done so, it would have immediately exposed itself to the converse question: Why do we need the verse dealing with lashes, since we can derive the law that the more severe penalty exempts from payment exclusively from the verse dealing with the pregnant woman? Hence the Gemara omitted this stage of the argument, and explained why both verses are needed.

Alternatively, *Ritva* explains that there is no question that if only one penalty is to be imposed, the death penalty takes precedence over any other penalty, because it is logically untenable to imagine that a person who has committed a capital offense should be exempt from the death penalty merely because his crime also involved a monetary offense. The only question is whether we impose both penalties or impose the death penalty alone. By contrast, when there is a conflict between lashes and a monetary penalty, there is room to speculate as to which penalty should take precedence, since they are of comparable severity, and the monetary penalty has the advantage of serving the interests of the injured party better than lashes.

TRANSLATION AND COMMENTARY

וּצְרִיכָא [1]**And,** continues the Gemara, **it was necessary** for the Torah **to teach** us these two laws in **two** separate **verses,** because we could not have inferred one from the other. [2]**For if we had been informed** only that a person who is subject to the **death** penalty does not pay **money** for the same offense, **we might have thought that** only a person who is executed is exempt from payment, [3]**because** the penalty involves **the loss of** his **life.** The death penalty is so severe that it is inappropriate to combine it with any other penalty. [4]**But regarding** a person who is subject to the penalty of **lashes and** to **monetary payment, which involve no loss of life,** [5]**I would say** that both penalties should be imposed, and that he should **not** be exempt from payment because of the more severe penalty of lashes.

וְאִי אַשְׁמְעִינַן [6]**And if we had been informed** only that a person who is subject to **lashes** does not pay **money** for the same offense, [7]**we might have thought that** only a person who is lashed is exempt from payment, **because prohibitions** that are punished by lashes **are not** as **severe** as prohibitions punished by death. And since the prohibition is not so severe, it is reasonable to exempt him from other penalties. [8]**But regarding** a person who is subject to the **death** penalty **and** to **monetary payment, where the prohibition is severe,** [9]**I would say** that the offender should **not** be exempt from payment. [10]**Therefore both verses were necessary,** so that the Torah could teach us these two laws.

וּלְרַבִּי מֵאִיר [11]But, the Gemara objects, this explanation is satisfactory according to the Sages, who maintain that a person does not receive lashes and pay a monetary penalty for the same offense. **But according to Rabbi Meir, who says that** a person who commits an offense punishable by lashes is not exempt thereby from any monetary penalty that he may have incurred at the same time, and that both penalties are imposed, so that the offender **is lashed and pays** the monetary penalty as well, [12]**why do we need two verses?** The Torah only needed to cite the verse dealing with the pregnant woman to inform us that the death penalty exempts from payment. What purpose is served, according to Rabbi Meir, by the verse dealing with lashes?

חֲדָא [13]The Gemara answers: **One** verse (dealing with the pregnant woman) informs us that a person who is subject to the **death** penalty does not pay **money** for the same offense, [37B] [14]**and one** verse (dealing with the judge who inflicts lashes) informs us that a person who is subject to the **death** penalty **and** to **lashes** is not lashed. For the verse dealing with lashes teaches us only that we do not impose "two

[1]וּצְרִיכָא. [2]דְּאִי אַשְׁמְעִינַן מִיתָה וּמָמוֹן, [3]מִשּׁוּם דְּאִיכָּא אִיבּוּד נְשָׁמָה. [4]אֲבָל מַלְקוּת וּמָמוֹן, דְּלֵיכָּא אִיבּוּד נְשָׁמָה, [5]אֵימָא לָא.

[6]וְאִי אַשְׁמְעִינַן מַלְקוּת וּמָמוֹן, [7]מִשּׁוּם דְּלָא חֲמִיר אִיסּוּרֵיהּ. [8]אֲבָל מִיתָה וּמָמוֹן, דַּחֲמִיר אִיסּוּרֵיהּ, [9]אֵימָא לָא. [10]צְרִיכָא. [11]וּלְרַבִּי מֵאִיר, דְּאָמַר לוֹקֶה וּמְשַׁלֵּם, [12]תַּרְתֵּי לָמָּה לִי? [13]חֲדָא בְּמִיתָה וּמָמוֹן, [37B] [14]וַחֲדָא בְּמִיתָה וּמַלְקוּת.

LITERAL TRANSLATION

[1]And it is necessary [that both verses be stated]. [2]For if it had informed us [about] death and money, [3][we might have thought that it is] because there is the loss of life (lit., "soul"). [4]But [regarding] lashes and money, where there is no loss of life, [5]I would say not.

[6]And if it had informed us [about] lashes and money, [7][we might have thought that it is] because its prohibition is not severe. [8]But [regarding] death and money, where its prohibition is severe, [9]I would say not. [10][Therefore both verses are] necessary.

[11]But according to Rabbi Meir, who said [that] he is lashed and pays, [12]why do I need two [verses]?

[13]One for death and money, [37B] [14]and one for death and lashes.

RASHI

משום דאיכא איבוד נשמה — יש כאן עונש חמור, ודיו בכך אם ענשתו לאבד נשמה, ליהרג. **אימא לא** — אין זה עונש יתירה, וליעביד ביה תרתי. **דלא חמיר איסוריה** — לא עבר עבירה חמורה, ודיו שתענשנו עונש אחד.

TERMINOLOGY

תַּרְתֵּי לָמָּה לִי Why do I need two? I.e., why do I need two statements, each of which teaches the same Halakhah? Or: "Why do I need two statements when one can be inferred from the other?"

NOTES

מִשּׁוּם דְּאִיכָּא אִיבּוּד נְשָׁמָה Because there is the loss of life. *Shittah Mekubbetzet* asks: We have seen above (35a) that the death penalty exempts from payment even if it is not actually inflicted. How, then, can the Gemara suggest that the death penalty exempts from payment only because it entails the loss of life?

Shittah Mekubbetzet answers that even if in practice there is no loss of life, the offense was so serious that it potentially involved the loss of life, and it is possible that only in such cases do we ignore other penalties incurred at the same time.

וַחֲדָא בְּמִיתָה וּמַלְקוֹת And one for death and lashes. The Rishonim ask: From where do the Sages who disagree with Rabbi Meir derive the law that someone who is subject to the death penalty is not lashed for the same offense?

There are two basic answers to this question given by the Rishonim. *Rashba* and *Ritva* explain that the Sages derive the law that lashes are set aside by the death penalty from

[1] וּצְרִיכָא. [2] דְּאִי אַשְׁמַעִינַן מִיתָה וּמָמוֹן, מִשּׁוּם דַּחֲדָא בְּגוּפֵיהּ וַחֲדָא בְּמָמוֹנֵיהּ לָא עָבְדִינַן. [3] אֲבָל בְּמִיתָה וּמַלְקוֹת, דְּאִידִי וְאִידִי בְּגוּפֵיהּ, [4] אֵימָא מִיתָה אֲרִיכְתָּא הִיא, וְנַעֲבֵיד בֵּיהּ. [5] וְאִי אַשְׁמַעִינַן מִיתָה וּמַלְקוֹת, [6] דְּתַרְתֵּי בְּגוּפֵיהּ לָא עָבְדִינַן. [7] אֲבָל מִיתָה וּמָמוֹן, דַּחֲדָא בְּגוּפֵיהּ וַחֲדָא בְּמָמוֹנֵיהּ, [8] אֵימָא נַעֲבֵיד בֵּיהּ. [9] צְרִיכָא.
[10] ״וְלֹא תִקְחוּ כֹפֶר לְנֶפֶשׁ רֹצֵחַ״ לָמָּה לִי?

LITERAL TRANSLATION

[1] And it is necessary [that both verses be stated]. [2] For if it had informed us [about] death and money, [we might have thought that it is] because we do not inflict (lit., "do") one [penalty] on his body and [another] one on his money. [3] But regarding death and lashes, where this [penalty] and that are [inflicted] on his body, [4] I would say [that] it is a long death, and we should inflict it on him.

[5] And if it had informed us about death and lashes, [6] [we might have thought that it is] because we do not inflict two [penalties] on his body. [7] But [regarding] death and money, where one [penalty] is [inflicted] on his body and [another] one on his money, [8] I would say [that] we should inflict [both] on him. [9] [Therefore both verses are] necessary.

[10] Why do I need [the verse]: "And you shall not take a ransom for the life of a murderer"?

RASHI

לא תקחו כופר – משמע נמי: אם תהרגנו – לא תענשנו ממון.

TRANSLATION AND COMMENTARY

wickednesses" in connection with lashes. It does not specify that the other "wickedness" is necessarily a monetary penalty, nor does it specify that the penalty of lashes takes precedence over this other penalty. Hence Rabbi Meir can interpret this verse as referring to an offense that is subject both to the death penalty and to lashes, and he can say that it teaches us that the death penalty is a more severe penalty that exempts from lashes.

וּצְרִיכָא [1] **And**, continues the Gemara, **it was necessary** for the Torah **to teach** us these two laws in **two** separate **verses**, because we could not have inferred one law from the other. [2] **For if we had been informed** that someone who is subject to the **death** penalty does not pay **money** for the same offense, but we had not been informed that he is also exempt from lashes, **we might have thought that** someone who has been sentenced to death is exempt from payment **because we do not impose one penalty on his person and another on his money.** Since death is a more severe penalty, the offender is exempt from other, unrelated penalties, such as monetary payments. [3] **But I would say that death and lashes, which are** both **inflicted on his person,** are not regarded as two unrelated penalties at all, but rather as **a** single **extended death** penalty, which begins with pain and ends with execution. [4] **On this basis, we should** perhaps **inflict** both penalties **on him**, and he should not be exempt from lashes because of the more severe death penalty.

וְאִי אַשְׁמַעִינַן [5] **And if we had been informed** that someone who is subject to the **death** penalty is not **lashed** for the same offense, but we had not been informed that the death penalty exempts the offender from monetary payment, [6] **we might have thought that** someone who is executed is exempt from lashes **because we do not impose two penalties on his person.** [7] **But I would say that** unrelated penalties, like **death and monetary payment, which are** inflicted, respectively, **on his person and on his money,** should not affect each other. [8] On this basis, **we should** perhaps **inflict both** penalties **on him**, and he should not be exempt from paying damages because of the more severe death penalty. [9] **Therefore it was necessary** for the Torah to teach us these two laws in **two** separate **verses**, even according to Rabbi Meir.

וְלֹא תִקְחוּ כֹפֶר [10] Having explained the two verses from which we learn the rule that an offender who is subject to a more severe penalty is exempt from a lesser penalty, the Gemara now examines a series of verses that also deal with a conflict between a monetary penalty and the death penalty. The Torah states

NOTES

the common factor between the two other cases — death and money, and lashes and money. Since lashes are not inflicted together with a monetary penalty, it follows that they are certainly not inflicted together with a more severe penalty, such as death. And if we argue that death, precisely because it is severe, should perhaps not set aside other penalties, we can prove that this is not so from the fact that death does set aside monetary penalties.

The second answer is given by *Tosafot*, who explains that the Sages derive both laws from the verse dealing with lashes — that the death penalty sets aside lashes, and that lashes set aside monetary penalties. For the verse teaches us only that lashes are not imposed together with another penalty, but it does not specify to which other penalties it is referring, nor does it specify which penalty takes precedence. Hence we can infer that lashes are not inflicted together with either a monetary penalty or the death penalty, and in both cases the more severe penalty is imposed. Therefore, if there is a conflict between lashes and a monetary penalty, the lashes take precedence, and if there is a conflict between lashes and the death penalty, the death penalty takes precedence.

¹דְּאָמַר רַחֲמָנָא: לָא תִּשְׁקוֹל מָמוֹנָא מִינֵּיהּ וְתִפְטְרֵיהּ מִקְּטָלָא.
²״לֹא תִקְחוּ כֹפֶר לָנוּס אֶל עִיר מִקְלָטוֹ״ לָמָּה לִי?
³דְּאָמַר רַחֲמָנָא: לָא תִּשְׁקוֹל מָמוֹנָא מִינֵּיהּ וְתִפְטְרֵיהּ מִן גָּלוּת.
⁴וּתְרֵי קְרָאֵי לָמָּה לִי?
⁵חַד בְּשׁוֹגֵג, ⁶וְחַד בְּמֵזִיד.
⁷וּצְרִיכִי. ⁸דְּאִי אַשְׁמְעִינַן מֵזִיד,

LITERAL TRANSLATION

¹Because the Torah said: You shall not take money from him and exempt him from being killed. ²Why do I need [the verse]: "You shall not take a ransom to flee to his city of refuge"? ³Because the Torah said: You shall not take money from him and exempt him from being exiled. ⁴But why do I need two verses? ⁵One [deals] with inadvertent [killing], ⁶and one [deals] with deliberate [killing]. ⁷And [both verses] are necessary. ⁸For if it had informed us [about] deliberate [killing],

TRANSLATION AND COMMENTARY

(Numbers 35:31): **"And you shall not take a ransom for** the life of a murderer, who is guilty of death." At first glance, this verse seems to be informing us that we do not impose a monetary penalty on a person who is subject to the death penalty. But we have already seen that this law is derived from the verse (Exodus 21:22) dealing with the pregnant woman. So **why do we need this verse** from Numbers?

דְּאָמַר רַחֲמָנָא ¹The Gemara answers: This verse is needed **because the Torah** wished to **say** to us: **You must not take money from him and** thereby **exempt him from being killed.** The purpose of the verse was not to inform us that a monetary penalty is not imposed *in addition to* the death penalty, but rather to inform us that a monetary penalty is not imposed *in lieu of* the death penalty.

לֹא תִקְחוּ כֹּפֶר ²But, the Gemara asks, the very next verse (Numbers 35:32) also seems to be informing us that we do not impose a monetary penalty on someone who inadvertently committed an offense subject to the death penalty. For the verse says: **"You shall not take a ransom to flee to his city of refuge."** Someone who has committed accidental homicide must go into exile in a city of refuge. The Gemara's question assumes that this verse is informing us that such a person is not punished by both exile and a monetary payment. But we have already seen that this law is derived from the verse dealing with the pregnant woman, in conjunction with the rule we learned above (35a) that the more severe penalty exempts from payment even if the offense was committed inadvertently. So **why do we need this verse?**

דְּאָמַר רַחֲמָנָא ³The Gemara answers: This verse is needed **because the Torah** wished to **say** to us: **You must not take money from him and** thereby **exempt him from being exiled.** The purpose of the verse was not to inform us that a monetary penalty is not imposed *in addition to* the penalty of exile, but rather to inform us that a monetary penalty is not imposed *in lieu of* the penalty of exile.

וּתְרֵי קְרָאֵי ⁴**But,** the Gemara asks, **why do we need two verses** to inform us that we do not impose a monetary penalty instead of death or exile? Surely we could extrapolate from one verse that the same law applies to the other case as well!

חַד בְּשׁוֹגֵג ⁵The Gemara answers: **One** verse **informs** us that we do not substitute a ransom when the **killing was inadvertent,** and the killer's punishment is exile, ⁶**and one** verse **informs** us that we do not substitute a ransom when the **killing was deliberate,** and the killer's punishment is death.

וּצְרִיכִי ⁷**And,** continues the Gemara, **it was necessary** for the Torah to state the law explicitly in **both cases**, because we could not have inferred one from the other. ⁸**For if we had been informed about** the unacceptability of a ransom after a **deliberate killing,** but not about its unacceptability after an inadvertent

RASHI

דאמר רחמנא — שניא הוא דמשנינן: לאו לאשמעינן דלא תעביד ביה תרתי, אלא לאשמועינן בחיוב מיתה לבדה, שלא יפדה בממון. **לא תקחו כופר לנוס** — קא סלקא דעתך: לא תעביד ביה תרתי להורג בשוגג, גלות וממון. **וצריכי דאי אשמעינן מזיד** — דלא ליפרוק נפשיה בממון, הוה אמינא: משום דחמיר איסוריה, אבל בשוגג — ליפרוק נפשיה בממון מגלות.

HALAKHAH

לָא תִּשְׁקוֹל מָמוֹנָא מִינֵּיהּ וְתִפְטְרֵיהּ מִקְּטָלָא You shall not take money from him and exempt him from being killed. "The court is forbidden to take a ransom from the murderer to spare him from being killed, even if he is willing to pay a huge sum of money. Even if the avenger of blood who is charged with killing the murderer is willing to spare him, the court must not agree to this. For the life of the murderer is not the property of the avenger of blood to keep or discard, but the property of God, who commanded that he be put to death," following our Gemara. (*Rambam, Sefer Nezikin, Hilkhot Rotze'aḥ* 1:4.)

לָא תִּשְׁקוֹל מָמוֹנָא מִינֵּיהּ וְתִפְטְרֵיהּ מִן גָּלוּת You shall not take money from him and exempt him from being exiled. "The court is forbidden to take a ransom from an inadvertent killer to spare him from being exiled," following our Gemara. (*Rambam, Sefer Nezikin, Hilkhot Rotze'aḥ* 5:1.)

TRANSLATION AND COMMENTARY

killing, [1] **we might have thought that** the Torah did not permit us to accept a ransom in lieu of execution **because the prohibition** violated by the killer **is severe,** and no ransom can possibly atone for his crime. [2] **But regarding inadvertent killing, where the prohibition** violated by the killer **is not** so **severe,** because he was guilty of negligence leading to death but not of deliberate murder, [3] **I would say** that the Torah's commandment prohibiting ransom does **not** apply. I might have thought that an appropriate ransom could serve as a substitute for the punishment of exile laid down in the Torah, were it not for the explicit statement of the Torah forbidding us to accept a ransom in lieu of exile.

וְאִי אַשְׁמַעִינַן [4] **And if we had been informed about** the unacceptability of a ransom after an **inadvertent killing,** but not about its unacceptability after a deliberate killing, [5] **we might have thought that** the Torah did not permit us to accept a ransom in lieu of exile **because there is no loss of life** involved if the killer is exiled. The Torah might have commanded us to send the inadvertent killer into exile and not permitted us to substitute some other penalty, because there is no compelling reason not to inflict the penalty laid down in the Torah. [6] **But regarding deliberate killing, where** the death penalty laid down in the Torah leads to the **loss of** the murderer's **life,** [7] **I would say** that the Torah's commandment prohibiting ransom does **not** apply. [8] **Therefore it was necessary** for the Torah to issue an explicit command in **both cases.**

וְלָאָרֶץ [9] The Gemara now considers the next verse in this passage (Numbers 35:33) which states: **"And the land shall not be atoned for the blood that was shed in it, except through the blood of him who shed it." Why do we need this verse?** If its purpose is to inform us that we do not accept a ransom in lieu of executing a murderer, surely we have already learned that law from the earlier verse: "And you shall not take a ransom for the life of a murderer"!

מִבָּעֵי לֵיהּ [10] The Gemara answers: This verse **is needed** as the basis for the law **that was taught** in the following Baraita, dealing with the laws governing the heifer whose neck is broken to atone for a murder when it is impossible to locate the murderer and punish him (Deuteronomy 21:1-9). [11] The Baraita asks: **"From where** in the Torah **do we know that if the killer was found after the heifer's neck was broken, we do not exempt him** from punishment? Perhaps the ritual of breaking the neck of the heifer is sufficient to atone for the crime." [12] The Baraita answers: "This is learned **from a verse** in the Book of Numbers [the very verse that the Gemara here is considering], which **says: 'And the land shall not be atoned for the blood that**

[1] מִשּׁוּם דַּחֲמִיר אִיסּוּרֵיהּ. [2] אֲבָל שׁוֹגֵג, דְּלָא חֲמִיר אִיסּוּרֵיהּ, [3] אֵימָא לָא.
[4] וְאִי אַשְׁמַעִינַן שׁוֹגֵג, [5] מִשּׁוּם דְּלֵיכָּא אִיבּוּד נְשָׁמָה. [6] אֲבָל מֵזִיד, דְּאִיכָּא אִיבּוּד נְשָׁמָה, [7] אֵימָא לָא. [8] צְרִיכָא.
[9] ״וְלָאָרֶץ לֹא יְכֻפַּר לַדָּם אֲשֶׁר שֻׁפַּךְ בָּהּ, כִּי אִם בְּדַם שֹׁפְכוֹ״ לָמָּה לִי?
[10] מִבָּעֵי לֵיהּ לִכְדְתַנְיָא: [11] ״מִנַּיִן שֶׁאִם נִתְעָרְפָה עֶגְלָה וְאַחַר כָּךְ נִמְצָא הַהוֹרֵג, מִנַּיִן שֶׁאֵין פּוֹטְרִין אוֹתוֹ? [12] שֶׁנֶּאֱמַר: ׳וְלָאָרֶץ לֹא יְכֻפַּר לַדָּם אֲשֶׁר שֻׁפַּךְ בָּהּ, וגו׳׳״.

LITERAL TRANSLATION

[1] [we might have thought that it is] because its prohibition is severe. [2] But [regarding] inadvertent [killing], where its prohibition is not severe, [3] I would say not.

[4] And if it had informed us about inadvertent [killing], [5] [we might have thought that it is] because there is no loss of life (lit., "soul"). [6] But [regarding] deliberate [killing], where there is loss of life, [7] I would say not. [8] [Therefore both verses are] necessary.

[9] Why do I need [the verse]: "And the land shall not be atoned for the blood that was shed in it, except through the blood of him who shed it"?

[10] It is needed for what was taught: [11] "From where [do we know] that if the heifer's neck was broken and afterwards the killer was found, from where [do we know] that we do not exempt him? [12] For it is said: 'And the land shall not be atoned for the blood that was shed in it, etc.'"

RASHI

ואי אשמעינן שוגג — דמשום דאין בגלותו איבוד נשמה, להכי לא לפטריה בממון אלא ליגלי. **אבל מזיד** — משום איבוד נשמה אימור ניסקול ממונא, ונקיים נפש בישראל. **כי אם בדם שופכו** — ולא בפדיון ממון, למה ליז מ״לא תקחו כופר״ נפקא. **שאין פוטרין אותו** — לומר: כבר נתכפר בעודו ספק, שהעגלה מכפרת על הספק.

CONCEPTS

עֶגְלָה עֲרוּפָה A heifer whose neck is broken. When a murdered person's body is found outside a town and it is not known who caused his death, the following procedure takes place (see Deuteronomy 21:1-9). First, judges from the Great Sanhedrin (סַנְהֶדְרִין גְּדוֹלָה) come to measure the distance between the corpse and the nearest town, to determine which town must perform the rite of the עֶגְלָה עֲרוּפָה. This measurement is carried out even if it is clear beyond any doubt which town is closest to the corpse. Afterwards, the elders of that town must bring a heifer that has never been used for any work and break its neck in a riverbed that is not tilled. The elders wash their hands and make a statement absolving themselves from guilt. If the murderer is discovered before the heifer has been killed, the rite of עֶגְלָה עֲרוּפָה is not performed.

HALAKHAH

שֶׁאִם נִתְעָרְפָה עֶגְלָה וְאַחַר כָּךְ נִמְצָא הַהוֹרֵג That if the heifer's neck was broken and afterwards the killer was found. "If the murderer is found, he is executed, even if the heifer has already been beheaded," following our Gemara. (*Rambam, Sefer Nezikin, Hilkhot Rotze'aḥ* 10:8.)

[1] ״וְאַתָּה תְּבַעֵר הַדָּם הַנָּקִי מִקִּרְבֶּךָ״ לָמָּה לִי? [2] מִיבָּעֵי לֵיהּ לְכִדְתַנְיָא: [3] ״מִנַּיִן לַמּוּמָתִים בְּסַיִיף שֶׁהוּא מִן הַצַּוָּאר? [4] תַּלְמוּד לוֹמַר: ׳וְאַתָּה תְּבַעֵר הַדָּם הַנָּקִי מִקִּרְבֶּךָ׳. [5] הוּקְשׁוּ כָּל שׁוֹפְכֵי דָמִים לְעֶגְלָה עֲרוּפָה. [6] מַה לְהַלָּן מִן הַצַּוָּאר, [7] אַף שׁוֹפְכֵי דָמִים מִן הַצַּוָּאר״.

אִי [8] מַה לְהַלָּן בְּקוֹפִיץ וּמִמּוּל עוֹרֶף, [9] אַף כָּאן בְּקוֹפִיץ וּמִמּוּל עוֹרֶף?

LITERAL TRANSLATION

[1] Why do I need [the verse]: "And you shall get rid of the [guilt of] innocent blood from among you"? [2] It is needed for what was taught: [3] "From where [do we know] concerning those who are executed by the sword that it is from the neck? [4] The verse states: 'And you shall get rid of the [guilt of] innocent blood from among you.' [5] All shedders of blood were compared to a heifer whose neck is broken. [6] Just as there it is [killed] from the neck, [7] so too shedders of blood are [killed] from the neck."

[8] If [so], just as there it is with a hatchet and from the back of the neck, [9] so too here it should be with a hatchet and from the back of the neck?

TRANSLATION AND COMMENTARY

was shed in it, except through the blood of him who shed it.'" This Baraita shows that the purpose of this verse was not to forbid accepting a ransom in lieu of execution, but rather to forbid accepting the ritual of the heifer whose neck is broken as being in lieu of execution.

וְאַתָּה תְּבַעֵר [1] The Gemara asks: If the law that breaking the neck of the heifer is not a substitute for execution is derived from the verse in Numbers, **why do we need the** last **verse** in the passage dealing with the ceremony of atonement involving the breaking of the heifer's neck (Deuteronomy 21:9): **"And you shall get rid of the guilt of innocent blood from among you"?** At first glance, it would seem that this verse is informing us that we must still hunt down and punish the killer, even after completing the ceremony of breaking the heifer's neck. But if that law is derived from the verse in Numbers, as was stated in the Baraita, what other law is this verse in Deuteronomy teaching us?

מִיבָּעֵי לֵיהּ [2] The Gemara answers: The verse in Deuteronomy **is needed** as the basis **for** the law **that was taught** in a Baraita which deals with the procedure to be followed when executing a criminal by the sword. We have seen above (30b) that there are four methods of execution that a Jewish court is authorized to mete out, depending on the crime: Stoning, burning, killing by the sword, and strangling. Two crimes are punished by the sword — murder, and idolatry practiced by an entire city (Deuteronomy 13:13-19.) [3] We are told in a Mishnah (*Sanhedrin* 52b) that execution by the sword is done by beheading, and the Baraita cites the Scriptural source for this law when it asks: **"From where do we know that** murderers and residents of an idolatrous city, **who are executed by the sword,** are killed by severing the head **from the neck,** rather than by some other method of killing with a sharp weapon?" [4] The Baraita answers: The Torah teaches us this law in **the verse** from Deuteronomy dealing with the heifer whose neck is broken, which **says: 'And you shall get rid of the guilt of innocent blood from among you.'"** [5] The Baraita explains: "In this verse the Torah introduces the punishment of those who shed blood in order **to compare all shedders of blood to the heifer whose neck is broken."** There is a traditional rule of Halakhic exegesis that when the Torah places two laws in juxtaposition in this way, its purpose is to teach us that the regulations governing the two laws are to be compared to the fullest degree possible. Thus in this case, the punishment meted out to murderers is to be compared with the fate meted out to the heifer whose neck is broken. [6] "Therefore," says the Baraita, "**just as there,** in the case of the heifer, the method of bringing about its death **is from the neck,** because the Torah commands (Deuteronomy 21:4) that the heifer must have its head cut off from the back of the neck, [7] **so too shedders of blood are** executed by severing their heads **from the neck."**

אִי [8] But, the Gemara objects, **if so,** if the execution procedure for murderers is the same as that followed in the case of the heifer whose neck is broken, then **just as there,** in the case of the heifer, the method of killing **is** to use **a hatchet and** to sever the head **from the back of the neck,** [9] **so too here,** when a murderer is executed by the sword, **it should be** done **with a hatchet and from the back of the neck?** But in the Mishnah (*Sanhedrin* 52b), the Sages state that when a criminal is executed by the sword, he stands erect, and his head is cut off at the neck with a fast stroke from the front, and their viewpoint is accepted as

RASHI

ואתה תבער — בתר עריפה כתיב.

LANGUAGE

קוֹפִיץ Hatchet. This word is derived from the Greek κοπίς, *kopis,* meaning "a large, wide knife."

REALIA

קוֹפִיץ Hatchet.

Part of a Roman picture depicting a hatchet. This was a large, slightly curved knife, used for cutting and chopping.

HALAKHAH

מַה לְהַלָּן מִן הַצַּוָּאר Just as there it is killed from the neck. "The heifer is beheaded with a blow of a hatchet to the back of the neck," following our Gemara. (*Rambam, Sefer Nezikin, Hilkhot Rotze'aḥ* 9:3.)

SAGES

רַבָּה בַּר אֲבוּהּ Rabbah bar Avuha. A Babylonian Amora of the second generation, Rabbah bar Avuha was a pupil of Rav, and transmitted many teachings in his name. Rabbah bar Avuha was a member of the Exilarch's family, and Rav Naḥman was his pupil and son-in-law.

TRANSLATION AND COMMENTARY

the normative Halakhah. How could the Sages rule this way, if there is an explicit verse in the Torah that teaches us that the same procedure should be followed as that used in the case of the heifer whose neck is broken?

אָמַר רַב נַחְמָן [1]In reply to this objection, **Rav Naḥman said in the name of Rabbah bar Avuha:** The Sages are of the opinion that there is a general principle that underlies all the rules governing execution.[2] **The verse** in the Torah **says** (Leviticus 19:18): **"And you shall love your neighbor as yourself."** [3]From this verse, says Rav Naḥman, we learn that we must show consideration toward a criminal who is about to be executed, and must **select a dignified death for him.** The Sages in tractate *Sanhedrin* maintained that the Torah could not have required that the execution of murderers should be carried out by a hatchet to the back of the neck, since this is an undignified death. Hence we interpret the verse dealing with the heifer whose neck is broken as teaching us that we must execute these criminals by beheading, and we then select the most dignified method of beheading that is available to us.

כָּל חֵרֶם [4]The Gemara now considers a related verse (Leviticus 27:29): **"Any condemned person who is condemned from among people shall not be redeemed;** he shall surely be put to death." This verse teaches us that a person who has been sentenced to death is not redeemed. But, asks the Gemara, if the purpose of **the verse** is to inform us that we must not accept a ransom to spare his life, **why do we need** it? We have already learned that law from the verse in Numbers (35:31) cited above: "And you shall not take a ransom for the life of a murderer."

[1]אָמַר רַב נַחְמָן אָמַר רַבָּה בַּר אֲבוּהּ: [2]אָמַר קְרָא: "וְאָהַבְתָּ לְרֵעֲךָ כָּמוֹךָ" — [3]בְּרוֹר לוֹ מִיתָה יָפָה.

[4]"כָּל חֵרֶם אֲשֶׁר יָחֳרַם מִן הָאָדָם לֹא יִפָּדֶה" לָמָּה לִי?

LITERAL TRANSLATION

[1]Rav Naḥman said in the name of Rabbah bar Avuha: [2]The verse said: "And you shall love your neighbor as yourself" — [3]select for him a dignified death.

[4]Why do I need [the verse]: "Any condemned [person] who is condemned from among people shall not be redeemed"?

RASHI

מיתה יפה — בסייף, ומלך הסימנים, שימות מהר. **כל חרם וגו׳** — משמע לשון חייבי מיתות, כמו "זובח לאלהים יחרם" (שמות כב).

NOTES

"וְאָהַבְתָּ לְרֵעֲךָ כָּמוֹךָ" "And you shall love your neighbor as yourself." The plain meaning of this verse is that we are commanded to have a feeling of love toward other people. Throughout Talmudic literature, however, this verse is interpreted as commanding us to show the same consideration toward other people that we wish to have shown toward ourselves.

Rav Naḥman's interpretation of the verse — that it teaches us to show consideration toward executed criminals — is cited in several places in the Talmud. *Remah* (*Sanhedrin* 52b) explains that Rav Naḥman is not interpreting the verse as referring specifically to this case. Rather, he is arguing that we should behave lovingly toward executed criminals, even though they are wicked. For although many of the laws regarding our treatment of other people apply only in relation to decent people, the term "your neighbor" is intended to include all Jews. *Remah* adds that the term "your neighbor" in Hebrew (רֵעֲךָ) is spelled the same way as "your evil" (רָעֲךָ), thus implying that even evil people are included in this category. *Shittah Mekubbetzet* adds that even if we say that there is no requirement to behave lovingly toward evil people, nevertheless, once a criminal has been punished, he is again considered to be "your brother" (*Sanhedrin* 10b), and consideration must be shown to him during the execution as well.

מִיתָה יָפָה A dignified death. *Remah* explains that cutting the head from the back with a hatchet is painful and undignified, because a hatchet is generally less sharp than a sword. Moreover, a hatchet is used for killing animals, whereas a sword is used for killing people. *Rashi* explains that cutting the head from the back prolongs death, since the key blood vessels and nerves are at the front of the neck.

"כָּל חֵרֶם אֲשֶׁר יָחֳרַם" "Any condemned person who is condemned." The verse reads: "Any condemned person who is condemned from among people shall not be redeemed; he shall surely be put to death." The Hebrew word חֵרֶם (translated here as "condemned person") has two meanings in the Torah: (1) Property that is dedicated to the Temple (see Leviticus 27:28); and (2) A person who is condemned to death (see Exodus 22:19). The first meaning is clearly not applicable to this verse, which commands that the condemned person must be executed; hence the Gemara assumes that the second meaning applies.

Ramban and *Ritva* suggest an alternative interpretation of the verse, which finds support in certain Midrashim, according to which the word חֵרֶם should be translated as "ban." If the governing authorities — the king or the Sanhedrin, with the consent of all Israel — declare a ban against any person who does a certain action, and someone dares to violate the ban, he is put to death, and must not be redeemed by any amount of payment, even though the action itself may have been a relatively minor monetary offense.

That this is the law is indisputable. It seems clear from our Gemara, however, that this is not the meaning of this verse. *Ritva* notes that there is a Midrash that explains the verse in this way, but according to our Gemara, this law must be derived from some other source.

TRANSLATION AND COMMENTARY

מִיבָּעֵי לֵיהּ [1]The Gemara answers: The redemption referred to in this verse does not mean a ransom paid in order to spare the condemned man's life. Rather, it refers to the topic discussed in the preceding verses of the same passage in Leviticus — the laws regarding a person who makes a dedication to the Temple. By Torah law, a person may dedicate the assessed value of any human being to the Temple, based solely on the assessed person's age and sex. The assessor then "redeems" his assessment by paying the assessed value to the Temple. Thus our verse is informing us that if a condemned person is assessed, the assessment cannot be "redeemed" (i.e., the assessment is invalid and no money need be paid to the Temple), since a person who is about to be put to death has no assessment value. Thus the verse **is needed** as the basis **for** the law that **was taught** in the following Baraita: [2]**"If someone is going out to be executed** (i.e., his trial has ended and he has been sentenced to death), [3]**and someone** else decides to dedicate this condemned person's assessed value to the Temple, **saying:** 'This person's **valuation is on me** (i.e., I vow to pay the assessed value of this person to the Temple),' [4]**his statement is of no effect,** the assessment is invalid, and no money need be paid to the Temple. **From where do we know** this? [5]From **the verse,** which **says: 'Any condemned person who is condemned from among people shall not be redeemed.'"** [6]But the Baraita limits on this law: "**I might have thought that this is** the law **even** if the assessment is made **before** the criminal's **trial ends,** if the criminal is ultimately sentenced to death. [7]Therefore **the Torah** adds the seemingly superfluous clause, 'who is condemned from among people,' to **teach** us that this is not so, and that this law applies to those who are condemned **'from among people,' and not** to **all the people** who are condemned. In other words, it applies to some condemned people and not to others. Thus we learn that the assessment of a condemned criminal is invalid only if it is made after he has been sentenced to death."

וּלְרַבִּי חֲנַנְיָא בֶּן עֲקַבְיָא [8]But, the Gemara objects, this law is the subject of a Tannaitic dispute (*Arakhin* 6b). The Baraita we have quoted reflects the viewpoint of the Sages, who maintain that a condemned criminal cannot be assessed. **But Rabbi Ḥananya ben Akavya** disagreed and **said:** "A condemned criminal **may be assessed,** even though he is valueless, **because his** assessed **value** is not based on his actual value, but **is fixed** in accordance with his age and sex." Hence even a condemned criminal has an assessed value, although he has no market value. [9]Now, argues the Gemara, **what use does** Rabbi Ḥananya ben Akavya **make of this** verse, **"Any condemned person"?** If the redemption referred to in the verse does not mean the assessment of human beings, it must be referring to a ransom that the criminal wishes to pay in order to

[1]מִיבָּעֵי לֵיהּ לְכִדְתַנְיָא: [2]"מִנַּיִן לַיּוֹצֵא לֵיהָרֵג, [3]וְאָמַר אֶחָד: 'עֶרְכּוֹ עָלַי', [4]מִנַּיִן שֶׁלֹּא אָמַר כְּלוּם? [5]שֶׁנֶּאֱמַר: 'כָּל חֵרֶם אֲשֶׁר יָחֳרַם מִן הָאָדָם לֹא יִפָּדֶה'. [6]יָכוֹל אַף קוֹדֶם שֶׁנִּגְמַר דִּינוֹ כֵּן. [7]תַּלְמוּד לוֹמַר: 'מִן הָאָדָם', וְלֹא כָּל הָאָדָם.

[8]וּלְרַבִּי חֲנַנְיָא בֶּן עֲקַבְיָא, דְּאָמַר: "נֶעֱרָךְ, מִפְּנֵי שֶׁדָּמָיו קְצוּבִין", [9]הַאי "כָּל חֵרֶם" מַאי עָבֵיד לֵיהּ?

LITERAL TRANSLATION

[1]It is needed for what was taught: [2]"From where [do we know] that [if] someone was going out to be executed, [3]and someone said: 'His valuation is on me,' [4]from where [do we know] that he has not said anything? [5]For it is said: 'Any condemned [person] who is condemned from among people shall not be redeemed.' [6]I might have thought that it is so even before his trial is completed. [7][Therefore] the verse states: 'From among people,' but not all the people.

[8]But according to Rabbi Ḥananya ben Akavya, who said: "He is assessed, because his value is fixed," [9]what does he do with this "any condemned [person]"?

RASHI

ערכו עלי — ואף על פי שערך אינו לפי דמים אלא לפי שנים — לא אמר כלום, דמעטיה קרא הכא. והאי "חרם" לשון הקדש הוא. שדמיו קצובין — בתורה, לפי שנים. ולא דמי לאומר "דמיו עלי" — דדמים אין לו, אבל ערך יש לו.

SAGES

רַבִּי חֲנַנְיָא בֶּן עֲקַבְיָא **Rabbi Ḥananya ben Akavya.** A fifth-generation Tanna, Rabbi Ḥananya ben Akavya (sometimes referred to as Rabbi Ḥanina ben Akiva) is mentioned twice in the Mishnah and on a few occasions in Baraitot. He was a colleague of Rabbi Yehudah and Rabbi Yose and during his long life he discussed Halakhic problems with the leaders of the following generation, Rabbi Yehudah HaNasi and Rabbi Natan. He lived in Tiberias and may have had his own academy there.

NOTES

נֶעֱרָךְ מִפְּנֵי שֶׁדָּמָיו קְצוּבִין **He is assessed, because his value is fixed.** The laws of assessment are stated in detail in the Torah (Leviticus, chapter 27) and in tractate *Arakhin*. The Torah states that if someone dedicates to the Temple property such as his house or a non-sacrificial animal, the value of the property is assessed by the priest, and the

HALAKHAH

לַיּוֹצֵא לֵיהָרֵג, וְאָמַר אֶחָד: "עֶרְכּוֹ עָלַי" **That if someone was going out to be executed, and someone said: "His valuation is on me."** "A dying person is not subject to the laws of assessment, because he has no value. Likewise, if someone has been convicted by a Jewish court and has been sentenced to death, he too is considered to have no

[1]מִיבָּעֵי לֵיהּ לְכִדְתַנְיָא: [2]"רַבִּי יִשְׁמָעֵאל בְּנוֹ שֶׁל רַבִּי יוֹחָנָן בֶּן בְּרוֹקָה אוֹמֵר: לְפִי שֶׁמָּצִינוּ לַמּוּמָתִים בִּידֵי שָׁמַיִם שֶׁנּוֹתְנִין מָמוֹן וּמִתְכַּפֵּר לָהֶן, [3]שֶׁנֶּאֱמַר: 'אִם כֹּפֶר יוּשַׁת עָלָיו', יָכוֹל אַף בִּידֵי אָדָם כֵּן. [4]תַּלְמוּד לוֹמַר: 'חֵרֶם מִן הָאָדָם לֹא יִפָּדֶה'. [5]וְאֵין לִי אֶלָּא מִיתוֹת חֲמוּרוֹת,

LITERAL TRANSLATION

[1]He needs it for what was taught: [2]"Rabbi Yishmael the son of Rabbi Yoḥanan ben Berokah says: Because we have found concerning those who are killed at the hands of Heaven that they give money and it atones for them, [3]as it is said: 'If a ransom is placed on him,' I might have thought that it is so even [for those who are executed] at the hands of man. [4][Therefore] the verse states: 'A condemned [person] from among people shall not be redeemed.' [5]And I only have [crimes punishable by] severe deaths,

TRANSLATION AND COMMENTARY

escape execution. But why do we need another verse to inform us that we must not accept a ransom to spare his life? We have already learned that law from the verse in Numbers cited above: "And you shall not take a ransom for the life of a murderer."

מִיבָּעֵי לֵיהּ [1]The Gemara answers: According to Rabbi Ḥananya ben Akavya, the verse is indeed referring to a criminal who attempts to escape execution by paying a ransom, and **it is needed** as the basis **for** the law that **was taught** in a Baraita dealing with an ox that killed a human being after its owner had been warned that it was behaving dangerously. The owner is considered morally culpable for having left such a dangerous ox unguarded, and the Torah commands that the owner must die (Exodus 21:29). This commandment is traditionally understood as meaning that the owner of the ox is not executed by the court, but is considered deserving of death at the hands of Heaven. However, the next verse requires him to pay a ransom to redeem his soul from this penalty. [2]On this point the Baraita states: "**Rabbi Yishmael the son of Rabbi Yoḥanan ben Berokah says: We have found that those who are** to be **killed at the hands of Heaven** [i.e., the owner of the ox] can **give money** instead as a ransom, **and it atones for them,** [3]**as the verse** (Exodus 21:30) **says: 'If a ransom is placed on him,** then he shall give the redemption of his life, in accordance with whatever is placed upon him.' Now, since this is so, **I might have thought that the same** law **should apply even** to offenders **who are killed at the hands of man,** and that condemned criminals should also be allowed to ransom themselves. [4]Therefore the Torah wrote **the verse** in Leviticus (27:29) to teach us that this is not so, **saying: 'Any condemned person** who is condemned **from among people shall not be redeemed.'** [5]**And** up to this point," the Baraita continues, **"I have only** proved that this is the law concerning the more **severe crimes** that are **subject to execution,** but it is still possible that an offender who has committed a less

RASHI

למומתין בידי שמים — כגון מי שהרג שורו את הנפש, דכתיב ביה "יומת". ולא מיתת בית דין, דנפקא לן בסנהדרין (טו,ב) "מות יומת המכה רוצח הוא" — על רציחתו אתה הורגו, ואי אתה הורגו על רציחת שורו. והאי "יומת" בידי שמים. **יכול אף** — חייבי מיתות בית דין יפדו בממון. **חרם מן האדם** — אדם שמחויב חרם.

NOTES

owner may then redeem it by paying the assessment figure plus twenty percent (Leviticus 27:11-15).

Human beings cannot be dedicated in this way. But someone may dedicate to the Temple the *actual market value* (דָּמִים) of himself or any other human being. In such a case, the person who has been dedicated does not become the property of the Temple, but the dedicator must pay the Temple the market value of the dedicated person. Alternatively, a person may dedicate the *assessed* value (עֵרֶךְ) of himself or of another human being. In such a case, the assessment is based solely on the assessed person's age and sex, in accordance with a fixed table given in the Torah.

If someone dedicates the *actual market value* of a person with no real market value — such as a severely diseased person, or a dying person, or a person who is about to be executed — his vow is null and void. But if he dedicates the *assessed* value of such a person, the vow is based solely on age and sex.

There is a Tannaitic dispute regarding the assessed value of a person who is about to be executed. Rabbi Ḥananya ben Akavya maintains that since the assessed value is based solely on age and sex, it makes no difference at all that a person about to be executed has no actual value; hence he is assessed in the usual way. But the first Tanna infers from the verse cited in our Gemara that a person who is about to be executed has no assessed value. The Halakhah is in accordance with the first Tanna.

HALAKHAH

לְפִי שֶׁמָּצִינוּ לַמּוּמָתִים בִּידֵי שָׁמַיִם שֶׁנּוֹתְנִין מָמוֹן וּמִתְכַּפֵּר לָהֶן Because we have found concerning those who are killed at the hands of Heaven that they give money and it atones for them. "Concerning an ox that killed a person

value. Hence, if he or someone else vows to assess his value and give it to the Temple, the vow is null and void," following the first Tanna against Rabbi Ḥananya ben Akavya. (*Rambam, Sefer Hafla'ah, Hilkhot Arakhin* 1:13.)

SAGES

רַבִּי יִשְׁמָעֵאל בְּנוֹ שֶׁל רַבִּי יוֹחָנָן בֶּן בְּרוֹקָה Rabbi Yishmael the son of Rabbi Yoḥanan ben Berokah. A fifth-generation Tanna, Rabbi Yishmael was the son of the important Tanna Rabbi Yoḥanan Ben Berokah, who was his teacher. In his youth Rabbi Yishmael studied in Yavneh. After the Bar Kochba revolt, when the seat of the Sanhedrin was in Usha, he was already one of the most prominent Sages of his generation.

CONCEPTS

חֵרֶם Ban, excommunication. The partial or complete removal of a person from the community of the Jewish people as a punishment or as a means of exerting pressure upon him to change his behavior. There are degrees of severity in the imposition of a ban. In its precise meaning, חֵרֶם refers to the most severe of these bans — excommunication from the Jewish people as a whole. A person in such a situation is no longer considered a member of the community. He is not included in a quorum for prayer or in any other religious activities. It is forbidden to stand within four cubits of him, or to have commercial dealings with him. The term חֵרֶם is also used with reference to the consecration of articles for Temple or priestly use (Leviticus 27:28-29).

[1] שֶׁלֹּא נִיתְּנָה שִׁגְגָתָן לְכַפָּרָה. [2] מִיתוֹת קַלּוֹת, שֶׁנִּיתְּנָה שִׁגְגָתָן לְכַפָּרָה, מִנַּיִן? [3] תַּלְמוּד לוֹמַר: 'כָּל חֵרֶם'". [4] וְלָא מִמֵּילָא מִ"לֹּא תִקְחוּ כֹפֶר" שָׁמְעַתְּ מִינָּהּ: [5] לָא תִּשְׁקוֹל מָמוֹנָא מִינֵּיהּ וְתִיפְטְרֵיהּ? [6] "כָּל חֵרֶם" לָמָּה לִי?

LITERAL TRANSLATION

[1] the inadvertent committing of which is not subject to atonement. [2] From where [do we know about crimes punishable by] light deaths, the inadvertent committing of which is subject to atonement? [3] [Therefore] the verse states: 'Any condemned [person].'" [4] But can you not infer automatically from "you shall not take a ransom" [that] you shall not take money from him and exempt him [from execution]? [5] Why do I need [the expression]: [6] "Any condemned [person]"?

TRANSLATION AND COMMENTARY

severe crime, but one that is still subject to execution, may be permitted to ransom himself." [1] The Baraita explains: "A severe crime is a crime **which, if committed inadvertently, is not subject to atonement."** The Torah inflicts capital punishment only for crimes or sins committed deliberately. If a capital crime is committed inadvertently, there are some cases in which the Torah prescribes a form of atonement — such as a sacrifice (if, for example, a person violated Shabbat or committed adultery) or exile (in the case of murder). In other cases (like kidnapping) the Torah prescribes no atonement at all. The Baraita is of the opinion that transgressions that are not subject to atonement — like kidnapping — are more severe, in some sense, than transgressions — like Shabbat violation and murder — which are subject to atonement. [2] "So," continues the Baraita, **"from where** in the Torah **do we know** the law that someone who commits a **less severe crime,** but one that is **subject to execution, which if committed inadvertently is subject to atonement,** is not permitted to ransom himself?" [3] The Baraita answers: "It was for this reason that the Torah wrote the extra word "any" in **the verse** in Leviticus (27:29), to inform us that this law applies to *any* case of execution, **saying: 'Any condemned person.'"**

וְלָא מִמֵּילָא [4] **But,** the Gemara objects, **can we not infer automatically from** the verse in Numbers (35:31), **"You shall not take a ransom** for the life of a murderer," [5] **that you must not take money from** a murderer **and exempt him from being killed.** But surely murder is a "less severe" offense, which if committed inadvertently is subject to atonement through exile. We see that even those who commit "less severe" offenses must not be ransomed. Therefore this is certainly the case with "severe" offenses. [6] So **why do we need the expression "*any* condemned person"** at all?

RASHI

אלא מיתות חמורות שלא ניתנה שגגתן לכפרה — כיון דקרא לא פריש כל מיתות, מיסתייך אי שדית הך חומרא דאין ממונו מצילו אמיתות חמורות, ומאי נינהו — כגון העושה חבורה באביו, או גונב נפש מישראל. שאין כפרה כתובה בשגגתו, שאין כרת בזדונו דליחייב חטאת בשגגתו. **מיתות קלות** — היינו כל מיתות האמורות בהן כרת על זדונו בלא התראה — יש כפרה בשגגתה בחטאת, כגון עבודה זרה ושבת ועריות. אי נמי, רוצח — שיש כפרה לשגגתו בגלות. **ולא ממילא** — שמעת לה מ"לא תקחו כופר" הא גבי רוצח כתיבא, וניתנה כפרה לשגגתו, ואשמעינן קרא שלא יציל את עצמו בממון. ולמה לי תו "כל חרם"?

NOTES

מִיתוֹת חֲמוּרוֹת, שֶׁלֹּא נִיתְּנָה שִׁגְגָתָן לְכַפָּרָה **Severe deaths, the inadvertent committing of which is not subject to atonement.** In many places in the Talmud, the various capital offenses are listed in order of severity, and the criterion for determining severity varies with the context. In some places, the capital offenses are arranged in order of the severity of the form of execution that is meted out. In our context, however, this is apparently not a factor. Indeed, our Gemara considers the most serious offenses in the Torah to be "light" — for example, idol worship, adultery, incest, and (according to *Rashi*) murder.

Rashba explains that our Gemara is discussing whether to permit a condemned offender to escape execution by paying a ransom, and for this purpose the seriousness of the offense itself is of no consequence, so long as it is subject to the death penalty. However, when it is possible to atone for an inadvertent offense, this may possibly be considered a precedent for permitting atonement for the deliberate offense as well. But when it is not possible to atone for the inadvertent offense, there is no precedent for permitting atonement for the deliberate offense.

מִמֵּילָא **Automatically.** There are two basic explanations of this passage given by the Rishonim. Our commentary follows *Rashi*, who explains that murder is considered a "mild" offense, since its inadvertent form is subject to atonement through exile. According to this explanation, the Gemara objects that we see from the verse in Numbers (35:31), which deals with murder, that ransom is not accepted for even "mild" capital offenses. Why, then, do we need a verse to teach us that ransom is not accepted for

HALAKHAH

after the owner was warned, the Torah states: 'The ox shall be stoned and its owner too shall be put to death.' This verse is understood to be referring to death at the hands of Heaven, and not to execution by the court. But if the ox's owner pays a ransom, his sin is atoned and he is not executed." (*Rambam, Sefer Nezikin, Hilkhot Nizkei Mamon* 10:4.)

SAGES

רָמִי בַּר חָמָא Rami bar Ḥama. A Babylonian Amora of the fourth generation. See *Ketubot,* Part II, p. 57.

TRANSLATION AND COMMENTARY

אֲמַר רָמִי בַּר חָמָא [1]**Rami bar Ḥama said** in reply: **It was necessary** for the Torah to write the verse in Leviticus as well as the verse in Numbers, because not all types of inadvertent murder are subject to atonement through exile. [2]Thus, if we only had the verse in Numbers, **it might have entered our minds to say** [38A] [3]that the verse in Numbers prohibiting ransom **applies** only to "severe" deliberate murders, **which, if committed inadvertently, are not subject to atonement;** but we might have argued that those who commit a deliberate murder which, if committed inadvertently, is subject to atonement through exile *can* be ransomed. In fact, not every inadvertent killer is exiled. Exile is imposed only if the death was caused by an accident that could have been prevented with reasonable care, but not if the killer behaved recklessly, nor if the death was caused by an accident that could not have been prevented with reasonable care. In general, **if** one man **kills** another with an accidental blow **while "going up"** (with an upstroke of an axe, or while climbing up a ladder), he is not subject to exile, but if he kills him with a blow delivered on the way down, he is subject to exile (see detailed explanation above, 35a). Thus a murderer who deliberately kills someone with an upstroke of an axe has committed a "severe" capital crime, which, had it been committed inadvertently, would not be subject to atonement, whereas if he kills him with a downstroke, it is a "less severe" capital crime, which if committed inadvertently *is* subject to atonement. Thus we might have thought that the prohibition in the verse in Numbers against accepting a ransom from a killer applies only to "severe" killing, [4]**but if** one man **kills** another in a "less severe" way, **which if committed inadvertently is subject to atonement,** such as if he kills him **while "going down,"** [5]**I might say** that **we** are permitted to **take money from him and exempt him** from the death penalty, since the prohibition in the verse in Numbers does not apply to this case. [6]**Therefore,** the Torah needed to write the verse in Leviticus in order to **inform us that this is not so.** From the verse in Leviticus we learn that there is in fact no distinction between "severe" and "less severe" capital offenses, and it is not permitted to accept a ransom from anyone who has been condemned to death.

[1]אֲמַר רָמִי בַּר חָמָא: אִיצְטְרִיךְ. [2]סָלְקָא דַּעְתָּךְ אָמִינָא: [38A] [3]הָנֵי מִילֵּי הֵיכָא דַּהֲרָגוֹ דֶּרֶךְ עֲלִיָּיה, שֶׁלֹּא נִיתְּנָה שִׁגְגָתוֹ לְכַפָּרָה. [4]אֲבָל הֲרָגוֹ דֶּרֶךְ יְרִידָה, דְּנִיתְּנָה שִׁגְגָתוֹ לְכַפָּרָה, [5]אֵימָא: נִישְׁקוֹל מָמוֹנָא מִינֵּיהּ וְנִיפְטְרֵיהּ. [6]קָא מַשְׁמַע לָן.

LITERAL TRANSLATION

[1]Rami bar Ḥama said: It was necessary. [2][For] it might have entered your mind to say: [38A] [3]This applies (lit., "these words") where he killed him while going up, the inadvertent committing of which is not subject to atonement. [4]But [where] he killed him while going down, the inadvertent committing of which is subject to atonement, [5]I would say: Let us take money from him and exempt him. [6][Therefore] it informs us [that this is not so].

RASHI

הני מילי – ד״לא תקחו כופר״ לפטור רוצח מזיד מקטלא. **היכא דהרגו** – במזיד, דרך עלייה. בהנפת ידו הכהו מאחריו, דכוותה בשוגג לא ניתן לכפרת גלות, כדכתיב ״ויפל״ – דרך נפילה.

NOTES

"severe" capital offenses? From the fact that ransom is not accepted for "mild" offenses, it should follow logically that the same applies to "severe" offenses. The Gemara answers that murder includes both "mild" and "severe" varieties, and we might have thought that the verse in Numbers was referring only to the "severe" ones, were it not for the verse in Leviticus.

Tosafot points out that this explanation is difficult to accept, because the Baraita derived both the "severe" and the "mild" cases from the verse in Leviticus, using the superfluous word "any."

Ramban suggests that, according to the Gemara's conclusion, it was not necessary for the Torah to write the word "any." But since the Torah needed to write the verse in Leviticus to teach us that "mild" cases may also not be ransomed, it wrote it in a way that included both types of case.

Ra'ah and *Ritva* suggest that, according to the Gemara's conclusion, the case of killing by an upward movement is an intermediate offense that is neither "severe" nor "mild," since it is a form of murder — which in principle is subject to atonement — but is itself not subject to atonement. Thus, according to the Gemara's conclusion, we need the verse in Numbers, as well as the verse in Leviticus together with the superfluous word "any," to teach us that a ransom must not be paid — neither for "severe" cases, nor for killing by an upward movement, nor for "mild" cases.

HALAKHAH

הֵיכָא דַּהֲרָגוֹ דֶּרֶךְ עֲלִיָּיה Where he killed him while going up. "If someone kills a person accidentally while 'going up' — for example, if he kills him with an upstroke of an axe, or if he falls off a ladder while climbing up and kills someone — he is exempt from exile. For it is most unusual for someone to be killed this way, and the killer is not considered to have been negligent." (*Rambam, Sefer Nezikin, Hilkhot Rotze'aḥ* 6:12-13.)

TRANSLATION AND COMMENTARY

אֲמַר לֵיהּ רָבָא [1]**Rava said to** Rami bar Ḥama: We do not need the verse in Leviticus to teach us that there is no distinction between "severe" and "less severe" murders, [2]for we can **derive it from** the Baraita **taught by the School of Ḥizkiyah,** from which we have already learned (above, 35a) that inadvertent killers are exempt from damage payments. From this very Baraita we can learn that the same laws apply both to "severe" murders and to "less severe" murders, and there is no need to invoke the verse in Leviticus.[3] **For the School of Ḥizkiyah taught** a Baraita commenting on the following verse (Leviticus 24:21): "And he that strikes an animal shall pay for it, and he that strikes a man shall be put to death." [4]The Baraita states: "The verse places the law **regarding someone who strikes a person** in juxtaposition to the law regarding **someone who strikes an animal.** According to traditional hermeneutic rules, when the Torah juxtaposes two different laws in this way, it teaches us that they are subject to the same rules. Hence we apply the same rules to the penalty imposed on someone who kills an animal as we do to the penalty imposed on someone who kills another human being, and we say: [5]**In the case of someone who strikes an animal we make no distinction between** cases in which the act **was done inadvertently and** those in which it was done **deliberately,** for the Mishnah (*Bava Kamma* 26b) rules that damage done directly by a human being is always culpable, even if it was entirely accidental. [6]And likewise we make no distinction **between** cases in which the animal was struck **intentionally and** cases in which the assailant intended to strike another animal but **unintentionally** struck this one. [7]Likewise we make no distinction **between** cases in which the animal was killed **while** the man was **"going down"** (i.e., when the blow was such that if it had killed a human being accidentally, the killer would be sent into exile) **and** cases in which the animal was killed **while** the man was **"going up"** (when an accidental homicide would not be subject to atonement through exile). [8]**Just as** in all these cases we do not **exempt** the man **from paying money** for the animal if he was not at fault, **and we oblige him to pay money** in all cases, [9]**so too in the case of someone who strikes a person, we should make no distinction between** cases in which the act **was done inadvertently and** those in which it was done

[1]אֲמַר לֵיהּ רָבָא: [2]הָא מִדְּתַנָּא דְּבֵי חִזְקִיָּה נָפְקָא. [3]דְּתָנָא דְּבֵי חִזְקִיָּה: [4]״מַכֵּה אָדָם וּמַכֵּה בְהֵמָה, [5]מַה מַּכֵּה בְהֵמָה לֹא חִלַּקְתָּ בּוֹ בֵּין שׁוֹגֵג לְמֵזִיד, [6]בֵּין מִתְכַּוֵּין לְשֶׁאֵין מִתְכַּוֵּין, [7]בֵּין דֶּרֶךְ יְרִידָה לְדֶרֶךְ עֲלִיָּיה, [8]לְפוֹטְרוֹ מָמוֹן, אֶלָּא לְחַיְּיבוֹ מָמוֹן, [9]אַף מַכֵּה אָדָם לָא תַּחֲלוֹק בּוֹ בֵּין שׁוֹגֵג לְמֵזִיד,

LITERAL TRANSLATION

[1]Rava said to him: [2]This is derived from what was taught in the School of Ḥizkiyah. [3]For the School of Ḥizkiyah taught: [4]"[Regarding] someone who strikes a person and someone who strikes an animal, [5]just as [in the case of] someone who strikes an animal you made no distinction between [doing it] inadvertently and deliberately, [6]between [doing it] intentionally and unintentionally, [7]between [doing it] while going down and while going up, [8]in order to exempt him [from paying] money, but to oblige him [to pay] money, [9]so too [in the case of] someone who strikes a person you should make no distinction between [doing it] inadvertently and deliberately,

RASHI

מדתנא דבי חזקיה נפקא – שאין חילוק בין דרך עלייה לדרך ירידה. **לחייבו ממון** – והוא הדין לפדותו, ו״לא יהיה אסון״ מיהא איצטריך, דאי מהיקישא הוה אמינא: אדרבה, לאידך גיסא: מה מכה בהמה – לעולם ישלם, אף מכה אדם – ישלם. והשתא דנפקא לן עכו׳ תשלומין למזיד מ״לא יהיה אסון״ על כרחך היקישא לפטור שוגג דרך עלייה.

NOTES

אֲמַר לֵיהּ רָבָא: הָא מִדְּתַנָּא דְּבֵי חִזְקִיָּה נָפְקָא Rava said to him: This is derived from what was taught in the School of Ḥizkiyah. Our commentary follows *Rashi,* who explains that the Baraita taught in the School of Ḥizkiyah is referring to the case of an inadvertent killer who incurs a damage payment at the same time (as explained above, 35a). According to *Rashi,* Rava's extrapolation from the Baraita's argument is as follows: Just as monetary penalties (i.e., incidental damage payments) may not be imposed *in addition to* the death penalty, regardless of whether the killing was deliberate or inadvertent, or done while "going up" or while "going down," so too monetary penalties (i.e., a ransom) may not be imposed *in lieu of* the death penalty, regardless of whether the killing was deliberate or inadvertent, or done while "going up" or while "going down."

Ramban asks: Since the Baraita's argument from juxtaposition applies only to damage payments, how can Rava extrapolate from the Baraita that we do not accept a ransom paid in lieu of the death penalty? What parallel is there between the ransom that we must not accept from a murderer and a monetary penalty that is demanded of the killer of an animal? *Ramban* answers that Rava is arguing that just as in the case of the animal, there is only one (monetary) penalty and no other penalty applies, so too in the case of murder there is only one (non-monetary) penalty, and no other penalty applies.

Ramban objects further: If the Baraita teaches us that no other penalty can be substituted in the case of a murderer,

[1]בֵּין מִתְכַּוֵּין לְשֶׁאֵין מִתְכַּוֵּין,
[2]בֵּין דֶּרֶךְ יְרִידָה לְדֶרֶךְ עֲלִיָּה,
[3]לְחַיְּיבוֹ מָמוֹן, אֶלָּא לְפוֹטְרוֹ
מָמוֹן".
[4]אֶלָּא אֲמַר רָמִי בַּר חָמָא:
אִיצְטְרִיךְ. [5]סָלְקָא דַּעְתָּךְ
אָמִינָא: הָנֵי מִילֵּי הֵיכָא דְּסִימֵּא
אֶת עֵינוֹ וַהֲרָגוֹ בָּהּ. [6]אֲבָל
הֵיכָא דְּסִימֵּא אֶת עֵינוֹ וַהֲרָגוֹ
בְּדָבָר אַחֵר, [7]אֵימָא: נִישְׁקוֹל
מָמוֹנָא מִינֵּיהּ.

LITERAL TRANSLATION

[1]between [doing it] intentionally and unintentionally, [2]between [doing it] while going down and while going up, [3]in order to oblige him [to pay] money, but to exempt him [from paying] money."

[4]Rather, Rami bar Ḥama said: It was necessary. [5][For] it might have entered your mind to say: This applies where he blinded his eye and killed him through it. [6]But where he blinded his eye and killed him by something else, [7]I would say: Let us take money from him.

RASHI

הכי גרסינן: אלא אמר רמי בר חמא כו׳ — איצטריך חד מהני קראי, לאשמועינן דלא ליעביד ביה תרתי, ואף על גב דנפקא לן מ"ולא יהיה אסון". הני מילי — דלא ענשינן ליה בתרתי — היכא דסימא את עינו והרגו בה באותה מכה ומת. בדבר אחר — במכה אחרת ובבת אחת. אימא — ניענשיה דמי עין, ומיתה בשביל ההריגה.

TRANSLATION AND COMMENTARY

deliberately. [1]Nor should we make a distinction **between** cases in which the person who was killed was struck **intentionally and** cases in which the assailant intended to strike another person but **unintentionally** struck this one. [2]Moreover, we should make no distinction **between** cases in which the person was killed **while** his killer was **"going down"** — in which case the killer is sent into exile for his negligence — **and** cases in which the person was killed **while** his killer was **"going up,"** in which case the killer was not even negligent and is not required to go into exile. [3]In all these cases we should not argue that the killer should be **obliged to pay** any sort of **monetary** penalty, either ransom or a damage payment, **and we must exempt him from paying money** in all cases." Rava argues that just as there is no distinction with regard to the monetary penalty imposed for killing an animal between a case in which the man killed it "going up" and a case in which he killed it "going down," there should likewise be no distinction with regard to the monetary penalty that must not be imposed for killing a person — the ransom — between a case in which one man killed another while "going up" and a case in which one man killed another while "going down." Thus we do not need the additional verse in Leviticus to inform us that a ransom must not be taken for a "less severe" murder.

אֶלָּא אֲמַר [4]**Rather, Rami bar Ḥama said:** According to Rabbi Ḥananya ben Akavya, the extra verse about ransom in Leviticus is indeed not needed in order to inform us that we do not accept a ransom, nor is it teaching us that a condemned criminal cannot be assessed, but **it is** still **necessary** in order to inform us that when an offense is subject to both the death penalty and a monetary penalty, the offender is always exempt from payment. For we have learned from the case of the pregnant woman that if the assailant killed the woman with the same blow that caused her to miscarry, he is exempt from paying compensation for the miscarriage. [5]But were it not for the verse in Leviticus, **it might have entered our minds to say** that the law we learned from the case of the pregnant woman **applies** only **where** one action incurred both the death penalty and a damage payment, such as a case in which the assailant struck a single blow which **blinded** the other person's **eye and killed him.** In such a case, the assailant is exempt from paying damages for the eye, just as an assailant is exempt from paying damages for the miscarriage if he killed a pregnant woman with the same blow that caused her to miscarry. [6]**But if he** committed two separate actions, one of which incurred the death penalty and the other a damage payment, such as a case in which he struck two blows, one of which **blinded** the other person's **eye,** while the other **killed him,** we cannot infer from the case of the pregnant woman that he is exempt from paying damages. [7]Rather, were it not for the verse in Leviticus, **I would have said** that **we should take money from him** to pay for the eye, even though he is subject to the death penalty.

NOTES

why do we need the verses in Numbers from which we learned that a ransom is not paid? *Ramban* replies that if the only guidance we had was the juxtaposition argument of the Baraita, we would have argued that a ransom *should* be paid, just as a damage payment is paid for a dead animal. But now that we have learned that a ransom may not be paid — at least in the "severe" cases — we can infer from the Baraita that the same applies to "less severe" cases as well. (*Rashi* also appears to explain the Baraita this way.)

TRANSLATION AND COMMENTARY

אָמַר לֵיהּ רָבָא [1]But **Rava** then **said to** Rami bar Ḥama: We do not need a special verse to teach us **this** law, because **this** law **too can be derived from another** Baraita **taught in the School of Ḥizkiyah.** [2]**For the School of Ḥizkiyah taught** the following Baraita. The Baraita is commenting on the verse (Exodus 21:24): **"An eye for an eye,"** from which we learn that an assailant must pay damages for the wounds he inflicts on another person. The Baraita explains how we know that this verse is not to be interpreted literally as commanding us to put out the eye of the assailant. [3]The Baraita argues as follows: "The verse authorizes us to take an eye from the assailant in exchange for the eye he put out, **but** it does **not** authorize us to take **an eye** *and* **a life for the eye** he put out. If the verse were to be interpreted literally, and we were to put out his eye, there would sometimes be cases in which putting out his eye might lead to his death. Thus the Torah must be understood as referring to monetary compensation equal in value to the eye that was put out, and this compensation can indeed be taken from the assailant without endangering his life." Now, says Rava, we can also apply the Baraita's reasoning to the exemption from a less severe penalty if a person is subject to a more severe penalty. For just as we are not authorized to take a man's life together with his eye, we are likewise not authorized to take his eye together with his life. In other words, we are permitted to demand compensation for the eye he put out only if we do not execute him, and no distinction is made between cases in which the victim's eye was put out by the same blow as the one that killed him or by a different blow. Thus we see that the law that a person who is subject to a more severe penalty is exempt from payment applies to all cases. So the verse in Leviticus is not needed to teach us this law, as Rami bar Ḥama suggested. What, then, do we learn from the verse in Leviticus, according to Rabbi Ḥananya ben Akavya, who maintains that it is not teaching us about assessment?

אֶלָּא אֲמַר [4]**Rather, Rav Ashi said:** According to Rabbi Ḥananya ben Akavya, the verse in Leviticus is indeed not needed to teach us that we do not accept a ransom, nor is it teaching us that a condemned criminal must not be assessed, but **it is** still **necessary** in order to inform us that when an offense is subject both to the death penalty and to a punitive damage payment, the offender is exempt from payment. For we learn from the case of the pregnant woman that if the assailant killed the woman at the same time

[1]אֲמַר לֵיהּ רָבָא: הָא נַמִי מֵאִידָךְ תַּנָּא דְּבֵי חִזְקִיָּה נָפְקָא. [2]דְּתָנָא דְּבֵי חִזְקִיָּה: "'עַיִן תַּחַת עַיִן', [3]וְלֹא עַיִן וְנֶפֶשׁ תַּחַת עַיִן". [4]אֶלָּא אֲמַר רַב אַשִׁי: אִיצְטְרִיךְ.

LITERAL TRANSLATION

[1]Rava said to him: This too is derived from another [statement] taught in the School of Ḥizkiyah. [2]For the School of Ḥizkiyah taught: "'An eye for an eye,' [3]but not an eye and a life for an eye."

[4]Rather, Rav Ashi said: It was necessary.

RASHI

הא — דסימא עינו והרגו בה. מאידך דבי חזקיה נפקא — דלא תיענשיה. ולא עין ונפש תחת עין — מייה קיימא לן ב"החובל" ד"עין תחת עין" לאו ממש. דאי אמרת ממש — דלמא בהדי דסמינן לעיניה מיית, והוה ליה עין ונפש תחת עין. מיהו, שמעינן מינה דלא תעביד ביה תרתי, לא שנא מת באותה מכה לא שנא לא מת.

NOTES

"עַיִן תַּחַת עַיִן", וְלֹא עַיִן וְנֶפֶשׁ תַּחַת עַיִן **"An eye for an eye," but not an eye and a life for an eye.** It is not entirely clear how the Gemara applies this Baraita to prove that an assailant who blinds someone with one blow and at the same time kills him with another is exempt from payment, and several explanations are given by the Rishonim. *Rashi* explains that the Gemara is proving from this Baraita that an assailant who kills someone and blinds him with the *same* blow is exempt from payment; hence the verse dealing with the pregnant woman is available to teach us that he is exempt even if the damage was not done by the same blow. *Rashi* explains that the Gemara's argument is that we see from the Baraita that we may never impose two penalties if an assailant puts out someone's eye, and this is true even if the victim was killed by the very blow that put out his eye. Hence we always impose only one penalty, and if the victim is killed, we kill the assailant, and if he is injured, we make the assailant pay damages (see also *Ra'ah*, *Shittah Mekubbetzet*).

Ritva explains that Rava is not inferring this law directly from the Baraita, but is rather extrapolating from the Baraita's argument. Just as the Baraita interprets the first "eye" in the phrase, "an eye for an eye," to mean "an eye and not a life and an eye," we may likewise interpret the second "eye," and say: "An eye for an eye, and not an eye for a life and an eye." The verse teaches us, therefore, that compensation for the eye is paid only if the victim was not killed. *Ritva* notes that some versions of the Talmud have a reading that explicitly supports this explanation.

Our commentary follows *Tosafot*, who explains that Rava is extrapolating a different point from the Baraita's argument. Just as the Baraita explained "an eye for an eye" to mean "an eye and nothing else," we may likewise interpret the next words in the verse, "a life for a life," to mean a life and nothing else. Thus we see that one person who kills another must give his life, but need not pay compensation for any other damage he caused at the same time, even if the damage was done by a separate blow.

אֶלָּא אֲמַר רַב אַשִׁי **Rather, Rav Ashi said.** According to Rav Ashi, the rule that the death penalty exempts from regular damage payments is inferred from the verse dealing with the pregnant woman, but the rule that the death penalty exempts from fines is inferred from the verse in Leviticus: "Any condemned person, etc." The Rishonim ask:

[1]סָלְקָא דַּעְתָּךְ אָמִינָא: [2]הוֹאִיל וְחִידּוּשׁ הוּא שֶׁחִידְּשָׁה תּוֹרָה בִּקְנָס, [3]אַף עַל גַּב דְּמִיקְּטִיל, מְשַׁלֵּם. [4]קָא מַשְׁמַע לָן.
[5]וּלְרַבָּה דַּאֲמַר: [6]חִידּוּשׁ הוּא שֶׁחִידְּשָׁה תּוֹרָה בִּקְנָס, [7]אַף עַל גַּב דְּמִיקְטִיל, מְשַׁלֵּם, [8]הַאי "כָּל חֵרֶם" מַאי עָבֵיד לֵיהּ?
[9]סָבַר לָהּ כְּתַנָּא קַמָּא דְּרַבִּי חֲנַנְיָא בֶּן עֲקַבְיָא.

LITERAL TRANSLATION

[1][For] it might have entered your mind to say: [2]Since it is an innovation that the Torah established regarding a fine, [3]although he is killed, he pays. [4][Therefore] it informs us [that this is not so].

[5]But according to Rabbah who said: [6]It is an innovation that the Torah established regarding a fine, [7][and therefore] although he is killed, he pays, [8]what does he do with this [expression], "any condemned [person]"?

[9]He agrees with the first Tanna of Rabbi Ḥananya ben Akavya.

TRANSLATION AND COMMENTARY

as he caused her to miscarry, he is exempt from paying for the miscarriage. [1]But were it not for the verse in Leviticus, **it might have entered our minds to say** that the law we learn from the case of the pregnant woman applies only to regular damage payments. But when an offense is subject to both the death penalty and a fine, we would not have applied the regular law, [2]**because fines are an innovation that the Torah established.** Normally, damage payments correspond to the loss suffered by the victim. But fines do not correspond to the loss suffered by the victim. Rather, they are imposed in order to punish the offender for his behavior, and this is an innovation that departs from the general practice of the Torah. Now, whenever the Torah states a novel requirement that is not consistent with the other laws of the Torah, we cannot assume that the regular laws apply, unless the Torah explicitly states that they do. Hence, in the case of fines imposed by the Torah as punishment in addition to normal damage payments (including the fines imposed on rapists and seducers discussed by our Mishnah), we might have thought that the rule that an offender who is subject to the death penalty is exempt from monetary payments does not apply, [3]and **even though** the offender **is killed, he must pay** the fine as well. [4]**Accordingly,** the Torah wrote the verse in Leviticus to **inform us that this is not so,** and that an offender who is subject to the death penalty is exempt from all monetary penalties, including fines.

וּלְרַבָּה דַּאֲמַר [5]**But,** the Gemara objects, **according to Rabbah, who said** (above, 34b) that even though an offender who is subject to the death penalty is exempt from regular damage payments, nevertheless if he raped his daughter or slaughtered a stolen animal on Shabbat, [6]he is punished with both penalties because **fines are an innovation that the Torah established** (as we explained above), how can we explain the verse in Leviticus? It cannot be informing us that the death penalty exempts from paying fines, because Rabbah is of the opinion that an offender who commits an offense that is subject both to the death penalty [7]and to a fine **pays** the fine **even though he is killed.** [8]So **what use does** Rabbah **make of the** verse in Leviticus that contains the **expression: "Any condemned person"?**

סָבַר לָהּ [9]The Gemara answers: Rabbah **agrees with the first Tanna** in **Rabbi Ḥananya ben Akavya's** Mishnah. Rabbah agrees with the anonymous first Tanna in the Mishnah in tractate *Arakhin* (6b), who disagrees with Rabbi Ḥananya ben Akavya, and maintains that a person who assesses the value of a condemned criminal does not pay the assessment to the Temple. We have seen above (37b) that this opinion is based on an interpretation of the verse in Leviticus. Hence the Tanna who disagrees with Rabbi Ḥananya ben Akavya is of the opinion that the verse in Leviticus is needed to teach us this law and is thus not available to teach us that the death penalty exempts from fines. On the basis of this opinion, Rabbah can argue that in fact a person subject to the death penalty is exempt only from regular damage payments, but not from fines.

RASHI

סלקא דעתך אמינא חידוש הוא שחידשה תורה — בכל תשלומי קנס, שאינו דין אלא גזרת מלך בעלמא, וכיון דחידוש הוא וגזירת חוק — אימא אף על גב דאיכא בהדיה מיתה — לשלם. **קא משמע לן** — חד מהנך קראי יתירא שאינו ענין לממון, תניהו ענין לקנס. **כתנא קמא** — ודריש ליה באומר "ערכו של יוצא ליהרג עלי".

NOTES

Our Mishnah (above, 36b) cites the verse dealing with the pregnant woman to prove that a man who rapes or seduces his daughter is exempt from paying, because he is subject to the death penalty. But the payment made by a rapist or a seducer is a fine. Why, then, according to Rav Ashi, did the Mishnah cite the verse dealing with the pregnant woman rather than the verse from Leviticus?

Tosafot answers that our Mishnah wished to include in its ruling all cases in which the death penalty exempts from payment, even if the monetary penalty is a regular damage payment and not a fine. *Maharam Schiff* adds that the rapist in our Mishnah is also exempt from paying for the *na'arah*'s lost virginity and lost reputation, and these are regular damage payments.

LITERAL TRANSLATION

MISHNAH [1] [Regarding] a *na'arah* who was betrothed and was divorced, [2] Rabbi Yose HaGelili says: She does not have a fine. [3] Rabbi Akiva says: She does have a fine, [4] and her fine [belongs] to her.

GEMARA [5] What is Rabbi Yose HaGelili's reason?

משנה [1] נַעֲרָה שֶׁנִּתְאָרְסָה וְנִתְגָּרְשָׁה, [2] רַבִּי יוֹסֵי הַגְּלִילִי אוֹמֵר: אֵין לָהּ קְנָס. [3] רַבִּי עֲקִיבָא אוֹמֵר: יֵשׁ לָהּ קְנָס, [4] וּקְנָסָהּ לְעַצְמָהּ.

גמרא [5] מַאי טַעֲמָא דְּרַבִּי יוֹסֵי הַגְּלִילִי?

RASHI

משנה שנתארסה ונתגרשה — דאילו ארוסה שלא נתגרשה חייב מיתה, ואין שם קנס. **אין לה קנס** — טעמא מפרש בגמרא. ורישא דקתני אשת אחיו ואשת אחי אביו דנתארסה ונתגרשה עסקינן, וקתני יש להן קנס — רבי עקיבא היא.

TRANSLATION AND COMMENTARY

MISHNAH נַעֲרָה [1] This Mishnah deals with the case of **a *na'arah* who was betrothed and was divorced.** In Jewish law, entry into marriage consists of two stages. After the first stage, called *kiddushin* ("betrothal"), the marriage is legally binding and cannot be dissolved without a bill of divorce. A betrothed woman who engages in extramarital intercourse is guilty of adultery. During the period of her betrothal, the bride lives apart from her husband, and their separation lasts until the second stage of marriage, *nissu'in*, when the marriage is consummated. If the husband dies or divorces his wife before the second stage of the marriage, she is considered a widow or a divorcee in certain respects (for example, if she was divorced, she is forbidden to marry a priest), but for most monetary purposes she is treated like a woman who has never been married. Thus she is considered a virgin, and is entitled to a full ketubah from her second husband (above, 10b), and if she is still a minor or a *na'arah*, her father is entitled to all the normal monetary prerogatives enjoyed by the father of a minor or a *na'arah* (below, 46b). Accordingly, if a virgin *na'arah* was betrothed and then divorced or widowed before *nissui'in*, and was subsequently raped or seduced, is she entitled to a fine, like a virgin *na'arah* who has never been married? Or is she not entitled to a fine, like a regular widow or divorcee? [2] **Rabbi Yose HaGelili says: She is not entitled to a fine.** Even though for most monetary purposes a virgin *na'arah* who was betrothed and divorced is treated like a virgin *na'arah* who has never been married, the rapist's fine is an exception. For the Torah specifically states that the fine has to be paid only if the virgin *na'arah* was not yet betrothed (Deuteronomy 22:28), but if she was already betrothed, this law does not apply at all. [3] **Rabbi Akiva says: She is entitled to a fine,** since a virgin *na'arah* who was betrothed and divorced is generally treated like a virgin *na'arah* who has never been married. And as for the Torah's requirement that the law applies only if the virgin *na'arah* was not yet betrothed, we interpret this narrowly as referring not to the entire law of the rapist's fine, but only to the requirement that the fine be paid to the *na'arah*'s father. Hence, although other financial benefits received by a minor or by a *na'arah* are the property of the father, even if his daughter was betrothed and divorced, [4] **the fine** paid by the rapist is not paid to the divorcee's father. Rather, it **is paid to the *na'arah* herself.**

GEMARA מַאי טַעֲמָא [5] The Gemara asks: **What is Rabbi Yose HaGelili's reason** for ruling that a betrothed and divorced *na'arah* who is later raped is not entitled to a fine?

SAGES

רַבִּי יוֹסֵי הַגְּלִילִי Rabbi Yose HaGelili. He was a Tanna of the generation following the destruction of the Second Temple, and is not to be confused with Rabbi Yose (ben Ḥalafta), a distinguished scholar of the following generation. We do not know who the teachers of Rabbi Yose HaGelili were, but when he arrived at Yavneh he was already an important Sage. We find him in the company of Rabbi Akiva, Rabbi Tarfon, and Rabbi Elazar ben Azaryah. On several occasions he disagrees with Rabbi Akiva, who treated him with great respect. Rabbi Akiva's students also regarded Rabbi Yose HaGelili as a great man capable of disagreeing with Rabbi Akiva on Halakhic matters. He applied special exegetical methods to the study of Halakhah. These methods were not unanimously accepted, but his views were followed where he lived. Most of the teachings cited in his name are Halakhic, but he was also the author of many Aggadic teachings. The Talmud in several places speaks of his virtues, especially in his relations with his fellowman, and also of his great righteousness.

Two of his sons, Rabbi Eliezer and Rabbi Ḥanina, were Sages in the following generation.

NOTES

נַעֲרָה שֶׁנִּתְאָרְסָה וְנִתְגָּרְשָׁה A *na'arah* who was betrothed and was divorced. The Mishnah deals explicitly only with a *na'arah* who was betrothed and divorced before she was raped. But from the language of the Mishnah it is not clear to what extent the dispute between Rabbi Akiva and Rabbi Yose HaGelili applies to a *na'arah* who was betrothed and widowed.

Shittah Mekubbetzet explains that Rabbi Yose HaGelili disagrees with Rabbi Akiva about this case as well. Thus the dispute in our Mishnah applies both to a betrothed *na'arah* who was widowed and to a betrothed *na'arah* who was divorced. Support for this view can be found in the *Sifrei*'s comment on Deuteronomy 22:28.

HALAKHAH

נַעֲרָה שֶׁנִּתְאָרְסָה וְנִתְגָּרְשָׁה A *na'arah* who was betrothed and was divorced. "A betrothed *na'arah* who was divorced before marriage, and who was subsequently raped while still a *na'arah*, is entitled to the fine, like any other virgin *na'arah*. The fine is paid to the *na'arah* herself, following Rabbi Akiva's ruling in the Mishnah. *Kesef Mishneh* explains that the Halakhah generally follows Rabbi Akiva when he disagrees with an individual Tanna.

"Regarding the compensation for pain, lost reputation, and lost virginity, there is a dispute among the authorities. *Rambam* rules that only the fine is paid to the *na'arah*, but these other payments are paid to her father, just like any other monetary benefit she receives while she is still a *na'arah*. *Kesef Mishneh* notes, however, that *Rosh* rules that the compensation for pain, lost reputation, and lost virginity is paid to the *na'arah* herself, together with the fine." (*Rambam, Sefer Nashim, Hilkhot Na'arah Betulah* 2:16.)

[1]אָמַר קְרָא: ״אֲשֶׁר לֹא אֹרָשָׂה״. [2]הָא אוֹרָסָה, אֵין לָהּ קְנָס. [3]וְרַבִּי עֲקִיבָא? [4]״אֲשֶׁר לֹא אֹרָשָׂה״, לְאָבִיהָ. [5]הָא אֹרָסָה, לְעַצְמָהּ. [6]אֶלָּא מֵעַתָּה, ״נַעֲרָה״ — וְלֹא בּוֹגֶרֶת — [7]הָכִי נַמִי דִּלְעַצְמָהּ? [8]״בְּתוּלָה״ — וְלֹא בְּעוּלָה — [9]הָכִי נַמִי דִּלְעַצְמָהּ? [10]אֶלָּא, לְגַמְרֵי. [11]הָכָא נַמִי לְגַמְרֵי!

LITERAL TRANSLATION

[1]The verse said: "Who has not been betrothed." [2]This [means that if] she has been betrothed, she does not have a fine.

[3]And Rabbi Akiva?

[4][In the case of a *na'arah*] "who has not been betrothed," [the fine belongs] to her father. [5]This [means that if] she has been betrothed, [it belongs] to her.

[6]But if so, does [the expression] "a *na'arah*" — [implying] but not an adult — [7]also [mean] that [the fine belongs] to her [the adult]? [8]Does [the expression] "a virgin" — [implying] but not a woman who has had intercourse — [9]also [mean] that [the fine belongs] to her [the non-virgin]? [10]Rather, [it means that they are] completely [excluded]. [11]Here too [they should be] completely [excluded]!

TRANSLATION AND COMMENTARY

אָמַר קְרָא [1]The Gemara answers: **The verse said** (Deuteronomy 22:28-29): "If a man finds a virgin *na'arah* **who has not been betrothed,** and seizes her and lies with her, and they are found, then the man who lay with her shall give to the father of the *na'arah* fifty pieces of silver." [2]**This implies that** the fine is paid only if the *na'arah* was not yet betrothed when the rape took place, but **if she was betrothed, she is not entitled to a fine,** even if she was divorced.

וְרַבִּי עֲקִיבָא [3]The Gemara asks: **And** how does **Rabbi Akiva** explain away the fact that the verse uses the expression, "who has not been betrothed"?

אֲשֶׁר לֹא אֹרָשָׂה [4]The Gemara answers: Admittedly, the verse stipulates that the law applies only **if the *na'arah* "has not been betrothed,"** and in such a case **the fine belongs to her father.** [5]**This means that if she has been betrothed,** the regular law does not apply. It does not follow, however, that the fine is not paid at all, as Rabbi Yose HaGelili claims. In fact, we interpret the Torah's stipulation that the fine for the rape of an unbetrothed *na'arah* is to be paid to the girl's father as limiting the father's right to the fine to the specific situation of an unbetrothed *na'arah*. But if the *na'arah* has been betrothed and then divorced the fine **is paid to** the *na'arah* **herself,** unlike other financial benefits accruing to a betrothed and then divorced *na'arah*, all of which are paid to her father.

אֶלָּא מֵעַתָּה [6]The Gemara objects to this way of interpreting the verse: **But if** we accept this form of interpretation, we are faced with problems in other verses in this passage. For example, the Torah stipulates that the raped woman must be a *na'arah*, and **from this we infer** that she may **not** be **an adult.** [7]**Does the expression *"na'arah"* also mean that** if the raped woman was an adult, **the fine is paid to the adult** woman **herself** rather than to her father? [8]Similarly, the Torah stipulates that the raped woman must be a virgin, **and from this we infer** that she may **not** be **a woman who has** already **had intercourse. Does the expression "a virgin"** [9]**also mean that** if the raped woman was not a virgin, **the fine is paid to the non-virgin herself** rather than to her father? [10]**Rather,** we interpret these verses literally — as **meaning** that adult women and non-virgins **are completely excluded** from this law, and are not entitled to any fine at all. [11]**Here too,** in the case of the betrothed and divorced *na'arah*, we should interpret the verse literally and say that **she is completely excluded** from this law, and is not entitled to any fine at all. Why does Rabbi Akiva not interpret this verse straightforwardly?

RASHI

גמרא אלא מעתה — לרבי עקיבא, הא דכתיב ״נערה״ למעוטי בוגרת, ו״בתולה״ למעוטי בעולה. הכי נמי — דלא ממעט לגמרי, ותדרוש: נערה — לאביה, הא בוגרת — לעצמה. הא לא אשכחן דאישתמיט תנא ומתני בוגרת יש לה קנס, ונימא רבי עקיבא היא.

NOTES

אֶלָּא מֵעַתָּה, ״נַעֲרָה״ — וְלֹא בּוֹגֶרֶת **But if so, does the expression "a *na'arah*" — implying but not an adult.** *Rashi* raises the following problem: The Gemara is asking why Rabbi Akiva did not interpret the Torah's stipulations that the raped girl must be a *na'arah* and a virgin in the same way that he interpreted the Torah's stipulation that the *na'arah* must not be betrothed — as teaching us that the fine is to be paid to the girl herself rather than to her father. But how does the Gemara know that Rabbi Akiva does not interpret these stipulations this way? Perhaps Rabbi Akiva maintains that a man who rapes an adult woman or a non-virgin pays a fine to the woman herself!

Rashi explains that this would have been such a radical departure from the accepted Halakhah that it would have been impossible for it to have remained unmentioned.

[1]אָמַר לָךְ רַבִּי עֲקִיבָא: [2]הַאי "לֹא אֹרָשָׂה" [3]מִיבָּעֵי לֵיהּ לְכִדְתַנְיָא: [4]"'אֲשֶׁר לֹא אֹרָשָׂה' — פְּרָט לְנַעֲרָה שֶׁנִּתְאָרְסָה וְנִתְגָּרְשָׁה, [5]שֶׁאֵין לָהּ קְנָס. [6]דִּבְרֵי רַבִּי יוֹסֵי הַגְּלִילִי. [7]רַבִּי עֲקִיבָא אוֹמֵר: יֵשׁ לָהּ קְנָס, [8]וּקְנָסָהּ לְאָבִיהָ. [9]וְהַדִּין נוֹתֵן: [10]הוֹאִיל וְאָבִיהָ זַכַּאי בְּכֶסֶף קִידּוּשֶׁיהָ, וְאָבִיהָ זַכַּאי בְּכֶסֶף

LITERAL TRANSLATION

[1]Rabbi Akiva can say to you: [2]This [expression] "has not been betrothed" [3]is needed for what was taught: [4]"'Who has not been betrothed' — to exclude a *na'arah* who was betrothed and was divorced, [5]who does not have a fine. [6][These are] the words of Rabbi Yose HaGelili. [7]Rabbi Akiva says: She has a fine, [8]and her fine [belongs] to her father. [9]And the logic is (lit., 'gives'): [10]Since her father is entitled to the money of her betrothal, and her father is entitled to the money

TRANSLATION AND COMMENTARY

אָמַר לָךְ [1]The Gemara replies: **Rabbi Akiva can say to you:** Normally, we would not interpret a verse in this way. [2]However, **this expression,** "who **has not been betrothed,"** was not intended to exclude a betrothed woman from the law. [3]Rather, it **is needed for** the law **that was taught** in the following Baraita (an expanded version of our Mishnah, including Scriptural exegesis). Hence we cannot use it to exclude betrothed women from the application of this law, and we can apply its plain meaning only in a restricted sense — to teach us that the fine is paid to the girl herself rather than to her father. (The Baraita presents a version of Rabbi Akiva's viewpoint that differs substantially from the version presented in our Mishnah, a problem which will be considered by the Gemara below.) [4]The Baraita states: "We learn from the expression, **'who has not been betrothed,'** that **a *na'arah* who was betrothed and was divorced is excluded** from the purview of this law, [5]and **is not entitled to a fine** at all. [6]**This is the opinion of Rabbi Yose HaGelili.** [7]**Rabbi Akiva says:** This *na'arah* **is entitled to a fine,** just like a *na'arah* who has never been betrothed, for reasons which will be explained below. [8]Moreover, says Rabbi Akiva, **her fine is paid to her father**, just like the fine of a *na'arah* who has never been betrothed, because there is no difference between a *na'arah* who has been betrothed and divorced and a *na'arah* who has never been betrothed at all." (This latter point conflicts with the version of Rabbi Akiva's viewpoint given in our Mishnah.) [9]The Baraita explains the reasoning underlying Rabbi Akiva's last statement: **"And logic dictates** that this is so. The Torah requires that all monetary benefits accruing to an unmarried *na'arah* should be paid to her father. [10]In particular, **her father is entitled to the money of her betrothal, and her father is entitled to the money of her fine.** One of the ways in which betrothal, the first stage of the marriage process, can be effected is by the bridegroom giving the bride money or an object

RASHI

וקנסה לאביה — ולקמן מקשינן דרבי עקיבא אדרבי עקיבא. **הואיל ואביה זכאי בכסף קידושיה** — שלו הוא בנערותה. ולקמן יליף לה בפרק "נערה שנתפתתה" (מו,ב).

NOTES

הַאי "לֹא אֹרָשָׂה" מִיבָּעֵי לֵיהּ לְכִדְתַנְיָא **This expression "has not been betrothed" is needed for what was taught.** The commentators have great difficulty explaining this passage. The Gemara explains that Rabbi Akiva's ruling in the Mishnah is based on a peculiar interpretation of the Torah's stipulation that the *na'arah* must not be betrothed. Rabbi Akiva argues that the verse should not be interpreted as altogether denying the fine to a betrothed *na'arah* but rather as teaching us that the fine is paid to the girl herself instead of to her father. And the Gemara explains that Rabbi Akiva does not interpret this stipulation literally because he needs this expression to construct the *gezerah shavah* presented in the Baraita. But surely, if Rabbi Akiva learns anything at all from this expression, it is no longer available to construct a *gezerah shavah*! And if he can construct a *gezerah shavah* even after learning from the expression that the fine is not paid to the betrothed *na'arah*'s father, why does he not interpret it literally as teaching us that the fine is not paid at all?

There are several explanations of this passage in the Rishonim. Our commentary follows *Rosh*, who explains that the expression "who has not been betrothed" is not in fact the source of Rabbi Akiva's ruling in the Mishnah that a betrothed and divorced *na'arah* receives the fine herself. Rabbi Akiva, as quoted in the Mishnah, argues that we know automatically that the fine is paid to the betrothed and divorced *na'arah* herself rather than to her father, and even though that law is not derived from this expression, we may interpret the expression in its plain meaning as referring to this law.

הוֹאִיל וְאָבִיהָ זַכַּאי בְּכֶסֶף קִידּוּשֶׁיהָ **Since her father is entitled to the money of her betrothal.** The Mishnah (*Kiddushin* 2a) rules that betrothal can be effected only through an act of acquisition. There are three possible acts of acquisition

HALAKHAH

הוֹאִיל וְאָבִיהָ זַכַּאי בְּכֶסֶף קִידּוּשֶׁיהָ **Since her father is entitled to the money of her betrothal.** "A father may marry off his daughter as long as she is a minor or a *na'arah*, and he may keep the betrothal money for himself. If she was betrothed, but not married, and was subsequently divorced or widowed, the father retains the authority to marry her off to someone else and to receive her betrothal money as long as she is still a *na'arah*." (*Rambam, Sefer Nashim, Hilkhot Ishut* 3:11.)

TRANSLATION AND COMMENTARY

of value and declaring that this payment is for the purpose of effecting a betrothal (*Kiddushin* 2a). As long as the girl is a *na'arah* and her father is alive, her father is entitled to marry her off to whomever he pleases, and the betrothal money is paid to him. Thus we see that before the *na'arah* is betrothed both betrothal money and the *na'arah*'s fine are paid to the father. [1]Now, if a *na'arah* was betrothed and divorced and subsequently remarried while still a *na'arah*, the **betrothal money is paid to her father, even though she has** already **been betrothed and divorced,** because in this regard a girl who is divorced before her marriage has been consummated is treated like a girl who has never been married. Since the two payments — the betrothal money and the fine — are treated in the same way by the Torah before the *na'arah* has been betrothed, it is reasonable to assume that they are also treated in the same way after she has been betrothed and divorced. [2]Hence **the money of her fine should also be paid to her father, even though she has been betrothed and divorced.** [3]But **if so,"** the Baraita continues, **"what is the Torah teaching us by using the expression: 'Who has not been betrothed?'** If the verse is not teaching us that a *na'arah* who was betrothed and divorced does *not* come within the purview of this law, what is it telling us?" The Baraita explains: [4]"This superfluous expression **is available** for exegetical interpretation. The Torah included a superfluous phrase in this verse for exegetical reasons, in order **to compare another verse with it, and to infer** the following ***gezerah shavah* from it.** According to this hermeneutic principle, when the Torah includes the same word in two different verses, we are entitled to transfer the laws of each verse to the other [see above, 29b]. In this case, the *gezerah shavah* is used to connect the laws concerning rape (Deuteronomy 22:29) with those concerning seduction (Exodus 22:15). [5]The verse **here** in Deuteronomy **says**:

קְנָסָהּ, [1]מַה כֶּסֶף קִידּוּשֶׁיהָ, אַף עַל פִּי שֶׁנִּתְאָרְסָה וְנִתְגָּרְשָׁה, לְאָבִיהָ, [2]אַף כֶּסֶף קְנָסָהּ, אַף עַל פִּי שֶׁנִּתְאָרְסָה וְנִתְגָּרְשָׁה, לְאָבִיהָ. [3]אִם כֵּן, מַה תַּלְמוּד לוֹמַר: 'אֲשֶׁר לֹא אֹרָשָׂה'? [4]מוּפְנֶה לְהַקִּישׁ לוֹ, וְלָדוּן הֵימֶנּוּ גְּזֵרָה שָׁוָה. [5]נֶאֱמַר כָּאן:

LITERAL TRANSLATION

of her fine, [1][then] just as the money of her betrothal, even if she was betrothed and was divorced, [belongs] to her father, [2]so too the money of her fine, even if she was betrothed and was divorced, [belongs] to her father. [3]If so, what is [the Torah] teaching us by saying: 'Who has not been betrothed'? [4]It is free to compare [another verse] with it, and to infer a *gezerah shavah* from it. [5]It says here:

RASHI

מה כסף קידושיה אף על פי שנתארסה ונתגרשה – מאחר, כשחוזרת ומתקדשת בתוך נערות. **לאביה הוי** – דהא כל קידושי נערות ילפינן לאביה, דגבי קידושין לא כתיב מיעוטא ד"אשר לא אורסה", כי הכא.

NOTES

that can be used, the most common method being the giving of money. The bridegroom gives the bride a sum of money or an object of value in the presence of witnesses and declares that by giving the money he wishes to effect a betrothal. If the bride accepts the money, it becomes her property absolutely, and the betrothal is valid. (Nowadays, this method is universally used, with a ring serving as the object of value.)

By Torah law, a minor girl may be married off by her father without her consent. If the marriage is effected by the giving of money, the bridegroom gives the bride's father the sum of money or object of value and declares that he wishes to effect a betrothal thereby. If the father accepts the money, the betrothal is valid. The money belongs to the father, and need not be given to the daughter.

It is not clear on what basis the Talmud rules that the father retains the prerogative to marry his daughter off even after she has been betrothed and divorced. *Rashi* explains that since the father retains his authority over his daughter in other respects, even after she has been betrothed, we assume that this applies to all matters.

Shittah Mekubbetzet asks: From *Rashi*'s explanation, it is clear that we may not assume that the father's rights to his daughter's fine are necessarily the same as his rights to her betrothal money. For if his rights were the same in both cases, we could have extrapolated from the verse in the case of the fine that the father loses his rights to the betrothal money as well, in the event that his daughter was betrothed and then divorced. How, then, can Rabbi Akiva as quoted in the Baraita extrapolate from the case of betrothal money and rule that the fine should be paid to the father?

Shittah Mekubbetzet answers that the law governing the fine and the law governing betrothal money are different, and we cannot assume that the Torah's requirement in one case necessarily applies to the other. However, when there is no source in the Torah, it stands to reason that there should be no distinction between them, unless we have some reason to think otherwise. Hence, according to Rabbi Akiva as quoted in the Mishnah, there is an explicit verse to teach us that the fine is not usually paid to the girl herself, and a logical argument to indicate that the betrothal money is paid to the father. But according to Rabbi Akiva as quoted in the Baraita, there is no explicit verse dealing with the fine, since the phrase "who has not been betrothed" is needed to construct the *gezerah shavah*. Hence we have no reason to make any distinction between the fine and betrothal money.

׳אֲשֶׁר לֹא אֹרָשָׂה׳, וְנֶאֱמַר לְהַלָּן: ׳אֲשֶׁר לֹא אֹרָשָׂה׳. [1]מַה כָּאן חֲמִישִּׁים, [2]אַף לְהַלָּן חֲמִישִּׁים. [3]וּמַה לְהַלָּן שְׁקָלִים, [4]אַף כָּאן שְׁקָלִים״.

[5]וְרַבִּי עֲקִיבָא מַאי חָזֵית דְּ״אֲשֶׁר לֹא אֹרָשָׂה״ לִגְזֵירָה שָׁוָה, [6]וּ״בְתוּלָה״ לְמַעוּטֵי בְּעוּלָה? [38B] [7]אֵימָא ״בְּתוּלָה״ לִגְזֵירָה שָׁוָה [8]וַ״אֲשֶׁר לֹא אוֹרָסָה״ פְּרָט לְנַעֲרָה שֶׁנִּתְאָרְסָה וְנִתְגָּרְשָׁה!

[9]מִסְתַּבְּרָא ״אֲשֶׁר לֹא אוֹרָסָה״ לִגְזֵירָה שָׁוָה, [10]שֶׁהֲרֵי אֲנִי קוֹרֵא בָּהּ ״נַעֲרָה בְּתוּלָה״.

LITERAL TRANSLATION

'Who has not been betrothed,' and it says there: 'Who has not been betrothed.' [1]Just as here [the fine] is fifty, [2]so too there it is fifty. [3]And just as there [the money] is shekalim, [4]so too here it is shekalim."

[5]But [according to] Rabbi Akiva, why do you decide (lit., "what did you see") that "who has not been betrothed" is [to be used] for a *gezerah shavah*, [6]and [that] "virgin" is to exclude a woman who has had intercourse? [38B] [7]Say [that] "virgin" is [to be used] for a *gezerah shavah* [8]and [that] "who has not been betrothed" [means] to the exclusion of a *na'arah* who was betrothed and was divorced!

[9]It stands to reason [that] "who has not been betrothed" is [to be used] for a *gezerah shavah*, [10]because I can [still] apply (lit., "call") to her [the expression] "a virgin *na'arah*."

TRANSLATION AND COMMENTARY

'If a man finds a virgin *na'arah* **who has not been betrothed,'** and the verse **there** in Exodus **says**: 'If a man seduces a virgin **who has not been betrothed,'** using the same wording. [1]Thus we apply the *gezerah shavah* principle and reason that **just as here** in Deuteronomy the Torah requires that the rapist pay **fifty** pieces of silver as a fine, [2]**so too there** in Exodus the fine that must be paid by the seducer **is fifty** pieces of silver. [3]**And just as there** in Exodus the Torah requires that **the coins** used for the seducer's fine **must be shekalim,** [4]**so too here** in Deuteronomy the coins used for the rapist's fine **must be shekalim**. Hence both the rapist and the seducer must pay a fine of fifty silver shekalim."

וְרַבִּי עֲקִיבָא [5]The Gemara asks: **But according to Rabbi Akiva, why do we decide that** the expression **"who has not been betrothed" was** included in the verse **to teach us a *gezerah shavah*,** [6]**and that** the word **"virgin" was** to be interpreted literally — **to exclude a woman who has** already **had intercourse?** [38B] [7]Could he not have **said that** the word **"virgin" was** included in the verse **to be used for a *gezerah shavah*,** [8]**and that** the expression **"who has not been betrothed" was** to be interpreted literally — **to exclude a *na'arah* who was betrothed and was divorced?** On the basis of this interpretation of the verse, we would say that a non-virgin should be entitled to a fine, but a *na'arah* who has been betrothed and later divorced is not!

מִסְתַּבְּרָא [9]The Gemara answers: **It stands to reason that** the expression **"who has not been betrothed" was** included in the verse **to be used for a *gezerah shavah*,** and was not meant to be interpreted literally, [10]**because** in the case of a betrothed *na'arah* who was divorced **the expression "a virgin *na'arah*" still applies.** Taken literally in its fullest sense, the verse requires that the fine be paid to every virgin *na'arah*, including a betrothed *na'arah* who was divorced, but not a *na'arah* who has had intercourse. Thus it is preferable

RASHI

נאמר כאן — באונס. **להלן** — במפתה. **מה להלן** — במפתה, שקלים, דכתיב ״ישקול״ **אימא בתולה לגזירה שוה** — ולאו למעוטי בעולה, ויהא קנס לבעולה. **מסתברא אשר לא אורסה לגזירה שוה** — ואפילו אורסה אית לה קנס. **שהרי אני קורא בה נערה בתולה** — אף על פי שנתארסה ונתגרשה, דהא נערה בתולה היא, כדכתיב קרא. אבל בעולה שאין אני קורא בה נערה בתולה — אין לה קנס.

NOTES

אֵימָא ״בְּתוּלָה״ לִגְזֵירָה שָׁוָה Say that "virgin" is to be used for a *gezerah shavah*. To understand the Gemara's question here, it is important to bear in mind that the Talmudic Sages were not permitted to construct a *gezerah shavah* arbitrarily to connect any two verses. Rather, a *gezerah shavah* had to be based on a tradition, and was considered part of the Oral Law that was passed down from generation to generation from the time of Moses (*Niddah* 19b). Hence most *gezerah shavah* interpretations are accepted by the Gemara without challenge. Indeed, *Tosafot* explains that this idea underlies this whole passage in the Gemara.

There are a few instances, however, which appear problematic. In our passage, for example, the Gemara questions why Rabbi Akiva did not use a different term to construct his *gezerah shavah*, and this question would seem to be meaningless if the *gezerah shavah* were based entirely on tradition, with no discretionary powers at all in the hands of the Sages.

Accordingly, *Tosafot* and *Ritva* explain that the tradition upon which *gezerah shavah* interpretations are constructed was not always fully detailed. Thus in our case there was a tradition that these two verses were to be connected by means of a *gezerah shavah*, but it was not clear to the Sages which particular words were to be used for this purpose.

[1]אַדְּרַבָּה, ״בְּתוּלָה״ לִגְזֵירָה שָׁוָה, [2]שֶׁהֲרֵי אֲנִי קוֹרֵא בָּהּ ״אֲשֶׁר לֹא אוֹרָסָה״!
[3]מִסְתַּבְּרָא, הָא אִישְׁתַּנֵּי גּוּפָהּ, [4]וְהָא לָא אִישְׁתַּנֵּי גּוּפָהּ.
[5]וְרַבִּי יוֹסֵי הַגְּלִילִי הַאי סְבָרָא מְנָא לֵיהּ?
[6]נָפְקָא לֵיהּ מִדְּתַנְיָא: [7]״׳כֶּסֶף יִשְׁקֹל כְּמֹהַר הַבְּתוּלֹת׳. [8]שֶׁיְּהֵא

LITERAL TRANSLATION

[1]On the contrary, [the word] "virgin" is [to be used] for a *gezerah shavah*, [2]because I can apply to her [the expression] "who has not been betrothed"! [3]It stands to reason, [because] this one's body has changed, [4]but that one's body has not changed.

[5]And from where does Rabbi Yose HaGelili infer this idea?

[6]He derives it from what was taught: [7]"'He shall pay money according to the dowry of virgins.' [8]That this should be

RASHI

אדרבה בתולה לגזירה שוה – ולאו למעוטי בעולה בזנות, אלא יש לה קנס לבעולה בזנות, שהרי אני קורא אותה ״נערה אשר לא אורסה״. **מסתברא** – ארוסה יש לה קנס, ובעולה אין לה. **דהא אישתני גופה** – ופגמה אין רב כל כך. **והא** – דנתארסה ונתגרשה לא נשתנה גופה. **הא סברא** – דחמשים כסף דאונס שקלים הן ו״כסף ישקול״ דמפתה יהו חמשים.

TERMINOLOGY

אַדְּרַבָּה On the contrary (lit., "on the greater side"). Where the Gemara presents an argument based on common sense, it sometimes seeks to refute this argument by showing that common sense actually tends to support the opposite view, and introduces the refutation with this term.

TRANSLATION AND COMMENTARY

to use the expression "who has not been betrothed" for a *gezerah shavah*, because this enables us to apply the word "virgin" literally in its fullest sense.

אַדְּרַבָּה [1]The Gemara objects: **On the contrary:** it is much more reasonable to suggest that **the word, "virgin" was** included in the verse **to be used for a *gezerah shavah*,** and was not meant to be interpreted literally, [2]**because** in the case of an unmarried *na'arah* who has had intercourse **the expression "who has not been betrothed" does apply.** Taken literally in its fullest sense, the verse requires that the fine be paid to every unbetrothed *na'arah*, including a non-virgin, but not a *na'arah* who was betrothed and divorced, even if she is still a virgin. Thus it is preferable to use the word "virgin" for a *gezerah shavah*, because this enables us to apply the expression "who has not been betrothed" literally, in its fullest sense. Why should we prefer to apply "virgin" in its fullest sense rather than "who has not been betrothed"?

מִסְתַּבְּרָא [3]The Gemara answers: **It stands to reason** that it is better to interpret "virgin" literally, in its fullest sense, than "who has not been betrothed," **because** by the loss of **her** virginity the girl's **body has changed,** [4]whereas the act of betrothal **does not change** the betrothed *na'arah's* **body** in any way. It is reasonable to assume that the rape of a virgin is a more serious crime than the rape of a non-virgin, whereas there is no inherent difference between the rape of a *na'arah* who has not been betrothed and the rape of a *na'arah* who has been betrothed and then divorced. Therefore, since only one of these expressions can be interpreted literally, we prefer to explain that the requirement that the *na'arah* be a virgin should be taken literally, in its fullest sense, whereas the requirement that she not be betrothed is intended for the purposes of a *gezerah shavah*.

וְרַבִּי יוֹסֵי הַגְּלִילִי [5]The Gemara asks: **From where does Rabbi Yose HaGelili infer this idea?** It is obvious that Rabbi Yose HaGelili does not accept Rabbi Akiva's *gezerah shavah*, because he explains both expressions in the verse about the rapist literally. But how does he know that the fines imposed on the seducer and on the rapist are to be compared, and in particular how does he know that the "fifty pieces of silver" mentioned in connection with the rapist and the shekalim mentioned in connection with the seducer refer to the same sum?

נָפְקָא לֵיהּ [6]The Gemara answers: Rabbi Yose HaGelili **derives** this law **from** a different *gezerah shavah,* **which was taught** in the following Baraita: "A man who seduces an unbetrothed *na'arah* must pay the girl's father a fine, as the verse says (Exodus 22:16): [7]**'He shall pay money according to the dowry of virgins.'** The 'dowry of virgins' mentioned in the verse refers to the fine of 'fifty pieces of silver' (Deuteronomy 22:29) imposed on a man who rapes an unbetrothed *na'arah.* The verse in Exodus does not explicitly state the amount of the fine imposed on the seducer, but stipulates that it must be paid in shekalim (*yishkol* — 'he shall pay shekalim'). Regarding the fine paid by the rapist, the verse in Deuteronomy does not specify the currency in which it must be paid, but sets the amount at fifty silver coins. [8]The *gezerah shavah* linking the fine imposed on a seducer to that imposed on a rapist teaches **that** the fine paid by the seducer **is**

NOTES

הָא אִישְׁתַּנֵּי גּוּפָהּ This one's body has changed. This line of the Gemara must be explained differently according to the various explanations of this passage given by the Rishonim. According to *Rashi* and *Rosh* (followed in our commentary), the Gemara has already explained that Rabbi Akiva did not interpret literally all the Torah's stipulations in the verses about the rapist and the seducer — because he needed one expression in order to construct a *gezerah shavah.* The Gemara is now asking a different question: Why did Rabbi Akiva construct the *gezerah shavah* using "who has not been betrothed" rather than "virgin," since both expressions appear in both verses? According to this

TRANSLATION AND COMMENTARY

similar to the 'dowry of virgins' paid by the rapist, which is expressly set at fifty silver coins. **And** at the same time it teaches that **the 'dowry of virgins'** paid by the rapist **is similar to** the fine paid by the seducer, which must be paid in shekalim." Thus the Baraita teaches us to apply the number fifty and the shekel coin to both cases, from which it follows that both the seducer and the rapist must pay a fine of fifty silver shekalim.

קַשְׁיָא דְּרַבִּי עֲקִיבָא [1]The Gemara explained above (38a) that Rabbi Akiva's ruling in the Mishnah was based on the exegesis presented by the Baraita it quoted on the same subject (ibid.). But this poses a new difficulty, because Rabbi Akiva as quoted in the Mishnah ruled that a *na'arah* who was betrothed and divorced is herself entitled to the fine, whereas Rabbi Akiva as quoted in the Baraita ruled that the fine is paid to her father. Thus **there is a contradiction between Rabbi Akiva's** viewpoint as presented in the Mishnah **and Rabbi Akiva's** viewpoint as presented in the Baraita!

תְּרֵי תַּנָּאֵי [2]The Gemara replies: **There are two Tannaim, and they disagree about the opinion of Rabbi Akiva.** The Mishnah and the Baraita reflect the viewpoints of disciples of Rabbi Akiva, who disagreed as to his opinion. In the transmission of Rabbi Akiva's opinion two differing reports were produced, one reflected in the Mishnah and the other in the Baraita. But the basic reasoning is the same in both versions: We do not interpret the expression "who has not been betrothed" literally, because an authoritative tradition maintains that this expression is to be used to construct a *gezerah shavah*. Rabbi Akiva as quoted in the Mishnah maintains that we nevertheless attempt to derive some information from the simple meaning of the expression, and we treat a *na'arah* who has been betrothed and divorced somewhat differently from a *na'arah* who has never been betrothed; whereas Rabbi Akiva as quoted in the Baraita maintains that we learn nothing at all from the simple meaning of the expression, and we treat a *na'arah* who has been betrothed and divorced exactly like a *na'arah* who has never been betrothed.

בִּשְׁלָמָא רַבִּי עֲקִיבָא [3]The Gemara objects to this explanation: **There is no problem** in understanding the ruling of **Rabbi Akiva in the Mishnah,** [4]**because** according to him **the *gezerah shavah* does not come and remove the verse entirely from its simple meaning.** There is an exegetical principle in Jewish law that regardless of what exegetical methods are applied to a verse, it must also have a straightforward meaning that is Halakhically correct. Hence, according to Rabbi Akiva as quoted in the Mishnah, the expression "who has not been betrothed" is primarily intended to teach us a *gezerah shavah*, but it can also be interpreted

זֶה כְּמוֹהַר הַבְּתוּלוֹת, וּמוֹהַר הַבְּתוּלוֹת כָּזֶה״.
[1]קַשְׁיָא דְּרַבִּי עֲקִיבָא אַדְּרַבִּי עֲקִיבָא!
[2]תְּרֵי תַּנָּאֵי, וְאַלִּיבָּא דְּרַבִּי עֲקִיבָא.
[3]בִּשְׁלָמָא רַבִּי עֲקִיבָא דְּמַתְנִיתִין, [4]לָא אָתְיָא גְּזֵירָה שָׁוָה וּמַפְּקָא לֵיהּ לִקְרָא

LITERAL TRANSLATION

like the dowry of virgins, and the dowry of virgins [should be] like this."

[1]There is a contradiction between Rabbi Akiva and Rabbi Akiva!

[2][There are] two Tannaim, and [they disagree] about the opinion of Rabbi Akiva.

[3]It is all right [according to] Rabbi Akiva of the Mishnah, [4][for] the *gezerah shavah* does not come and take the verse

RASHI

כמוהר הבתולות — מנין המפורש אצל אונס, דהיינו חמשים. **ומוהר הבתולות** — יהיו שקלים. **כזה** — שכתוב בו "ישקול". **קשיא דרבי עקיבא** — דברייתא, דאמר קנסה לאביה. **אדרבי עקיבא** — דמתניתין. **לא אתיא גזירה שוה ומפקא לקרא מפשטיה לגמרי** — דאתא פשטיה לאשמועינן הא ארוסה לעצמה, וחד מתרוייהו לאפנויי. אי נמי לא מופני — ליכא למיפרך מידי.

NOTES

explanation, the Gemara answers that we prefer to interpret "virgin" literally and leave "who has not been betrothed" for the *gezerah shavah*, since it seems more likely that the Torah is concerned about bodily changes, such as loss of virginity, than about changes in marital status.

קַשְׁיָא דְּרַבִּי עֲקִיבָא אַדְּרַבִּי עֲקִיבָא There is a contradiction between Rabbi Akiva and Rabbi Akiva. *Shittah Mekubbetzet* asks: Since the contradiction between the Mishnah and the Baraita is obvious, why did the Gemara not raise this point immediately, when the Baraita was introduced? *Shittah Mekubbetzet* answers that the texts of Baraitot are sometimes inaccurate, and when a Baraita contradicts a Mishnah, the Gemara normally assumes that it is the result of an error. But having explained this Baraita in detail, and having argued that it is the basis of Rabbi Akiva's reasoning in the Mishnah as well, the Gemara can no longer dismiss it, and must seek to account for the contradiction between it and the Mishnah.

וּמַפְּקָא מִפְּשָׁטֵיהּ לְגַמְרֵי And takes it away entirely from its simple meaning. In several places in the Talmud, the Gemara states that "a verse never departs from its simple meaning" (אֵין מִקְרָא יוֹצֵא מִידֵי פְשׁוּטוֹ). This means that regardless of whatever hermeneutic rules we may apply to a verse in order to derive Halakhic information, the verse also has a simple meaning which is Halakhically correct.

TRANSLATION AND COMMENTARY

as teaching us that a *na'arah* who has been betrothed and divorced is treated differently from a *na'arah* who has never been betrothed, in that she receives the fine herself. [1] **But according to Rabbi Akiva in the Baraita, the *gezerah shavah* comes to remove** this verse **from its simple meaning entirely.** How are we supposed to understand the verse's explicit statement that the law regarding the fine applies to a *na'arah* who has not been betrothed, if the very same law applies to a *na'arah* who has been betrothed and divorced?

אָמַר [2] **Rav Naḥman bar Yitzḥak said** in reply: For the purposes of understanding the straightforward meaning of the verse, [3] we must **read** this expression as though it said: **"Who *is* not betrothed"** rather than "who *has not been* betrothed." (The two expressions are spelled the same way in Hebrew; they differ only in their pronunciation.) Thus the verse informs us that the law regarding the fine applies specifically to *ne'arot* who were not betrothed at the time of the rape. Thus it excludes a betrothed *na'arah*, but it does not exclude a *na'arah* who has previously been betrothed but was divorced before she was raped.

אֲרוּסָה [4] **But**, the Gemara objects, the Torah cannot be informing us that a man who rapes a *na'arah* who is currently betrothed need not pay the fine. **Surely** a man who rapes **a betrothed woman is subject to stoning!** There is no need to inform us that the fine is not paid if the woman was betrothed at the time of the rape, because the rapist is subject to the more severe penalty of death. Rather, we must conclude that the purpose of the verse is to exclude a *na'arah* who has been betrothed and divorced from receiving the fine.

סָלְקָא דַּעְתָּךְ אָמִינָא [5] The Gemara answers: According to Rabbi Akiva as quoted in the Baraita, the verse is intended to exclude *ne'arot* who were betrothed at the time of the rape from receiving the fine, but it does not exclude *ne'arot* who were betrothed but subsequently divorced. And it was necessary for the Baraita to inform us that betrothed *ne'arot* are not entitled to a fine, even though the rapist is subject to the death penalty, and an offender who is subject to the more severe penalty does not normally pay damages as well, because **it might have entered our minds to say** that the law exempting an offender who is subject to the more severe penalty from paying damages applies only to regular damage payments. But if an offense is subject to the death penalty and to a fine, such as the fine for rape, we do not apply the regular law, [6] because **fines are an innovation established by the Torah.** Normally, damage payments correspond to the loss suffered by the victim. But fines do not correspond to any specific loss incurred by the victim. Rather, they are imposed in order to punish the offender for his behavior, and this is a novel

SAGES

רַב נַחְמָן בַּר יִצְחָק **Rav Naḥman bar Yitzḥak.** A Babylonian Amora of the fourth generation. See *Ketubot*, Part I, p. 52.

מִפְּשָׁטֵיהּ לְגַמְרֵי, [1] אֶלָּא לְרַבִּי עֲקִיבָא דְּבָרַיְיתָא אָתְיָא גְּזֵירָה שָׁוָה וּמַפְּקָא מִפְּשָׁטֵיהּ לְגַמְרֵי. [2] אֲמַר רַב נַחְמָן בַּר יִצְחָק: [3] קְרִי בֵּיהּ "אֲשֶׁר לֹא אֲרוּסָה". [4] אֲרוּסָה בַּת סְקִילָה הִיא! [5] סָלְקָא דַּעְתָּךְ אָמִינָא: [6] הוֹאִיל וְחִידּוּשׁ הוּא שֶׁחִידְּשָׁה תּוֹרָה

LITERAL TRANSLATION

away entirely from its simple meaning, [1] but [according] to Rabbi Akiva of the Baraita the *gezerah shavah* comes and takes it away entirely from its simple meaning.

[2] Rav Naḥman bar Yitzḥak said: [3] Read in it: "Who *is* not betrothed."

[4] [But surely] a betrothed woman is subject to stoning!

[5] It might have entered your mind to say: [6] Since it is an innovation that the Torah established

RASHI

אלא לרבי עקיבא דברייתא וכו׳ אתיא גזירה שוה ומפקא מפשטיה לגמרי – דלא דריש פשטא ד"אשר לא אורשה" כלל, ומשוי אורשה כלא אורשה, ואם כן מיעקר משמעותיה! **קרי ביה** – בפשטיה אשר לא ארוסה – למעוטי ארוסה. **בת סקילה היא** – ומ"לא יהיה אסון" נפקא פטורא מתשלומין.

NOTES

There must be some way of understanding the verse that accords with its grammar and context and presents Halakhically correct information. Hence our Gemara seeks to find a way to understand the expression "who has not been betrothed" in the context of the verse in a Halakhically correct way, even according to Rabbi Akiva as quoted in the Baraita, who definitely does not interpret it literally.

קְרִי בֵּיהּ: "אֲשֶׁר לֹא אֲרוּסָה" **Read in it: "Who *is* not betrothed."** According to the Masoretic text of the Torah, the word "betrothed" (אֹרָשָׂה) in the verse appears in the past tense ("has been betrothed" or "was betrothed"), and the text clearly excludes both a girl who has previously been betrothed and a girl who is currently betrothed. Rav Naḥman bar Yitzḥak is proposing that the word should be read instead as a participle (אֲרֻשָׂה — "is betrothed"). According to this explanation, no fine need be paid if the *na'arah* is currently betrothed. But the verse does not exclude an unmarried *na'arah* who has previously been betrothed but was subsequently divorced.

There is no difference in spelling in the Bible between אֹרָשָׂה ("she was betrothed") in the past tense and אֲרֻשָׂה ("is betrothed") in the form of the feminine participle. The difference is only in the vowels, which are not written down

TRANSLATION AND COMMENTARY

idea that departs from the general practice of the Torah. Now, we have a principle that whenever the Torah issues a novel commandment that is not consistent with the other laws of the Torah, we cannot assume that the regular laws apply, unless the Torah explicitly states that they do. Hence in the case of fines imposed by the Torah as punishment in addition to normal damage payments (including the fines imposed on rapists and on seducers, which are discussed by our Mishnah), we might have thought that the rule that an offender who is subject to the death penalty is exempt from monetary payments does not apply, [1]and **although** the offender **is put to death** for committing adultery, **he must pay** the fine for rape as well. Hence the Torah explicitly informed us that this is not so, and a *na'arah* who was betrothed at the time of the rape is not entitled to a fine. On the other hand, a *na'arah* who has been betrothed and divorced is treated just like a *na'arah* who has never been betrothed.

בִּקְנָס, [1]אַף עַל גַּב דְּמִיקְטִיל, מְשַׁלֵּם.
[2]וּלְרַבָּה דַּאֲמַר: [3]חִידּוּשׁ הוּא שֶׁחִידְּשָׁה תּוֹרָה בִּקְנָס, אַף עַל גַּב דְּמִיקְטִיל, מְשַׁלֵּם, [4]מַאי אִיכָּא לְמֵימַר?
[5]סָבַר לָהּ כְּרַבִּי עֲקִיבָא דְּמַתְנִיתִין.
[6]תָּנוּ רַבָּנַן: ״קְנָסָהּ לְמִי? לְאָבִיהָ. [7]וְיֵשׁ אוֹמְרִים: לְעַצְמָהּ״.
[8]לְעַצְמָהּ אַמַּאי?
[9]אֲמַר רַב חִסְדָּא: הָכָא בְּנַעֲרָה שֶׁנִּתְאָרְסָה וְנִתְגָּרְשָׁה עָסְקִינַן.

LITERAL TRANSLATION

regarding a fine, [1]although he is killed, he pays.
[2]But according to Rabbah who said: [3]It is an innovation that the Torah established regarding a fine, [and therefore] although he is killed, he pays, [4]what is there to say?
[5]He agrees with Rabbi Akiva of the Mishnah.
[6]Our Rabbis taught: "To whom [is] her fine [paid]? [7]To her father. But some say: To herself."
[8]Why to herself?
[9]Rav Ḥisda said: Here we are dealing with a *na'arah* who was betrothed and was divorced.

RASHI

קנסה למי — קא סלקא דעתך בסתם אנוסה קאי.

וּלְרַבָּה [2]**But**, the Gemara objects, **according to Rabbah, who said** (above, 34b) that although an offender who is subject to the death penalty is exempt from regular damage payments, nevertheless if he raped his daughter or slaughtered a stolen animal on Shabbat, [3]he is punished with both penalties, **and even though he is killed, he pays,** because **fines are an innovation established by the Torah,** how can we explain the ruling of Rabbi Akiva as quoted in the Baraita? According to Rabbah, a man who rapes a virgin *na'arah* who is currently betrothed must pay a fine, just like a man who rapes a *na'arah* who has been betrothed and divorced, because the more severe penalty (of death) does not exempt a rapist from the fine. How, then, can Rabbah explain the straightforward meaning of the verse, which stresses the fact that the *na'arah* under discussion was *not* betrothed? [4]**What is there** for him **to say?**

סָבַר לָהּ [5]The Gemara answers: On this matter Rabbah **agrees with Rabbi Akiva** as quoted **in the Mishnah.** Rabbah rejects as inaccurate the version of Rabbi Akiva's viewpoint given in the Baraita. Rabbah maintains that the verse, according to its straightforward meaning, is teaching us that a *na'arah* who has been betrothed (regardless of whether she was later divorced) is treated differently from a *na'arah* who has never been betrothed, in that she receives the fine herself (as Rabbi Akiva ruled in the Mishnah). Thus the verse can be explained according to its straightforward meaning in a Halakhically accurate manner even according to Rabbah, who is of the opinion that the more severe penalty (of death) does not exempt from the fine.

תָּנוּ רַבָּנַן [6]Before concluding its analysis of Rabbi Akiva's viewpoint, the Gemara cites a Baraita on a related topic. **Our Rabbis taught** the following Baraita: "If a virgin *na'arah* is raped, **to whom is her fine** to be **paid?** [7]It must be paid **to her father,** as stated explicitly in the verse (Deuteronomy 22:29). **But some** authorities **say** that the fine is paid **to the** *na'arah* **herself."**

לְעַצְמָהּ אַמַּאי [8]The Gemara asks: **Why** is the fine paid **to the** *na'arah* **herself?** How can anyone maintain that the fine is paid to the *na'arah* herself, when the Torah explicitly states that it is paid to her father?

אֲמַר רַב חִסְדָּא [9]**Rav Ḥisda said** in reply: Even though the Baraita appears to be referring to all cases involving the rape of a *na'arah,* in fact **we are dealing here with** one special case — that of **a *na'arah* who**

NOTES

in Hebrew and are passed on by tradition. It should be noted that in our texts of the Talmud, the auxiliary consonant vav was inserted in the words אֲרוּסָה — אוֹרָסָה, to indicate where the vowel is supposed to be placed and to facilitate pronunciation, but in the Torah itself the vav does not appear, and both words are spelled ארשׂה. It also should be noted that the Talmud substitutes the letter ס for שׂ, again to facilitate pronunciation.

BACKGROUND

מִלְּתָא דִּפְשִׁיטָא לֵיהּ The thing that was obvious. This expression occurs frequently in the Gemara, and reflects a difference of opinion between Amoraim. Sometimes one Sage reaches a clear-cut conclusion on a certain issue, whereas another sees the matter as an insoluble problem. The expression "the thing that was obvious to X was problematic to Y" has Halakhic significance, because in such a situation we abandon the standard rules for Halakhic decision-making (according to which, for the sake of example, the law follows Y rather than X). We conclude that a clear-cut ruling is preferred to a state of indecision, and we decide in accordance with X.

TRANSLATION AND COMMENTARY

was betrothed and was divorced. The Baraita is ruling that the fine must be paid in such a case. According to the first opinion expressed in the Baraita, it is paid to the *na'arah*'s father; according to the second, it is paid to the *na'arah* herself. Rav Ḥisda explains: [1]The two opinions in the Baraita **disagree about the dispute between Rabbi Akiva** as quoted **in the Mishnah and Rabbi Akiva** as quoted **in the Baraita.** The first opinion cited in the Baraita being analyzed by Rav Ḥisda corresponds to the opinion of the disciple of Rabbi Akiva reflected in the Baraita we considered above. According to this opinion, a *na'arah* who has been betrothed and divorced is treated exactly like a *na'arah* who has never been betrothed. The second opinion cited in the Baraita being analyzed by Rav Ḥisda corresponds to the opinion of the disciple of Rabbi Akiva reflected in the Mishnah. According to this opinion, a *na'arah* who has been betrothed and divorced is entitled to a fine, but she is treated somewhat differently from a *na'arah* who has never been betrothed in that the fine is paid to the *na'arah* herself rather than to her father.

אָמַר אַבַּיֵי [2]**Abaye said: If** the rapist or the seducer **has intercourse with** the *na'arah,* **and** before he is ordered by the court to pay the fine, **she dies, he is exempt** from paying, even though the girl's father, who was supposed to receive the fine, is still alive. [3]**For the verse says** (Deuteronomy 22:29): **"And he shall give** the fine **to the father of the *na'arah*."** The verse could have simply said: "To her father." The extra mention of "the *na'arah*" is intended to teach us that the rapist must pay the fine to the father only if he is still the father of a *na'arah,* [4]**but not** if he is **the father of a dead girl.**

מִלְּתָא דִּפְשִׁיטָא לֵיהּ [5]The Gemara notes that this **matter, which was obvious to Abaye, was problematic**

[1]וְקָמִיפַּלְגִי בִּפְלוּגְתָּא דְּרַבִּי עֲקִיבָא דְּמַתְנִיתִין וְרַבִּי עֲקִיבָא דְּבָרַיְיתָא.

[2]אָמַר אַבַּיֵי: בָּא עָלֶיהָ וּמֵתָה, פָּטוּר, [3]שֶׁנֶּאֱמַר: "וְנָתַן לַאֲבִי הַנַּעֲרָה", [4]וְלֹא לַאֲבִי מֵתָה.

[5]מִלְּתָא דִּפְשִׁיטָא לֵיהּ לְאַבַּיֵי מִיבָּעֲיָא לֵיהּ לְרָבָא.

LITERAL TRANSLATION

[1]And they disagree about the dispute between Rabbi Akiva of the Mishnah and Rabbi Akiva of the Baraita.

[2]Abaye said: [If] he had intercourse with her and she died, he is exempt, [3]as it is said: "And he shall give to the father of the *na'arah,*" [4]but not to the father of a dead [girl].

[5]The thing that was obvious to Abaye was problematic to Rava.

RASHI

בא עליה ומתה — לא הספיק האב להעמידו בדין, עד שמתה.

NOTES

וְלֹא לַאֲבִי מֵתָה But not to the father of a dead girl. The Rishonim ask: How can Abaye infer from the expression "the father of the *na'arah*" that the law applies only if she is still alive when the rapist is sued in court? Later in the Gemara (below, 45b), we infer from the expression "and they shall take the *na'arah* out," which appears in the verse dealing with a betrothed *na'arah* who committed adultery (Deuteronomy 22:21), that the girl is executed by stoning even if she is no longer a *na'arah*, provided that she was a *na'arah* at the time of the offense. Thus we see that the expression "the *na'arah*" refers to the time of the offense, not the time of the penalty.

Tosafot and *Rosh* explain that the expression "the *na'arah*" is superfluous in both verses, because the verse dealing with the rapist could have said "her father" instead of "the father of the *na'arah,*" and the verse dealing with the adulteress could have said "they shall take her out" instead of "and they shall take the *na'arah* out." Hence we infer from the superfluous language that the law is not as we might perhaps have imagined. In the case of the *na'arah* who committed adultery, we learn from the superfluous word that she is executed by stoning even if she is no longer a *na'arah*, since we might perhaps have thought that she should be executed by strangulation like other adults guilty of adultery. In the case of the rapist's fine, by contrast, we learn from the superfluous word that the rapist is exempt from the fine if the *na'arah* died, since we might have imagined that her death is not a reason for the rapist to be exempt (see also *Ritva*).

מִלְּתָא דִּפְשִׁיטָא לֵיהּ לְאַבַּיֵי מִיבָּעֲיָא לֵיהּ לְרָבָא The thing that was obvious to Abaye was problematic to Rava. The Gemara presents three versions of Rava's problem. The first version: If the *na'arah* dies after being raped and the rapist is not brought to court until six months have passed since the dead girl became a *na'arah*, is the fine paid to the girl's father or to her heir? The Gemara rejects this

HALAKHAH

בָּא עָלֶיהָ וּמֵתָה If he had intercourse with her and she died. "If a man rapes a *na'arah* but she dies before the charge against the rapist can be pressed in court, he is exempt from paying the fine, following Abaye. *Kesef Mishneh* explains in the name of *Rosh* that in this matter we follow Abaye, even though we normally follow Rava in his disputes with Abaye, and Rava's question was left unanswered. For according to the Gemara's final version of Rava's question, he did not necessarily disagree with Abaye, but rather was in doubt about the matter. Thus, in effect, Abaye was resolving Rava's doubt, and in such cases the Halakhah follows Abaye." (*Rambam, Sefer Nashim, Hilkhot Na'arah Betulah* 1:15; *Tur, Even HaEzer* 177.)

[1] דְּבָעֵי רָבָא: יֵשׁ בֶּגֶר בַּקֶּבֶר אוֹ אֵין בֶּגֶר בַּקֶּבֶר? [2] יֵשׁ בֶּגֶר בַּקֶּבֶר, וְדִבְנָהּ הָוֵי? [3] אוֹ דִלְמָא אֵין בֶּגֶר בַּקֶּבֶר, וּדְאָבִיהָ הָוֵי?

LITERAL TRANSLATION

[1] For Rava asked: Is there coming of age in the grave or is there no coming of age in the grave? [2] Is there coming of age in the grave, and it [the fine] belongs to her son? [3] Or perhaps is there no coming of age in the grave, and it belongs to her father?

TRANSLATION AND COMMENTARY

in the eyes of **Rava.** [1] **For Rava posed the** following **problem: Does one reach adult status in the grave or does one not reach adult status in the grave?** A woman's legal status changes twice: Once, when she ceases to be a minor and becomes a legally competent *na'arah*, and a second time, when she becomes a full adult. The first change in status is dependent upon the girl's physical development, but the second change takes place automatically, regardless of physical development, as soon as six months have passed since she became a *na'arah*. What, then, is the law if a *na'arah* dies before attaining adulthood? Is she considered an adult six months after becoming a *na'arah*, or does the entire process cease with her death?

יֵשׁ בֶּגֶר בַּקֶּבֶר [2] Rava explains that this seemingly theoretical question has practical consequences. If we say that **a person reaches adult status in the grave, and** a man raped a *na'arah*, but before he was ordered by the court to pay the fine, the *na'arah* died leaving a son who inherited her legal claims, then **the fine is awarded to her son,** if it is paid more than six months after she became a *na'arah*. For the Mishnah rules (below, 41b) that if the rapist was not taken to court until after the *na'arah* became an adult, the fine is paid to the girl herself rather than to her father. Hence, in this case, the *na'arah*'s infant son, who has inherited her legal claims, can sue the rapist six months after his late mother became a *na'arah*, and is entitled to the fine. [3] On the other hand, **it is possible that a person does not reach adult status in the grave, and the fine belongs to the** *na'arah*'s **father,** even if the rapist is not fined until after six months have passed. Thus we see that, unlike Abaye, who was certain that the fine need not be paid after the *na'arah*'s death, Rava raised questions about this matter that he could not resolve.

RASHI

יש בגר בקבר — אם מתה בנערותה עד שלא עמדה בדין, והגיע זמן בגרותה בקבר, מי חשיב בגר או לא? ולקמיה מפרש ואזיל למאי הלכתא. **יש בגר בקבר** — וכי היכי דאם לא הספיקה לעמוד בדין עד שבגרה, תנן לקמן בפרק "נערה שנתפתתה" (מא,ג) דהרי הן לעצמה ולא לאביה, והשתא נמי בגר בקבר מפקיע כח האב, ובנה ירית לה, אם יש לה בן.

NOTES

version because of an internal difficulty and presents a second version: If the *na'arah* dies after being raped and the rapist is not brought to court until six months have passed since the dead girl became a *na'arah*, need the fine be paid at all? According to both of these versions, Rava clearly disagrees with Abaye. For Abaye is of the opinion that the fine need not be paid at all if the *na'arah* dies, whereas Rava maintains that the fine must be paid — at least during the first six months following the girl's death.

At the end of this passage, the Gemara presents a third version of Rava's problem, in the name of Mar bar Rav Ashi: If the *na'arah* dies after being raped and the father sues the rapist immediately, is the fine paid to her father, or is a dead *na'arah* considered to be an adult, so that the fine need not be paid at all? It was because of this latter version that the Gemara described Rava as being in doubt about "something that was obvious to Abaye." According to the first two versions, Rava clearly disagrees with Abaye, and his problem concerns a different matter (*Rashi*). *Maharam Schiff* explains that the Gemara considered Mar bar Rav Ashi's version to be authoritative, because, apart from two instances, the Halakhah always follows Mar bar Rav Ashi (see *Tosafot,* below, 84b).

וְדִבְנָהּ הָוֵי And it belongs to her son. According to Jewish law, the order of inheritance is as follows: (1) A husband takes precedence over all other heirs in inheriting the property of his wife, provided that the marriage was completed through *nissu'in* and that the husband is still alive when his wife dies. (2) The sons of the deceased take precedence over all other heirs in inheriting his or her property (except in the case of a married woman whose heir is her living husband, as above). (3) If the deceased left no living sons, the estate is inherited by his sons' children or his sons' grandchildren. (4) If the deceased left no sons at all, the estate is inherited by his daughters, or their children or their grandchildren. (5) If the deceased left no sons or daughters at all, the estate is inherited by his father. (6) If the deceased's father is not alive, the estate is inherited by his father's heirs, in accordance with rules 2 to 5 above (see *Rambam, Hilkhot Naḥalot* 1:1-9).

On the basis of these rules of inheritance, the Gemara finds the first version of Rava's problem difficult to understand. For Rava is asking whether the fine of a dead *na'arah* is collected by her father or by her own heirs, and we can see from the rules given above that if the *na'arah* left no children, her father *is* her heir. Accordingly, the Gemara tries to find a case in which a *na'arah* can have had a son after being raped, and can still have died before becoming a full adult. But since it is impossible for a girl to become pregnant and to give birth in the six months between becoming a *na'arah* and becoming an adult, the Gemara is forced to reject the first version of Rava's problem and to present the second and third versions.

וְדִבְנָהּ הָוֵי And it belongs to her son. According to Talmudic law, monetary claims are inherited but debts are not. Thus, if a creditor dies, his heirs may claim the money on his behalf; but if a debtor dies, the debt is canceled,

TRANSLATION AND COMMENTARY

וּמִי מְעַבְּרָא [39A] [1]The Gemara now objects to Rava's problem as presented. According to Rava, the problem arises only if the *na'arah* has a child. But Rava is referring to a case in which the daughter died while she was still a *na'arah*. Thus she must have given birth while still a *na'arah*, and she must have become pregnant nine months earlier, while still a minor. **But, asks the Gemara, can** a minor **become pregnant?** [2]**Surely Rav Bivi taught** a Baraita **before Rav Naḥman** that proves that this is impossible. [3]The Baraita states: **"The following three women** are permitted and even required to **have intercourse while using an** absorbent **cloth** as a contraceptive device to prevent pregnancy, although the use of such a device is usually forbidden: [4]**A minor, and a pregnant woman, and a nursing mother.** In all these cases, pregnancy would pose a serious health risk.

[39A] [1]וּמִי מְעַבְּרָא? [2]וְהָתָנֵי רַב בִּיבִי קַמֵּיהּ דְּרַב נַחְמָן: [3]״שָׁלֹשׁ נָשִׁים מְשַׁמְּשׁוֹת בְּמוֹךְ. [4]אֵלּוּ הֵן: קְטַנָּה, וּמְעוּבֶּרֶת, וּמֵנִיקָה.

LITERAL TRANSLATION

[39A] [1]But can she become pregnant? [2]But surely Rav Bivi taught before Rav Naḥman: [3]"Three women have intercourse while using (lit., 'with') a cloth. [4]These are they: A minor, and a pregnant woman, and a nursing woman.

RASHI

ומי מעברא — בקטנות או בנערות כשהיא בת קנס שתלד בנערות.
משמשות במוך — מותר להן לשמש במוך, ואינן כמשחיתות זרע.

NOTES

unless it was covered by a lien on the debtor's real estate. Accordingly, Rava assumes that if the *na'arah* were to die before pressing her claim to the fine, her heirs could sue the rapist in court on her behalf.

The Rishonim have difficulty in accepting this idea. For if we are referring to a case in which the rapist was sued in court before the *na'arah* died but failed to pay the fine until she died, Rava's problem would not exist. For according to the Mishnah (below, 41b), the father does not lose his right to the fine, even if his daughter dies. On the other hand, if we are referring to a case in which the rapist was not sued in court before the *na'arah* died, Rava's problem would also not exist. For we have a rule that fines cannot be collected by the claimant's heirs unless the claim was already pressed in court before the claimant died. How, then, could Rava have suggested that the *na'arah*'s son can press her claim on her behalf?

There are several answers to this problem given by the Rishonim. *Ra'ah* cites *Ba'al HaMa'or,* who explains that Rava's problem is based on the viewpoint of Rabbi Shimon, who disagrees with the other Sages in the Mishnah, and maintains that the father loses his right to collect the fine if the *na'arah* becomes an adult or marries before it can be collected, even if he has already sued the rapist in court. In such a case, Rabbi Shimon would argue that the rights of collection pass to the daughter and to her son, if we accept that the *na'arah* is considered to have come of age in the grave.

Tosafot explains that Rava is referring to the compensation paid to the *na'arah* for her lost virginity and lost reputation, which are not fines and can be inherited. Alternatively, *Tosafot* suggests that the Gemara may not have gone to the trouble of pointing out this difficulty with the first version of Rava's problem, because it is rejected for other reasons in any case (see also *Ra'avad* cited by *Ramban*).

Some Rishonim (*Ritva, Meiri*) suggest a different interpretation of the Mishnah (below, 41b), according to which the Mishnah's ruling applies only to one special case — where the father died before suing the rapist in court, and the father's heirs wished to claim the rapist's fine on his behalf. According to this interpretation, the right to collect other fines is inherited by the claimant's heirs, and even the right to collect the rapist's fine is inherited by the *na'arah*'s heirs in those cases in which she is entitled to collect the fine herself.

Ritva adds that this question appears to be the subject of an Amoraic dispute in the Jerusalem Talmud at the beginning of the fourth chapter, and even if we interpret the Mishnah (below, 41b) in the traditional way — as excluding any possibility of the right to collect a fine being inherited by a claimant's heirs — it is possible that Rava follows the opposing view.

שָׁלֹשׁ נָשִׁים מְשַׁמְּשׁוֹת בְּמוֹךְ Three women have intercourse while using a cloth. Our commentary follows *Rashi*, who explains that the topic of this Baraita is the prohibition against contraception. According to *Rashi*, a woman is forbidden to prevent pregnancy by inserting an absorbent cloth into her vagina, because ejaculation onto the cloth is considered a form of masturbation. In the case of these three women, however, Rabbi Meir permits the use of this form of contraception in order not to endanger their lives, whereas the Sages insist that they have intercourse normally.

In contrast to *Rashi*, most other Rishonim explain that the topic of this Baraita is the commandment to preserve one's life (see *Ramban, Rashba, Ra'ah, Ritva*). According to this explanation, it is *permitted* for any woman to prevent pregnancy in this way, but Rabbi Meir *requires* these three women to do so in order not to endanger their lives, whereas the Sages permit them to have intercourse normally.

Rabbenu Tam agrees with *Rashi* that inserting an absorbent cloth into the vagina to prevent pregnancy is forbidden, but he follows the explanation of the other Rishonim, that the topic of this Baraita is the commandment to preserve one's life. He explains that the Baraita is not referring to an absorbent cloth inserted into the vagina before intercourse (which is forbidden even according to Rabbi Meir) but rather to a cloth used after intercourse to wipe away the semen. This method of contraception is permitted to everyone, but Rabbi Meir maintains that these three women are required to do so, whereas the Sages permit them to have intercourse without taking this precaution.

TRANSLATION AND COMMENTARY

[1] We permit **a minor** to take steps to prevent pregnancy, **lest she become pregnant and die.** A minor is not sufficiently developed physically to be able to take the strain of pregnancy, and it may well be fatal for her to become pregnant and give birth. [2] Likewise, we permit **an** already **pregnant woman** to take steps to prevent a second pregnancy, **lest her existing fetus become** crushed until it looks like **a flat fish.** [3] Likewise, we permit **a nursing mother** to take steps to prevent pregnancy, **lest she wean her son** prematurely. Once a woman becomes pregnant, she ceases to produce milk properly and she can no longer nurse. Hence we fear for the life of the child she is nursing." [4] The Baraita goes on to explain the first case in greater detail: **"Who is** considered **a 'minor'** for the purposes of this law? [5] **A girl from eleven years and one day old to twelve years and one day old.** [6] But if she is **less than** eleven or **more than** twelve, **she may have intercourse in the normal way.** For a girl under the age of eleven cannot possibly become pregnant, and a girl over the age of twelve is in no special danger if she does become pregnant." [7] The Baraita points out: "Everything that has been said until now reflects **the viewpoint of Rabbi Meir.** [8] **But the Sages say: In all cases,** whether the minor is under eleven or between eleven and twelve, **she may have intercourse in the normal way** — and similarly, the pregnant woman and the nursing mother may have intercourse in the normal way — because there is virtually no danger of pregnancy in any case, [9] **and** we are confident that God **in Heaven will have mercy** on these women. If a danger is very remote, and the means to avert it is very disruptive, we are permitted to take risks and rely on God's mercy. [10] We learn this principle from the following verse (Psalms 116:6) which **says: 'The Lord protects the simple.'"**

[1] קְטַנָּה — שֶׁמָּא תִּתְעַבֵּר וְתָמוּת. [2] מְעוּבֶּרֶת — שֶׁמָּא תַּעֲשֶׂה עוּבָּרָהּ סַנְדָּל. [3] מֵנִיקָה — שֶׁמָּא תִּגְמוֹל אֶת בְּנָהּ. [4] וְאֵיזוֹהִי 'קְטַנָּה'? [5] מִבַּת אַחַת עֶשְׂרֵה שָׁנָה וְיוֹם אֶחָד עַד שְׁתֵּים עֶשְׂרֵה שָׁנָה וְיוֹם אֶחָד. [6] פָּחוֹת מִיכֵּן וְיָתֵר עַל כֵּן, מְשַׁמֶּשֶׁת כְּדַרְכָּהּ וְהוֹלֶכֶת. [7] דִּבְרֵי רַבִּי מֵאִיר. [8] וַחֲכָמִים אוֹמְרִים: אַחַת זוֹ וְאַחַת זוֹ מְשַׁמֶּשֶׁת כְּדַרְכָּהּ וְהוֹלֶכֶת, [9] וּמִן הַשָּׁמַיִם [10] יְרַחֲמוּ, מִשּׁוּם שֶׁנֶּאֱמַר: 'שֹׁמֵר פְּתָאיִם ה׳'"!

LITERAL TRANSLATION

[1] A minor — lest she become pregnant and die. [2] A pregnant woman — lest she make her fetus a flat fish. [3] A nursing woman — lest she wean her son. [4] And who is a 'minor'? [5] [A girl] from eleven years and one day old to twelve years and one day old. [6] Less than that and more than that, she goes on having intercourse in her [normal] way. [7] [These are] the words of Rabbi Meir. [8] But the Sages say: In all cases (lit., 'one this and one this') she goes on having intercourse in her [normal] way, [9] and from Heaven they will have mercy, [10] because it is said: 'The Lord protects the simple.'"

RASHI

שמא יעשה עוברה סנדל — שאם תתעבר עובר שני, פוחת השני את צורת הראשון, ודומה לסנדל שהוא דג שנים. **שמא תגמול את בנה** — מפני שהחלב נעכר כשמתעברת, ואינו טוב ליונק, ותצטרך להעתיקו משדים, וימות. **פחות מכאן** — מבת אחת עשרה שנה, משמשת כדרכה, לפי שלא תתעבר. **ויתר על כן** — על בת שתים עשרה שנה משמשת כדרכה, שאם תתעבר — לא תמות. אלמא בקטנות לא מיעברא, שיבא לכלל לידה, דהא "ותמות" קתני.

BACKGROUND

שֶׁמָּא תִּתְעַבֵּר וְתָמוּת Lest she become pregnant and die. Even though young girls generally cannot conceive, women apparently reached puberty at an earlier age in ancient times than they do now, and hence the Gemara's assumption that a young girl might become pregnant. (Even today, cases have been documented where girls have conceived and given birth before reaching their teens.) However, such pregnancies are very risky to the mother, even though they are not necessarily fatal. Hence the Gemara permitted contraception here, in order to protect the girl's life.

שֶׁמָּא תַּעֲשֶׂה עוּבָּרָהּ סַנְדָּל Lest she make her fetus a flat fish. Sometimes, when a woman is pregnant with twins (or close multiple pregnancies — a rare but nevertheless possible condition), one of the fetuses may develop faster than the other, thereby preventing the second fetus from continuing to develop. In such cases, the second fetus will leave the womb at birth as an unformed piece of flesh ("a flat fish" in the Gemara's terminology) next to the live baby.

NOTES

שֶׁמָּא תִּתְעַבֵּר וְתָמוּת Lest she become pregnant and die. Our commentary follows *Rashi*, who explains that the Gemara's objection to Rava's problem is based on Rabbi Meir's position. Rava refers to a *na'arah* who has a son. Thus she must have become pregnant as a minor. But Rabbi Meir is of the opinion that a minor who becomes pregnant inevitably dies before or in giving birth. Hence it is impossible for a *na'arah* to have given birth to a son.

This Baraita is also cited in tractate *Yevamot* (12b). There the Gemara concludes that some minors do in fact survive pregnancy, and that the correct reading in the Baraita is: "Lest she become pregnant and lest she die." According to the Gemara there, Rabbi Meir maintains that a minor should take steps to avoid pregnancy because pregnancy is extremely dangerous for a minor, although not invariably fatal.

The conclusion of the Gemara in *Yevamot* presents a problem for us, since our Gemara is clearly inferring from the Baraita that there is no possibility whatsoever of a *na'arah* giving birth to a live son. In *Yevamot*, *Meiri* explains that our Gemara's objection to Rava's problem is not that it is impossible for a *na'arah* to give birth, but that it is so extremely unlikely that Rava should not have built a question around it. Here in *Ketubot*, *Meiri* explains that our Gemara's objection to Rava's problem is based on the Sages' position: Since the Sages are not concerned about the possibility of a minor becoming pregnant, even though this would be extremely dangerous; we can conclude that this is not a realistic possibility.

Most Rishonim attempt to reconcile our Gemara with the conclusion of the passage in *Yevamot* — that it is possible for a minor to become pregnant and to give birth. They note that the Gemara concludes in *Yevamot* that if a minor does give birth, she is considered from that moment to have become a *na'arah*, regardless of her age. These Rishonim explain that the Gemara means that a minor who

[1] וְכִי תֵּימָא דְּאִיעַבְּרָא כְּשֶׁהִיא נַעֲרָה [2] וְאוֹלִידָה כְּשֶׁהִיא נַעֲרָה — [3] וּבְשִׁיתָּא יַרְחֵי מִי קָא יָלְדָה? [4] וְהָאָמַר שְׁמוּאֵל: אֵין בֵּין נַעֲרוּת לְבַגְרוּת אֶלָּא שִׁשָּׁה חֳדָשִׁים!

[5] וְכִי תֵּימָא: בְּצִיר הוּא דְּלֵיכָּא, [6] הָא טְפֵי אִיכָּא — [7] הָא "אֶלָּא" קָאָמַר!

[8] אֶלָּא הָכִי קָמִיבָּעֲיָא לֵיהּ: [9] יֵשׁ בֶּגֶר בַּקֶּבֶר, [10] וּפָקַע אָב?

LITERAL TRANSLATION

[1] And if you say that she became pregnant while she was a *na'arah* [2] and she gave birth while she was a *na'arah* — [3] but can she give birth within six months? [4] But surely Shmuel said: Between *na'arut* and adulthood there are only six months!

[5] And if you say: It is less that there are not, [6] but there are more — [7] but surely he said "only"!

[8] Rather, this was what he asked: [9] Is there coming of age in the grave, [10] and [the right of] a father ceases?

TRANSLATION AND COMMENTARY

וְכִי תֵּימָא [1] We see from this Baraita that there is no possibility of a *na'arah* giving birth. For even Rabbi Meir, who is concerned about the possibility of a minor becoming pregnant, states that if she were to become pregnant, she would die. How, then, can Rava be referring to a case in which a girl became pregnant as a minor and gave birth as a *na'arah*? **And if we say that** Rava is perhaps referring to a case where **she became pregnant** on or after her twelfth birthday, **when she was** already **a *na'arah*, [2] and gave birth while she was** still **a *na'arah***, this is impossible, [3] because **she cannot** become pregnant and **give birth** to a live baby **within a six-month period. [4] Surely Shmuel said: Between *na'arut* —** נַעֲרוּת (the period when a girl is a *na'arah*) **and adulthood only six months** pass and no more!

וְכִי תֵּימָא [5] **And,** continues the Gemara, **if we say** that Shmuel meant that **there is no** possibility of a *na'arah* becoming an adult in ***less* than** six months, [6] **but there is** a possibility of a *na'arah* taking ***more*** than six months, and that it is therefore possible for her to conceive and to give birth before becoming an adult, this argument too is untenable. [7] For Shmuel **said** that **"only"** six months pass and no more, thereby clearly indicating that all girls become adults six months after becoming *ne'arot*.

אֶלָּא [8] **Rather,** concludes the Gemara, we must amend Rava's question slightly, and say that **the problem he was posing is as follows:** Does a child reach adult status in the grave or not? What is the law if a *na'arah* is raped and happens to die before attaining adulthood? Is she considered an adult six months after becoming a *na'arah*, or does the entire process cease with her death? [9] If we say that **a person reaches adult status in the grave, and** a man raped a *na'arah*, but before he was ordered by the court to pay the fine, the *na'arah* died, [10] then **the father's rights cease,** if he has not yet pressed his claim against the rapist within six months after his daughter became a *na'arah*. For the Mishnah rules (below, 41b) that the father must take the rapist to court before his daughter becomes an adult, but if he delays longer than that, the fine is paid to the girl herself rather than to her father. Hence, in this case, where the *na'arah* is dead, there is no one who can sue the rapist, and he is therefore exempt from paying the fine.

RASHI

וכי תימא — מבת שתים עשרה ויום אחד שהגיעו ימי הנעורים נתעברה, וילדה בנערות ומתה בנערות — הא נמי ליתא, דאמר שמואל: אין בין נערות לבגרות אלא ששה חדשים. **משתביא שתי שערות** — הויא נערה באותן שתביא משתים עשרה שנה והלאה, ומשתביאם עד שתבגור — ששה חדשים ותו לא. ומתניתא דקתני מבת שתים עשרה ואילך אי מעברא לא מתה — במביאה שתי שערות קודם שתתעבר קאמר. אבל כל זמן שלא הביאה — קטנה היא. והאי דנקט מנין שנים — משום דבציר משתים עשרה ויום אחד, אפילו הביאה שערות אינו אלא שומא, כדאמרינן במסכת נדה ובקדושין. **ופקע אב** — פקעה תביעת אב, וזכה הלה במה שבידו, שאין בעל דינו קיים. וקנס לאו ממון הוא להורישו לאביה בתורת ירושה, כל כמה דלא גבתיה.

NOTES

gives birth is considered to have become a *na'arah* retroactively — from the time she became pregnant. Hence she would be an adult six months later — before she gave birth (*Ramban*, *Rashba*, *Ritva*, and others).

יֵשׁ בֶּגֶר בַּקֶּבֶר, וּפָקַע אָב? **Is there coming of age in the grave, and the right of a father ceases?** The Rishonim ask: Why should the father be prevented from collecting the fine merely because his deceased daughter is considered an adult? The Mishnah (below, 41b) does not exempt a man who rapes a *na'arah* from paying the fine if he is not sued until she becomes an adult; rather, it rules that he must pay the fine to the girl herself instead of to her father. Hence, if the girl dies, the fine should be collected by her heir. But in this case her heir is none other than her father. Why, then, should he not collect the fine on her behalf?

There is a dispute among the Rishonim as to whether the right to collect a fine passes to the claimant's heirs like other monetary claims. *Tosafot* and other Rishonim cite our Gemara as proof that a fine cannot be inherited. According to this explanation, if the daughter became an

HALAKHAH

אֵין בֵּין נַעֲרוּת לְבַגְרוּת אֶלָּא שִׁשָּׁה חֳדָשִׁים **Between *na'arut* and adulthood there are only six months.** "A girl at least twelve years old who has produced two pubic hairs is called a *na'arah*, and six full months later she becomes an adult," following Shmuel. (*Rambam, Sefer Nashim, Hilkhot Ishut* 2:2; *Shulḥan Arukh, Yoreh De'ah* 234:1, in *Rema*.)

[1] אוֹ דִּלְמָא אֵין בֶּגֶר בַּקֶּבֶר, [2] וְלָא פָּקַע אָב? [3] מָר בַּר רַב אַשִׁי בָּעֵי לָהּ הָכִי: [4] מִיתָה עוֹשָׂה בַּגְרוּת, אוֹ אֵין עוֹשָׂה בַּגְרוּת? [5] תֵּיקוּ. [6] בָּעֵי מִינֵּיהּ רָבָא מֵאַבַּיֵי: [7] בָּא עָלֶיהָ וְנִתְאָרְסָה, מַהוּ?

LITERAL TRANSLATION

[1] Or perhaps is there no coming of age in the grave, [2] and [the right of] a father does not cease? [3] Mar bar Rav Ashi asked it thus: [4] Does death effect adulthood, or does it not effect adulthood? [5] Let [the question] remain [undecided]. [6] Rava asked [the following question] of Abaye: [7] [If] he [forcibly] had intercourse with her and she became betrothed, what is [the law]?

TRANSLATION AND COMMENTARY

[1] On the other hand, **it is possible that a person does not reach adult status in the grave,** [2] **and the father's rights do not cease** even after six months have passed. Under such circumstances, the father can sue the rapist for the fine without any time limit.

מָר [3] **Mar bar Rav Ashi** had yet another version of Rava's **problem,** which he **posed as follows:** [4] **Does death bring about adulthood, or does it not bring about adulthood?** According to the two versions of Rava's question presented above, it applies only if the father fails to press charges until the six months have passed, but if he presses charges immediately, he is certainly entitled to the fine, because the *na'arah* has not yet had a chance to attain "adulthood in the grave." According to these versions of Rava's question, he disagrees with Abaye's exegetical argument that if the *na'arah* is dead, the rapist is automatically exempt from payment. However, according to Mar bar Rav Ashi's version, Rava is asking whether or not the father loses his prerogatives as soon as his daughter dies, as if she has become an adult. According to this version, Rava does not necessarily reject Abaye's exegetical argument, but merely questions whether or not it is correct.

תֵּיקוּ [5] The Gemara concludes that Rava's **question remains undecided.** The Gemara is unable to determine whether a father's prerogatives cease if his daughter dies while she is a *na'arah,* as Abaye ruled, or whether they continue until the time when the *na'arah* would have become an adult — or even longer, as suggested in the first version of Rava's question.

בָּעֵי מִינֵּיהּ [6] The Gemara now considers a related problem. The Mishnah (below, 41b) rules that the fine is paid to the father only if the rapist was sued in court while the girl was still under her father's authority. But if the girl was an unbetrothed virgin *na'arah* when she was raped, and before the rapist could be sued in court her father died or she became an adult, the fine is paid to the girl herself rather than to her father or to his heirs. The Mishnah does not explicitly deal with a case in which the girl married before the rapist was sued in court, but the Gemara cites a Baraita below, which rules that here too the fine is paid to the girl herself rather than to her father or to his heirs. **Rava asked the following question of Abaye:** [7] **If** the man **raped** the *na'arah*, **and** before he could be sued **she became betrothed,** but not married, **what is the law?** Is the fine paid to the father, as for an unmarried *na'arah*, or is it paid to the girl herself, as for a married woman?

RASHI

או אין בגר בקבר — לאפקועי תביעת אב. **מר בר רב אשי** — לא בעי לה בעיא דרבא משום בגר בקבר, אלא אם מתה בנערותה מי פקעה כי בגרות דמחייס, או לא. ולהאי לישנא דמר בר רב אשי אליבא דרבא אמרו לעיל: מילתא דפשיטא ליה לאביי מיבעיא ליה לרבא. דאילו ללישנא קמא — מפשט פשיטא ליה לרבא דמיתה לא מפקעא, ודלא כאביי, כל זמן שלא בגרה. וכי קא מיבעיא ליה — בבגר בקבר קמבעיא ליה, אבל במיתה, כל זמן שלא בגרה פליג אדאביי ואמר: לא מפקעא, וחייב. **מיתה עושה בגרות** — עושה דין בגרות, דמפקעא כח אב כי בגרות.

TERMINOLOGY

תֵּיקוּ Let the question remain undecided. I.e., the question raised in the previous passage remains unresolved (lit., "standing"), because we have no sources enabling us to resolve it, and there is no logical proof tending toward one solution rather than another. From a theoretical standpoint, therefore, the question remains "standing" in its place. However, in Halakhic decision-making there are various principles as to what action is to be taken in such cases. If the unresolved problem relates to a Rabbinic decree, the decision leans toward leniency. In matters of civil law, where absolute degrees of stringency or leniency have no place, the decision is to leave the existing situation in place.

NOTES

adult and died before claiming the fine, her heirs have no right to the fine, and the rapist is exempt from paying it. This explanation was followed by *Rashi* as well, and has been adopted in our commentary.

According to the other Rishonim, *Tosafot* explains that the father would indeed retain the right to collect the fine, even if his dead daughter were considered an adult. But he would be collecting it on his daughter's behalf, rather than in his own right. *Tosafot* explains that there is a difference between collecting as an heir and collecting in one's own right. For if the daughter owed money and her creditor wished to collect the debt from the fine paid to the daughter's estate, then, if the fine was owed to the daughter and the father collected it as the heir, the creditor could seize it in payment, but if the father collected the fine in his own right, the creditor would have no claim on it.

בָּא עָלֶיהָ וְנִתְאָרְסָה, מַהוּ If he forcibly had intercourse with her and she became betrothed, what is the law? It is not entirely clear why this question was inserted here. Our commentary follows *Tosafot,* who explains that the question is based on the viewpoint of Rabbi Akiva as quoted in the Mishnah, who maintains that if a *na'arah* is raped after she has already been betrothed, the fine is paid to the *na'arah* herself rather than to her father. Thus we see that, for the purposes of the fine, the father loses his prerogatives when his daughter becomes betrothed, even though for other purposes he retains his prerogatives until

[1] אֲמַר לֵיהּ: מִי כְּתִיב: [2] ״וְנָתַן לַאֲבִי הַנַּעֲרָה אֲשֶׁר לֹא אֲרוּסָה״?

[3] וּלְטַעֲמִיךְ, הָא דְּתַנְיָא: [4] ״בָּא עָלֶיהָ וְנִשֵּׂאת, [5] לְעַצְמָהּ״ — [6] מִי כְּתִיב: ״וְנָתַן לַאֲבִי הַנַּעֲרָה אֲשֶׁר לֹא נְשׂוּאָה״?

[7] הָכִי הָשְׁתָּא? [8] הָתָם, הוֹאִיל וּבַגְרוּת מוֹצִיאָה מֵרְשׁוּת אָב, [9] וְנִישּׂוּאִין מוֹצִיאִין מֵרְשׁוּת אָב, [10] מַה בַּגְרוּת, בָּא עָלֶיהָ וּבָגְרָה,

LITERAL TRANSLATION

[1] He said to him: Is it written: [2] "And he shall give to the father of the *na'arah* who is not betrothed"? [3] But according to your reasoning, [regarding] what was taught: [4] "[If] he [forcibly] had intercourse with her and she became married, [5] [it belongs] to [the girl] herself" — [6] is it written: "And he shall give to the father of the *na'arah* who is not married"? [7] Now is this so? [8] There, since adulthood removes [the daughter] from the authority of the father, [9] and marriage removes [the daughter] from the authority of the father, [10] just as [in] adulthood, [if] he had [forcible] intercourse with her and she became an adult,

TRANSLATION AND COMMENTARY

אֲמַר לֵיהּ [1] Abaye **said to** Rava: Why should the fact that the *na'arah* became betrothed after the rape make any difference in this context? Rabbi Akiva ruled in our Mishnah that the father loses his prerogatives if the girl was already betrothed at the time of the rape, but it does not follow that the father loses his prerogatives if the girl was betrothed at the time of payment. For Rabbi Akiva derives his ruling from a verse which states that the fine is given to the father only if the *na'arah* was not betrothed at the time of the rape. But **is it written** in the verse: [2] **"And he shall give to the father of the *na'arah* who is not betrothed"** at the time of payment? Surely not! Thus there is no reason to doubt the father's prerogatives in this matter.

וּלְטַעֲמִיךְ [3] **But**, Rava objects, **according to your reasoning,** how do we know the law **that is taught** in the following Baraita: [4] **"If** a man **rapes** a *na'arah*, **and she** subsequently **becomes married** through *nissu'in*, before the rapist can be sued in court, [5] the fine **belongs to the girl herself** rather than to her father, because she ceased to be under her father's authority when she married"? But, says Rava to Abaye, why, according to your argument, should her marriage make any difference in this context? [6] **Is it written** in the verse: **"And he shall give to the father of the *na'arah* who *is* not married"** at the time of payment? Surely not! Thus there should be no reason to doubt the father's prerogatives in this matter. Yet we see from the Baraita that the father does lose his prerogatives in this case. So perhaps the same is true of betrothal as well!

הָכִי הָשְׁתָּא [7] Abaye replied: **How can you compare** the two cases? In the case of marriage, we do not need a verse to teach us explicitly that the father loses his prerogatives. [8] For we see in other contexts that **adulthood removes a daughter from the authority of her father,** [9] **and** that **marriage** too **removes a daughter from the authority of her father.** A father has a number of monetary prerogatives vis-à-vis his daughter — some of them based on Scriptural authority — but they all cease as soon as she becomes an adult or becomes married. Thus we see that marriage has the same effect as adulthood regarding the father's prerogatives, and we may assume that the same applies to the father's right to the rapist's fine. [10] Hence, **just as regarding adulthood** the Mishnah ruled, on the basis of an exegetical argument, that **if** a man **raped her and she became an adult** before suing him in court, the fine **belongs to the girl herself** rather than to

RASHI

מהו — מי הוי לאביה או לעצמה. **בגרות מוציאה מרשות אב** — דלא מצינו שזכתה לו תורה בבתו אלא מכר בקטנות, ושאר שבח כגון קנסה ומעשה ידיה בנערות, כדילפינן בפרק ״נערה״ (כתובות מו,ב), אבל בבגרות לא אשכחן. וכיון דלא זיכתה לו תורה — אנן מהיכא תיתי לן לזכותו בשלה? **ונשואין מוציאין מרשות אב** — כדאשכחן בהפרת נדרים, דכל זמן דלא ניסת — אביה מיפר, ומשניסת — אין יכול להפר. **בא עליה** — כשהיא נערה ובגרה.

NOTES

she is married. What, then, is the law if the *na'arah* was not yet betrothed when she was raped, but became betrothed before the fine could be collected?

בָּא עָלֶיהָ וְנִשֵּׂאת **If he forcibly had intercourse with her and she became married.** The Gemara assumes that if the *na'arah* marries after the rape, the fine is paid to the *na'arah* herself rather than to her father. It should be noted, however, that the Jerusalem Talmud disagrees with the Babylonian Talmud on this matter, ruling that even if the *na'arah* marries after the rape the fine is still paid to the father. But even the Jerusalem Talmud agrees that if she becomes an adult after the rape, or her father dies, the fine is paid to her.

HALAKHAH

בָּא עָלֶיהָ וְנִשֵּׂאת **If he forcibly had intercourse with her and she became married.** "If a girl is raped or seduced, and before her father can collect the fine she becomes an adult or becomes married, the rapist or the seducer pays the fine to the girl herself. But if she is merely betrothed, the father collects the fine, because betrothal has no effect

לְעַצְמָהּ, [1] אַף נִישּׂוּאִין, בָּא עָלֶיהָ וְנִשֵּׂאת, לְעַצְמָהּ. [2] אֶלָּא אֵירוּסִין מִי קָא מַפְּקֵי מֵרְשׁוּתָא דְּאָב לְגַמְרֵי? [3] הָא תְּנַן: ״נַעֲרָה הַמְאוֹרָסָה, אָבִיהָ וּבַעְלָהּ מְפִירִין לָהּ נְדָרֶיהָ״.

LITERAL TRANSLATION

[it belongs] to [the girl] herself, [1] so too [in] marriage, [if] he had [forcible] intercourse with her and she became married, [it belongs] to [the girl] herself. [2] But does betrothal remove [the daughter] from the authority of the father entirely? [3] Surely we have learned: "[In the case of] a betrothed *na'arah*, her father and her husband annul her vows for her."

RASHI

לעצמה — דכתיב ״ונתן האיש השוכב עמה לאבי הנערה״, אם נערה היא בשעת נתינה. **אביה ובעלה** — ואינו מופר עד שיפרו שניהם.

TRANSLATION AND COMMENTARY

her father, [1] **so too regarding marriage** we may infer that **if** the man **raped her and she became married** before suing him in court, the fine **belongs to the girl herself** rather than to her father. [2] **But**, continues Abaye, **does betrothal remove a daughter from her father's authority entirely** in any context other than the payment of the fine? The only other prerogative of the father that is affected by his daughter's betrothal is his right to annul her vows, and even in this case the father retains some authority. [3] For **surely the Mishnah** (*Nedarim* 66b) **teaches: "In the case of a betrothed *na'arah*, her father and her husband** may jointly **annul her vows for her."** The Torah (Numbers, chapter 30) states that the father of a girl who is a minor or a *na'arah* may annul his daughter's vows on the day he learns of them, and a husband has a similar authority over his wife. If the girl was betrothed as a minor or a *na'arah*, the Gemara (*Nedarim* 67a) derives from a verse in the Torah that the father and the husband must both agree to annul the vow. Thus we see that even in this case the father retains some authority over his betrothed daughter, until she is married. Hence we have no right to assume that betrothal affects the father's prerogative of receiving the rapist's fine, except when we have an explicit verse restricting his prerogative — as in the case of a *na'arah* who was betrothed and divorced at the time of the rape considered by our Mishnah. But if the *na'arah* became betrothed after the rape, there is no explicit verse restricting the father's prerogative, and we must assume that the ordinary rules apply.

NOTES

אֶלָּא אֵירוּסִין מִי קָא מַפְּקֵי מֵרְשׁוּתָא דְּאָב לְגַמְרֵי **But does betrothal remove the daughter from the authority of the father entirely?** At first glance, it is not clear why Abaye introduced the law concerning vows into the discussion at this point. *Ritva* explains that Abaye is citing the law concerning vows because this is the only case, other than the rapist's fine itself, in which betrothal has any effect on the father's prerogatives. Abaye is saying, as it were: Regarding regular monetary matters, the father retains his authority even after his daughter is betrothed. However, even if you wish to say that the rapist's fine is special according to Rabbi Akiva as quoted in the Mishnah, because he rules that betrothal does affect the father's right to collect it if the *na'arah* was already betrothed at the time of the rape, betrothal should still not have more effect on the laws of fines than it does on the laws of vows. We see in the case of vows that the father does not actually lose his prerogatives, but merely gains a partner. Hence it follows that the father should not lose his prerogatives regarding the rapist's fine either.

נַעֲרָה הַמְאוֹרָסָה, אָבִיהָ וּבַעְלָהּ מְפִירִין לָהּ נְדָרֶיהָ **In the case of a betrothed *na'arah*, her father and her husband annul her vows for her.** The laws concerning vows are based on the Scriptural commandments found in Numbers, chapter 30, and are described in detail in *Rambam, Hilkhot Nedarim,* chapters 11 and 12.

The Torah requires a man, and a single adult woman, to keep their vows scrupulously. But a minor girl or a *na'arah* is subject to the authority of her father in these matters. If her father learns that his daughter has made a vow, he has one day to decide whether to confirm it or to annul it. If he says nothing within that time, the vow is automatically confirmed. A similar rule applies to a married woman of any age: Her husband has the power to confirm or annul her vow, within one day of hearing of it.

As long as the daughter is an unmarried minor or *na'arah*, she is subject to her father's authority in these matters. Once she becomes an adult, any vows she makes while still unmarried cannot be annulled at all. If she was betrothed but not married while still a *na'arah*, her father and husband have joint authority over her vows, which may be annulled only if both parties agree to annul them on the very day one of them hears of them for the first time. The vows of a betrothed woman may not be annulled by her husband alone, even if she is an adult or her father has died.

If a betrothed *na'arah* is widowed or divorced before becoming married, she returns to her father's authority as

HALAKHAH

on the father's prerogatives," following the conclusion of our Gemara. (*Rambam, Sefer Nashim, Hilkhot Na'arah Betulah* 2:15-16; *Tur, Even HaEzer* 177.)

נַעֲרָה הַמְאוֹרָסָה, אָבִיהָ וּבַעְלָהּ מְפִירִין לָהּ נְדָרֶיהָ **In the case of a betrothed *na'arah*, her father and her husband annul her vows for her.** "The vows of a betrothed *na'arah* can be annulled only by her father and her husband acting jointly. But if one of them declares that it is his wish to annul the vow, it is not annulled," following the Mishnah cited in our Gemara. (*Rambam, Sefer Hafla'ah, Hilkhot Nedarim* 11:9; *Shulhan Arukh, Yoreh De'ah* 234:5.)

מִשְׁנָה [1]הַמְפַתֶּה נוֹתֵן שְׁלֹשָׁה דְּבָרִים, וְהָאוֹנֵס אַרְבָּעָה. [2]הַמְפַתֶּה נוֹתֵן בּוֹשֶׁת וּפְגָם וּקְנָס. [3]מוֹסִיף עָלָיו אוֹנֵס שֶׁנּוֹתֵן אֶת הַצַּעַר. [4]מַה בֵּין אוֹנֵס לִמְפַתֶּה? [5]הָאוֹנֵס נוֹתֵן אֶת הַצַּעַר, [6]וְהַמְפַתֶּה אֵינוֹ נוֹתֵן אֶת הַצַּעַר. [7]הָאוֹנֵס נוֹתֵן מִיָּד, [8]וְהַמְפַתֶּה לִכְשֶׁיּוֹצִיא. [9]הָאוֹנֵס שׁוֹתֶה

LITERAL TRANSLATION

MISHNAH [1]The seducer gives three things, and the rapist four. [2]The seducer gives [payments for] shame and blemish and the fine. [3]A rapist adds to it in that he gives the [payment for] pain.

[4]What is [the difference] between a rapist and a seducer? [5]The rapist gives the [payment for] pain, [6]but the seducer does not give the [payment for] pain. [7]The rapist gives immediately, [8]but the seducer [gives] when he sends [her] away. [9]The rapist drinks

RASHI

משנה בושת ופגם – במתניתין לקמן מפרש להו. **האונס נותן מיד** – לאביה, אף על פי שכונסה. **לכשיוציא** – בגמרא פריך: אטו אשתו היא? ומפרש לה: לכשלא יכנוס. דאם כנסה – אינו נותן קנס, כדכתיב "מהר ימהרנה לו...ואם מאן ימאן וגו' כסף ישקול". אבל אונס – כתיב "ונתן...חמשים כסף ולו תהיה לאשה".

TRANSLATION AND COMMENTARY

MISHNAH הַמְפַתֶּה [1]We have seen that the fines paid by the seducer and the rapist are identical, and that, in general, similar laws apply to both. However, there are a few differences between these two situations, and these are now considered by the Mishnah. A man who **seduces** a virgin *na'arah* must **give** her father **three things** in compensation, **whereas** a man who **rapes** a virgin *na'arah* must give her father **four.** [2]The Mishnah explains: **The seducer pays** the *na'arah*'s father compensation **for** her **shame and blemish, in addition to the** fifty-shekel **fine** set by the Torah. [3]**A rapist must do more, in that he must pay for the pain** she suffered, in addition to the other three payments. The fifty-shekel fine is a fixed sum set by the Torah as a penalty for the crime itself, and it applies only if the girl was a virgin *na'arah*. But the Mishnah rules that, in addition to this fine, the seducer must also pay damages for the girl's ruined reputation ("shame") and for her loss of virginity ("blemish"). In addition, a rapist must also pay for the pain suffered by the girl during the rape. A later Mishnah (below, 40a) will explain that these additional payments are assessed on an individual basis just as for any other assault. Hence they may also apply to an adult woman or to a non-virgin.

מַה בֵּין אוֹנֵס לִמְפַתֶּה? [4]The Mishnah continues: **What are the differences between** the laws governing **rape and seduction?** The Mishnah lists three such differences. (1) [5]**The rapist pays for** the *na'arah*'s **pain,** as we explained above, [6]**whereas the seducer does not pay for** the *na'arah*'s **pain.** (2) [7]**The rapist pays** the fine **immediately,** as soon as the court convicts him of rape, [8]**whereas the seducer pays** the fine only **when he sends her away.** (The Gemara will explain this clause.) (3) [9]**The rapist drinks from his pot.** The Torah

NOTES

it existed before she was betrothed. But if she was married and then was divorced or widowed, she does not return to her father's authority, even if she is still a minor. Such a widow or divorcee is called "an orphan in the lifetime of her father," because she is subject to the same laws as an orphaned minor or a *na'arah*.

שׁוֹתֶה בַּעֲצִיצוֹ Drinks from his pot. The term עָצִיץ (translated here as "pot") refers to a rough earthenware vessel, not suitable for drinking (*Rambam*). It usually appears in the Talmud in the sense of a flowerpot (*Talmidei Rabbenu Yonah*). Thus the Mishnah is comparing a man who rapes a lame or blind girl and is forced to marry her to a man who drinks out of a flowerpot and is now compelled to use it as his personal goblet.

The law that the rapist must marry his victim and must not divorce her is somewhat puzzling. It would appear highly unlikely that in most cases the *na'arah* or her father would wish her to be married to him. *Sefer HaḤinnukh* explains that the Torah made this requirement in order to deter potential rapists, as well as to give an option to a

HALAKHAH

הַמְפַתֶּה נוֹתֵן שְׁלֹשָׁה דְּבָרִים, וְהָאוֹנֵס אַרְבָּעָה The seducer gives three things, and the rapist four. "A man who seduces a virgin *na'arah* must pay for her lost virginity and for her shame, in addition to the fifty-shekel fine set by the Torah. A rapist must in addition compensate her for her pain." (*Rambam, Sefer Nashim, Hilkhot Na'arah Betulah* 2:1; *Shulḥan Arukh, Even HaEzer* 177:1.)

הָאוֹנֵס נוֹתֵן מִיָּד The rapist gives immediately. "The rapist must pay the four things he owes immediately, whether or not the *na'arah* agrees to marry him. The seducer, by contrast, pays for the *na'arah*'s lost virginity and for her shame immediately, but he pays the fine only if he fails to marry her. But if he marries her, he must write her a full ketubah as for a virgin." (*Rambam, Sefer Nashim, Hilkhot Na'arah Betulah* 2:7; *Tur, Even HaEzer* 177.)

הָאוֹנֵס שׁוֹתֶה בַּעֲצִיצוֹ The rapist drinks from his pot. "A man who rapes a virgin *na'arah* must marry her — provided that both she and her father agree to the marriage. He must marry her even if she is blind or lame or a leper. After he marries her, he may never divorce her, except with her permission. If he does divorce her, we compel him to remarry her." (*Rambam, Sefer Nashim, Hilkhot Na'arah Betulah* 1:3; *Shulḥan Arukh Even HaEzer* 177:3.)

TRANSLATION AND COMMENTARY

states (Deuteronomy 22:29) that the rapist must marry the *na'arah* he has raped and can never divorce her. This requirement binds the rapist but not the *na'arah*. Thus, if she wishes, she can compel him to marry her and can refuse to allow him to divorce her; but she is under no compulsion to marry him, and the couple are permitted to divorce if she consents. Thus the rapist is punished for forcing the girl to have intercourse with him against her will by himself being forced to live with her as husband and wife against his will. This punishment is described as "drinking from the pot" from which he had forced his victim to drink.

[1]**The seducer,** on the other hand, is not bound by this law. The Torah urges the seducer to marry the girl he seduced (Exodus 22:15), but no compulsion is involved, and either party may refuse to marry the other. Moreover, if the seducer does marry the girl, there are no special restrictions on his prerogatives as a husband, and **if he wishes to divorce her, he may divorce her** in the normal way.

כֵּיצַד [2]The Mishnah notes that the duty of marriage imposed on the rapist is described as "drinking from his pot" — rather than "from his cup" or some other term. The Mishnah uses a word that suggests a rough earthenware container not normally used for drinking, thereby suggesting an additional dimension to the penalty. The Mishnah asks rhetorically: **How does he drink from his pot?** [3]The Mishnah answers that the rapist **is compelled to marry** the *na'arah* **even if she is lame, even if she is blind, and even if she is afflicted with boils.** No matter how unattractive she may be, he is commanded to marry his victim and he is forbidden to divorce her. The Mishnah points out, however, that there is one exception to this rule: It is not permitted to override any other law of the Torah. [4]Thus, **if it was found that she had acted adulterously** (if, for example, after he married her she was found to have acted in such a way that she was suspected of committing adultery), [5]**or if she is** one of the women who are **not fit to marry a Jew** (if, for example, she is a *mamzeret* and the rapist is an ordinary Jew, or if she is a woman who is disqualified from marrying a priest and the rapist is a priest), [6]the rapist **is not permitted to keep her** in the first case, or to marry her in the second. [7]The Mishnah explains that this law is derived from **the verse** dealing with the rapist (Deuteronomy 22:29) which **says: "And she shall be his wife."** The Mishnah notes that the Hebrew word לוֹ (literally, "to him" — "and *to him* she shall be a wife") is superfluous, [8]and its purpose is to teach us that this law applies only to **a wife who is fit for him** according to the laws of the Torah.

בַּעֲצִיצוֹ, [1]וְהַמְפַתֶּה, אִם רָצָה לְהוֹצִיא, מוֹצִיא.
[2]כֵּיצַד שׁוֹתֶה בַּעֲצִיצוֹ? [3]אֲפִילּוּ הִיא חִיגֶּרֶת, אֲפִילּוּ הִיא סוּמָא, וַאֲפִילּוּ הִיא מוּכַּת שְׁחִין. [4]נִמְצָא בָּהּ דְּבַר עֶרְוָה, [5]אוֹ שֶׁאֵינָהּ רְאוּיָה לָבֹא בְּיִשְׂרָאֵל, [6]אֵינוֹ רַשַּׁאי לְקַיְּימָהּ, [7]שֶׁנֶּאֱמַר: "וְלוֹ תִהְיֶה לְאִשָּׁה" — [8]אִשָּׁה הָרְאוּיָה לוֹ.

LITERAL TRANSLATION

from his pot, [1]but the seducer, if he wishes to send [her] away, he sends [her] away.

[2]How does he drink from his pot? [3][He must marry her] even if she is lame, even if she is blind, and even if she is afflicted with boils. [4][If] a matter of adultery was found about her, [5]or if she is not fit to enter [by marriage] into [the community of] Israel, [6]he is not permitted to keep her, [7]for it is said: "And she shall be his wife" — [8]a wife who is fit for him.

RASHI

שותה בעציצו – בכלי שבחר לו לשתות בו. כלומר, על כרחו ישאנה, כדכתיב "לא יוכל לשלחה" (דברים כב).

LANGUAGE

עָצִיץ Pot. This word is related to the Arabic أصيص, meaning "flowerpot." The Hebrew letter ayin in our word may reflect the fact that flowerpots were used for growing trees (עֵצִים, which also begins with the letter ayin).

REALIA

עָצִיץ A pot

A relief of a decorated flowerpot from the Talmudic period.

The Talmudic sources imply that pots were earthenware containers (although wooden flowerpots might also have been used), which were generally not finished carefully or fully fired. Hence, these flowerpots were generally not fit for display, and were used instead for growing plants, or as toilets and urinals. Occasionally, the bottom part of a broken jug was used as a flowerpot.

NOTES

na'arah who feels that her marriage possibilities have been ruined. *Ramban*, in his commentary on the Torah (Exodus 22:15) explains that it is intended to deter members of powerful families from raping women from the lower classes with impunity, as was all too common in other societies.

אֵינוֹ רַשַּׁאי לְקַיְּימָהּ He is not permitted to keep her. *Rashba* explains that the Mishnah used this language — "to keep her" — primarily for the sake of the first case, in which the girl is suspected of adultery. In such a case, the rapist is permitted to divorce his wife only if she commits adultery after he has married her, but he may not excuse himself from marrying her on the basis of her previous behavior. However, rather than using repetitive language, and saying that the rapist must divorce his wife if she commit adultery, and may not marry her if she is forbidden to him, the Mishnah selected the verb "to keep," which has the connotation of not marrying as well as of divorcing.

HALAKHAH

נִמְצָא בָּהּ דְּבַר עֶרְוָה If a matter of adultery was found about her. "If the rapist rapes a woman whom he is forbidden to marry — even if she is forbidden only by Rabbinic decree — he may not marry her. Likewise, if the rapist marries the woman he raped, and she later commits adultery or is suspected of committing adultery, and she thereby becomes forbidden to him, he must divorce her." (*Rambam, Sefer Nashim, Hilkhot Na'arah Betulah* 1:5; *Shulḥan Arukh, Even HaEzer* 177:4.)

SAGES

אֲבוּהּ דִּשְׁמוּאֵל The father of Shmuel. See *Ketubot,* Part II, p. 150.

רַבִּי שִׁמְעוֹן בֶּן יְהוּדָה Rabbi Shimon ben Yehudah. A member of the last generation of Tannaim, Rabbi Shimon ben Yehudah was the closest disciple of Rabbi Shimon (ben Yoḥai) and almost all the statements attributed to him in the Talmud are rulings transmitted to him by his teacher, Rabbi Shimon.

Rabbi Shimon ben Yehudah came from Kefar Acco in Upper Galilee. His teachings are recorded in the Babylonian and Jerusalem Talmuds and in Halakhic and Aggadic Midrashim.

BACKGROUND

צַעַר Pain. Such pain may result from insufficient moistening of the vagina, or from contraction of the vaginal muscles (these problems generally do not exist when a woman has intercourse of her own free will). Moreover, a woman who was raped usually finds even minor pain intolerable, since she did not want to have intercourse (which might even cause physical injury) in the first place. The Gemara is apparently not referring to the pain caused by the rupture of the hymen, which is generally minimal, and no worse than that of a minor wound in a sensitive area, as the Gemara states.

גמרא [1]צַעַר דְּמַאי? [2]אָמַר אֲבוּהּ דִּשְׁמוּאֵל: צַעַר שֶׁחֲבָטָהּ עַל גַּבֵּי קַרְקַע. [3]מַתְקִיף לַהּ רַבִּי זֵירָא: אֶלָּא מֵעַתָּה, [4]חֲבָטָהּ עַל גַּבֵּי שִׁירָאִין, [5]הָכִי נַמִי דְּפָטוּר? [6]וְכִי תֵּימָא הָכִי נַמִי, [7]וְהָתַנְיָא: ״רַבִּי שִׁמְעוֹן בֶּן יְהוּדָה אוֹמֵר מִשּׁוּם רַבִּי שִׁמְעוֹן: [8]אוֹנֵס אֵינוֹ מְשַׁלֵּם אֶת הַצַּעַר, מִפְּנֵי [39B] שֶׁסּוֹפָהּ לְהִצְטַעֵר תַּחַת בַּעְלָהּ.

LITERAL TRANSLATION

GEMARA [1]Pain from what?

[2]The father of Shmuel said: Pain [caused] when he knocked her down onto the ground.

[3]Rabbi Zera objected to it: But if so, [4][if] he knocked her down onto silk garments, [5]would he really be exempt? [6]And if you say it is indeed so, [7]but surely it was taught: "Rabbi Shimon ben Yehudah says in the name of Rabbi Shimon: [8]A rapist does not pay [for] the pain, because [39B] she will ultimately have pain from her husband.

RASHI

גמרא שסופה להצטער כו׳ — ואי חיבוט על גבי קרקע הוא, וכי סופה ליחבט על גבי קרקע תחת בעלה?

TRANSLATION AND COMMENTARY

GEMARA צַעַר דְּמַאי [1]The Gemara begins by considering the first clause of the Mishnah, which stated that the rapist must pay compensation for the pain suffered by the *na'arah* during the rape — pain that is not suffered by a *na'arah* who is seduced. The Gemara asks: **Pain from what?** What kind of pain is suffered by a virgin *na'arah* who was raped, but is not suffered by a virgin *na'arah* who engaged in intercourse voluntarily?

אָמַר אֲבוּהּ דִּשְׁמוּאֵל [2]**The father of Shmuel said** in reply: He must pay compensation for the **pain** he **caused** her **when he knocked her down onto the ground** as he forced her to submit. In other words, according to the father of Shmuel, the payment is not for the pain suffered during the act of intercourse itself, but rather for the incidental pain suffered during the course of the violent assault that resulted in the rape.

מַתְקִיף [3]**Rabbi Zera objected to** this explanation: **But if so,** if the payment for pain is not for the pain of the rape itself but for the incidental violence that accompanied it, surely there is no certainty that the rapist hurt his victim in this way! [4]Thus, according to the explanation offered by Shmuel's father, **if he knocked her down onto silken garments** (i.e., if he raped her without harming her in any way other than through the act of rape itself), [5]**is he exempt** from paying for her pain? [6]**And if we argue that this is indeed the case,** and the Mishnah mentioned this payment not because it is inherently part of the law governing rape, but rather because it applies in most rape situations, **surely** such an explanation is untenable. For it is clear from an authoritative Baraita explaining this Mishnah (found in almost identical language in Tosefta *Ketubot* 3:6) that the pain is caused by the intercourse itself and not by the incidental violence that may accompany it. [7]For **it was taught** in this Baraita: "A rapist pays compensation for pain, whereas a seducer does not. **Rabbi Shimon ben Yehudah said in the name of Rabbi Shimon:** [8]**A rapist does not pay** compensation **for pain, because** [39B] **she will ultimately have pain** during her first intercourse **with her husband.** No compensation needs to be paid for the pain suffered during rape, for had the girl not been raped, she would have suffered

NOTES

צַעַר דְּמַאי? Pain from what? At first glance, the Gemara's question appears astonishing. The Mishnah is referring to a virgin *na'arah* whose first experience of sexual intercourse was when she was raped. Surely it is obvious that she suffered pain from the rupture of her hymen!

Tosafot gives two answers to this question. The first answer (followed by *Ritva* and other Rishonim) is as follows: Under Talmudic law, an assailant pays compensation for pain caused at the time of the assault, but not for pain suffered by the victim subsequently. Since the pain caused by the rupture of the hymen is usually felt most strongly after the act of intercourse, the assailant is not liable for it.

Our commentary follows *Tosafot*'s second answer (followed also by *Rosh*): The Gemara is seeking to find a category of pain that is suffered by a woman who is raped but not by a woman who is seduced. Hence it is obvious that we cannot be referring to the rupture of the *na'arah*'s hymen, since this pain is suffered equally during any first intercourse, whether voluntary or not. Therefore the Gemara asks what other pain is suffered by a raped woman, and answers: "The pain caused by being knocked to the ground."

שֶׁסּוֹפָהּ לְהִצְטַעֵר תַּחַת בַּעְלָהּ Because she will ultimately have pain from her husband. The Jerusalem Talmud also cites this Baraita and states that our Mishnah follows the viewpoint of the Sages. In the version cited in the Jerusalem Talmud, Rabbi Shimon compares the pain caused by the rupture of the virgin's hymen to the pain caused by the cutting off of a wart that was about to be cut out anyway. The Sages argue against him that there is a big difference between intercourse on the ground in an alleyway and intercourse on a bed.

The Jerusalem Talmud adds that Rabbi Shimon agrees that if the rapist hurt the virgin in a way unconnected to the pain of the intercourse itself (for example, by laying her down on thorns), he must pay compensation for the pain he caused. *Pnei Moshe* explains that, according to the Jerusalem Talmud, the case in dispute between Rabbi Shimon and the Sages is if he knocked her to the ground: The Sages hold him liable to pay in this case as well, and only exempt him if he placed her down on a bed, whereas

TRANSLATION AND COMMENTARY

this pain later, when she married. [1]But the other Sages **said to** Rabbi Shimon ben Yehudah: Even though it is true that the girl was bound to suffer some pain when she married, the rapist must still pay compensation. For the pain suffered by **a woman who is forced to have intercourse is not the same as** the pain suffered by **a woman who has intercourse voluntarily,** and the rapist must pay compensation for the difference between the two levels of pain." Thus we see from this Baraita that the pain suffered by the raped girl is inherently connected with the act of intercourse itself, and not with the incidental violence of the rapist's assault.

אֶלָּא [2]**Rather, Rav Naḥman said in the name of Rabbah bar Avuha: The pain** to which the Mishnah refers — which is caused by the intercourse itself but is suffered only by a woman who is raped and not by a woman who engages in intercourse voluntarily — comes **from spreading the legs** apart. [3]**And** support for this interpretation of the Mishnah is found in **the** Biblical **verse** (Ezekiel 16:25) which **says** of a woman who engaged in prostitution: **"And you have spread your legs for every passerby."**

אִי הָכִי [4]The Gemara rejects Rav Naḥman's explanation: **If,** as Rav Naḥman claims, the pain was caused by spreading the legs apart, **a seduced woman** should **also** be compensated for this pain!

[1]אָמְרוּ לוֹ: אֵינוֹ דּוֹמֶה נִבְעֶלֶת בְּאוֹנֶס לְנִבְעֶלֶת בְּרָצוֹן״!
[2]אֶלָּא אָמַר רַב נַחְמָן אָמַר רַבָּה בַּר אֲבוּהָ: צַעַר שֶׁל פִּיסּוּק הָרַגְלַיִם. [3]וְכֵן הוּא אוֹמֵר: ״וַתְּפַשְּׂקִי אֶת רַגְלַיִךְ לְכָל עוֹבֵר״.
[4]אִי הָכִי, מְפוּתָּה נַמִּי!

LITERAL TRANSLATION

[1]They said to him: A woman who has intercourse by force is not similar to a woman who has intercourse voluntarily"!

[2]Rather, Rav Naḥman said in the name of Rabbah bar Avuha: The pain of spreading the legs. [3]And so [the verse] says: "And you have spread your legs for every passerby."

[4]If so, a seduced woman also!

NOTES

Rabbi Shimon holds him liable to pay only if he knocked her down onto thorns, but not if he knocked her to the ground. *Yefeh Enayim* notes that the Jerusalem Talmud appears to follow Shmuel's father in our Gemara, who explains that the Mishnah is referring to the pain caused by knocking the *na'arah* to the ground. For the Jerusalem Talmud declares that our Mishnah follows the Sages and disagrees with Rabbi Shimon; hence it must be referring to the case in dispute between them. *Korban HaEdah*, however, attempts to reconcile the Jerusalem Talmud with our Gemara.

שֶׁסּוֹפָהּ לְהִצְטַעֵר תַּחַת בַּעְלָהּ **Because she will ultimately have pain from her husband.** *Ḥatam Sofer* asks: How can Rabbi Shimon ben Yehudah be so certain that this virgin *na'arah* will suffer this pain during her first act of intercourse with her husband? Perhaps she will never get married! There is no commandment in the Torah requiring women to get married (although there is such a commandment addressed to men), and a woman is perfectly entitled to remain unmarried all her life if she prefers. How, then, can we reduce the rapist's liability, on the assumption that his victim will marry?

Ḥatam Sofer answers that the entire law of the rapist is based on the assumption that most women wish to get married. For *Ramban* (in his commentary on Exodus 22:15) explains that the fifty-shekel fine is essentially compensation for the *na'arah*'s reduced marriage prospects following her loss of virginity.

וַתְּפַשְּׂקִי אֶת רַגְלַיִךְ **"And you have spread your legs for every passerby."** In the chapter from which this verse is quoted, the Prophet Ezekiel castigates the behavior of the Jews in Eretz Israel toward the end of the First Temple period, when idolatry was widespread. The prophets often compared the straying of the Jewish people from the worship of their own God to the worship of idols with the straying of an adulterous wife from her own husband to a chance lover. In this verse, Ezekiel declares that idolatry has become so commonplace that it is to be likened to an adulterous wife who engages in indiscriminate prostitution.

Ritva notes that it is not entirely clear what the Gemara is seeking to prove by citing this verse. What do we know about the pain of intercourse that we did not know before this verse was cited? *Ritva* suggests that it may simply be a reference to help the reader understand the expression "spreading the legs."

Alternatively, *Ritva* explains that we see from the verse in Ezekiel that spreading the legs is painful. For Ezekiel is castigating the adulterous wife for showing no restraint in her enthusiasm for prostitution. Thus he mentions the spreading of the legs, because this causes a certain amount of pain, and yet the prostitute does not hesitate to do it constantly.

אִי הָכִי, מְפוּתָּה נַמִּי **If so, a seduced woman also.** According to the plain meaning of the text, the Gemara is objecting that a seduced woman too should be entitled to compensation for pain, if the pain is caused by the spreading of the legs. The Rishonim have difficulty in understanding the Gemara's objection. If the pain of spreading the legs is the same in all acts of intercourse, why should the seducer be liable? On the contrary, both the seducer and the rapist should be exempt, since the girl will eventually suffer this pain anyway during her first act of intercourse with her husband!

Ramban explains that this argument is part of the Gemara's objection: It is possible that the Mishnah maintains that the rapist is held liable for the pain caused by spreading his victim's legs apart, even though she will ultimately suffer this pain from her husband, in accordance with those Tannaim who argue that even if other damage is prevented from occurring later, the payment is not reduced. But if so, why does the Mishnah exempt the seducer?

[1] אָמַר רַב נַחְמָן אָמַר רַבָּה בַּר אֲבוּהּ: [2] מָשָׁל דִּמְפוּתָּה, [3] לְמָה הַדָּבָר דּוֹמֶה? [4] לְאָדָם שֶׁאָמַר לַחֲבֵירוֹ: ״קְרַע שִׁירָאִין שֶׁלִּי וְהִפָּטֵר״.

[5] ״שֶׁלִּי״? דַּאֲבוּהּ נִינְהוּ!

[6] אֶלָּא אָמַר רַב נַחְמָן אָמַר רַבָּה

TRANSLATION AND COMMENTARY

אָמַר רַב נַחְמָן [1] In reply to this objection, **Rav Naḥman said in the name of Rabbah bar Avuha:** The reason why a seducer is not required to pay for the pain he caused is not because the seduced woman does not feel it, but because she does not care about it. [2] **As an illustration of the case of a seduced woman** we can say: [3] **To what is the matter similar?** [4] **To a man who said to another: "Tear my silken garments and be exempt** from paying for them." In such a case, the other person is indeed exempt from paying damages, even though he definitely caused the owner of the garments a financial loss. Similarly the seduced girl was clearly not concerned about the pain she would suffer, and submitted to it voluntarily.

״שֶׁלִּי״ [5] But the Gemara rejects this explanation: What analogy is there between seduction and a case in which the owner of a garment tells someone else, "Tear ***my*** garment"? Since the seduced girl is a *na'arah* or a minor and her father is alive, the right to receive compensation for her loss of virginity **is her father's,** and she can no more waive her father's right than can the daughter of the owner of a garment tell someone to tear her father's garment and be exempt!

אֶלָּא [6] **Rather,** we must reject this explanation and look for pain caused by the act of intercourse itself, but suffered only by a virgin *na'arah* who was raped and not by a virgin *na'arah* who engaged in intercourse

LITERAL TRANSLATION

[1] Rav Naḥman said in the name of Rabbah bar Avuha: [2] [As] an illustration [of the case of] a seduced woman, [3] to what may the matter be compared? [4] To a man who said to his fellow: "Tear my silk garments and be exempt."

[5] "My"? They are her father's!

[6] Rather, Rav Naḥman said in the name of Rabbah

RASHI

שלי – בתמיה. **דאבוה הוא** – דהא כל שבח נעורים ילפינן לקמן (מו,ב) לאביה, והיאך היא יכולה למחול?

NOTES

Tosafot explains that spreading the legs is painful even for a non-virgin. But Rabbi Shimon ben Yehudah only exempts the rapist from compensation for pain that his victim is destined to suffer once in her lifetime. He does not exempt the rapist from paying compensation for pain which his victim is destined to suffer every time she has intercourse. Hence the Gemara does not object that the rapist should be exempt from compensating her for this pain, but objects instead that the seducer should also be liable, since this pain is felt even in voluntary intercourse.

״קְרַע שִׁירָאִין שֶׁלִּי וְהִפָּטֵר״ "Tear my silk garments and be exempt." The straightforward meaning of the text is that Rav Naḥman is of the opinion that the seduced *na'arah* is not entitled to compensation for her pain, because she is considered to have waived her right to it when she consented to the intercourse. This explanation is difficult to accept, for it assumes that Rav Naḥman overlooked the explicit Mishnah (below, 41b) that rules that the payment for pain goes to the father and not to the *na'arah* herself. Moreover, the Torah explicitly states that the fine for a seduced *na'arah* is paid to the father. But if a *na'arah* is considered to have waived her right to compensation for pain, why is she not considered to have waived her right to the fine as well, like an orphan *na'arah* who was seduced (above, 32a)?

Ritva explains that Rav Naḥman is of the opinion that a distinction should be made between the rights of the father to payment for pain and shame, and his right to the fine. The fine is a simple monetary right which belongs to her father, and she cannot waive it. But pain and shame are compensation for what she personally experienced, and although they too are paid to the father, Rav Naḥman maintains that they should not be paid where she voluntarily submitted to them. The Gemara rejects this argument, ruling that pain and shame are no different from other rights in this regard.

Rashba explains that even in Rav Naḥman's initial explanation — when he says that seduction is similar to a case in which a person says: "Tear my silken garments" — he does not mean that the *na'arah* is considered to have waived her claims. Rather, he means that spreading the legs need not hurt if the intercourse is voluntary and the *na'arah* is careful. Hence whatever pain she suffers if she is careless is her own concern and does not affect her father, just like a person's decision to have his garments torn is his own concern. The father is entitled to compensation for those damages inflicted on his daughter that he himself would indirectly have inflicted by marrying her off. But pain suffered by the seduced *na'arah* through her own carelessness does not "belong" to her father. The Gemara, however, does not understand Rav Naḥman's argument in this way, and thinks that Rav Naḥman is referring to the seduced *na'arah* waiving her claims. Hence the Gemara objects that a *na'arah* cannot waive her father's claims, and Rav Naḥman responds by explaining his reasoning explicitly.

אֶלָּא אָמַר רַב נַחְמָן Rather, Rav Naḥman said. Our translation and commentary follow the standard Talmud edition, which introduces Rav Naḥman's explanation with the word "rather" (אֶלָּא — a technical term implying that the previous explanation has been withdrawn in the face of the objection raised against it. This reading is satisfactory according to *Rosh*, who argues that the discussion in the Gemara was based on a false assumption that was not overcome until this point. According to *Rosh*, Rav Naḥman is now withdrawing his explanation that the Mishnah is referring to the pain caused by spreading the legs, and is explaining instead that the Mishnah is referring to the pain caused by the rupture of the hymen.

But according to the other Rishonim, Rav Naḥman is still

TRANSLATION AND COMMENTARY

voluntarily. Accordingly, **Rav Nahman said in the name of Rabbah bar Avuha:** [1]I asked some **clever women** about this matter and they **said: A seduced woman does not** suffer **pain** from her first intercourse.

וְהָא קָא [2]**But surely,** objects the Gemara, **we see that** a seduced woman **does** experience pain when the seduction is the first time she has ever had intercourse!

אֲמַר אַבַּיֵי [3]The Gemara answers that although women do suffer some pain when they engage — even voluntarily — in intercourse for the first time, this pain is negligible. For **Abaye said:** My foster **mother said to me:** [4]The pain felt by a virgin who voluntarily engages in intercourse feels **like hot water on the head of a bald man.** [5]**Rava said:** My wife, **the daughter of Rav Ḥisda, said to me:** It feels **like the** momentary **pain caused by a bloodletter's lancet.** [6]**Rav Pappa said:** My wife, **the daughter of Abba of Sura, said to me:** It feels **like hard bread on the gums.** This very slight discomfort is accepted as part of the normal course of a first act of sexual intercourse. But the pain suffered by a victim of rape is much greater — even if there is no attendant violence — and the rapist must pay compensation for it.

הָאוֹנֵס [7]The Gemara now considers the next clause of the Mishnah, which ruled that one of the differences between the rapist and the seducer is that **"the rapist pays** the fine to the father **immediately,** as soon as the court convicts him of rape, **whereas the seducer pays** the fine only **when he divorces her."** [8]The Gemara objects: How can the Mishnah say that the seducer pays the fine **"when he divorces her"! Is she his wife?** He did not marry the girl, he seduced her!

בַּר אֲבוּהּ: [1]פִּקְחוֹת שֶׁבָּהֶן אוֹמְרוֹת: מְפוּתָּה אֵין לָהּ צַעַר. [2]וְהָא קָא חָזֵינַן דְּאִית לָהּ! [3]אֲמַר אַבַּיֵי: [4]אָמְרָה לִי אֵם: כְּמַיָּא חֲמִימֵי עַל רֵישֵׁיהּ דְּקָרְחָא. [5]רָבָא אֲמַר: אָמְרָה לִי בַּת רַב חִסְדָּא: כִּי רִיבְדָּא דְּכוּסִילְתָּא. [6]רַב פַּפָּא אֲמַר: אָמְרָה לִי בַּת אַבָּא סוּרָאָה: כִּי נַהֲמָא אַקּוּשָׁא בְּחִינְכֵי. [7]"הָאוֹנֵס נוֹתֵן מִיָּד, הַמְפַתֶּה לִכְשֶׁיּוֹצִיא וכו׳". [8]"לִכְשֶׁיּוֹצִיא"? אִשְׁתּוֹ הִיא?

LITERAL TRANSLATION

bar Avuha: [1]The clever women among them say: A seduced woman does not have pain.
[2]But surely we see that she does!
[3]Abaye said: Mother said to me: [4]Like hot water on the head of a bald [man]. [5]Rava said: The daughter of Rav Ḥisda said to me: Like the prick of a bloodletter's lancet. [6]Rav Pappa said: The daughter of Abba of Sura said to me: Like hard bread on the gums.
[7]"The rapist gives immediately, [but] the seducer [gives] when he sends [her] away, etc." [8]"When he sends [her] away"? Is she his wife?

RASHI

ריבדא דכוסילתא = *פולטוייר"א דפלמוא"ה בלעז. **ריבדא** = ניקור. **כוסילתא** — כלי אומן מקיז, ואית דגרסי: כי תרפתא דסיכורי, והיא היא. **אמרה לי אם** — אומנתו היתה. **בת רב חסדא** — אשתו של רבא. **בת אבא סוראה** — דביתהו דרב פפא. **נהמא אקושא בחינכי** — כלחם קשה שגורר את החיך. **אשתו היא** — וכי אשתו היא כבר דקאמר "לכשיוציא"?

LANGUAGE

רִיבְדָּא דְּכוּסִילְתָּא Prick of a blood-letter's lancet. The word רִיבְדָּא is cognate to the Arabic رَبْذ, "puncture, prick," while כּוּסִילְתָּא is Aramaic for "blood-letting."

LANGUAGE (RASHI)

***פורצטוייר"א דפלמוא"ה (read: פוינטור"א דיפלימא"ה).** From the Old French *pointure de flemie,* meaning "knife puncture" (from blood-letting).

NOTES

explaining the Mishnah as referring to the pain caused by the spreading of the legs. Hence we must say that he has withdrawn his original explanation — that the seducer is exempt from payment for pain because seduction is like asking another person to tear one's own clothes — and that he is now substituting the explanation that the rape victim suffers more pain from the spreading of the legs than she does during voluntary intercourse. *Ritva* explains that Rav Nahman is of the opinion that a distinction can be made between the *na'arah*'s right to waive payment for pain and her right to waive other payments, but that he accepts the Gemara's viewpoint that the *na'arah* has no authority to waive any of her father's claims.

According to *Rashba*, however, Rav Nahman maintains throughout the discussion that a victim of rape suffers more pain from the spreading of the legs than she would during voluntary intercourse, and it is the Gemara that does not understand what he meant when he said: "Tear my garments." Accordingly, *Rashba* removes the word "rather" from the text, since Rav Nahman is not withdrawing his previous explanation but merely elucidating it.

פִּקְחוֹת שֶׁבָּהֶן אוֹמְרוֹת The clever women among them say. According to the plain meaning of the Gemara, the women described here are "clever" because they know how to answer the Gemara's question. *Shittah Mekubbetzet*, however, has a different explanation, according to which it is the clever women themselves who suffer no pain during voluntary intercourse. *Shittah Mekubbetzet* asserts that there is a technique involved in achieving painless intercourse. According to this explanation, the Gemara cites three different "clever women," each of whom showed a different level of skill, and had a different level of pain.

אִשְׁתּוֹ הִיא Is she his wife? Our translation and commentary follow *Rashi* and most Rishonim, who explain that the Gemara is objecting to the Mishnah's language by means of a rhetorical question: Why does the Mishnah say that the seducer pays the fine when he divorces the *na'arah*? Why do we assume that he married her? *Ra'avad* has a different explanation, according to which the Gemara is not asking a rhetorical question but making a statement of fact: We see that the Mishnah is referring to a case in which the seducer married the *na'arah* and then divorced

[1] אָמַר אַבַּיֵי: אֵימָא: [2] "לִכְשֶׁלֹּא יִכְנוֹס".
[3] תַּנְיָא נַמִי הָכִי: [4] "אַף עַל פִּי שֶׁאָמְרוּ הַמְפַתֶּה נוֹתֵן לִכְשֶׁלֹּא יִכְנוֹס, [5] בּוֹשֶׁת וּפְגָם נוֹתֵן מִיָּד".
[6] "וְאֶחָד הָאוֹנֵס וְאֶחָד הַמְפַתֶּה, בֵּין הִיא וּבֵין אָבִיהָ יְכוֹלִין לְעַכֵּב".
[7] בִּשְׁלָמָא מְפוּתָּה: [8] "כְּתִיב: 'אִם מָאֵן יְמָאֵן אָבִיהָ'. [9] אֵין לִי אֶלָּא אָבִיהָ, [10] הִיא עַצְמָהּ מִנַּיִן? [11] תַּלְמוּד לוֹמַר: 'יְמָאֵן', מִכָּל מָקוֹם". [12] אֶלָּא אוֹנֵס,

LITERAL TRANSLATION

[1] Abaye said: Say: [2] "When he does not marry [her]." [3] It was also taught thus: [4] "Although they said [that] the seducer gives when he does not marry [her], [5] [payments for] shame and deterioration he gives immediately."
[6] "And regarding both the rapist and the seducer, both she and her father can prevent [it]."
[7] Granted [in the case of] the seduced woman [it was taught]: [8] "It is written: 'If her father will surely refuse.' [9] I have only [the case of] her father. [10] From where [do I know that] she herself [may also refuse]? [11] The Torah says: 'will [surely] refuse,' [implying] either of them (lit., 'any way')." [12] But [in the case of] a rapist,

TRANSLATION AND COMMENTARY

אָמַר אַבַּיֵי [1] **Abaye said** in reply: We must emend the language of the Mishnah slightly and **say:** [2] "The seducer pays the fine only **if he does not marry her,**" but if he marries her, he need not pay the fine, because the Torah (Exodus 22:16) requires the fine to be paid only "if her father refuses to give her to him in marriage," but not if he agrees to marry her. The rapist, by contrast, must pay the fine immediately, whether or not he marries the girl.

תַּנְיָא נַמִי הָכִי [3] The Gemara notes that the following authoritative Baraita **also teaches** the law of the Mishnah, as emended by Abaye: [4] **"Even though** the Sages **said that the seducer pays** the fine to the girl's father only **if he does not marry her,** [5] nevertheless the **payments for** her **shame and deterioration he must give immediately,** regardless of whether he actually marries the girl." Thus we see that Abaye's emendation is supported by the Baraita just quoted.

וְאֶחָד הָאוֹנֵס [6] Having mentioned the Baraita's explanation of our Mishnah, the Gemara cites its next clause: **"Regarding the rapist and the seducer, both** the girl **and her father can prevent** the marriage."

בִּשְׁלָמָא מְפוּתָּה [7] The Gemara now explains this clause of the Baraita. **There is no problem in the case of the seduced girl,** for it is clear that both she and her father have the right to refuse the marriage, as we can see from another Baraita, which says: [8] **"It is written** in the verse (Exodus 22:16): **'If her father surely refuses** to give her to him, he shall pay, etc.' The verse states explicitly that her father has the right to refuse permission. [9] So far **I have** learned **only** that **her father** has the right to refuse permission. [10] **From where do I know that she herself may do so,** even though a *na'arah* does not normally have the right to refuse her father's choice of a husband?" The Baraita answers that the verse uses the double verb form *"ma'en yema'en"* (מָאֵן יְמָאֵן). [11] "By using this form," says the Baraita, **"the Torah** is teaching us to expand the scope of the term 'refuse' and to **say** that the expression **'will surely refuse' implies** that the refusal may come from **either** the father or the daughter." Thus we see from this Baraita that the daughter too has the right to refuse to marry her seducer. [12] **But,** continues the Gemara, what about **the case of a rapist?** The first Baraita ruled that the right of refusal is the same both for rape and for seduction, but the second Baraita's exegetical argument applies only to seduction. How do we know that both the girl and her father have the power to prevent her marriage to the rapist? The Gemara notes that in this case our problem

RASHI

לכשלא יכנוס — שתמאן היא, או אביה, או המפתה עצמו. **יכולין לעכב** — שלא יכניסנה.

NOTES

her. But if so, why does he pay the fifty-shekel fine? The Torah imposes this fine only if the seducer does not marry the *na'arah*, but if he marries her and subsequently divorces her, he is exempt from paying it!

HALAKHAH

אֵימָא: "לִכְשֶׁלֹּא יִכְנוֹס" Say: "When he does not marry her." "The seducer must pay for the seduced *na'arah*'s deterioration and shame immediately, but he does not pay the fine unless he fails to marry her." (*Rambam, Sefer Nashim, Hilkhot Na'arah Betulah* 2:7; *Shulḥan Arukh, Even HaEzer* 177:1.)

בֵּין הִיא וּבֵין אָבִיהָ יְכוֹלִין לְעַכֵּב Both she and her father can prevent it. "If either the girl or her father oppose the marriage, they are permitted to prevent it, both in cases of rape and in cases of seduction. If the *na'arah* or her father reject the marriage, or if the seducer refuses to go through with it, the rapist or the seducer pays the fine and the other penalties and is exempt from marrying her." (*Rambam, Sefer Nashim, Hilkhot Na'arah Betulah* 1:3; *Shulḥan Arukh, Even HaEzer* 177:3.)

TRANSLATION AND COMMENTARY

concerns the father, not the daughter. [1] **There is no doubt that she may** refuse permission, **for it is written** in the verse dealing with the rapist (Deuteronomy 22:29): [2] **"And *she* shall be his** wife." [3] This implies that she marries him only **of her own free will.** [4] **But from where do we know that her father,** too, **may** refuse permission for the rapist to marry his daughter, even if she is willing to marry the rapist?

אָמַר אַבַּיֵי [5] **Abaye said:** There was no need for the Torah to state this explicitly. Obviously the rapist cannot marry the *na'arah* without her father's permission, because the Torah's intention was **that the sinner should not be rewarded** for his crime. If the rapist had wished to marry this *na'arah* legally, he could not have done so without her father's permission. Hence it is obvious that he cannot do so merely because he sinned by raping her.

רָבָא אָמַר [6] **Rava said:** We can deduce that the father has the power to prevent his daughter's marriage to the rapist from his power to prevent her marriage to a seducer by using the exegetical argument called ***kal vaḥomer***. According to this argument, when the Torah explicitly commands us to be lenient regarding one law, the leniency necessarily applies to all laws that are more lenient than this one, and when the Torah explicitly commands us to be severe regarding one law, the severity necessarily applies to all laws that are more severe than this one. In this case, the Torah explicitly commands us to be severe with regard to the law of seduction, and not to permit the marriage unless both the girl and her father consent. Therefore we can argue that this severity necessarily applies to the more severe law of rape, although the Torah does not mention this point explicitly. [7] For **just as in the case of a seducer, who** obtained the *na'arah*'s consent to the intercourse and **acted only against the will of her father,** [8] nevertheless **both she and her father can prevent** the marriage, [9] so too in the case of **a rapist, who** did not obtain the *na'arah*'s consent and **acted against both her father's will and her own will** by raping her, [10] **how much more so** should both she and her father have the power to refuse the marriage.

[1] בִּשְׁלָמָא אִיהִי, [2] כְּתִיב: ״וְלוֹ תִהְיֶה״ — [3] מִדַּעְתָּהּ. [4] אֶלָּא אָבִיהָ מְנָלַן?

[5] אָמַר אַבַּיֵי: שֶׁלֹּא יְהֵא חוֹטֵא נִשְׂכָּר.

[6] רָבָא אָמַר: קַל וָחוֹמֶר. [7] וּמַה מְפַתֶּה, שֶׁלֹּא עָבַר אֶלָּא עַל דַּעַת אָבִיהָ בִּלְבַד, [8] בֵּין הִיא וּבֵין אָבִיהָ יְכוֹלִין לְעַכֵּב, [9] אוֹנֵס, שֶׁעָבַר עַל דַּעַת אָבִיהָ וְעַל דַּעַת עַצְמָהּ, [10] לֹא כָּל שֶׁכֵּן.

LITERAL TRANSLATION

[1] granted [that] she [may do so], [2] [for] it is written: "And to him she shall be" — [3] of her own [free] will. [4] But from where [do we know that] her father [may do so]?

[5] Abaye said: So that the sinner will not be rewarded.

[6] Rava said: It is a *kal vaḥomer*. [7] Just as [in the case of] a seducer, who acted only against the will of her father, [8] both she and her father can prevent [it], [9] a rapist, who acted against her father's will and against her own will, [10] how much more so?

RASHI

תהיה — משמע: היא מהוה את עצמה לו.

NOTES

בִּשְׁלָמָא אִיהִי Granted that she may do so. The Gemara explains that in the case of the seducer the verse explicitly teaches us that both she and her father may refuse permission, but in the case of the rapist there is a verse that teaches us that the daughter may refuse permission, but there is no verse that refers to her father. Accordingly, Abaye infers this law by means of an argument based on common sense, and Rava uses a *kal vaḥomer*.

Tosafot asks: We have seen above (38a) that there is a *gezerah shavah* that teaches us that all the rules applying to rape apply also to seduction and vice versa. Why, then, do we need any exegetical argument at all in the case of the rapist? Why do we not simply infer it from the case of the seducer?

Tosafot explains that the *gezerah shavah* does not apply at all to the commandment to marry the *na'arah*, since the rapist's obligations under the terms of this commandment are entirely different from those of the seducer. Hence we cannot transfer any of the laws regarding this commandment from the seducer to the rapist by using the *gezerah shavah* (see also *Ritva* and *Rosh*).

Tosafot asks: Why do we need an explicit verse to teach us that the *na'arah* may refuse to marry the rapist? Why do we not infer this law from the case of the seducer by using Rava's *kal vaḥomer*, or apply Abaye's argument that it is logically untenable that the sinner should be rewarded, just as we do in connection with her father?

Tosafot answers that we do in fact infer the law that the *na'arah* has the right to refuse to marry the rapist from Rava's *kal vaḥomer* or from Abaye's argument, and the verse is needed to teach us some other law. The Gemara is merely saying that it would be possible to infer this law from this verse if there were no other source.

Yam Shel Shlomo explains that even though we infer the law that the father may refuse permission from Rava's *kal vaḥomer* or from Abaye's logical argument, the law that the *na'arah* herself may refuse must be inferred from the verse. For if the verse had not explicitly stated that the

TRANSLATION AND COMMENTARY

רָבָא [1]Having cited these two solutions to the original problem, the Gemara now explains why **Rava did not** solve it **as Abaye did** — by arguing that it is obvious that the rapist cannot be allowed to obtain an additional prerogative by committing rape. The Gemara explains: The law that the rapist must marry the rape victim needs to be seen in the wider context of the other penalties imposed on him; and even if in one detail the penalty gives him a certain advantage, in its totality it is clearly a penalty. [2]In the case of rape, **he must pay a fine** to the father of the *na'arah* for raping his daughter. So even if this punishment were to give him the right to marry her without the father's permission, [3]**it would** still **not be a case of a sinner being rewarded.** Therefore Rava preferred to use the *kal vaḥomer* exegetical argument in order to prove that in this respect the laws of rape and of seduction are the same.

אַבַּיֵי [4]The Gemara now explains why **Abaye did not** solve the problem **as Rava did** — by arguing that a *kal vaḥomer* inference can be drawn from seduction to rape. [5]The Gemara explains: **In the case of seduction** the seducer himself **is able to prevent** the marriage. For the Gemara (below, 40a) infers from a verse in the Torah that the seducer is urged but not compelled to marry the *na'arah*. Therefore it is essentially a normal marriage, and the girl's **father is also able to prevent it,** just as he can refuse his permission to any marriage proposal to his daughter until she is an adult. [6]**In the case of rape,** by contrast, the rapist himself **is not able to prevent** the marriage, because the Torah commands him to marry his victim whether he wishes to or not, and he is forbidden to divorce her. Therefore it is not a normal marriage, and we might have imagined that the *na'arah*'s **father would not be able to prevent it,** were it not for the argument that the Torah did not intend the rapist to be rewarded for his sin.

[1]רָבָא לָא אֲמַר כְּאַבַּיֵי: [2]כֵּיוָן דְּקָא מְשַׁלֵּם קְנָס, [3]לָאו חוֹטֵא נִשְׂכָּר הוּא.

[4]אַבַּיֵי לָא אֲמַר כְּרָבָא: [5]מְפַתֶּה, דְּאִיהוּ מָצֵי מְעַכֵּב, אָבִיהָ נַמִי מָצֵי מְעַכֵּב. [6]אוֹנֵס, דְּאִיהוּ לָא מָצֵי מְעַכֵּב, אָבִיהָ נַמִי לָא מָצֵי מְעַכֵּב.

LITERAL TRANSLATION

[1]Rava did not say as Abaye [did]: [2]Since he pays a fine, [3]it is not [a case of] a sinner being rewarded. [4]Abaye did not say as Rava [did]: [5][In the case of] a seducer, where he is able to prevent [it], her father is also able to prevent [it]. [6][In the case of] a rapist, where he is not able to prevent [it], her father may also not be able to prevent [it].

RASHI

מצי מעכב — שאם רצה אינו כונס, כדאמרינן לקמן: ימהרנה לו — מדעתו. **אביה נמי לא מצי מעכב** — אי לאו שלא יהא חוטא נשכר.

NOTES

na'arah is permitted to refuse, we would have said that the Torah commands the rapist to marry her, and neither he nor she nor her father can refuse permission — by decree of the Torah. However, since the Torah explicitly allows her to refuse her consent, we learn that the Torah's commandment is addressed only to the rapist. Hence we can apply Rava's *kal vaḥomer* or Abaye's argument from common sense to prove that her father too may refuse his consent (see also *Rosh* and *Shittah Mekubbetzet*).

מְפַתֶּה, דְּאִיהוּ מָצֵי מְעַכֵּב In the case of a seducer, where he is able to prevent it. Rava argues that a case of rape is more severe than a case of seduction. Therefore we can construct a *kal vaḥomer* and can argue that any severity that applies to seduction applies *a fortiori* to rape as well. Hence, if the father has the right to prevent his daughter marrying the seducer, he must also have the same right in the case of the rapist. Abaye responds that it is possible that the father has the right to prevent the marriage only in the case of seduction, where the seducer has the same right, but not in the case of rape.

Ostensibly, Abaye appears to be arguing that the *kal vaḥomer* is invalid because it is possible that the severity in the case of the seducer — that the father can prevent the marriage — is in compensation for the fact that the law is lenient, and the seducer is not required to marry her. But surely this undermines the very basis of the *kal vaḥomer* exegesis! For if it is possible to say that the law is more severe in a lenient case in compensation for the leniency, we can never argue that a severity that applies to a lenient case applies *a fortiori* to a severe case as well!

Rabbenu Tam explains that Abaye is arguing that the fact that the girl's marriage to a seducer can be prevented is not a severity at all but a leniency. For the Torah compels the rapist to marry the *na'arah*, whereas it permits the seducer to refuse to do so. Hence it is possible that the father's right to refuse applies only to the seducer, where the command to marry is essentially voluntary, but not to the rapist, where the command to marry is treated more strictly.

Tosafot explains that Abaye is not disputing Rava's *kal vaḥomer* in itself, but is arguing that we cannot transfer laws from the seducer to the rapist by using a *kal vaḥomer*, just as we cannot do so by using a *gezerah shavah*. For the Torah compels the rapist to marry the *na'arah*, whereas it does not insist that the seducer do so. Hence we cannot assume that restrictions on the seducer's voluntary marriage apply equally to the rapist's forced marriage, because these two laws are entirely distinct. (Our commentary follows *Tosafot*'s explanation.)

[1] תַּנְיָא אִידָךְ: [2] "אַף עַל פִּי שֶׁאָמְרוּ אוֹנֵס נוֹתֵן מִיָּד, [3] כְּשֶׁיּוֹצִיא הוּא, אֵין לָהּ עָלָיו כְּלוּם". [4] "כְּשֶׁיּוֹצִיא"? [5] מִי מָצֵי מַפֵּיק לָהּ? [6] אֵימָא: "כְּשֶׁתֵּצֵא הִיא, [7] אֵין לָהּ עָלָיו כְּלוּם". [8] "מֵת, יָצָא כֶּסֶף קְנָסָהּ בִּכְתוּבָּתָהּ. [9] רַבִּי יוֹסֵי בְּרַבִּי

LITERAL TRANSLATION

[1] Another [Baraita] was taught: [2] "Although they said [that] a rapist gives immediately, [3] when he sends [her] away, she has no [claim] against him." [4] "When he sends [her] away"? [5] Can he send her away? [6] Say: "When she goes out, [7] she has no [claim] against him." [8] "[If] he died, the money of her fine is in lieu of (lit., 'went out in') her ketubah. [9] Rabbi Yose the son of Rabbi

RASHI

אף על פי שאמרו אונס נותן מיד כשיוציאנה אין לה עליו כלום — ולא אמרינן אין קנסה תחת כתובתה, שהרי לאביה נותן מיד. אלא כסף קנסה הוא כתובתה, וכן אם מת — יצא כסף קנסה בכתובתה. מי מצי מפיק לה — "לא יוכל לשלחה" כתיב. כשתצא היא — אם יצתה מאליה, ותבעה הימנו גט.

TRANSLATION AND COMMENTARY

תַּנְיָא אִידָךְ [1] In connection with the clause of our Mishnah requiring the rapist to pay the fine "immediately," there is **another Baraita** in which the following ruling **was taught:** [2] **"Although** the Sages **said that a rapist pays** the fine to the *na'arah*'s father **immediately,** as soon as the court convicts him of rape, nevertheless **if** the rapist subsequently **divorces** the girl, [3] **she has no claim against him,** because a rapist who marries the girl he raped does not write a ketubah for her."

כְּשֶׁיּוֹצִיא [4] The Gemara interrupts the quotation from the Baraita to object: The Baraita said that the girl has no claim **"if he divorces her"!** [5] But **can he divorce her?** Surely the Torah states that he is not permitted to divorce her!

אֵימָא [6] The Gemara answers that we must emend the Baraita slightly and **say: "If she goes out** of her own free will, [7] **she has no claim against him,"** because a rapist who marries his victim does not write a ketubah for her. Although the Torah forbids the rapist to divorce his wife, he is permitted to do so with her consent, just as he is not required to marry her if she does not agree to the marriage. However, if they do divorce by mutual consent, the rapist does not need to pay his wife the usual ketubah, according to the first Tanna in this Baraita.

מֵת [8] "Likewise," continues the Baraita, **"if** the rapist husband **dies,** the wife is also not entitled to a ketubah. For in such a case, **the money from her fine is in lieu of her ketubah."** The fine was set at fifty shekalim of silver precisely because this is "the virgin's dowry." In other words, it is equal to the value of the ketubah paid when the wife is a virgin (two hundred Talmudic zuzim are equal in value to the fifty shekalim mentioned in the Torah). Hence the rapist is considered to have paid the ketubah before he married the girl, and neither he nor his estate are required to pay anything more when the marriage ends. [9] The Baraita continues: **"Rabbi Yose the son of Rabbi Yehudah,** however, disagrees with the first Tanna and

NOTES

אֵין לָהּ עָלָיו כְּלוּם **She has no claim against him.** The Baraita rules that if the rapist divorces his wife, she has no claim against him, and if she is widowed, her fine is in lieu of her ketubah. Why does the Baraita not simply say that she is not entitled to a ketubah, irrespective of whether she is widowed or divorced?

Tosafot and *Rosh* note that the primary reason for instituting a ketubah for a divorcee is to make it more difficult for the husband to divorce her. Hence, in the case of the rapist, the Baraita informs us that the divorcee has no claim against her husband, for it is she who initiated the divorce. By contrast, the primary reason for instituting a ketubah for a widow is to enable her to remarry more easily. Hence the Baraita informs us that in the case of the rapist the Rabbis saw no need to institute a ketubah for her, since she has already received it in the form of the fine.

Ritva adds that the argument that a woman is entitled to a ketubah in order to make it easier for her to remarry applies primarily to a widow and not to a divorcee. Hence the wife of a rapist who initiates divorce proceedings has no claim at all, since we are not concerned about her ability to remarry. A widow, by contrast, does have a certain claim, since she needs the money to remarry; but the Rabbis did not institute a ketubah for her, since she has already received her ketubah in the form of the fine.

Tosafot adds that in cases other than that of the rapist, the Rabbis extended the ketubah to all wives, even if there is no question of making it more difficult for him to divorce her or making it easier for her to remarry. It is only because the rapist's wife has already, in a sense, received her ketubah that the Rabbis made a distinction in this case.

HALAKHAH

יָצָא כֶּסֶף קְנָסָהּ בִּכְתוּבָּתָהּ **The money of her fine is in lieu of her ketubah.** "The Rabbis did not institute a ketubah if the rapist married the *na'arah*, since in any case he is not permitted to divorce her. Therefore, if he dies, she is not entitled to a ketubah," following the view of the Sages in the Baraita. (*Rambam, Sefer Nashim, Hilkhot Na'arah Betulah* 1:4 and 2:7; *Shulhan Arukh, Even HaEzer* 177:3.)

SAGES

רָבָא מִפַּרְזַקְיָא Rava from Parzakya. A Babylonian Amora of the sixth generation, Rava from Parzakya was one of the members of Rav Ashi's academy and is usually mentioned in the Talmud in the context of discussions with Rav Ashi. Rava's son, Huna Mar, was also a Sage and was a disciple of Rav Ashi. The location of Parzakya is not known.

TRANSLATION AND COMMENTARY

says: Even though she is not entitled to the full ketubah of a virgin, since that has already been covered by the fine, **she *is* entitled to** the **ketubah** instituted by the Rabbis for non-virgins — **a maneh,** which equals one hundred zuz."

בְּמַאי קָמִיפַּלְגִי [1] The Gemara asks: What is the issue **about which** Rabbi Yose the son of Rabbi Yehudah and the other Sages **disagree?** All agree that the regular ketubah that is awarded to a virgin by Torah law is not applicable here, since the Torah intended the fine to take its place. But the Rabbis enacted that a ketubah worth half the amount given to virgins should be given in all marriages to which the full ketubah instituted by Torah law is not applicable. Why, then, should the rapist's wife not be entitled to this reduced ketubah, like any other wife?

רַבָּנַן סָבְרִי [2] The Gemara answers: **The Rabbis** (the first Tanna of the Baraita) **maintain** that **the reason why the Rabbis instituted the ketubah was in order that** it **should not be a light matter** for a man **to divorce** his wife. By Torah law, a man can divorce his wife at any time without her consent and without giving any reason for his action. Therefore, in order to deter a husband from abusing this prerogative in a moment of anger, the Rabbis instituted that he must pay his wife a sum of money if he divorces her. He is thus forced to consider his situation carefully and not to take precipitate action. [3] **But** the rapist **cannot divorce** his wife anyway without her consent. Hence there was no need for the Rabbis to institute a ketubah to protect her. And since the full ketubah to which she was entitled by Torah law as a virgin was paid to her father at the time of the marriage in the form of the fine, the Rabbis did not institute any further payments when the husband died or the couple divorced by mutual consent. [4] On the other hand, **Rabbi Yose the son of Rabbi Yehudah maintains** that the rule that the rapist cannot divorce his wife without her consent is true only theoretically. [5] In practice, a rapist who is determined to divorce his wife **can make** her **suffer** so much that **she** consents to the divorce and **says: "I do not want you."** Because of this possibility, Rabbi Yose the son of Rabbi Yehudah considered that there was a need for the Rabbis' institution of the reduced ketubah, so as to force the rapist to consider carefully before trying to persuade or intimidate his wife into agreeing to a divorce.

אוֹנֵס שׁוֹתֶה בַּעֲצִיצוֹ [6] The Gemara now considers the next clause of the Mishnah, which ruled that one of the differences between the rapist and the seducer is that a seducer may refuse to marry the girl, whereas **"a rapist drinks from his pot"** and must marry her, whether he wishes to or not. The Torah does not explicitly state that the seducer has the right to refuse to marry the girl; on the contrary, the Torah states that "he shall surely make her his wife," which is understood by the Sages as being a strong recommendation rather than a binding requirement. [7] On this point, **Rava from Parzakya said to Rav Ashi:** How do we know that

יְהוּדָה אוֹמֵר: יֵשׁ לָהּ כְּתוּבָּה מָנֶה״.

[1] בְּמַאי קָמִיפַּלְגִי?

[2] רַבָּנַן סָבְרִי: טַעֲמָא מַאי תַּקִּינוּ רַבָּנַן כְּתוּבָּה כְּדֵי שֶׁלֹּא תְּהֵא קַלָּה בְּעֵינָיו לְהוֹצִיאָהּ. [3] וְהָא לָא מָצֵי מַפֵּיק לָהּ. [4] וְרַבִּי יוֹסֵי בְּרַבִּי יְהוּדָה סָבַר: [5] הָא נַמִי מְצַעֵר לָהּ עַד דְּאָמְרָה הִיא: ״לָא בָּעֵינָא לָךְ״.

[6] ״אוֹנֵס שׁוֹתֶה בַּעֲצִיצוֹ״. [7] אֲמַר לֵיהּ רָבָא מִפַּרְזַקְיָא לְרַב אַשִׁי:

LITERAL TRANSLATION

Yehudah says: She has a ketubah [of] a maneh."

[1] About what do they disagree?

[2] The Rabbis maintain: The reason why the Rabbis instituted the ketubah [was] in order that she should not be easy in his eyes to send her away. [3] But this one he cannot send away. [4] And Rabbi Yose the son of Rabbi Yehudah maintains: [5] This one too he can make suffer until she says: "I do not want you."

[6] "A rapist drinks from his pot."

[7] Rava from Parzakya said to Rav Ashi:

RASHI

טעמא מאי תקינו רבנן כתובה — לשאר נשים.

NOTES

יֵשׁ לָהּ כְּתוּבָּה מָנֶה She has a ketubah of a maneh. The Rishonim are unanimous that the Halakhah is in accordance with the Sages, who rule that the wife of a rapist is not entitled to any ketubah at all (see *Rambam, Hilkhot Na'arah Betulah* 1:4).

In the fourth chapter of *Ketubot* (below, 54a), the Gemara considers the aspects of the ketubah beyond the basic sum of two hundred zuz. Normally a man has an obligation under the ketubah to feed and clothe his daughters from his estate after he dies until they reach adulthood or are betrothed. Does this law apply to the daughters of a rapist, according to the Sages who rule that the rapist need not write a ketubah? The Gemara leaves this question unanswered. Therefore the Rishonim rule that the daughters of a rapist are not entitled to this privilege (*Rambam, Hilkhot Ishut* 19:14), in accordance with the general principle that when the Gemara leaves a question unanswered the benefit of the doubt favors the person from whom money is being demanded — in this case, the rapist's estate.

TRANSLATION AND COMMENTARY

this is so? [1]**Since** the laws governing rape and seduction **are inferred from each other** through a *gezerah shavah* (as explained above, 38b), the general rule is that the two situations are treated in the same way. [40A] [2]Therefore, **on this point too let** the laws governing rape and seduction **be inferred from each other,** and let us say that just as the Torah requires the rapist to marry the *na'arah*, even if he does not want to, and forbids him from divorcing her, so too must the seducer marry the *na'arah* and never divorce her. How do we know that on this point the laws are different, with the seducer merely being urged, but not compelled, to marry her?

אֲמַר קְרָא [3]Rav Ashi answered: We learn from the *gezerah shavah* that the laws governing rape and seduction are the same unless we have a Scriptural text informing us otherwise. In the case of seduction **the verse says** (Exodus 22:15): **"He shall surely marry her to him as a wife."** [4]The text contains the seemingly superfluous word לו, meaning **"to him,"** and from it we infer that the seducer marries her **of his own free will.** He is urged to marry the *na'arah*, but is not compelled to do so.

כֵּיצַד שׁוֹתֶה בַּעֲצִיצוֹ [5]The Gemara now considers the next clause of the Mishnah, which explains **how** the Mishnah's ruling that the rapist must **"drink from his pot"** is to be understood. The Mishnah explains that the rapist cannot refuse to marry the *na'arah*, even if she is blind or lame. But if he is forbidden to marry her by some other law of the Torah, this ruling does not apply. [6]On this point **Rav Kahana said: I** was studying this Mishnah when I was a student and I **recited this passage** in the presence of my teacher, **Rav Zevid from Neharde'a**, and I said to Rav Zevid: **Let the positive commandment set aside the negative commandment!** There is a Halakhic principle that when a positive commandment of the Torah conflicts with a negative commandment so that they cannot both be fulfilled, the positive commandment takes precedence. For example, there is a positive Torah commandment to circumcise by removing the foreskin, and there is a negative Torah commandment forbidding the surgical removal of leprous lesions. Thus, if an

[1]מִכְּדִי מִיגְמַר גָּמְרֵי, מֵהֲדָדֵי, [40A] [2]לְהָא מִילְּתָא נַמִי לִיגְמְרוּ מֵהֲדָדֵי!
[3]אֲמַר קְרָא: ״מָהֹר יִמְהָרֶנָּה לּוֹ לְאִשָּׁה״. [4]״לוֹ״ — מִדַּעְתּוֹ.
[5]״כֵּיצַד שׁוֹתֶה בַּעֲצִיצוֹ, כו׳״.
[6]אֲמַר רַב כָּהֲנָא: אָמְרִיתָא לִשְׁמַעְתָּא קַמֵּיהּ דְּרַב זְבִיד מִנְּהַרְדְּעָא: נֵיתֵי עֲשֵׂה וְנִדְחֶה לֹא תַעֲשֶׂה!

LITERAL TRANSLATION

[1]Now since they are derived from each other, [40A] [2]for this matter too let them be inferred from each other!

[3]The verse said: "He shall surely marry her to him as a wife." [4]"To him" — of his own free will.

[5]"How does he drink from his pot, etc." [6]Rav Kahana said: I said [this] statement before Rav Zevid from Neharde'a: Let the positive commandment come and set aside the negative commandment!

RASHI

מיגמר גמרי מהדדי — אונס ממפתה — לשקלים, ומפתה מאונס — לחמשים. **להא מילתא** — שיהיה מפתה נושא על כרחו. **עשה** — ״לו תהיה לאשה״. **ונדחה את לא תעשה** — דאינה ראויה לבא בישראל, כגון ממזרת.

SAGES

רַב זְבִיד מִנְּהַרְדְּעָא Rav Zevid of Neharde'a. A fifth-generation Babylonian Amora, Rav Zevid of Neharde'a is to be distinguished from the more frequently cited "Rav Zevid." The latter was probably from Pumbedita. Virtually nothing is known about Rav Zevid of Neharde'a, although Amemar and Rav Kahana were apparently his students, and both of them cite his teachings. After his death, he was eulogized by Rav Kahana.

NOTES

״לוֹ״ — מִדַּעְתּוֹ "To him" — of his own free will. The Gemara is apparently inferring from the superfluous expression "to him" that appears in the verse dealing with seduction that the seducer marries the *na'arah* only if he wishes to do so. *Tosafot* objects: In the verse dealing with the rapist the same superfluous expression "to him" appears. Yet the rapist cannot withhold his consent!

Tosafot explains that since the Torah forbids the rapist to divorce the *na'arah*, the superfluous expression cannot be informing us that his consent is required for the marriage. Rather, the expression "to him" in this case informs us that he may not marry a woman who is forbidden to him.

Alternatively, says *Tosafot*, in the case of the rapist the expression "to him" appears in the clause, "and to him she shall be a wife," in which the verb "to be" is emphasized, with the woman the subject of the verb. Hence the expression "to him" relates to the woman, and we infer from it that her consent is required. But in the case of the seducer, the expression "to him" appears in the clause, "he shall surely marry her to him as a wife," in which the verb is "to marry" and the man is the subject. Hence the expression "to him" relates to him, and we infer from it that his consent is required.

נֵיתֵי עֲשֵׂה וְנִדְחֶה לֹא תַעֲשֶׂה Let the positive commandment come and set aside the negative commandment. This principle is mentioned in several places in the Talmud, and is discussed in detail in tractate *Yevamot* (3b-7a). The Gemara notes there that there is a Halakhic tradition that whenever a positive commandment conflicts with a negative commandment, the positive commandment takes precedence. The purpose of the discussion in *Yevamot* is to determine two questions: (1) What is the Scriptural source of this tradition? (2) Does it apply only when a positive commandment conflicts with an ordinary negative commandment, or does it apply even when a positive commandment conflicts with a severe negative commandment punishable by excision or death?

The Gemara concludes (4b) that the Scriptural source of this tradition is a pair of verses that appear one after the other in Deuteronomy (22:11-12): "You shall not wear a mixture, wool and linen together. You shall make fringes

TRANSLATION AND COMMENTARY

uncircumcised male develops leprosy in his foreskin, there is clash between the positive commandment to circumcise and the negative commandment not to remove the lesion, and the law is that in such a case the circumcision is performed. The Mishnah considered a case in which the rapist's victim was forbidden to him by a negative commandment, and the Mishnah ruled that the negative commandment takes precedence, and the rapist does not marry the girl. But, says Rav Kahana, why do we not apply our regular principle and give precedence to the positive commandment?

אֲמַר לִי [1]Rav Kahana relates that Rav Zevid from Neharde'a **said to him** in response: It is not true that positive commandments always take precedence over negative commandments. **Where do we say** that **the positive commandment comes and sets aside the negative commandment?** [2]Only **in cases** like the clash between **circumcision and leprosy, for example, where it is impossible to fulfill the positive commandment** at all, except by violating the negative commandment. If there is some way of fulfilling both commandments, we interpret the Torah as commanding us to follow that procedure and not to violate either. Here, in the case of the rapist, he is commanded to marry the girl only if she consents. [3]**But if she says that she does**

[1]אֲמַר לִי: הֵיכָא אָמְרִינַן: נֵיתֵי עֲשֵׂה וְנִידְחֵי לֹא תַעֲשֶׂה? [2]כְּגוֹן מִילָה בְּצָרַעַת, דְּלָא אֶפְשָׁר לְקִיּוּמֵיהּ לַעֲשֵׂה. [3]אֲבָל הָכָא,

LITERAL TRANSLATION

[1]He said to me: Where do we say: Let the positive commandment come and set aside the negative commandment? [2]For example, [in a case of] circumcision on leprosy, where it is impossible [otherwise] to fulfill the positive commandment. [3]But here,

NOTES

for yourself on the four corners of your garment with which you cover yourself." The Gemara notes that these two verses are essentially repetitions of laws that have already been mentioned in Leviticus (19:19) and in Numbers (15:37-41). Moreover, the word "mixture" is superfluous. Hence we may infer that the Torah repeated these laws and placed them together to teach us the principle that where the positive commandment to wear fringes conflicts with the negative commandment not to wear wool and linen together, the positive commandment takes precedence. The Gemara also explains that the Torah (Numbers 15:38) requires that the fringe contain a thread of blue wool. Thus a four-cornered linen garment cannot have proper fringes without the commandment against mixing wool and linen being violated.

The Gemara (8a) also concludes that this rule applies only to ordinary negative commandments, but not to a severe negative commandment that is punishable by excision or death. In addition, the Gemara mentions (5a) that this rule does not apply if the positive commandment conflicts with a negative commandment *and* with another positive commandment.

There are other cases in which the Torah sets aside one commandment in favor of another, because of the relative importance of the favored commandment (e.g., *Yevamot* 7b). But the Gemara notes (7a) that the rule that a positive commandment takes precedence over a negative commandment has nothing to do with the relative importance or severity of the positive and negative commandments involved. Indeed, negative commandments are generally more severe than positive commandments, in that violation of a negative commandment is generally punishable by lashes, whereas failure to observe a positive commandment is not punishable at all. Moreover, it is forbidden to violate a negative commandment even under pressing circumstances, unless there is a danger to life, whereas a positive commandment may be violated if it will cost more than a fifth of a person's wealth to fulfill it. In the light of all these factors, this rule must be regarded as a special decree of the Torah, which does not impose the negative commandment when it conflicts with a positive commandment.

וְנִדְחֶה לֹא תַעֲשֶׂה And set aside the negative commandment. Rav Kahana does not specify to which negative commandment he is referring. But it is clear that he cannot be referring to all the cases discussed in the Mishnah.

Rashi and *Tosafot* explain that Rav Kahana is referring to a case in which the *na'arah* is a *mamzeret.* In such a case, there is an ordinary negative commandment forbidding the rapist from marrying the *na'arah*, but Rav Kahana proposes that it be set aside by the positive commandment requiring the rapist to marry the girl he raped. *Ramban* observes that this explanation is difficult to accept, because the Mishnah inferred from an explicit verse that the rapist is forbidden to marry the *mamzeret.* There should thus be no room for Rav Kahana's question.

Ramban explains that Rav Kahana is referring to the second case discussed by the Mishnah, in which the rapist marries the *na'arah* and later she commits adultery. The Gemara rules (*Makkot* 15a) that the positive commandment to marry the *na'arah* continues for the rest of the rapist's life, so that if he divorces her he still has a positive

HALAKHAH

מִילָה בְּצָרַעַת Circumcision on leprosy. "Circumcision takes place on Shabbat and sets it aside only if it is performed, as commanded, on the eighth day of the infant boy's life. If circumcision is delayed for some reason, it does not set aside Shabbat. However, even if it is delayed, it does set aside the prohibition against the removal of leprous lesions. Hence, if there is a leprous lesion in the foreskin, it may be removed as part of the circumcision, since the positive commandment to circumcise sets aside the negative commandment prohibiting the removal of the lesion." (*Rambam, Sefer Ahavah, Hilkhot Milah* 1:9; *Shulḥan Arukh, Yoreh De'ah* 266:1.)

TRANSLATION AND COMMENTARY

not want to marry **him,** [1]**is there a positive commandment at all?** Surely her refusal eliminates the positive commandment completely! Therefore, if a man rapes a *mamzeret* or the like, we interpret the Torah as instructing the girl to refuse the marriage. The result is that the rapist is not permitted to marry the girl, if she is forbidden to marry him by another law of the Torah, even though there is a positive commandment requiring him to marry her if she is not forbidden to him.

MISHNAH יְתוֹמָה שֶׁנִּתְאָרְסָה וְנִתְגָּרְשָׁה [2]The previous Mishnah listed three differences between the laws governing rape and those governing seduction. Our Mishnah notes that there is one more difference, and it **concerns** a *na'arah* who was **an orphan** when she was raped or seduced, **or** a *na'arah* **who had been betrothed and was** already **divorced** at the time of the rape or seduction. In both these situations, if the fine is payable, it is paid to the *na'arah* herself rather than to her father. [3]**Rabbi Elazar says:** In these cases **the rapist is liable** to pay the fine and the other payments to the *na'arah* herself, **but the seducer is exempt** altogether, because the *na'arah* had intercourse voluntarily, and is therefore considered to have waived all her claims. If the payment is owed to the father, she cannot waive her father's claims (as the Gemara explained above, 39b), but if the payment is owed to the *na'arah* herself, her waiver is valid, and the seducer is exempt.

אִי אָמְרָה דְּלָא בָּעֵינָא, [1]מִי אִיתֵיהּ לַעֲשֵׂה כְּלָל?

משנה [2]יְתוֹמָה שֶׁנִּתְאָרְסָה וְנִתְגָּרְשָׁה, [3]רַבִּי אֶלְעָזָר אוֹמֵר: הָאוֹנֵס חַיָּיב וְהַמְפַתֶּה פָּטוּר.

LITERAL TRANSLATION

if she says that she does not want [him], [1]is there a positive commandment at all?

MISHNAH [2][Regarding] an orphan [or one] who was betrothed and was divorced, [3]Rabbi Elazar says: The rapist is liable and the seducer is exempt.

RASHI

מי איתיה לעשה כלל — השתא נמי, מלמדין אותה לומר ״איני רוצה״.

משנה יתומה שנתארסה ונתגרשה האונס חייב והמפתה פטור — דכיון דיתומה היא, וקנס שלה היא, ואחילתיה, דמדעתה נתפתתה לו — פטור. ובגמרא מפרש ד״נתארסה ונתגרשה״ מילתא אחריתי היא, ולא א״יתומה״ קאי.

SAGES

רַבִּי אֶלְעָזָר (בֶּן שַׁמּוּעַ) Rabbi Elazar (ben Shammu'a). Rabbi Elazar ben Shammu'a was a Tanna of the fifth generation and is usually referred to as Rabbi Elazar. He was a priest, one of the most prominent disciples of Rabbi Akiva, and lived to a great age. During the period after the Bar Kokhba revolt, Rabbi Elazar was one of the leaders of the generation and attracted many disciples. Among these was Rabbi Yehudah HaNasi, the editor of the Mishnah.

NOTES

commandment to remarry her. Hence, if the *na'arah* commits adultery, there is a negative commandment forbidding the rapist to remain married to her, and a positive commandment commanding him to remain married to her.

מִי אִיתֵיהּ לַעֲשֵׂה כְּלָל Is there a positive commandment at all? Our commentary follows *Rashi,* who explains that the *na'arah* is in effect commanded to refuse permission for the marriage. This explanation poses problems, because it is theoretically possible that she will disobey the Torah's commandment and not refuse permission. *Ramban* explains that in such a case we would compel her to say "I refuse" — by force, if necessary — just as we do in other cases in which the Torah commands a person to give his or her consent to something.

Most Rishonim, however, explain that Rav Zevid from Neharde'a is saying that since the *na'arah* has the power to refuse permission, the positive commandment is set aside even if she says nothing at all. *Tosafot Yeshanim* explains that since the girl can refuse permission, the positive commandment applies only to him but not to her. But the negative commandment applies to both parties; hence the positive command does not set it aside.

Tosafot and most other Rishonim explain that the positive commandment is inherently incapable of setting aside the negative commandment. The rule that a positive commandment sets aside a negative commandment is extrapolated from the case of woolen fringes on a linen garment, or from the case of circumcision on leprosy, in which there is no other way of fulfilling the positive commandment. But if it is possible to fulfill the positive commandment without violating the negative commandment, the case cannot be extrapolated from the cases that serve as paradigms. Hence the negative commandment is not set aside, even if the parties concerned refuse to take advantage of the approved method of avoiding the conflict.

יְתוֹמָה שֶׁנִּתְאָרְסָה וְנִתְגָּרְשָׁה An orphan or one who was betrothed and was divorced. The Aḥaronim ask: Why does this Mishnah appear here, between the two Mishnayot dealing with the additional payments for loss of virginity and shame? It should have appeared before the previous Mishnah, immediately after the Mishnah (above, 38a)

HALAKHAH

יְתוֹמָה שֶׁנִּתְאָרְסָה וְנִתְגָּרְשָׁה An orphan or one who was betrothed and was divorced. "If the raped *na'arah* was an orphan, she is entitled to receive all the payments herself. If a *na'arah* was already betrothed and divorced at the time of the rape, she is entitled to receive the fine herself, but the other payments are given to her father. But *Rosh* rules that all the payments are given to her in this case as well." (*Rambam, Sefer Nashim, Hilkhot Na'arah Betulah* 2:14,16; *Tur, Even HaEzer* 177.)

הָאוֹנֵס חַיָּיב וְהַמְפַתֶּה פָּטוּר The rapist is liable and the seducer is exempt. "If a man rapes a *na'arah* who has already been betrothed and divorced, he must pay the fine to the *na'arah* herself. But if he seduces her, he is exempt from the fine altogether, because she consented to the intercourse," following Rabbi Elazar. (*Rambam, Sefer Nashim, Hilkhot Na'arah Betulah* 1:9; *Tur, Even HaEzer* 177.)

SAGES

רַבָּה בַּר בַּר חָנָה **Rabbah bar Bar Ḥanah.** An Amora of the third generation, he was a student of Rabbi Yoḥanan. He was apparently born in Babylonia, emigrated to study Torah in Eretz Israel, and wandered in many lands. He transmitted teachings in the name of Rabbi Yoḥanan, his teacher, as well as in the name of Rabbi Yehoshua ben Levi, Resh Lakish, and Rabbi Elazar; he was also a student of Rabbi Yoshiyah of Usha. One of his sons, Rabbi Yitzḥak, was a Sage. Rabbah bar Bar Ḥanah tells many stories of the wonders he saw in his travels.

TRANSLATION AND COMMENTARY

GEMARA אָמַר [1] **Rabbah bar Bar Ḥanah said in the name of Rabbi Yoḥanan: Rabbi Elazar made the statement** quoted in his name in the Mishnah **in accordance with the opinion of Rabbi Akiva, his teacher.** Rabbi Elazar ben Shammu'a was one of Rabbi Akiva's five outstanding disciples (*Yevamot* 62b), and his statement in our Mishnah is merely an application of the opinion expressed by Rabbi Akiva in the Mishnah (above, 38a), [2] **when he said:** "A virgin *na'arah* who was betrothed and was divorced **is entitled to a fine,** like a *na'arah* who has never been married at all." Rabbi Yose HaGelili disagreed with Rabbi Akiva in that Mishnah and said that a *na'arah* who was betrothed and divorced is not entitled to a fine, because the Torah specifically commanded that the rapist's fine was to be paid only if the virgin *na'arah* was not yet betrothed (Deuteronomy 22:28). But Rabbi Akiva responded that we interpret this verse as referring not to the entire law of the rapist's fine, but only to the requirement that the fine be paid to the *na'arah*'s father. Hence Rabbi Akiva stated that although other financial benefits received by a minor or a *na'arah* are the property of the father, even if his daughter was betrothed and divorced," **the fine** paid by the rapist is not paid to the divorcee's father. Rather, it **is paid to** the *na'arah* **herself.**"

מְמַאי [3] The Gemara asks: **From what** Tannaitic source **is this inferred?** How do we know that Rabbi Elazar supports the viewpoint of Rabbi Akiva as expressed in the Mishnah?

גמרא [1] אָמַר רַבָּה בַּר בַּר חָנָה אָמַר רַבִּי יוֹחָנָן: רַבִּי אֶלְעָזָר בְּשִׁיטַת רַבִּי עֲקִיבָא רַבּוֹ אֲמָרָהּ, [2] דְּאָמַר: ״יֵשׁ לָהּ קְנָס, וּקְנָסָהּ לְעַצְמָהּ״. [3] מִמַּאי?

LITERAL TRANSLATION

GEMARA [1] Rabbah bar Bar Ḥanah said in the name of Rabbi Yoḥanan: Rabbi Elazar said it in accordance with the opinion of Rabbi Akiva, his teacher, [2] who said: "She does have a fine, and her fine belongs to her."

[3] From what [is this inferred]?

RASHI

גמרא בשיטת רבי עקיבא רבו אמרה – דלאמר במתניתין: נערה שנתארסה ונתגרשה – קנסה לעצמה. והך ״נתארסה ונתגרשה״ דרבי אלעזר – כשאביה קיים, וקרי לה ״יתומה״ משום דפקע זכות אב מינה לגבי קנסא. ממאי – דכרבי עקיבא סבירא ליה.

NOTES

dealing with the dispute between Rabbi Akiva and Rabbi Yose HaGelili about a *na'arah* who was betrothed and was divorced.

Our commentary follows *Melekhet Shlomo*, who explains that the previous Mishnah listed three differences between the laws governing rape and those governing seduction, and Rabbi Elazar is noting that there is one more difference, concerning a *na'arah* who was an orphan when she was raped or seduced, or a *na'arah* who was betrothed and then divorced at the time.

Yam Shel Shlomo explains that Rabbi Elazar wished to emphasize that the ruling of Rabbi Akiva — that the fine is paid to the *na'arah* herself — applies to the compensation for her lost virginity and for her shame as well as to the fine.

רַבִּי אֶלְעָזָר בְּשִׁיטַת רַבִּי עֲקִיבָא רַבּוֹ אֲמָרָהּ **Rabbi Elazar said it in accordance with the opinion of Rabbi Akiva, his teacher.** At first sight, Rabbi Yoḥanan's point seems obvious. Clearly Rabbi Elazar follows Rabbi Akiva and not Rabbi Yose HaGelili, since he rules that the betrothed and divorced *na'arah* is entitled to compensation for rape, whereas Rabbi Yose HaGelili maintains that she is entitled to nothing. Why, then, does Rabbi Yoḥanan feel the need to prove this point?

Ramban and *Ritva* explain that Rabbi Yoḥanan was not concerned so much with Rabbi Yose HaGelili's viewpoint, as with the variant version of Rabbi Akiva's opinion found in the Baraita (above, 38b), according to which a *na'arah* who has been betrothed and divorced is treated exactly like a *na'arah* who has never been betrothed, and the rapist pays the fine to her father. Rabbi Yoḥanan is arguing that Rabbi Elazar's ruling that the betrothed and divorced *na'arah* is not entitled to compensation for seduction is presumably because she is considered to have waived her claim when she consented to the intercourse. But according to Rabbi Akiva as quoted in the Baraita, she cannot waive her claim, since the fine is paid to her father (see above, 39b). Hence it is clear that Rabbi Elazar follows Rabbi Akiva as quoted in the Mishnah, who maintains that the fine is paid to the *na'arah* herself.

This argument is not so obvious, because it is based on the assumption that the cases of the orphan and of the betrothed and divorced *na'arah* in the Mishnah are two separate cases. But it is theoretically possible to understand Rabbi Elazar as referring to the one case of an orphan who has also been betrothed and divorced. If we follow this interpretation, Rabbi Elazar is teaching us that an orphan is not entitled to compensation for seduction, but that she is entitled to compensation for rape, even if she has been betrothed and divorced, in spite of the verse that mentions that the *na'arah* had not yet been betrothed at the time of the rape. On the basis of this interpretation there is no proof that Rabbi Elazar follows Rabbi Akiva as quoted in the Mishnah, because the same ruling could have been issued according to Rabbi Akiva as quoted in the Baraita. Hence Rabbi Yoḥanan feels the need to prove his point by showing that the alternative interpretation is untenable.

מִמַּאי? **From what is this inferred?** The Rishonim differ in their explanations of Rabbi Yoḥanan's proof. *Ritva* explains that Rabbi Yoḥanan is arguing that if Rabbi Elazar were to maintain that the fine for a betrothed and divorced *na'arah* is paid to the father, unless he is no longer alive, the only reason for mentioning the betrothed and divorced *na'arah* at all would be to inform us that she is entitled to a fine if she is raped, contrary to the viewpoint of Rabbi Yose HaGelili, and this point could have been made more briefly

TRANSLATION AND COMMENTARY

מִדְּקָתָנֵי [1]The Gemara answers: We must conclude that Rabbi Elazar could not have been referring to an orphan who has also been betrothed and divorced **from what** our own **Mishnah says.** For if Rabbi Elazar were referring to such a case, the stipulation that the orphan must also have been betrothed and divorced would add nothing to the law that an orphan is not entitled to compensation for seduction, because the same law would apply to an unbetrothed orphan as well. Thus for all intents and purposes the Mishnah would be teaching us that in the case of **an orphan Rabbi Elazar says** that **the rapist is liable and the seducer is exempt,** since the orphan has no father. [2]But surely this law **is obvious** in the case of **the orphan!** It goes without saying that if an orphan has been raped, the fine is paid to the orphan herself, and it is clear that she is not entitled to compensation if she engaged in intercourse willingly. Thus the only important point Rabbi Elazar would be making would be that a *na'arah* who has been betrothed and divorced is entitled to a fine, and this point could have been made far more clearly and concisely without mentioning the case of the orphan at all. [3]**Rather**, says the Gemara, we must interpret Rabbi Elazar's statement as referring to an orphan *or alternatively* to a *na'arah* who has been betrothed and divorced. When Rabbi Elazar informs us that neither of these two *ne'arot* is entitled to compensation for seduction, **he is telling us** something that is far from obvious — **that a *na'arah* who has been betrothed and divorced** is treated **like an orphan** in the context of this law. [4]**Just as an orphan** is entitled to a fine if she is raped, and the fine **is paid to** the girl **herself,** [5]**so too is a *na'arah* who has been betrothed and divorced** entitled to a fine if she is raped, **and it is paid to** the girl **herself,** as Rabbi Akiva ruled in the Mishnah. And it therefore follows that these *ne'arot* are not entitled to compensation if they are seduced.

אָמַר רַבִּי זֵירָא [6]**Rabbi Zera said in the name of Rabbah bar Shela who said in the name of Rav Hamnuna**

[1]מִדְּקָתָנֵי: ״יְתוֹמָה, רַבִּי אֱלְעָזָר אוֹמֵר: הָאוֹנֵס חַיָּיב וְהַמְפַתֶּה פָּטוּר״. [2]יְתוֹמָה פְּשִׁיטָא! [3]אֶלָּא הָא קָא מַשְׁמַע לָן — דְּנַעֲרָה שֶׁנִּתְאָרְסָה וְנִתְגָּרְשָׁה כִּיתוֹמָה. [4]מָה יְתוֹמָה לְעַצְמָהּ, [5]אַף נַעֲרָה שֶׁנִּתְאָרְסָה וְנִתְגָּרְשָׁה, לְעַצְמָהּ.

[6]אָמַר רַבִּי זֵירָא אָמַר רַבָּה בַּר שֵׁילָא אָמַר רַב הַמְנוּנָא סָבָא אָמַר רַב אַדָּא בַּר אַהֲבָה

LITERAL TRANSLATION

[1]From what [the Mishnah] teaches: "[Regarding] an orphan, Rabbi Elazar says: The rapist is liable and the seducer is exempt." [2]An orphan is obvious! [3]Rather this is what he is telling us — that a *na'arah* who was betrothed and was divorced is like an orphan. [4]Just as [in the case of] an orphan, [it belongs] to her, [5]so too [in the case of] a *na'arah* who was betrothed and was divorced, [it belongs] to her.

[6]Rabbi Zera said in the name of Rabbah bar Shela who said in the name of Rav Hamnuna the Elder who said in the name of Rav Adda bar Ahavah

RASHI

מדקתני אונס חייב ומפתה פטור — אלמא יש לה קנס, ולעצמה. הלכך מפתה פטור — דמדעתה עבד, ואונס חייב. ואפילו אביה קיים. דאי יתומה כדקתני — פשיטא דמפתה פטור, אלא הא קא משמע לן כו׳. **יתומה פשיטא** — מסקנא דמילתא דרבי יוחנן היא.

SAGES

רַבָּה בַּר שֵׁילָא **Rabbah bar Shela.** A Babylonian Amora of the third and fourth generations, Rabbah bar Shela was a disciple of Rav Ḥisda, whose teachings he cites. He seems to have lived near Meḥoza, and is usually associated with Rava, who came from Meḥoza. Rabbah bar Shela apparently served as a Rabbinic judge where he lived, and he may have had a small academy of his own there.

רַב הַמְנוּנָא סָבָא **Rav Hamnuna the Elder.** A Babylonian Amora of the second and third generations, Rav Hamnuna the Elder was given the title "the Elder" to distinguish him from another Rav Hamnuna, who, like Rav Hamnuna the Elder, was a disciple of Rav. Rav Hamnuna the Elder was one of the most junior of Rav's disciples and most of the teachings he transmits in the Talmud are in the names of Rav's senior disciples.

NOTES

without mentioning the orphan. The only additional point Rabbi Elazar makes by mentioning the orphan together with the betrothed and divorced *na'arah*, is that a seduced orphan is considered to have waived her rights when she consented to the intercourse, and this point is not worth mentioning, since it is obvious that the fine belongs to the orphan herself. Rather, Rabbi Elazar must maintain that the fine for a betrothed and divorced *na'arah* is paid to the *na'arah* herself, even if the father is alive, and the orphan was mentioned only by way of comparison. *Tosafot* and *Rashi* appear to explain the passage in a similar way.

יְתוֹמָה פְּשִׁיטָא **An orphan is obvious!** According to the explanation of *Ritva*, *Rashi*, and *Tosafot*, the Gemara is saying that it is obvious that an orphan who was seduced is entitled to absolutely nothing. Indeed, it is so obvious that it need not even have been mentioned in the Mishnah.

In the Jerusalem Talmud, however, there is a dispute about this matter. According to one Amora, a seduced orphan is considered to have waived her claim to compensation for shame and deterioration, but not to the fine itself, whereas another Amora maintains that she is considered to have waived her claim to the fine as well. The Jerusalem Talmud explains that the seducer is liable for the other payments from the time of the seduction, whereas the fine is not awarded until he is sued in court, and the first Amora maintains that a person cannot waive a monetary benefit that he or she has not yet been awarded.

It is not entirely clear why the Babylonian Talmud considers it so obvious that the seduced *na'arah* is considered to have waived her right to the fine. *Ran* cites *Ramban,* who proves that the Babylonian Talmud maintains that a person can refuse in advance to receive a monetary benefit that will come to him later.

Ritva explains that being seduced is not a simple waiver of a monetary claim. Rather, the *na'arah* gave the seducer permission to use her body, and therefore she cannot demand compensation for his having used it, just as a person who is given permission to tear a garment cannot be sued for it.

TRANSLATION AND COMMENTARY

the Elder who said in the name of Rav Adda bar Ahavah who said in the name of Rav: The Halakhah is in accordance with Rabbi Elazar, whose ruling reflects the viewpoint of Rabbi Akiva as expressed in the Mishnah. [1]The Gemara notes that **Rav** praised **Rabbi Elazar's** wisdom and learning, and **called** him **the happiest of the Sages,** a Sage whose Halakhic rulings are soundly based and reliable.

MISHNAH אֵיזֶהוּ בּוֹשֶׁת [2]This Mishnah returns to the topic of the payments made by the seducer and the rapist in addition to the fine. We have seen (above, 39a) that there are two payments applicable to both of them — payments for shame and blemish. In addition, there is compensation for pain, but this is paid by the rapist alone. Our Mishnah discusses how these payments are assessed. **How,** asks the Mishnah, do we assess **the payment for** the **shame** suffered by the *na'arah* as a result of the illicit intercourse? [3]The Mishnah answers: **Everything is** assessed **in accordance with** the status of **the man who did the shaming and the girl who was shamed.**

אָמַר רַב: הֲלָכָה כְּרַבִּי אֶלְעָזָר. [1]קָרֵי רַב עֲלֵיהּ דְּרַבִּי אֶלְעָזָר טוּבִינָא דְּחַכִּימֵי.

מִשְׁנָה [2]אֵיזֶהוּ בּוֹשֶׁת? [3]הַכֹּל לְפִי הַמְבַיֵּישׁ וְהַמִּתְבַּיֵּישׁ.

LITERAL TRANSLATION

who said in the name of Rav: The Halakhah is in accordance with Rabbi Elazar. [1]Rav called Rabbi Elazar the happiest of the Sages.

MISHNAH [2]What is [the payment for] shame? [3]Everything is according to the shamer and the shamed.

RASHI

טובינא דחכימי = מאושר שבחכמים. אשרי מתרגמינן טובאי. רבי אלעזר הוא רבי אלעזר בן שמוע, ותלמידו של רבי עקיבא היה, כדאמרינן ביבמות ב״הבא על יבמתו״ (סב,ב): והיה העולם שמם, עד שבא רבי עקיבא אצל רבותינו שבדרום ושנה להם: רבי מאיר, ורבי יהודה, ורבי יוסי, ורבי שמעון, ורבי אלעזר בן שמוע.

משנה הכל לפי המבייש — אדם בינוני המבייש, בושתו קשה מאדם זולל ומאדם חשוב. **והמתבייש** — לפי חשיבותו בושתו.

NOTES

הֲלָכָה כְּרַבִּי אֶלְעָזָר **The Halakhah is in accordance with Rabbi Elazar.** *Ritva* asks: Since Rabbi Elazar is reflecting the viewpoint of Rabbi Akiva, why does the Gemara not simply rule in favor of Rabbi Akiva? *Ritva* answers that if the Gemara had ruled in favor of Rabbi Akiva, it would not be clear whether the Halakhah is in accordance with Rabbi Akiva as quoted in the Mishnah or in accordance with Rabbi Akiva as quoted in the Baraita. Hence the Gemara rules in favor of Rabbi Elazar, who clearly follows Rabbi Akiva as quoted in the Mishnah.

Yam Shel Shlomo explains that Rabbi Akiva ruled only that if the *na'arah* was betrothed and divorced *the fine* is paid to the *na'arah* herself. It is not clear from his statement whether the same applies to the compensation for shame and blemish, or whether these are paid to the father. But from Rabbi Elazar's statement that the seducer is completely exempt if the *na'arah* was betrothed and divorced — since she is considered to have waived her claims by consenting to intercourse — it is clear that the shame and blemish payments are also paid to the *na'arah* herself.

This question is the subject of a disagreement between Rishonim. *Rambam* (*Hilkhot Na'arah Betulah* 2:16) rules that someone who rapes a *na'arah* who was betrothed and divorced pays only the fine to the *na'arah*, whereas the compensation for shame and deterioration are paid to her father. *Rambam*'s reason is that betrothal normally has no effect on the father's prerogative to receive monetary benefits accruing to his daughter, and Rabbi Akiva's exegetical argument that the payment should be made to the *na'arah* herself applies only to the fine. Hence there is no reason to depart from the normal procedure regarding these other payments. *Tosafot* and *Rosh* argue that the Torah hints at these other payments in the same verse in which it requires that the fine be paid (see below, 40b), and this teaches us that these payments are always made to the party that receives the fine.

Ritva notes that *Rashi* appears to explain Rabbi Elazar's statement as referring only to the fine and not to any other payment — in accordance with *Rambam*'s ruling. *Ritva* notes further that the Jerusalem Talmud supports *Rambam*'s ruling.

טוּבִינָא דְּחַכִּימֵי **The happiest of the Sages.** In two other places in the Talmud (*Gittin* 26b and *Keritot* 13b) the Gemara rules in favor of Rabbi Elazar and mentions that Rav called him "the happiest of the Sages." *Ritva* explains that Rav called Rabbi Elazar "the happiest of the Sages" because he showed wisdom in making difficult decisions in cases which confused lesser men. In this case, he decided in favor of Rabbi Akiva as quoted in the Mishnah, against the variant version of Rabbi Akiva as quoted in the Baraita, and against the seemingly more logical argument advanced by Rabbi Yose HaGelili.

Moreover, when Rabbi Akiva issued his ruling, the Gemara had difficulty in understanding it, because it appeared to contradict the explicit requirement of the Torah that the law of the rapist should apply only if the *na'arah* was not betrothed. Rabbi Elazar, however, addressed this point by comparing the *na'arah* who was betrothed and divorced to an orphan.

הַכֹּל לְפִי הַמְבַיֵּישׁ וְהַמִּתְבַּיֵּישׁ **Everything is according to the shamer and the shamed.** The Mishnah rules that the

HALAKHAH

הַכֹּל לְפִי הַמְבַיֵּישׁ וְהַמִּתְבַּיֵּישׁ **Everything is according to the shamer and the shamed.** "The compensation for shame depends on the social status of the rapist and of the girl. If she comes from a very important family, she is

TRANSLATION AND COMMENTARY

פְּגָם [1]The Mishnah continues: **Regarding** the *na'arah*'s **blemish,** brought about by her loss of virginity, **we view her as if she were a female slave being sold in the market.** [2]**We estimate how much she would have been worth** as a virgin, **and how much she is** now **worth** as a non-virgin, and the rapist or the seducer pays the difference.

קְנָס [3]By contrast, continues the Mishnah, **the** fifty-shekel **fine is the same for everyone.** Provided that the *na'arah* is entitled to a fine, she is paid fifty silver shekalim, regardless of her social status.

וְכָל שֶׁיֵּשׁ לוֹ [4]The Mishnah adds that the same rule applies to **every** payment imposed **by the Torah that has a fixed value** — for example, the hundred-shekel fine imposed on a husband who falsely accuses his wife of adultery (Deuteronomy 22:19), or the thirty-shekel fine imposed on the owner of an ox that killed a slave (Exodus 21:32). In all such cases, the payment **is the same for everyone,** regardless of the person's social status or his value on the slave market.

GEMARA וְאֵימָא [5]Before discussing the assessment procedure laid down by the Mishnah, the Gemara considers the additional payments themselves. The Torah requires the rapist or the seducer to pay fifty silver shekalim. How do we know that the other payments mentioned in the Mishnah are in addition to this sum? Why should we not **say** that the **fifty sela'im** (the Talmudic sela was equal in value to the Torah shekel) that **the Torah said** must be paid by the rapist or the seducer **was intended to cover everything** normally associated with rape or seduction? Fifty shekalim is a significant sum of money. Perhaps the Torah intended it to cover the *na'arah*'s shame and blemish as well. How do we know that the Torah intended the fifty shekalim to be paid in addition to the other damage payments?

[1]פְּגָם, רוֹאִין אוֹתָהּ כְּאִילּוּ הִיא שִׁפְחָה נִמְכֶּרֶת בַּשּׁוּק, [2]כַּמָּה הָיְתָה יָפָה וְכַמָּה הִיא יָפָה.

[3]קְנָס שָׁוֶה בְּכָל אָדָם.

[4]וְכָל שֶׁיֵּשׁ לוֹ קִצְבָּה מִן הַתּוֹרָה שָׁוֶה בְּכָל אָדָם.

גמרא [5]וְאֵימָא: חֲמִשִּׁים סְלָעִים אָמַר רַחֲמָנָא מִכֹּל מִילֵּי!

LITERAL TRANSLATION

[1][Regarding] blemish, we view her as if she were a female slave being sold in the market, [2][and we estimate] how much she was worth and how much she is worth.

[3]The fine is equal for everyone.

[4]And everything that has a fixed amount from the Torah is equal for everyone.

GEMARA [5]But say: The Torah said fifty sela'im for everything!

RASHI

כאילו היא שפחה — כגמרא מפרש מאי גריעותא מחמת בעילה.

NOTES

payment for shame depends on the social status of the rapist and of the *na'arah*. The Mishnah in *Bava Kamma* (83b) issues a similar ruling regarding ordinary cases of assault. But neither of these Mishnayot clarify what they mean by this ruling. Obviously, a victim of rape or assault who comes from a very dignified family will suffer more shame than would someone from the lower classes. It is not clear, however, how the social status of the rapist or the assailant should affect his liability. *Rambam* (*Hilkhot Na'arah Betulah* 2:4 and *Hilkhot Ḥovel U'Mazzik* 3:1) rules that the shame caused by rape or assault by an important person is less than the shame caused by an ignoble person. Thus the maximum degree of shame occurs when a highly dignified person is raped or assaulted by a very lowly person. *Meiri* notes that the Jerusalem Talmud's explanation of our Mishnah supports *Rambam*'s ruling.

Rashi, in his explanation of the Mishnah in *Bava Kamma* (83b) dealing with ordinary assault, appears to agree with *Rambam*. In his explanation of our Mishnah, however, which deals with rape and seduction, *Rashi* insists that contempt shown by a very lowly person is less humiliating than contempt shown by one's peers. Thus the maximum degree of shame occurs when it is caused by a person of average social status. *Ran* takes the opposite position, insisting that in the case of rape a woman feels more shamed when raped by a lowly person than by an average person, whereas in other cases of shame, such as when one person spits on another or slaps him in the face, the maximum degree of shame occurs when it is caused by a person of average social status.

HALAKHAH

entitled to more than if she comes from a very lowly family. And if he comes from a very important family, he pays less than if he comes from a very lowly family. *Sma* notes that *Rashi* maintains that a man of average importance pays more than either of the others. But *Ran* argues that this applies only to other forms of assault but not to rape." (*Rambam, Sefer Nashim, Hilkhot Na'arah Betulah* 2:4; *Shulḥan Arukh, Ḥoshen Mishpat* 420:24.)

קְנָס שָׁוֶה בְּכָל אָדָם **The fine is equal for everyone.** "The fine itself is fixed at fifty silver shekalim, regardless of whether the victim was the daughter of the High Priest or a *mamzeret*. But the payments for shame, blemish, and pain vary from case to case." (*Rambam, Sefer Nashim, Hilkhot Na'arah Betulah* 2:3; *Tur, Even HaEzer* 177.)

LANGUAGE

הֶדְיוֹט **Private person.** This word is derived from the Greek ἰδιώτης, *idiotes*, meaning "common man," "layman," or "private person."

מַרְגָּלִיּוֹת **Pearls.** From the Greek μαργηλίς, *margelis*, or μαργαρίτης, *margarites*, meaning "pearl."

REALIA

נוֹקֵב מַרְגָּלִיּוֹת **Who pierces pearls.** Since pearls were generally strung in necklaces, they had to be perforated. Only skilled craftsmen could do this work in such a way that the pearls would not be damaged. Obviously, such workers were paid more for their services (or were sold at higher rates, if they were slaves) than ordinary workers (or slaves).

[1]אָמַר רַבִּי זֵירָא: יֹאמְרוּ: [2]"בָּעַל בַּת מְלָכִים, חֲמִשִּׁים; [3]בָּעַל בַּת הֶדְיוֹטוֹת, חֲמִשִּׁים?!"

[4]אֲמַר לֵיהּ אַבַּיֵי: אִי הָכִי, גַּבֵּי עֶבֶד נַמִּי יֹאמְרוּ: [5]"עֶבֶד נוֹקֵב מַרְגָּלִיּוֹת, שְׁלֹשִׁים; [6]עֶבֶד עוֹשֶׂה [40B] מַעֲשֵׂה מַחַט, שְׁלֹשִׁים?!"

[7]אֶלָּא אָמַר רַבִּי זֵירָא: אִילּוּ בָּאוּ עָלֶיהָ שְׁנַיִם, [8]אֶחָד כְּדַרְכָּהּ

LITERAL TRANSLATION

[1]Rabbi Zera said: They will say: [2]"[If] he had intercourse with the daughter of kings, [he pays] fifty; [3][if] he had intercourse with the daughter of commoners, [he also pays] fifty?!"

[4]Abaye said to him: If so, concerning a slave they will also say: [5]"[If he was] a slave who pierces pearls, [he pays] thirty; [6][if he was] a slave who does [40B] needlework, [he also pays] thirty?!"

[7]Rather, Rabbi Zera said: If two had intercourse with her, [8]one naturally (lit., "in her way")

TRANSLATION AND COMMENTARY

אָמַר רַבִּי זֵירָא [1]**Rabbi Zera said** in reply: If the assumption on which this question is based were true, there would be no difference at all in the payments made for the rape of any *na'arah*. But if so, people **will say:** [2]**"If he had intercourse with the daughter of kings, he** must **pay fifty** shekalim, [3]but **if he had intercourse with the daughter of commoners, must he also pay fifty?"** Surely the Torah cannot ignore the greater humiliation suffered by a princess! Thus there must be a payment for shame in addition to the fine, and it stands to reason that the same applies to the payments for blemish and for pain.

אֲמַר לֵיהּ אַבַּיֵי [4]**Abaye said to** Rabbi Zera: The Torah (Exodus 21:32) requires the owner of an ox that has killed a slave to pay a fixed fine of thirty shekalim to the owner of the slave. But **if** your reasoning is **correct,** people will say the same thing **about a slave** who was fatally gored by an ox. **They will say:** [5]**"If he was a slave who pierced pearls** (a highly skilled slave who was extremely valuable), the owner of the ox must **pay thirty** shekalim, [6]but **if he was an** ordinary **slave who did** [40B] **needlework, must he also pay thirty** shekalim?" Surely the Torah cannot ignore the greater loss suffered by the owner of the more valuable slave! Yet we see that the Torah does precisely that. Hence we cannot assume that damage payments will necessarily correspond to the damage actually done, and it is possible that where the Torah requires a fixed fine to be paid no other payment is required, even though it sometimes happens that this fine is inadequate to compensate for the loss. So our original question returns: How do we know that the fifty-shekel fine was not the only payment required?

אֶלָּא [7]**Rather, Rabbi Zera** withdrew his original explanation and **said:** If the fifty-shekel fine had been intended to cover the entire damage caused, there would be no difference at all in the payments made for raping a real virgin and for raping a *na'arah* who had already had intercourse but whose hymen had not been ruptured. But on this basis **if two** rapists **had intercourse with her,** one after the other, [8]the second **one naturally** (i.e., by regular intercourse, that ruptured the hymen) **and the** first **one unnaturally**

RASHI

גמרא יאמרו כו' — והיכן הוא חילוק שביניהן אלא בושת? הלכך יהיב בושת. **גבי עבד** — שנגחו שור, שנתנה תורה קצבה שלשים שקלים. **מעשה מחט** — חייט, תופר. **אלא אמר רבי זירא** — מהכא מסתברא שאין בושת בכלל חמשים, דאם כן — אין הפרש בין בעל שלימה לבעל פגומה שנבעלה שלא כדרכה, והיכן הוא הפרש שביניהם? שמע מינה גבי בושת, כיון שנפגמה כבר — אין בושתה רב כשלימה.

NOTES

אֶלָּא אָמַר רַבִּי זֵירָא **Rather, Rabbi Zera said.** Since the Gemara introduces Rabbi Zera's second argument with the word "rather," it would appear that Rabbi Zera withdrew his first argument because of Abaye's objection. But his second argument is not different in substance from the first. He began by arguing that it stands to reason that the Torah would take individual differences into account in determining compensation for shame, and Abaye responded by citing the example of the slave who was killed. Why, then, does Rabbi Zera believe that his second explanation is an improvement on his first?

Ritva explains that Rabbi Zera's two arguments are really quite different. In his first argument, Rabbi Zera reasoned that the Torah always takes social status into account when determining compensation for shame. Against this, Abaye cited the example of the slave who pierces pearls and the slave who does needlework. The expensive slave is likely to be owned by a more important person, yet the Torah did not take this into account when fixing the fine. Rabbi Zera accepted this objection and presented a second argument. If we assume that the fifty-shekel fine is intended to cover the *na'arah*'s shame as well, then it follows that part of the fifty shekalim is essentially a damage payment, and only the remainder is a true fine imposed as a punishment. But if so, it would follow that the greater the shame the less the fine, and if the *na'arah* was a true virgin, the fine would be small, because most of the fifty shekalim would be a damage payment for shame, whereas if the *na'arah* had already had anal intercourse, the fine would be larger. Surely this is illogical! To this Abaye responded that the same is true of a slave killed by an ox. The true fine is the part of the thirty shekalim that is more than the actual value of the slave. Thus it follows that if the slave was healthy, the fine is small, since most of the thirty shekalim would be a damage payment, and if the slave was sick, the fine would be larger.

Shittah Mekubbetzet suggests a different explanation of

TRANSLATION AND COMMENTARY

(i.e., by anal intercourse), both would pay the same amount. [1]But if so, people **will say:** "How can it be that the first one, who **had intercourse with an undamaged** virgin who had never had intercourse **pays fifty** shekalim, [2]but the second one who **had intercourse with a damaged woman** who had already had anal intercourse **pays** the same **fifty** shekalim?" Surely the Torah cannot ignore the greater shame suffered by the *na'arah* the first time! Thus we see that there must be a separate payment for shame, and it stands to reason that the same applies to the payments for blemish and pain.

אֲמַר לֵיהּ [3]But here too **Abaye said to** Rabbi Zera: **If** your reasoning **is correct,** people **will say** the same thing **about a slave** who was fatally gored by an ox: [4]**"If he was a healthy slave,** the owner of the ox **must pay thirty** shekalim, [5]and **if he was a slave struck with boils, must he also pay thirty** shekalim?" Surely the Torah cannot ignore the greater loss suffered by the owner of the healthy slave! Yet we see that the Torah does precisely that. Hence we cannot assume that damage payments will necessarily correspond to the damage actually done, and it is possible that where the Torah requires a fixed fine to be paid no other payment is required, even though it sometimes happens that this fine is inadequate to compensate for the loss. So our original question returns: How do we know that the fifty-shekel fine was not the only payment required?

אֶלָּא [6]**Rather,** says the Gemara, we cannot prove by logic alone that the fine is not the only payment required, and we must seek an explicit Scriptural source for the payments for blemish and shame. Two such sources are cited, the first by **Abaye,** who **said:** [7]**The verse says** (Deuteronomy 22:29) that the rapist must pay the father of the *na'arah* fifty shekalim, **"for he has humbled her."** Why does the Torah need to explain again the reason for the fine? [8]It is in order to teach us that *this* fifty-shekel fine **is paid** only **"for he has humbled her,"** and for no other reason. In other words, rape involves many different culpable offenses, and the fifty-shekel fine is in compensation for only one — the illicit intercourse itself. All other penalties that may be incurred by the rapist are in addition to the fifty shekalim, and are assessed as for any other assault. [9]**This proves by implication that** a man who rapes or seduces a virgin *na'arah* is held liable to **pay** for her **shame and blemish,** in addition to paying the fifty-shekel fine.

וְאֶחָד שֶׁלֹּא כְּדַרְכָּהּ, [1]יֹאמְרוּ: "בָּעַל שְׁלֵימָה, חֲמִשִּׁים; [2]בָּעַל פְּגוּמָה, חֲמִשִּׁים?!"

[3]אֲמַר לֵיהּ אַבַּיֵי: אִי הָכִי, גַּבֵּי עֶבֶד נַמִי יֹאמְרוּ: [4]"עֶבֶד בָּרִיא, שְׁלֹשִׁים; [5]עֶבֶד מוּכֵּה שְׁחִין, שְׁלֹשִׁים?!"

[6]אֶלָּא אֲמַר אַבַּיֵי: [7]אָמַר קְרָא: "תַּחַת אֲשֶׁר עִנָּהּ". [8]הָנֵי "תַּחַת אֲשֶׁר עִנָּהּ". [9]מִכְּלָל דְּאִיכָּא בּוֹשֶׁת וּפְגָם.

LITERAL TRANSLATION

and the other unnaturally (lit., "not in her way"), [1]they will say: "[If] he had intercourse with an undamaged woman, [he pays] fifty; [2][if] he had intercourse with a blemished woman, [he also pays] fifty?!"

[3]Abaye said to him: If so, concerning a slave they will also say: [4]"[If] he was a healthy slave, [he pays] thirty; [5][if] he was a slave struck with boils, [he also pays] thirty?!"

[6]Rather, Abaye said: [7]The verse says: "For he has humbled her." [8]These [are payable] "for he has humbled her." [9][This proves] by implication that there are [payments for] shame and blemish.

RASHI

תחת אשר עינה — גבי "חמשים כסף" כתיב. **מכלל דבושת ופגם** — שאינם משום עינוי, שהרי ישנן בשאר חובלין — אינו בכלל זה. פגם הוא נזק הנישום נמי בשאר חבלות.

NOTES

Rabbi Zera's second argument. Granted that the Torah does not always take social status into account, as Abaye proved with the case of the slave. But it is surely clear that in the case of the rapist's fine the Torah took the *na'arah*'s virginity into account, since no fine at all is imposed if she was not a virgin. But if the Torah distinguishes between a virgin and a non-virgin, surely it must also make a distinction between a complete virgin and a damaged virgin. To this Abaye responded that the same is true of a slave killed by an ox. The Torah definitely distinguished between a living slave and a dead slave, but the Torah did not distinguish between a healthy slave and a slave who was so sick that he was worthless.

וְאֶחָד שֶׁלֹּא כְּדַרְכָּהּ **And the other unnaturally.** In general, the Torah considers anal intercourse to be the equivalent of normal intercourse for all Halakhic purposes.

There is a dispute among the Rishonim as to whether this general principle applies also to the rapist's fine. *Tosafot* and *Ra'avad* maintain that here too a man who rapes or seduces a virgin *na'arah* unnaturally must pay the fine, just as he would if he had had regular intercourse with her. *Rambam* (*Hilkhot Na'arah Betulah* 1:8) and *Rashi* are of the opinion that this law is exceptional, and that only regular intercourse, which destroys the girl's virginity, is subject to the rapist's fine.

According to these viewpoints, there are different explanations for the case referred to by Rabbi Zera. *Rashi* explains that Rabbi Zera is comparing two different girls who were both raped, one of whom had never had intercourse before, whereas the other had previously been raped unnaturally. In such a case, Rabbi Zera objects to the idea that the fine should be the same for both rapists,

[1] רָבָא אֲמַר: [2] אָמַר קְרָא: "וְנָתַן הָאִישׁ הַשֹּׁכֵב עִמָּהּ לַאֲבִי הַנַּעֲרָה חֲמִשִּׁים כָּסֶף". [3] הֲנָאַת שְׁכִיבָה חֲמִישִּׁים. [4] מִכְּלָל דְּאִיכָּא בּוֹשֶׁת וּפְגָם.

[5] וְאֵימָא לְדִידָהּ!

[6] אָמַר קְרָא: "בִּנְעֻרֶיהָ בֵּית אָבִיהָ". [7] כָּל שֶׁבַח "נְעוּרֶיהָ" לְאָבִיהָ.

LITERAL TRANSLATION

[1] Rava said: [2] The verse says: "And the man who lay with her shall give the father of the *na'arah* fifty [pieces of] silver." [3] [For] the pleasure of lying [he pays] fifty. [4] [This proves] by implication that there are [payments for] shame and blemish.

[5] But say [that] it is [paid] to her!

[6] The verse says: "While she is a *na'arah* in her father's house." [7] All the benefit of "while she is a *na'arah*" [belongs] to her father.

TRANSLATION AND COMMENTARY

רָבָא אֲמַר [1] The second source is provided by **Rava,** who pointed to a different part of the verse cited by Abaye as the Scriptural source for the payments for blemish and shame, **saying:** How do we know that the fifty-shekel fine is not all that the offender must pay? [2] **The verse says: "And the man who lay with her shall give the father of the *na'arah* fifty pieces of silver."** Why does the Torah need to repeat the fact that it is "the man who lay with her" who pays the fine? [3] It is in order to teach us that these **fifty** pieces of silver **are** to be **paid** in compensation **for the** illicit **pleasure** he had when **lying with her,** and for nothing else. All other penalties that may be incurred by the rapist are in addition to the fifty shekalim, and are assessed as for any other assault. [4] **This proves by implication that** a man who rapes or seduces a virgin *na'arah* is held liable to **pay for** her **shame** (i.e., lost reputation) **and blemish** (i.e., lost virginity), in addition to paying the fifty-shekel fine. Thus we see that, according to both Abaye and Rava, the Torah explicitly requires that the fifty-shekel fine be in addition to the regular penalties for assault.

וְאֵימָא לְדִידָהּ [5] **But,** asks the Gemara, if we learn from the verse that the fine is separate and distinct from regular damage payments, why do we not **say that** these payments **must be made to her?** The verse requires that the fine be paid to the *na'arah*'s father, but it says nothing about these other damage payments. Thus they should presumably be subject to the same laws that apply in other cases of assault. Yet the Mishnah (below, 41b) rules that these payments are made to the *na'arah*'s father. Why, asks the Gemara, are they not treated like regular compensation for assault?

אָמַר קְרָא [6] The Gemara first suggests an exegetical argument. **The verse says** (Numbers 30:17) concerning the laws of the annulment of vows: "These are the statutes that the Lord commanded Moses between a man and his wife, between a father and his daughter **while she is a *na'arah* in her father's house."** From this verse we learn that a father has the power to annul his daughter's vows as long as she is a *na'arah*. [7] However, from the fact that she is described as being part of her father's household as long as she is a *na'arah*, we also learn that **all the** monetary **benefits** she may receive **while she is a *na'arah* belong to her father.** Thus, according to this exegesis, someone who assaults a *na'arah* or a minor must pay all the

RASHI

ואימא לדידה הוי – דבשלמא קנס כתיב ביה "ונתן לאבי הנערה" אלא הני – ליהוו לדידה. **בנעוריה בית אביה** – גבי נדרים כתיב. ומיהו, איכא למשמע מינה דבימי נעוריה תלאה הכתוב בבית אביה.

NOTES

רָבָא אֲמַר: אָמַר קְרָא: "וְנָתַן הָאִישׁ הַשֹּׁכֵב עִמָּהּ" **Rava said: The verse says: "And the man who lay with her shall give."** *Shittah Mekubbetzet* explains that Rava rejects Abaye's explanation because he needs Abaye's verse to construct the *gezerah shavah* presented above (32b), which teaches us that monetary penalties take precedence over lashes if the two penalties clash. Abaye, by contrast, maintains that lashes take precedence.

וְאֵימָא לְדִידָהּ **But say that it is paid to her!** *Shittah Mekubbetzet* asks: The Gemara is essentially asking a question about the Mishnah below (41b). Why did the Gemara ask this question here instead of there?

Shittah Mekubbetzet answers that the Gemara's question

arguing that the girl who was raped for the first time should receive more.

According to *Tosafot* (followed by our commentary), Rabbi Zera's statement can be explained as referring to one girl, in accordance with its plain meaning. *Tosafot* explains that Rabbi Zera described the cases out of order. In fact, Rabbi Zera was referring to a case where the girl was first raped unnaturally and then raped naturally. *Tosafot* explains that when the Talmud mentions two terms, one phrased in positive language ("naturally") and the other in negative language ("unnaturally"), the Talmud usually puts the positive term first, even when this is chronologically inaccurate.

HALAKHAH

הֲנָאַת שְׁכִיבָה חֲמִשִּׁים **For the pleasure of lying he pays fifty.** "The fifty-shekel fine paid by a rapist or a seducer is compensation only for the pleasure of lying illicitly with the girl. It does not encompass the regular damage payments that he owes her," following Rava. (*Rambam, Sefer Nashim, Hilkhot Na'arah Betulah* 2:1.)

כָּל שֶׁבַח "נְעוּרֶיהָ" לְאָבִיהָ **All the benefit of "while she is a *na'arah*" belongs to her father.** "The four payments

TRANSLATION AND COMMENTARY

damages to her father, and the same applies in the case of a rapist or a seducer.

וְאֶלָּא [1]**But** the Gemara rejects this exegesis. It is not the case that all monetary benefits received by a *na'arah* go automatically to her father. **Let us consider what Rav Huna said in the name of Rav** (below, 47a): [2]**From where do we know that the work of a daughter** (anything she makes or earns) **belongs to her father?** [3]Rav answers that **the verse** (Exodus 21:7) **says: "And if a man shall sell his daughter as a maidservant."** The word "maidservant" was inserted in this verse in juxtaposition to the word "daughter" so that we would compare the two situations and say: [4]**Just as the work of a maidservant** obviously **belongs to her master,** [5]**so too does the work of a daughter belong to her father.** [6]But if all the monetary benefits that a girl may receive while she is a *na'arah* belong to her father, **why do we need** a special exegetical argument to prove that her wages also belong to her father? [7]All we need to do is to **derive** this law **from** the general exegetical argument provided by the text, **"while she is a *na'arah* in her father's house"!**

אֶלָּא [8]**Rather,** says the Gemara, the exegetical argument presented above is incorrect. The verse in Numbers **deals** specifically **with the annulment of vows,** and it teaches us that a father has the power to annul his daughter's vows as long as she is a *na'arah*. We cannot infer from the fact that the *na'arah* is described as being "in her father's house" that her father is entitled to all monetary benefits that she may receive. In fact, the father is entitled only to those benefits that the Torah explicitly awards him: The rapist's fine, the right to annul her vows, the right to marry her off to whomever he pleases (all of which apply while she is a minor or a *na'arah*), and the right to sell her as a maidservant (which applies only as long as she is a minor), as well as the rights that are derived indirectly from these explicit rights (e.g., the right to take her wages), and a few rights awarded by Rabbinic decree (e.g., to keep objects she finds). But the father is not entitled to take the compensation she receives if she is assaulted, and it is not clear why he should be entitled to receive her shame and blemish payments if she is raped.

וְכִי תֵּימָא [9]**And,** continues the Gemara, **if you say** that **we should derive from** the fact that the father has the power to annul his daughter's vows that he is also entitled to keep any monetary benefits she receives,

[1]וְאֶלָּא הָא דְּאָמַר רַב הוּנָא אָמַר רַב: [2]מִנַּיִן שֶׁמַּעֲשֵׂה הַבַּת לְאָבִיהָ? [3]שֶׁנֶּאֱמַר: "וְכִי יִמְכֹּר אִישׁ אֶת בִּתּוֹ לְאָמָה". [4]מָה אָמָה מַעֲשֵׂה יָדֶיהָ לְרַבָּהּ, [5]אַף בַּת מַעֲשֵׂה יָדֶיהָ לְאָבִיהָ. [6]לָמָּה לִי? [7]תֵּיפּוֹק לֵיהּ מִ"בִּנְעֻרֶיהָ בֵּית אָבִיהָ"!

[8]אֶלָּא הַהִיא בַּהֲפָרַת נְדָרִים הוּא דִּכְתִיב.

[9]וְכִי תֵּימָא: נֵילַף מִינֵּיהּ,

LITERAL TRANSLATION

[1]But [let us consider] what Rav Huna said in the name of Rav: [2]From where [do we know] that the work of the daughter [belongs] to her father? [3]For it is said: "And if a man shall sell his daughter as a maidservant." [4]Just as the work of a maidservant's hands [belongs] to her master, [5]so too [does] the work of a daughter's hands [belong] to her father. [6]Why do I [need this]? [7]Let him derive it from "while she is a *na'arah* in her father's house"!

[8]Rather, that is written about the annulment of vows.

[9]And if you say: Let us derive from it,

RASHI

בתו לאמה הקיש בת לאמה. **תיפוק ליה כו׳** – אלא על כרחך מהתם לא מצי למילף, דההוא בהפרת נדרים כתיב.

NOTES

was prompted by the explanations of Abaye and Rava. According to Rabbi Zera's initial explanation, it is obvious that the additional payments are given to the father whenever the fine is given to him. For Rabbi Zera infers the additional payments from the fact that the fine is a fixed sum, and it stands to reason that it should be adjusted to the status of the girl. Thus these payments are essentially adjustments in the fine itself, and it is clear that they should be made to the person who receives the fine. But Abaye and Rava infer from the verse that the fifty-shekel fine is unconnected with the regular damage payments. Thus they maintain that the shame and blemish payments are essentially regular damage payments independent of the fine. Hence the Gemara asks: How does the Mishnah know that these payments are not made to the daughter, like other forms of compensation for assault?

HALAKHAH

made by the rapist, and the three payments made by the seducer, are all paid to the father, since all the benefits received by a *na'arah* belong to her father." (*Rambam, Sefer Nashim, Hilkhot Na'arah Betulah*, 2.14.)

אַף בַּת מַעֲשֵׂה יָדֶיהָ לְאָבִיהָ So too does the work of a daughter's hands belong to her father. "Anything made or any wages earned by a girl belong to her father, until she becomes an adult." (*Rambam, Sefer Nashim, Hilkhot Ishut 3:11; Shulḥan Arukh, Even HaEzer* 37:1.)

BACKGROUND

מְנוּוָּל **Someone repulsive.** The term מְנוּוָּל generally serves to indicate, as here, the flawed and repellent physical condition of a person or an object, but by extension it is sometimes applied to ethical defects.

מוּכֵּה שְׁחִין **Someone afflicted with boils.** The term שְׁחִין (translated here as "boils") is used in the Talmud as a general description of skin ailments. Such conditions are characterized by changes in skin coloring and in particular by an accumulation of pus beneath the skin's surface. This results both in pain suffered by the victim and in a repulsive facial appearance.

TRANSLATION AND COMMENTARY

[1] we can object that **we do not derive monetary laws from ritual laws.** The laws governing ritual matters are different from those governing monctary matters. Hence we cannot extrapolate from the father's power to annul his daughter's vows that he also has authority over her in monetary matters.

וְכִי תֵּימָא [2] **And,** continues the Gemara, **if you say** that **we should derive from the** father's right to the rapist's **fine** that he is also entitled to keep any monetary benefits she receives, including all payments for assault, [3] we can object that **we do not derive** regular **monetary laws from fines.** Fines are an innovation that the Torah originated, and the laws governing them are different from those governing regular monetary payments. Hence we cannot extrapolate from the father's power to collect the rapist's fine that he also has authority over his daughter in regular monetary matters.

אֶלָּא [4] **Rather**, says the Gemara, we must reject this line of argument, and we must accept that the father has no right to monetary benefits received by his daughter, except in those cases where the Torah or the Rabbis awarded them to him. But in cases of assault the payment is made to the daughter herself and not to her father. Why, then, does the Mishnah (below, 41b) rule that the compensation for the seduced or raped *na'arah*'s blemish and shame, as well as the compensation for the raped *na'arah*'s pain, are paid to her father? The Gemara explains: **It is reasonable that** these payments should be made **to her father,** because his right to receive them can be derived indirectly from his power to marry her to whomever he pleases, even without her consent. [5] **For** the father has the power to bring his daughter's virginity to an end at his own discretion, by marrying her off. Moreover, **if he wishes, he can hand her over** in marriage **to someone repulsive or afflicted with boils,** causing her shame and humiliation. Thus the father in effect "owns" his daughter's virginity and reputation as long as she is a *na'arah*. Hence the rapist or the seducer is considered to have encroached upon a prerogative of the *na'arah*'s father, and he must therefore pay compensation for her blemish and shame to the father.

פְּגָם [6] The Gemara now considers the next clause of our Mishnah, which rules that in assessing the **blemish** suffered by a *na'arah* **we view her as if she were a female slave sold** in the slave market. [7] The Gemara asks: **How do we assess her** value?

[1] מָמוֹנָא מֵאִיסּוּרָא לָא יָלְפִינַן.
[2] וְכִי תֵּימָא: נֵילַף מִקְּנָסָא,
[3] מָמוֹנָא מִקְּנָסָא לָא יָלְפִינַן.
[4] אֶלָּא מִסְתַּבְּרָא דְּאָבִיהָ הָוֵי.
[5] דְּאִי בָּעֵי, מָסַר לָהּ לִמְנוּוָּל וּמוּכֵּה שְׁחִין.
[6] "פְּגָם, רוֹאִין אוֹתָהּ כְּאִילּוּ הִיא שִׁפְחָה נִמְכֶּרֶת". [7] הֵיכִי שָׁיְימִינַן לָהּ?

LITERAL TRANSLATION

[1] we do not derive monetary [laws] from ritual [laws].

[2] And if you say: Let us derive [it] from the fine, [3] we do not derive monetary [laws] from fines.

[4] Rather, it is reasonable that it is her father's. [5] For if he wished, he could have handed her over to someone repulsive or afflicted with boils.

[6] "[Regarding] blemish, we view her as if she were a female slave being sold." [7] How do we assess her?

RASHI

נילף מקנסא – מה קנסה לאביה – אף שאר שבח ממון נעורים לאביה:

אלא מסתברא – דבושת ופגם דאב הויא, שהרי בידו לביישה בבושת בעילה, ולפוגמה בפגם בעילה. **דאי בעי מסר לה** – לקדשה בביאה. **למנוול ומוכה שחין** – כדתנן לקמן: האב זכאי בבתו בקידושין בכסף ובשטר ובביאה, וכיון דבידו ליטול ממון לפוגמה ולביישה בושה זו – השתא אפסדיה האי דפגמה.

NOTES

דְּאִי בָּעֵי, מָסַר לָהּ לִמְנוּוָּל **For if he wished, he could have handed her over to someone repulsive.** *Rashi* explains that it was in the father's power to blemish and shame his daughter in a manner analogous to rape. Moreover, he could theoretically have made a profit from this power, by demanding money from the prospective husband in exchange for his permission. Hence the *na'arah*'s virginity and shame are considered to be her father's property, as it were, and the rapist or the seducer is considered to have damaged the father by taking advantage of the *na'arah* without obtaining the father's permission.

Rosh explains that the father is entitled to marry off his daughter in the regular way, through betrothal money, keeping that money for himself. But now that his daughter has been raped or seduced, he will probably receive less money if he marries off his daughter. Hence the seducer or

HALAKHAH

פְּגָם, רוֹאִין אוֹתָהּ כְּאִילּוּ הִיא שִׁפְחָה נִמְכֶּרֶת **Regarding blemish, we view her as if she were a female slave being sold.** "The payment for blemish is assessed as follows: We view the girl as if she were being sold as a female slave to a master who wished to give her to his slave as a reward for faithful service. The rapist or the seducer must pay the difference between her value as a virgin and her value as a non-virgin," in accordance with the Gemara's conclusion here. (*Rambam, Sefer Nashim, Hilkhot Na'arah Betulah* 2:6.)

TRANSLATION AND COMMENTARY

אָמַר [1]**Shmuel's father said: We estimate** the difference between **how much a person is willing to give for a virgin slave to serve him, and** how much he is willing to give **for a non-virgin slave.** The difference between these two estimates is the value of her virginity on the slave market.

שִׁפְחָה בְּעוּלָה [2]But, the Gemara objects, Shmuel's father suggests that a prospective buyer would give less for **a non-virgin slave to serve him.** [3]But **what difference does it make to him** if the slave serving him is a virgin or a non-virgin?

אֶלָּא [4]**Rather,** says the Gemara, **we** must **estimate the difference between** how much a person is willing to give for **a virgin slave** in order **to marry her to his slave, and** how much he would be willing to give for **a non-virgin slave** for the same purpose.

וּלְעַבְדּוֹ [5]**But,** the Gemara objects, **what difference does it make to him** if his slave is given a virgin or a non-virgin? All that interests the master is that the two slaves should produce more slaves for him.

בְּעֶבֶד [6]The Gemara answers: We are referring to **a slave with whom his master is** particularly **satisfied.** The master bought the female slave as a reward for his own slave's faithful service, and he was careful to buy a female slave who would please his own slave. In such a case, the master is willing to pay more money to buy a virgin than a non-virgin, and the difference in price is the value of virginity on the slave market.

MISHNAH כָּל מָקוֹם [7]This Mishnah considers which girls are entitled to a fine. The Gemara ruled (above, 32a) that compensation for a girl's blemish, shame, and pain are paid to a girl of any age. However, the Torah explicitly commands that the fine be paid to a girl who was a virgin *na'arah* — between the age of twelve, when she becomes legally competent, and the age of twelve-and-a-half, when she achieves full sexual maturity. Hence a fully mature woman who has been raped or seduced is not entitled to a fine, according to all opinions. But there is a Tannaitic dispute regarding laws such as this, which the Torah stipulates apply to a *na'arah* and not to an adult. Does such a law apply all the more so to a minor under the age of twelve, or does it apply only to a *na'arah*, by decree of the Torah? The author of our Mishnah maintains that the rapist's fine and similar laws apply only to a *na'arah*, as he indicates through the following general rule: **Wherever there is a sale, there is no fine,** [8]**and wherever there is a fine, there is no sale.** The Mishnah compares the law that a man who seduces or rapes a *na'arah* must pay a fine with

[1]אָמַר אֲבוּהּ דִּשְׁמוּאֵל: אוֹמְדִין כַּמָּה אָדָם רוֹצֶה לִיתֵּן בֵּין שִׁפְחָה בְּתוּלָה לְשִׁפְחָה בְּעוּלָה לְשַׁמְּשׁוֹ.

[2]״שִׁפְחָה בְּעוּלָה לְשַׁמְּשׁוֹ״? [3]מַאי נָפְקָא לֵיהּ מִינָּהּ?

[4]אֶלָּא, בֵּין שִׁפְחָה בְּעוּלָה לְשִׁפְחָה שֶׁאֵינָהּ בְּעוּלָה לְהַשִּׂיאָהּ לְעַבְדּוֹ.

[5]וּלְעַבְדּוֹ, מַאי נָפְקָא לֵיהּ מִינָּהּ?

[6]בְּעֶבֶד שֶׁיֵּשׁ לוֹ לְרַבּוֹ קוֹרַת רוּחַ הֵימֶנּוּ.

מִשְׁנָה [7]כָּל מָקוֹם שֶׁיֵּשׁ מֶכֶר, אֵין קְנָס, [8]וְכָל מָקוֹם שֶׁיֵּשׁ קְנָס, אֵין מֶכֶר.

LITERAL TRANSLATION

[1]Shmuel's father said: We estimate how much a person is willing to give for a virgin slave and for a non-virgin slave to serve him.

[2]"A non-virgin slave to serve him?" [3]What difference does it make to him?

[4]Rather, [we estimate the difference] between a virgin slave and a non-virgin slave to marry her to his slave.

[5]But for his slave, what difference does it make to him?

[6]For a slave from whom his master has satisfaction.

MISHNAH [7]Wherever there is a sale, there is no fine, [8]and wherever there is a fine, there is no sale.

RASHI

[מאי נפקא ליה — לכל אדם בבעילתה, אם בעולה היא, הואיל ולמלאכה קיימא]. **ולעבדו מאי נפקא ליה** — למריה מינה אם בעולה היא, מי קפיד מריה אלא שיהו להן ולדות. **קורת רוח** — שזהיר בעבודתו. ואף הוא רוצה לעשות לו נחת רוח, להטעימו טעם בתולה.

משנה כל מקום שיש מכר — לאו דדחו, דהייגו דקוווחה

NOTES

the rapist must pay damages to the father. According to this explanation, the Gemara mentioned the repulsive person only by way of illustration, since such a person would probably give the father the largest sum of money.

בֵּין שִׁפְחָה בְּתוּלָה לְשִׁפְחָה בְּעוּלָה **For a virgin slave and for a non-virgin slave.** *Tosafot* asks: How can this method adequately measure the value of the *na'arah*'s virginity? She is not a slave at all, but may well be a dignified woman from an important family.

Tosafot answers that the assessment takes this factor into account. We assess how much a person would pay to buy a slave from an important family. *Talmidei Rabbenu Yonah* explains that the *na'arah*'s dignity was already covered in the payment for shame. The blemish payment is intended only to cover her basic virginity, and this is the same for a dignified woman as for a slave.

כָּל מָקוֹם שֶׁיֵּשׁ מֶכֶר, אֵין קְנָס **Wherever there is a sale, there is no fine.** *Tosefot Yom Tov* asks: Normally, when a

LITERAL TRANSLATION

[1]A minor girl is subject to (lit., "has") sale, but she does not have a fine. [2]A *na'arah* has a fine, but she is not subject to sale. [3]The adult woman is neither subject to sale nor does she have a fine.

GEMARA [4]Rav Yehudah said in the name of Rav: These are the words of Rabbi Meir. [5]But the Sages say: She has a fine in the place of sale. [6]For it was taught: "A minor girl, from one day old until she produces two [pubic] hairs, [7]is subject to sale, but she does not have a fine. [8]From when she produces two [pubic] hairs until she becomes mature, [9]she has a fine, but she is not subject to sale. [10][These are] the words of Rabbi Meir. For Rabbi Meir used to say: Wherever there is a sale, there is no fine, [11]and wherever there is a fine, there is no sale.

[1]קְטַנָּה יֵשׁ לָהּ מֶכֶר, וְאֵין לָהּ קְנָס. [2]נַעֲרָה יֵשׁ לָהּ קְנָס, וְאֵין לָהּ מֶכֶר. [3]הַבּוֹגֶרֶת אֵין לָהּ לֹא מֶכֶר וְלֹא קְנָס.

גמרא [4]אָמַר רַב יְהוּדָה אָמַר רַב: זוֹ דִּבְרֵי רַבִּי מֵאִיר. [5]אֲבָל חֲכָמִים אוֹמְרִים: יֵשׁ לָהּ קְנָס בִּמְקוֹם מֶכֶר. [6]דְּתַנְיָא: "קְטַנָּה, מִבַּת יוֹם אֶחָד וְעַד שֶׁתָּבִיא שְׁתֵּי שְׂעָרוֹת, [7]יֵשׁ לָהּ מֶכֶר, וְאֵין לָהּ קְנָס. [8]מִשֶּׁתָּבִיא שְׁתֵּי שְׂעָרוֹת עַד שֶׁתִּיבָּגֵר, [9]יֵשׁ לָהּ קְנָס, וְאֵין לָהּ מֶכֶר. [10]דִּבְרֵי רַבִּי מֵאִיר. שֶׁהָיָה רַבִּי מֵאִיר אוֹמֵר: כָּל מָקוֹם שֶׁיֵּשׁ מֶכֶר, אֵין קְנָס, [11]וְכָל מָקוֹם שֶׁיֵּשׁ קְנָס, אֵין מֶכֶר.

RASHI

אין לו בה קנס – דאין קנס לקטנה.
כל מקום שיש קנס – משהיא נערה.
אין מכר – דתניא (ערכין כט,ב): יכול ימכור אדם בתו כשהיא נערה – אמרת מכורה כבר יוצאה עכשיו, שאינה מכורה אינו דין שלא תימכר?
גמרא זו דברי רבי מאיר – דאמר: אין קנס לקטנה.

TRANSLATION AND COMMENTARY

the law that a father who is under great financial pressure can sell his daughter into semi-slavery, on the understanding that his daughter's master will either marry her himself or marry her to his son (Exodus 21:7-11). The general rule laid down in the Mishnah teaches us that these two laws are mutually exclusive, and never apply to the same girl. But the Gemara (*Nedarim* 76a) proves from a Biblical verse that the sale applies only to minors, but not to *ne'arot* or to mature girls. [1]Thus it follows that **a minor girl,** who **is subject to sale** by her father, **is not entitled to a fine** if she is raped or seduced. [2]**A *na'arah*,** on the other hand, **is entitled to the fine, but is not subject to the sale.** However, although these laws are mutually exclusive, it does not follow that every woman is subject to one of these laws. [3]For **an adult woman is not subject to sale** by her father, **and is** also **not entitled to a fine** if she is raped or seduced.

GEMARA אָמַר רַב יְהוּדָה [4]**Rav Yehudah said in the name of Rav:** Even though the Mishnah was written anonymously, **it represents the viewpoint of Rabbi Meir.** [5]**But the Sages** disagree with him **and say:** A girl **can be entitled to a fine** if she was raped or seduced, even **when there is a sale** (i.e., even if she is a minor who is subject to sale by her father). [6]**For** the following **was taught in** a Baraita: "**A minor girl, from one day old until she produces two pubic hairs** (at about the age of twelve), [7]**is subject to sale** by her father, **but is not entitled to a fine** if she is raped or seduced. [8]A *na'arah*, on the other hand, **from** the time **when she produces two pubic hairs** (at the age of twelve) **until she becomes mature** (at twelve-and-a-half), [9]**is entitled to the fine, but is not subject to sale.** [10]**This is the opinion of Rabbi Meir, for Rabbi Meir used to say: Wherever there is a sale** — whenever the girl is of an age that entitles her father to sell her — **there is no fine** if she is raped or seduced, [11]**and wherever there is a fine, there is no sale.** According to Rabbi Meir, the fine and the sale are mutually exclusive. Just as the sale does not apply to *ne'arot*, so too does

NOTES

Mishnah states a general rule like this, it is intended to cover situations that are not explicitly listed in the Mishnah itself. But in this case the rule covers only those cases explicitly mentioned — the *na'arah* and the minor. What, then, is the point of the general rule?

Tosefot Yom Tov explains that in this case the rule was inserted simply as a mnemonic device. *Tosefot Yom Tov* adds that the Mishnah departed from its usual practice on this occasion because this rule appears verbatim in the last Mishnah of the first chapter of *Ḥullin* (26b), together with a list of other mutually exclusive pairs of laws, and in *Ḥullin* the Mishnah simply states the rule without listing the cases in detail.

Melekhet Shlomo adds that it is possible that the Mishnah wished to emphasize with this rule that the mutual exclusivity of these two laws applies only to the fine itself, but not to the compensation for blemish and shame, which is paid to women of any age.

HALAKHAH

קְטַנָּה...יֵשׁ לָהּ קְנָס A minor...has a fine. "A girl is entitled to a fine if she was seduced or raped at any time from her third birthday until she becomes an adult," following the Sages. (*Rambam, Sefer Nashim, Hilkhot Na'arah Betulah* 1:8; *Shulḥan Arukh, Even HaEzer* 177:1.)

¹וַחֲכָמִים אוֹמְרִים: קְטַנָּה, מִבַּת שָׁלֹשׁ שָׁנִים וְיוֹם אֶחָד וְעַד שֶׁתִּיבָּגֵר, יֵשׁ לָהּ קְנָס.
²קְנָס אִין; מֶכֶר לָא?
³אֵימָא: אַף קְנָס בִּמְקוֹם מֶכֶר.
⁴אָמַר רַב חִסְדָּא: מַאי טַעֲמָא דְּרַבִּי מֵאִיר? ⁵אָמַר קְרָא: ״וְלוֹ תִהְיֶה לְאִשָּׁה״. ⁶בִּמְהַוָּה עַצְמָהּ הַכָּתוּב מְדַבֵּר. ⁷וְרַבָּנַן? ⁸אֲמַר רֵישׁ לָקִישׁ: אָמַר קְרָא: ״נַעֲרָ״. ⁹אֲפִילּוּ קְטַנָּה בְּמַשְׁמָע.

LITERAL TRANSLATION

¹But the Sages say: A minor girl, from three years and one day old until she becomes mature, has a fine."

²A fine yes; a sale no?

³Say: [There is] also a fine where there is a sale.

⁴Rav Ḥisda said: What is Rabbi Meir's reason? ⁵The verse says: "And to him she shall be a wife." ⁶The verse is speaking of where she causes herself to be [married]. ⁷And the Rabbis? ⁸Resh Lakish said: The verse says: "A *na'arah*." ⁹Even a minor girl is within the meaning.

RASHI

מבת שלש שנים — שביאתה ביאה, ואין בתוליה חוזרין. **מכר לא** — בתמיה. **אף קנס במקום מכר** — משתהא ראויה לביאה עד שתביא שתי שערות הוו תרוייהו, ומשהביאה שערות עד שתבגר — קנס ולא מכר. **מאי טעמא דרבי מאיר** — דאמר: קטנה אין לה קנס. **דאמר קרא** — גבי קנס "ולו תהיה לאשה". **במהוה עצמה** — במי שיש בידה להקנות עצמה לאישות הכתוב מדבר.

TRANSLATION AND COMMENTARY

the fine not apply to minors. ¹**But the Sages say:** The two laws are not mutually exclusive. Rather, **a minor girl, from three years and one day old until she becomes mature** at the age of twelve-and-a-half, **is entitled to the fine,** even though she can no longer be sold by her father once she reaches the age of twelve." Thus we see from this Baraita that there is a dispute between Rabbi Meir and the Sages as to whether a minor girl is entitled to a fine, and that our Mishnah reflects the viewpoint of Rabbi Meir.

קְנָס ²Before continuing its analysis of our Mishnah, the Gemara seeks to clarify the language of the Baraita it has just quoted. The Sages say that a minor girl from the age of three is entitled to the **fine.** But does this mean that she is **not** subject to **sale?** Surely everyone agrees that a minor girl is subject to sale until she becomes a *na'arah!*

אֵימָא ³The Gemara answers: We cannot infer anything about the sale of a young girl from the wording of this Baraita, because the topic of the Baraita was the fine, and the issue of the sale was only introduced for the sake of comparison. Rabbi Meir ruled that the fine applies only when the sale is not applicable, whereas the Sages **said** that the two laws are not connected, and that a minor girl and a *na'arah*, from the age of three until the age of twelve-and-a-half, is entitled to **a fine, irrespective of whether there is a sale**. Thus the ages of three and twelve-and-a-half, given by the Sages in the Baraita, relate only to the fine, and in fact the Sages agree with Rabbi Meir that the girl may be sold by her father from birth until the age of twelve.

אָמַר רַב חִסְדָּא ⁴The Gemara now returns to the dispute between Rabbi Meir and the Sages, as reflected in our Mishnah. **Rav Ḥisda said: What is Rabbi Meir's reason?** Why does Rabbi Meir interpret the word *"na'arah"* in the Torah so narrowly, instead of arguing that any law that applies to a *na'arah* and not to an adult should apply all the more to a minor? Rav Ḥisda explains: ⁵**The verse says** (Deuteronomy 22:29): **"And to him she shall be a wife."** ⁶**The verse is speaking of** a situation in which a girl **can cause herself to be married,** where she has the independent right to accept an offer of marriage. Since a minor is not legally competent to contract a marriage, we see that this law applies specifically to *ne'arot*. The Gemara asks: ⁷**And the** other **Rabbis?** How can they say that the law applies to a minor when the Torah stipulates that it applies to a *na'arah?* ⁸In answer to this question, **Resh Lakish said:** According to the Rabbis, whenever **the Torah uses** the expression ***"na'arah,"*** ⁹**a minor girl is** also **included** in the application of the law, unless the Torah specifically teaches us otherwise.

NOTES

״נַעֲרָ״ אֲפִילּוּ קְטַנָּה בְּמַשְׁמָע "A *na'arah.*" Even a minor girl is within the meaning. The word *"na'arah"* (נַעֲרָה) appears in many places in the Torah. Almost invariably, it is spelled without the final letter (נַעֲרָ). This is one of several words in which the Torah systematically deviates from conventional spelling. Thus, when the Torah spells the word out in full, this itself is considered to be a deviation that calls for exegetical analysis.

There are four laws that the Torah applies specifically to virgin *ne'arot*. (1) The law of the rapist. (2) The law of the seducer. (3) The law of the betrothed virgin *na'arah*. The Torah requires (Deuteronomy 22:23-27) that a virgin *na'arah* who committed adultery after she was betrothed be executed by stoning, whereas other cases of adultery are punished by strangulation. In addition, the man who committed adultery with her is also stoned. In a case of rape, the man is stoned, whereas the raped betrothed *na'arah* is exempt. (4) The law of the husband who accuses his wife of adultery. The Torah requires (Deuteronomy 22:13-21) that a man who marries a virgin *na'arah* and, after consummating the marriage, accuses his wife of committing adultery while betrothed, must have his claim

SAGES

רַב פַּפָּא בְּרֵיהּ דְּרַב חָנָן מִבֵּי כְּלוֹחִית Rav Pappa the son of Rav Ḥanan from Bei Keloḥit. This Babylonian Amora is mentioned only here, but it is possible that the reference is to Rav Pappa the son of Rav Ḥanin who was Rava's scribe. The reference to Bei Keloḥit is also unclear, but it is mentioned on a number of occasions in the Talmud as a place where certain Sages had made their home.

רַב שִׁימִי בַּר אַשִׁי Rav Shimi bar Ashi. A Babylonian Amora of the fifth generation. See *Ketubot*, Part II, p. 91.

[1]שְׁמָעָהּ רַב פַּפָּא בְּרֵיהּ דְּרַב חָנָן מִבֵּי כְּלוֹחִית. [2]אֲזַל אֲמָרָהּ קַמֵּיהּ דְּרַב שִׁימִי בַּר אַשִׁי. [3]אֲמַר לֵיהּ: אַתּוּן אַהָא מַתְנִיתוּ לָהּ. [4]אֲנַן אַהָא מַתְנִינַן לָהּ: [5]אָמַר רֵישׁ לָקִישׁ: הַמּוֹצִיא שֵׁם רַע עַל הַקְּטַנָּה פָּטוּר, [6]שֶׁנֶּאֱמַר: "וְנָתְנוּ לַאֲבִי הַנַּעֲרָה". [7]"נַעֲרָה" מָלֵא דִּיבֵּר הַכָּתוּב.

LITERAL TRANSLATION

[1]Rav Pappa the son of Rav Ḥanan from Bei Keloḥit heard it. [2]He went [and] said it before Rav Shimi bar Ashi. [3]He said to him: You taught it about that. [4]We taught it about this: [5]Resh Lakish said: Someone who puts out a bad name about a minor is exempt, [6]for it is said: "And they shall give to the father of the *na'arah.*" [7]The verse was speaking [about] a *"na'arah"* [spelled] in full.

TRANSLATION AND COMMENTARY

שְׁמָעָהּ [1]**Rav Pappa the son of Rav Ḥanan from Bei Keloḥit heard** Resh Lakish's explanation. [2]**He went and repeated it before Rav Shimi bar Ashi.** [3]Rav Shimi bar Ashi **said to him: Your tradition is** that Resh Lakish made this remark **about the** verse dealing with the rapist. According to you, Resh Lakish was discussing the case of the rapist's fine, and simply said that, according to the Sages, the word *"na'arah"* includes minors. [4]**We have a tradition** that he made this remark **about** the following verse, dealing with a husband who accuses his wife of adultery, and according to our tradition Resh Lakish gave a more detailed exegetical argument. The Torah (Deuteronomy 22:13-21) considers the case of a man who marries a virgin *na'arah*, and after consummating the marriage he announces that he has discovered that his wife was not a virgin, and that he has proof that she committed adultery while she was betrothed to him. In such a case, the Torah commands the court to investigate the matter, and if it is found that the man was lying, he is lashed, and he is required to pay the father of the *na'arah* a fine of one hundred silver shekalim, and he is forbidden to divorce his wife without her consent. If, on the other hand, his complaint is found to be justified, his wife is stoned to death, in accordance with the law (Deuteronomy 22:23-24) regarding a betrothed virgin *na'arah* who committed adultery. [5]Concerning this case, **Resh Lakish said:** If the wife was **a minor** and her husband **falsely accused her** of adultery, the husband **is exempt** from the lashes and the fine, [6]**for the verse says** (Deuteronomy 22:19): **"And they shall give it to the father of the *na'arah*"** — and not to the father of a minor. [7]Resh Lakish explains: We know that the term *"na'arah"* is to be understood narrowly in this case, because **the verse was speaking about a *"na'arah"* spelled in full.** The word *"na'arah"* (נַעֲרָה) is usually spelled in the Torah without its final Hebrew letter heh (ה). In this verse, however, the word is spelled in full, and this informs us that the Torah was being very specific when it referred to this *na'arah*, and did not intend the law to apply to a minor or to an adult.

RASHI

אהא מתניתו לה — אהא דריש לקיש, דאמר כל מקום שנכתב "נער" בלא ה' וקרינן נערה — ללמד על הקטנה בא. **שם רע** — "לא מצאתי לבתך בתולים." **פטור** — ד"וענשו אותו מאה כסף ונתנו לאבי הנערה" מלא כתיב.

NOTES

investigated by the court. If the claim is found to be justified, the *na'arah* is stoned in front of her father's house. But if the husband is found to be lying, he is lashed and fined one hundred silver shekalim. He is also forbidden ever to divorce his wife without her consent.

In all four of these cases, the law applies to a *na'arah*, but not to a full adult. In the case of the husband who falsely accuses his wife, the law does not apply to a minor, since she cannot be punished if found guilty, as the Gemara explains below. In the other three cases, there is a dispute between Rabbi Meir and the Sages: According to Rabbi Meir, these laws apply only to *ne'arot* and not to minors, whereas the Sages maintain that the term *"na'arah"* includes minors.

"נַעֲרָה" מָלֵא דִּיבֵּר הַכָּתוּב The verse was speaking about a *"na'arah"* spelled in full. The Jerusalem Talmud asks: The word *"na'arah"* appears several times in the Biblical passage dealing with the false accuser (Deuteronomy 22:13-21), and only once does it appear spelled in full. In the other cases, it is spelled without the final letter. But if the word *"na'arah"* spelled in full means a *na'arah* and not a minor, whereas the word spelled without the final letter includes a minor, why was it not spelled in full throughout the passage?

The Jerusalem Talmud answers that by spelling the word without the final letter, the Torah is teaching us that this law applies even if the wife was accused of committing adultery through anal intercourse, as if she were a male (the word *"na'arah"* spelled without the final letter is spelled the same way as the word for a young man).

HALAKHAH

הַמּוֹצִיא שֵׁם רַע עַל הַקְּטַנָּה Someone who puts out a bad name about a minor. "A husband who falsely accuses his wife of adultery is exempt from lashes and from the fine if she was a minor or a full adult. He is liable only if she was a *na'arah*, because the verse wrote *'na'arah'* in full." (*Rambam, Sefer Nashim, Hilkhot Na'arah Betulah* 3:2; *Tur, Even HaEzer* 177.)

[1]מַתְקִיף לָהּ רַב אַדָּא בַּר אַהֲבָה: [2]טַעֲמָא דִּכְתַב רַחֲמָנָא ״נַעֲרָה״. [3]הָא לָאו הָכִי, הֲוָה אָמִינָא אֲפִילּוּ קְטַנָּה? [4]וְהָא כְּתִיב: ״וְאִם אֱמֶת הָיָה הַדָּבָר הַזֶּה, לֹא נִמְצְאוּ בְתוּלִים לַנַּעֲרָה, [5]וְהוֹצִיאוּ אֶת הַנַּעֲרָה אֶל פֶּתַח בֵּית אָבִיהָ וּסְקָלוּהָ״. [6]וּקְטַנָּה לָאו בַּת עוֹנָשִׁין הִיא! [7]אֶלָּא, כָּאן ״נַעֲרָה״. [8]הָא כָּל מָקוֹם שֶׁנֶּאֱמַר ״נַעֲרָ״, [9]אֲפִילּוּ קְטַנָּה בְּמַשְׁמָע.

[41A] **מִשְׁנָה** [10]הָאוֹמֵר: ״פִּתִּיתִי אֶת בִּתּוֹ שֶׁל פְּלוֹנִי״,

LITERAL TRANSLATION

[1]Rav Adda bar Ahavah objected to it: [2]The reason is that the Torah wrote *"na'arah"* [in full]. [3]But if this were not so, would I have thought [that] even a minor [was meant]? [4]But surely it is written: "But if this thing was true, [and the signs of] virginity were not found in the *na'arah* [spelled defectively], [5]then they shall bring the *na'arah* [spelled defectively] out to the door of her father's house and stone her." [6]But a minor is not subject to punishment!

[7]Rather, here [it is spelled] *"na'arah"* [in full]. [8]But wherever *"na'arah"* is said [spelled defectively], [9]even a minor girl is within the meaning.

MISHNAH [41A] [10][If] someone says: "I seduced the daughter of so-and-so,"

TRANSLATION AND COMMENTARY

מַתְקִיף לֵיהּ [1]When **Rav Adda bar Ahavah** heard Resh Lakish's explanation, he **objected to it:** [2]We see from Resh Lakish's explanation that **the reason** why the law of the husband who falsely accuses his wife of adultery does not apply to a minor **is because the Torah wrote the word *"na'arah"* in full.** [3]**But** the implication is that **if this were not so we would have thought that** the verse **was referring even to a minor.** [4]**But surely** this is impossible, for the following **is written** in the next two verses: **"But if this thing was true, and the signs of virginity were not found in the *na'arah*** [spelled defectively], [5]**then they shall bring the *na'arah*** [spelled defectively] **out to the door of her father's house and stone her."** [6]**But** surely the second verse cannot apply to a minor, since **a minor is not subject to punishment!** Even if his minor wife had committed adultery, she would still not be stoned to death, since as a minor she was not legally competent. Hence the first verse must also not be referring to a minor. Why, then, do you need to learn this law from the spelling of the word *"na'arah"* in this verse?

אֶלָּא [7]**Rather,** Rav Adda bar Ahavah amended Resh Lakish's explanation to read as follows: **Here,** in the case of the husband who falsely accused his wife of adultery, where we know that the law does not apply to minors, the Torah (Deuteronomy 22:19) writes ***"na'arah"* spelling it in full.** [8]Thus we can infer that only if the word *"na'arah"* is spelled in full does the law not apply to minors, **but wherever** the word ***"na'arah"* is spelled defectively,** [9]without its last letter, we may infer that **a minor girl is** also **implied.** Therefore the Sages maintain that in the case of the rapist's fine the word *"na'arah,"* spelled defectively, includes a minor, and this rule applies in any other case where the word *"na'arah"* is spelled defectively.

MISHNAH הָאוֹמֵר [41A] [10]This Mishnah returns to the subject of the payments for shame and blemish that

RASHI

אלא כאן נערה — האי דכתיב ״נערה״ מלא — לאו לגלויי עליה אתא, אלא על כל מקום שנאמר ״נער״ חסר. ויליף הכי: כאן שאי אפשר אלא בנערה — כתיב ״נערה״ מלא, וללמדך דכל מקום שנאמר ״נער״ — אפילו קטנה במשמע.

משנה פתיתי — בגמרא מפרש אמאי לא תנא ״אנסתי״.

NOTES

וּקְטַנָּה לָאו בַּת עוֹנָשִׁין הִיא But a minor is not subject to punishment! The Rishonim disagree as to how to explain the objection raised by Rav Adda bar Ahavah. Our commentary follows *Ramban,* who explains that Rav Adda bar Ahavah is pointing out that we already know, even without the inference from the spelling of the word *"na'arah,"* that the law of the husband who falsely accuses his wife of adultery does not apply if the wife was a minor. For this law applies only if the husband made an accusation that would have caused the wife to be executed, if it were found to be true, and a minor is not legally competent and cannot be punished.

Tosafot objects to this explanation, because it would appear from a passage in *Sanhedrin* (8b) that the husband is fined, even when his accusation could not possibly have led to her execution.

In order to avoid this problem, *Tosafot* offers another explanation of our Gemara. Rav Adda bar Ahavah is not objecting that the husband's accusation of his minor wife could not have led to her execution in practice because the husband is fined if he falsely accuses his wife of adultery, even if she could not have been executed. However, the Gemara rules (*Yevamot* 33b) that a minor wife who commits adultery is permitted to remain with her husband, since the seduction of a minor is considered to be the equivalent of rape. Thus, if the accused wife was a minor, the husband would not be accusing her of any crime at all, and in such a case there is no fine if the accusation was false.

הָאוֹמֵר: ״פִּתִּיתִי״ If someone says: "I seduced." The

HALAKHAH

הָאוֹמֵר: ״פִּתִּיתִי״ If someone says: "I seduced." "If someone confesses to seducing or to raping a *na'arah*, he does not pay the fifty-shekel fine, because fines cannot be imposed on the basis of a confession; but he does pay compensation

CONCEPTS

תַּשְׁלוּמֵי כֶפֶל The double payment. A thief must repay twice the value of a stolen article (Exodus 22:3), i.e., he must restore the article itself to its legal owner and must make an additional payment equal to the value of the article. This obligation is considered a fine (קְנָס). Accordingly, a thief is required to make this payment only if he is apprehended by others. If he voluntarily admits his wrongdoing and desires to restore the stolen article or its value, he does not make the additional payment. Similarly, a person who swears that something placed in his care was stolen is also obligated to pay כֶפֶל if the object is found to be still in his possession.

TRANSLATION AND COMMENTARY

the rapist and seducer must make, in addition to paying the fifty-shekel fine. There are some situations in which the rapist or the seducer is exempt from paying the fine, but is still liable for the other payments. For example, **if someone** comes to court of his own volition and **says: "I seduced the daughter of so-and-so,"** [1]**he must pay** compensation **for her shame and blemish by his own admission,** on the basis of his confession, **but he does not pay the fine.** We have seen above (34b) that fines are considered an innovation. One of the novel aspects of fines is that they cannot be imposed on the basis of a confession. Regular damage payments, by contrast, are subject to the normal rules of civil law, and confessions with regard to them are believed. Accordingly, if someone confesses to a sin that is subject to a regular damage payment, he is liable to pay the compensation on the basis of his own confession; but if he confesses to a sin that is subject to a fine, he is exempt from paying the fine. Hence, if a man admits to the rape or the seduction of a *na'arah*, he is held liable to pay the compensation for her shame and blemish, since these are regular damage payments, but he is not held liable to pay the fifty-shekel fine.

הָאוֹמֵר [2]The Mishnah gives another example of this distinction: **If someone says: "I stole** a cow from so-and-so and later slaughtered it," **he must pay the principal** — the value of the cow itself — **by his own admission,** because the principal is a regular damage payment; [3]**but he does not pay the double payment** that is imposed as a fine on a thief, **and** he does not pay **the fourfold and fivefold payment** that is imposed as a fine on a thief who steals a sheep or an ox and slaughters it or sells it.

"הֵמִית שׁוֹרִי אֶת פְּלוֹנִי" [4]Likewise, the Torah states (Exodus 21:29-30) that if an ox that has already done three acts of malicious goring and has the status of an animal whose owner must guard it closely — known in Hebrew as a *mu'ad* (מוּעָד) — and this ox then gores a man and causes his death, the owner of

[1]מְשַׁלֵּם בּוֹשֶׁת וּפְגָם עַל פִּי עַצְמוֹ, וְאֵין מְשַׁלֵּם קְנָס. [2]הָאוֹמֵר: "גָּנַבְתִּי", מְשַׁלֵּם אֶת הַקֶּרֶן עַל פִּי עַצְמוֹ, [3]וְאֵין מְשַׁלֵּם תַּשְׁלוּמֵי כֶפֶל וְתַשְׁלוּמֵי אַרְבָּעָה וַחֲמִשָּׁה. [4]"הֵמִית שׁוֹרִי אֶת פְּלוֹנִי"

LITERAL TRANSLATION

[1]he pays [for her] shame and blemish by his own admission, but he does not pay the fine.

[2][If] someone says: "I stole," he pays the principal by his own admission, [3]but he does not pay the double payment or the fourfold and fivefold payments.

[4][If someone says:] "My ox killed so-and-so,"

RASHI

ואינו משלם קנס — בבבא קמא נפקא לן מודה בקנס פטור מ"אשר ירשיען אלהים" — פרט למרשיע את עצמו. **המית שורי את פלוני** — והריני חייב בכופר.

NOTES

Mishnah lists three kinds of fines: The fine paid by a seducer (and by implication a rapist), the double, fourfold, and fivefold fines paid by a thief, and the fine paid by the owner of an ox that gored a slave. The Mishnah does not mention the hundred-shekel fine paid by a man who falsely accuses his wife of adultery (Deuteronomy 22:19), nor the law that a master who injures his slave must set him free (Exodus 21:26-27), which is also considered to be a fine. *Tosafot* explains that the Mishnah was not attempting to give an exhaustive list, and the other fines are clearly covered by the general rule at the end of the Mishnah.

The Aharonim attempt to explain why the Mishnah selected these three fines. *Tosefot Yom Tov* explains that the seducer's fine was mentioned in order to teach us that we believe the seducer and hold him liable to make the shame and blemish payments, even though the girl's reputation may be ruined as a result. The double, fourfold, and fivefold fine paid by the thief was selected in order to teach us that if the thief confesses, he is held liable to pay the principal but not the fine, even though the Torah links them together in a single payment. The case of the goring ox was selected in order to teach us that the ransom paid when the ox gores a free man is treated as a regular damage payment.

Melekhet Shlomo explains that the Mishnah listed these three cases in ascending order of novelty. It is a greater novelty that the thief who confesses is exempt from paying the fine than that the seducer is exempt, because the Gemara explains that we do not entirely accept the seducer's confession, in order not to ruin the girl's reputation. And it is a still greater novelty that the owner of the ox is exempt from paying the fine for killing the slave, because he does not pay anything at all, whereas the seducer pays for the maiden's shame and blemish, and the thief pays the principal.

"הֵמִית שׁוֹרִי אֶת פְּלוֹנִי" "My ox killed so-and-so." The Torah states (Exodus 21:29-30): "If it was a goring ox in time past and its owner was warned but he did not guard

HALAKHAH

for her shame and blemish, since these are regular damage payments," in accordance with the Mishnah. (*Rambam, Sefer Nashim, Hilkhot Na'arah Betulah* 2:12.)

הָאוֹמֵר: "גָּנַבְתִּי" If someone says: "I stole." "If someone confesses to stealing an object or to selling or slaughtering a stolen ox or sheep, he must pay the principal on the basis of his own confession, but not the double or fourfold and fivefold payments, since these are fines." (*Rambam, Sefer Nezikin, Hilkhot Genevah* 3:9; *Tur, Hoshen Mishpat* 348.)

"הֵמִית שׁוֹרִי אֶת פְּלוֹנִי" "My ox killed so-and-so." "If someone confesses that his *mu'ad* ox has killed a person,

TRANSLATION AND COMMENTARY

the ox must pay a ransom to the family of the victim; and if an ox that has already been attested to be a *mu'ad* by reason of three acts of malicious goring kills an ox (Exodus 21:36), the owner of the goring ox must pay for the dead ox in full. These payments are considered to be regular damage payments. Therefore, **if someone says: "My ox killed so-and-so," or "my ox killed the ox of so-and-so,"** [1]**he pays** the ransom for the dead person, or the value of the dead ox, **by his own admission,** because these payments are not fines. But the Torah states (Exodus 21:32) that if the person killed by the *mu'ad* was a slave, a fixed fine of thirty shekalim is paid to the slave's owner, and this payment is considered to be a fine. [2]Therefore, **if someone says: "My ox killed so-and-so's slave,"** [3]**he does not pay by his own admission** the thirty-shekel fine set by the Torah.

אוֹ: ״שׁוֹרוֹ שֶׁל פְּלוֹנִי״, [1]הֲרֵי זֶה מְשַׁלֵּם עַל פִּי עַצְמוֹ. [2]״הֵמִית שׁוֹרִי עַבְדּוֹ שֶׁל פְּלוֹנִי״, [3]אֵין מְשַׁלֵּם עַל פִּי עַצְמוֹ.

LITERAL TRANSLATION

or: "[My ox killed] the ox of so-and-so," [1]he pays by his own admission. [2][If someone says:] "My ox killed so-and-so's slave," [3]he does not pay by his own admission.

RASHI

הרי זה משלם על פי עצמו — קסבר: כופרא ממונא. עבדו של פלוני — והריני חייב שלשים סלע. אינו משלם — דקנס נינהו, שאפילו אין יפה דינר נותן שלשים.

BACKGROUND

אֵינוֹ מְשַׁלֵּם עַל פִּי עַצְמוֹ **He does not pay by his own admission.** There is an important principle in Talmudic jurisprudence that a person's confession to a crime has no legal validity. For this reason, when there are no witnesses to a crime, even if someone voluntarily confesses his guilt, he is not punished. In such a case atonement for the crime is a private matter between the perpetrator and his Maker and is of no concern to an earthly court. This principle applies to all areas of criminal law, and physical punishment is inflicted only on the basis of the testimony of witnesses. Fines, too, come under the category of such punishments, and this is why a person is not fined on the basis of his own admission. The law that a person can obligate himself to pay in civil matters on the basis of his own admission is founded on the fact that a person's money is his own property, and he can choose to obligate himself of his own free will. Thus a person's admission that he is guilty of a financial crime cannot incriminate him; it is merely an acceptance on his part to give a certain sum of money.

NOTES

it, and it killed a man or a woman, the ox shall be stoned and its owner shall also be put to death. If a ransom is set for him, he shall give the redemption money for his life in accordance with whatever is set for him." The Gemara explained above (37b) that the owner of the ox is subject to death at the hands of Heaven, from which he can redeem himself by paying a ransom. The ransom is not an optional matter, however, and if the owner fails to pay it voluntarily, the court compels him to do so (*Bava Kamma* 40a).

There is a Tannaitic dispute (*Bava Kamma* 40a) as to whether the ransom is set at the slave-market value of the dead person, or at the slave-market value of the owner of the ox. According to Rabbi Yishmael the son of Rabbi Yoḥanan ben Beroka, the ransom is set at the slave-market value of the owner of the ox, since the Torah calls it "redemption money for his life." The Sages, however, infer by means of a *gezerah shavah* that it is set at the slave-market value of the dead person. Commenting on this Baraita, Rav Ḥisda explains that Rabbi Yishmael the son of Rabbi Yoḥanan ben Beroka is of the opinion that the ransom money is a form of atonement, similar to a sacrifice, whereas the other Sages maintain that it is a form of damage payment. Rav Pappa, however, insists that even the Sages maintain that the ransom is a form of atonement and not a damage payment.

Tosafot asks: According to Rabbi Yishmael, the ransom money is not equal in value to the damage done. Why, then, is it paid by the admission of the owner of the ox? *Tosafot* answers that, according to Rabbi Yishmael, the ransom is intended to serve as an atonement for the ox owner's person. Hence it is sufficient for it to be equal to his own slave-market value.

Rashi, however, explains that our Mishnah follows the opinion — attributed by Rav Ḥisda to the Sages — that the ransom is in fact a damage payment and not a form of atonement (see *Shittah Mekubbetzet*). According to this explanation, Rabbi Yishmael would disagree with our Mishnah's ruling. *Rabbi Akiva Eger* notes that, according to *Rashi*, it would seem that an atonement is subject to the same rules as a fine and cannot be imposed on the basis of a confession. This, however, is clearly contradicted by a passage in *Bava Kamma* (41b), which explicitly states that the ransom is paid by his own admission, even under circumstances where it takes the form of a fine, *because* it is an atonement. *Rabbi Akiva Eger* notes, however, that *Rashi's* explanation is supported by the Jerusalem Talmud, commenting on our Mishnah, which explains that the ransom is considered a fine according to Rabbi Yishmael.

״הֵמִית שׁוֹרִי עַבְדּוֹ שֶׁל פְּלוֹנִי״ **"My ox killed so-and-so's slave."** The Jerusalem Talmud asks: Is the entire payment a fine, or is the fine only the amount beyond the value of the slave himself? The Jerusalem Talmud concludes that the entire thirty shekels is a fine. Hence the owner of the ox pays absolutely nothing if he confesses to the killing of the slave — not even the market value of the slave.

But in the Babylonian Talmud there is a long discussion (*Bava Kamma* 43a-b) as to whether the owner of the ox is required to pay damages for the value of the slave himself, if the fine is not applicable. The Gemara does not arrive at a clear conclusion, and the Rishonim are divided on this matter. According to *Ra'avad*, whenever the owner of the ox is exempt from the ransom or the fine, he must pay damages for the dead free man or slave. Thus, if the owner of the ox confesses that his ox killed a slave, he need not pay the thirty-shekel fine, but he must pay the market value of the slave. According to *Rambam*, this rule applies only if the ox was a *tam* (תָּם — an animal that is not known to cause damage with the intent to injure), and killed a slave by accident (*Hilkhot Nizkei Mamon* 10:9,14). But according to *Tosafot* (*Bava Kamma* 41b), this rule does not apply to a *tam* at all.

HALAKHAH

he must pay the ransom. If, however, he confesses that it has killed a slave, he need not pay the thirty-shekel fine on the basis of his own confession. Likewise, if he confesses that his *mu'ad* ox has killed an ox, he must pay damages. If, however, his ox is a *tam* and it kills an ox, he need not pay the half-damages on the basis of his confession," following Rav Huna's opinion in the Gemara. (*Rambam*, *Sefer Hafla'ah*, *Hilkhot Shevuot* 8:2,4; and *Sefer Nezikin*, *Hilkhot Nizkei Mamon* 2:8; and *Sefer Shofetim*, *Hilkhot Sanhedrin* 5:14.)

LITERAL TRANSLATION

[1] This is the rule: [2] Whoever pays more than he damaged does not pay by his own admission.

GEMARA [3] But let [the Tanna] teach "I raped"! [4] He is speaking [in the style of] "there is no need." [5] There is no need [to teach] "I raped," [6] where he does not damage her [reputation], [and to say] that he pays [for her] shame and blemish

[1] זֶה הַכְּלָל: [2] כָּל הַמְשַׁלֵּם יָתֵר עַל מַה שֶּׁהִזִּיק אֵינוֹ מְשַׁלֵּם עַל פִּי עַצְמוֹ.

גמרא [3] וְלִיתְנֵי "אָנַסְתִּי"! [4] לָא מִבָּעֲיָא קָאָמַר. [5] לָא מִבָּעֲיָא "אָנַסְתִּי", [6] דְּלָא קָא פָּגֵים לָהּ, דִּמְשַׁלֵּם בּוֹשֶׁת וּפְגָם

RASHI

גמרא **דלא פגים לה** — אין לעז של אנוסה גדול כלעז של מפותה. וכיון דלאו פגם דילה הוא — מהימנינן ליה למשקל מיניה בושת ופגם על פיו.

TRANSLATION AND COMMENTARY

זֶה הַכְּלָל [1] We have seen that the rules governing fines are different from the rules governing regular damage payments. The Mishnah now informs us of the way to distinguish between a fine and a regular damage payment. **This is the rule:** A regular damage payment is assessed as being equal in value to the damage done. [2] Thus **whenever someone** is required by the Torah to **pay more than** the value of **the damage he did,** we know that the payment is a fine imposed to punish him, and he **does not make this payment by his own admission.**

GEMARA וְלִיתְנֵי אָנַסְתִּי [3] The Gemara begins its analysis by considering the first clause of the Mishnah, which ruled that a seducer is not required to pay the fine on the basis of his own confession, but must pay the compensation for shame and blemish. The Gemara asks: **But surely the Mishnah can inform** us of this law by using the rapist's fine as the illustration, rather than the seducer's fine! Why does the Mishnah use the expression: "If someone says: 'I seduced the daughter of so-and-so,'" rather than: "If someone says: **'I raped** the daughter of so-and-so'"? Surely it would be a more striking illustration of the rule that a person need not pay a fine on the basis of his own confession if the Mishnah were to inform us that a rapist, who has committed an assault against the girl, is exempt from punishment, instead of concentrating on the seducer, who did nothing without the girl's consent!

לָא מִבָּעֲיָא קָאָמַר [4] The Gemara answers: Even though the principal topic of the Mishnah — the law that an offender who confesses to a deed punishable by a fine is exempt from paying the fine — would be better served if the Mishnah had selected the case of the rapist, the Mishnah mentions the case of the seducer because **it is following a stylistic** form called: **"There is no need."** According to this stylistic device, the Mishnah illustrates its ruling by using a case that poses an additional problem, rather than by using a more-or-less straightforward case. In this context, the additional problem relates to the shame and blemish payments which the rapist or the seducer is required to pay on the basis of his own confession. If we require the rapist or the seducer to make these payments on the basis of his own confession, it shows that we accept his statement that he raped or seduced this *na'arah*, even though there are no witnesses. But in addition to the financial aspects of this case there is a moral problem with accepting such a statement, because the result may well be the destruction of the *na'arah*'s reputation. It might perhaps be preferable not to accept his statement at all, unless witnesses come forward. [5] Therefore the Mishnah says that **there is no need to state** the law that someone who says, **"I raped** the daughter of so-and-so," [6] need not pay the fine **by his own admission,** but **must pay** the compensation **for her shame and blemish.** For even

NOTES

כָּל הַמְשַׁלֵּם יָתֵר עַל מַה שֶּׁהִזִּיק **Whoever pays more than he damaged.** *Yam Shel Shlomo* points out that in some cases the fine is set at more than the damage done (e.g., the double fine of the thief), and in other cases it is set at a fixed amount (e.g., the rapist's fine or the fine for an ox that killed a slave). Thus a fine may conceivably be less than the amount of the damage, or even equal to the amount of the damage. But a fixed amount is also considered to be more than the damage done, since it is possible for it to be more, whereas a regular damage payment is always equitable.

וְלִיתְנֵי "אָנַסְתִּי" **But let the Tanna teach: "I raped"!** *Ritva* explains that the Gemara is asking why the Mishnah illustrated its ruling only in the case of the seducer, rather than mentioning *both* the seducer and the rapist. Our commentary follows *Tosafot*, who explains that the Gemara is asking why the Mishnah did not select the case of rape to illustrate its ruling instead of the case of seduction. For the law that the rapist or the seducer is exempt if he confesses is more striking in the case of the rapist, who committed an assault against the maiden, than in the case of the seducer, who conspired with the maiden to engage in illicit intercourse. But the Gemara answers that the Mishnah preferred to illustrate its ruling by using the case of the seducer, because it wished to emphasize that we believe him regarding the shame and blemish payments, even though this may ruin her reputation, and this point is more striking in the case of the seducer than in the case of the rapist.

לָא מִבָּעֲיָא "אָנַסְתִּי" **There is no need to teach "I raped."** Our translation and commentary is in accordance with the standard Vilna Talmud, which follows *Rashi*. There is

TRANSLATION AND COMMENTARY

if we accept his statement that he raped her, **he does not damage her reputation** very much, because everyone realizes that she is not to blame for having been raped. [1] **But if** someone **says, "I seduced** the daughter of so-and-so," **he will damage her reputation** if we believe him without supporting testimony, because people will blame her for acquiescing in the seduction. [2] Therefore, **we might** have **argued that** a seducer **does not pay** compensation for shame and blemish **by his own admission**. For even though these payments are regular damage payments, and theoretically a confession is acceptable proof in such cases, nevertheless we might have thought that we do not accept his uncorroborated story that she voluntarily engaged in intercourse with him. [3] **Therefore** the Mishnah selected the case of seduction to **inform us that this is not so,** and that even in a case of seduction we require the seducer to make the damage payments he has confessed to owing.

עַל פִּי עַצְמוֹ; [1] אֲבָל ״פִּתִּיתִי״, דְּקָא פָּגֵים לָהּ, [2] אֵימָא לָא מְשַׁלֵּם עַל פִּי עַצְמוֹ. [3] קָא מַשְׁמַע לָן.
[4] מַתְנִיתִין דְּלָא כִּי הַאי תַּנָּא, [5] דְּתַנְיָא: ״רַבִּי שִׁמְעוֹן בֶּן יְהוּדָה אוֹמֵר מִשּׁוּם רַבִּי שִׁמְעוֹן: [6] אַף בּוֹשֶׁת וּפְגָם אֵינוֹ מְשַׁלֵּם עַל פִּי עַצְמוֹ. [7] לֹא כָּל הֵימֶנּוּ שֶׁיִּפְגּוֹם בִּתּוֹ שֶׁל פְּלוֹנִי״.
[8] אֲמַר לֵיהּ רַב פַּפָּא לְאַבַּיֵי: [9] נִיחָא לָהּ לְדִידָהּ, מַאי?
[10] דִּלְמָא לָא נִיחָא לֵיהּ לְאָבִיהָ.
[11] נִיחָא לֵיהּ לְאָבִיהָ, מַאי?

LITERAL TRANSLATION

by his own admission; [1] but [if he said] "I seduced," where he damages her [reputation, [2] I might] say [that] he should not pay by his own admission. [3] [Therefore] he informs us [that this is not so].

[4] Our Mishnah is not like this Tanna, [5] for it was taught: "Rabbi Shimon ben Yehudah says in the name of Rabbi Shimon: [6] Even [for] shame and blemish he does not pay by his own admission. [7] It is not in his power to damage [the reputation] of so-and-so's daughter."

[8] Rav Pappa said to Abaye: [9] [If] she herself agrees, what [is the law]?

[10] Perhaps her father does not agree.

[11] If her father agrees, what [is the law]?

RASHI

אימא לא – נהימניה להחזיק את הלעז. **לא כל הימנו** – שיוציא עליה לעז מזנה בעיר. **ניחא לה לדידה** – לשאת את הלעז כדי להשתכר הממון.

מַתְנִיתִין [4] The Gemara notes that **the Mishnah does not reflect the viewpoint of the following Tanna,** Rabbi Shimon, who maintains that we do not believe the seducer's confession at all, since we are not willing to damage the girl's reputation. [5] **For it was taught** in a Baraita: **"Rabbi Shimon ben Yehudah said in the name of Rabbi Shimon:** In a case of seduction, not only does the seducer not pay the fine on the basis of his confession, [6] **he does not even pay** the compensation **for** her **shame and blemish by his own admission.** [7] For **it is not in his power to damage the reputation of so-and-so's daughter** without corroborating testimony."

אֲמַר לֵיהּ [8] **Rav Pappa said to Abaye:** According to Rabbi Shimon, we do not believe the seducer regarding the shame and blemish payments, because this would damage the girl's reputation. [9] But **what is the law if she herself is satisfied** to accept the money at the expense of her reputation? Would Rabbi Shimon agree that in such circumstances the seducer must pay for her shame and blemish?

דִּלְמָא [10] Abaye replied: Even if she is willing to ruin her reputation for the sake of the money, **perhaps her father is not satisfied** with such an outcome. Not only is the girl's personal reputation at stake; her father's reputation is also threatened. Therefore we do not accept the seducer's confession, whose consequence will be the ruin of her father's reputation, unless we have corroborating testimony. And according to Rabbi Shimon, we do not even believe him regarding the shame and blemish payments.

נִיחָא לֵיהּ [11] But, Rav Pappa continued to ask, **what is the law if her father *is* satisfied** to accept the money at the expense of his daughter's and his own reputation? Would Rabbi Shimon agree that in such circumstances the seducer must pay for the girl's shame and blemish?

NOTES

a variant reading, cited by *Shittah Mekubbetzet* in the name of the Geonim, according to which the Gemara is concerned with the fine itself, rather than with the payments for shame and blemish.

According to this reading, the Gemara says: "There is no problem with the law that a man who said 'I raped' is exempt from paying the fine, for his confession does not damage her reputation. Hence, he is exempt from the fine if he confesses, and pays only the shame and blemish payments. But if he said: 'I seduced,' he damages her reputation by his confession. Hence we might have thought that he should be liable to pay the fine, even if he confessed. Therefore the Mishnah selected the case of seduction to inform us that this is not so."

[1] דִּלְמָא לָא נִיחָא לְהוּ לִבְנֵי מִשְׁפָּחָה.
[2] נִיחָא לְהוּ לִבְנֵי מִשְׁפָּחָה, מַאי?
[3] אִי אֶפְשָׁר דְּלֵיכָּא חַד בִּמְדִינַת הַיָּם דְּלָא נִיחָא לֵיהּ.
[4] ״הָאוֹמֵר: ׳גָּנַבְתִּי׳, מְשַׁלֵּם אֶת הַקֶּרֶן, וכו׳״. [5] אִיתְּמַר פַּלְגָא נִיזְקָא: [6] רַב פַּפָּא אֲמַר: פַּלְגָא נִיזְקָא מָמוֹנָא. [7] רַב הוּנָא בְּרֵיהּ דְּרַב יְהוֹשֻׁעַ אֲמַר: פַּלְגָא נִיזְקָא קְנָסָא.
[8] רַב פַּפָּא אֲמַר: פַּלְגָא נִיזְקָא מָמוֹנָא. [9] קָסָבַר: סְתָם שְׁוָורִים לָאו בְּחֶזְקַת שִׁימּוּר קָיְימִי,

LITERAL TRANSLATION

[1] Perhaps the members of the family do not agree. [2] If the members of the family agree, what [is the law]?

[3] It is impossible that there should not be one [person] overseas who does not agree.

[4] "[If] someone says: 'I stole,' he pays the principal, etc." [5] It was said [about] half-damages: [6] Rav Pappa said: Half-damages is a monetary [obligation]. [7] Rav Huna the son of Rav Yehoshua said: Half-damages is a fine.

[8] Rav Pappa said: Half-damages is a monetary [obligation]. [9] He maintains: Ordinarily oxen are not presumed to be under control,

TRANSLATION AND COMMENTARY

דִּלְמָא [1] Abaye replied: Even if she and her father are willing to ruin their reputations for the sake of the money, **perhaps the members of her family are not satisfied** with such an outcome. Not only is the father's personal reputation at stake; the whole family's reputation is threatened. Therefore we do not accept the seducer's confession, whose consequence will be the ruin of her family's reputation, unless we have corroborating testimony. And according to Rabbi Shimon, we do not even believe him regarding the shame and blemish payments.

נִיחָא לְהוּ [2] But, Rav Pappa continued to ask, **what is the law if the members of the family are** all **satisfied** with the outcome? Would Rabbi Shimon agree that in such circumstances the seducer must pay for the girl's shame and blemish?

אִי אֶפְשָׁר [3] Abaye replied: Even if all the members of the family here do not care about their reputation, **it is inconceivable that there should not be one member** of the family somewhere far away **overseas who is not satisfied.** And since the reputation of that remote member of the family is also threatened, we do not accept the seducer's confession, whose consequence will be the ruin of this family member's reputation, unless we have corroborating testimony. And according to Rabbi Shimon, we do not even believe him regarding the shame and blemish payments. Thus, according to Rabbi Shimon, we never accept the seducer's confession under any circumstances, and he does not pay the shame and blemish payments by his own admission.

הָאוֹמֵר: ׳גָּנַבְתִּי׳ [4] The Gemara now considers the rest of the Mishnah, beginning with the clause, **"If someone says: 'I stole,' he pays the principal, etc."** From here to the end of the chapter, the Gemara cites a passage from tractate *Bava Kamma* (15a-b), in which the various clauses of our Mishnah play a crucial role.

אִתְּמַר [5] The Torah states (Exodus 21:35) that if a hitherto placid ox — known in Hebrew as a *tam* — suddenly fatally gores another ox, the owner pays for half the damage caused. **It was related** that there is an Amoraic dispute **about** the principle of paying **half-damages:** [6] **Rav Pappa said:** The payment of **half-damages is a monetary obligation.** [7] **Rav Huna the son of Rav Yehoshua said:** The payment of **half-damages is a fine.**

רַב פַּפָּא אֲמַר [8] The Gemara explains the dispute: From the fact that the Torah imposed half-damages we can see that the responsibility for the damage is not clear-cut. The owner of the goring ox obviously bears some responsibility for the damage it caused, even though it had never hitherto acted maliciously, and it is equally obvious that he should not bear full responsibility, since there was no reason for him to have anticipated that the ox would act as it did. Nevertheless, this matter can be regarded in two ways. **Rav Pappa,** who **said** that the payment of **half-damages is a monetary obligation,** [9] **maintains** that we should view the hitherto placid ox that gored as follows: **Ordinarily oxen are not presumed to be under control.** Even

RASHI

לא ניחא להו לבני משפחה — ובית דין אין עליהם לעשות דבר להחזיק בושתם. **פלגא ניזקא** — שחייבה תורה שור תם. [**ממונא** — ומשלם על פי עצמו]. **לאו בחזקת שימור קיימי** — אם לא ישמרום בעלים שלא יזיקו — [אינם בחזקת משתמרים מאליהם שלא יזיקו], אלא מזיקין אפילו ניזקא דלאו אורחיה. הלכך על מרייהו רמיא לנטורינהו. וזה שלא שמרו — בדין הוא דלישלם כולה, אלא דרחמנא חס עליה. ומיהו, מה שמשלם — בדין משלם.

NOTES

סְתָם שְׁוָורִים לָאו בְּחֶזְקַת שִׁימּוּר קָיְימִי **Ordinarily oxen are not presumed to be under control.** Ostensibly, Rav Pappa's explanation — that the ox's owner should have assumed that his ox was liable to gore another ox —

[1] וּבְדִין הוּא דִּמְשַׁלֵּם כּוּלֵּיהּ, [2] וְרַחֲמָנָא הוּא דְּחָיֵיס עִלָּוֵיהּ, דְּאַכַּתִּי לָא אִיַּעַד תּוֹרָא.
[3] רַב הוּנָא בְּרֵיהּ דְּרַב יְהוֹשֻׁעַ אֲמַר: פַּלְגָא נִיזְקָא קְנָסָא. [4] קָסָבַר: סְתָם שְׁוָורִים בְּחֶזְקַת שִׁימּוּר קַיְימֵי, [5] וּבְדִין הוּא דְּלָא לִישַׁלֵּם כְּלָל, [6] וְרַחֲמָנָא הוּא דְּקָנְסֵיהּ, [7] כִּי הֵיכִי דְּנִינְטְרֵיהּ לְתוֹרֵיהּ.
[8] סימן: היזיק מה והמית כלל.
[9] תְּנַן: "הַנִּיזָּק וְהַמַּזִּיק בְּתַשְׁלוּמִין". [10] בִּשְׁלָמָא לְמַאן דַּאֲמַר פַּלְגָא נִיזְקָא מָמוֹנָא — [11] הַיְינוּ דְּשַׁיָּיךְ נִיזָּק בְּתַשְׁלוּמִין.

LITERAL TRANSLATION

[1] and by right he should pay all of it, [2] but it was the Torah that spared him, because his ox had still not been forewarned.

[3] Rav Huna the son of Rav Yehoshua said: Half-damages is a fine. [4] He maintains: Ordinarily oxen are presumed to be under control, [5] and by right he should not pay at all, [6] but it was the Torah that fined him, [7] so that he should guard his ox.

[8] Mnemonic: Damaged — what — and he killed — the rule.

[9] We have learned: "The damaged [party] and the damager [share] in the payment." [10] [This] is satisfactory according to the one who said [that] half-damages is a monetary [obligation] — [11] this is why the damaged [party] is involved in the payment.

TRANSLATION AND COMMENTARY

though the behavior of this ox was hitherto placid, such an animal is by its nature unpredictable, and the owner must anticipate that its behavior may become aggressive. [1] Therefore **by right** the owner of the goring ox **should pay for all** the damage the animal caused, just like the owner of an ox known to be vicious. [2] **But** in view of the fact that the damage done by the goring ox was indeed unanticipated, **the Torah spared** its owner because **the ox had not yet been attested** as dangerous. Thus the half-damage payment is a concession to the owner of the ox, and should be viewed as half of a regular damage payment. This payment should be subject to the same rules as govern the full-damage payments, which are a monetary obligation.

רַב הוּנָא בְּרֵיהּ דְּרַב יְהוֹשֻׁעַ [3] By contrast, **Rav Huna the son of Rav Yehoshua,** who **said** that the payment of **half-damages is a fine,** [4] **maintains** that we should view the hitherto placid ox that gored as follows: **Ordinarily oxen are presumed to be under control.** Since the behavior of this ox was hitherto placid, the owner was entitled to anticipate that it would not do any malicious damage. [5] Therefore **by right** the owner of the ox **should not pay** damages **at all,** since the damage was not his fault. [6] **But** in view of the fact that animals do on occasion behave unpredictably, [7] **the Torah fined him** half the damage, **so that he would guard his ox** more carefully in the future. Thus the half-damage payment was imposed as a fine to punish the owner of the ox, just like any other payment that goes beyond the damage actually done.

סִימָן [8] The Gemara now raises four objections against the viewpoint of Rav Huna the son of Rav Yehoshua that the payment of half-damages is a fine — two from Mishnayot in tractate *Bava Kamma* and two from our Mishnah. These objections are introduced by a **mnemonic,** in which the four words that begin each of these Mishnayot are arranged in a sort of sentence: **Damaged — what — killed — the rule.**

תְּנַן [9] The first objection is as follows: **We have learned** in a Mishnah (*Bava Kamma* 14b): **"The damaged party and the damager** sometimes **share in the payment."** It sometimes happens that the damaged party does not receive full satisfaction for the damage done, and is required to absorb some of the loss himself. The Mishnah does not specify to which case it is referring. [10] However, **this** ruling in the Mishnah **is satisfactory according to** Rav Pappa, **who said that** the payment of **half-damages is a monetary obligation.** For we have seen that, according to Rav Pappa, the fact that the owner of the goring ox pays half of the damage is a concession to him at the expense of the owner of the dead ox, [11] and **this is how the damaged**

RASHI

כי היכי דנינטריה — שיוסיף שמירה על שמירתו. **תנן** — בבבא קמא. **הניזק והמזיק בתשלומין** — שניהם מפסידין בדבר. חלוקא דינתך דהכי קאמר: תרוייהו נגעי להו בהאי פסידא, דניזק מפסיד פלגא, ומזיק פלגא. **היינו דשייך ניזק בתשלומין** — דמפסיד פלגא בממוניה.

NOTES

seems to contradict our accepted tradition that half-damages are imposed where the damage was unusual and unpredictable. *Rashi* explains that there is no contradiction. Goring is considered to be unusual behavior for oxen, and for that reason Rav Huna the son of Rav Yehoshua maintains that they can be relied upon not to do so. But even so, Rav Pappa is of the opinion that the owner is required to guard his ox, since oxen that are not guarded are liable to do unusual things from time to time, and according to Rav Pappa it is the owner's responsibility to prevent this from happening (see also *Ritva*).

[1] אֶלָּא לְמַאן דַּאֲמַר פַּלְגָא נִיזְקָא קְנָסָא — [2] הָשְׁתָּא דְּלָאו דִּידֵיהּ קָא שָׁקֵיל, [3] בְּתַשְׁלוּמִין אִיתֵיהּ? [4] לָא נִצְרְכָא אֶלָּא לִפְחַת נְבֵילָה.

LITERAL TRANSLATION

[1] But according to the one who said [that] half-damages is a fine — [2] now what he is taking is not his, [3] is he [involved] in the payment? [4] It is needed only for the depreciation of the carcass.

TRANSLATION AND COMMENTARY

party becomes involved in and bears a share of the payment. [1] **But according to** Rav Huna the son of Rav Yehoshua, **who said that** the payment of **half-damages is a fine,** this Mishnah is difficult to understand. According to Rav Huna the son of Rav Yehoshua, the fact that the owner of the ox that was killed receives half the damage goes beyond the normal demands of the Torah. [2] **Now** the owner of the dead ox **is taking** money that **is not his,** since the proper damage payment in this case is nothing, and the half-damage payment is in a sense beyond the call of duty. [3] So how can the Mishnah say that the owner of the dead ox **is involved in the payment?** What has he contributed? He has already received more than he deserves!

לָא נִצְרְכָא [4] The Gemara replies: According to Rav Huna the son of Rav Yehoshua, the Mishnah is not referring to the law of half-damage at all. Rather, **it is needed only** to teach us that even in cases where the damage done must be paid for in full, the owner of the dead ox must bear **the depreciation of the carcass** from the moment the ox was killed until the carcass was sold. The Gemara (*Bava Kamma* 10b) infers from a Biblical verse that the owner of the goring ox need only pay for the damage caused — for the difference in value between a live ox and a dead ox. The task of disposing of the dead ox and selling it is the responsibility of its owner. Moreover, if during the time it takes to arrange the sale, the carcass deteriorates and its value drops, the owner of the goring ox is not responsible, even though this loss was clearly caused by his ox. Thus we see that the damaged party does not always receive full satisfaction for the damage done, and is required to bear some of the loss himself.

RASHI

דלאו דידיה שקיל — דמה שנוטל — בחנס נוטל. **בתשלומין איתיה** — בתמיה. **לא נצרכא אלא לפחת נבילה** — הא דקתני "ניזק בתשלומין", לאו בפלגא דקא שביק קאמר, אלא בההוא פלגא ניזקא נמי דקני ליה רחמנא — מפסיד כל פחת שפחתה נבילה מדמיה משעת מיתה עד שעת העמדה בדין. שמשין את הנבלה כמה היה יפה השור בחייו, וכמה היתה נבילה יפה בשעת מיתה, ומשלם החצי. אבל מה שהוזלו דמי נבילה משעת מיתה עד שעת מכירה — אין המזיק משלם כלום באותו פחת. ובבבא קמא (י,ב) יליף לה מקראי. ואשמעינן האי תנא דפחת נבילה דניזק הוי.

NOTES

לָא נִצְרְכָה אֶלָּא לִפְחַת נְבֵילָה **It is needed only for the depreciation of the carcass.** The Gemara explains that, according to Rav Huna the son of Rav Yehoshua, when the Mishnah states that the damaged party must sometimes absorb part of the loss, it is not referring to the half of the damages he does not receive if his ox was gored by a *tam*, since the half-damages that he *does* receive are themselves more than he deserves. Rather, it is referring to the loss he must sustain if the dead ox depreciates before it is sold. The Gemara does not specify if, at this stage in the argument, it is referring to a *mu'ad*, whose owner pays full damages, or if it is still referring to a *tam*, whose owner pays half-damages.

Our commentary follows *Rashba*, who explains that the Gemara is not referring to half-damages at all at this stage in the argument. The Gemara has just stated that, according to Rav Huna the son of Rav Yehoshua, anything the owner pays the damaged party is beyond what is due. Thus the depreciation of the carcass cannot be described as a loss, any more than the half of the damages that is not paid at all.

This interpretation is difficult to accept. The Gemara concludes that the Mishnah mentioned this law twice — once in connection with a *tam* and once in connection with a *mu'ad*. But if the depreciation of the carcass cannot be described as a loss to the damaged party, than we must explain that the expression in the Mishnah that says, "The damaged party and the damager share in the payment," is referring to the *mu'ad*, whereas the expression in the Mishnah that says, "Payment for damage," refers to the *tam*. But *Rashi* points out that the Mishnah that mentions "payment for damage" concludes that the "payment for damage must be paid from the best of the land," and "the best of the land" is a rule that applies to payments for damage caused by a *mu'ad* and to payments for other damage, but not to a *tam*, as the Gemara explains below. *Ritva* attempts to address this problem.

Accordingly, *Rashi* and *Tosafot* explain that the Gemara is still at this stage of the argument referring to a *tam*, whose owner pays half-damages. This is problematic, because the Gemara has just stated that, according to Rav Huna the son of Rav Yehoshua, anything the owner pays the damaged party is beyond what is due. Nevertheless, *Tosafot* explains that the depreciation of the carcass can still be described as a loss. The fact that the Torah granted the owner of the dead ox half his damages is not a loss, according to Rav Huna the son of Rav Yehoshua, since by rights he should have received nothing at all. But once the Torah granted the owner of the dead ox half his damages, it is considered an absorption of losses for him to receive less than he could have received because he did not succeed in selling the carcass before it depreciated. *Shittah Mekubbetzet* cites alternative explanations in the name of *Ra'avad* and *Or Zarua*.

TRANSLATION AND COMMENTARY

פְּחַת נְבֵילָה תְּנֵינָא [1] But, the Gemara objects, the Mishnah cannot be referring to the **depreciation of the carcass,** because **we have already learned** this law in a previous Mishnah (*Bava Kamma* 9b), as interpreted by a Tosefta (*Bava Kamma* 1:1). The Mishnah mentions that the damager makes **"payment for damage."** The Tosefta explains that "with these words the Mishnah is **teaching us that the owner** of the dead ox **must dispose of the carcass,"** as we explained above. Thus, says the Gemara, since we already know from the previous Mishnah that the owner of the dead ox must dispose of the carcass, when the later Mishnah mentioned that the owner of the dead ox must sometimes absorb some of the loss, it must have been referring to a loss other than the depreciation of the carcass. Hence it must have been referring to the half of the damage that the owner of the dead ox does not receive if the goring ox had hitherto been placid, and this contradicts the viewpoint of Rav Huna the son of Rav Yehoshua.

חֲדָא בְּתָם [2] The Gemara replies: The Mishnayot in tractate *Bava Kamma* are indeed referring to the loss that the owner of the dead ox must bear in disposing of the carcass, and it was necessary to mention this law twice: **Once** to inform us that the owner of the dead ox disposes of the carcass if the ox was killed by **a *tam*** (an ox that does not have a history of causing malicious damage), **and once** to teach us that the owner of the dead ox disposes of the carcass if the ox was killed by **a *mu'ad*** (an ox whose owner has already been warned that his ox has already caused malicious damage on three previous occasions). If a *mu'ad* kills another ox, the owner of the *mu'ad* cannot claim that the damage was unanticipated and he must pay for the damage in full. Thus the Mishnah teaches us that the rule that the owner of the dead ox disposes of the carcass applies both to the full damage paid by the owner of a *mu'ad* and the half-damages paid by the owner of a *tam*. In both cases, the depreciation of the carcass after the goring must be absorbed by the damaged party. [3] **And** the Mishnah **needed** to inform us of this law in **both** cases. [4] **For if we had only been informed about a *tam***, but not about a *mu'ad*, **we might have said** that the reason why the owner of the dead ox disposes of the carcass is **because** the goring ox **has not yet been attested** as a *mu'ad*. Just as the Torah did not impose the payment of full damages in such a case, so too did the Torah not impose responsibility for the carcass on the owner of the goring ox. [5] **But** if the dead ox was gored by **a *mu'ad***, where the ox's vicious behavior **has already been attested,** and the owner bears full responsibility for it, [6] **we might say** that the owner of the dead ox need **not** bear any of the loss at all.

[1] פְּחַת נְבֵילָה תְּנֵינָא: ״׳תַּשְׁלוּמֵי נֶזֶק׳ מְלַמֵּד שֶׁהַבְּעָלִים מְטַפְּלִין בַּנְּבֵילָה״.
[2] חֲדָא בְּתָם וַחֲדָא בְּמוּעָד.
[3] וּצְרִיכָא. [4] דְּאִי אַשְׁמוּעִינַן תָּם, מִשּׁוּם דְּאַכַּתִּי לָא אִיַּעַד, [5] אֲבָל מוּעָד דְּאִיַּעַד, [6] אֵימָא לָא.

LITERAL TRANSLATION

[1] Depreciation of the carcass we have [already] learned: "'Payment of damage' teaches [us] that the owner must dispose of the carcass."

[2] One [refers] to a *tam* and one [refers] to a *mu'ad*.

[3] And [both are] necessary. [4] For if it had [only] informed us [about] a *tam*, it might have been because it has not yet been forewarned, [5] but [in the case of] a *mu'ad* which has already been forewarned, [6] [I might] say no.

RASHI

תשלומי נזק מלמד שהבעלים מטפלין בנבילה – תנא דברייתא דריש לישנא דמתניתין, דתנן בבבא קמא: משלם תשלומי נזק במיטב הארץ. ותנא עלה בברייתא, דהאי דנקט תנא דמתניתין "תשלומי נזק", ולא תנא "משלם את הנזק" – לאשמועינן אתא, שהניזק נוטל את נבילתו ומטפל בה ומוכרה, והמזיק משלים עליה מה שחייבתו תורה, אם תם – חצי, ואם מועד – הכל. ותרתי למה ליה לרבי למיתנא במתניתין דבעלים מטפלין בנבילה?

CONCEPTS

תָּם *Tam,* innocent. An animal that is not known to cause damage with the intent to injure. The first three times an animal causes an injury of this nature, its owner is required to pay only half the damage it has caused (חֲצִי נֶזֶק). Afterwards it becomes an attested dangerous animal, an animal with a history of causing injury. The owner of a מוּעָד animal is required to pay for all the damage it causes. An animal can be considered a תָּם with regard to certain kinds of damage and a מוּעָד with regard to others. For example, an ox that has a history of goring other oxen is still considered תָּם with regard to goring humans. Similarly, if it is established that the animal causes injury only on certain days, for example, on Shabbat and Festivals, it may be considered a מוּעָד on those days alone and a תָּם during the rest of the week. An animal that is a מוּעָד can regain the status of תָּם if, on three separate occasions, animals that it was accustomed to attacking passed by and it refrained from attacking them.

מוּעָד *Mu'ad,* forewarned. In its more limited sense, this expression is used to refer to a שׁוֹר מוּעָד — "an ox whose owner has been forewarned," i.e., an ox that has gored three times. If an ox causes damage by goring, or, in general, any animal causes *malicious* damage, the first three times that it gores, the owner is liable for only half of the resulting damage. If, however, the ox gores a fourth time, and the owner was officially notified that it had gored three times previously, the animal is considered a שׁוֹר מוּעָד, and the owner must pay in full for the resulting damage.

NOTES

תַּשְׁלוּמֵי נֶזֶק Payment for damage. This particular Mishnah (*Bava Kamma* 9b) is written in a unique style. The Mishnah lists a series of laws applying to damages without explaining them or even forming them into proper sentences. Thus this Mishnah is to be seen as a sort of outline, and every word in it carries special significance.

The Mishnah states: "I am liable for the payment for his damage." The Gemara notes (*Bava Kamma* 10b) that the word "payment" serves no purpose, since the Mishnah could simply have written, "I am liable for his damage." The Gemara cites a Tosefta which explains that the Mishnah is hinting at the law that the owner of the dead

HALAKHAH

שֶׁהַבְּעָלִים מְטַפְּלִין בַּנְּבֵילָה That the owner must dispose of the carcass. "We do not give the damager the carcass and make him pay for the entire dead ox. Rather, the carcass remains in the possession of the damaged party, and we assess the difference in value between a live ox and a dead ox and make the damager pay the difference. Moreover, if the carcass depreciates after the animal was killed, the loss is borne by the damaged party. For example, if the ox was worth two hundred zuz alive and one hundred freshly killed, and by the time it was assessed by the court, it had depreciated and was worth only eighty zuz, the owner of the goring ox is not liable for the twenty

CONCEPTS

חֲצִי נֶזֶק **Half-damages.** The Sages explained that the owner of an ox (or any other animal) which has had no history of causing malicious damage is required to pay only one-half of such damage maliciously caused by his animal to other animals or to human beings (see Exodus 21:35). The Sages debated whether the reason for the half-damages was that the owner should really have been obligated to pay the entire sum and the Torah reduced his liability, or that no payment should really have been required at all and the Torah obligated him to pay this amount as a fine. The owner of an animal which indirectly damaged property by causing clods of dirt or pebbles (צְרוֹרוֹת) to fly while walking in its usual way must also pay half of the damage caused. This is an oral law transmitted to Moses at Sinai (הֲלָכָה לְמֹשֶׁה מִסִּינַי), and all agree that it is a case of reduced liability and not a fine.

TRANSLATION AND COMMENTARY

[1] **And conversely, if we had been informed only about a _mu'ad_,** but not about a _tam_, **we might have said** that the reason why the owner of the dead ox disposes of the carcass is **because** the owner of the goring ox is already **paying for all** the direct damage his ox caused, and he should not be made to bear responsibility for the indirect damage caused by the depreciation of the carcass. [2] **But if the dead ox was gored by a _tam_,** where the owner is required to pay only half-damages, **we might say** that the owner of the goring ox should **not** be exempted from paying half of all the loss he caused, both direct and indirect. [3] **Therefore it was necessary** for the Mishnah **to teach** us this law explicitly in **both** cases. Hence Rav Huna the son of Rav Yehoshua can explain that the Mishnah is referring to the law about the depreciation of the carcass when it rules that the damaged party must sometimes absorb some of the loss, and no proof can be brought against the viewpoint of Rav Huna the son of Rav Yehoshua regarding the law of half-damages.

תָּא שְׁמַע [4] The Gemara now raises a second objection against Rav Huna the son of Rav Yehoshua, from another Mishnah in _Bava Kamma_ (16b): **Come and hear** what this Mishnah says: **"What is the difference between** the laws governing **a _tam_ and** the laws governing **a _mu'ad_?"** [5] The Mishnah answers **"that** there are two differences: (1) **The owner of the _tam_ pays half-damages whereas the owner of the _mu'ad_ pays full damages;** and (2) **The owner of the _tam_ pays damages from** the **body** of the goring ox, **whereas the owner of the _mu'ad_ pays from the best** of his property." Concerning a _tam_ whose owner pays half-damages, the Torah states (Exodus 21:35) that the parties must sell the living ox and the carcass of the dead ox, and divide the difference. From here we learn that the damage payment may come only from the proceeds of the sale of the goring ox. Accordingly, if the goring ox was worth much less than the dead ox, the owner of the goring ox need pay only up to the value of the goring ox and no more. The owner of a _mu'ad_, by contrast, bears unlimited personal liability, and must — if necessary — sell even his most cherished property to pay for the damage. The Mishnah listed only two differences between the rules governing a _tam_ and those governing a _mu'ad_. [6] **But** according to Rav Huna the son of Rav Yehoshua, there is a third difference

LITERAL TRANSLATION

[1] And if it had [only] informed us [about] a _mu'ad_, it might have been because he pays for all of it, [2] but [in the case of] a _tam_, [I might] say no. [3] [Therefore] it was necessary [to state both].
[4] Come [and] hear: "What [is the difference] between a _tam_ and a _mu'ad_? [5] That [in the case of] the _tam_ he pays half-damages from its body, and [in the case of] the _mu'ad_ he pays the full damage from the best." [6] But it does not teach that [in the case of]

[1] וְאִי אַשְׁמוּעִינַן מוּעָד, מִשׁוּם דְּקָא מְשַׁלֵּם כּוּלֵיהּ, [2] אֲבָל תָּם, אֵימָא לָא. [3] צְרִיכָא. [4] תָּא שְׁמַע: "מַה בֵּין תָּם לְמוּעָד? [5] שֶׁהַתָּם מְשַׁלֵּם חֲצִי נֶזֶק מִגּוּפוֹ, וּמוּעָד מְשַׁלֵּם נֶזֶק שָׁלֵם מִן הָעֲלִיָּיה". [6] וְלָא קָתָנֵי

RASHI

דקא משלם כוליה — וְדָיו בְּהֶפְסֵד זֶה. מגופו — אֵינוּ גוֹבֶה אֶלָּא מְגּוּף הַשּׁוֹר, וְאִם אֵין בּוֹ כְּדֵי חֲצִי נִזְקוֹ — יַפְסִיד הַמּוּתָר. מן העלייה — מִן הַמֵּיטַב שֶׁבְּנִכְסֵי מַזִּיק. דְּגַבֵּי תָּם כְּתִיב (שמות כא) "וּמָכְרוּ אֶת הַשּׁוֹר כַּפְּפוּ", וְגַבֵּי מוּעָד כְּתִיב (שם) "שַׁלֵּם יְשַׁלֵּם שׁוֹר". וְאִם אִיתָא דִּפְלַגָּא נִיזְקָא קַנְסָא — נִיתְנֵי נַמִי שֶׁהַתָּם אֵינוֹ מְשַׁלֵּם עַל פִּי עַצְמוֹ, וּמוּעָד מְשַׁלֵּם עַל פִּי עַצְמוֹ. דְּמוּעָד וַדַאי דִּין מְשַׁלֵּם, שֶׁהֲרֵי הִתְרוּ בוֹ וְהֵעִידוּ בּוֹ לִשְׁמוֹר שׁוֹרוֹ.

NOTES

ox must dispose of the carcass. _Rashi_ explains that the Hebrew word for payment — "תַּשְׁלוּמֵי" — can also mean "making up the difference" (from the root לְהַשְׁלִים instead of לְשַׁלֵּם). Thus the Mishnah is stating that the owner of the goring ox is liable to make up the difference caused by the damage — the difference between the value of the ox alive and its value dead — but he bears no responsibility for the carcass itself. The Gemara explains that this law is inferred from the verse (Exodus 21:36): "And the carcass shall be his."

HALAKHAH

zuz the damaged party lost through the carcass's depreciation. Rather, he pays one hundred zuz if the goring ox was a _mu'ad_ or fifty zuz if the goring ox was a _tam_, because it is the responsibility of the dead ox's owner to sell the carcass as quickly as possible, following the Gemara.

"_Rema_ adds that this law applies only to depreciation that occurred after the owner of the dead ox heard that it had been gored. But if he did not hear about it for some time, and by the time he heard about it, the carcass had already depreciated, the owner of the goring ox bears responsibility.

"_Rema_ adds that there is a dispute if the carcass did not depreciate, but its market value went down as a result of a general change in prices. _Tur_ maintains that the law is the same as for depreciation, whereas _Nimmukei Yosef_ maintains that the loss is always borne by the owner of the dead ox, even if he did not hear that his ox had been gored." (_Rambam, Sefer Nezikin, Hilkhot Nizkei Mamon_ 7:8; _Shulḥan Arukh, Ḥoshen Mishpat_ 403:1–2.)

מַה בֵּין תָּם לְמוּעָד **What is the difference between a _tam_ and a _mu'ad_?** "In most cases of damage, including damage

TRANSLATION AND COMMENTARY

that this Mishnah **did not teach — that the** owner of the ***tam* does not pay** damages at all **by his own admission,** if there are no witnesses to attest to the damage, [1] whereas the owner of **the *mu'ad* does pay by his own admission.** According to Rav Huna the son of Rav Yehoshua, the payment of half the damage is a fine. Hence it should be subject to the rules governing fines, and the owner of the *tam* should not be required to pay damages on the basis of his own confession. By contrast, the owner of the *mu'ad* is required to pay regular damages, and can be obligated to pay on the basis of his own confession, without any corroborating testimony. From the fact that the Mishnah did not list this third very important difference, it would appear that the Mishnah agrees with Rav Pappa, who maintains that the half-damage payment is merely a reduced version of regular damages, and is subject to the same rules that govern regular monetary obligation. Thus this Mishnah appears to refute the viewpoint of Rav Huna the son of Rav Yehoshua.

תָּנָא וְשַׁיֵּיר [2] The Gemara replies: It is true that, according to Rav Huna the son of Rav Yehoshua, the owner of the *tam* need not pay on the basis of his own confession, whereas the owner of the *mu'ad* does pay. However, the Mishnah **taught** only some of the differences between the rules governing the *tam* and the *mu'ad*, **and omitted** others. The Mishnah did not explicitly state that it was listing all the differences; it merely stated that it was listing some of them. And in such cases, the Mishnah does not give an exhaustive list.

מַאי שַׁיֵּיר [3] But, the Gemara objects, although it is true that the Mishnah is sometimes not exhaustive, in such cases the Mishnah never omits only one case; it always omits at least two. So if you say that the Mishnah was not giving an exhaustive list, we must find another difference between the *tam* and the *mu'ad*, apart from the rule that the owner of a *tam* need not pay on the basis of his own confession, that was also omitted by the Mishnah. So **what other** difference **did it omit, that** you say that **it** also **omitted this** difference?

שַׁיֵּיר [4] The Gemara answers: The Mishnah **omitted** the rule that the owner of a *mu'ad* that killed a person must pay a ransom (Exodus 21:30), whereas the owner of a *tam* that killed a person pays nothing (Exodus 21:28), not even **half a ransom.** Thus we see that the Mishnah omitted another difference between a *tam* and a *mu'ad*. Accordingly, it also omitted the difference between them regarding confessions.

שֶׁהַתָּם אֵינוֹ מְשַׁלֵּם עַל פִּי עַצְמוֹ, [1] וּמוּעָד מְשַׁלֵּם עַל פִּי עַצְמוֹ!

[2] תָּנָא וְשַׁיֵּיר.

[3] מַאי שַׁיֵּיר דְּהַאי שַׁיֵּיר?

[4] שַׁיֵּיר חֲצִי כּוֹפֶר.

LITERAL TRANSLATION

the *tam* he does not pay by his own admission, [1] but [in the case of] the *mu'ad* he does pay by his own admission!

[2] He taught and left out.

[3] What [else] did he leave out that he left this out?

[4] He left out the half ransom.

RASHI

שייר חצי כופר — לא שנה כל החילוקים שביניהם, שהרי אף יש חילוק זה ביניהם: שהמועד שהמית את האדם משלם כופר שלם, ותם שהמית — אפילו חצי כופר, כדינו בניזקין, לא משלם. דכתיב "בעל השור נקי" ודרשינן: (בבא קמא מא,ב), נקי מחצי כופר.

TERMINOLOGY

תָּנָא וְשַׁיֵּיר He taught and left out. An expression used when suggesting that a list given in a Mishnah or a Baraita is incomplete: "The Mishnah taught certain cases, and left other cases to be added."

NOTES

תָּנָא וְשַׁיֵּיר He taught and left out. In many places the Gemara explains that lists given in the Mishnah are not necessarily exhaustive. In tractate *Kiddushin* (16b) the Gemara states that if a Mishnah summarizes a list with the words: "These are the cases," the list must be presumed to be exhaustive, but *Tosafot* (*Ketubot* 29a) points out that there are circumstances under which the Mishnah omits part of a list, even though it uses these words to summarize. In any case, in a Mishnah such as the one in *Bava Kamma*, where these words do not appear, there is no reason to assume that the Mishnah's list is exhaustive. Hence no objection can be raised against Rav Huna the son of Rav Yehoshua because the Mishnah did not mention "confession" in its list of differences between a *tam* and a *mu'ad*.

However, the Gemara always insists that whenever the Mishnah gives a list that is not exhaustive, it always omits at least two cases. Hence the Gemara objects: Rava Huna the son of Rav Yehoshua is entitled to explain that the Mishnah was not giving an exhaustive list, but if so, he must find another difference between a *tam* and a *mu'ad* that was also omitted by the Mishnah — in addition to the rule that the owner of a *tam* need not pay on the basis of his own confession. And the Gemara replies that the Mishnah omitted the fact that the owner of a *mu'ad* that kills a person pays a ransom, whereas the owner of a *tam* pays nothing.

HALAKHAH

caused by a *mu'ad*, the damager must pay for the damage in full from the best of his property. The case of a *tam* that gored is exceptional. Its owner pays only half-damages, and only from the body of the goring ox." (*Rambam, Sefer Nezikin, Hilkhot Nizkei Mamon* 1:2-3; *Shulḥan Arukh, Ḥoshen Mishpat* 389:2,9.)

חֲצִי כּוֹפֶר Half ransom. "If a *tam* kills a person, its owner pays nothing, although the ox itself is killed," following the opinion of the Rabbis who disagree with Rabbi Yose HaGelili. (*Rambam, Sefer Nezikin, Hilkhot Nizkei Mamon* 10:2.)

TRANSLATION AND COMMENTARY

אִי מִשּׁוּם [1]The Gemara's rejoinder to this objection is so effective, that it poses a problem for Rav Pappa. It would seem that the Mishnah omitted the difference between a *tam* and a *mu'ad* that the owner of the *mu'ad* pays a ransom and the owner of the *tam* does not. But we know that the Mishnah never omits only one case; it always omits at least two. Thus, if the Mishnah omitted this difference, it would appear that there is yet another difference between a *tam* and a *mu'ad*, and this difference must be the fact that the owner of a *tam* need not pay on the basis of his own confession, as Rav Huna the son of Rav Yehoshua argued. But Rav Pappa now explains that it is not necessary to explain that the Mishnah omitted any case at all. For **if** the only omission that has definitely been established **is the** case of **half ransom,** [2]**it is not** necessarily **an omission** at all. [41B] For the rule that the owner of a *tam* that killed a person pays nothing is the subject of a Tannaitic dispute. [3]Thus it is possible that **this** Mishnah **reflects the viewpoint of Rabbi Yose HaGelili,** [4]**who said:** The owner of ***a tam*** that killed a human being **pays half the ransom** that is paid by the owner of a *mu'ad*, just as he would pay half-damages if his animal had killed an ox. According to Rabbi Yose HaGelili, the only difference between a *tam* that killed a person and a *mu'ad* that killed a person is that the owner of the *tam* pays half the amount paid by the owner of the *mu'ad*, and this difference has already been mentioned in the Mishnah. Thus there are only two differences between the *tam* and *mu'ad*, and the Mishnah has mentioned them both. Thus, according to the Gemara's conclusion, this Mishnah can be explained satisfactorily both according to Rav Pappa and according to Rav Huna the son of Rav Yehoshua. Rav Pappa can explain the Mishnah as reflecting the viewpoint of Rabbi Yose HaGelili and as giving an exhaustive list, whereas Rav Huna the son of Rav Yehoshua can explain it as reflecting the viewpoint of the other Sages, and as omitting two differences: (1) that the owner of a *mu'ad* that killed a human being pays a ransom whereas the owner of a *tam* pays nothing; and (2) that the owner of a *mu'ad* pays on the basis of his own confession whereas the owner of a *tam* does not.

[1]אִי מִשּׁוּם חֲצִי כּוֹפֶר, [2]לָאו שִׁיּוּרָא הוּא. [41B] [3]הָא מַנִּי? רַבִּי יוֹסֵי הַגְּלִילִי הִיא, [4]דְּאָמַר: תָּם מְשַׁלֵּם חֲצִי כּוֹפֶר.

LITERAL TRANSLATION

[1]If it is because of the half ransom, [2]it is not an omission. [41B] [3]Whose [opinion] is this? It is [that of] Rabbi Yose HaGelili, [4]who said: [In the case of] a *tam* he pays a half ransom.

RASHI

הא מני רבי יוסי הגלילי היא דאמר תם משלם חצי כופר — דדריש להאי "נקי" לדרשא אחריתי, לדמי ולדות — אם נגח אשה ויצאו ילדיה. הלכך לא הוה ליה לפלוגי בינייהו בכופר. וכי תימא: הוה ליה לפלוגי, דהאי פלגא והאי כוליה — ההיא בכלל רישא היא, דקתני: תם משלם חצי נזק ומועד נזק שלם, ותנא בניזקין, והוא הדין לכופר.

NOTES

אִי מִשּׁוּם חֲצִי כּוֹפֶר לָאו שִׁיּוּרָא הוּא If it is because of the half ransom, it is not an omission. This line of the Gemara is difficult to understand. On the surface, it is an objection by Rav Pappa against the answer given by Rav Huna the son of Rav Yehoshua. Rav Huna argues that the Mishnah omitted a second difference between a *tam* and *mu'ad* — the law of the ransom, which applies only to a *mu'ad* and not to a *tam*. But Rav Pappa counters that the law of the ransom is not a valid second omission, because the Mishnah may be in accordance with the opinion of Rabbi Yose HaGelili, who maintains that the owner of a *tam does* pay a ransom.

This explanation appears illogical. The fact that it is possible to explain that the Mishnah follows a minority view is no reason to object to the explanation offered by Rav Huna the son of Rav Yehoshua. How does Rav Pappa know that the Mishnah follows Rabbi Yose HaGelili? What is wrong with Rav Huna's explanation — that the Mishnah follows the other Tannaim and omitted the law of the ransom?

Ra'avad cites an opinion that Rav Pappa is arguing that it is better to explain a Mishnah in accordance with a minority view rather than to say that it omitted cases from its list, because the latter explanation is forced.

Most Rishonim, however, explain this line of the Gemara not in accordance with its simple meaning. Our commentary follows *Tosafot* and other Rishonim (*Rosh*, *Ritva*), who explain that this entire line of the Gemara is not an objection by Rav Pappa at all, but rather Rav Pappa's response to a counter-objection raised against him by Rav Huna the son of Rav Yehoshua. Rav Huna has just proved that the Mishnah omitted the ransom from its list of differences between a *tam* and a *mu'ad*, and we know that the Mishnah always omits at least two cases when it gives a list that is not exhaustive. Thus, if the Mishnah omitted the ransom from its list, there must be another difference between a *tam* and a *mu'ad*, and that must be the rule that the owner of a *tam* need not pay on the basis of his own confession, as Rav Huna the son of Rav Yehoshua argued. But Rav Pappa responds that it is not necessary to explain that the Mishnah omitted any case at all, because the Mishnah may reflect the viewpoint of Rabbi Yose HaGelili, who maintains that the owner of a *tam* pays a ransom. *Ritva* notes that there is a variant reading which supports this explanation.

הָא מַנִּי? רַבִּי יוֹסֵי הַגְּלִילִי הִיא Whose opinion is this? It is that of Rabbi Yose HaGelili. According to the explanation given by most Rishonim, this line is Rav Pappa's response to a counter-objection raised against him by Rav Huna the son of Rav Yehoshua. Rav Pappa is saying that the Mishnah can be explained as reflecting the viewpoint of Rabbi Yose HaGelili, in which case it did not omit any

TRANSLATION AND COMMENTARY

תָּא שְׁמַע [1]The Gemara now raises a third objection against Rav Huna the son of Rav Yehoshua from our Mishnah in *Ketubot*: **Come and hear** what this Mishnah says. The Mishnah rules that **"if someone says: 'My ox killed so-and-so,'** [2]**or 'my ox killed the ox of so-and-so,'** [3]**he pays** the ransom for the dead person, or the value of the dead ox, **by his own admission,** because these payments are considered regular damage payments, not fines." [4]**Is this** Mishnah **not referring to** an ox of any kind — even **a *tam*** that killed a person or another ox? And can we not infer from here that the payment for the damage caused by the ox is always considered a regular damage payment, as Rav Pappa argued, and not a fine, as Rav Huna the son of Rav Yehoshua maintained?

לָא בְּמוּעָד [5]**No,** replies the Gemara, Rav Huna the son of Rav Yehoshua can explain that the Mishnah is referring specifically **to a *mu'ad*.** In such a case, the owner must pay a ransom for the dead person, and must pay regular damages for the dead ox. These payments are considered regular damage payments, but the half-payment made by the owner of a *tam* is considered a fine.

אֲבָל בְּתָם מַאי? [6]**But** the Gemara does not accept this explanation, for according to it **what** is the law if the owner of **a *tam*** confesses that his ox has killed another ox? [7]**Does he not** in fact **pay by his own admission?** But if so, why did the Mishnah not mention this point? [8]**Instead of teaching in the last clause of the Mishnah,** [9]"If someone says: 'My ox killed **so-and-so's slave,' he does not pay** the thirty-shekel fine set by the Torah by **his own admission,"** [10]the author of the Mishnah **should have made a distinction** within the case it was already discussing, **and** should have **taught us about that case itself**, as follows: [11]**"In what case are these things said** — that the owner of an ox that has killed another ox pays damages by his own admission? [12]Only **in the case of a *mu'ad*. But in the case of a *tam*** the owner **does not pay by his own admission"!** From the fact that the author of the Mishnah did not mention this case, we may infer that there is no difference between a *tam* and a *mu'ad* for this purpose, as Rav Pappa argued, and the Mishnah is referring to both cases.

[1]תָּא שְׁמַע: ״׳הֵמִית שׁוֹרִי אֶת פְּלוֹנִי׳, [2]אוֹ: ׳שׁוֹרוֹ שֶׁל פְּלוֹנִי׳, [3]הֲרֵי זֶה מְשַׁלֵּם עַל פִּי עַצְמוֹ״. [4]מַאי לָאו בְּתָם? [5]לָא, בְּמוּעָד. [6]אֲבָל בְּתָם מַאי? [7]אֵינוֹ מְשַׁלֵּם עַל פִּי עַצְמוֹ? [8]אַדְּתָנֵי סֵיפָא, [9]״׳עַבְדּוֹ שֶׁל פְּלוֹנִי׳, אֵינוֹ מְשַׁלֵּם עַל פִּי עַצְמוֹ״, [10]נִיפְלוֹג וְנִיתְנֵי בְּדִידָהּ: [11]״בַּמֶּה דְּבָרִים אֲמוּרִים? [12]בְּמוּעָד, אֲבָל תָּם אֵינוֹ מְשַׁלֵּם עַל פִּי עַצְמוֹ״!

LITERAL TRANSLATION

[1]Come [and] hear: "[If someone says:] 'My ox killed so-and-so,' [2]or: '[My ox killed] the ox of so-and-so,' [3]he pays by his own admission." [4]Is it not [referring] to a *tam*?

[5]No, to a *mu'ad*.

[6]But what about a *tam*? [7]Does he not pay by his own admission? [8]Instead of teaching [in] the last clause [of the Mishnah], [9]"'so-and-so's slave,' he does not pay by his own admission," [10]let him distinguish and teach it in [this case] itself: [11]"In what [case] are these things said? [12]About a *mu'ad*, but [in the case of] a *tam* he does not pay by his own admission"!

RASHI

מאי לאו בתם — ואי משום דקתני בה ״המית שורי את פלוני״ דחיובו כופר, ותם לאו בר כופר הוא — הא מני רבי יוסי הגלילי היא. **אדתני עבדו של פלוני כו׳** — דלא אשכח פטור על פי עצמו אלא בעבד. **ניפלוג בדידה** — בבן חורין. ובבהמה נמי הוה מצי לשנויי חילוק, ולמיתני דאיכא דלא משלם על פי עצמו. **במה דברים אמורים** — דמשלם על פי עצמו במועד כו׳

NOTES

differences at all, since Rabbi Yose HaGelili maintains that the owner of a *tam* pays a ransom just like the owner of a *mu'ad*.

Rashi objects: Even according to Rabbi Yose HaGelili, the Mishnah omitted an important difference between a *tam* and a *mu'ad*. For the owner of a *mu'ad* pays a full ransom, whereas the owner of a *tam* pays only half. *Rashi* answers that this difference is included in the Mishnah's statement that the owner of a *tam* pays only half-damages.

Tosafot objects: There is still one more important difference between a *tam* and a *mu'ad*, even according to Rabbi Yose HaGelili. The owner of a *mu'ad* pays the full ransom if the ox is stoned to death (Exodus 21:29), whereas the half ransom is paid (according to Rabbi Yose HaGelili) only if the ox is not stoned, for technical reasons; but if the ox is stoned, Rabbi Yose HaGelili agrees that no ransom at all need be paid, since half-damages are paid only from the animal's own body, and if the animal is stoned, there is nothing from which to pay. *Tosafot* answers that this difference is included in the Mishnah's statement that the owner of a *tam* pays only from its body.

¹כּוּלָּהּ בְּמוּעָד קָמַיְירֵי.
²תָּא שְׁמַע: ³״זֶה הַכְּלָל: כָּל הַמְשַׁלֵּם יָתֵר עַל מַה שֶּׁהִזִּיק אֵינוֹ מְשַׁלֵּם עַל פִּי עַצְמוֹ״. ⁴הָא פָּחוֹת מִמַּה שֶּׁהִזִּיק, מְשַׁלֵּם עַל פִּי עַצְמוֹ!
⁵לָא תֵּימָא: ״הָא פָּחוֹת מִמַּה שֶּׁהִזִּיק, ⁶אֶלָּא אֵימָא: ״הָא כְּמַה שֶּׁהִזִּיק, מְשַׁלֵּם עַל פִּי עַצְמוֹ״.
⁷אֲבָל פָּחוֹת מַאי? ⁸אֵינוֹ מְשַׁלֵּם עַל פִּי עַצְמוֹ? ⁹לִיתְנֵי: ״זֶה הַכְּלָל: ¹⁰כָּל שֶׁאֵינוֹ מְשַׁלֵּם כְּמַה שֶּׁהִזִּיק אֵינוֹ מְשַׁלֵּם עַל פִּי עַצְמוֹ״, ¹¹דְּמַשְׁמַע פָּחוֹת וּמַשְׁמַע יָתֵר!

LITERAL TRANSLATION

[1]All of it is all dealing with a *mu'ad*.

[2]Come [and] hear: [3]"This is the rule: Whoever pays more than he damaged does not pay by his own admission." [4]Thus, [if the payment is] less than he damaged, he does pay by his own admission!

[5]Do not say: "Thus, [if the payment is] less than he damaged," [6]but say: "Thus, [if the payment is] as much as he damaged, he does pay by his own admission."

[7]But [if the payment is] less, what [is the law]? [8]Does he not pay by his own admission? [9]Let him teach: "This is the rule: [10]Whoever does not pay as much as he damaged does not pay by his own admission," [11]which implies less and implies more!

TRANSLATION AND COMMENTARY

כּוּלָּהּ בְּמוּעָד קָמַיְירֵי [1]The Gemara replies: Rav Huna the son of Rav Yehoshua can argue that our Mishnah preferred to select the case of the slave, because **it is dealing entirely with** cases involving **a** ***mu'ad***. The Mishnah prefers to show that the owner of a *mu'ad* sometimes does not pay by his own admission — namely, if the ox killed a slave — rather than turning to the case of a *tam*.

תָּא שְׁמַע [2]The Gemara now raises a fourth objection against Rav Huna the son of Rav Yehoshua from our Mishnah in *Ketubot*: **Come and hear** what our Mishnah says. [3]The last clause of the Mishnah states: **"This is the rule** to determine how to distinguish between a fine and a regular damage payment: **Whenever someone** is required by the Torah to **pay more than** the value of **the damage he did,** we know that the payment is a fine imposed to punish him, and he **does not make this payment by his own admission,** whereas a regular damage payment is never more than the value of the damage done. [4]This implies that **if the payment is** equal in value to the damage done or **less than the damage done,** it is considered a regular damage payment, which **he** ***does*** **pay by his own admission.** Thus we see that half-damages are considered a regular damage payment, as Rav Pappa argued.

לָא תֵּימָא [5]The Gemara replies: Rav Huna the son of Rav Yehoshua can argue that the Mishnah merely stated that if someone pays more than the value of the damage done, the payment is considered a fine. The Mishnah did not explicitly state the converse. It is **not** necessary to **say** that the Mishnah is implying that **if someone pays less than** the value of **the damage done,** it is considered a regular damage payment. [6]We can **say** that the Mishnah is implying that **if someone pays as much as** the value of **the damage done,** it is considered a regular damage payment, which **he** ***does*** **pay by his own admission.** But the case where someone pays less than the value of the damage done was not considered by the Mishnah.

אֲבָל פָּחוֹת מַאי [7]**But** the Gemara rejects this explanation, for according to it **what is the law if he pays less** than the value of the damage? [8]**Does he not** in fact **pay by his own admission?** But if so, why did the Mishnah not mention this? Why did the Mishnah mention only the case of someone who paid more than the value of the damage done, if the same law applies if he paid less? The Mishnah could have taught us both cases quite easily, merely by changing a few words. Instead of saying, "This is the rule: Whenever someone pays more than the value of the damage he did, he does not pay by his own admission," [9]the Mishnah **should have said: "This is the rule:** [10]**Whoever does not pay as much as** the value of **the damage he did does not pay by his own admission"!** [11]If the Mishnah had been phrased in this way **it would have meant** that both when he pays **less and** when he pays **more,** the payment is considered a fine. Is it not clear, therefore, that the Mishnah was phrased in the way it was, because the sole case in which someone pays less than the value of the damage done — the case of half-damages — is not a fine at all, as Rav Pappa argued?

RASHI

כולה במועד קמיירי — במועד אתא לאשמועינן, דאף הוא יש בו חילוק, דאיכא ביה מידי דלא משלם על פי עצמו, ומאי ניהו — נגיחת עבד. ואי הוה תני כדקאמרת — הוה שביק נמי לאורחיה, דרישא איירי במועד וסיפא ניתני תם. ומה לי שבקה תנא לאורחיה גבי ניזק לדלג מבן חורין לעבד, מה לי שבקה במזיק ולדלג ממועד לתם. **יתר על מה שהזיק** — כגון נגיחת עבד. וכן אונס, ומפתה, ומוציא שם רע, ותשלומי כפל, ותשלומי ארבעה וחמשה. **הא פחות ממה שהזיק** — כגון חצי נזק דתם. הכי גרסינן: **ליתני כל שאינו משלם כמה שהזיק אינו משלם על פי עצמו.**

TRANSLATION AND COMMENTARY

תְּיוּבְתָּא [1]The Gemara concludes that this fourth objection **is** indeed **a** valid **refutation** of the explanation given by Rav Huna the son of Rav Yehoshua, and his explanation must therefore be rejected.

וְהִלְכְתָא [2]**And** the Gemara follows this statement by remarking that **the Halakhah is** that **half-damages are** in fact **a fine,** in accordance with the ruling of Rav Huna the son of Rav Yehoshua.

תְּיוּבְתָּא וְהִלְכְתָא [3]The Gemara's last two remarks are a cause for astonishment. The Gemara has just said that the objection from our Mishnah in *Ketubot* **is a refutation** of the viewpoint of Rav Huna the son of Rav Yehoshua, and his viewpoint must therefore be rejected, **and** now the Gemara has reversed its decision and said that **the Halakhah** *does* follow his viewpoint! How can this contradiction be reconciled?

אִין [4]The Gemara answers: **Yes,** the decision that the Halakhah is in accordance with the viewpoint of Rav Huna the son of Rav Yehoshua is correct, because the Gemara's initial conclusion that the Mishnah in *Ketubot* is a refutation of his viewpoint was too hasty. [5]In fact, it is possible to answer the objection from this Mishnah as follows: **The reason why** the viewpoint of Rav Huna the son of Rav Yehoshua **was refuted was because the author of the Mishnah did not teach** us that, both when a person pays less than the value of the damage he did and when he pays more, the payment is considered a fine, by saying: [6]"Whoever does not pay **as much as** the value of **the damage he did** does not pay by his own admission." We therefore interpreted the Mishnah as implying that if he pays less, it is in fact a regular damage payment. But it is possible that the Mishnah means to imply not that if he pays less, it is *necessarily* a regular damage payment, but rather that if he pays less, it *may be* a regular damage payment or it may be a fine. [7]For the author of our Mishnah **did not** wish to **determine** that half-damages are **always** a fine, **since there is**

[1]תְּיוּבְתָּא.
[2]וְהִלְכְתָא: פַּלְגָא נִיזְקָא קְנָסָא.
[3]תְּיוּבְתָּא וְהִלְכְתָא?!
[4]אִין. [5]טַעֲמָא מַאי אִיתּוֹתַב מִשּׁוּם דְּלָא קָתָנֵי: [6]"כְּמַה שֶׁהִזִּיק". [7]לָא פְּסִיקָא לֵיהּ, כֵּיוָן דְּאִיכָּא חֲצִי נֶזֶק צְרוֹרוֹת,

LITERAL TRANSLATION

[1]It is a refutation.
[2]And the Halakhah is: Half-damages is a fine.
[3]It is a refutation and it is the Halakhah?!
[4]Yes. [5]The reason why he was refuted was because [the Tanna] did not teach: [6]"As much as he damaged." [7][But this] was not [an] absolute [ruling] for him, since there is [the case of] half-damages of pebbles,

RASHI

והלכתא פלגא ניזקא קנסא — דהואיל וכל חצי נזק אינו אלא בניזקא דלאו אורחיה, לאו על מריה הוא רמיא למינטריה בהכי, אלא קנסא הוא, כי היכי דלוסיף ביה נטירותא. **טעמא מאי איתותב** — כלומר, תיובתא מאי היא? **משום דלא קתני כל שאינו משלם כמה שחזיק אינו משלם על פי עצמו** — דלישתמע מינה נמי חצי נזק — הא לאו תיובתא היא. **כיון דאיכא חצי נזק** — דמשתלם בנזקי בהמה במהלכת והתיזה צרורות מתחת רגליה והזיקה, דתנן בבבא קמא (יז,א) דמשלמת חצי נזק. וההוא חצי נזק קיימא לן בבבא קמא דהלכתא גמירי לה מסיני שהוא תולדה של רגל, ופטורה ברשות הרבים כי רגל. וניזקי רגל לאו קנסא נינהו אלא ממונא, שהרי מועדת מתחילתה, וגבי צרורות הוא דאקיל רחמנא. וכיון דממונא הוא, משלם על פי עצמו, משום הכי לא פסיקא ליה למיתני: כל שאינו משלם כמה שהזיק, דהא איכא הא.

TERMINOLOGY

תְּיוּבְתָּא וְהִלְכְתָא It is a refutation and it is the Halakhah?! Sometimes, after an Amora's view is rejected (with the expression תְּיוּבְתָּא), the Talmud nevertheless rules that the Halakhah is in accordance with his view. In such cases the Talmud may then ask: "A refutation of this Amora was just offered, yet the Halakhah is in accordance with his viewpoint?!" The Talmud then proceeds to solve this problem.

NOTES

תְּיוּבְתָּא **It is a refutation.** When the Gemara offers no response to an objection, it usually concludes with the term תְּיוּבְתָּא ("it is a refutation") or קַשְׁיָא ("it is difficult"). These terms are not synonyms. Rather, when the Gemara says that something is refuted, it means that this viewpoint must be rejected. But when the Gemara says that something is difficult, it means that there is an answer to the question, but it is not completely satisfactory. Indeed, the commentators often devote considerable effort to finding the missing solutions to problems that remained as "difficult," and entire books, such as *Kashot Meyushav* of *Rabbi Yeshayahu Berlin*, have been written for this purpose.

Usually, when the Gemara ends with "it is difficult" the Halakhah does not follow the difficult opinion, although there are a few exceptions. But where the Gemara ends with "it is a refutation" the Halakhah never follows the refuted view. Hence the Gemara's astonishment in our case.

HALAKHAH

וְהִלְכְתָא פַּלְגָא נִיזְקָא קְנָסָא **And the Halakhah is: Half-damages is a fine.** "Damage payments equal in value to the damage done may be collected on the basis of the damager's own confession. Damage payments greater in value to the damage done, or the half-damage payment of the owner of a *tam*, are considered fines, and may be collected only on the basis of witnesses, not on the basis of the damager's own confession." (*Rambam, Sefer Nezikin, Hilkhot Nizkei Mamon* 2:8.)

חֲצִי נֶזֶק צְרוֹרוֹת **Half-damages of pebbles.** "If an animal is walking in a neighbor's field or on the public road, and while walking it causes some pebbles to fly and cause damage in a neighbor's field, this is considered to be a regular damage payment. It is paid from the best property of the owner of the animal, and is paid on the basis of his own confession. However, it is a Halakhah passed down by Moses on Sinai that indirect damage like this is compensated by the payment of half-damages only." (*Rambam, Sefer Nezikin, Hilkhot Nizkei Mamon* 2:2-4; *Shulḥan Arukh, Ḥoshen Mishpat* 390:3-4.)

REALIA

נִזְקֵי כֶּלֶב וְחָתוּל Damages caused by cats and dogs. From Talmudic sources it seems that cats were frequently not trained or domesticated; even cats kept at home (to keep mice and other animals away) often attacked domesticated birds (and even children).

Most dogs in the Talmudic period were shepherd dogs or watchdogs (cf. below, 61b, which implies that dogs were generally not raised as pets). Some people even raised vicious guard dogs who were trained to attack and kill intruders. It is no wonder, then, that such dogs occasionally attacked and killed other animals.

TRANSLATION AND COMMENTARY

the case of half-damages caused by pebbles. [1] In that case **we have a tradition that there is a** special **Halakhah** passed down by Moses **that** the payment for damage caused by pebbles **is a monetary obligation** and not a fine, and this tradition is, of course, accepted by Rav Huna the son of Rav Yehoshua. The case of half-damages under the heading of "pebbles" occurs when an animal causes damage indirectly. For example, if an animal walks through a neighbor's field, and kicks up a pebble as it walks, and the pebble damages the crops, the owner of the animal pays only half-damages. This is not because the damage is unusual or unanticipated, like the case of the *tam* that gores another ox. Rather, it is a separate Halakhah, traditionally handed down by Moses as part of the Oral Law, that only half-damages are to be paid for indirect damage of this sort. Thus, in this case, Rav Huna the son of Rav Yehoshua agrees that the damage payment is not a fine. The owner of the animal should by right have paid for the full damage, since he should have anticipated the problem; but the Torah had mercy on him, because the damage was indirect, and waived half the payment. [2] And **because** the case where someone pays less than the value of the damage done is sometimes a fine (e.g., where a *tam* gores) and is sometimes a regular damage payment (in the case of pebbles), **the author of the Mishnah did not teach** us about this case, and restricted himself to the case where the defendant pays more than the value of the damage done. Therefore our Mishnah is not a refutation of Rav Huna the son of Rav Yehoshua, and the Gemara's ruling stands: The Halakhah is that half-damages are a fine, and are not paid by the damager's own admission.

וְהָשְׁתָּא דְּאָמְרַתְּ [3] The Gemara concludes by noting another practical difference between fines and regular damage payments — a difference that did not arise until after the Mishnah was completed. According to Torah law, monetary questions may be judged only by a court of three judges, all of whom have been ordained according to the full ordination procedure. But if ordained judges are not available, it is permitted to decide pressing and uncomplicated monetary questions, such as debts and loans, in a court of unordained judges. Such judges are considered to be acting as the representatives of the true court, in its absence. Questions of property damage may also be decided this way (though not questions of bodily damage), but fines may not be imposed by an unordained court. Over time the ordination procedure fell into disuse, as fewer and fewer scholars attained the degree of excellence to receive it. In Talmudic times, however, full ordination still existed in Eretz Israel, but not in Babylonia. Accordingly, the Gemara notes that **now that we have established that half-damages are a fine,** it follows that half-damages may be collected only by an ordained court, and not by a Babylonian court. [4] Therefore, if a **dog eats** someone's **lamb, or a cat eats**

[1] דְּהִלְכְתָא גְּמִירִי לָהּ דְּמָמוֹנָא הוּא. [2] מִשּׁוּם הָכִי לָא קָתָנֵי. [3] וְהָשְׁתָּא דְּאָמְרַתְּ פַּלְגָא נִיזְקָא קְנָסָא, [4] הַאי כַּלְבָּא דַּאֲכַל אִימְרֵי, וְשׁוּנְרָא דְּאָכֵיל תַּרְנְגוֹלֵי

LITERAL TRANSLATION

[1] where we have this Halakhah as a tradition that it is a monetary [obligation]. [2] Because of this [the Tanna] did not teach [it].

[3] And now that you have said [that] half-damages is a fine, [4] this dog that ate lambs, or a cat that ate large chickens,

RASHI

דאכיל אימרי — שחנק טלאים חיים ואכלם.

NOTES

וְהָשְׁתָּא דְּאָמְרַתְּ פַּלְגָא נִיזְקָא קְנָסָא And now that you have said that half-damages is a fine. By Torah law, all monetary cases must be decided by a court of three judges, all of whom must have been ordained with the full ordination originally passed down by Moses to Joshua (Numbers 27:23). The conditions for ordination are very strict, and as time passed it became harder and harder to find ordained judges. One of the rules posed special problems: Ordination can be done only in Eretz Israel. And although an ordained judge from Eretz Israel can judge cases elsewhere as well, this restriction obviously made it difficult to find such judges.

Accordingly, in Talmudic times it was accepted that ordained judges officiated only in Eretz Israel, whereas in Babylonia unordained judges officiated. The principle justifying this practice was that the Babylonian judges were acting as the representatives of the true court in Eretz Israel, on an ad hoc basis. But the judges in Babylonia were not authorized to judge all monetary cases. Only loans and other cases in which the injured party suffered financial loss and the problem was commonplace were judged in this way. Cases involving fines could not be judged in Babylonia.

Rif (*Bava Kamma* 84b) reports a Geonic tradition that the courts should use the power of excommunication to order the damager to appease the injured party, and should release him from the excommunication if he succeeds in coming to terms with the injured party, or if he pays the fine. But it is forbidden to use the power of excommunication to issue a direct order to pay the fine.

HALAKHAH

הַאי כַּלְבָּא דַּאֲכַל אִימְרֵי This dog that ate lambs. "If a wild animal kills a domestic animal and eats it, it is considered to be normal behavior, and the owner of the wild animal must pay full damages. But if a dog kills and eats a lamb,

TRANSLATION AND COMMENTARY

someone's **large chickens,** [1] **we do not collect compensation in Babylonia for** such damage. Causing damage of this sort **is unusual** and unanticipated **behavior**, and is therefore subject to half-damages, just like the behavior of a *tam* that gores. [2] **But if** the cat **ate** the other person's **small** chicks, **it is** considered **normal** behavior. [3] Therefore the owner of the cat is held liable to pay full damages, **and we may collect** such compensation in Babylonia.

וְאִי תָּפַס [4] Having mentioned the rule that we do not collect fines in Babylonia, the Gemara adds that **if the owner** of the animals that were killed takes the law into his own hands and **seizes** the property of the owner of the cat or the dog in payment of the half-damages to which he is in principle entitled, the courts **do not take it away from him.** For although the courts in Babylonia do not have the authority to impose a fine, the injured party is certainly entitled to the money. Therefore the court does not intervene — neither to force the damager to pay, nor to prevent the damaged person from seizing the

רַבְרְבֵי, [1] מְשׁוּנֶּה הוּא, וְלָא מַגְבִּינַן בְּבָבֶל. [2] אֲבָל זוּטָרֵי, אוֹרְחֵיהּ הוּא, [3] וּמַגְבִּינַן.

[4] וְאִי תָּפַס, לָא מַפְּקִינַן מִינֵּיהּ.

LITERAL TRANSLATION

[1] is unusual [behavior], and we do not order collection [of it] in Babylonia. [2] But [if it ate] small ones, it is its [normal] way, [3] and we do order collection.

[4] But if he [the damaged party] seized [it], we do not take [it] away from him.

RASHI

משונה הוא — אין דרכו בכך, וכל נזק משונה בבהמה הוי תולדה דקרן תמה, שאף היא משונה, שאין דרכה בכך, וחצי נזק הוא דמשלם. וכיון דקנסא הוא — לא מגבינן ליה בדייני בבל, שאין שם סמיכה בזקנים ולא מקרו מומחים, וגבי קנס כתיב (שמות כב) "ירשיעון אלהים". **אורחיה הוא** — והוו להו נזקי דשן, ושן משלמת נזק שלם, וממונא הוא וגובין אותו בבבל. **ואי תפס** — ניזק ממונא דמזיק גבי קנסא דחצי נזקו, דאין צריך לצעוק לפנינו. **לא מפקינן מיניה** — וגבי פלגא נזקיה.

NOTES

תַּרְנְגוֹלֵי רַבְרְבֵי **Large chickens.** It is commonplace for a cat to attack and eat a small chick, but a full-grown chicken is not normally attacked by cats. *Rambam* explains that this distinction applies only to a cat. But a dog does not attack lambs at all, and if it does so, it is considered unusual, even if the lamb was quite small. *Rashi* (*Bava Kamma* 15b) does not distinguish between dogs and cats in this connection, and our commentary follows his opinion.

מְשׁוּנֶּה הוּא **Is unusual behavior.** There are three basic types of damage that can be done by an animal: Eating, trampling, and goring. (These three terms are described in Hebrew as שֵׁן — "tooth," רֶגֶל — "foot," and קֶרֶן "horn.") The Gemara explains (*Bava Kamma* 2b-3a) that whenever an animal does damage in order to derive some benefit from the damage, it is a form of "eating." Whenever it does damage incidentally in the course of doing something else, it is a form of "trampling." And whenever it does damage deliberately, purely for the sake of doing the damage itself, it is a form of "goring." Thus, if one animal bites another, it is a form of "goring," not eating. And if an animal cleans its horns on something, thereby spoiling it, it is a form of "eating" not goring.

In general, tame animals are expected to do damage to derive some benefit, or to do damage incidentally in the course of doing something else, but they are not expected to do damage deliberately. Hence the Gemara interprets the Torah's commandment that the owner of an ox that gores is held liable to pay half-damages, as applying to any sort of damage that could not have been anticipated. Thus, if a dog kills and eats something that dogs do not ordinarily kill and eat (such as a lamb), it falls under the category of "goring" rather than of "eating." Hence the dog's owner is held liable only to pay half-damages.

וְלָא מַגְבִּינַן **And we do not order collection.** *Rashba* explains that even though the Babylonian courts cannot collect half-damages, they can force the owner of the dog to pay for the benefit he derived when his dog ate the lamb (i.e., the dog food he saved because his dog had already eaten). The source of this ruling is a passage in *Bava Kamma* (20a) which rules that the owner of an animal that ate a neighbor's crops in the public domain, who is not required to pay full damages, must nevertheless pay for the benefit it derived from the crops (i.e, the fact that it does not need to be fed).

וְאִי תָּפַס, לָא מַפְּקִינַן מִינֵּיהּ **But if he seized it, we do not take it away from him.** There is a dispute among the Rishonim as to whether the injured party in a case of a fine was permitted to seize the damager's property up to the value of the fine. Most Rishonim cite our Gemara as

HALAKHAH

even if the lamb is small, or if a cat eats a large chicken, it is considered unusual behavior, and the owner of the dog or the cat pays only half the damage." (*Rambam, Sefer Nezikin, Hilkhot Nizkei Mamon* 3:7; *Shulḥan Arukh, Ḥoshen Mishpat* 391:6.)

לָא מַגְבִּינַן בְּבָבֶל **We do not order collection of it in Babylonia.** "Fines, such as the half-damages paid by the owner of a *tam*, may be collected only by a court of fully ordained judges, who were ordained in Eretz Israel. Such courts no longer exist today. *Rema* says that this law applies only to the fines laid down in the Torah, such as the rapist's fine, or the fines established by the Rabbis, such as the fine imposed on a person who slaps someone. But courts today are empowered to enact local decrees and to enforce them by means of fines." (*Rambam, Sefer Shofetim, Hilkhot Sanhedrin* 5:8,9; *Shulḥan Arukh, Ḥoshen Mishpat* 1:1,5.)

וְאִי תָּפַס, לָא מַפְּקִינַן מִינֵּיהּ **But if he seized it, we do not take it away from him.** "Even in the absence of ordained judges, the courts may place the damager under a ban

SAGES

רַבִּי נָתָן **Rabbi Natan.** One of the greatest Tannaim during the generation before the completion of the Mishnah. See *Ketubot,* Part II, p. 71.

TRANSLATION AND COMMENTARY

payment. [1]Moreover, **if** the damaged person appeals to the Babylonian court and **says:** "Since you do not have the authority to impose half-damages on him, **fix a time for me to attend a court hearing in Eretz Israel,** so that if the defendant does not agree to pay the fine of his own volition, he must go with me to Eretz Israel to be judged by a competent court," [2]**we** accept this appeal and **fix** a time **for him** to go to Eretz Israel. [3]**And if the owner of** the dog or the cat **does not** pay the fine of his own volition by that time, or **go** to Eretz Israel to be judged by a competent court, **we place him under a ban** for showing contempt by refusing to go to Eretz Israel as ordered.

[1]וְאִי אֲמַר: ״אַקְבְּעוּ לִי זִימְנָא לְאֶרֶץ יִשְׂרָאֵל״, [2]מַקְבְּעִינַן לֵיהּ. [3]וְאִי לָא אָזֵיל, מְשַׁמְּתִינַן לֵיהּ. [4]בֵּין כָּךְ וּבֵין כָּךְ, מְשַׁמְּתִינַן לֵיהּ. [5]דְּאָמְרִינַן לֵיהּ: ״סָלֵיק הֶיזֵּיקָךְ״, [6]מִדְּרַבִּי נָתָן. [7]דְּתַנְיָא: ״רַבִּי נָתָן אוֹמֵר: [8]מִנַּיִן שֶׁלֹּא

LITERAL TRANSLATION

[1]And if he said: "Fix a time for me [for a court hearing] in Eretz Israel," [2]we fix [it] for him. [3]And if he [the damager] does not go, we place him under a ban. [4]Whether like this or whether like that, we place him under a ban. [5]For we say to him: "Remove your damager," [6]in accordance with what Rabbi Natan [said]. [7]For it was taught: "Rabbi Natan says: [8]From where [do we know] that a

RASHI

בין כך ובין כך — בין שרוצה ניזק לילך לארץ ישראל, בין שאינו רוצה. **משמתינן ליה** — למזיק, מיהא להרוג אותו כלב ולסלק היזיקיה.

הדרן עלך אלו נערות

בֵּין כָּךְ וּבֵין כָּךְ [4]The Gemara notes that, in the case of the dog, **whether** the defendant pays the fine or goes to Eretz Israel, **or** refuses to pay the fine, **we** threaten him anyway with being **placed under a ban,** for another reason. [5]**For we say to him:** "It is forbidden to keep a vicious dog, even in your own home, and if you do not **remove your damager** (your dog that has caused damage), we will place you under a ban." [6]The Gemara notes that our power to impose such a ruling on pain of excommunication, is **in accordance with what Rabbi Natan said** in the following Baraita, [7]**for it was taught: "Rabbi Natan said:** [8]**From where do we**

NOTES

proof that seizure is permitted for all fines. But *Rabbenu Tam* insists that our Gemara was referring only to half-damages, but not to other fines. *Rabbenu Tam* explains that since half-damages are paid from the damaging animal's body, the injured party is permitted to seize the dog or the cat that did the damage. But the damager's other property must not be seized, even in a case of half-damages; and for any other fine, no seizure at all is allowed.

The dispute revolves around the idea that the Babylonian courts were not allowed to use the power of excommunication directly to compel the damager to pay the fine, as this would be tantamount to judging a case of fines. *Rabbenu Tam* argues that, according to the other Rishonim, the Babylonian courts were effectively judging cases of fines in Babylonia by permitting the injured party to seize the damager's property. For the court could not simply step aside; it had to oversee the seizure, in order to be certain that the injured party did not seize more than he was permitted. But *Rivan* explains that the court does not oversee the seizure itself. Rather, it gets involved only after the property has been seized, if the damager complains that too much was taken; and in such a case, the matter becomes a question of theft, which the Babylonian courts are authorized to judge.

Radbaz adds that *Rabbenu Tam*'s explanation is difficult to accept, because our Gemara concludes that the owner of the dog or the cat must kill it. What good does it do for the owner of the chicken to seize the cat, since it must be killed anyway? Rather, the Gemara must mean that the injured party is permitted to seize the damager's other property, as the other Rishonim explained.

There is a related question — whether there is a moral obligation to pay the fine in a case where one is exempt for technical reasons. The Jerusalem Talmud rules that if an offender confesses to a deed punished by a fine, he does not even have a moral obligation to pay it. But *Rashi* connects the right to seize with the moral obligation. Accordingly, it would appear that since our Gemara permits the injured party to seize, there is also a moral obligation on the damager to pay the fine.

״סָלֵיק הֶיזֵּיקָךְ״ **"Remove your damager."** *Rashi* explains that the owner of the dog is required to kill it. This explanation is supported by a passage in *Bava Kamma* (46a) which

HALAKHAH

until he appeases the damaged party. If he offers to pay the equivalent of the fine, and the damaged party refuses to accept this, the ban is lifted. Likewise, if the damaged party seizes the damager's property up to the value of the fine, we do not interfere — following the Gemara here. But *Rema* notes that we do not assist the damaged party in taking the law into his own hands by telling him how much the fine is worth. Rather, we look at what he has seized after he seizes it, and if it is worth more than the fine, we make him return the balance." (*Rambam, Sefer Shofetim, Hilkhot Sanhedrin* 5:17; *Shulḥan Arukh, Ḥoshen Mishpat* 1:5.)

TRANSLATION AND COMMENTARY

know that a person must not raise a vicious dog, even **within his** own **house,** [1]**and that he must not stand a defective ladder,** even **within his** own **house?** [2]**For it is said** in the verse (Deuteronomy 22:8): 'When you build a new house, you shall make a railing for your roof, **and you shall not put blood in your house,** if someone falls from it.'" Rabbi Natan infers from the clause about putting blood in the house that this law applies to all dangerous situations, and not merely to the case of the railing on the roof. Thus we see that the Torah commanded us not to allow a dangerous situation to develop, even in our private domains. Hence the court has the power to enforce this law, just as it has the power to enforce the other laws of the Torah.

יְגַדֵּל אָדָם כֶּלֶב רַע בְּתוֹךְ בֵּיתוֹ, [1]וְלֹא יַעֲמִיד סוּלָם רָעוּעַ בְּתוֹךְ בֵּיתוֹ? [2]שֶׁנֶּאֱמַר: ׳וְלֹא תָשִׂים דָּמִים בְּבֵיתֶךָ׳״.

הדרן עלך אלו נערות

LITERAL TRANSLATION

person must not raise a vicious dog within his house, [1]and [that] he must not stand a defective ladder within his house? [2]For it is said: 'And you shall not put blood in your house.'"

NOTES

infers from Rabbi Natan's ruling that the only effective way to prevent a dangerous ox from doing further harm is to slaughter it. *Ritva*, however, notes that the Torah did not command the owner of the dangerous ox to kill it. Rather, it required him to guard it carefully, and penalized him if it did damage. *Ritva* explains that Rabbi Natan was referring only to dangerous objects in a house that serve no essential purpose, such as a vicious dog or a defective ladder. But it is permitted to keep a dangerous object, such as an ox, that is needed for one's livelihood, provided that it is guarded carefully.

HALAKHAH

כֶּלֶב רַע A vicious dog. "It is forbidden to raise a vicious dog in one's house, unless it is tied up with iron chains. *Rambam* says that this ruling applies to any dog. In a border town that is subject to raids, it is permitted to let such a dog loose at night. *Rema* adds that where the Jews are living as a minority among hostile non-Jews, it is permitted to have an unchained watchdog, but if it is so vicious that it is liable to cause damage to innocent passersby, it is forbidden," following our Gemara and the Gemara in *Bava Kamma*. (*Rambam, Sefer Nezikin, Hilkhot Nizkei Mamon* 5:9; *Shulḥan Arukh, Ḥoshen Mishpat* 409:3.)

סוּלָם רָעוּעַ A defective ladder. "It is a positive commandment to build a railing on one's roof, as the verse (Deuteronomy 22:8) says: 'You shall make a railing for your roof.' This law applies equally to any other dangerous place or object, such as an open pit or the like. It is a positive commandment to avoid dangerous obstacles oneself, as the verse (Deuteronomy 4:9) says: 'Take heed to yourself and guard your life,' and we are required to remove them from our houses. Anyone who keeps such an obstacle in his house violates the positive commandment to make a railing for his roof, and violates the negative commandment (Deuteronomy 22:8): 'And you shall not put blood in your house.'" (*Rambam, Sefer Nezikin, Hilkhot Rotze'aḥ U'Shemirat HaNefesh* 11:1,4; *Shulḥan Arukh, Ḥoshen Mishpat* 427:1,7,8.)

Conclusion to Chapter Three

In this chapter it is established that if someone rapes or seduces a *na'arah* whom he is not permitted to marry, whether the prohibition of such a marriage is by Torah law or by Rabbinic law, he is neither required to marry her nor is he allowed to. However, he must pay her father the fine stipulated by the Torah. Nevertheless, if sexual intercourse between the rapist or the seducer and his victim is a transgression punishable by execution administered by the court, then even if he is not in fact sentenced to death, he is exempt from paying the fine.

These Halakhot are based on several principles that are clarified in this chapter. One is that a person is not punished twice for the same transgression; instead, he receives the more severe of the applicable punishments (קִים לֵיהּ בִּדְרַבָּה מִינֵּיהּ). Furthermore, if someone commits a transgression that involves both a monetary obligation and the penalty of lashes, he fulfills the monetary obligation and is not lashed. The monetary obligation takes precedence even if the transgressor is subject to the penalty of excision.

From a precise reading of the Biblical text, the Sages conclude in this chapter that the rapist must pay the fine only if his victim is a virgin, but not if his victim is presumed not to be a virgin — such as in the case of a freed slave, or of someone who has already been married. However, the rapist must also pay the fine if his victim was a minor and not just a *na'arah*. According to the Halakhah, even if the offender raped a *na'arah* who had been betrothed and was widowed, he must pay the fine. And even though the Torah speaks of a *na'arah* whose father is living, an orphan girl is also entitled to the fine. In this respect, however, there is a difference between a rape victim and a girl who was seduced. The seducer of an orphan girl is exempt from paying the fine, because the girl had agreed to the act. Regarding the right of refusal to marry the man who committed the act, the Sages established that this right applies both to a seduced girl and to a rape victim. Both the father and the daughter have the right to refuse.

It is established that the sum stipulated in the Torah is a fine. The rapist pays it to *ne'arot* of all kinds. But in addition, like anyone else who has committed assault, he must pay damages for pain, shame, and blemish. The fine is for the sexual act alone. Since the sum stipulated is a fine (and not a monetary obligation), it may be collected, like all other fines, only on the basis of testimony by witnesses, and not by the transgressor's admission, and it may be collected only by ordained judges.

List of Sources

Aḥaronim, lit., "the last," meaning Rabbinic authorities from the time of the publication of Rabbi Yosef Caro's code of Halakhah, *Shulḥan Arukh* (1555).

Arukh, Talmudic dictionary, by Rabbi Natan of Rome, 11th century.

Ba'al Ma'or, Rabbi Zeraḥyah ben Yitzḥak, Spain, 12th century. Author of *HaMa'or*, Halakhic commentary on *Hilkhot HaRif*.

Baḥ (Bayit Ḥadash), commentary on *Arba'ah Turim*, by Rabbi Yoel Sirkes, Poland (1561–1640).

Bet Shmuel, commentary on *Shulḥan Arukh, Even HaEzer*, by Rabbi Shmuel ben Uri Shraga, Poland, second half of the 17th century.

Bet Ya'akov, novellae on *Ketubot*, by Rabbi Ya'akov Lorberboim of Lissa, Poland (1760–1832).

Bet Yosef, Halakhic commentary on *Arba'ah Turim* by Rabbi Yosef Caro (1488–1575), which is the basis of his authoritative Halakhic code, *Shulḥan Arukh*.

Even HaEzer, section of *Shulḥan Arukh* dealing with marriage, divorce, and related topics.

Geonim, heads of the academies of Sura and Pumbedita in Babylonia from the late 6th century to the mid-11th century.

Gra, Rabbi Eliyahu ben Shlomo Zalman (1720–1797), the Gaon of Vilna. Novellae on the Talmud and *Shulḥan Arukh*.

Hafla'ah, novellae on *Ketubot*, by Rabbi Pinḥas HaLevi Horowitz, Poland and Germany (1731–1805).

Ḥatam Sofer, responsa literature and novellae on the Talmud by Rabbi Moshe Sofer (Schreiber), Pressburg, Hungary and Germany (1763–1839).

Ḥelkat Meḥokek, commentary on *Shulḥan Arukh, Even HaEzer*, by Rabbi Moshe Lima, Lithuania (1605–1658).

Ḥokhmat Shlomo, novellae on the Talmud by Rabbi Shlomo Luria, Poland (1510–1573).

Ḥoshen Mishpat, section of *Shulḥan Arukh* dealing with civil and criminal law.

Kashot Meyushav, a work devoted to solving "difficulties" that remained unresolved in Talmudic discussions, by Rabbi Yeshayahu Pik Berlin, Breslau (1725–1799).

Kesef Mishneh, commentary on *Mishneh Torah*, by Rabbi Yosef Caro, author of *Shulḥan Arukh*.

Ketzot HaḤoshen, novellae on *Shulḥan Arukh, Ḥoshen Mishpat*, by Rabbi Aryeh Leib Heller, Galicia (1754?–1813).

Korban HaEdah, commentary on the Jerusalem Talmud by Rabbi David ben Naftali Frankel, Germany (1707–1762).

Kovetz Shiurim, novellae on the Talmud by Rabbi Elḥanan Wasserman, Lithuania (1875–1941).

Leḥem Mishneh, commentary on *Mishneh Torah*, by Rabbi Avraham di Boton, Salonica (1560–1609).

Maggid Mishneh, commentary on *Mishneh Torah*, by Rabbi Vidal de Tolosa, Spain, 14th century.

Maharam Schiff, novellae on the Talmud by Rabbi Meir ben Ya'akov HaKohen Schiff (1605–1641), Frankfurt, Germany.

Maharsha, Rabbi Shmuel Eliezer ben Yehudah HaLevi Edels, Poland (1555–1631). Novellae on the *Talmud*.

Maharshal, Rabbi Shlomo ben Yeḥiel Luria, Poland (1510–1573). Novellae on the Talmud.

Meiri, commentary on the Talmud (called *Bet HaBeḥirah*), by Rabbi Menaḥem ben Shlomo, Provence (1249–1316).

Mekhilta, Halakhic Midrash on the Book of Exodus.

Melekhet Shlomo, commentary on the Mishnah by Rabbi Shlomo Adeni, Yemen and Eretz Israel (1567–1626).

Mishnah Berurah, commentary on *Shulḥan Arukh, Oraḥ Ḥayyim*, by Rabbi Yisrael Meir HaKohen, Poland (1837–1933).

Mishneh LeMelekh, commentary on *Mishneh Torah*, by Rabbi Yehudah ben Shmuel Rosanes, Turkey (1657–1727).

Nimmukei Yosef, commentary on *Hilkhot HaRif*, by Rabbi Yosef Ḥaviva, Spain, early 15th century.

Or Sameaḥ, novellae on *Mishneh Torah*, by Rabbi Meir Simḥah HaKohen of Dvinsk, Latvia (1843–1926).

Or Zarua, collection of Halakhic rulings of German and French Rabbis by Rabbi Yitzḥak ben Moshe of Vienna (c. 1180 - c. 1250).

Oraḥ Ḥayyim, section of *Shulḥan Arukh* dealing with daily religious observances, prayers, and the laws of the Sabbath and Festivals.

Pnei Moshe, commentary on the Jerusalem Talmud by Rabbi Moshe ben Shimon Margoliyot, Lithuania (c. 1710-1781).

Pnei Yehoshua, novellae on the Talmud by Rabbi Ya'akov Yehoshua Falk, Poland and Germany (1680-1756).

Ra'ah, see *Rabbi Aharon HaLevi.*

Ra'avad, Rabbi Avraham ben David, commentator and Halakhic authority. Wrote comments on *Mishneh Torah.* Provence (c. 1125-1198?).

Rabbenu Ḥananel (ben Ḥushiel), commentator on Talmud, North Africa (990-1055).

Rabbenu Tam, commentator on the Talmud, Tosafist, France (1100-1171).

Rabbi Aharon HaLevi, Spain, 13th century. Novellae on the Talmud.

Rabbi Cresdas Vidal, Spanish Talmudist and commentator, 14th century.

Radbaz, Rabbi David ben Shlomo Avi Zimra, Spain, Egypt, Eretz Israel, and North Africa (1479-1574). Commentary on *Mishneh Torah.*

Rambam, Rabbi Moshe ben Maimon, Rabbi and philosopher, known also as Maimonides. Author of *Mishneh Torah,* Spain and Egypt (1135-1204).

Ramban, Rabbi Moshe ben Naḥman, commentator on Bible and Talmud, known also as Naḥmanides, Spain and Eretz Israel (1194-1270).

Ran, Rabbi Nissim ben Reuven Gerondi, Spanish Talmudist (1310?-1375?).

Rashash, Rabbi Shmuel ben Yosef Shtrashun, Lithuanian Talmud scholar (1794-1872).

Rashba, Rabbi Shlomo ben Avraham Adret, Spanish Rabbi famous for his commentaries on the Talmud and his responsa (c. 1235-c. 1314).

Rashbam, Rabbi Shmuel ben Meir, commentator on the Talmud, France (1085-1158).

Rashi, Rabbi Shlomo ben Yitzḥak, the paramount commentator on the Bible and the Talmud, France (1040-1105).

Rav Hai Gaon, Babylonian Rabbi, head of Pumbedita Yeshivah, 10th-11th century.

Rema, Rabbi Moshe ben Yisrael Isserles, Halakhic authority, Poland (1525-1572).

Remah, novellae on the Talmud by Rabbi Meir ben Todros HaLevi Abulafiya, Spain (c. 1170-1244). See *Yad Ramah.*

Ri, Rabbi Yitzḥak ben Shmuel of Dampierre, Tosafist, France (died c. 1185).

Rid, see *Tosefot Rid.*

Rif, Rabbi Yitzḥak Alfasi, Halakhist, author of *Hilkhot HaRif,* North Africa (1013-1103).

Rishonim, lit., "the first," meaning Rabbinic authorities active between the end of the Geonic period (mid-11th century) and the publication of *Shulḥan Arukh* (1555).

Ritva, novellae and commentary on the Talmud by Rabbi Yom Tov ben Avraham Ishbili, Spain (c. 1250-1330).

Rivam, Rabbi Yitzḥak ben Mordekhai, Tosafist, France, 11th-12th century.

Rosh, Rabbi Asher ben Yeḥiel, also known as Asheri, commentator and Halakhist, Germany and Spain (c.1250-1327).

Sefer HaḤinnukh, anonymous work on the 613 Biblical commandments, 14th century.

Shakh (Siftei Kohen), commentary on *Shulḥan Arukh* by Rabbi Shabbetai ben Meir HaKohen, Lithuania (1621-1662).

Shittah Mekubbetzet, a collection of commentaries on the Talmud by Rabbi Betzalel ben Avraham Ashkenazi of Safed (c. 1520-1591).

Shulḥan Arukh, code of Halakhah by Rabbi Yosef Caro, b. Spain, active in Eretz Israel (1488-1575).

Talmidei Rabbenu Yonah, commentary on *Hilkhot HaRif* by the school of Rabbi Yonah of Gerondi, Spain (1190-1263).

Tosafot, collection of commentaries and novellae on the Talmud, expanding on Rashi's commentary, by the French-German Tosafists (12th and 13th centuries).

Tosefot Rid, commentary on the Talmud by Rabbi Yeshayahu ben Mali di Trani, Italian Halakhist (c. 1200-before 1260).

Tosefot Sens, the first important collection of *Tosafot,* by Rabbi Shimshon of Sens) late 12th-early 13th century).

Tosefot Yom Tov, commentary on the Mishnah by Rabbi Yom Tov Lipman HaLevi Heller, Prague and Poland (1579-1654).

Tur, abbreviation of *Arba'ah Turim,* Halakhic code by Rabbi Ya'akov ben Asher, b. Germany, active in Spain (c. 1270-1343).

Yad Ramah, novellae on the Talmud by Rabbi Meir ben Todros HaLevi Abulafiya, Spain (c. 1170-1244).

Yefeh Enayim, cross-references and notes to the Jerusalem Talmud, by Rabbi Yeshayahu Pik Berlin, Breslau (1725-1799).

Yam Shel Shlomo, novellae on the Talmud and Halakhic decisions, by Rabbi Shlomo ben Yeḥiel Luria, Poland (1510-1573).

Yoreh De'ah, section of *Shulḥan Arukh* dealing mainly with dietary laws, interest, ritual purity, and mourning.

About the Type

This book was set in Leawood, a contemporary typeface designed by Leslie Usherwood. His staff completed the design upon Usherwood's death in 1984. It is a friendly, inviting face that goes particularly well with sans serif type.